THE GRINDING MILL.
2 THE SLIP KILNS.
FORMING ON THE WHEEL.
5 TURNING.
6 MODELLING.
7 THE BISCUIT KILN.
8 DIPPING OR GLAZING.
9 THE GLAZE KILN.
10 PAINTING.
11 ENAMELLING KILN.
12 BURNISHING.

b

Only 1 volume printed in this format.

£ 38-00

The Dictionary of

WORCESTER PORCELAIN

VOLUME I

1751-1851

Frontispiece. A magnificent Barr, Flight and Barr vase, the shell theme extenuated by gilt dolphin and scallop handles, the painting by a distinctive hand believed to be John Barker, 13in. (33cm), impressed mark. (Phillips.)

(Opposite) A mug decorated with the Beckoning Chinaman *pattern which should be compared with the example illustrated as Colour Plate 8 on page 56. Although the treatment of the painting is similar, during the early 1750s the factory was not too concerned with consistency and the composition of patterns can vary considerably. 3½in. (9cm), c.1754. (Phillips.)*

The Dictionary of

WORCESTER PORCELAIN

VOLUME I

1751-1851

John Sandon

The Antique Collectors' Club

ISBN 1 85149 156 2

British Library Cataloguing-in-Publication Data
A catalogue record for this book is available from the British Library.

Printed in England
on Consort Royal Satin from Donside Mills, Aberdeen,
by the Antique Collectors' Club, Woodbridge, Suffolk, IP12 1DS

The Antique Collectors' Club

The Antique Collectors' Club was formed in 1966 and quickly grew to a five figure membership spread throughout the world. It publishes the only independently run monthly antiques magazine, *Antique Collecting*, which caters for those collectors who are interested in widening their knowledge of antiques, both by greater awareness of quality and by discussion of the factors which influence the price that is likely to be asked. The Antique Collectors' Club pioneered the provision of information on prices for collectors and the magazine still leads in the provision of detailed articles on a variety of subjects.

It was in response to the enormous demand for information on 'what to pay' that the price guide series was introduced in 1968 with the first edition of *The Price Guide to Antique Furniture* (completely revised 1978 and 1989), a book which broke new ground by illustrating the more common types of antique furniture, the sort that collectors could buy in shops and at auctions rather than the rare museum pieces which had previously been used (and still to a large extent are used) to make up the limited amount of illustrations in books published by commercial publishers. Many other price guides have followed, all copiously illustrated, and greatly appreciated by collectors for the valuable information they contain, quite apart from prices. The Price Guide Series heralded the publication of many standard works of reference on art and antiques. *The Dictionary of British Art* (now in six volumes), *Oak Furniture* and *Early English Clocks* were followed by many deeply researched reference works such as *The Directory of Gold and Silversmiths*, providing new information. Many of these books are now accepted as the standard work of reference on their subject.

The Antique Collectors' Club has widened its list to include books on gardens and architecture. All the Club's publications are available through bookshops world wide and a full catalogue of all these titles is available free of charge from the addresses below.

Club membership, open to all collectors, costs little. Members receive free of charge Antique Collecting, the Club's magazine (published ten times a year), which contains well-illustrated articles dealing with the practical aspects of collecting not normally dealt with by magazines. Prices, features of value, investment potential, fakes and forgeries are all given prominence in the magazine.

Among other facilities available to members are private buying and selling facilities, the longest list of 'For Sales' of any antiques magazine, an annual ceramics conference and the opportunity to meet other collectors at their local antique collectors' clubs. There are over eighty in Britain and more than a dozen overseas. Members may also buy the Club's publications at special pre-publication prices.

As its motto implies, the Club is an organisation designed to help collectors get the most out of their hobby: it is informal and friendly and gives enormous enjoyment to all concerned.

For Collectors — By Collectors — About Collecting

ANTIQUE COLLECTORS' CLUB
5 Church Street, Woodbridge Suffolk IP12 1DS, UK
Tel: 01394 385501 Fax: 01394 384434
— or —
Market Street Industrial Park, Wappingers' Falls, NY 12590, USA
Tel: 914 297 0003 Fax: 914 297 0068

For Elizabeth and Robert

Contents

Preface and Acknowledgements

This *Dictionary* tells the story of Worcester porcelain through its first hundred years, up to the year 1851. The second century, and right up to the present day, will be told in a second volume. My father and I initially thought of including all in a single book, but this would have reached unrealistic proportions. Dividing our work by date seemed natural, and fitted into place easily as 1851 did indeed mark a watershed in the history of Worcester china.

It is no coincidence that the period I have set out to cover in my part of the *Dictionary* is the same as Richard Binns' classic work *A Century of Potting in the City of Worcester.* Binns wrote his book in 1865. He had spent the previous thirteen years transforming the factory from what he described as 'a degenerate and almost moribund establishment' into the thriving Worcester Royal Porcelain Company of which he was Art Director. His limitless energy still left him time to research the full history of the ceramic world, and through his scholarship he was able to establish Worcester's position as one of the great porcelain centres of Europe.

Richard Binns has been an invaluable inspiration to me since I was a boy. In my involvement with the Worcester porcelain works I have felt humble following in his footsteps in the present day factory which he had largely re-built in the nineteenth century. The porcelain made under his direction will be covered in the further volume of this *Dictionary.* For my part, Binns' great contribution was to preserve the old works collection of special pieces which remained from the two great factories of Flight and Chamberlain. Considering the severe financial situation he faced on his arrival at Worcester, Binns must have fought to prevent the collection from being sold in 1852. Instead he added to it with all the enthusiasm of a great Victorian art collector, and thankfully he realised the importance of the old records, pattern books and copper printing plates which remained on the works. Thank goodness he had the great foresight to preserve these for the benefit of all future students.

Sadly most of the Flight factory records and those from Worcester's earliest days had been destroyed, probably a decade before, with the result that Binns had to begin as a pioneer. He met many of the old work-force and recorded their details and the stories they remembered. They told him the names of some of the painters of pieces in the works collection and these he faithfully recorded in his catalogue. In short, I am only continuing what R.W. Binns began and, in acknowledging his work as a primary source, I must also stress that he is but one of the giants on whose shoulders I have stood to write this *Dictionary.*

Amongst the wealth of material presented here, I have attempted to list all of the managers, principal artists and craftsmen as far as are known, and also all of the primary shapes, named patterns and forms of decoration, for each of the different factories over a hundred year period. While some information is presented here for the first time, most of this history of Worcester porcelain is contained in other classic reference books which have been by my side constantly. These are listed in the Bibliography and my task has been to study and correlate the masses of facts and comments each contain, and to draw new conclusions. R.L. Hobson, H. Rissik Marshall and Charles Dyson Perrins were all well before my time, but I feel I know them from their writings and from the first-hand accounts of the many collectors and writers whom I have been fortunate to meet over the last twenty-five years. All have, without exception, been so generous with their time and knowledge, willing to tolerate the enquiring nature of a Worcester schoolboy, visiting with my father some of the greatest collections. I could never thank them all, but if I have to single out a few names who particularly stirred my own enthusiasm, not least by letting me handle priceless examples in their collections, I would have to remember my visits to Sir Anthony Tuke, Dr Severne Mackenna, Dr Paul Riley, Gilbert Bradley, Henry Clay Hoffheimer, Milton and Jeanne Zorensky and particularly Tom Burn at Rous Lench Court.

This *Dictionary* is the culmination of my lifelong study of Worcester porcelain. I could not possibly begin to thank everyone who has helped as this would inevitably include almost every collector and museum curator I know. I have always been observing pieces, gathering little bits of information here and there, collecting photographs and noting unusual patterns and marks. I know that those who have assisted me will understand why I cannot list all their names here, but my gratitude goes out to them all. I cannot leave out mention of a few special people whose help has been crucial to this book. Simon Spero, Bernard Watney, Geoffrey Godden, Tony Stevenson and Norman Stretton have all helped in many ways, including supplying photographs, and especially by being available to answer questions and discuss points that did not quite make sense.

The photographs which make this *Dictionary* possible have taken me twenty years to assemble, and so I ask to be forgiven if not every source is fully acknowledged in this introduction. The largest number come from the archives of Phillips where I have worked since 1975. I have been fortunate to have had available the skills of Chris Halton, Phillips' senior photographer, who took most of these, often at very short notice as a rare or interesting piece passed through my department. His work, particularly some of the colour groups he has taken specially for this *Dictionary,* deserves the highest recognition. Other photographs have been kindly provided by other leading auction houses, including Bonhams, Christie's and Sotheby's, and I am particularly grateful to Letitia Roberts at Sotheby's in New York for her help. Many other photographs were taken by John Beckerley for my father, Henry Sandon, when he was Curator of the Dyson Perrins Museum and he has kindly provided me with full access to these and others in his files. In addition my father has provided transparencies of some fine pieces in the Cheekwood Fine Art Centre, Nashville, Tennessee, the important collection of Worcester porcelain of which he is honorary curator. I must also thank Lawrence Branyan for photographs taken for our joint book *Worcester Blue and White Porcelain, 1751-1790,* and also the third member of our team, Professor Neal French, for permission to use several of his line drawings of blue and white patterns which have not previously been published.

Many of my colleagues at Phillips in London have helped with odd bits of information or checking historical facts. I especially want to thank Diana Kay and Nicole Murray who run the photographic library, our Oriental specialist Desmond

Healey, and my immediate colleagues in the European Ceramics Department, Jo Marshall and Frances Lynas who have helped me in so many different ways. I am especially grateful to Jo Marshall for access to the important research notes and photographs left in her care by the family of the late and much respected A.J.B. Kiddell, former director of Sotheby's ceramics department.

A book as wide-ranging as this does not write itself and would not have been possible without the teamwork of the Antique Collectors' Club who have transformed my mountain of text and photographs. I must also thank my wife Kristin and my good friend Michael Poulson who took the time to read every single entry to make sure it made sense, and to make invaluable suggestions and offer advice at every stage. My children Elizabeth (aged six) and Robert (two) had difficulty understanding why Daddy spent so much time shut away from them working on 'the Book' and I hope that their patience will be rewarded when they are old enough to understand the *Dictionary* and that they will grow up to love Worcester porcelain just as I have done.

For this reason, my final and most heartfelt thanks go to my father, not only for the enormous help he has given me in providing information and photographs for what became my part of our *Dictionary*. Much more than this, his patient teaching when I was a boy, letting me help with the excavations on the early factory site, allowing me to help him at all times on chores within the porcelain factory, to search through the factory archives for him, and accompany him on visits to collectors — all this moulded me into a scaled-down 'chip off the old pot', something I will never be able properly to repay. Dad taught me to appreciate all the qualities of Worcester porcelain, and I could have asked for no greater gift than this.

John Sandon

Historical Survey

If their earliest biographer is to be believed, William Davis and Dr John Wall made the first Worcester porcelain in the fireplace of Davis' apothecary shop in Broad Street, using an iron pot around which the fire was heaped. I see no reason for this not being the case although it was not reported by Chambers until the early nineteenth century. Clearly they would not have been able to attract backers to finance the building of a porcelain factory without first providing evidence that they had the technology and materials available, and no doubt they could have achieved the necessary temperature in their cauldron to fuse a primitive form of porcelain. Just what they did produce has long remained a mystery, however.

John Wall was certainly not the complete quack he has been made out to be. He wrote serious medical tracts (as well as believing totally in his Malvern water miracle cures), and was also an influential businessman, able to persuade thirteen acquaintances to put up the sum of £4,500 to finance the new venture. On 4 June 1751 the 'Articles for carrying on the Worcester Tonquin Manufacture' were drawn up as a partnership agreement. These survive, still kept by the present-day factory, and can be seen on display in the Dyson Perrins Museum. They were first published in full by R.W. Binns (Worcester, 1883) and subsequently reproduced by Franklin Barrett (*Worcester Porcelain and Lund's Bristol*, 1953). In addition an extract of the more important details was published by Henry Sandon (*Worcester Porcelain*, 1969). It is therefore necessary only to summarise the articles here.

The original partners and their subscriptions to the capital of the new company were as follows:

William Baylies of Evesham, Worcs., Doctor of Physic	£675
Edward Cave of St Johns Gate, London, Printer	£562.10s.
Richard Holdship of Worcester, Glover	£562.10s.
Richard Brodribb of Bevere, Worcs., Esquire	£225
John Brodribb and John Berwick of Worcester, Woollen Drapers, as Co Partners	£225
Josiah Holdship of Worcester, Malster	£450
John Thorneloe of Worcester, Gent	£337.10s.
Doctor John Wall of Worcester, Doctor of Physic	£225
William Davis of Worcester, Apothecary	£225
Edward Jackson of Worcester, Merchant	£225
Samuel Bradley of Worcester, Goldsmith	£225
John Doharty of Cathedral Precincts, Worcester, Gent	£225
Samuel Pritchett of Knightwick, Worcs., Clerk	£225
William Oliver of Worcester, Gent	£112.10s.

John Wall and William Davis are given as inventors of the 'new Manufacture of Earthen Ware.... under the denomination of Worcester Porcelain'. They agreed as part of the Articles 'to discover for the benefitt of themselves and the other subscribers the real true and full art mystery and secret' of their invention and to find out 'further improvements and secrets.... for the making, finishing or perfecting of the said ware'. They were not to disclose their secret to any other persons under a penalty of £4,000 each, and the secret was to remain the property of the subscribers. Any further discoveries by Wall and Davis were to be reported, if required by a majority of the subscribers, under oath before a magistrate at a monthly meeting of subscribers. The entire process, together with any improvements, was to be written down and deposited in a box with three separate locks and keys, one key kept by Wall and Davis, the other two keys by persons appointed by the subscribers. Although John Wall and William Davis were subscribers themselves, they were to receive £500 in shares as a reward for discovering the secret, with the remaining forty £100 shares divided amongst the subscribers in proportion. In addition, as soon as the manufacture showed a clear profit of £10 per centum per annum, a further £100 would be paid to the inventors.

The articles record that a twenty-one year lease had already been taken out by Richard Holdship (from 16 May 1751) on behalf of the subscribers, in Warmstry House and its gardens and other buildings, although precise details of the premises are not given in the agreement. A committee made up of at least three subscribers appointed by the others would meet at ten o'clock every Tuesday to direct the erection of new buildings, employment of workmen, purchase of materials and to make any other decisions concerning carrying on the manufacture. The committee would report to a monthly meeting of all the subscribers and proper books and accounts were to be kept, inspected from time to time by the subscribers who would receive a full report on the general state of the accounts every six months. The committee would appoint a superintendent to oversee the works and would make known to him the secret art of manufacture. Richard Brodribb was appointed Treasurer.

The Articles contain evidence that some kind of manufacture had been carried on by Dr Wall and William Davis for some time. Provision was made for the 'materialls and utensills [*sic*] that the inventors are now possessed of and which are proper to carry on the work' to be purchased from them at their just and real value. In addition 'the workmen and boys now employed by the inventors' were 'deemed to have entered into the service of the subscribers.... from the eleventh day of May last'. Robert Podmore and John Lyes are specifically mentioned as 'workmen who have for some time been employed by the inventors in the said manufacture'. It was agreed that, in addition to their wages, once the manufacture showed a profit Podmore and Lyes would receive a gratuity from the subscribers to 'better engage their fidelity to keep such part of the secret as may be intrusted to them'. Any payment made to them in this way would be forfeited if they disclosed any part of the secret or deserted the service of the subscribers.

Secrecy was clearly felt to be of the utmost importance. No strangers were to be admitted into the works, and to keep an eye on the employees a clerk of the works was to be appointed to act also as doorkeeper. There was to be an inner door with a different lock, this key kept by Robert Podmore and John Lyes, 'so that they and the clerks may be checks upon each other'. In due course it was hoped that success in the manufacture would enable the subscribers to apply for a patent from the crown to fully secure and protect their secrets. In the meantime all the subscribers had to agree to the same penalty as the inventors, £4,000 to be forfeited if any one of them disclosed knowledge of the secret to any other persons. Likewise all subscribers were obliged to disclose to the others any new discoveries they might make. The deed was duly signed by all fifteen partners.

Richard Holdship had leased Warmstry House on 16 May 1751 for twenty-one years at a rent of £30 per annum. The owner was a glover, William Evett, and it could be that the partners chose Holdship to negotiate the lease because, as a glover himself, he would have been able to use his influence to get the best terms.

It has been assumed that Dr Wall's and William Davis' claims to have invented porcelain were spurious and that instead they intended all along to make use of the formula already worked with some success at Bristol. There could be a certain amount of truth in this, but recent evidence does rather support the Worcester inventors. Some finds from the lowest levels of occupation on the Warmstry House site are illustrated here for the first time (Colour Plate 1) and these reveal types of porcelain hitherto unknown but very different from the products of Bristol. About thirty fragments of flatware (plates or dishes) in different stages of production seem related and composed of a somewhat underfired body decorated in underglaze blue. When these were first discovered in 1979, preliminary examination led me to assume that this underfired, non-vitreous biscuit ware, still soft and very porous, would have gone on to be glazed and fired at a higher temperature rather in the Chinese 'true porcelain' manner. Instead, however, examination of the glazed fragments from the same levels show these to be still porous and not really porcellaneous, part of an experimental production which failed to achieve translucence. One exception, a larger fragment in blue and white (shown in the centre of Colour Plate 1) has reached a higher temperature and is translucent, albeit only just. This has distorted and adhered to kiln debris. Three other fragments appear to be decorated with the same pattern as this piece, a blue painted design of long leaves issuing from circular hollow rocks or roots with tufts of vegetation.

No finished piece of this pattern is known, but the search is now on for a plate or dish, possibly masquerading as Bow. Other decoration in blue occurring on these shards includes a sampan which is not unlike Bristol porcelain, and a fragment of the border of a plate painted with a leaf in thick cobalt oxide, the veins scratched through to the white, a technique copied from delftware. One undecorated piece of a dish with a sharply slice-cut shaped rim is also shown in Colour Plate 1. A preliminary X-ray analysis of a fragment from this group indicates that it is probably neither phosphatic nor steatitic, different from all other known types of early English porcelain. Most importantly, this suggests that there is no soaprock present. The possibility of course exists that these finds are evidence of Dr Wall and William Davis' invention. R.W. Binns wrote in his *Century of Potting in the City of Worcester* (1865) that Worcester made a frit porcelain before their soaprock body, and Binns may at length be proved right in this, even though his own arguments are far from convincing.

Not all of the fragments from this early level show signs of having failed and it is possible, therefore, that some of this body was finished and sold. A plate in an American private collection appears to match most of the potting characteristics of the shards from Worcester. This extraordinary piece is painted in blue with an incredibly naïve pattern (Plate 1) which gives the appearance of being a trial. If this is an example which survived the kiln, then it illustrates clearly the difficulty of painting on such an underfired and thus highly absorbent body. It is most likely that this newly invented porcelain was not the commercial success that the subscribers had hoped for. Instead, faced with ruin, they had to look urgently elsewhere for a new formula to save their investment. I do not believe, as other authors have claimed, that the Worcester manufacture was set up with the intention all along to take over the Bristol works. In desperation, however, taking over the modest successes of Bristol must have seemed their only option.

Richard Holdship bought the process of manufacture, entire stock, utensils and effects of the Bristol porcelain factory on 21 February 1752 on behalf of the Worcester partners, and arrangements were made for the transfer of all the equipment to

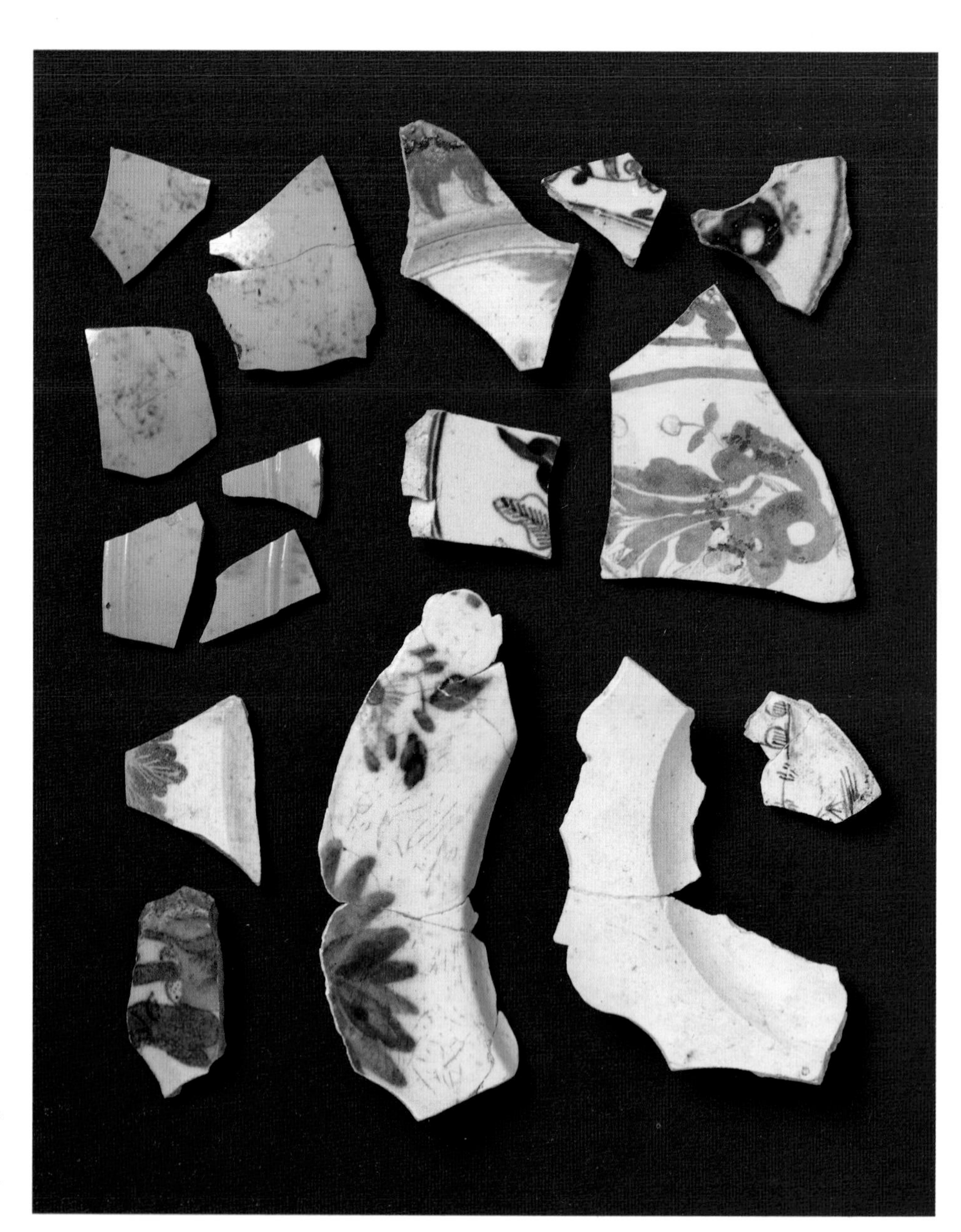

Colour Plate 1. An important group of shards from the very lowest levels of the excavations on the Warmstry House site. The fragments top left are sponged in manganese underglaze and appear to be porcellaneous. c.1751-2.

Worcester. The lease of soaprock mines was bought by Holdship personally at the same time from Benjamin Lund. Holdship agreed to provide the Worcester partners with soaprock as from the previous Christmas, which suggests that this vital material was being sent to Worcester for at least two months before the actual purchase of the Bristol factory. It is unlikely that any porcelain containing soaprock was manufactured at Worcester before the beginning of 1752 and, indeed, the *Gentleman's Magazine* for August 1752 states that 'the sale of this manufacture will begin at the Worcester Music Meeting on 20 September 1752'. Edward Cave, one of the original subscribers, was proprietor of this important monthly journal and understandably, therefore, significant space was given in this issue to a print of the Porcelain Manufactory at Worcester together with an explanation of the buildings (Plate 2). This is not quite the first contemporary reference to the Worcester factory, as the *Bristol Intelligencer* described on 24 July 1752 how the china manufactory in Bristol was 'now united with the Worcester Porcelain Company where for the future the whole business will be carried on'.

A delightful early ribbed bowl, the enamelled pattern combining Japanese, Chinese and Meissen influences in a purely Worcester way, c.1752-3, 4¾in. (12.1 cm) diameter. (Cheekwood Botanical Gardens and Museum of Art, Nashville, Tennessee.)

Just how this early Worcester porcelain differed from Bristol is unclear. Three glazed, blue and white fragments were found at Worcester identical in appearance to known Bristol wares, including the base of a sauceboat embossed with the 'OL' of the Bristol mark (*see* illustration on page 83). These pieces, of course, could have been part of the stock and utensils brought from Bristol, but it is likely that early Worcester blue and white was very similar to Bristol.

The bankruptcy papers of Richard Holdship, discovered by Aubrey Toppin, provide a clue to production at the time of the acquisition of the Bristol works, although they were not drawn up until several years later. These refer to the Bristol factory as a 'porcelain manufactory in imitation of Indian China ware', while Worcester was a 'porcelain manufactory in imitation of Dresden ware'. The purpose of uniting the two manufactories was so that both kinds of ware could be made. This has been interpreted to mean that Bristol was making only blue and white porcelain, while Worcester made coloured ware only. Evidence of earlier production of blue and white at Worcester does contradict this notion, however. Alternatively Worcester could merely have been decorating white porcelain obtained from Bristol or even from elsewhere, following the failure of their own invention.

The Bristol factory, under the direction of Benjamin Lund with backing from William Miller, was established in 1749 by 'one of the principal manufacturers at Limehouse which failed'. The wares do have some similarity to what we now know to have been made at Limehouse. The largest output seems to have been sauceboats, with pickle dishes and a certain range of teawares also made, all decorated in blue in Chinese style. In addition some sauceboats were sold just in white, as well as white figures of Lu Tung-Pin which were marked 'Bristoll 1750'. Underglaze manganese

Plate 1. An early blue and white plate appearing to correspond with wasters from the earliest levels at Worcester, although this precise pattern was not found on the site; 9in. (23cm.), c.1751. (Private collection, photograph Simon Spero.)

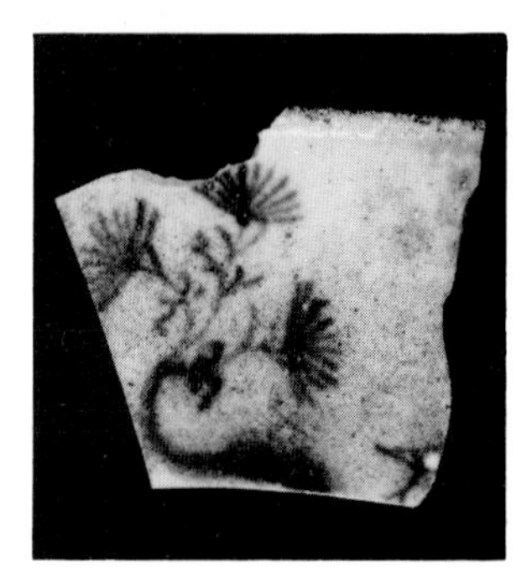

A newly discovered waster from an early bowl or large mug, c.1751-2, with blue painting in a mood similar to that on Plate 1. The shard is glazed, but was badly burnt in what was probably a failed firing. Reproduced actual size.

was also attempted but with little success. For a contemporary account of a visit by Richard Pocock see the entry for **Bristol Porcelain Manufactory**.

Undoubtedly some Bristol workmen moved to Worcester, including Benjamin Lund himself. Dr Watney discovered bankruptcy papers of February 1753 which described Lund as 'late of.... the County of Gloucester, Dealer in Copper and Brass, but now of Worcester, China Maker'. The Bristol style of underglaze painting known as the Three Dot Painter style continued to be made, incorporating distinctive 'Long Eliza' figures and boats. The earliest identified Worcester coloured wares, from 1752 to 1753, fall into three main groups. One comprises plain wheel-thrown and turned shapes such as teawares and larger jugs, while the second includes press-moulded creamboats and sauceboats with rococo panels, in both cases types previously made at Bristol. The third group comprises press-moulded, primarily ornamental shapes in an entirely new style influenced not by Chinese porcelain but by European metalwork. In all cases, however, the enamelling is in oriental style, ranging from simple flower motifs to elaborate bird and figure subjects. Direct copying of Chinese is rare. Instead the factory developed its own distinctive style and palette which combines Chinese *famille rose* with Japanese elements, influenced to a certain extent by Meissen's 'Indian' style of foliate decoration.

It is somewhat curious that many of these shapes are known only in colours, while others are only very occasionally seen in blue and white. This suggests that the output of blue and white Worcester porcelain in the early 1750s was far smaller than coloured wares. Of course this is hardly surprising when you consider that the quality of early

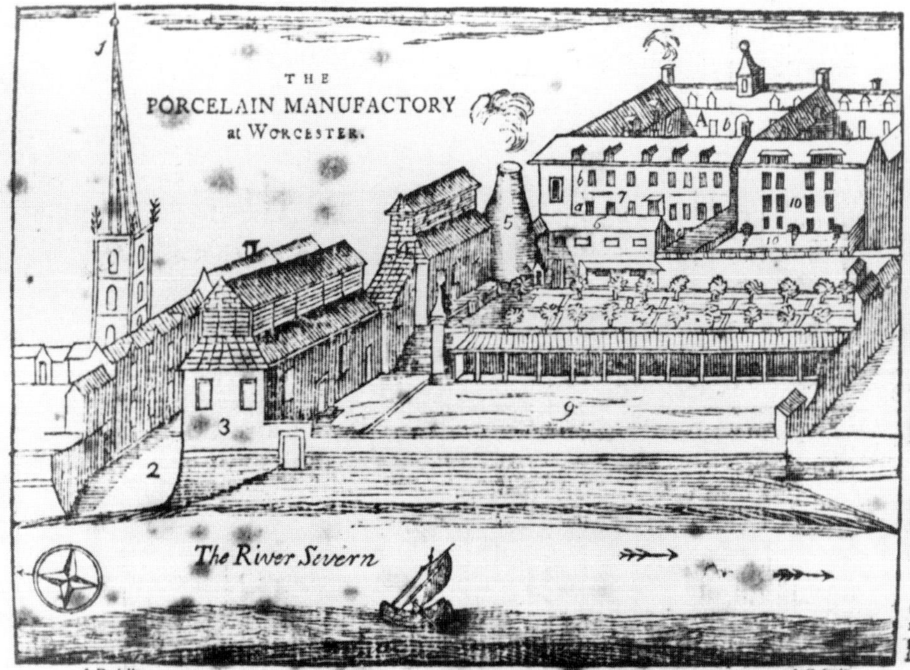

EXPLANATION.

1 St Andrews. 2 Warmſley ſlip. 3 Biſcuit kilns. 4 Glaſing kilns. 5 Great kiln for ſegurs. 6 Preſſing and modelling gallery.— 7 Rooms for throwing, turning, and ſtove drying the ware on the firſt floor *a*, of the chamber floors. 8 The garden. 9 The yard for coals. 10 Mr Evett's houſe and garden, landlord of the premiſes. *b* The eight windows in two large chambers, in which the ware is placed on ſtallions, on the Eaſt and North, where are the painters rooms.——All the beginning of the proceſs is carried on under the quadrangular building ground floor, mark'd A; in its N. W. angle is the great rowl and ring; in the N. E. the horſes turn the ſame, and the levigators near to the rowl. The next (on the ground floor) is the ſlip and treading rooms, behind Number 4 is the glaſing room, behind 5 is the ſecret room on the ground floor.

N. B. A ſale of this manufacture will begin at the *Worceſter* muſic meeting, on *Sept.* 20, with great variety of ware, and, 'tis ſaid, at a moderate price.

Plate 2. This page from The Gentleman's Magazine *of August 1752 is the earliest known announcement of the new porcelain factory at Worcester. Although clumsy, the illustration is in fact surprisingly accurate. (Dyson Perrins Museum.)*

Worcester blue and white was not nearly good enough to compete realistically with Chinese imports. A blue-painted Worcester coffee cup in the British Museum is dated 1753 and this is certainly not a credit to the factory. Gradually this was to change as they achieved better control of their blue painting, but it is for this reason that blue and white Worcester creamboats, for example, usually appear to be later in date than their coloured counterparts. This includes the 'Wigornia' type creamboats embossed with Chinese landscapes, which occur both in colours and in blue. Only one single, coloured example is known with the embossed mark Wigornia moulded on to the base, in the same manner as the embossed Bristol marks. It is tempting to repeat the long-held belief that this is a commemorative piece, the mark (the Latin name for the city of Worcester) celebrating the new factory, but, in spite of its early date, the creamboat is far too sophisticated to be the very first piece made at Worcester.

Sadly no documents survive to identify any of the craftsmen responsible for early Worcester decoration. The factory's success was due in part to the skilful modellers of the ornamental forms, one of whose work is distinguished by a particular style of flower modelling which adorns the rococo ornament on sauceboats, cornucopias and a variety of other forms (*see* Colour Plate 96). Related modelling does not occur on other English porcelain but instead is found on Staffordshire saltglazed stoneware, suggesting the modeller either came to Worcester from Staffordshire or else moved there subsequently when styles at Worcester changed in the mid-1750s.

Most early moulded forms used at Worcester are described as silver shapes and this is clearly where Worcester took their inspiration, although not to the same extent as Chelsea, for example. Instead Worcester seems to have themselves adapted shapes from English rococo silver just as they combined oriental influences into their own style of coloured decoration. Worcester must have been well aware of having to compete with imported Chinese wares and chose not to follow the path of the Bow factory making exact copies, preferring to find its own niche in the market-place by making shapes which could not be obtained from China — hence the contradiction of oriental decoration on European rococo shapes.

Plate 3. A selection of unglazed wasters from levels of the factory site excavations datable to the mid-1750s. The distinctive embossed patterns are fresh and crisp without any covering of glaze. Finds such as these have proved essential in identifying and dating corresponding finished porcelain.

The wonderful teapot (Colour Plate 69) represents the triumph of Worcester's early style, c.1753-4. Generally the factory's decorators knew when to stop and never let coloured enamelling detract from the modelled form, the embossed cartouche panels remaining white for a more subtle effect. Transcribed to blue and white this is seen at its best on the incredible large tureens which presented the factory with such difficulty controlling the shapes during firing.

The marketing of Worcester porcelain was very important and, according to the custom of the time, much was sold by auction in London. To handle the ware sent from Worcester to London for these sales the company established a warehouse in Aldersgate Street, the first mention of which appeared on 1 March 1754, in an advertisement in *The Public Advertiser* discovered by Nancy Valpy:

> For SALE by the CANDLE, At the Royal Exchange Coffee-house, Threadneedle-Street, *On Friday the 15th Inst. at Five in the Afternoon*, ABOUT 40,000 Pieces of China Ware of the Worcester Manufactory; the Commodity will speak for itself. They will be shewn at London House in Aldersgate-Street ...

The following year a further sale was announced, discovered by Geoffrey Wills in the pages of the *General Evening Post*. The issue of 9-12 August 1755 carried an advertisement for a three-day auction sale also at the Royal Exchange Coffee House in Threadneedle Street, on 17-19 September 1755. This was to offer:

> A Large Assortment of **Worcester China-Ware**. This early Advertisement is given that Country Traders may have timely Notice to give their Orders to those whom they deal with in London, as the Proprietors of this Manufactory do not send Riders to vend their Ware

> by Pattern or Description, making London their only Mart of Sale, where their Goods will be shewn open at London-House in Aldersgate-Street. N.B. Sold among the Trade only.

This sale was in fact postponed until 8-10 October 1755 'on account of the large Quantity of Goods which could not be got ready so soon'. A further advertisement for the new sale mentioned:

> About 300 lots of **Worcester China-Ware**, lotted for Traders. The said Goods will be on Shew, in the Worcester-China Ware-House in London-House, in Aldersgate-Street, the 6th and 7th [October].; and such lots as shall remain unsold will be shewn till the Time of Sale on the succeeding Days of Sale.

In addition to auctions, the Worcester company decided to sell direct to the trade through their same London warehouse. They announced in *The Public Advertiser* for 20 March 1756:

> The Proprietors of the Worcester China Manufacture, for the better accommodation of Merchants and Traders, have open'd a Warehouse at London House, Aldersgate Street, London, where they may be supplied every day, between the hours of nine in the morning and three in the afternoon, with a Sortment of Goods, wholesale on the most reasonable terms. Orders are likewise taken, and executed with Despatch, for Home and Foreign Trade.

One very important document survives which gives considerable insight into the goods on offer at Aldersgate Street. This is a wholesale price list of the London Warehouse which, although undated, would appear to be from c.1755-6. This list, preserved in the Dyson Perrins Museum, is reproduced under **London Shops** and is frequently referred to in this *Dictionary*. It gives useful contemporary names to certain shapes which indicate how they were used, as well as listing the price per dozen for the different sizes of each shape. The same items could be bought direct from the factory, as *Aris's Birmingham Gazette* of 27 February 1758 gave notice:

> all Dealers may be supplied with WORCESTER PORCELAIN, in Variety of assortments, at the Warehouse, in Aldersgate-Street London; and at the Manufactory in the City of Worcester.

Sadly there is little to indicate how the shapes on offer in the London warehouse were decorated. Styles were changing and, instead of almost total dependence on oriental designs, by the mid-1750s European styles began to be of greater importance in overglaze decoration, though initially not so much in painted designs but primarily in the area of transfer printing.

The earliest use of printing on Worcester occurs on moulded creamboats and sauceboats as well as plain teawares of 'Scratch Cross' type datable to c.1754. There is reason to believe that some of these so-called 'Smoky Primitive' prints were added to white Worcester pieces by Birmingham enamellers using similar copper plates to those used at the Worcester factory at the same time. Robert Hancock was probably responsible for engraving some of these earliest prints while he was living in Birmingham (or possibly London) prior to his arrival at Worcester c.1756. The designs for these smoky primitives were transferred from the copper plates using a special oil on tissue paper and the finely powdered colour dusted on to the surface of the porcelain where it adhered to the oil. Whereas printing on enamel probably predates similar printing on porcelain, it is likely that Worcester was the first china factory to make use of the technique. Josiah Holdship claimed to have invented printing on porcelain, and this may well be so, although his brother Richard was also likely to have been very much involved at the same time. Early transfer printing at Worcester is

Plate 4. An 18th century watercolour based on a view of Worcester by Paul Sandby. The porcelain factory occupied the central buildings on the left. The unknown artist has corrected the view slightly by omitting a large bottle kiln which Sandby had somewhat imaginatively included in his version. The painting shows the sloping shoreline of the river where the factory was to dump vast quantities of waste material, enabling them to expand their premises after 1770. (Author's collection.)

discussed at greater length elsewhere in this *Dictionary*, especially in the entries for the Holdship brothers and Robert Hancock.

There is still much to be learnt before we can understand fully the important role played by Richard and Josiah Holdship in the early years of the Worcester factory. Richard had spent a great deal of his own money buying the Bristol factory (on behalf of the other subscribers) and the soaprock licence, and in way of compensation the factory had agreed to buy from him a minimum of twenty tons of soaprock per year at £18 per ton. The original lease of Warmstry House was also in his name and when the leasehold became available in 1759 it was Richard Holdship who bought the site, with his brother Josiah providing some of the capital. Richard Holdship was clearly a speculator. In 1756 he bought some small houses next door to the factory and in their place built a 'large commodious dwelling house' for himself. This palatial home can be seen in the superb print of the factory which was engraved by Robert Hancock in 1757 (*see* **Warmstry House**) entitled 'A West Prospect of the Worcester Porcelain Works with Mr Holdship's New Building'. Although Hancock moved the position of Warmstry House itself some way to the north in order to accommodate the mast and rigging of the 'Severn trow' riverboat, this engraving is the most accurate representation of any English china factory surviving from the eighteenth century and our excavations on the site were later able to confirm many of Hancock's details.

Richard Holdship is believed to have left Worcester just two years later in 1759 and in 1761 was declared bankrupt. His movements after leaving Worcester are unclear but when he entered into an agreement with Duesbury and Heath in Derby in 1764 he agreed to provide them with full details of the secret of making soaprock porcelain together with a regular supply of the stone. He was able to provide detailed recipes showing that he had a considerable understanding of porcelain manufacture as well as the process of transfer printing.

Although Holdship was in breach of the original Articles of 1751, he was not the first person to defect with the secret of soaprock porcelain. In spite of the subscribers' 'gratuities' to maintain his fidelity, Robert Podmore left Worcester and on 14 June 1755 signed an agreement with Richard Chaffers and Philip Christian in Liverpool. In return for a guinea a week and one twelfth share in any net profits, Podmore was to reveal the secret of 'making earthenware in imitation of or to resemble china ware'. In 1756 Chaffers was in Cornwall to arrange his own regular supply of soaprock which he was to use to make a very similar material to that made at Worcester. The Worcester subscribers had never applied for their patent and now had lost the monopoly they had taken such pains to protect. There is no evidence, however, that either Podmore or Holdship were pursued for breaking their agreements.

One reason the Worcester company may not have been unduly worried about the defections is that they had been able to make significant improvements in the quality and output of their own porcelain and their fame was spreading as a result. By 1755 their blue and white porcelain was far superior to any other of English manufacture and could now be regarded as a reasonable alternative to Chinese porcelain, both in terms of quality and price. A Bristol china dealer announced in the *Bath Advertiser* on 31 January 1756:

> This is to give notice that I have lately purchased a large assortment of enamel'd and Blue and White useful Worcester China ware which will be sold, at the Warehouse in Castle Green, cheaper, better in quality and in greater variety than has hitherto been exposed to sale there. The lowest price will be marked on each piece of ware according as it is more or less perfect, without Abatement, unless to wholesale dealers who shall be allowed a discount for present money... which will make it greatly their interest to deal for this ware, with their humble servant Robert Carpenter, N.B. Good Blue and White Tea Cups and Saucers, at 3s 6d per set, Quart Basons 10d, Half Pints 7d, and all other sorts in proportion.

Complete tea services were becoming far more important to the factory than sauce-boats and ornamental shapes. Production increased significantly, especially in blue and white, and there must have been a shortage of trained painters. In order to keep up with demand the factory introduced patterns for tea services which were quick and unexacting to paint, so that their better artists could concentrate on the more costly coloured wares. Even so there was always a need for more painters. On 10-12 December 1761 the London *General Evening Post* carried a notice:

> **Worcester** *Porcelain Manufacture.*
> *WANTED*
> **Painters** in Blue and White: Good Workmen, who are sober and diligent, will meet with proper Encouragement, by applying to the Manufactory in Worcester

The shortage of blue painters was partly alleviated by transfer printing in underglaze blue, although sadly very little is known about its introduction. There is little doubt that Worcester were the first to make use of blue printing and that it was not employed until several years after overglaze printing had been perfected. The King of Prussia prints show the superb quality that could be achieved in onglaze black printing by 1757, but it was impossible to print in such detail directly on to the biscuit porcelain and prevent heavy blurring when glazed. Some copper plates with finely etched detail for use overglaze were partly smoothed and re-cut deeper to produce stronger images suitable for blue printing. Other patterns were specifically designed for use underglaze, strongly engraved without delicate shading. These earliest Chinese

Plate 5. A cabbage leaf moulded mask spouted jug or 'Dutch Jug'. The decoration comprises panels of Chinese riverscapes in puce monochrome, with Japanese style chrysanthemums and red scrollwork bands on a yellow ground, and a border of European coloured flowers. Such a combination, which is actually quite successful, can only have originated at Worcester; c.1758-60. (Sotheby's/Kiddell Papers.)

riverscape and floral prints occur in blue and white on shapes which normally can be dated to c.1756-8. Certainly by 1760 underglaze blue printing had been perfected and the factory was well on its way to mass-production.

While blue and white designs remained exclusively oriental in style, the influence of Meissen had altered the direction of Worcester's coloured wares. Import restrictions meant that German porcelain was not openly sold in England, although a certain amount was privately owned and had been made available to the Chelsea factory. Although we like to think of Worcester painters copying fine Meissen, it is probably more correct to think of them imitating Chelsea in order to compete in the London market. Worcester employed several fine landscape painters, possibly from Chelsea originally, and many fine presentation jugs and mugs were made in the late 1750s. Surprisingly, Chelsea had not discovered a market for armorial decoration, but instead Worcester was to fill this gap with some of the most remarkable of all English porcelain. The Brodribb jugs (*see* **Brodribb, John and Richard**) with their stunning rococo cartouches and detailed landscapes, are perfect evidence of why the factory by this time should have had no fears of serious competition.

The painter responsible for pieces like these has been the subject of much discussion, centred around a mug in the British Museum signed by I. Rogers and dated 1757. Initial publication of a photograph of this mug led collectors to attribute most Worcester bird and landscape painting and some flower painting from the late 1750s to the mysterious Rogers, but more detailed study, initiated by Franklin Barrett, shows that many different workmen were responsible. The hand of the signed I. Rogers mug does occur on other pieces and, while competent, is not the finest of the artists; meanwhile other hands who painted in the same style are far inferior.

The Meissen influence (via Chelsea) can sometimes be very direct, as for example certain vase shapes and flower painting. The Worcester factory's first ground colour, yellow, which was in use by 1757, was certainly inspired by Meissen. In addition there

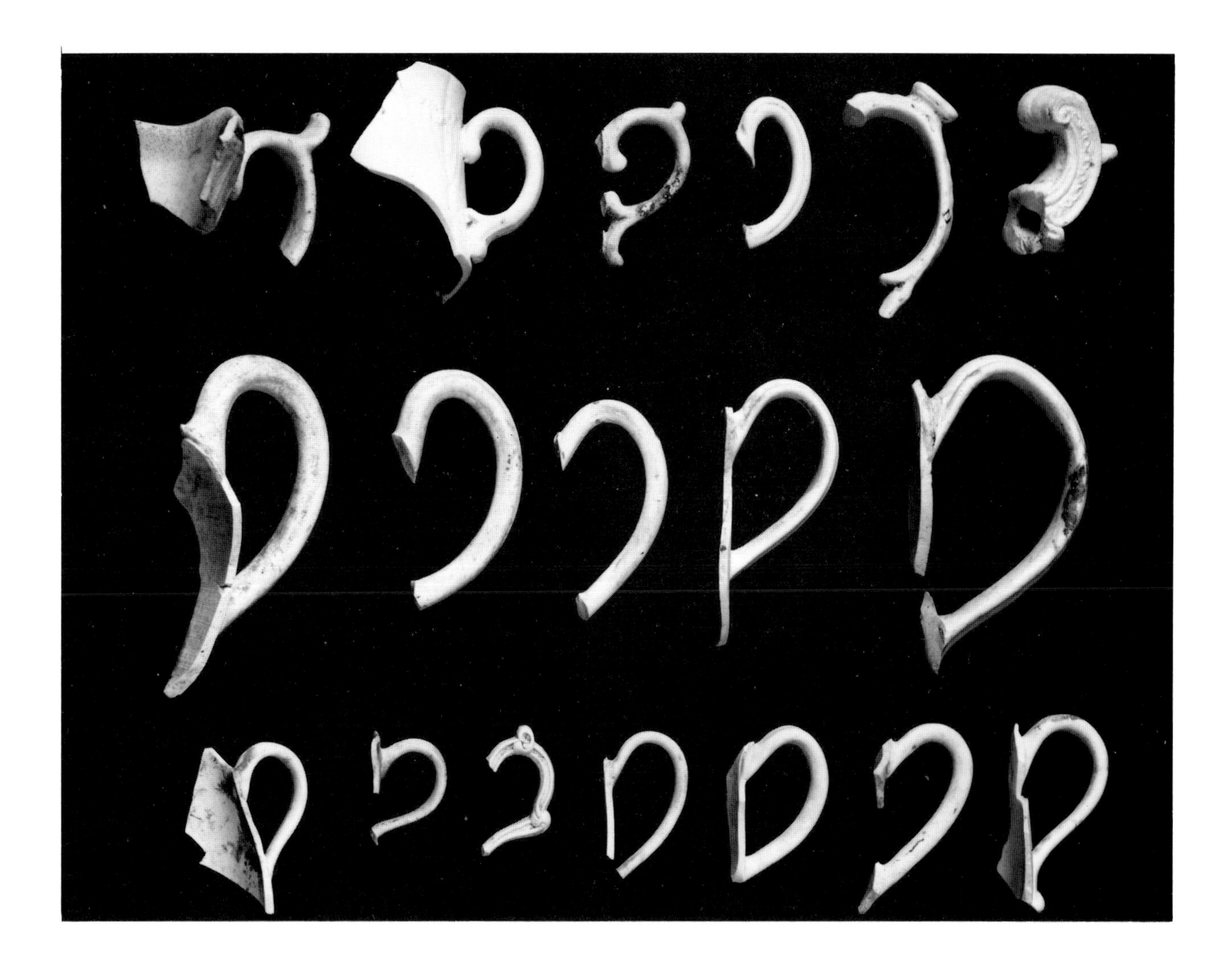

Plate 6. Worcester handles were always formed with great care and many are distinctive. These examples are all unglazed and were excavated on the factory site, 1750s-70s.

is a less direct influence which, none the less, has origins in early Meissen painting. Worcester had rarely copied Chinese or Japanese porcelain exactly in their early designs, although by the 1760s a certain number of oriental patterns were introduced with little or no adaptation. Meissen had followed a similar course and created its own style of floral landscape decoration which became known as *indianische Blumen* or *Indian Flowers*. This combined Chinese and Japanese elements into altogether more splendid compositions. Worcester copies of this Meissen style are rare, but instead Worcester created its own style which borrows heavily from a combination of Japanese *Kakiemon* and Meissen *Indian Flowers*. I prefer to call this Worcester style 'Rich Kakiemon' and it is typified by patterns such as *Jabberwocky*. The style is seen at its most splendid on a series of large hexagonal vases dating from c.1765-70 (*see* **Rich Kakiemon**), a style which can rightly be claimed as a Worcester invention.

Various claims have been made over the years as to the origin of Worcester's scale blue ground, with suggestions that it is based on Chinese porcelain or Meissen, but I prefer to think of this also as a purely Worcester creation. To overcome the difficulty of controlling a solid underglaze blue ground the factory initially tried powder blue for a softer mottled ground, and then hit upon the idea of painting fine scales in two different strengths of colour. After glazing a most successful effect was achieved and was to prove very popular. Amongst the earliest examples known is a teapot in the Frank Lloyd Collection in the British Museum which combines a scale blue ground with *Rich Kakiemon* flowering chrysanthemums. Beneath the spout is gilded 'No. 45' which refers to issue No. 45 of the *North Briton*, published in April 1763 and of special significance to the supporters of the social reformer John Wilkes. A date of 1763 has been given to this teapot which has been used as evidence that these two important styles of decoration were firmly established by then, but the use of No. 45 as a sign of support for Wilkes continued for several years and c.1765-6 is probably a more realistic date for the introduction of scale blue.

The high standards of Worcester's enamelled and gilded decoration during the 1760s tend to overshadow the importance of the factory's run-of-the-mill production. An increased output of blue and white tea services and the opening up of an export trade brought prosperity to the factory and meant that they did not have to rely for their income on the much more difficult, albeit prestigious top end of the ornamental market. Several contemporary newspaper accounts reflect the popularity of Worcester porcelain for everyday use. The *Annual Register* of 1763 discussed foreign and Chelsea ornamental porcelain and the high cost of their useful china. It goes on:

> We have indeed, here, many other manufactories of porcelain, which are sold at a cheaper rate than any that is imported; but except the Worcester, they all wear brown, and are subject to crack, especially the glazing, by boiling water; the Worcester has a good body, scarce inferior to that of Eastern china; it is equally tough, and its glazing never cracks or scales off. But this is confined comparatively to few articles; the tea-table indeed it completely furnishes; and some of it is so well enamelled as to resemble the finest foreign china so that costly sets which are broken it makes up without a palpable difference. Yet somehow or another, this manufacture has not found its way to the dining-table except perhaps in sauce boats, toys for pickles, and hors d'oeuvres; but by communicating this defect to the public, some remedy may probably be found for it...

The *Gentleman's Magazine* published a very similar account in the same year, and in May 1763 the *Oxford Journal* was equally complimentary, adding:

> ...The great abuse of it is the selling of other far inferior kinds of ware for Worcester, by which both the buyer is deceived to his loss and the credit of the manufacture is injured. The most valuable part of all, and which principally calls for notice, is the extraordinary strength and cheapness of the common sort of blue and white Worcester porcelain; and let any person but impartially consider the difference, in these respects, between this and that of an equil degree, though hardly of equil beauty, imported from abroad, and he will find the advantage is considerable and in favour of the former, that if he has any degree of candour, he must see and acknowledge his obligations to a manufacture which not only supplies an ornament fitted for the homes and cabinets of the rich and curious, but affords an elegant and desirable furniture calculated by its ease of purchase, for general and ordinary use.

In order to increase production of this 'common sort of blue and white', emphasis was put on certain painted patterns which were made up of solid blocks of colour and plain lines. Patterns such as *Cannonball* and *Mansfield* did not require any skill with perspective and a large team of junior painters must have worked on these two patterns alone. At the same time the use of printing was increased still further, enabling the factory to decorate a blue and white printed service in a fraction of the time it would have taken to paint. Finds from different levels of the factory site excavations were recorded in table form by Lawrence Branyan, Neal French and myself for our *Worcester Blue and White Porcelain*. By counting the number of painted and printed shards in each level we found that during the 1760s there was a steady rise in the use of blue printing, followed by a very sharp rise indeed after c.1770. Many underglaze blue painters probably changed over to painting scale blue which was still growing in popularity. R.W. Binns reported, however, that a strike in 1770 by blue painters against the increased use of printing led to many painters leaving the factory. No evidence has

Plate 7. A selection of blue and white Worcester porcelain, all c.1765-70. During this period the factory's output was enormous as well as being remarkably consistent both in quality and design. (Dyson Perrins Museum.)

been found to confirm this account, but there is no doubt that some Worcester painters went to Plymouth and Derby at about this time.

Public taste had changed considerably in the decade after 1760. Simple Meissen styles were somewhat old-fashioned and had been replaced by richer, more colourful wares such as the *Rich Kakiemon* vases already alluded to. The new influence of French rococo, and especially the porcelain of Sèvres, had led the Chelsea factory to change direction with Worcester following soon after. The important features of the new French style were partly asymmetrical rococo shapes and strongly coloured grounds. Deep 'mazarine' blue and claret became the important ground colours at Chelsea during the Gold Anchor period in the 1760s. Worcester's wet blue and scale blue grounds were in many respects technically advanced on Chelsea, although Worcester lacked the courage to introduce any of the exciting ornamental vase shapes for which Chelsea is justly famous. Worcester believed much more in the decoration and kept to plain shapes on which to display their 'Fancy Birds' and new, more formal style of flower painting reserved against scale blue, or apple green borders. These rich tea services and vases had to sell in the competitive London market, offered alongside Chelsea and other English factories, and at the same time had to compete with Worcester porcelain decorated in London at the workshop of James Giles.

Giles came from a family of china painters who had been decorating Chinese porcelain in London since the 1720s. The family seems to have had some sort of connection with the City of Worcester and probably decorated Worcester as well as Chinese and Bow porcelain, fired in their kilns in Kentish Town from 1756 and subsequently by James Giles in Berwick Street, Soho, from at least 1763. Giles was a retailer as well as a decorator and in 1767 he drew up a formal agreement with the Worcester factory for them to supply him with white porcelain. It has been claimed that Giles became the sole 'Enamelling Branch' of the Worcester factory from this date with no significant coloured ware at all decorated at Worcester. A study of surviving pieces, however, as well as advertisements by Giles and the Worcester company, does not begin to support such a suggestion.

The continuing importance of London as a market for fine porcelain is suggested by an advertisement placed by the Worcester factory and their London manager, John Spurling, in the *Public Advertiser* of 19 December 1767:

> The chief Proprietor and acting manager for the Proprietors of the Worcester Porcelain Manufactory having moved some thousand Pounds worth of their best Wares, from their Warehouse in the City to the large Exhibition Room, Spring Gardens, Charing Cross, the chief Manager....hath marked the Lowest prices on each sample of the said Ware, the same as at their Manufactory at Worcester, with the usual Discount to Trades. This Manufactory is more esteemed by real Judges than any other making in this Kingdom, being arrived at such great Beauty and Perfection. The Nobility and Gentry, who want particular Patterns of fine Goods made, are desired to leave their Orders in Time at the said Room, as the Reasonableness of the Prices makes them have so great a Demand, that they have now more to execute than they can perform for some Time.

The Spring Gardens exhibition rooms also sold Chelsea porcelain and was only around the corner from the shop premises of James Giles which he called the 'Worcester Porcelaine Warehouse' in his advertisement in the same journal on 28 January 1768, just the following month. There is no doubt from the wording that Giles was responding directly to the factory's announcement.

> J.GILES, China and Enamel Painter, Proprietor of the *Worcester Porcelaine Warehouse,* up one Pair of Stairs in Cockspur Street, facing the lower end of the Haymarket, begs Leave to acquaint the Nobility, Gentry &c., that the said Warehouse is daily opened with a great Variety of articles of the said Manufactory, useful and ornamental, curiously painted in the Dresden, Chelsea and Chinese Tastes, superior to anything before exhibited to the Public on that Porcelaine.
> As the enamelling Branch is performed in London by the said J.Giles, and under his Inspection, this Warehouse will be daily supplied with a Variety of new Goods, which will be sold as cheap as at the Manufactory, or any Place in Town, with the usual Discount to the Trade. As the Proprietor has a great Variety of white Goods by him, Ladies and Gentlemen may depend upon having their Commands executed immediately, and painted to any Pattern they shall chuse.

Giles repeated this notice three months later but omitted 'Proprietor of the Worcester Porcelain Warehouse', possibly in the face of a complaint from John Spurling. Three weeks later the factory retaliated with a further announcement, worded even more strongly and confirming that a very unhappy alliance existed between the manufactory and Mr Giles:

> *Exhibition Room, Spring Gardens, Charing Cross.* As several of the Nobility and Gentry &c. have lately been disappointed of seeing the large and curious Collection of the *Worcester China Manufactory*; as some of their Ware is advertised at another Room, painted in London, the chief Proprietor and acting Manager has sent some thousand Pounds Worth of the said Ware from their late Warehouse in Aldersgate Street, to be sold in the same Exhibition Room, where will be sent every Week, new Variety of the finest Goods. Curious Patterns that are wanted will be made in a short time not to be distinguished from the Original, as the Proprietors have engaged the best Painters from Chelsea &c. Any orders will be executed in the highest taste and much cheaper than can be afforded by any Painters in London.

It is difficult to know just what to make of all these rival claims. Giles' surviving account book shows that he purchased white porcelain until 1771 when the agreement was effectively terminated, although at this time he presumably held a large stock. He would have continued as a decorator until 1776 when, faced with difficulties, the remaining stock of James Giles, Chinaman, was sold by auction. The catalogue survives of a previous sale of Giles' stock at Christie's in March 1774 and this has provided vital clues to identifying the London styles. A previous London auction, held at Christie's in December 1769, appears to have contained only wares sent from the Worcester factory or their London warehouse, again providing important information.

What is clear is that from the early to mid-1760s until 1776 Giles and his decorators sold a great deal of Worcester porcelain which they had painted. Certain styles, patterns and painting characteristics have been positively identified as Giles' work, in contrast to decoration which undoubtedly continued to be carried out within the Worcester factory. There will probably be many pieces which can never be attributed, and at all times care has to be taken in labelling any piece as the work of a London decorator.

When the factory claimed in 1768 to have 'engaged the best painters from Chelsea &c.', these would have included two very significant artists whose work can be identified from signed vases. John Donaldson was an accomplished figure painter who was engaged on a series of impressive vases with wet blue grounds. Mythological and rustic subjects were treated in a spirited manner, if lacking in delicacy. Rare chinoiserie or Watteau-style figures on vases and chocolate cups are also likely to be his work although Donaldson's stay at the Worcester factory was clearly only short. Jefferyes Hammett O'Neale probably remained at Worcester longer and in his turn had considerable influence on other painters at the factory.

Large panels on vases gave him the opportunity to paint dramatic equestrian figures, but his best work was majestic studies of exotic animals on the reverses of these vases. Because they are more readily available, O'Neale is best known for fable subjects painted on a number of dessert services c.1770. Most, but not all, fables on Worcester porcelain are by O'Neale, for it must be remembered that there was at least one other accomplished animal painter who tended to use more intricate vegetation in his landscape vignettes, on a white ground rather than in full landscape panels. No records survive, but Donaldson and O'Neale had both probably left the factory by 1772. Other less accomplished hands continued to work in the same styles, having learnt from O'Neale particularly his method of painting landscapes using solid washes of colour on foreground rocks and curious purple and yellow colouring to present atmosphere in the clouds and sky.

While the influence of Chelsea is strongly felt, another London style introduced at Worcester at about the same time was to have even greater impact on the factory's output. The mark of a letter 'T' which occurs on Bow figures from the 1760s is the first clue to the origin of a modeller and so-called 'repairer', who had joined Worcester by c.1768. The impressed or embossed marks 'T', 'To' or 'IT' occur on a very different style of Worcester shapes including added decoration similar to that previously used at Bow.

The new style can best be seen on dessert baskets. In addition to the simple circular shapes made since the 1750s, new oval moulded baskets were introduced. The handles were gnarled twigs with flower and leaf terminals, similar in modelling to elaborate decoration applied to the covered cream bowls and stands which have incorrectly become known as chestnut baskets. Versions of other shapes known previously at Bow were so-called 'Frill Vases' encrusted with elaborate porcelain flower garlands hung from mask heads; also shell salts and multiple centrepieces for pickle, and tubs of modelled flowers. All these shapes occur with the 'T' or 'To' mark which used to be attributed to a modeller called Tebo. Instead research by Geoffrey Godden has followed this potter's career after leaving Worcester c.1770-2, to Bristol, then to Caughley, ending his days back in Worcester at Chamberlain's factory in the 1790s. He can now be identified almost certainly as John Toulouse.

Toulouse would have modelled some shapes as his mark sometimes appears embossed, having been cut directly into the moulds. In other cases he probably assembled the complicated shapes from moulded parts and applied the hand-made flowers, an important role known as 'repairing'. Needless to say he would have had others working for him and not every flower will be by his own hands, but John Toulouse's influence on Worcester's productions was widespread.

One feature closely associated with the new style of flower modelling is the 'Hot Cross Bun Bud', a cross cut into a tiny ball of clay to form a flower bud. This occurs on many baskets and vases and was the first clue which led to the identification of the very rare Worcester figures. Mrs Powys and Captain Roach both visited the factory in 1771 and their different accounts (quoted in full in Appendix 2) both mention watching figures being made there. Only eight models have so far been identified, among them a pair of Turks which have been recorded with the impressed 'IT' mark. If one believes these to be the work of John Toulouse, then his training at Bow is apparent. By this period, however, Bow figure making had been in decline and the Worcester figures were far inferior to contemporary Derby. Strong colours and gilding are the only redeeming features which distinguish Worcester figures. Worcester must have been aware of their limitations and did not persevere in this direction.

John Toulouse's apparent departure for Bristol, at about the same time as Donaldson and O'Neale, coincided with a very serious phase in the factory's history. Its lease was due to expire and several of the partners wished to retire. Because there was no obvious agreement between these and the few who wanted to continue the business, it was decided that the whole factory should be put up for sale. The announcement of the sale appeared in *Berrow's Worcester Journal* of 5 December 1771:

> To be Sold by Public Auction, in one lot, to the best bidder, on Thursday, the Second day of January 1772, at Eleven o'clock in the Forenoon, at.... the Hop Pole Inn in the city of Worcester-
>
> The genuine process of making Worcester Porcelain, together with the stock, estate, and effects of the Worcester Porcelain Company, comprehending the stock of materials, moulds, models, tools, utensils, kilns, &c., employed in the said manufacture; the household goods and furniture in the manufactory house at Worcester, and the stock of ware, finished and unfinished, lying in the warehouses and rooms of the said manufactory house..... Also the leases of the said manufactory house in Worcester, and of the mills at Astley, in the County of Worcester, now occupied by the Company....., and the Company's interest in the lease of a mine of clay in Cornwall.
>
> Further particulars may be known by applying to the principal clerk at the manufactory house in Worcester aforesaid, or to the agent at the Company's warehouse, No. 12, in Gough Square, Fleet Street, London.
>
> N.B. The stock of ware and goods in the said warehouse in London will be sold separately in London, some time after the above sale in Worcester, of which due notice will be given: in the meantime, the trade will be carried on there without interruption, and all orders duly attended to and supplied.

The sale took place and the company was sold for £5,250. The vendors were given as 'John Wall Sr, John Salway, David Henry, Germain Lavie, Rev. Thomas Pritchett, Rev. Thomas Vernon, Rev. Benjamin Blayney, Mary Blayney, Richard Cook, Henry Cook, William Davis, William Oliver, John Thorneloe, Samuel Bradley* (*by assignee Robert Blayney). Following some kind of prior arrangement, however, the purchasers were a consortium of previous shareholders. The buyer in the auction was Thomas Vernon who then temporarily signed over the company for a further 10s. to Dr Wall's son, John Wall jun. Soon afterwards the transfer of ownership was completed with payment to Wall jun. of a further 5s. From 3 March

1772 the new partners were John Wall sen., William Davis sen., William Davis jun., Robert Hancock, Thomas Vernon and Richard Cook.

This also proved to be only a temporary arrangement. Richard Cook died and his widow Catherine inherited his share. Then on 31 October 1774 the deeds of Warmstry House record that:

> ...reciting that controversies, disputes, and differences having arisen between the said co-partners touching the said Robert Hancock's share of said stock, they the said J Wall, Thomas Vernon, W Davis, W Davis, and C Cook, for preventing all such controversies, touching the matter aforesaid, had agreed with the said Robert Hancock for the purchase of all of his share and interest therein for the price of 900 pounds, being an equal share of one sixth.

It is almost certain that behind this disagreement was Hancock's involvement with Thomas Turner. Turner had probably begun as a fellow engraver alongside Hancock at Worcester and seems to have attained a position of some authority within the factory. The account records kept by Giles in London show that purchases of white porcelain were made from Mr Thos. Turner in Worcester, and Turner must have had access to the process of making soaprock porcelain. By 1775 and probably earlier, Turner was firmly established at Caughley in Shropshire, in direct competition with Worcester. Robert Hancock joined him, not as an engraver but apparently to manage the Salopian China Warehouse in Bridgnorth. It is reasonable to assume that a number of workmen accompanied Turner to Caughley, where blue and white transfer printing was to succeed at the expense of Worcester's declining blue and white production.

In 1774 Dr John Wall retired. In spite of his support for the virtues of Malvern water, he chose to live out his final years in Bath. He retained his shares in the china works and seemed happy to leave the running of the factory to his long-standing friend William Davis. In order to tidy up his affairs, just two weeks before his death, on 10 June 1776, Dr Wall sold his share of one fifth of the company to Davis for £1,100, approximately what it had cost him in 1772 but now well below its true value. Dr Wall died on 27 June 1776 and was interred in Bath Abbey. In December of the same year Catherine Cook sold her one-fifth share to the remaining three partners for £2,000. The company continued to trade as William Davis and Co. and had clearly increased in value since its sale in 1772.

Blue and white continued to be made in great quantity, much of it for the increasingly important export trade, but from comparison of pieces surviving from the 1770s the factory was clearly less particular about quality. Maybe they let the copper plates become worn which resulted in blurred impressions, but, whatever the reason, they did not seem to mind selling vastly inferior pieces, probably as 'seconds' or even third quality for a reduced price. These cannot have helped their reputation, however.

At the other extreme, though, some of Worcester's coloured wares made under William Davis' direction deserve the greatest respect. There were still many customers willing to pay the price for top quality porcelain and Worcester had found its place in the market for richly decorated teawares and the increasingly important area of dessert services. Coloured grounds of apple green and turquoise were popular, but underglaze blue continued to dominate their production. Wet blue was still difficult to control and used mostly on flatware — dessert plates and dishes where there was less problem with the ground running. Considering the time it must have taken to painstakingly paint the fine scale blue, the sheer quantity of this form of decoration which survives today is evidence of the size of Worcester's market in wares which would have been very expensive.

Because of the costly labour the factory had to put into the painting and gilding of these pieces, they chose to complete only pieces which had survived the glaze kiln in reasonable state without bad blemishes or blurred and dribbled underglaze blue grounds. Any substandard pieces were put on one side and a sizeable stock of reject blue-ground pieces seems to have been built up. These appear to have been disposed of to an outside decorator, either at the time of the sale of the factory in 1772 or just a few years later. Because they were cheaper, these did not merit the kind of quality afforded by the Giles workshop and instead only a limited palette was used without gilding. The painting is mostly in *Kakiemon* style and the rims and panels are usually edged in red enamel instead of gold. For this reason I have designated these pieces the 'Red Line Bordered Group', as it is not known where they were decorated.

The 1770s saw several changes in public taste which become noticeable in Worcester's productions. Oriental decoration became far less important than previously, possibly because of cheaper Chinese imports with which the factory chose not to compete. Blue and white patterns of European flowers and landscape prints became their main production, with even the popular Chinese style patterns such as the 'Fence' print adopting a more English flavour. In coloured wares the *Rich Kakiemon* style of oriental-inspired foliage and Jabberwocky-type beasts was mostly replaced with European landscapes and, in particular, ever more elaborate 'Fancy Birds'. The direct influence on these, as with most of the factory's productions in the 1770s, came not from Meissen as previously but from France and the porcelain of Sèvres.

Finely painted panels on coloured grounds epitomised the Sèvres style. Giles in London was directly influenced by the coloured grounds to a much greater extent than the Worcester factory, but other influences from Sevres become very apparent in factory decorated wares. The most important although seldom appreciated influence was in the style of flower painting used on the cheaper productions. A formal style developed at Worcester, carefully painted in bright colours with stylised details and a flat appearance with little sense of depth to the painting. This lacks the delicacy of Sèvres, caused by the very soft French glaze, but the design is far removed from the more realistic German style used previously at Worcester.

A new kind of pattern copied from Sèvres was introduced c.1772 and remained popular at Worcester until the early 1780s. The variety of designs known as 'Hop Trellis' were not unique to Worcester but no other English factory attempted such a wide range of different patterns and with such care and general elegance. There is evidence that some *Hop Trellis* patterns were decorated by Giles in London, but most were produced at the factory. Worcester was famed for local hop growing, hence the name given by collectors later on, but in reality the berried vegetation festooned on coloured poles owes its origins to Sèvres from the 1750s. Coloured borders with scale, herring-bone or caillouté (pebble) effects were used on other designs such as the *Earl Manvers* pattern, and can be particularly successful, combining rococo with just a hint of the new classical styles which were dominating public taste in London in the 1770s.

Worcester's principal English rivals, the now combined factories of Chelsea-Derby, and Richard Champion's factory in Bristol, were influenced by the neo-classical movement in art to a much greater extent than Worcester ever was. Although Giles painted dessert services with classical urns and borders of palmettes as early as 1774, and also gilded services with husk festoons, rams' heads and *paterae*, the Worcester factory were slow to pick up on this new taste and their share of the market undoubtedly suffered as a result. William Davis was himself growing old and the factory started to sink into a very serious decline, both in terms of artistry and general quality. Worcester's few

Plate 8. Part of a typical tea service from the 1780s featuring popular fluted shapes. Wares of this type are usually given earlier dates but the bright tone of the underglaze blue border indicates a true date nearer 1785. Crescent marks. (Phillips.)

classical patterns date from the late 1770s and 1780s and, with the almost sole exception of the Lord Stormont service, were lacking in original design.

The blue grounds which had been so successful in the previous decade had grown old-fashioned. After c.1775 the production of scale blue and wet blue was greatly reduced in favour of a new style which was more in keeping with the new classical ideals of the time. Deep underglaze blue was used for borders only, enriched with gilding and combined with a great many patterns, principally on strongly fluted teaware shapes and scalloped dessert wares. These blue bordered patterns are typified by the patterns associated with the names of Lord Henry Thynne and Earl Dalhousie, confusing titles as there are a great many variations of these designs. All are painted with landscapes, usually in panels framed with turquoise husk patterns as a token classical element. The painting owed much to the influence of J.H. O'Neale, but had become very formal and to some extent almost childlike. The blue-bordered patterns can mostly be attributed to the period c.1778-85 (a date of 1784 appears under a mug in the Godden Reference Collection), although this whole class has in the past been given dates far too early. The designs are strong, the gilding usually good, but on the whole the quality of decoration on what were Worcester's most expensive products at the time can often be very disappointing.

The factory continued to live in the shadow of its former glory while Caughley, its principal rival for the blue and white market, produced much higher quality printed tea services. The decline of the Worcester company is reflected in its value, set at £10,000 in 1776 when the Widow Cook sold her share, but having shrunk to only £3,000 in 1783. Thomas Vernon and William Davis and his son decided to sell up completely and on 10 April 1783 the price was agreed between them and their London agent, Thomas Flight, the £3,000 to be paid in instalments over one year, suggesting that Flight was the only interested buyer at the time. Thomas Flight bought the company for his two sons, hoping that their experience of the London retail market could breathe new life into the works and reverse its fortune.

Thomas Flight seems to have done little, however, until his sons John and Joseph

Plate 9. Typical productions of the early Flight period, c.1785-92. The printed teawares are in bright underglaze blue only, while the Royal Lily pattern mug and shanked teabowl are painted in blue with added gilding, crescent and disguised numeral marks. (Dyson Perrins Museum.)

were old enough to assume control. Standards at Worcester continued to decline, with Thomas Flight in London seemingly more interested in purchasing French porcelain for sale there. Any fine decoration that was carried out at Worcester had for some time been under the direction of Robert Chamberlain sen. and his son Humphrey sen. Robert Chamberlain had been apprenticed to Richard Holdship as a 'pot painter' more than thirty years earlier and had ascended to this most senior position leaving the company vulnerable. In 1786 the Chamberlains set up on their own as decorators, with an agreement to continue to decorate for Flights. Most of the painters and gilders had been employed by the Chamberlains and when, two years later in c.1788, the Chamberlains appear to have broken away completely, Flights' factory was suddenly left in a desperate position without any fine decorators, and a blue and white production which was poorly controlled and out of date.

John Flight came to Worcester in July 1788 to take charge and he recorded in his diary the desperate situation the factory was in. Finally unable to agree with the Chamberlains, John Flight brought Charlotte Hampton from London to take charge of decorating and 'teach us the gilding & assist us for 3 years'. With her help Flights' factory began the slow road to recovery, but had to cope with other serious problems. The works foreman, named Shaw, had been defrauding the firm, but Flights relied on his knowledge of the processes. When he died John Flight had to buy his papers from Shaw's widow in order to carry on. Whole kiln loads of ware were being spoilt and John Flight had to set about building new kilns. Very gradually things started to improve.

The visit of George III to Worcester in August 1788 gave Flights great encouragement. The King visited their factory and spoke with John Flight about the future. Assisted by the Royal Warrant, on the King's advice they opened a new retail shop in London at 1 Coventry Street where initially they sold more French porcelain than their own. From this they learnt what styles the public wanted to buy. In September 1788 John Flight visited France to see porcelain factories there principally to 'improve our shapes', and he also went to Newcastle in Staffordshire to 'seek after a modeller'. He found one and engaged him for three years. Amongst the many French styles introduced at this time, their most important new teaware shape, called 'shanked' with moulded spiral flutes, was put into production by 1790 (Plate 9).

Flights were forced by economic pressures to move in a new direction. Unable to compete with cheap Chinese imported porcelain and Staffordshire creamware and pearlware, John Flight made the important decision to move up-market. All underglaze blue printing was abandoned and simple copies of Chinese patterns were left to Staffordshire porcelain makers such as New Hall. Instead all Flight porcelain was decorated to a very high standard using fine gold, even the simple sprig patterns, in puce and gold for example, which looked very elegant on the sharply moulded French shapes. On plainer shapes bright underglaze blue was successfully combined with the very finest gilding to produce some very rich patterns.

Two important orders from the Duke of Clarence in 1789 confirmed that Flights were well on the road to recovery. An armorial dessert service was followed by a most important dinner service painted with female figures in monochrome panels representing Hope. These were mostly by John Pennington, a fine figure painter who had been working in London and was engaged by James Flight, the first of many accomplished artists who were to join the Worcester factory. The Duke of Clarence order had been won by Flights against competition from the Derby factory. Derby had moved in a similar direction to Flights, employing fine artists to paint their expensive porcelain rather than relying on more traditional factory decorators, a formula which was to bring success to both enterprises.

Flights' main competition came from much closer to home, however. Having severed their arrangement to decorate for Flights, Robert Chamberlain and his family entered instead into an agreement with Thomas Turner at Caughley. Turner had concentrated on blue and white to the total exclusion of coloured wares. Instead the Chamberlains acted as retailers and decorators for Caughley. They took over Flights' old shop at 33 High Street, Worcester, which had formerly been managed by Samuel Bradley. Bradley had died and John Flight found these premises too small, but the Chamberlains were keen to capitalise on the reputation Bradley's old shop would have built up. From 1788 they sold blue and white Caughley (as well as a certain amount of Flight blue and white) alongside coloured and gilded Caughley which they had decorated themselves.

Chamberlains quickly learnt from their competitors and, while they were happy to sell blue-printed Caughley in Chinese style, they realised many of Caughley's designs were now out of date. They added gilding to blue-printed services to liven them up, and were provided with Caughley porcelain decorated with simple underglaze blue borders or designs which Chamberlain combined into rich blue and gold patterns, just as Flight had done. Copies of some of the correspondence between Ann Chamberlain and Thomas Turner survive and show that Chamberlain had difficulty obtaining all the shapes and wares they wanted, and often had reason to complain about the quality. But the two firms seem to have managed to work together for several years. In July 1790, for instance, Chamberlain sent Thomas Turner a complete set of Flights' new 'shanked' shape which was possibly meant to be copied. Certainly by the end of 1792 Chamberlain were selling Caughley's 'new shankered' shape which they decorated in French style with patterns such as *L'Amitie* with doves and pretty borders. In October 1791 the artist Fidelle Duvivier was employed to paint in the Continental manner on these shanked shapes, but apparently stayed for only one week.

The Chamberlain account books and other extensive archives survive at Worcester and provide a great deal of information about this early period. There is evidence that the Chamberlains began to experiment with their own porcelain manufacture in 1791, employing at least two modellers and purchasing regular supplies of clay and other raw materials. To begin with they sold their own porcelain alongside Caughley which they continued to decorate until at least the end of 1793. The early Chamberlain porcelain was of a so-called hybrid hard paste type, much more advanced than the Caughley soaprock formula and better suited to compete with Flights' improved whiter porcelain which was generally much more finely potted. One of the earliest modellers employed by Chamberlains was John Toulouse and there are many similarities to his work for Worcester twenty years earlier.

On the whole Chamberlains set their sights much lower than Flights. They produced copies of cheaper Chinese export patterns, in the traditions of Staffordshire, and some early Chamberlain wares have in the past been mistaken for New Hall. Some of their patterns did not use gold, something which would have been almost unheard of at Flights, for instance. Chamberlains even seem to have attempted underglaze blue printing, but just for a short time on shanked wares in the 1790s and with little success. Apparently they had learnt from the mistakes of the other Worcester factory in the 1770s and 1780s, and did not produce these cheaper ranges at the expense of quality. They saw a market for this type of inexpensive ware in Worcester and were happy to supply it, while at the same time they continued the traditions which they had learnt at the upper end of the decorating trade.

Chamberlains' artists had mostly moved with the family from Flights and brought with them certain styles which had become firmly established. Several well-known patterns from the 1770s were continued by Chamberlain, such as the designs we now call *Jabberwocky, Sir Joshua Reynolds* and *Rich Queens*. The painter George Davis (known as Doctor Davis) is specifically mentioned as a painter of *Fancy Birds* at Chamberlains in the 1790s and his work, as well as fruit and flower painting associated with these birds, is a direct continuation of Worcester painting from the earlier period. A new style of painting was introduced to Chamberlains by the painter John Wood who copied classical figure subjects from a stock of engravings which were bought by the factory. Their work is exceptional, however, as on the whole Chamberlains did not employ the expensive trained artists who migrated to Flights. The Chamberlains continued their factory as a family business and amongst their most accomplished painters were to be the sons of Humphrey Chamberlain, Humphrey jun. and Walter.

The progress of Flights' factory had been severely affected by the tragic death of John Flight in July 1791 when he was only about twenty-five years of age. His father Thomas had little interest in the business himself and a new partner was needed to help John's brother James. Martin Barr was the partner of John Flight's father-in-law in a firm of general merchants in Worcester and his background was as a salesman, not as a potter. Barr became the senior and most active partner in the new firm of Flight and Barr from 1792, and was able to guide the factory as its fortunes continued to grow. They maintained the course of quality above all else as public taste moved towards the splendours of the Regency.

The style known as 'Japan' dominated the first years of the nineteenth century. The colourful designs, also known as Imari and sometimes Indian, were inspired by Japanese porcelain of a hundred years earlier, although updated by the use of even brighter colours. True to form, Flight and Barr took greater care over their Japan patterns than any other factory, but were probably unrealistically expensive. Although less careful, the overwhelming effect of richness presented by Chamberlains' patterns such as *Dragon in Compartments* and *Finger and Thumb* cannot really be surpassed. The taste may have been vulgar and over the top to many people's eyes, but was undeniably popular and brought a lot of business to the Worcester factories. When

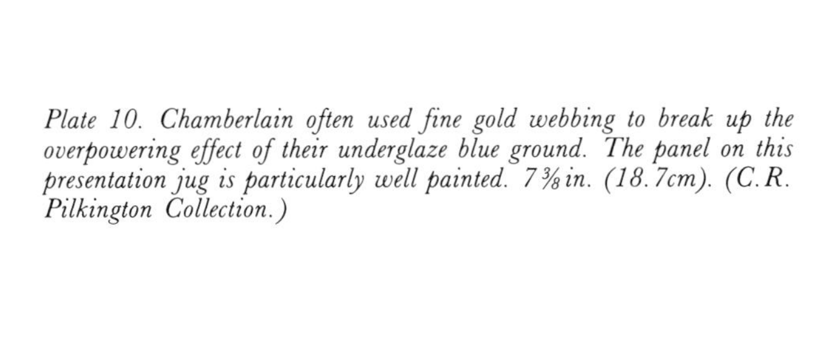

Plate 10. Chamberlain often used fine gold webbing to break up the overpowering effect of their underglaze blue ground. The panel on this presentation jug is particularly well painted. 7⅜ in. (18.7cm). (C.R. Pilkington Collection.)

Plate 11. Chamberlain's most popular design, called 'Fine Old Japan', used to decorate a magnificent soup tureen, script mark Chamberlains Worcester and pattern no. 240, c.1800-5. (Phillips.)

Plate 12. A wonderfully dramatic and superbly detailed painting of the interior of a moonlit ruin, framed with a gilded border also of the highest quality. This Barr, Flight and Barr plate would have been from a very costly dessert service, c.1810, 8in. (20.5cm). (Phillips.)

Lord Nelson came to Worcester in August 1802 he chose to honour Chamberlains with a visit and placed a most important order for an armorial service based on their most popular pattern 240, called *Fine Old Japan* (Plate 11). The order was so costly that only part of it was ever completed.

Martin Barr brought the first of his sons formally into the business in 1804. Martin Barr sen. worked alongside his father and James Flight, the company trading as Barr, Flight and Barr until the death of Martin Barr jun. on 10 November 1813. His other son, George, then became a full partner with his brother Martin and James Flight and the company traded as Flight, Barr and Barr until 1840.

During the Barr, Flight and Barr period the careful attention to quality really paid off and some incredibly fine porcelain was produced. The main influences were still classical, inspired now by Empire and Biedermeier porcelain from Paris, Berlin and Vienna. Gilding was still of paramount importance, used to set off well-controlled ground colours and to frame painted panels. Fine hand painting took on a new dimension under Barr, Flight and Barr. Incredible landscapes fulfilled the ideals of the picturesque style in English art, while the same care was taken over the painting of flowers, birds, shells, feathers or figure subjects. The high standards of decoration achieved at Flights' factory between 1805 and 1820 were quite superb and no other English factory ever really came near.

In 1808 one of the most important of all English porcelain decorators arrived at Worcester almost destitute and was taken on by Barr, Flight and Barr. William Billingsley had fled from creditors and assumed the alias of William Beeley, but his reputation was well known to Martin Barr who took advantage of his enormous talent, both as a painter and as a ceramic chemist. Initially employed for the wages of a 'common hand' along with his daughters and future son-in-law Samuel Walker, Billingsley probably painted at Worcester for at least a year before devoting his time to perfecting a new porcelain body. Martin Barr paid Billingsley handsomely for his work on the understanding that the new formula remained a secret. Billingsley broke his agreement and fled one night in 1813 taking the knowledge he had learnt to Swansea. Barr threatened to pursue him in law but decided not to trouble, choosing instead to warn Dillwyn at Swansea not to attempt to use the formula as it could never be made commercially. Ultimately Barr was proved right, and there is no evidence that Flights ever attempted to make use of the Billingsley recipe. William Billingsley seems to have

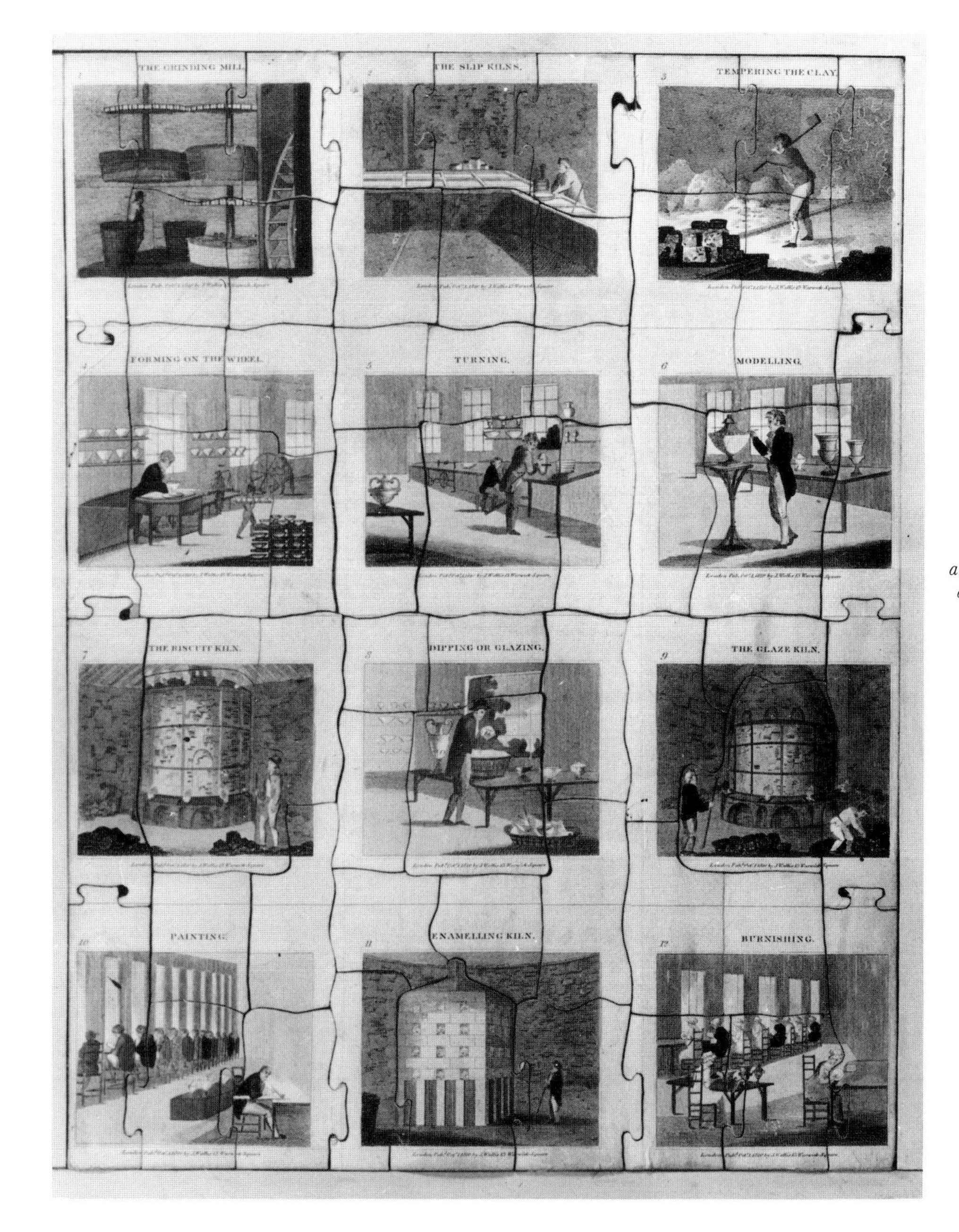

Plate 13. A wooden jigsaw puzzle of 'The Process of Making China – for the information of youth' published in 1810. The accompanying booklet identifies the illustrations as Messrs. Barr, Flight and Barr's factory. Considering the confined space the firm occupied at Warmstry House, these light and spacious rooms, uncrowded and orderly, must be very fanciful depictions of working conditions. (Dyson Perrins Museum.)

had a much greater influence on other flower painters at Worcester, and identifying any actual pieces by Billingsley himself is understandably controversial as well as difficult.

The names of some of the other painters have been preserved and further artists can be identified by signed pieces. Many vital clues are contained in an account given to William Chaffers by Solomon Cole, a painter at Flights, recording the artists who worked for Flight, Barr and Barr in 1819. It was written in the 1870s, however, when Cole was a very old man, and so has to be regarded with some degree of caution. Cole wrote:

> At the same time that Thomas Baxter was engaged in painting Classical figure subjects... John Pennington was devoting his talent to rustic figures, while Samuel Astles and Henry Stinton were painting groups of flowers. There were also flower painters subordinate to them. Then there were also Messrs. Thomas Rogers, John Barker and John Smith painting landscapes. Barker excelled in painting shells..; William Doe painted natural birds, feathers, insects &c.; Charles Stinton painted Fancy Birds &c.; Thomas Crowther painted flowers; The celebrated bird painter George Davis, usually called Dr. Davis. added his brilliant colouring in the rich plumage of his birds.

Plate 14. A Barr, Flight and Barr service of c.1812 combining several different teaware shapes. The vignettes of rustic figures are delicately bat-printed on a fawn ground, impressed marks. (Phillips.)

Solomon Cole added that he was himself a figure painter along with Thomas Lowe, and among the other pupils of Thomas Baxter were Moses Webster who painted flowers and John Pitman who did animals. This is virtually the complete record we have of these artists and their subjects. The difficulty is that only a handful of signed pieces are known to back up Cole's list.

Early collectors read these descriptions and assumed that all shells were by Barker or Baxter, all feathers by William Doe, all animals by Pitman and all 'Fancy Birds' by Davis. The reality is not nearly so simple, however, and readers should refer to each artist listed alphabetically in this *Dictionary* as well as the entries on some of the subjects.

Cole failed to mention Samuel Smith as a painter, and yet from a number of signed pieces it is clear that he was of great importance as a painter of landscapes and shells. The treatment of his shell painting, using a background of fine dendritic weed, differs from the hand of Thomas Baxter who painted with a stipple technique, often with landscapes behind, and also differs from another hand whose many fine shell paintings feature a background of weed gathered together into tiny oval clusters. This latter is probably the fine shell painter named by Solomon Cole as John Barker.

Thomas Baxter was undoubtedly the most important and influential painter at Worcester during the Regency period and considerable space is given to his biography in this *Dictionary*. Baxter received his training in London at his father's decorating studio where mostly Coalport and not Worcester porcelain was painted. To escape the polluted air of London Thomas Baxter arrived in Worcester in 1814. As well as working for Flight, Barr and Barr, he also ran a school for china painting at his house in Edgar Street, teaching many other artists his distinctive mannerisms. Baxter could try his hand at almost any subject and it is therefore increasingly difficult to make firm attributions.

Thomas Baxter left Flights to go to Swansea in 1816, returning in 1819. This time he joined Chamberlains and shortly afterwards he wrote to a friend in London concerning an article about Flight, Barr and Barr which had praised them for their

Plate 15. Various Grainger tea and coffee cups, their identification confirmed by finds from the factory site excavations. Some are unique to this factory while others follow closely popular shapes of their competitors. (Henry Sandon Collection.)

painting. Baxter complained to his old friend:

> Five year's banishment from all that is great [i.e. London] has rather increased if possible my love of the arts. My health of body is very much better for my removal. I cannot say much for my mind as I am employed here on little things and the ''littler and prettier'', the *dear* little things and the *dearer* they are the better.... The two plates which are noticed are my painting, and their figure painting is now done by a pupil of mine named Lowe. It is not very likely that I will paint anything more for them, as the people I am now engaged with [i.e. Chamberlains] are more liberal minded and would be much more likely to bring forward what is good if there was a choice of encouragement....

Baxter must have painted many 'littler and prettier' pieces for Chamberlains, such as inkwells or pin trays with views of Worcester and Malvern. Some have been attributed to Baxter and are remarkably fine, but great care needs to be taken before any small painting can be attributed. He was only at Chamberlains for two years before his death in 1821, his last work being a series of cabinet plates painted with still-life subjects with very great care and accuracy.

Amongst the pupils of Thomas Baxter from Edgar Street and Chamberlains' factory were Enoch Doe and George Rogers. During the 1820s they broke away to found their own china decorating business, trading as Doe and Rogers at 93 High Street, Worcester, buying blanks principally from Coalport. There were other independent decorators in Worcester, and by this time a third major porcelain factory had become well established in the city, founded initially by two other former Chamberlain artists who decided to become independent decorators and then manufacturers.

Thomas Grainger was in fact the grandson of Robert Chamberlain sen. and had been apprenticed to the Chamberlain family in 1798 as a china painter. Grainger seems to have been far more than just a decorator during his apprenticeship as he is recorded in the Chamberlain archives as going on business journeys for the firm. Having completed his term and become a Freeman of Worcester on 9 September 1805,

Plate 16. Grainger biscuit porcelain vases with finely modelled and coloured flowers, unmarked but corresponding with a page from the factory shape book recording the original cost prices, c.1832-5. Central vase 12in. (31cm). (Vases private collection, book Worcester Royal Porcelain Co.)

Plate 17. The classical influence on Flight vase shapes is well represented by this yellow ground pot-pourri of c.1795, flanked by a sacred presentation bowl and a pot-pourri with eagle and ring handles, both 1825. The central vase 10⅜in. (26.5cm). (Phillips.)

Thomas Grainger left to set up in partnership with John Wood and Stephen Wilkins in premises at St Martin's Gate, Worcester. They probably decorated Coalport blanks until new porcelain kilns had been built and their own models were ready. The first Grainger porcelain was probably produced in 1806. Thomas Grainger and John Wood were both listed as china painters although no pieces have been positively attributed to either hand. In spite of a serious fire which destroyed the Grainger works on 25 April 1809, the firm was rebuilt and continued to produce porcelain of hybrid hard paste type in competition with Flights and Chamberlains.

At their best early Grainger wares exhibit fine potting and gilding, especially when decorated with Japan patterns or finely gilded presentation ciphers. Generally, however, Grainger avoided the fine ornamental market and stuck to everyday teawares, mostly copied from Coalport (Plate 15). Their shanked and oval shapes were copied from Coalport forms of several years earlier and consequently did not find such a ready market.

John Wood withdrew on 7 March 1811, and the factory then traded as Thomas Grainger and Co. In October 1814 the firm became Grainger, Lee and Co, with the arrival of James Lee, the son of John Lee, an earlier backer of the company. James Lee was also probably Thomas Grainger's brother-in-law. The new partnership commenced on 10 October 1814, although it is just possible that the new name was not fully adopted until 1 January 1817 when Joseph Gillam withdrew as a further backer of the partnership. Certainly from January 1817 until 1837 the firm traded as Grainger, Lee and Co. They had introduced bone china by c.1812 but at times the quality of their body was very poor. Generally the firm supplied the lower end of the fine porcelain market in Worcester. They tried to compete with Coalport and Staffordshire factories rather than with Flights or Chamberlains, and in this respect they were actually more alert to changes in fashion. Taste changed in the 1820s away from classical symmetry towards a revival of the rococo. Graingers had never been much influenced by classical styles and easily adapted to rococo ideals. In the 1830s they introduced flower-encrusted porcelain in the manner of Coalbrookdale and Rockingham, the modelling finely detailed and delicately coloured (Plate 16). Chamberlains' attempts to compete in a similar fashion were far more clumsy, however. Graingers were also successful figure makers, more in the traditions of Staffordshire porcelain than the finer factories of Derby or Minton, but still far superior to Chamberlain figures. Flights avoided figure making altogether.

James Lee remained at the Grainger factory until 1837 when he left Worcester. Thomas Grainger was then the sole proprietor of the factory which traded as Thomas Grainger and Co. until his death on 28 December 1839. His widow, Mary Ann Grainger, sold her interest in the factory to her son, George, in 1843. George Grainger was to be the firm's driving force for the next forty-five years, until his death on 14 July 1888.

It is ironic that the factory which was so reluctant to introduce neo-classical designs in the 1770s should suffer from a similar reluctance to give up classical styles once rococo had come back into fashion. Flights stuck stubbornly to their established styles to such an extent that in the late 1830s they were still making the same shapes and some similar patterns that they had sold twenty-five years earlier. Such a policy is fine as long as the products keep selling, but the result in Flights' case was a complete inability to change once the market rejected their traditional designs. Chamberlains suffered equally from a decline in the number of customers for their richest porcelain, and attempted to combat the problem by moving down market, into areas where they had no experience. Cheap dinner services, door furniture, and floor tiles were all products which had their place in potteries geared to mass-production but were totally unsuited to a factory like Chamberlains with traditions of maintaining quality. The result here was an inability to make cheap items cheaply enough.

Joseph Flight died in 1838 and left his share in the company to his younger partners, George Barr and Martin Barr jun. They would have liked to sell the business, but found it impossible to agree terms. Instead they entered into a very uncomfortable alliance with Walter Chamberlain, the last surviving member of the Chamberlain family. Humphrey Chamberlain sen. had retired in 1827 and his son-in-law, John Lilly, had been brought in as a new partner. Chamberlain and Lilly became senior

Plate 18 A publicity tile for the 'Worcester Encaustic Tile Works' of Chamberlain and Co., c.1850. Large pavements would have been 'signed' by placing such a tile somewhere in the design. (Dyson Perrins Museum.)

figures in the new joint stock company formed in 1840 called the Worcester Royal Porcelain Company. They were advised to continue to trade using a family name in the interests of business and so remained as Chamberlain and Co.

Things went from bad to worse. R.W. Binns' much quoted description of the amalgamation as a marriage of convenience and not of love proved to be apt, with great disagreements over the value of the stock of the two London shops. Full details of the break-up of the new partnership and the other problems they faced are given in the *Dictionary* entry for Chamberlain and Co. Martin Barr and George Barr terminated their involvement in 1844. They continued to live with their widowed sister at Henwick Hall and all three died in 1848. Walter Chamberlain and John Lilly continued to run the previous Chamberlain factory at Diglis in Worcester and some fine porcelain was made there during the 1840s. On the whole, however, their products were either old-fashioned or simply unimaginative. Other ventures, such as the production of porcelain buttons, and beads to trade with far away natives, proved to be financial disasters. Other former partners continued to use the Warmstry House site for the manufacture of encaustic floor tiles which were well received but costly to make and could not compete with other tile manufacturers (Plate 18). The tile works were eventually taken over by Maw and Co. in 1850 and then transferred to Benthall, near Ironbridge.

John Lilly retired in 1850 in favour of his son Frederick and W.H. Kerr, a china dealer from Dublin. They exhibited at the Great Exhibition in 1851 under the name of Chamberlain and Co. but mostly showed fine pieces from the past drawn from the works collection. The only praise they received was for their new reticulated or pierced porcelain which was unusual in England although directly copied from the Sèvres factory. Walter Chamberlain retired the same year, ending his family's involvement one hundred years after his grandfather had been apprenticed to Richard Holdship. Without a Chamberlain at its head the firm became W.H. Kerr and Co. and desperately needed a new guiding spirit. In 1852 Kerr invited Richard William Binns to join him and the new firm of Kerr and Binns led the revival of the company's fortunes as Worcester porcelain began its second century.

Abergavenny, Marquis of
See **Nevill, Lord**

Absolon, William
A china dealer in Yarmouth, well known for his decoration on English creamware and gilding on glass. His somewhat amateur attempts at landscape painting are very distinctive, mostly in tones of brown and green and using green rims. Between December 1791 and September 1801 William Absolon bought a certain quantity of Chamberlain porcelain, mostly tea sets for re-sale, but included in the orders are white undecorated wares. Absolon seemed content to buy seconds and damaged goods, such as '12 dozn cups and saucers small shank(ed) 2nd White' in September 1800 and '36 Toy mugs & 74 pints white 2nds' five months earlier. So far no signed examples of Absolon's painting have been noted on Chamberlain porcelain and it will be worth looking out for unmarked Chamberlain shapes which might be attributable to his hand or other members of the Absolon family.

Account Books
Due largely to the great insight of R.W. Binns*, most of the Chamberlain factory* records have been preserved. Unfortunately, though, Binns arrived too late to save the Flight factory* records. When Chamberlain and Flight, Barr and Barr amalgamated in 1840 the business was transferred to the Diglis factory. All the records relating to Flight's factory and its predecessors at Warmstry House* must have been burnt at this time as they were considered unimportant. The records of Chamberlain's productions are probably the most complete of any English 19th century factory and form the basis of Geoffrey Godden's *Chamberlain-Worcester Porcelain, 1788-1852.* The records include order books and invoice books for the Worcester and London shops, lists of stock, wages books and letter books. These are housed now in the Dyson Perrins Museum and it is hoped that a programme of preservation work will be possible, as many are in poor condition. A smaller number of Grainger* account books survive but again most were destroyed in 1902 when the works were finally closed.
See also **Pattern Books.**

Acrobats Pattern
One of the most appealing of the early Chinese figure patterns. The design of two acrobats balancing with a table between them occurs only on small hexagonal bottle-shaped vases painted in Worcester's version of *famille rose**. The pattern suits the shape very well and is usually carefully painted, with a house and fence on the reverse. Examples date from c.1753.

Aggressive Birds
A distinctive form of bird painting associated with the Giles* studio in London. Thickly applied in strong colours, the style is, as a rule, much more lively than the formal and rather

Acrobats Pattern. *A delightful hexagonal bottle-shaped vase painted in bright colours, c.1753, 4¾in. (12cm). (Wallace Elliot Collection.)*

harmless bird painting practised at the Worcester factory. Very similar bird painting occurs on Chinese porcelain painted in London. Related decoration is also found on Chelsea and Bow, which further confirms a London attribution.

Agitated Birds
The Worcester factory's equivalent of the Giles* workshop's *Aggressive Birds** are the so-called agitated birds, popular from c.1765-70. These occur usually in panels on either powder blue* or scale blue* grounds and are rather less elaborate than full *Fancy Birds**. They are placed amongst very tightly packed leafy foliage, often containing berries. They are seen at their best on a series of cabbage leaf dishes against plain white grounds and these usually include smaller birds in branches behind. In spite of red anchor marks often seen on these dishes, there is a marked difference between the Giles and Worcester factory versions of these painted birds.

Anchor Marks
The mark associated with the Chelsea factory was never used directly as a Worcester mark but does occur on certain pieces as a natural emblem for the Holdship* brothers (*see* **Anchor Rebus**). An anchor mark painted in red occurs on some Worcester porcelain in the 1770s and has been associated with

Animal Models. *A pair of Chamberlain models of a stag and doe, on characteristic matt blue bases, script marks, Chamberlains Worcester, 3in. (7.5cm) wide. (Phillips.)*

the Giles* workshop. While a London association via Giles to Chelsea can be assumed, this seems unlikely as there are very few direct links between these two London styles. Instead the pieces of Worcester with red anchor marks seem to relate more closely to factory decoration. Leaf dishes with *Agitated Birds** often bear the mark and differ from Giles' interpretation of the same subject. These seem to have contemporary decoration from the late 1760s but the red anchor mark on *Blind Earl** plates is usually accompanied by considerable spit-out* and suggests the work of an outside decorator or later redecoration*. Most anchor marks on Worcester pieces, especially in gold, should be treated with great suspicion.

Anchor Rebus

The mark of an anchor occurs on several early Worcester transfer printed designs alongside the initials 'RH'. The sign is an obvious choice for a rebus for the name Holdship and clearly relates to Richard Holdship* who continued to use the same mark at Derby. There were of course two Holdships connected with transfer printing at Worcester, and it was Josiah Holdship* who claimed to have invented the process. One print of the *Milkmaids** is known with the mark of two anchors crossed over one another along with a reversed 'RH' monogram. It is likely from the positioning of these two anchors and slight differences in form between them that the second anchor was added to the engraving slightly later, possibly by Josiah Holdship at the time he was in disagreement with his brother. After Richard's departure in 1759, all anchor marks were probably removed from existing copper plates. There is no connection here with Chelsea where an anchor was used as a factory mark.

Animal Models

Cheap to make and greatly appealing, it is no wonder so many porcelain factories produced small animal models as ornaments and toys. In the early period Worcester strangely avoided this market although the cow* finial to a bowl shows that they could have made successful models if they had tried. Chamberlain began by decorating Caughley porcelain and pairs of lambs are listed in 1789. A biscuit waster of a small lamb has been found near the Caughley site and matches an example which has been attributed to Chamberlain's early porcelain. Records show that these were being produced at Chamberlain in 1798. The only other Chamberlain model known from the 1790s is the celebrated kingfisher (*see* **Toulouse, John**).

During the 19th century Chamberlain and Grainger both made large numbers of animals, especially dogs of all kinds, and examples from both factories are usually marked which helps identification. The Grainger shape drawing books record many distinctive models. Chamberlain favoured plain bases, usually simple mounds in one colour of enamel edged in gold, with strong matt blue enamel being the most distinctive colour used. The Chamberlain animals themselves are frequently white with just the slightest painting of details to pick out features such as eyes, ears and paws. Their finest model, a crouching poodle, is sometimes found in biscuit porcelain* with the name mark incised into the base, the dog's coat being formed of finely shredded clay. Some models are incredibly rare or known only from the factory lists, such as lions, peacocks and peahens, geese, swans and even an elephant.

Grainger animals mostly date from around 1830-5 and are usually placed on irregular rockwork bases which can be heightened in gold. Their most remarkable models are a pair of giraffes introduced c.1836 when the first giraffes were brought to London Zoo. Listed as 'Giraff or Camel L'pard', they sold for 3s. 6d. coloured in a most imaginary way. Grainger also made a fine biscuit poodle and a wonderful model of a dog looking at a mouse in a cage made of fine wire.

Animal Models. *A selection of small dog models from the 1820s. From left: a Chamberlain coloured poodle on blue base; an unusual Chamberlain biscuit poodle; a Grainger, Lee and Co. biscuit poodle; and a Chamberlain coloured pug, all marked. (Barbara Sandon Collection.)*

Animal Models. *A Grainger, Lee and Co. model of a 'Giraff or Camel L'pard', c.1836, impressed mark*, 4½in. (11.5cm). These sold for 2s.6d. white or 3s.6d. coloured. (Sotheby's.)*

Most have the mark 'Grainger, Lee and Co. Worcester' impressed lightly into the base but the thick glaze makes the marks very difficult to see. Certain Staffordshire animal models can be very similar to Worcester and great care has to be taken in attributing unmarked examples.

Apple Green

This distinctive ground colour, named after the celebrated *pomme verte* of Sèvres*, was much used at the Worcester factory rather than in London. The enamel is remarkably thick and opaque and can be felt well above the surface. As a ground it tended to dribble and consequently was used mostly around rococo panels where such irregularities did not matter. One feature is that Worcester's apple green could not take gold directly on top and therefore gilding followed the outline of the ground and never overlapped it. Introduced in the late 1760s, the ground colour continued into the Flight period and was subsequently modified so that gilding could be applied to it (*see* Colour Plate 13). The best known pattern using apple green is the so-called Marchioness of Huntley* service of about 1770.

A great many surviving pieces with apple green grounds show evidence of redecoration*. This could have been contemporary but is most likely to be of much later date. Because the later green is indistinguishable from the original, the only way of identifying the fakes is evidence elsewhere on the piece of refiring as well as of uncharacteristic painting.

Patterns with apple green borders seem on the whole to be perfectly acceptable as a contemporary form of decoration. On the other hand, the use of green as a ground around panels of birds or fruit is in almost every case highly suspect. *See* **Redecoration,** *Group VIg,* and page 46.

***Apple Green.** A teapot showing the influence of Sèvres* with panels of* Fancy Birds*, *the porcelain c.1765, the decoration probably later, 5¼in. (13.3cm). (Kenneth Klepser Collection.)*

Argument Pattern
A curious design in Chinese style, the busy landscape is named after the two figures who appear to be fighting in a window in the principal building. Occasionally, however, these figures are omitted. Popular from c.1778-90, the pattern has its own border and usually bears a disguised numeral* mark. Like most from this period, the *Argument* pattern was for a long time believed to be Caughley but was re-attributed following factory site excavations* at Worcester. Listed in Branyan, French and Sandon as II.B.10.

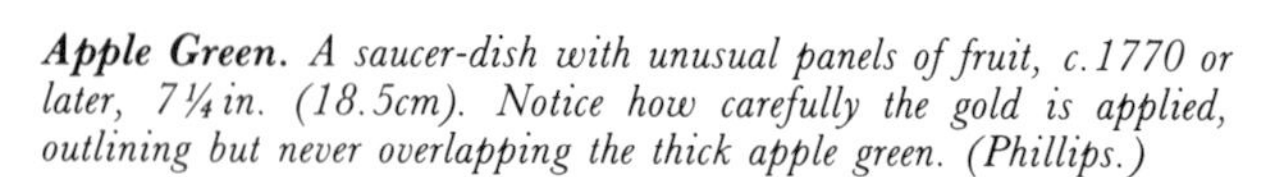

***Apple Green.** A saucer-dish with unusual panels of fruit, c.1770 or later, 7¼in. (18.5cm). Notice how carefully the gold is applied, outlining but never overlapping the thick apple green. (Phillips.)*

Armorial Decoration

A major market in Chinese armorial porcelain had developed in England by the middle of the 18th century. Dinner services painted with the owner's coat of arms took a considerable time to arrive from China and it is therefore surprising that generally very little armorial porcelain was made in England. Chelsea derived most of its designs from silver where armorial decoration is commonplace, so it is very curious that they chose to leave this potentially lucrative market to Worcester. Unfortunately Worcester's soaprock* body was not controlled sufficiently to make good plates and dishes and they were unable to compete with the Chinese. Worcester made some fine tea services with armorials (Colour Plate 2) but mostly they excelled in producing presentation jugs and mugs (Colour Plate 3) and other shapes not so readily available from China.

The earliest Worcester armorial piece is the celebrated Tracy mug* (*see* Colour Plate 86) painted in the early 1750s to commemorate the disputed election of 1749. The arms of the Tracy family appear on a pillar above an inscription. Generally on the earlier armorial pieces the shield is contained within a rococo cartouche and stands against a painted landscape background in colours or in puce. Other pieces have elaborate moulding with reserved armorial panels or else white grounds with coloured flowers and borders of puce rococo scrollwork. Blue or other coloured grounds are rare but were occasionally used after 1765, although in the case of the yellow ground jug with the arms of Mary Countess of Eroll (illustrated by H. Rissik Marshall as item 652 in *Coloured Worcester Porcelain*) did occur as early as 1757-8.

Transfer printing* was used from the later part of the 1750s to assist the painters who had to draw complicated rococo cartouches. Instead these scrollwork panels were printed and the different shield designs were painted in for each service. Other armorials were completely printed in black and merely coloured in by hand. Between c.1768-75 Giles* painted many elaborate armorial tea services and occasional dessert sets which can be distinguished by characteristic flower sprigs and gilded borders. Amongst the rarer shapes in armorial Worcester porcelain are cutlery handles*, a snuff box*, a vase and a pair of sauceboats. Harry Rissik Marshall made a special study of Worcester armorials and many examples can be seen in his collection in the Ashmolean Museum in Oxford.

Armorial decoration is not restricted to the 18th century, however. The termination of the Chinese export trade meant that English factories found a new market for their dinner and dessert services. Flight and Chamberlain between them dominated the market in rich armorial services and a very large number of sets were made, ranging from simple plain crests to wonderfully elaborate services emblazoned with full arms, supporters and mottoes (*see* Colour Plate 79). These were usually incorporated into the central panels of standard patterns (*see* Colour Plate 54). The Duke of Clarence service* of 1789 was the first royal armorial service followed by a whole succession of impressive royal commissions for each succeeding monarch. It is not possible to identify the work of any individual artists although Solomon Cole* recorded that at Flight, Barr and Barr John Bly*

> excelled in shading the gold in arms, and was unequalled in giving a natural expression to the lion in the royal arms or wherever it occurred, and took that part in the grand service made for his Majesty William IV*.

Arrow and Annulet Marks

Painted designs used in blue c.1756, *see* **Workmen's Marks.** These signs also occur in coloured enamel and are always an indication of an early date.

Armorial Decoration. *A large jug painted in colours with scattered flowers and the arms of Cocks, c.1758-60, 7¼in. (18.5cm). The jug was possibly made for Lord Somers, Baron of Evesham, Worcestershire. (Phillips.)*

Armorial Decoration. *A Flight, Barr and Barr vase and cover painted with wonderful flowers, probably by Thomas Baxter*, the reserved panels with the arms of Best of Packhouse, Kent and Kilkenny, Ireland, full circular printed mark, c.1815, 7½in. (19cm). (Phillips.)*

Artichoke Cups
Small covered cups moulded with fine scales to resemble an artichoke are first known in the Flight and Barr period c.1800. The shape probably derives from the French porcelain of St Cloud where they were popular at the beginning of the 18th century, although examples were made by many other factories. The cups came in sets of six placed on a tray, decorated simply in gold. It has been assumed that they were probably for a custard or other dessert rather than for a preparation using artichokes; however, the Chamberlain order books list in May 1795 '6 Artichoke butter cups and 1 Stand'. These are probably similar to the Flight set but no finished examples have been recorded. Similar shapes were used much later at Graingers and also at Royal Worcester, c.1880.

Asparagus Servers. *A Worcester asparagus server painted in blue with the* Gillyflower* *pattern, crescent mark, c.1775-80, 3½in. (9cm). The underside is fully glazed. (Phillips, Bath.)*

Asparagus Servers
Small fan-shaped holders with flat bottoms and tapering sides were made extensively in silver, earthenware and porcelain from the 1770s. Much confusion exists today over a number of blue and white porcelain asparagus servers painted with a narcissus sprig and loop border, c.1775-80. Although they have usually been attributed to Worcester, it is now strongly believed that most are of Derby origin. Worcester did make slightly larger and wider asparagus servers, normally painted with the *Gillyflower** pattern or printed with the *Fisherman** pattern, c.1780-5. Worcester asparagus servers are surprisingly rare, especially as Caughley produced a very great many with the popular *Fisherman* or *Pleasure Boat* pattern. A single entry in the Chamberlain books for 7 May 1799 lists '2 Asparagus servers, lily'. This is several years after Chamberlain's trade with Caughley and no Caughley asparagus servers have been seen with the *Royal Lily** pattern, so it is, therefore, reasonable to assume that these were in Chamberlain's own porcelain even though no finished examples have been seen.

Astles, Samuel
A superb painter of flowers employed at Flight's factory. He was probably born in 1792. He studied at Thomas Baxter's* china painting school c.1812 and remained at the factory until at least 1840. His work, known from a small number of signed plaques, testifies to his great skill in building up colour in his compositions, with a background in thick enamel that has a distinctive incised texture. One of these fine plaques was exhibited at the Royal Accademy in 1827. Recognising any unsigned work is very difficult as most of his painting would have been flower sprays without any textured background. Much tends to be ascribed to Samuel Astles without any evidence (*see* Colour Plate 20). R.W. Binns* recorded that the flowers in the services made for the Earl of Plymouth* and the Prince of Wales (*see* **Regent, Prince, Services**) were by Astles, and he quotes James Knight who knew Astles and recorded that he had a cork leg. Astles probably continued to work into the Chamberlain and Co. period and left Worcester some time during the 1840s. He died of typhoid in Smethwick on 13 April 1853, aged sixty-one.

Astley Pattern
The name, given in the 20th century, belongs to an early Worcester pattern also known to collectors as *Harvest Bug*. Directly copying a Chinese *famille rose** original, the peony and branch design includes a fanciful insect and a red loop and dot border. Thick white enamel is often included. Dating from about 1765-70, the pattern was reintroduced in the 1930s, probably at the request of Dyson Perrins. It remained popular into the 1970s.

Astley Pattern. *A teapot painted in thick enamels with the* Astley *or* Harvest Bug *pattern, c.1768-70, 6⅛in. (15.5cm). (Phillips.)*

Colour Plate 2. **Armorial Decoration.** *A full tea service of* Rich Queen's* *pattern, the central panel replaced by the coat of arms and crest of Fry. The service includes a* Blind Earl* *shaped 'sweetmeat dish' which possibly served as a stand for the teapot. Note also the two different cup handle shapes in use together, c.1765. (Phillips.)*

Colour Plate 3. **Armorial Decoration.** *A remarkable and most amusing mug painted with a fake armorial, c.1757-60. The supporters are tabby cats while the shield has three black mice. The crest is a bowl of cream. The motto reads* La Nuit Tous Chats Sont Gris *(at night all cats are grey). The history of why the mug was made is sadly not recorded. (Private Collection.)*

B

'B' Mark, Incised

A distinctive form of the letter 'B' was incised into the bases of Worcester porcelain as a factory mark from c.1792. Its introduction probably coincides with the arrival at Worcester of Martin Barr* in 1792, although there remains some uncertainty. Only a handful of pieces are known with the incised initials 'F & B' which would seem a much more likely mark for the partnership which lasted until 1804. The incised letter 'B' mark usually has a small top loop and large lower loop and is occasionally accompanied by an incised cross or single stroke as some form of workmen's tally marks. The incised letter was replaced by an impressed mark of the letters 'BFB' on the commencement of the Barr, Flight and Barr partnership in 1804. Certain old stock left in the white by the factory and bearing the incised 'B' mark could have been decorated after 1804 and pieces are known with incised 'B' marks as well as painted Barr, Flight and Barr marks.

Banded Hedge Pattern

A confusing term which refers to a decorative motif derived from Japanese *Kakiemon* porcelain. It is likely that the porcelain painters were trying to represent reeds bound together for use as wind-breaks although the motif became very stylised by the time it had been copied in Europe. Several patterns include such a motif, the most distinctive Worcester version dating from about 1753-4 with flowering chrysanthemums, bamboo and a phoenix. It has been suggested that this represents the symbolic 'Three Friends' from Oriental art, but there is no pine tree in Worcester's version. From the later 1760s banded hedges are often included in rich *Kakiemon* panels on deep blue grounds. These have variously been referred to as the *Wheatsheaf* pattern although it is probably correct to use this term only for the version with alternate panels between wide deep blue stripes reserved with *mons*. Certain 19th century Flight and Chamberlain patterns also include banded hedges.

Barbar, Lewis

A painter at the Worcester factory, known only from a reference in *The London Gazette,* 14 April 1761:

> Insolvent and in debtor's prison in Worcester, Lewis Barbar, formerly of St Mary Le Bow, Middlesex, late of the parish of St Alban's in the City of Worcester, China-Painter.

St Albans was right next door to the porcelain works in Worcester. From his former residence, it would seem likely that Lewis Barbar had previously worked at the Bow China factory, but there is no evidence to support this.

Barker, John

Solomon Cole's* account of the painters at Flight's factory records John Barker as a painter of landscapes who also 'excelled in painting shells, and was engaged in that part of the celebrated service made for Watson Taylor Esq.'. No signed pieces are known by John Barker, although R.W. Binns attempted to attribute some pieces in the Porcelain Works Museum to him. From signed pieces by Thomas Baxter* and Samuel Smith* it has been possible to identify their respective shell painting. There remains a large group of pieces, mostly from the Barr, Flight and Barr period, painted with shells seemingly by a single hand (*see* Colour Plates 76 and 77). The fine weed in the background of these compositions is grouped into tiny clumps of filaments in contrast to the more dendritic treatment by Samuel Smith. It is reasonable to conjecture that these pieces are the work of John Barker.

Banded Hedge Pattern. *An early scallop-shaped pickle dish, an unusual example in* Kakiemon* *style, c.1754, 3¾in. (9.5cm). (Phillips.)*

Barr, Flight and Barr

Martin Barr* had been very much the senior partner since 1792, although his name only acceded to first position in the factory's trading name in 1804 when his son, Martin Barr jun.* became a Freeman of Worcester and joined his father as a full partner. Joseph Flight* remained but his name moved into second place in the firm's title. Martin jun. had been an apprentice to his father and was admitted Freeman on 13 August 1804. The following month *Berrow's Worcester Journal* was already referring to the new name Barr, Flight and Barr and James Ross* was once again asked to engrave a bill-head in the new name in December 1804. During the Barr, Flight and Barr period William Billingsley* and Samuel Walker* were engaged to improve the porcelain body but left taking the results of their researches to Swansea. It is unlikely that any real change was made to Flight's soaprock* body as a result of their experiments. Martin Barr sen. died on 10 November 1813, leaving his interest in the firm to his two sons Martin jun. and George Barr*. The impressed mark of the initials 'BFB' replaced the incised 'B' mark in 1804 although from painted marks it is clear the London shop* at 1 Coventry Street remained solely in the names of Martin Barr sen. and Joseph Flight as Flight and Barr.

Barr, Martin jun.
The eldest son of Martin Barr*, partner in the firm of Flight and Barr, porcelain manufacturers, Martin jun. was apprenticed to his father and became a Freeman of Worcester on 13 August 1804. By September 1804 Martin jun. had become a full partner and the firm became Barr, Flight and Barr. On the death of Martin Barr sen. in 1813 Martin jun. and George Barr* inherited their father's shares in the business and finally were left also Joseph Flight's* shares following his death in 1838. Martin jun. was clearly heavily involved in the running of the factory. Michael Faraday recorded in his diary in 1819 how he was shown around the factory by Martin Barr and taken to Malvern ten miles away for lunch in the family home with his mother, Hannah Barr. Solomon Cole* wrote that Martin and George went round the painting-room twice a day, frequently saying to the painters 'We want you to consider this as jewellery — we wish you to take all possible pains'. Later, though, Martin and George lost interest and virtually sold out to Chamberlain and Co.* in 1840, retaining shares in the joint stock company. By 1844 their involvement was terminated and Martin retired to Henwick Hall near Worcester which he shared with George and their widowed sister Maria. Martin Barr died on 28 January 1848 and his brother and sister later the same year.

***Barr, Flight and Barr.** A garniture of vases representing the finest neo-classical* and picturesque* traditions which were so dominant during this period, script marks, c.1810, central vase 10⅝in. (27cm). (Phillips.)*

Barr, George
Like his elder brother, George was apprenticed to his father Martin Barr sen.* He became a Freeman of Worcester in 1808, but only became a partner in the Porcelain Company following his father's death in November 1813. Joseph Flight* left the two brothers to manage the firm jointly (*see* **Barr, Martin jun.***) and on his death in 1838 Joseph Flight left his shares in the company to them also. Following the amalgamation with Chamberlains in 1840, George Barr remained involved far more than his brother and was awarded a salary of £200 per year in 1841 for his work for the company. George continued to assist in running the business until 1844 when the partnership was dissolved. He died at Henwick Hall on 21 July 1848, six months after the death of his brother.

Colour Plate 4. ***Baskets.*** *A matching pair of oval baskets with pierced trellis sides, the twig handles with modelled flower terminals, square marks*, c.1770, 8¼ in. (21cm). The combination of scale blue* and birds produces a very rich effect. (Phillips.)*

Colour Plate 5. ***Bat Printing.*** *A Barr, Flight and Barr coffee pot of the extraordinary flattened shape unique to Flight's factory, decorated with simple bat prints of classical subjects, impressed mark*, c.1805, 8½ in. (22cm). (Dyson Perrins Museum.)*

(Opposite) Colour Plate 7. ***Baxter, Thomas.*** *Two plates from the service made for Lord Valentia*, painted by Thomas Baxter after drawings by W. Page who accompanied his lordship on his travels in the East. The quality of the raised gold work is as remarkable as the painting. Printed marks, c.1815, 9½ in. (24cm). (Dyson Perrins Museum.)*

Colour Plate 6. ***Bat Printing.*** *Chamberlain teawares bat printed with different classical figures copied from engravings in use at the factory, on a rich orange ground, c.1805-10. (Phillips.)*

***Baskets.** A massive dessert basket or table centrepiece, heavily moulded with a vine trellis and pierced, painted in underglaze blue* with the* Boating Lake *pattern, workmen's marks*, c.1755-7, 15⅛ in. (38.5cm). (Sotheby's, Chester.)*

Barr, Martin, sen.

Born c.1756, Martin Barr was a businessman in Worcester who became involved in the porcelain firm initially through the marriage of his partner's daughter to John Flight*. Gillam and Barr were 'Drapers, Salesmen, Mercers and Undertakers' in Worcester High Street. John Flight married Ann Gillam in 1790 and became acquainted with Martin Barr, for Barr was appointed as one of John Flight's executors following his untimely death in July 1791. In a letter to R.W. Binns in 1877, James Knight told the story of how Martin Barr is said to have come into the money to buy his way into the porcelain company. While putting up the shutters of his humble drapers shop one evening a drunken dragoon officer picked a fight with him and cut Barr's head with his sword. To keep him quiet the officer paid a sizeable sum to Martin Barr and this, according to Knight, enabled him to buy his partnership from Thomas Flight. While to be taken with a great pinch of salt, the account does confirm Barr's lack of any form of ceramic training, instead representing him as someone with skill as a salesman. He had not previously become a Freeman of the City of Worcester and did so on 2 January 1792 on payment of £20. Martin Barr remained as the senior partner of Joseph Flight* from 1792 until Barr's death in 1813. He had introduced his two sons Martin jun.* and George Barr* to the business and seems to have been far more active in the running of the firm than his partner, evidenced by letters from Martin Barr preserved in the Wedgwood archives.

Martin Barr also remained active in city life in Worcester where he was auditor of the Royal Infirmary, a director of the House of Industry (a form of workhouse) and served on the committee of Worcester Library. James Ross* noted in his account book at the end of his dealings with Barr, Flight and Barr: 'Mr Barr died of Appoplexy, Nov. 10th 1813, in his 57th Year, and was buried at the Angel Street Chapel (north and south) on the 18th following.' He left considerable bequests to his wife, Hannah, and his share in the porcelain works to his two sons, Martin jun. and George.

Barr's Orange

A popular ground colour developed c.1800. The flame red colour was used by many factories, but only Flights achieved such a rich depth of colour.

Basins

Early bowls in the 1750s were referred to as basons (*sic*) and listed according to their capacity (*see* **Bowls**). Washbowls or basins were made with matching ewers or water bottles, usually in blue and white with elaborate painted Chinese landscapes. The price list of the London warehouse (*see* **London Shops**) c.1755-6 includes two sizes of 'Wash hand Basons'. Later examples c.1765-70 were blue-printed or, rarely, decorated with blue grounds or coloured flowers. Plain

Baskets. *An oval dessert basket printed in blue with the* Pine-cone* *pattern, the handles applied with very unusual modelled cherries, crescent mark*, c.1772-5, 8⅝in. (22cm) wide. (Phillips.)*

or wide-fluted versions were made, always circular with strengthened or everted rims. From the 1780s onwards it was usual for wash basins to be made in pottery rather than porcelain and only occasional references to porcelain examples occur in the Chamberlain records, sold with matching water ewers.

Baskets

Baskets made of porcelain have always had considerable appeal and were staple products of most English porcelain factories. The exact purpose of many forms of basket is uncertain and it was probably left to the original owner to decide if they should be for fruit or purely ornamental. A small bowl or basket with an overhead handle and matching tiny spoon was made at Bristol but does not appear to have been continued at Worcester. The price list of Worcester's London warehouse (*see* **London Shops**) c.1755-56 makes no mention of baskets but some very large examples were certainly being made at this time. By c.1758 the factory had introduced a popular shape of small circular basket with sides made of interlaced circles which were cut out while the clay was still wet. Close examination shows that the shapes for cutting out were drawn on the baskets with a compass. After piercing, small florets were applied on the outside both as decoration and to strengthen the intersections where the clay was prone to crack in the kiln. This standard circular form originated at Chelsea and remained in production at Worcester until the 1770s, with wide tapering sides or occasionally more upright. Oval baskets with rounded sides pierced in the same way were introduced c.1765-68, and from the same period a taller form of oval basket was moulded with diagonal trellis sides. These also came in many different sizes and were applied with florets at the intersections.

It is clear from the patterns used as well as the early auction sale catalogues that most baskets were made as accompaniments to dessert services*. Some were sold separately, however, and very occasionally sets of four small baskets are encountered. The large covered shapes now known as chestnut baskets* were probably for sugar and cream or sauce for dessert. The oval baskets from c.1765-75 were applied with twisted rope or gnarled twig handles with modelled leaves and flowers (Colour Plate 4). Some can be very elaborate with finely detailed flowers and sometimes 'hot-cross-bun buds'*. Similarity to the flower modelling on Worcester figures* and frill vases* suggests the work of John Toulouse*, at least as a supervisor, and the initial mark 'T' or 'To'* is sometimes embossed on the base of an oval basket. A rare variant has modelled oak leaves and acorns.

Baskets are unusual in Flight's factory although several versions with overhead handles date from the 1820s and 1830s, probably intended as card trays*. Early Chamberlain examples are also rare but some round baskets for fruit were made c.1800. Some dessert services in the 1790s included elaborate quatrelobed footed baskets with arcaded sides and matching stands, the last time such shapes were included with dessert sets. Later shapes included many forms of ornamental baskets, either with pierced covers for pot-pourri or dried violets, or open with overhead handles as card trays. The term 'card basket' is used in the 1840s. Both Chamberlain and Grainger from c.1820 specialised in making baskets containing finely modelled flowers. Most were issued in biscuit porcelain with glass domes called 'shades' for protection. Others were fully coloured and were costly productions. These

Colour Plate 8. ***Beckoning Chinaman Pattern.*** *A very carefully painted example on a large mug, the reverse with flowers in Meissen style*, workman's mark* of an anchor, c.1754-6, 5½in. (14cm). (Phillips.)*

Colour Plate 9. ***Billingsley, William.*** *A Barr, Flight and Barr dessert service, each piece painted with a different flower specimen in Billingsley's distinctive style, impressed* and printed marks, c.1808-10. (Phillips.)*

Colour Plate 10. ***Blind Earl Pattern.*** *A Chamberlain and Co. dessert service using moulds first used by Flight, Barr and Barr and supplied to the Earl of Coventry c.1815. These examples use richer colours and very carefully observed butterflies and insects. Impressed* marks Chamberlains, c.1840-2. (Phillips.)*

baskets of flowers were probably intended to be sprinkled with perfume to add scent to a room. Some flower baskets from both factories could include modelled cupids amongst the flowers and Chamberlain also made baskets filled with modelled shells in the 1840s. All of the Worcester factories, including Flights, made miniature baskets with finely painted scenes or flowers, made purely as novelties and pretty ornaments. Some were filled with modelled flowers and rare Grainger examples can have modelled mushrooms instead of flowers.

Bat Pattern

A blue printed design in Chinese style, although no exact parallel has been seen. This is one of a few patterns which were printed in outline with solid washes of blue added as shading. Occasionally certain details of the pattern were heightened in gold. Produced c.1785, the pattern usually bears disguised numeral marks* and seems to have been unique to Worcester. Listed in Branyan, French and Sandon as II.B.26.

Bat Printing

A form of printing on ceramics where the design is transferred to the surface of the vessel not by means of ink on paper but as tiny droplets of oil on a bat of a semi-solidified glue-like substance. The engraved copper plate is filled with the oil and the prepared bat is pressed carefully on to the surface. When peeled off the oil adheres to the bat which is rubbed down on to the glazed surface. When peeled off for a second time the pattern remains in tiny oil droplets on the glaze. Fine powdered enamel colour is then dusted on with a cloth and adheres to the oil, leaving a perfect impression ready to be fired in the kiln. The advantage over transfer printing is the degree of fine detailed shading which can be achieved by bat printing, although heavy coloured areas can become blotchy.

The same engraved copper plates can be used for both paper transfers and bat transfers, with the result that there has been much discussion in the past as to which technique was practised at Worcester. When Lady Shelburne visited Mr Taylor's enamel factory in Birmingham she saw printing on enamel boxes using paper to transfer the sticky impression and then dusting on colour as a powder. It is likely that this method was used for the Smoky Primitive* printing at Worcester c.1754. When Charles Hatchett visited Flight and Barr's factory in 1796 he gave a vivid account of printing, having seen 'rollers take off the impression on a sort of soft tissue

Bat Pattern. *A large dessert dish printed and washed-in in bright underglaze blue*, disguised numeral mark*, c.1785, 10in. (26.5cm). (Dyson Perrins Museum.)*

Bat Printing. *A Barr, Flight and Barr coffee can showing clearly the stipple engraving used with bat printing, impressed mark* BFB and crown, c.1810, 2⅜in. (6cm). (Private Collection.)*

paper which they then apply to the ware'. No contemporary account of early bat printing on porcelain has been passed down but it is understood to have been used for printing enamels. By the end of the Flight and Barr period and up until c.1820 it was certainly practised at the Worcester factory.

Prints were restricted by the size of glue bat which could be easily handled. Therefore most Flight bat prints are of small vignettes, such as a series of farm labourers and other rustic figures. Classical gods and goddesses (Colour Plate 5), groups of shells and flowers are regularly seen in a style which is remarkably close to Flight painted compositions, suggesting that the engravings were prepared at the works also. Thomas Baxter* had experience as an engraver and etcher for book illustrations and it has to be noted that some of the Flight bat prints are in his style. It is too dangerous to draw any conclusions from this, however, especially as Samuel Smith* also published signed etchings of the city of Worcester. Flights used bat printing for a series of border designs such as vines or classical masks. Later on the factory used the technique to produce delicate outlines on subjects such as the portraits of Futteh Ali Shah* and Abbas Mirza, and the central design for the Imaum of Muscat service*. These were hand coloured and in most cases give the appearance of having been fully hand painted.

Chamberlain did very little bat printing but a series of prints of classical figures were used c.1800-10 (Colour Plate 6). These follow exactly compositions which were painted on to Chamberlain vases and attributed to John Wood*, so again it is likely that the copper plates were prepared at the Chamberlain factory. Grainger used a curious pair of engravings of rustic scenes which were printed on teapots c.1805-10. These prints, which appear to have been bat printed, include a signpost inscribed 'To Worcester'. Most Grainger printing would seem to have been done with paper transfers, however.

Baxter, Thomas

Thomas Baxter was born in 1782 in Worcester where his father was probably a painter at the porcelain factory. Thomas Baxter jun. received his artistic training in London, however, as his family had moved there in 1797. The young Thomas learned the skills of china painting from his father at their decorating workshop off Fleet Street where French, Chinese and Coalport blanks were decorated in the latest French styles. Yet it was the Royal Academy school and in particular the teaching of the eccentric genius Henry Fuseli which was to influence Thomas Baxter above all else. Baxter joined the Academy school at the age of eighteen and exhibited his work at the Academy in thirteen different years from 1802 until his death in 1821.

In 1811 he exhibited the famous watercolour which now hangs in the Ceramics Gallery in the Victoria and Albert museum. This shows the interior of the Baxter family workshop and Thomas Baxter jun. is shown supervising other hands. The majority of the white porcelain decorated there was Coalport and it is indeed fortunate that so many signed pieces survive as these enable easy recognition of many styles unique to this workshop. Some pieces signed T. Baxter will be by his father, while Baxter jun. usually signed with a cursive 'TB' monogram.

Thomas Baxter could try his hand at almost any subject but he was primarily a figure painter. Many of his pieces depicted

Baxter, Thomas. *A portrait in watercolour of Lady Hamilton, inscribed on the reverse in the hand of the artist 'Drawn at Merton by TB, 1804'. Baxter paid many visits to Emma Hamilton at Merton, the house she shared with Nelson. Baxter much preferred to paint portraits rather than porcelain, but sadly never received the patronage he needed. (Private Collection.)*

Colour Plate 11. ***Blue and White.*** *A small cream jug in three dot painter* style, similar to Bristol but probably made very early at Worcester, c.1752, 2⅝in. (6.7cm). (Phillips.)*

Colour Plate 13. ***Botanical Decoration.*** *A Flight, Barr and Barr plate painted with a delicately observed spray of blossom, the apple green* border only slightly influenced by the rococo revival*. Impressed* and printed marks, c.1830, 9ins. (23cm). (Dyson Perrins Museum.)*

Colour Plate 12. ***Blue Grounds.*** *A collection of Worcester porcelain decorated with the three principal forms of blue ground — a teapot with wet blue* bands, a teapot and a cup and saucer with powder blue* and fan-shaped panels, the remainder with scale blue* grounds, all c.1765-75. The saucer-dish in the centre was decorated in the Giles* workshop. (Phillips.)*

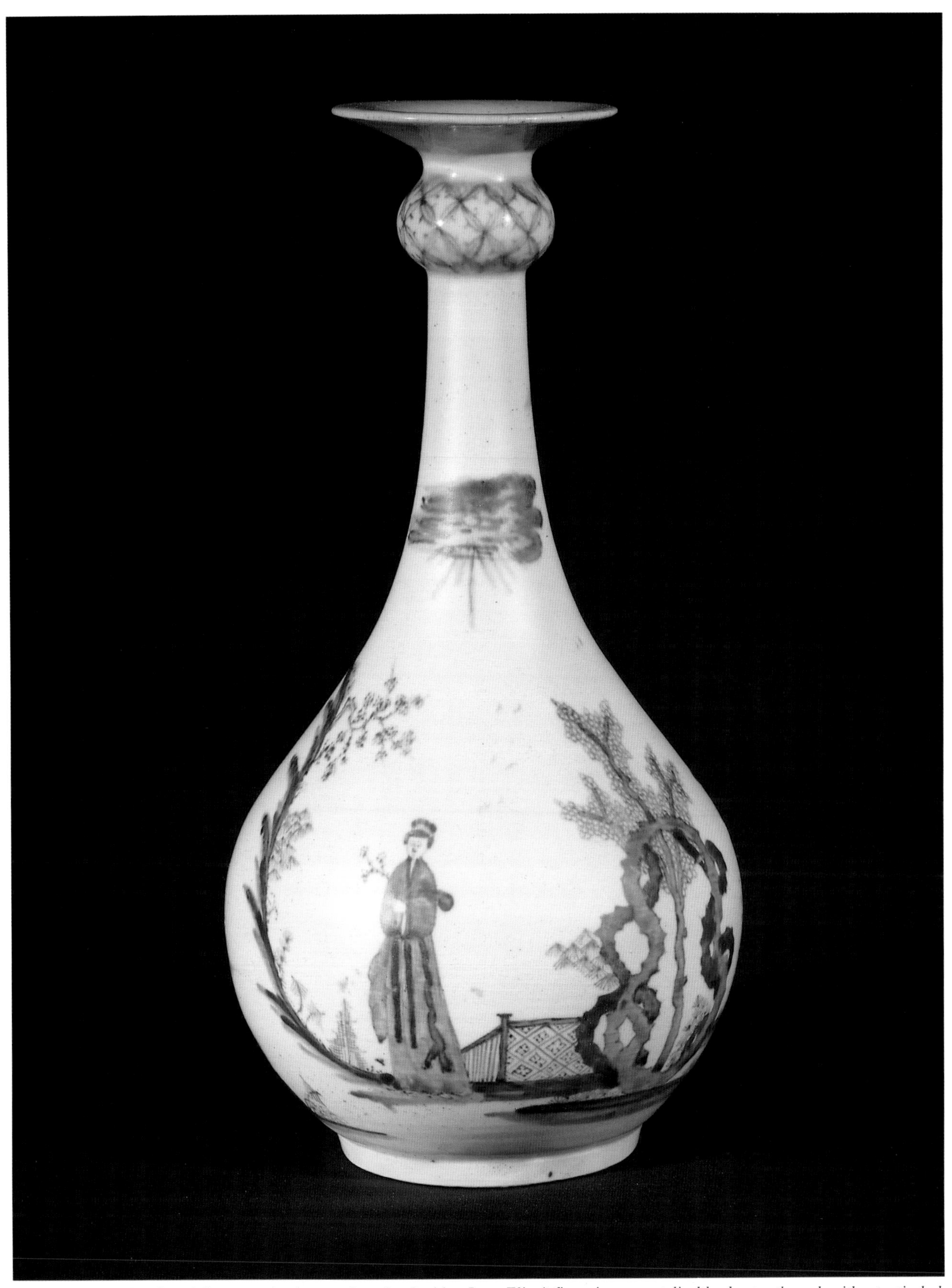

Colour Plate 14. ***Bottles.*** *A fine water bottle or guglet painted with a Long Eliza* figure in a very stylised landscape, the neck with a particularly elegant rim, c.1753-4, 10in. (25.5cm). (Private Collection.)*

Baxter, Thomas. *A Flight, Barr and Barr cabinet plate inscribed 'Mrs Siddons in the character of the Tragic Muse after the original by Sir J. Reynolds PRA', painted soon after Baxter arrived in Worcester in 1814. Impressed* and printed marks, 9in. (23cm). The companion plate sold at the time for an incredible 50 guineas. (Dyson Perrins Museum, photograph Phillips.)*

classical themes as, in his own words, 'it is to the Greeks that we owe nearly all that is elegant or dignified in art'. Many popular illustrations of Grecian ladies seen around 1800 are said to represent Lady Hamilton. Artists such as Romney painted her in these classical 'attitudes' and Baxter was certainly not alone in copying some of these famous poses on to porcelain. It is believed that Nelson bought a set of vases by Baxter for the home he shared with Emma Hamilton at Merton and this led to Baxter being invited to Merton to paint. Thomas Baxter did indeed make several visits to Merton as Emma's guest while Nelson was away at sea.

Preserved in the library of the National Maritime Museum is a fascinating album of drawings by Thomas Baxter, many dated either 1802, 1803 or 1804. They range from quick pen and ink and pencil sketches of Lady Hamilton, her daughter Horatia and other guests at Merton, to finished watercolours of parts of the house and grounds. It is tempting to see in these watercolours many similarities to Baxter's work on porcelain. Indeed, one of the sketches, depicting Emma Hamilton as Britannia, was adapted as the central subject on a Coalport plate signed by Thomas Baxter in 1806. The plate itself must have been important to Thomas Baxter as he placed it proudly in the foreground of the watercolour of his workshop painted in 1810. The plate was recently bought by the Victoria and Albert Museum and it can now be seen alongside the watercolour.

Baxter, Thomas. *The 'harlequin' panels on this Flight, Barr and Barr* déjeuner* *service presented a perfect opportunity for Thomas Baxter to illustrate the variety of his subjects. These comprise scenes from Shakespeare, named landscapes, shells 'from nature', flowers, feathers and insects. Script marks, c.1815. (Sotheby's.)*

It seems that the air of London seriously affected Thomas Baxter's health. He painted less and eventually in 1814 he was forced to leave London for the clean air of Worcester. He bought a house in Edgar Street just a stone's throw from the cathedral and close to the two great china factories. Here he established a china painting school of his own. One of his pupils, the figure painter Solomon Cole*, recorded that among his other pupils were Samuel Astles* and Moses Webster* (flowers), Thomas Lowe* (figures), William and Enoch Doe* (various subjects) and John Pitman* (animals).

Baxter was a very fine teacher and it is not difficult to see his influence in the work of any of these pupils when they can be identified, such as the plaque by Enoch Doe illustrated in Colour Plate 31. It is inscribed on the reverse:

> Painted by E Doe... Worcester, From the original painting by T Baxter. In the possession of R Lawrence Esq.

With pupils so closely emulating the work of their teacher, it is naturally going to be difficult to ascribe unsigned pieces to Thomas Baxter. Baxter himself only painted for Flight, Barr and Barr for three years at the same time as running his school. Yet during this time he was enormously prolific and there are many pieces which can be attributed with certainty. In the Dyson Perrins Museum, for instance, there is a signed mug with a self portrait in silhouette and fine flower painting. This can help the recognition of Baxter's flower painting which is generally little known.

The Worcester museum also exhibit one of the Sarah Siddons plates where Baxter carefully copied Reynolds' painting of *The Tragic Muse.* Baxter had seen and sketched Mrs Siddons on the London stage and Solomon Cole tells us that Baxter painted two such plates, one of which sold in 1816 for fifty guineas to the Marquis of Stafford. Plates from the services made for Lord Valentia* (Colour Plate 7) and the Nabob of Oude* are well documented by Binns* and others as by Baxter and these are remarkable works. From these it is certain that several large ice pails in the Worcester museum are undoubtedly by Baxter and these pieces link with some of his painting on Welsh porcelain. His shell painting, either in large panels on these ice pails or else in a much smaller scale on teawares, is distinctive in the use of perspective and fine stippled details which is a very different technique from the shell painting of Samuel Smith* and a hand believed to be John Barker* (*see* Colour Plate 76). The remarkable *déjeuner* service illustrated is important in showing many different subjects all by Thomas Baxter. The Shakespearian* figures are painted with the same sense of spontaneity which can be seen in many of the sketches of theatrical scenes Baxter had painted in his earlier days in London.

Thomas Baxter had moved to Worcester in 1814, which is after the change-over from Barr, Flight and Barr to Flight, Barr and Barr. Therefore only pieces marked 'FBB' impressed, or Flight, Barr and Barr in full, can be by Thomas Baxter. Pieces marked Barr, Flight and Barr are often ascribed to Baxter but these have to be by other hands such as John Pennington* or Samuel Smith.*

While engaged with Flight, Barr and Barr, Thomas Baxter showed also his skills as a modeller. He was responsible for four different portrait medallions, finely cast in biscuit porcelain within circular jewelled frames. Two depict Thomas Baxter himself and his father and these are known signed and dated 1815. A third subject of Nelson on a medallion in the Dyson Perrins Museum is signed 'TB 1805', even though it was not made until 1815. Another titled version of the Nelson medallion is in Southend Museum along with a companion medallion of the Duke of Wellington. Binns recorded that

Baxter, Thomas. *A portrait medallion* of Nelson showing Baxter's skill as a modeller, made in biscuit* porcelain with a jewelled deep blue surround, incised on the reverse 'TB 1805' but produced c.1815, 3in. (7.5cm). (Formerly Rous Lench Collection, now in the Dyson Perrins Museum.)*

Baxter, Thomas. *A Chamberlain cabinet cup painted with 'Cupid in a Glass', a subject designed as a test of any artist's skill. Baxter had painted the same subject previously on Swansea porcelain. Chamberlains Regent China mark, c.1820, 3½in. (9cm). (Phillips.)*

Colour Plate 15. ***Bristol Porcelain Manufactory.*** *A large mug of characteristic form with a very wide spreading base, c.1750-1, 4½in. (11.5cm). (Phillips.)*

Colour Plate 16. ***Bristol Porcelain Manufactory.*** *An early Bristol mug showing the typical thick opaque glaze and kiln spit-out* on the handle, c.1750. The primitive shape and decoration have no other parallels in English porcelain. 4½in. (11.3cm). (Phillips.)*

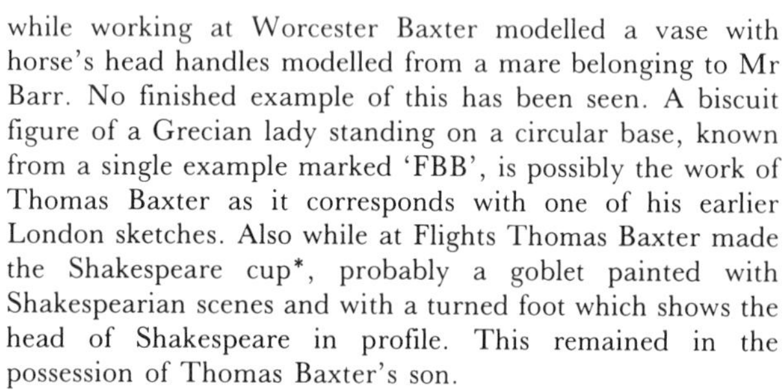

while working at Worcester Baxter modelled a vase with horse's head handles modelled from a mare belonging to Mr Barr. No finished example of this has been seen. A biscuit figure of a Grecian lady standing on a circular base, known from a single example marked 'FBB', is possibly the work of Thomas Baxter as it corresponds with one of his earlier London sketches. Also while at Flights Thomas Baxter made the Shakespeare cup*, probably a goblet painted with Shakespearian scenes and with a turned foot which shows the head of Shakespeare in profile. This remained in the possession of Thomas Baxter's son.

Thomas Baxter probably was not always in agreement with the management at Flight, Barr and Barr, in spite of producing most of his finest work there. In 1816 Baxter left Worcester for the quiet town of Swansea where he seems to have lived very humbly and felt even more isolated from the artistic life he used to know in London. With little work at the Swansea China Factory and unable to live as a portrait painter, he returned to Worcester once again in 1819, this time joining Chamberlains after a short engagement at Flights.

Following his return he wrote to the artist B.R. Haydon concerning an article about Flight, Barr and Barr which had appeared in the *Annals of the Fine Arts* including praise for a plate 'with a miniature copy of Mrs Siddons as the Tragic muse which would grace the cabinet of a prince'. Baxter complained to his old friend:

> Five year's banishment from all that is great [i.e. London] has rather increased if possible my love of the arts. My health of body is very much better for my removal. I cannot say much for my mind as I am employed here on little things and the "littler and prettier", the *dear* little things and the *dearer* they are the better...

Baxter goes on to mention the previous article and criticises the praise afforded to Flights:

> The two plates which are noticed are my painting, and their figure painting is now done by a pupil of mine named Lowe. It is not very likely that I will paint anything more for them, as the people I am now engaged with [i.e. Chamberlain] are more liberal minded and would be much more likely to bring forward what is good if there was a choice of encouragement....

While working for Chamberlains Baxter must have painted many of these 'littler and prettier' pieces with landscape views, especially Worcester and Malvern. Some which can with reasonable certainty be attributed to Baxter are remarkably fine, but great care needs to be taken before any small painting can be attributed. He was only at Chamberlains for two years, his last work being a series of cabinet plates painted with still-life subjects with very great care and accuracy (*see* illustration on page 97). The detailed account in Michael Faraday's diary of his visit on 2 August 1819 gives a useful insight into Baxter's position at this time. After spending some time being shown around Flight's factory by George Barr, Faraday...

> went to seek out Mr. Bagster, an artist employed at Chamberlains to whom I had words of introduction from several friends. I had found out at Barr's manufactory that he lived in Edgar Street and...I found out his habitation. The maid would fetch him from the works and I was forced to submit, though quite a stranger to him, but when he came he brought a large stock of goodwill and good nature and so we were soon familiar acquaintances. I went with him to Chamberlains, the Manufactory of Porcelain, where I believe he superintended the painting department and as Mr Bagster professed to be but a bad showman for all the operations, he placed me in the hands of another person.....the place looked much fitter and more lively than Flight Barrs had done.
>
> When I had seen all there Mr Bagster would take me home to lunch and on the way showed me the outside of the Cathedral and other old buildings. At home he showed me various paintings and drawings of his own admirably done and a specimen on porcelain entirely the work of his own hands. After lunch he again walked with me and set me on the river side where we parted having promised to meet together in the Cathedral in the afternoon, he to draw and I to see...

Thomas Baxter seems to have had a reasonably peaceful life at Chamberlains, being able to take whatever time he wished to sketch and draw. He probably did supervise or at least instruct other painters. Binns learnt from one of Baxter's pupils that there were frequent discussions in the work rooms as to the merits of Humphrey Chamberlain jun.'s* painting. Baxter regarded this as wonderful for its manipulative power but nothing else, with little to approve from an artistic point of view. Thomas Baxter still regarded himself as a great artist and must have been saddened to think back over his life, missing out on the success he felt he deserved as a painter in London.

Sadly Thomas Baxter's continued poor health led to his untimely death in 1821 at the age of thirty-nine. Fortunately we are left with many signed pieces which help chronicle his career, and his influence on the work of his pupils helped set the course of so much later porcelain painting at Worcester.

Baylies, Dr William

One of the original partners in the Worcester manufactory, Baylies was a physician who had similar interests to Dr John Wall*, having worked at Bath and made a study of the use of medicinal waters. He moved to Evesham, sixteen miles from Worcester, and must have been a close business associate of Wall and Davis, for he was persuaded to put up the largest single share, £675.10s., in the porcelain company. In spite of this considerable investment, there is no reason to suppose that he was involved in the day to day running of the works, however. Baylies had interests in politics and stood unsuccessfully for election at Evesham. He moved to Germany and died in Berlin in 1787.

Beads

It is traditionally believed that Worcester's production of beads during the 1840s was with the intention that they would be used by missionaries to trade with natives in far-off countries. It is intriguing to think of North American Indians and tribal warriors in remote jungles proudly parading about with Worcester porcelain around their necks. Spherical and oval beads were made in many sizes, with coloured glazes or fine printed patterns. Few records survive as to the extent of Chamberlain and Co.'s bead production, but it was probably short lived. A certain quantity has survived at the Worcester factory but it is unlikely that any other Worcester beads could ever be identified.

Beakers

See **Tumblers**

Beckoning Chinaman Pattern

The first really popular overglaze enamelled pattern used at Worcester from about 1753-7, on variously shaped mugs (Colour Plate 8) and on teapots. The primary subject of a standing Oriental waving to a flock of birds bears on the reverse either a Chinese lady and child or a spray of formal flowers in Meissen rather than oriental style. A rare variant on larger Worcester pieces includes a smaller child beside the Chinaman, waving his hands in the air.

The precise origin of the pattern is unkown, but an early mug, c.1752, in the Klepser Collection (Spero's catalogue no. 4), includes a related standing figure. The fluted globular teapots of this pattern were copied exactly at Christian's factory in Liverpool and these are frequently mistaken for Worcester.

The *Beckoning Chinaman* was not used in underglaze blue except for a unique design on a tureen which bears similarities. (See Branyan, French and Sandon, pattern I.A.23.)

Bell Pulls

These small egg-shaped porcelain handles for attaching to a rope or curtain cord were first made at Worcester c.1775. The very few examples known are all decorated with rich Japan

Bell Pulls. *One of a pair of Flight period bell handles in deep blue and gold, c.1785, 4in. (10.5cm) overall. In this case the bell pulls have been mounted in ormolu to form miniature vases. (Author's Collection.)*

Billingsley, William. *A Barr, Flight and Barr bowl painted in the distinctive style of William Billingsley against a pale blue ground, the salmon border with rich gilding, impressed* BFB mark, c.1808-10, 6⅝in. (17cm). (Lawrence Fine Art of Crewkerne.)*

foliate panels between deep underglaze blue and gold bands. Most of the examples attributed to early Worcester appear in fact to be Chamberlain from the 1790s. These were made in the same rich Japan pattern which Chamberlain called *Queen's**, as well as in blue and gold and other popular designs. All examples are unmarked, of course, and hard to attribute, so it is possible some will be from Flight's factory.

A few Flight 'bell handles' are known dating from c.1785-90. These are of double-ogee moulded shape and decorated in deep blue and gold. One pair (illustrated here) is known mounted in ormolu to form vase-shaped ornaments. The mounts seem to be contemporary and so it is possible that this shape of porcelain section was supplied by the factory to be mounted and was never intended to be used on a cord.

Bengal Tyger Pattern
(Also sometimes spelt Bengal Tiger.) *See* **Dragon in Compartments Pattern**

Billingsley, William
William Billingsley is justifiably regarded as the finest flower painter on English porcelain and yet his life was pathetically sad. He travelled the country in pursuit of dreams which always eluded him. Some regard Billingsley as a genius, others as a charlatan, but few can deny not only his great talent but also the enormous influence he was to have over the industry. His career began in Derby where he was born in October 1758 and worked as a painter at the porcelain factory. At the same time he experimented with all branches of the manufacturing process. By 1795 he felt ready to set up on his own and by 1796 he had moved to Pinxton where he was provided with backing from John Coke to build the necessary kilns to make his own fine porcelain. Heavy kiln losses and little profit led to disagreement and in April 1799 Billingsley had left Pinxton, setting up instead at Belvedere Street in Mansfield where he ran a decorating establishment, buying white porcelain from wherever he could, principally Staffordshire. It is interesting to note that on 8 July 1799 the Chamberlain order books record the sale of a small amount of white Worcester porcelain to Billingsley at his address in Mansfield.

After his attempts to make porcelain at Torksey had also led

Billingsley, William. *A Barr, Flight and Barr spill vase painted with pink and white roses on a grey marbled ground, attributed to William Billingsley, impressed* mark, c.1808-10, 3⅛in. (8cm). (Phillips.)*

Billingsley, William. *The painting on this salmon-ground Barr, Flight and Barr cup and saucer is much closer to Derby in style than traditional Flight flower painting. The technique strongly suggests that Billingsley was responsible, impressed and printed marks, c.1808-10. (Private Collection.)*

to failure and near bankruptcy, he set out for Wales in 1808. He travelled with his two daughters, Sarah and Lavinia, and Samuel Walker*, who had become his partner, with a shared interest in developing new kilns. Billingsley's wife returned to Derby and he was destined never to see her again. Having been unable to find financial backing or other work at Nantgarw at this time, Billingsley sent word to Barr, Flight and Barr* who advanced him a small amount of money to finance his journey to Worcester. Billingsley, Walker and the two girls walked all the way, arriving in Worcester in the late summer of 1808. A most pathetic letter was sent by Sarah Billingsley to her mother on 24 October 1808, quoted originally by Haslem and repeated by Henry Sandon in *Flight and Barr Worcester Porcelain.* In this letter Sarah dares not mention any names for fear of being found out by creditors, but she recounts that William Billingsley had been employed for 'wages very low for a good hand, indeed he has not any more at present than the Common hands'. They could not even afford to pay for their lodgings even though they were 'reckoned the cheapest rooms in the town'. The two daughters were working from seven in the morning until seven at night, on a kind of work unknown to their mother (probably printing). Samuel Walker had not yet found work, although according to Sarah 'the person who we work for has promised to think of a place for him as soon as he can'.

The situation changed over the next few years as Martin Barr sen.* realised how useful Billingsley could be. Billingsley probably painted for at least a year and then joined Walker in working on improvements to Flight's body and kilns. Billingsley and Walker were paid various sums while working on these improvements and then in November 1812 they received £200 as part of an agreement in return for having 'imparted and disclosed ... the knowledge of a certain secret relating to a new method of composing porcelain'. They were bound by this agreement not to disclose this secret to any other parties under penalty of £1,000. Binns* tells us that Walker had made significant improvements to Flight's kilns, and built for them a 'reverberating enamel kiln'. According to Binns he built a similar kiln for Chamberlains. The Chamberlain account books record for 30 May 1812 a payment of £5 to 'Billingsley, Worcester for a Plan of Building standing Kiln'.

Notwithstanding the agreement, in November 1813 William Billingsley and Samuel Walker, who by this time was married to Sarah Billingsley, left Worcester suddenly without notice, returning once more to Wales where they entered into an agreement first with William Weston Young at Nantgarw and subsequently with Messrs Dilwyn and Bevington at Swansea. Flight, Barr and Barr* wrote to Samuel Walker on 12 November 1814 threatening to use legal redress to prevent Billingsley and Walker using the formula for which they had been paid so handsomely. Instead of taking this action, however, Flights wrote to Lewis Dilwyn warning him not to employ Walker and 'Beeley' (the alias Billingsley was then using), while at the same time advising him that the granulated body they had developed could never be made any use of, and was not worth Flight's while pursuing.

Bird and Snail Pattern. *The base of the mug illustrated. Note the single incised stroke inside the footrim by the handle, confirming its attribution to the Scratch Cross class. (Sotheby's.)*

Bird and Snail Pattern. *A bell-shaped mug of Scratch Cross class*, painted in enamel colours and dated under the base 'E * L 1754', 4¾in. (12cm). (Sotheby's.)*

Although Billingsley did manufacture some beautiful porcelain at Swansea and subsequently at Nantgarw, he remained destined to fail, living most of the time near to poverty and seeing both of his daughters die through illness brought on by their wretched existence. He and Walker eventually walked once more to Coalport and were taken on through the kindness of John Rose. Billingsley worked on Coalport's body but he was old and worn out by this time. He did little further in the porcelain industry and died in January 1828, aged seventy. He was buried under the name William Beeley in a church near Coalport.

Two principal questions remain unanswered concerning Billingsley's time at Worcester. What painting can be attributed to him and did Flights introduce his improved porcelain composition? Martin Barr would not have employed the finest flower painter of his day and not put him to work right away. If the accounts in the agreement of November 1812 are correct Billingsley had worked for three years on improving the porcelain. This gives at least a year following his arrival in Worcester in the summer of 1808, when he would have been just a painter. Someone who had boasted at Derby that he could paint 'a spray of six fine large roses with twelve buds and delicate leaf foliage' in just one hour, could have painted a very great deal of porcelain in one year. There are pieces of Barr, Flight and Barr which exhibit Billingsley's mannerisms and must be his work, although it is difficult to know the extent to which Martin Barr encouraged Billingsley to follow the factory's own decorating styles rather than continuing the style he had developed at Derby. The pieces illustrated here and in Colour Plate 9 are, in my opinion, the work of Billingsley but such attributions are always controversial. No flower painters could have worked in a factory alongside a master like Billingsley and not have been influenced by him. The other artists undoubtedly adopted some of his mannerisms. Billingsley had left Worcester during the Barr, Flight and Barr period in 1813. There are many pieces marked Flight, Barr and Barr too late in date to be by Billingsley, but which very closely follow his style. These were by Samuel Astles*, Henry Stinton* or even Moses Webster*, yet many will continue to be incorrectly ascribed to the great Billingsley himself.

Martin Barr wrote in 1810 to the editor of *The London Miscellany:*

> It affords me considerable gratification to inform you that perseverance has accomplished very great improvements in the texture, whiteness and beauty of our porcelain.

This could have been due to Billingsley's labours but more likely it was just a selling ploy. The factory continued to use soaprock* until the end of the Flight, Barr and Barr period and there appears to have been no significantly different body in use during the time of Barr, Flight and Barr — certainly nothing approaching the bodies used at Swansea and Nantgarw. The letter from Worcester to Lewis Dilwyn warning him not to manufacture the new composition was therefore probably sent in good faith by a firm who knew that this beautiful invention could never be manufactured profitably.

Binns, Richard William

The important role played by R.W. Binns in the history of Worcester porcelain cannot be emphasised too greatly. Little is known about his early career except that he had worked as Art Director for Messrs Apsley Pellatt and Company at the

Bird in a Ring Pattern. *A teapot painted in dark underglaze blue*, crescent mark*, c.1765-70, 5¾in. (14.5cm). (Sotheby's.)*

Birmingham Printing. *A South Staffordshire enamel watch-back or lid from a snuff box, the print of* The Tea Party* *(version number 1) signed R.H.f (for Robert Hancock* fecit). An identical print was used on Worcester porcelain. (Dyson Perrins Museum.)*

Falcon Glass Works, where he would have learnt a great deal about marketing both glass and ceramics. Apsley Pellatt were major exhibitors at the Great Exhibition in 1851, where Worcester under Chamberlain and Co. put on such a feeble display. Following the departure of Walter Chamberlain*, W.H. Kerr* was in need of a new partner to attempt to revive the fortunes of the once great factory, and looked to Mr Binns to provide the necessary drive. From 1852 the Worcester factory traded as Kerr and Binns and passes beyond the period covered by this book. However, Binns' contribution to the history of earlier Worcester porcelain began on his arrival in the city when he realised the factory owned a superb collection of their finest products going back to the eighteenth century. He lovingly preserved and catalogued these, as well as all archives which remained, and established a museum of ceramic art which inspired and instructed his own workmen and new generations of students. Today we all owe a very great deal to Binns' researches and his principal publication, *A Century of Potting in the City of Worcester,* remains as a work of classic scholarship and enthusiasm for the traditions which he loved.

Bird and Snail Pattern
Probably copied directly from Chinese porcelain, this very rare design is known only on a single water bottle and basin and a series of three bell-shaped mugs. The mugs are all dated underneath the base 'E * L 1754'. This is important as it confirms a date for the type of Worcester porcelain known as the Scratch Cross* class. The pattern is finely painted, mostly in tones of brown, the bird looking alertly at a rather stylised snail. There is no evidence that the pattern represents a fable although this has been suggested. The celebrated bottle and basin, formerly in the Rous Lench Collection, was donated to the Dyson Perrins Museum following the death of Tom Burn.

Bird in a Ring Pattern
An underglaze blue pattern used on teawares from c.1758-70. Always exactly painted, the primary motif of a bird perched on a suspended hoop was possibly derived from an earlier overglaze design of figures and objects used on jugs and bottles. Large quantities of wasters have been found on the factory site, although the pattern is relatively uncommon today. Branyan, French and Sandon list the pattern as I.C.14.

Birds in Branches Pattern
A printed pattern finely engraved for use on teawares from about 1770 until the 1790s. The design appears to have been copied exactly from an earlier pattern of the *Mobbing Birds** type, used on vases in the late 1750s, although it is curious why the factory should have waited so long to introduce their printed version. The pattern was referred to as *Birds* in the Chamberlain account books when they sold the Caughley version, which is indistinguishable from Worcester. It was also made elsewhere, principally in pearlware. Branyan, French and Sandon list the pattern as II.B.21.

Birmingham Printing
During the 1750s Birmingham became the centre for the manufacture of English enamel on metal, especially small patch boxes, snuff boxes and bonbonnières. Many pieces were decorated with transfer printing and there are direct links between printing on enamel and some porcelain. Certain signed prints by Robert Hancock* are recorded on enamel and other less sophisticated prints have been noted on early Worcester porcelain which relate directly to enamel printing. The Birmingham enameller John Brooks applied for a patent in 1751 for a method of 'printing, impressing and reversing upon enamel and china'. Porcelain is very unlikely to have been made in Birmingham and any china decorated there will be either Chinese or quite likely Worcester, sold in the white or decorated under licence. Some of the 'Smoky Primitives'* could have been printed at Birmingham, although some sauceboats* bearing these prints are known with enamelled borders in typical Worcester factory style. This tends to suggest that these at least were decorated at the factory.

Biscuit Porcelain. *A pair of fine quality Chamberlain biscuit figures of children with the unusual incised marks 'H. Chamberlain & Sons, Worcs.' and 'Chamberlain's China Works, Worcester', c.1825-30, 6¼in. (16cm). (Phillips.)*

Biscuit Porcelain. *A remarkable Grainger, Lee and Co. vase known as the Arabian vase. Fortunately, the delicate handles and modelled vines have been preserved by the original glass dome which was sold with the vase, c.1832-5. (Private Collection.)*

Biscuit Porcelain

The term biscuit is used in the industry for a ceramic body which has been fired once but is not glazed. Porcelain can be sold in an unglazed state to show the delicate modelling but is porous and prone to get dirty. Biscuit figures were a speciality of the Derby factory, but Worcester were not figure makers and sold no biscuit porcelain in the 18th century. Thomas Baxter* introduced the first biscuit productions to Worcester with a series of portrait medallions* dated 1815. A single biscuit figure of a classical female standing on a circular plinth is known from the Barr, Flight and Barr period and could also be the work of Thomas Baxter, especially as it resembles a much earlier sketch drawn by Baxter in London. Chamberlain used biscuit porcelain for elaborate cottage pastille burners* c.1820. These were encrusted with sieved clay vegetation and must have been difficult to keep clean as they would not function as pastille burners inside a glass dome. Such domes or 'shades' were sold with many biscuit models to protect the delicate pieces. Chamberlain made a number of biscuit figures as well as vases with applied modelled biscuit flowers and inkstands surmounted by biscuit figures of Cupid. Grainger, Lee and Co. specialised in biscuit porcelain from c.1825, producing a great range of different figure and animal subjects. Their finest creations were bower groups* of cupids within incredibly elaborate modelled flowers. Some of these flowers were delicately enamelled in colours. Other larger figures were applied with real lace which had been dipped in liquid clay and burnt away in the kiln, leaving incredibly fine china lacework on their costumes. Unless protected by a glass shade since they were made, these figures will have retained very little of this lacework today. Ewers and vases with applied flowers and vines were another speciality of the Grainger factory in the 1830s. The development of parian*, a refined form of biscuit porcelain which was easier to keep clean, brought about the end of traditional biscuit in the 1840s.

Bishop Sumner Pattern

This striking design directly copies a Chinese *famille verte** original from the *Kangxi* period, showing a fight between a flying phoenix and a kylin. The border includes a variety of fanciful beasts within panels. For some unknown reason the pattern is almost invariably marked with a crescent in gold. It is uncertain which bishop gave the pattern its name. There was a John Sumner who became Archbishop of Canterbury and a Charles Sumner who was Bishop of Winchester, but both were 19th century figures and so the pattern, which dates from the 1770s, would not have been made for either originally, even though rare examples were made as replacements in the Flight, Barr and Barr period. The pattern was used only for dessert wares and from the large number of pieces surviving many sets must have been produced. A rare cylindrical mug of the pattern c.1780 is in the National Museum of Wales. The *Bishop Sumner* pattern has been confused with the Bengal Tyger design (*see* **Dragon in Compartments pattern**), also copied from *famille verte,* although there is little similarity between the two.

Bleeding Bowls

Small circular bowls roughly 5in. (13cm) in diameter with rounded sides and single flat side handles with elaborate moulded designs. As most of the known Worcester examples

Bishop Sumner Pattern. *Even the shape of this Worcester plate copies a Chinese original from the* Kanxi *period, although the colouring has been adapted slightly, gold crescent mark*, c.1775, 8⅞in. (22.5cm). (Phillips.)*

are decorated with Chinese patterns it is probable that the shape was also based on Chinese porcelain rather than the European silver or pewter prototypes. There will always be arguments as to whether these objects were bleeding bowls or porringers*. Worcester did make a bowl of similar size with either one or two shell-shaped side handles which had matching covers and will have been porringers. The bleeding bowls have handles set higher up level with the rims which are also thick and everted. Worcester bleeding bowls are great rarities and most which do survive are painted with the *Squirrel and Vine* pattern copying Chinese. They date from the mid-1750s.

Bleeding Bowls. *A 'bleeding bowl' painted in blue with the* Squirrel and Vine *pattern, a curiously primitive rarity from c.1756, workman's mark*, 5⅜in. (13.5cm). (Dyson Perrins Museum.)*

Blind Earl Pattern

This design of embossed rose leaves and buds is probably the best known of all the early Worcester patterns. It is named after the Earl of Coventry who lost his sight in a hunting accident and asked the factory to make him a design he could feel. The date of the accident is variously given as 1770 or 1780. Research at Croome Court, the seat of the Earls of Coventry, suggests two generations of the family suffered in this way but none as early as the mid-1750s when the design was introduced. A very similar shape was made at Chelsea during the Red Anchor period but we shall never know which came first. The pattern is known from just three early shapes — scalloped dessert plates, twig-handled 'sweetmeat dishes', and oval spoon trays*. The latter two shapes would have been sold with conventional teawares, the dishes possibly serving as teapot stands (*see* Colour Plate 2). The pitcher block mould for a bowl was found during early excavations* on the Worcester factory site but no finished example has been seen.

The earliest examples of the pattern remaining in the family of the Earls of Coventry date from the Flight, Barr and Barr period and it is likely that the Coventrys ordered a set at this time, which gave the pattern its popular name. The pattern continued to be made by Chamberlain and Co. (Colour Plate 10) and Kerr and Binns and remains popular today in both painted and photolitho printed versions. In the 18th century the usual form of decoration was for the rose leaves to be naturalistically coloured. Underglaze blue versions were painted with fancy insects between the leaves. In addition the twig-handled dishes and spoon trays were painted to match any teaware decoration without reference to the moulded pattern underneath. Some plates were coloured in the Giles* workshop with distinctive insects and a rare version is painted with a full blown rose issuing from the moulded stem (illustrated on page 72). A series of lobed circular dishes is known where the *Blind Earl* pattern is not moulded but entirely painted in enamels. A set of eight is in a collection in Ireland, but without the dessert plates which would probably originally have accompanied them.

Blind Earl Pattern. *A small dish known as a sweetmeat dish, the embossed decoration picked out in underglaze blue*, crescent mark*, c.1765, 6in. (15cm). (Phillips.)*

Blind Earl Pattern. *Two embossed dessert plates with contrasting decoration. The example on the right is decorated in the typical style of the Worcester factory, while the plate on the left bears an additional painted rose enamelled in the Giles* workshop. Both c.1770, 7⅝in. (19.5cm). (Phillips.)*

Blue and White

Chinese porcelain decorated in blue was treasured in Europe in the 16th century and keenly collected by the end of the 17th. By the middle of the 18th century so much had been shipped to Europe that it was virtually in everyday use in the wealthy homes where tea was served. Nankin ware, as Chinese blue and white porcelain was known, was trusted whereas early English porcelain was new and treated with suspicion. There is little doubt that early Bow and Worcester teawares were painted in Chinese style to be passed off as true Nankin.

Although blue and white had been the principal product at Limehouse* and Bristol*, Worcester had discovered a more important market for its enamelled wares. A certain amount of blue and white was made at Worcester during the first few years (Colour Plate 11), but most of the earliest shapes are known just from coloured examples or the very occasional example painted in blue. This suggests that the output of blue and white in the 1750s was surprisingly small, and limited mostly to teawares and sauceboats*. Generally Bow was better at blue and white and Worcester could not compete with the Chinese. Instead at Worcester they concentrated on their own rather different style of enamelled decoration. Gradually the factory became firmly established and introduced a far greater range of blue and white designs by the later 1750s. In 1757 the Worcester Porcelain Warehouse placed an advertisement in the *Whitehall Evening Post:*

> Good blue and white painters wanted — none else will be employed.

while in December 1761 the London *General Evening Post* carried the following advertisement:

> WANTED, PAINTERS in Blue and White: Good Workmen, who are sober and diligent, will meet with proper encouragement, by applying to the manufactory in Worcester.

Possibly the Worcester factory was unable to obtain enough painters to meet the demand for their blue and white porcelain. By c.1757 underglaze transfer printing was introduced, followed by a tendency during the 1760s to make painted patterns less complicated and exacting. The *Oxford Journal* wrote a glowing account of the factory and its wares in May 1763:

> ...The most valuable part of all, and which principally calls for notice, is the extraordinary strength and cheapness of the common sort of blue and white Worcester porcelain; and let any person but impartially consider the difference... between this and that of an equal degree, though hardly of equal beauty, imported from abroad, and he will find the advantage is considerable and in favour of the former, that if he has any degree of candour, he must see and acknowledge his obligations to a manufactory which .... affords an elegant and desirable furniture calculated by its ease of purchase for general and ordinary use.

The few contemporary records which do survive indicate that Worcester blue and white was able to match cheap Chinese imported Nankin sets more or less evenly on price. Demand grew, especially for export to Europe. The only evidence for Worcester's important trade with Holland is the enormous amount of Worcester blue and white porcelain which survives there in old family homes. English dealers in antiques are now regularly travelling to Holland to bring back some of the sets which were traded there in the 18th century. The toy* tea service illustrated was discovered in Holland and contains a

Blue and White. *A fine hexagonal vase, the design adapted from a Japanese* Kakiemon* *original but producing a very different effect in underglaze blue*, workmen's marks*, c.1760, 15½in. (39.5cm). (L.O. Branyan Collection.)*

Blue and White. *Decoration in underglaze blue* rarely blurs on a flat shape such as this dessert plate, a particularly striking example of a hitherto unrecorded pattern copied from the Chinese. The border is a popular design inspired by early French porcelain, crescent mark*, c.1770, 8¼in. (21cm). (Phillips.)*

shape of tea kettle stand which is purely Dutch and unknown in full size for the English market.

To supply the export trade greater emphasis was placed on transfer printing, possibly leading to a strike among the blue painters at Worcester in 1770 (recorded by Binns* but not confirmed). Some Worcester blue painters went to Plymouth and Derby, while those who remained at Worcester mostly painted scale blue*. Blue painting declined at Worcester and gradually, along with a change to a new brighter blue colour (*see* **Underglaze Blue**), the quality of blue printing also declined. By 1775 the factory had lost Thomas Turner* to Caughley and he took with him his expertise as well as a compete understanding of the market. Worcester's heavy blue prints of the Davis period and Flight period could not compete and by 1788 Chamberlain was selling blue and white Caughley alongside Worcester in the High Street. Even greater competition from Staffordshire blue printed earthenware, along with trouble controlling blue printing in the kiln, led to Flight abandoning blue and white by c.1792. The full story of blue and white is told by Lawrence Branyan, Neal French and John Sandon in *Worcester Blue and White Porcelain, 1751-1790.*

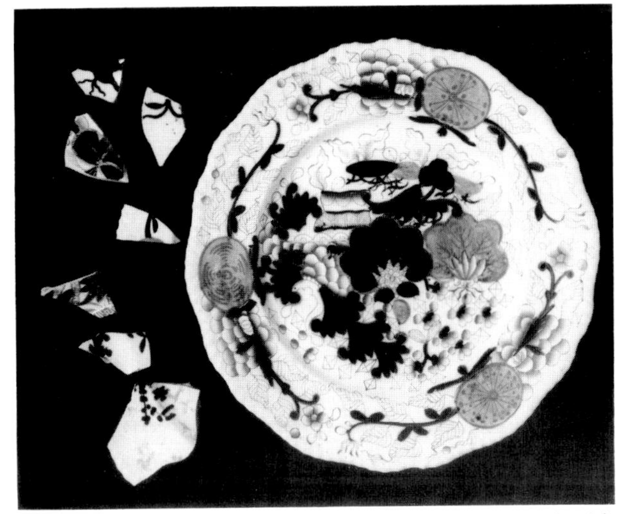

Blue Ball Japan Pattern. *A gadroon-edged dinner plate painted in the Imari* style, shown with matching wasters* from the Grainger factory site, pattern number* 1472, c.1825, 10¼in. (26cm). (Henry Sandon Collection.)*

***Blue and White.** A selection of unglazed, biscuit* 'wasters'* found during factory site excavations* in a level dating from c.1770. All have been fired once to harden on the colouring which remains black. Only after glazing will the cobalt oxide turn blue.*

Blue Ball Japan Pattern
A popular pattern at Graingers around 1820-5. The distinctive ball shapes are painted in underglaze blue with colours and gold added in the Imari* style. The pattern usually has a gadroon rim* and was used on dinner and dessert wares with the pattern number 1472. (Illustrated on pages 73 and 130.)

Blue Bordered Patterns
As taste and styles changed during the 1770s, the heavy all-over wet blue* and scale blue* grounds of Worcester became less popular and were replaced with patterns on white grounds with dark blue borders. The blue borders have variously been described as royal blue* and said to be overglaze, but in actual fact only a very small number of pieces use overglaze blue and these tend to be decorated outside the factory. There has always been a tendency to date Worcester's deep blue bordered patterns far too early. Geoffrey Godden drew attention to this in the introduction of his *Chamberlain-Worcester Porcelain,* showing that the fluted shapes so often used were mostly of the late 1770s and 1780s. I do not feel any blue bordered patterns can be dated before c.1775. Indeed, the bright tone of the underglaze cobalt blue in most examples suggests at least 1780. One jug illustrated by Godden (op.cit., colour pl. 1) is dated underneath 1784. Popular designs such as *Lord Henry Thynne**, *Earl Dalhousie**, *Lord Rodney** and the Kew* service will all date from c.1775-85, and are therefore from the Davis and early Flight periods after the death of Dr Wall. Importantly, no biscuit* fragments of blue borders were found on the factory site except in levels alongside Flight period blue-printed patterns.

Blue Dragon Pattern
A printed design used at the Grainger factory. *See* **Dragon Pattern.**

Blue Grounds
Underglaze blue was popular as a ground colour from the mid-1760s and appears in four different forms at Worcester (Colour Plate 12). Solid cobalt blue is very heavy and dark and difficult to control. Worcester's solid blue is usually known as wet blue*. In the 18th century, the factory used grounds of powder blue*, scale blue* or cracked ice* to break up the heavy effect of the solid cobalt. A few simple printed patterns in bright blue were subsequently used as backgrounds in Chamberlain and Grainger services from c.1820.

Blue Printing
Although Worcester may not have invented the process of transfer printing*, there is no doubt that they were the first to use printing in underglaze blue. Having mastered the printing process, there were additional problems to overcome before the technique could be adapted for use underglaze. The early process of transferring the design in oil and then dusting on the colour was only possible on top of glaze and could not be used

on biscuit porcelain. When using paper transfers underglaze, the main difficulty was with blurring. Overglaze prints were very finely engraved and this detail became smudged together below the runny glaze. Instead new copper plates had to be engraved in a very different style of strong outlines with only limited shading. By c.1757 their experiments were completed and the first blue printed porcelain was put on sale.

A shard from an experimental trial teabowl found during the excavations is illustrated (*see* **Josiah Holdship**). It is printed with part of the *Man in Pavilion** pattern which is amongst the earliest Worcester blue prints. The trial is identified with certain Worcester factory code symbols including the letters 'i.h.' which just possibly could relate to Josiah Holdship who claimed to have invented printing at Worcester. The small range of early floral and landscape prints was followed by a few rare attempts to adapt overglaze transfer prints for use in underglaze blue. Portraits of George III and Charlotte were printed in blue from the same copper plates which had been engraved for overglaze printing. Two of these copper plates survive at the factory and show that the original finely detailed engraving was partly smoothed and deeply re-engraved around the outline in order to be suitable for blue printing. The *Parrot Pecking Fruit** and the *Tea Party** patterns were both re-cut in this way. The blue print of Queen Charlotte was accompanied on the mug illustrated by a very rare print of Venus and Cupid and it is interesting to record that this is the same print as was used on a trial shard signed 'IH' found during the excavations.

By the 1760s underglaze printing had been perfected at Worcester and its use became widespread. Modern engravers and painters estimate that a painted saucer, for example, would have taken fifteen times as long on average to decorate as a printed saucer. This discovery made Worcester blue and white cheap enough to sell in enormous quantities, even if, as Binns* recorded, the increased use of printing led to a strike within the Worcester factory among the blue painters, many of whom left the factory, c.1770. Richard Holdship* had taken the secret of printing to Derby but in terms of quality blue printed Derby was no competition to Worcester. On the other hand, Thomas Turner* who had trained as an engraver at Worcester, left together with Robert Hancock* to set up the Caughley factory where underglaze blue printing became the principal form of decoration. This was eventually to bring about the downfall of blue printing at Worcester. John Flight's diary* recorded that in 1788 and 1789 the factory was having great problems controlling their blue printing. They used patterns which combined printing with hand painting to prevent blurring of closely shaded areas. Gradually, however, Worcester had to admit defeat and left the process of blue printing to Staffordshire potters who had copied the Worcester invention and eventually bettered it.

Chamberlains had probably learnt from Flight's failure and as a result seem to have avoided this market. As retailers the Chamberlains had sold a great deal of Caughley blue-printed porcelain but clearly felt that it would not be commercial to try to compete. Recently one tea service has been discovered which indicates that they did at least make an attempt at underglaze blue printing. The shanked* shapes illustrated here seem to conform to other known Chamberlain teawares and the print itself has not been identified on the wares of any other factory. The only reference in the Chamberlain account books which might relate to this is in the Wages book for March 1797, where the words 'blue-print' are written against Joseph Yeates jun. The shanked set illustrated would tie in with this date, but is generally unsuccessful due to the great difficulty of printing on a tramline shanked shape. It is certainly inferior to the printed porcelain of other makers and

Blue Printing. *An early example of underglaze blue printing, the design deeply engraved with little fine detail which would have blurred and spoilt the effect. This saucer of the* Boathouse *pattern dates from c.1757-9, 4⅝in. (11.75cm). (L.O. Branyan Collection.)*

Blue Printing. *An example of a print designed for use overglaze and adapted for underglaze printing. Fine details have been removed while the outlines have been deeply strengthened. This rare print of Venus and Cupid accompanies a portrait of Queen Charlotte, c.1762, about 3⅜in. (8.5cm). (Present whereabouts unknown.)*

Chamberlain were probably wise to abandon their attempts.

Grainger made considerable use of blue printing from c.1810 when they used a number of patterns on their early bone china. Many of the original copper plates survive and Grainger's versions of popular patterns such as Broseley* or Dragon* can be identified from the many examples marked Grainger & Co. and Grainger, Lee and Co.

Blue Printing. *A part tea service apparently conforming to Chamberlain shanked* shapes of c.1795-1800. This is the only recorded instance of blue printing used at the Chamberlain factory, an unsuccessful form of decoration on such finely fluted shapes. (Phillips.)*

Blue Scale
See **Scale Blue**

Bly, John
According to Solomon Cole's* account of workmen at Flight's factory, John Bly 'excelled in shading the gold in arms, and was unequalled in giving a natural expression to the lion in the Royal Arms'. Cole records that Bly decorated the important armorial service for William IV*, although it is not known which other armorial services he worked on. Like many Worcester decorators, John Bly also worked for Chamberlain and his name appears in the wages books during two periods around 1800 and 1808-9. Geoffrey Godden, in his *Lowestoft Porcelains,* has shown that he was born in Lowestoft in 1779 and apprenticed at the Lowestoft china works, even though armorial decoration was a very minor product of the East Anglian factory. John Bly's son, also John, worked for Flight, Barr and Barr as a landscape painter and the latter's son, Jabez Bly, is known from several signed watercolours. It is possible Jabez Bly also painted at Graingers.

Bodenham Pattern
A teaware design with rococo-shaped panels of coloured Chinese figures framed with gold scrolls on a clear blue scale ground. Always finely potted, the decoration is associated with the Giles* workshop and dates from c.1768. While Giles' artists frequently copied Chinese patterns, the combination of blue scale is very unusual. The pattern is named after a set which was included in the sale of the Bodenham Collection in 1872, although it is likely that other services were made at the same time.

Bodenham Pattern. *This teabowl and saucer is very thinly potted with very delicate enamelling, unmarked, c.1768. (Phillips.)*

Bodies
The various Worcester factories generally used very few different ceramic bodies. Some are discussed here under **Bone China, Chemical Porcelain, Granite China, Regent China,** and **Soaprock.**

Boitard, L.P.
A French artist who worked in London and had connections with the Battersea enamel works. Robert Hancock* engraved a number of copper plates for the London printseller Robert Sayer and these included several designs after Boitard. One series was published in 1754. Some of these included the

Boscawen, Admiral. A cylindrical mug printed in black to commemorate the Admiral's victory at Louisburg in 1758, c.1758-60, 3¼ in. (8.4cm). (Phillips.)

inscription 'L.P. Boitard *delin*' as well as Hancock's name as engraver. Boitard had no connection with the Worcester factory but some of these prints were used on Worcester porcelain. A small number of sauceboats* with Hancock's engravings of *The Four Ages of Man* include the 'signature' 'L.P. Boitard *delin*' in reverse, showing that the same plates engraved for Robert Sayer were used for the porcelain. These were probably brought to Worcester by Hancock and used by him c.1756. It is also possible, however, that these had been printed prior to 1756 by Josiah or Robert Holdship* or else printed in Birmingham (*see* **Birmingham Printing**).

Bonbonnières
See **Snuff Boxes**

Bone China
A porcelain body which contains up to fifty per cent animal bone, although the amount of bone used in different formulas can vary greatly. It is uncertain when Worcester first made bone china but undoubtedly it was some time after the technique was invented in Staffordshire. Flights used their soaprock* body until 1840 and Chamberlain also persisted with a hybrid hard paste well into the 1810s. Their Regent China* introduced in 1811 was a refined white porcelain which probably contained some bone, but they did not make bone china as such until probably some time in the 1830s. Grainger changed from their hybrid hard paste to bone china c.1812 and it was initially very much a change for the worse. Grainger's early bone china is thick, unevenly glazed and very prone to staining. By the 1820s they had perfected the material, however, and continued to produce bone china until their closure in 1902.

Bostock Service. A heart-shaped dish from the well-known service, c.1785, 10¼ in. (26cm). (Phillips.)

Boscawen, Admiral
Edward Boscawen (1711-1761) achieved fame as commander-in-chief at the siege of Louisburg in 1758 when the British fleet helped Col. Amherst to capture the harbour and fortress which commanded the entrance to the St Lawrence in Nova Scotia. Hancock's* engraving used on Worcester was taken from an earlier portrait by Ramsay which had been engraved by John Faber in 1747. This depicts the admiral three-quarter length and was printed in black on cylindrical mugs. Very rare examples are known with the addition of the name Louisburg to the chart held by the admiral and the fronts of these mugs are printed with the arms of Boscawen impaling Glanville, presumably as a special commission from the admiral himself. Boscawen was successful at Lagos in 1759 but his acclaim was short lived and he died in 1761.

Bostock Service
One of the best known armorial services, this actually dates from c.1785 although it is usually credited with an earlier date. The bright tone of the underglaze blue border and heavily blued glaze confirms the late date and as such the service is important in confirming the factory's own style of rich fruit painting. This differs from fruit painting found on many redecorated pieces in similar style (*see* **Redecoration**). The arms are of Bostock with Rich in pretence, although it is not known exactly when or for what occasion the dessert service was made. *See* Colour Plate 29.

Botanical Decoration
While flower painting was a feature of some of the earliest Worcester porcelain, careful copies of actual specimens are uncommon (*see* Colour Plate 61). The earliest truly botanical services date from the 1790s on Flight and Barr spiral fluted shapes, the centres copied from published sets of botanical prints, each titled on the reverse of the pieces. Named botanical specimens are more common in Flight, Barr and Barr in the 1820s and 1830s (Colour Plate 13) but usually in small panels and lacking the excitement of Derby botanical painting. Chamberlain copied a popular Derby pattern c.1800

Bottles. *Three water bottles or guglets, the central example a great rarity bearing a workman's mark*, c.1753. This is flanked by slightly less elegant forms from the 1760s, painted with the popular* Willow Bridge Fisherman *pattern, 10in. and 11in. (25.5cm and 28cm). (Sotheby's.)*

with yellow borders and named specimens painted with great accuracy, and later dessert services can be very dramatic, although again rarely seen. Their most important botanical service was for the Nabob of the Carnatic* ordered in 1820, a vast set which contained more than one thousand pieces. To economise, Chamberlains used transfer printed outlines of the flowers which were then painted in colours. The titles of the flower specimens were also printed in this service. Although David Evans* painted delicate wild flowers at Graingers, no strictly botanical decoration has been noted.

Bottles

Elegant pear-shaped bottles were made from c.1753-60 with knopped necks and flared rims which copy Chinese porcelain shapes (Colour Plate 14). The earliest examples have remarkably wide rims which, although graceful, must have been impractical and were probably just ornamental, even though the price list of the London Warehouse c.1755-6 includes 'Decanters' made in one pint, quart and three pint (.57, 1.14 and 1.7 litre) sizes. By c.1756-60 the rim became a simple trumpet shape and these bottles are found only in patterns which are otherwise used on wash basins, confirming their purpose. Later examples, usually in the same patterns but from c.1765, have abandoned any attempt at a flared rim and, although more practical, these lack the elegance of the earlier forms. The word guglet is frequently used for these water bottles and, while some authors have specified that guglets should have narrow necks without the presence of a flared rim, the usage remains confused and for the purpose of this *Dictionary* the word bottle is preferred.

Small onion-shaped bottles with hexagonal sections were popular in the early 1750s but these were probably vases rather than any form of serving bottles. Similarly Grainger and Chamberlain made larger bottle-shaped vases purely as ornaments. Both made scent bottles* and Grainger also made curious shaped bottles for Cheltenham College Sauce (*see* **Sauce Bottles**).

Bough Pots

The arguments will always continue as to whether these popular objects were for growing flowers from bulbs or for displaying cut flowers. Basically they could serve either purpose and were designed to sit on a mantelpiece with a flat section against the wall. Of the two shapes from the early period, the more commonly seen is strongly rococo with heavy scroll edging and was probably introduced c.1765. Its decoration ranges from underglaze blue flower prints to rich coloured grounds such as the wonderful yellow ground* specimen in the Klepser Collection and many can be seen with scale blue*. A rarer fluted shape of bough pot was made c.1770 in the French style. Both shapes are pierced at the back for suspension on a wall. By about 1790 the popular semi-circular form of bough pot had been adopted by most factories. Flight and Barr examples are rarely seen and follow a simple panel-moulded form with a flat cover. Chamberlain made at least five different shapes, all illustrated by Geoffrey Godden in *Chamberlain-Worcester Porcelain,* pp.267-70. The Chamberlain account books refer to these as 'Ornaments' and show that they were sold separately, as pairs or as sets of three, either all of the same shape or with beaker-shaped side vases or spill vases*. Early examples c.1800 are of a waisted vase shape and can have flat or high domed covers. All subsequent straight-sided examples have high covers which are frequently missing today. Most have an artichoke finial which is very distinctive. Some are plain-sided while others have panels divided by rounded columns and were referred to at the time as 'half-circle pillar ornaments'. Classical decoration suits the bough pots remarkably well and the factory always seems to have reserved its finest decoration for these most splendid articles. The fashion for bough pots seems to have died out around 1810.

Bough Pots. *A Flight and Barr semi-circular bough pot, the cover with three apertures for bulbs, decorated with dramatic yellow and black grounds, painted script mark, c.1795-1800, 2⅜in. (16cm). (Phillips.)*

Bough Pots. *An unusual form of bough pot probably copied from French pottery. The shape is designed to stand or hang on a wall. Printed in underglaze blue*, crescent mark*, c.1768-70, 6⅝in. (17cm). (Dyson Perrins Museum.)*

Bouillion Cups
See **Broth Bowls**

Bourdaloues
Henry Sandon illustrates a bourdaloue or female chamber pot in his *Flight and Barr Worcester Porcelain,* pl.22, but this example in *Dragon in Compartments Pattern** is unmarked and is now thought to be of Coalport origin. Caughley made bourdaloues which were called coach pots when sold by Chamberlain, but no Worcester examples are known.

Bower Groups
The triumph of the Grainger factory's figure modelling was a series of bower groups made in the 1830s. One or two chubby Cupids were placed within an arbour of incredibly finely modelled flowers and vines, in white biscuit porcelain* or with delicate colouring to the flowers. Another version was titled 'Cupids Building a Gothic Bower' and depicts three putti placing flowers over a ruined Gothic window arch. Related bower groups were made at Derby but the superior quality of the flower work sets the Grainger examples apart.

Bower Groups. *A colourful biscuit* group of 'Cupids Building a Gothic Bower', showing the skill and delicacy of Grainger's modelling. Impressed Grainger, Lee & Co., c.1835, 9½in. (24cm). (Private Collection.)*

***Bowls.** An early bowl painted with a combination of* famille rose* *and* Kakiemon* *decoration producing a most attractive design, c.1755, 6¼in. (15.8cm). (Phillips.)*

***Bowls.** A rare covered bowl following a Chinese shape, the cover reversing to form another shallow bowl or a stand, painted in blue with the* Plantation *pattern, workman's mark*, c.1756, 9in. (23cm). (Sotheby's.)*

***Bowls.** An impressive large presentation bowl with a wet blue ground* and panels of* Fancy Birds*, *c.1770. (Phillips.)*

Bowls

The price list of the London Warehouse (*see* **London Shops**), c.1755-6 refers to bowls as basons and lists them as half-pint, pint and quart sizes (.28, .57 and 1.14 litres). No use is specified and so it is necessary to be careful in assuming that all bowls of a certain size were intended as slop bowls from tea services or that all large bowls were for punch. Most tea services did include at least one bowl, roughly 4¾-6in. (12-15cm) in diameter to be used as a slop or waste bowl, never for sugar. Expensive sets always included a covered sugar bowl or sucrier, but cheaper sets, basically in blue and white, often included a smaller open bowl as a sugar bowl. Larger bowls or basins could be used as the owner wished. 18th century blue and white bowls were often decorated with patterns which do not occur on teawares, such as the *Precipice** and *Brigand**, and these can seem rather too small for punch. At the other extreme some of the finest punch bowls were made in the 1770s and into the Regency period. Decorations of grapes and vines and hunting scenes give a clue to their purpose. Contemporary records usually refer to bowls by their capacity, such as one gallon or two quart (4.5 or 2.2 litres), rather than by their diameter or intended use.

Bowls. *The interior of the presentation bowl opposite, showing the arms of Fry painted in the bottom. (Phillips.)*

Boy on a Buffalo Pattern

A confusing name because it has been applied to many differing designs at numerous factories. The Worcester 'Boy on a Buffalo' pattern is seemingly the earliest English version and also appears to be unique to Worcester, even though it was copied directly from a Chinese prototype. Pencilled* in black monochrome, the design features a single figure riding on a cow or buffalo under a pine tree, with a lake or river at the side housing two sampans with masts that resemble modern-day pylons. The pattern is always consistently painted, mostly c.1755-6 although a few cups and saucers do appear to be up to ten years later. The porcelain is normally of Scratch Cross* type wth a creamy glaze, thinly cast and with small footrims. Curiously, teapots of plain, globular shape are surprisingly common, while milk jugs and larger jugs also survive far more frequently than cups and saucers. The pattern was also used, rarely, on mugs. Four badly fired fragments of the pattern were found on the Warmstry House* excavations, giving proof, if it was needed, that the decoration was carried out at the factory. Examples often carry workmen's marks* in black enamel.

Bradley, Samuel

In the original partnership deeds of the Worcester Porcelain Company one of the subscribers was 'Samuel Bradley of the City of Worcester, Goldsmith'. Little is known about his activities except for a reference in Valentine Green's* *History of Worcester* written in 1795:

> ...This manufactory was first established in 1751, by the late Dr Wall, Mr William Davis and several other gentlemen, under the firm of the Worcester Porcelain Company, and by their appointment, the late Mr Samuel Bradeley [*sic*] vended the china when finished.

This was through his shop and house at 33 High Street, Worcester. Valentine Green adds that on the death of Bradley the place was found to be too small and the trade removed to 43 High Street in 1788-9, so Bradley died just before this. In the Dyson Perrins Museum is a longcase clock, the dial engraved with the name Samuel Bradley, Worcester, either made by him or also retailed through his shop. Bradley's premises at 33 High Street were taken over in 1789 by the Chamberlain family for their retail shop, in direct competition with Flights.

R.W. Binns* found evidence in the form of apprenticeship indentures which suggests that Samuel Bradley was of greater importance to the day to day running of the factory, acting alongside William Davis* as some kind of managing director.

Boy on a Buffalo Pattern. *Two teapots 'pencilled'* in black with the popular design, c.1755-6, about 4¾in. (12cm). Both have workmen's marks*. The example on the right has the correct cover for the period, while the teapot on the left has a later replacement cover. (Phillips.)*

Eight indentures discovered by Binns from the 1760s were in the name of Samuel Bradley, listed as a China Manufacturer or as a Goldsmith and China manufacturer. Five other indentures give William Davis' name as manager, while none lists Dr John Wall* in any capacity.

Bread Plates
Flat, circular dishes with embossed borders of Gothic lettering were made by Grainger from c.1850. Many factories made similar items and the Grainger examples can be distinguished by the inscription 'Eat Thy Bread with Joy and Thankfulness'. Other bread plates were made by Kerr and Binns and Royal Worcester.

Breakfast Cups
It became fashionable from the early 19th century to supply somewhat larger than normal teacups with breakfast services* although most breakfast sets also included smaller tea and coffee cups. Some oversized cups can date as early as c.1775-80 in blue and white patterns and Chamberlain order books for 1794 include mention of large handled cups and saucers, called '¼ pints and stands', included with normal teawares. Although unpopular with collectors, early breakfast cups are in fact great rarities.

Breakfast Services
Extended tea and coffee services known as breakfast sets originated in the early 19th century. In addition to the usual range of teaware shapes they included large breakfast cups* and saucers as well as muffin dishes*, egg cups* and egg stands*, butter pots or tubs* and honey pots*. While tea services did not include side plates at this period, plates were often supplied with breakfast services, usually a little smaller than dessert plates.

***Brigand Pattern.** A bowl carefully painted in dark blue, pseudo Chinese character mark, c.1765, about 7¾in. (20cm). (Sotheby's/ Kiddell Papers.)*

Brigand Pattern
A direct copy of a Chinese pattern painted in blue on bowls around 1765. The design after a *Kangxi* original probably tells the story of Yong Kwei-Fei and Ming Hwang. On one side the princess is pushed in a rickshaw while a horseman on the reverse holds a banner inscribed with imaginary initials. The centre is painted with Li T'ai Po, a drunken poet, seated by a wine jar. The imitation Chinese four-character mark found on these bowls is particularly elaborate but, like the flying banner held by the horseman, has no apparent meaning. The pattern is listed by Branyan, French and Sandon as I.A.21.

Bristol or Bristoll Marks
In his catalogue of the Klepser Collection (1984), Simon Spero records thirty-two examples of marked Bristol porcelain. The mark is embossed under the base of sauceboats and creamboats as well as moulded on the back of the figures of Lu Tung-Pin*. It has been wondered why the mark never occurs on any teawares or bowls and the simple explanation is that the lettering was incised into the plaster of the mould and any plain round shapes were thrown on a wheel and turned, not moulded. The mark is mostly found on blue and white or plain white pieces although eight of the examples listed by Spero have been enamelled. In these cases a green leaf-like blob has been painted over the Bristoll mark in a crude attempt to disguise it. The logical explanation for this is that pieces marked in this way were potted at Bristol and enamelled at Worcester, either before or just after the merger of the companies early in 1752. A fragment from the base of a glazed blue and white creamboat with the 'OL' of Bristoll embossed on it was found in the lowest levels of the Worcester factory site excavations*, although it was too small to show any evidence of being a kiln waster. It is hard to believe that any pieces marked 'Bristol' were cast from moulds at Worcester.

***Bristol Porcelain Manufactory.** A sauceboat painted in blue with many of the characteristics of the Three Dot Painter style* which originated at Bristol, c.1749-51. The blue painting is typically blurred. Note the exaggerated thumb-rest on the handle, a feature found on most Bristol sauceboats. About 6¼in. (16cm) long. (Private Collection.)*

Bristol Porcelain Manufactory (Miller & Lund)
The extent to which the Bristol factory was a direct continuation of Limehouse* is subject to much investigation. Dr Pocock* tells us that the Bristol China factory had been founded by 'one of the principal manufacturers at Limehouse which failed' and this reference is presumed to be to Benjamin Lund*, although there is no further evidence to link him to Limehouse. Indeed the evidence is conflicting, as Lund was possibly in partnership in Bristol with William Miller*, a grocer and banker, at the same time as the Limehouse factory was flourishing.

Lund and Miller's premises at Bristol had previously been used for the manufacture of glass by William Lowdin* and the conical glassmaking kiln could have been adapted in some way for producing experimental porcelain. Lowdin's glassworks

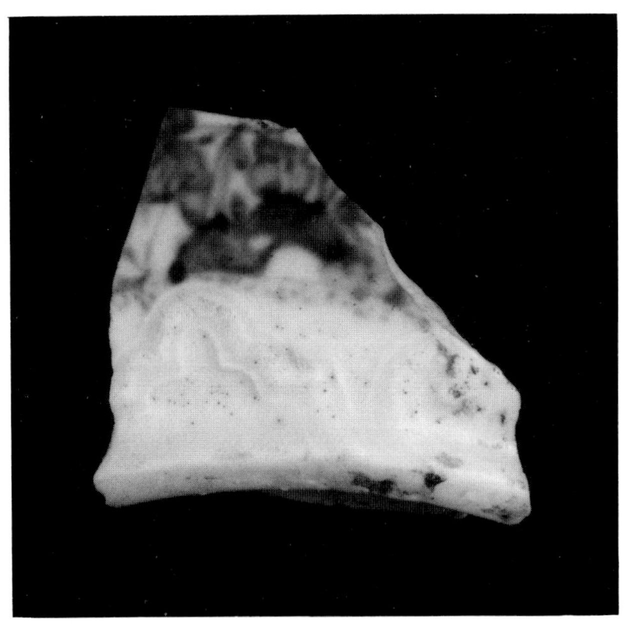

Bristol/Worcester. *A fragment of a sauceboat, apparently a waster*, found during excavations* on the lowest levels of the Worcester factory site. The base is embossed with the letters 'OL', part of the mark 'BRISTOL', about 1⅛ in. (3cm) wide. Although this piece was almost certainly made at Bristol, the excavations show that Bristol type porcelain probably continued in production for a short time at Worcester.*

Bristol/Worcester. *A cream jug painted in the so-called Three Dot Painter* style and clearly of early date. It is, however, impossible to determine whether this was made at Bristol or during the earliest period of production at Worcester, c.1751-2, 2⅝ in. (6.7cm). (Phillips.)*

were sold at auction on 27 June 1745, but Lund and Miller occupied only part of the buildings.

The earliest date for the commencement of experimental porcelain production at Bristol is March 1749, as it was at that time that Benjamin Lund was granted a licence to mine soaprock*. The first Bristol porcelain, however, was probably not offered for sale until the end of 1749. The celebrated figures of Lu Tung-Pin* are dated 1750 and in November 1750 the factory was advertising for apprentices to learn 'the art of pottery as practised in Staffordshire'.

The most important record of the Bristol factory is given by Dr Richard Pocock who wrote a letter to his mother dated 2 November 1750, giving an account of his visit to the porcelain works. He mentions that it was at Lowdn's (*sic*) Glass House and 'lately established' by one of the manufacturers at Limehouse. He tells us:

> They made two sorts of ware, one called stone china which has a yellow cast, both in the ware and the glazing that I suppose is made of pipe clay and calcin'd flint. The other they call old china that is whiter and I suppose this is made of calcin'd flint and the soapy rock at Lizard point which 'tis known they use; this is painted blue and somewhat like old china of a yellowish cast, another kind is white with a bluish cast, and both called fine ornamental white china.

Some important bankruptcy proceedings discovered by Aubrey Toppin and quoted in the *ECC Transactions,* vol. 3, pt 3, refer to the purchase of the Bristol factory. The document calls the Worcester partnership a 'porcelain manufactory in imitation of Dresden ware' while the Bristol works were a 'porcelain manufactory in imitation of Indian China ware'. Dr Watney, probably correctly, interprets this to mean that Bristol was producing only blue and white porcelain while Worcester was making enamelled wares. White Bristol porcelain may have been enamelled at Worcester prior to February 1752. Under a complicated agreement Richard Holdship* purchased the stock, utensils, effects and process of manufacture from Miller & Lund as well as the rights to the soaprock licence. Holdship agreed to provide the Worcester partnership with a minimum of twenty tons of soaprock per year at £18 per ton.

No further porcelain was made at Bristol after this takeover and Benjamin Lund was described in a further bankruptcy document of 23 February 1753 as a 'china maker now of the City of Worcester'. The Bristol porcelain factory probably made porcelain for only two years, mostly blue and white (Colour Plates 15 and 16) with a few pieces left just in white. Marked examples of Bristol help identify the early products and we believe that the same manufacturing process was continued at Worcester for a very short time before the firing methods were altered and the wares perfected. No unmarked piece can be attributed to Bristol with total confidence as the wares made at Worcester early in 1752 will be virtually indistinguishable (*see* **Bristol/Worcester**).

Bristol/Worcester

A term coined by Henry Sandon in 1968 to refer to the controversial class of wares indistinguishable between Bristol and Worcester manufacture. It is likely that only blue and white porcelain was made at Bristol, as well as some white porcelain which was sent for decoration at Worcester. Initially Henry Sandon included many early Worcester coloured wares in his Bristol/Worcester group as well, but recent research has shown that, with the exception of Bristol marked pieces, all of these coloured creamboats and wares would probably have been made at Worcester. The term Bristol/Worcester is still valid for blue and white porcelain as a very similar production was continued for a short time at least at Worcester (*see* Colour Plates 11 and 83). It is unlikely that many collectors would ever admit to the possibility of their Bristol porcelain having been made at Worcester, however, and so the term is destined for oblivion.

Brocade Pattern

A striking design inspired partly by Japanese *Arita* porcelain, but very much adapted in colouring. Indeed, the strong green colour used suggests that Worcester were copying Meissen to some extent. The name derives from the 1769 Sale Catalogue where 'brocade' is used to describe a number of the lots. It is, however, impossible to determine whether this was the actual 'brocade' pattern referred to. The design was used on standard dessert shapes, c.1768-70, as well as on fluted teawares of possibly slightly later date, c.1770-5. The dessert wares are usually marked with a gold crescent*, while the teawares are unmarked. Examples have been seen from the Flight, Barr and Barr period, presumably made as replacements.

Brodribb, John and Richard

Two of the original partners in the Worcester Tonquin Manufacture were Richard Brodribb of Berere in the county of Worcester, Esquire, and John Brodribb of the City of Worcester, woollen draper. Richard Brodribb was appointed treasurer of the new company but does not appear to have played any further active role. John Brodribb is only otherwise known to collectors from a magnificent pair of jugs which were made for his marriage in 1760. These cabbage-leaf moulded mask jugs, in the Dyson Perrins and Victoria and Albert Museums, are painted with extensive landscapes including figures taken from a design by Johann Nilson of Augsburg. The arms of Brodribb impaling Barrow on the front of the jugs were apparently created only for these jugs as John Brodribb was not entitled to bear arms. He died in 1761.

Brodribb, John and Richard. *One of a pair of magnificent cabbage leaf moulded mask jugs made for the marriage of John Brodribb, one of the original partners in the Worcester porcelain company, c.1760, 10½in. (27cm). (Dyson Perrins Museum.)*

Brooches

During the 1840s Grainger and Co. produced numerous brooches which were mounted in gold or pinchbeck. The oval porcelain plaques were mostly decorated with coloured engravings of Worcester or Malvern while others were painted with birds or flowers. The most elaborate Grainger brooch I have seen was painted with Leda and the Swan. In the mid-1840s Grainger used their fine parian* body to model sprays of flowers in the glazed ware called 'Cryolite'. The Union Brooch was formed of a spray of rose, thistle and shamrock. None was marked and few have survived. Chamberlain made similar plaques for brooches during the 1840s and were selling two sizes each of square and crescent-shaped brooches. They also sold modelled flowers for brooches in Dresden style and apple blossom for brooches at 14s. per dozen. These were almost certainly made at Chamberlain's factory. Flight's factory does not appear to have made brooches.

Broseley

The contemporary name used at several English factories for what was undoubtedly the most popular of all underglaze blue* printed patterns used on porcelain teawares. Broseley is a village close to Caughley and the name was used in the Chamberlain account books for a common teaware shape as well as patterns supplied from Caughley. In time it became the established name for the blue printed Chinese landscape pattern, first used at Caughley, featuring a prominent zig-zag wall. Grainger used the name Broseley for their version of the pattern, which they had introduced by c.1810, on the distinctive partly fluted shape which they also referred to as Broseley.

Brooches. *A Grainger and Co. brooch decorated with a coloured-in print of Worcester from the north-west, marked 'Worcester' c.1840, 2⅜in. (6cm). (The late Dorothy Howell Collection.)*

Broth Bowls. *A rare form of broth bowl or bouillon cup, the shape adapted from the mould for a sucrier* by the addition of scroll handles, decorated in the* Gold Queen's* *pattern, c.1775. (Dyson Perrins Museum.)*

Broth Bowls. *A Barr, Flight and Barr broth bowl with distinctive eagle and ring handles, the painting probably by a pupil of Thomas Baxter*, printed marks, c.1815-20, 7ins. (18cm). (Phillips.)*

Broth Bowls

Bowls with covers are often referred to as broth bowls or by the continental term *écuelle.* There is no evidence to suggest how these were used and it is hard to know whether all types of covered bowl should have had a stand. Some bowls probably served as tureens, but the circular bowls with two side handles were likely to be for broth. Early blue and white examples are known painted with birds in landscapes or with flowers but always in the European or Meissen style rather than Chinese. One shape of circular covered bowl and stand copied Meissen with spiral moulding and embossed basket weave border. It does not have handles but in other respects was probably intended for broth. These were painted with Meissen flowers in underglaze blue, c.1760, and I know of two examples which have had added colouring and yellow grounds. By about 1765-70 the popular shape of broth bowl was round with ogee sides, a reasonably flat cover and scroll-shaped handles. Rich scale blue examples are well known and blue and white printed flower patterns were also used. The Chamberlain and Flight factories both made broth bowls although no Grainger examples have been recorded. A smaller shape of two-handled bowl was made c.1775 using the mould for a fluted sugar bowl but with added scroll handles and a circular stand. These have variously been called broth bowls, porringers or bouillon cups but their precise use is uncertain. An example in *Gold Queen's* pattern* is illustrated here.

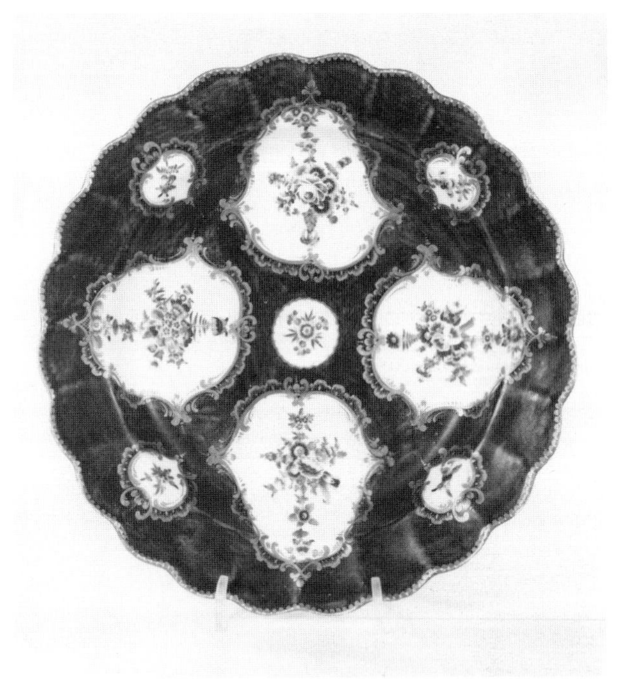

Burdett Coutts Service. *A scallop bordered dessert plate, the unusual shaped panels reserved on a wet blue* ground, square mark*, c.1770, 8½in. (21.5cm). (Phillips.)*

Burdett Coutts Service

A dessert service of this unique design belonged to Baroness Burdett Coutts who died in 1906 and was sold by the Burdett Coutts family in 1922. Made about 1770, each piece features four unusual lobed panels of formal coloured flowers elaborately framed in gold on a deep wet blue* ground with five smaller flower panels producing a particularly splendid effect. The flower painting is typical of factory-decorated pieces, although the design might suggest otherwise. An example from the Klepser Collection is illustrated by Simon Spero, op. cit., item 134.

Butter Coolers

The earliest form of Worcester butter tub* is usually pierced all around the sides and base with small round holes. Examples are known in silver and in Chelsea porcelain and it

Butter Coolers. *A butter cooler with typical ill-fitting cover, decorated with scattered sprigs and yellow bands, c.1756, 5½in. (14cm) wide. (Phillips.)*

is believed that these were to stand in water. The tubs are oval with moulded staves and ropework hoops and lug handles. They stand on four scroll feet and have apple and leaf finials. They probably date from around 1756 and are known only in coloured examples with either puce or yellow bands. A single example in blue and white appears to be slightly later and is not pierced.

Butter Tubs

The early Worcester vessels called potting pots* were probably for potted meat preparations but it is likely some were used also for butter. The earliest definite butter pot or tub is datable to c.1760 and used the same mould as a butter cooler* but without pierced holes. Only one example is recorded with underglaze blue flowers. By the late 1760s all Worcester butter tubs followed the same conventional form derived from Meissen via Chelsea. Worcester chose not to put feet on their butter tubs, however, and the fruit finials were deemed inappropriate. Instead the dairy theme is preserved in the two lug handles based on wooden cream pails. The plain circular drum shapes have fairly flat covers with flower finials and plain circular stands. Oval tubs with covers and stands from about 1770 are larger and unlikely to be for butter. Chamberlain made a similar drum shaped butter tub c.1810-15 and Flight also made butter tubs as part of breakfast

Butter Tubs. *The popular shape of Worcester butter tub decorated with a version of the* Quail* *pattern, marked with a gold crescent*, c.1770, 4in. (10cm). (Phillips.)*

services*. Grainger made a more elaborate version around 1840 with moulded hoops and staves like a barrel, and a 'Primrose Butter pot' was made in the 1840s with moulded leaves all around.

Buttons

A single waster of a stud-like button painted with a blue flower sprig was found by Kristin Sandon on the factory site in a level dating from c.1755-60. Only just over ⅜in. (1cm) in diameter, it is edged in manganese. Sadly no finished examples have survived. A slightly larger stud in an American collection is painted with initials in dark blue. Early Flight period buttons are also unknown except from the excavations*. Made in three sizes up to 1⅜in. (3.5cm) diameter, they have a single loop attached to the undersides. The blue bands would have been gilded and possibly jewelled in the manner of Caughley buttons which have survived from the same period c.1790. Many Caughley buttons were decorated by Chamberlain. Later, in the late 1830s Chamberlain bought a button press and began the manufacture of buttons under licence of the patentee Richard Prosser. The products were of high quality but could not be sold for very much and had to be sewn on to display cards by hand in a very time-consuming process. Binns* was convinced that button manufacture had contributed to the factory's decline and straight away abandoned the process in 1851. Grainger's first *Ornamental Shape Book* of the 1830s includes eight designs for buttons but it is unlikely that buttons represented any sizeable part of that factory's output.

***Buttons.** A card of 'Patent Agate' buttons, inscribed 'Manufactured by W. Chamberlain & Co. Worcester', each button sewn on by hand, c.1840-50. (Private Collection.)*

Cabaret Sets
See **Déjeuner Sets**

Cabbage Leaf Jugs
The origin of Worcester's famous shape of large jug is presumed to be English silver, although the earliest reference to the shape in the price list of the London Warehouse (*see* **London Shops**), c.1755-6 lists them as 'Dutch Jugs', made in two sizes. The Chamberlain records include many references to Caughley Dutch jugs sold by them in the late 1780s, showing that the name survived for some thirty-five years, as long as the jugs were made. The moulded ovoid bodies have a design of overlapping cabbage leaves extending into the straight necks which are embossed with a border of small leaves. The earliest Worcester examples have a plain leaf-moulded loop handle but these are rare and the standard scroll ring handle had been introduced by at least 1757. During the 1750s most Dutch jugs were made without lips but the moulded mask lip was also in production at the same time as the plain versions. Each factory where mask-spouted jugs were made had their own distinctive face which remained constant over long periods. Worcester's own bearded man is moulded with slit eyes which appear closed, even though coloured examples were painted with the eyes open. Large numbers of Worcester cabbage leaf jugs were made continuously until c.1785, in a great variety of styles, both in blue and white and colours. The finest examples date from the late 1750s, however, with extensive coloured landscapes, birds or armorials. Benjamin Franklin bought a blue and white mask spouted jug in 1758 and sent it to his wife Deborah with a note that it was

> A large fine jug for beer, to stand in the cooler. I fell in love with it at first sight; for I thought it looked like a fat jolly dame, clean and tidy, with a neat blue and white calico gown on, good natured and lovely, and put me in mind of somebody.

Chamberlain sold Caughley Dutch jugs and decorated these with crests and initials as well as with rich fruit and birds. They did not make a mask jug in their own porcelain but one of the earliest Chamberlain jugs has a cabbage leaf-moulded body below a spiral fluted or 'shanked'* neck and leaf lip. The shape of Dutch jugs had gone out of fashion by this time, however, and these early Chamberlain jugs are great rarities. New Hall and other Staffordshire factories made small cabbage leaf jugs and matching mugs c.1790 but no mugs were made at Worcester.

Cabbage Leaf Jugs. *A very large jug designed without a lip, painted with a continuous floral design in blue, workman's mark*, c.1758, 11¼in. (28.5cm). (Private Collection.)*

Cabinet Cups
While most cups and saucers were parts of tea and coffee services, in the 19th century it became increasingly popular to collect single expensive cups and saucers as art objects to keep in a display cabinet, hence the name cabinet cup. Quality mattered above all else and the best painting and gilding was used, often to very great effect. The initial idea of rich cabinet wares decorated in this way came from France where single Paris cups and saucers were painted at decorating workshops. Most of the Worcester cabinet cups of the Regency period are based on French shapes, with intricate handles and frequently raised on paw or hoof feet. Flight's factory frequently further embellished their cups with rows of simulated pearls, a custom only rarely used at Chamberlains. It is generally assumed that cabinet cups always came with saucers, called stands, but several entries in the Chamberlain archives refer just to cabinet cups by themselves. Chamberlain specialised in cups with views of popular towns such as Worcester itself, Cheltenham and Bath. Others were painted with historical and Shakespearian* subjects, particularly by Humphrey Chamberlain jun.* In only very few other cases is it possible to identify the painters of cabinet cups, even though a great many are still incorrectly attributed to Thomas Baxter*. The Chamberlain order books include several references to 'Cabinet cups, Swansea make' but I believe this refers to the

shape and does not indicate that Chamberlain were decorating white Swansea porcelain after the demise of the Welsh factory, for few shapes other than cabinet cups are so described. Cabinet cups were usually very expensive and only a few continued to be made after about 1850.

Cache Pots
See **Jardinières**

Caddy Spoons
While Caughley and Derby both made caddy spoons, no early Worcester examples have been recorded. The Chinese shape rice spoons* made in the 1770s have been called caddy spoons but this seems unlikely. Caddy spoons were mentioned in Chamberlain's stock-taking list in 1795 but these may not be porcelain. Grainger made medicine spoons on leaf-like feet in their Chemical Porcelain* around 1845-50 but these had a very different specific purpose.

Candle Extinguishers
Although mentioned in Chamberlain and Grainger records, no Worcester examples have been seen dating to before the Kerr and Binns period. Chamberlain orders for 1821 include examples in matt blue enamel or with views of Worcester and Malvern, all inscribed *Bon Soir.* Others are listed on trays. These were conical, probably with a small handle. Grainger made a chamber candlestick in 1830 with a matching conical extinguisher. The Flight factory, which made very few candlesticks, is unlikely to have made extinguishers.

Candle Fence Pattern
A simple underglaze blue landscape pattern inspired by Chinese porcelain and featuring a prominent fence with flame-like points on each post giving the design its name. Unlikely to date much before 1770, the pattern was used on teawares and various sizes of bowl. Numerous wasters* of this pattern were found on the factory site including the complete unglazed saucer illustrated. The pattern is listed by Branyan, French and Sandon as I.D.18.

Candlesticks. *A Flight and Barr candlestick in French style, painted with coloured feathers on a gold ground, incised 'B'* mark, c.1800-4, 5¾in. (14.5cm) wide. (Phillips, Leeds.)*

Candlesticks
The two basic forms of candlestick are tall or low, the latter generally known as chamber candlesticks or chambersticks. Very small candlesticks are called tapersticks.

Tall candlesticks are great rarities in any period but particularly in the 18th century. Two different models are known, however, both dating from c.1760. One of these is circular in section with gadroon moulded rims around the

Candle Fence Pattern. *Two apparently similar saucers, the example on the left an unglazed waster* found during the factory site excavations,* crescent marks*, c.1768-70, 4¾in. (12cm). (Author's Collection.)*

Candlesticks. *One of a pair of Barr, Flight and Barr candlesticks on hexagonal bases, painted with attractive picturesque* landscapes, script marks, c.1810, 5⅛in. (13cm). (Phillips.)*

foot, shoulder and nozzle. These are represented by a single surviving pair in the Marshall Collection in Oxford, painted in underglaze blue with Meissen style flowers. The other shape has a fluted column and is raised on a stepped cruciform foot with leaf moulded corners. Only coloured flower painting is recorded on this shape, once again in European style on a shape inspired by English silver. A pair of these was donated to the Dyson Perrins Museum from the Rous Lench Collection. Both of these Worcester candlestick shapes were made in three sections joined by metal bands in exactly the same way as South Staffordshire enamel sticks of similar date. The Worcester candlesticks were probably sent to Birmingham to be fitted up and are likely to have had enamel sconces.

Barr, Flight and Barr tall candlesticks are known from c.1806-10 and a bill surviving in the papers of the Earls of Coventry records the purchase on 9 April 1813 of '1 Pair Music candlesticks — French grey and gold roses' which cost £1.11s.6d. The term 'Music Candlesticks' probably means that these were intended to be placed on a piano. Most Flight examples have octagonal bases although some are square. Other rare Flight, Barr and Barr sticks are shaped like small urns on top of tall cylindrical plinths. A single pair of somewhat crude circular tall candlesticks has been recognised as Grainger, c.1815. Chamberlain did not make many tall candlesticks and only very few of plain pillar shape have survived. The Chamberlain account books refer to the tall shape as 'bracket' candlesticks.

Chambersticks were first made c.1765 in a basic shape which has a saucer-shaped dish moulded with a grotesque mask underneath the applied scrolling handle. The leaf-moulded nozzle rises from the centre and the rim, which is moulded with 'C'-scrolls, is occasionally pierced. Examples are usually in underglaze blue or scale blue although simple flowers, monochrome flowers and a very rare yellow ground example have been recorded. A Flight and Barr chamberstick of c.1800 is particularly elegant with a crossed-over flat scroll handle inspired by Sèvres. Another model of similar date is of an almost conical spreading shape with a gilded ring handle applied on the side.

In the 19th century the three main Worcester factories all made many different shapes of chamberstick and an equally large range of taperstick shapes. Most take the form of a nozzle set into the centre of a saucer-shaped base with a moulded rim. Some were applied with modelled flowers or shells while others can be very finely painted. Views of Worcester and Malvern were particularly popular and many must have been sold locally. Amongst the more elaborate Chamberlain shapes were models of mermaids, dolphins and griffins, some with added figures of boys in biscuit or bronze. Grainger were making 'Flat gaddaroons candlestick with extinguishers' in three sizes in June 1826 and Chamberlain also made candle extinguishers* to accompany some of their chambersticks. These are great rarities today.

Finally we should not forget that certain figures were sold fitted up as candlesticks. In the Dyson Perrins Museum is a figure of a gardener from c.1770 with elaborate bocage supporting a flower nozzle (*see* **Figures**). Also the group of canaries in apple blossom from the same period was designed with a candle nozzle set into the top of the tree. Chamberlain made candlestick figures also but it is not certain what form these took.

Canisters

Although usually referred to today as tea caddies, this is strictly incorrect as a caddy is a box to contain canisters. All surviving 18th century records show that Worcester used the name canister and sold these either as part of a complete tea equipage or as a pair of canisters on their own. There is surprisingly little variation in the shape of Worcester tea canisters. The plain oval shape with short neck was in use from c.1760 although earlier examples tend to be more globular with wider domed circular feet instead of slightly spreading feet. Reeded and wide fluted versions were made but surprisingly none has been seen with rococo moulding even though other teaware shapes are well known, presumably from an earlier date than the introduction of canisters at Worcester. The ovoid canisters have loosely fitting domed covers with flower finials. They were made as additions to more expensive services and blue and white tea canisters are surprisingly rare. In the late the 1770s certain special services such as the Duchess of Kent* and Stormont* services were supplied with a tapering cylindrical canister shape slanting inwards at the neck and with a flat cover with flower knop. This shape continued, albeit rarely, until c.1790. One remarkable pair in this shape, c.1775, is recorded with a combination of a *Hop Trellis** type pattern and the *Gold Queen's** pattern, one inscribed 'Green' and the other 'Bohea'. These two types of tea were kept in different canisters and usually were mixed only by the lady of the house. A very rare square shape of tea canister from c.1780 copies German porcelain and is known with an underglaze landscape print. Tea canisters went out of fashion c.1785 and are not known in Chamberlain, Grainger or later Flight porcelain.

Cannonball Pattern. A teapot painted with one of the most popular blue and white patterns, crescent mark, c.1768-75, 5⅛in. (13cm). (Dyson Perrins Museum.)*

Cannonball Pattern
Worcester's most popular blue and white pattern, introduced in the late 1750s and continued until c.1785. Presumably copied from Chinese porcelain, the pattern was made up of solid blocks of colour and line and required no understanding of perspective. It could therefore be left to junior painters and was inexpensive. The *Cannonball* pattern was used on the full range of teaware shapes as well as large bowls, cylindrical mugs and mustard pots. It was also subsequently used at most other English factories, in some cases copied so exactly that identification can be difficult. The name 'Blue Rock' pattern has also been used for this design which is listed by Branyan, French and Sandon as I.D.6.

Canton Style
The port from which most of the Chinese export trade was shipped has given its name to various kinds of Chinese porcelain. This leads to considerable confusion, although generally Worcester collectors have used the term Canton to refer to a single style of figure painting. Many exact copies of Chinese *famille rose** figure patterns were made, ranging from some sparsely painted to others with very thick enamel colours. Certain rare examples combine Canton figure panels with a wet blue* ground. The Canton style was mostly used on teawares and was popular from c.1765-75. Most pieces appear to be factory decorated and usually include the Chinese figures in panels within a formal background. In certain cases, where the pattern is particularly full and detailed, the term 'Mandarin style' has been used, but no clear definition for either Canton or Mandarin has been established.

Card Cases
Small leather cases for visiting cards. *See* **Card Trays**

Card Racks
See **Card Trays**

Card Trays
Flat open baskets with overhead handles and various other shapes of ornamental tray were used as card trays. The custom was for a visitor to place a visiting card on such a tray on a

Canton Style. A cabbage leaf moulded mask jug painted in bright colours with a copy of a Chinese export pattern, c.1770, 8¼in. (21cm). (Bonhams.)

Canton Style. A saucer-dish unusually combining Canton style figures with a wet blue ground, crescent mark*, c.1768-70, 7½in. (19cm). (Phillips.)*

Card Trays. *A Chamberlain basket intended to be used as a card tray, with modelled shell border and view of Malvern Abbey, script mark, c.1835, 10½in. (27cm). (Phillips.)*

Card Trays. *A Chamberlain card tray painted with the 'New Houses of Parliament', based on the original design for Westminster which was subsequently modified, marked Chamberlains Worcester and 155 New Bond Street, London, c.1840-5, 13in. (33cm). (Phillips.)*

hall table and a servant would convey this on the tray to the master or mistress of the house. These trays gave the host a perfect opportunity to impress his or her guests and certain very rich examples were made. Few can be dated before the 1830s. Flight, Barr and Barr favoured the handled type with various moulded borders of leaves or classical palmettes. Care has to be taken as the handles are very vulnerable and many trays have now lost them and been expertly altered to become trays without handles. The usual Chamberlain shape made around 1840 is roughly rectangular with heavy scroll-moulded borders. Some were further ornamented with remarkably realistic modelled shells placed all around the border. The centres were usually painted with views, in particular the Houses of Parliament and the suspension bridge at Clifton, near Bristol. Curiously both of these views on Chamberlain are copied from original designs which were never built and such trays sold in 1841 and 1843 for five guineas.

The small hanging china troughs which today tend to be called letter racks were referred to in the 1820s account books as card racks. Made by Chamberlain with flowers or views, they would have held visiting cards or possibly small envelopes. Card cases were also made in the 1840s. Examples of these in the Dyson Perrins Museum show that they were made of leather and set with Chamberlain porcelain plaques. It is little wonder that few of these fragile objects survive.

Carnatic, Nabob of the, Service
A truly magnificent service was ordered by His Highness Willajah Nabob Auzum Jar, Nabob of the Carnatic, from Chamberlains via the importers Griffiths & Co. in Madras. The order was placed in 1820 but not completed until 1823 when it was shipped on the *Windsor Castle.* The list in the factory's invoice book takes up four whole pages and the order comprised several different shapes and designs with anything up to eighteen dozen dinner plates, seven dozen soup plates and eighty hot water plates in one design alone. The service comprised two principal patterns: one with a deep blue border with reserved white and gold 'C' scrolls and different botanical plants painted in the centre of each over printed outlines; the other with a pink border and formal gilding. Both sets included on every piece a medallion in Islamic script including the date 1236 which relates to 1820. The climate in India has not been kind to the service and many surviving pieces have become stained or have lost some of their enamel. Even so the examples which are offered for sale each year give only a very slight taste of what this incredible service must have looked like when it arrived in Madras.

Cassolettes
Mantelpiece vases which also served as candlesticks were popular in the 18th century, although porcelain examples have rarely survived. One pair and one other single Worcester example are known, apparently dating from c.1775, although a later date has also been suggested. The bodies are of goblet shape on square feet and the tops can be inverted to reveal either a neck tapering in to a pointed finial, or a 'U' shaped candle nozzle with leaf-moulded surround. The pair, decorated with the Jabberwocky* pattern, are illustrated by H. Rissik Marshall, *Coloured Worcester Porcelain,* item 614.

Catherine Wheel
See **Charlotte, Queen, Pattern**

Caudle Cups
References to these cups in the Chamberlain records give very few clues to the age-old problem of differentiating between caudle and chocolate cups. Both came with either one or two handles although two are most usual. Interestingly, covers are mentioned with some but not with others and from surviving examples it would seem that many of the two-handled cups never had covers when they were originally sold. In his *Caughley and Worcester Porcelain 1775-1800,* Geoffrey Godden notes from the Chamberlain records that caudle cups were taller with plain upright sides while chocolate cups were of ogee shape and wider. Examples in Chamberlain's own porcelain are quite rare and some rich surviving examples with two handles and covers were probably intended as cabinet cups* rather than for actual use. Earlier Worcester porcelain caudle cups from the late 1770s or 1780s are also uncommon and usually decorated in very simple patterns or popular blue prints. The most usual form is of a large coffee* cup with two double-twisted handles. Some Flight period cups of c.1790 are of tall beaker shape with covers and stands and were probably for caudle as the stands have deep wells acting as trembleuse stands*. Certain oversized cups from the mid-1760s in blue and white or with blue grounds have been called caudle cups. These do not appear to have had stands and must be regarded as of uncertain use. The large ogee-shaped cups popular around 1770 are discussed under **Chocolate Cups***.

Caughley Porcelain, Chamberlain Decorated. A tea service of shanked shape decorated in the French style adopted by Chamberlain c.1790, the porcelain of Caughley manufacture. (Phillips.)*

Caughley Porcelain, Chamberlain Decorated
The Chamberlain family left the employment of the Flights c.1786 to decorate for them on a free-lance basis. Robert Chamberlain sen.* must have been thinking ahead and would have considered other suppliers of white porcelain on which to decorate. French porcelain was hardly available in England at that time and Staffordshire porcelain represented by New Hall was still in its infancy. Derby had its own decorators and this left only the Penningtons in Liverpool and Caughley with any tradition for porcelain making and no ability to do their own fine overglaze decoration. Caughley had never tried to compete with Worcester in the area of rich enamelled porcelain, preferring instead to make a serious attempt to capture the trade in blue-printed porcelain. Robert Chamberlain would have worked alongside Thomas Turner* at Worcester before 1775 and looked to Turner not just as a supplier of white wares but as a backer, providing funding for the venture in return for a regular supply of enamelled goods for Turner to sell in his London shop. It is possible that the Chamberlains initially decorated for Thomas Turner alongside Flight and felt able to make a complete break in 1788, becoming the principal enamelling branch of the Caughley factory. Chamberlains' own shop in Worcester High Street supplied their own customers and Turner was presumably happy with this arrangement, although evidence from the letters copied into the factory archives shows that the relationship became somewhat strained. Supplies of white goods to decorate were in short supply and Chamberlain owed interest payments on their financial arrangements. When they began to manufacture their own porcelain in 1791 Chamberlain obviously felt that this was to the mutual benefit of Thomas Turner as a backer, even though they suspected that Turner would regarded this as deceit and ingratitude. Caughley porcelain was still preferred for Chamberlain's more important customers up until 1793 when the supply was finally terminated.

The Chamberlain account and order books covering the five years from 1788 give an invaluable clue to the decoration carried out at Worcester. Gilded borders were added to blue and white patterns while designs partly in blue were left purposely unfinished at Caughley for gilding to be added. Simple patterns in the French style were preferred with little attention to fine painting. George Davis* painted some elaborate fancy birds* and fruit while John Wood* may have executed some figure subjects. Fidelle Duvivier* was engaged for a very short time by Chamberlain to paint figures (*see* Colour Plate 36) but probably proved too expensive.

Part of the agreement with Thomas Turner must have been to prohibit the Chamberlains from marking any pieces with their own name. This must have been frustrating to Chamberlains in direct competition with Flights in Worcester High Street, and yet no Caughley porcelain is known with the name Chamberlain upon it. The only marked piece in the extensive Marquis of Donegal service* of 1793 (*see* Colour Plate 33) was a stand of Chamberlain's own make. One Caughley cabbage leaf jug in an American private collection has had rich *Fancy Birds** and the *Dragon in Compartments** pattern added to cover up blue printed flowers. The 'S' mark of Caughley has become the letter 'S' in the middle of the name Worcester in gold under the base. Probably this was old stock decorated at a later date when such ingenuity could pass unchallenged.

Cauliflower Tureens
Based on Meissen originals although very much in the tradition of vegetable forms made as tureens at Chelsea and Longton Hall in the 1750s. The Worcester models seem to date from the late 1750s and are press moulded very thinly and often misshapen, which adds to their great charm. Most were naturalistically coloured and seem to have been sold with leaf-shaped stands although the leaf stands were sold as dishes in their own right. Some cauliflower tureens were further decorated with transfer printed butterflies and insects on the tureens and stands, either in black or filled in with colours. (*See* illustration on page 94.)

Cave, Edward
One of the original partners in the Worcester Porcelain Company in 1751, Edward Cave was listed as a printer of St Johns Gate, London, and as such was the only partner not to live in or near Worcester. Instead Cave was in an ideal position to help the factory market its wares. He had founded the influential *Gentleman's Magazine* and was able to insert a complimentary review which appeared in August 1752. This comprised an engraving of the factory complete with

Cauliflower Tureens. A tureen in the Meissen style with its matching leaf-shaped stand, c.1758-60, the tureen 4⅛ in. (10.5cm), the stand 8in. (20.5cm). (Phillips.)*

descriptions and the note that 'A sale of this manufacture will begin at the Worcester Music Meeting, on September 20th, with a great variety of ware, and 'tis said at a moderate price'. Unfortunately Edward Cave died less than two years' later, on 18 June 1754.

Centrepieces
See **Dessert Centrepieces**

Chamber Pots
There is a curious reference to chamber pots selling in the London warehouse (*see* **London Shops**) of the Worcester factory in c.1755-6 for 3s.6d. per dozen. No existing Worcester chamber pots can be dated before c.1765-70, however, and even then only very few have survived. The known examples are all in blue and white with floral prints and match a small number of wasters found on the factory site. No

***Chamber Pots.** One of the more utilitarian items made at Worcester, decorated with a popular blue print, the interior showing evidence of considerable use in its day, crescent mark*, c.1770, 6⅝ in. (17cm) diameter; shown with a matching waster* from the factory site excavations*. (Dyson Perrins Museum.)*

Flight or Grainger chamber pots are known and although Chamberlain sold examples with French sprig decoration in 1796, production must have been limited and none has been recognised. Probably the Worcester factories believed that such mundane items were better left to Staffordshire pottery makers.

Chamberlain and Co.
The difficult decade following the death of Joseph Flight* is fully chronicled in Henry Sandon's *Flight and Barr Worcester Porcelain* and Geoffrey Godden's *Chamberlain-Worcester Porcelain.* In simple terms the two former great Worcester factories, Flight, Barr and Barr and Chamberlain were finding business very bad and could no longer survive in competition. Martin Barr jun.* and George Barr* would have liked to sell out completely but were only able to agree to a form of amalgamation where they retained shares in a joint stock company called the Worcester Royal Porcelain Company but which was to trade as Chamberlain and Co. The assets of the company, comprising the two factories and the extensive stock in their respective London shops*, were valued and financial backers brought in to re-establish the company with a firm financial footing. Instead all remained unwell as much of the stock was found to be old-fashioned and proved difficult to dispose of.

The principal partners in 1840 were John Lilly* (eight shares), Walter Chamberlain* (seven shares), Fleming St John* (five shares), Martin Barr* (three shares) and George Barr* (two shares). The London stock held by James Yates* was exchanged for a further five shares. Other money was advanced in return for shares by George Allies, Jabez Allies, John Brook Hyde and Henry Douglas Carden. Failure to agree with James Yates about the value of the stock led to his resignation and his shares were bought by Walter Chamberlain and John Lilly. The factory buildings of Flight, Barr and Barr (the old Warmstry House* factory) proved difficult to sell and it was unproductive as a tile works (*see* **Tiles**). A new salesman was appointed to try to sell the

***Chamberlain and Co.** A bottle-shaped vase, possibly intended for toilet water, painted with a view of Malvern Abbey Church, the matt blue ground remaining popular. Printed mark Chamberlain and Co., c.1845-50, 6½in. (16.5cm). (Phillips.)*

***Chamberlain Factory.** A Caughley cabbage leaf mask jug decorated with a view of Worcester from the south west, leaving no doubt as to where the decoration was carried out. A riverboat known as a Severn trow can be seen on the river at the left of the panel; c.1788-90, 7½in. (19cm). (Dyson Perrins Museum.)*

London stock. Disagreement over the valuing of the stock and other aspects of business in Worcester led to three of the backers — Hyde, Carden and Jabez Allies — wishing to withdraw. In January 1844 it was decided to dissolve the partnership and agreement was reached to divide the assets. Walter Chamberlain and John Lilly took the Diglis factory and everything connected with the manufacture of porcelain except for the tile works. They also kept the stock of the High Street, Worcester shop. The other partners took the two London shops with their entire stocks as well as the tile business. This was not the end of the matter as disagreement over the true value of the even more old-fashioned stock continued to divide the partners. Some of the old stock was eventually offered for sale by auction. By 1848 Walter Chamberlain and John Lilly were the only partners remaining and they continued to manufacture traditional wares as well as new innovations. Mostly the porcelain productions of Chamberlain and Co. from the 1840s were totally unoriginal, although they were generally of very high quality (Colour Plate 17). New products such as door furniture* and buttons* did little to revive the company's former reputation.

In 1850 John Lilly retired, his place being taken by his son Frederick Lilly and W.H. Kerr*, a Dublin china dealer and principal retailer of Worcester porcelain. They remained as Chamberlain and Co., exhibiting under this name at the Great Exhibition*. The Jury at the Exhibition was barely complimentary about any of their products and offered only slight praise for their reticulated porcelain* which was not at all original. 1851 marked the end of a great era when Walter Chamberlain finally retired, the last member of his family to be involved in the business. W.H. Kerr was left in sole charge and pieces marked W.H. Kerr & Co. Worcester date from this time. Kerr was a businessman, not a potter, and he needed a new partner to be responsible for the artistic and manufacturing side. He invited Richard William Binns* to join him, trading as Kerr and Binns. So began a new century in the history of Worcester porcelain and the start of what Binns was to call its 'Awakening'.

Chamberlain Factory

It seems likely that Robert Chamberlain sen.* and Humphrey Chamberlain sen.* left the direct employment of Flight c.1786 but continued to decorate for them until c.1788. They then completely severed their relationship with their Worcester rivals, setting up in direct competition with Flight in Worcester, even to the extent of taking over Flight's old shop at 33 High Street and employing most of their decorators. The Chamberlains did not have the ability to manufacture their own porcelain at this stage but instead entered into an agreement with Thomas Turner*, proprietor of the Caughley factory. The Chamberlains decorated white

Chamberlain Factory. *A 'Regent Vase' painted with a view of Worcester seen from the Bath Road tollgate. Chamberlain's prominent advertising sign greeted every visitor to the city. This vase was probably for display in the London showroom and remained in the factory's own collection, c.1815, 10¼ in. (26cm). (Dyson Perrins Museum.)*

Chamberlain Factory. *A selection of pieces made by Chamberlains. Left: a reticulated* jug shown at the Great Exhibition,* 1851; a cabinet plate by Thomas Baxter*, c.1820; a model of a cat, c.1820; and a mermaid cream bowl, c.1815. (Dyson Perrins Museum.)*

Caughley porcelain* for Turner to sell in London as well as for their own shop in Worcester. In addition they sold blue and white Caughley porcelain, some glass and possibly the products of other factories. The extensive archives which survive at Worcester have made it possible to identify many of these Caughley products decorated by the Chamberlains. Their speciality was fine gilding and individual pieces with crests or ciphers made for the local trade. The visit of the King to their shop while they were still fitting it out gave the family encouragement and soon they felt able to expand into the much more difficult area of porcelain manufacture.

By 1791 they were certainly making their own porcelain although to begin with they continued to decorate Caughley wares alongside. The harlequin dessert service made for the Marquis of Donegal* in September 1793 was mostly of Caughley porcelain with a single centrepiece of Chamberlain's own make. At the end of 1791 the factory had employed at least two modellers and regular supplies of clay and other raw materials were obtained. The relationship with Thomas Turner became understandably strained and gradually Chamberlain's own porcelain was produced in sufficient quantity to deem it unnecessary for any further trade in Caughley white ware after 1793. The employment of John Toulouse* as the factory's own modeller led in a way to a revival of earlier Worcester styles although French forms had become of great importance. Chamberlain were now established and in 1796 won their first important royal order, a dessert service for the Prince of Orange, decorated in blue and gold with different figures. This was possibly the set which later became known as the King of Hanover service*, or else another set of similar design was made for the King. Chamberlain had become an important maker of armorial services by 1800. The choice by Lord Nelson* to visit Chamberlain's factory in 1802 rather than the rival Flight and Barr must have given them publicity as well as confidence.

Chamberlain remained as a family company and was still controlled by Humphrey sen. and Robert jun.* Humphrey's sons Humphrey jun.* and Walter Chamberlain* played an increasingly important part in the day-to-day activities of the factory from the early 1820s. Humphrey jun. was himself one of the finest china painters in the country at this time and his tragic death in 1824 must have come as quite a blow to the family business. Porcelain by the very young Humphrey Chamberlain had been particularly requested by the Prince Regent in 1807 when he visited the factory and gave the Chamberlains the honour of his Appointment. Vases by Humphrey Chamberlain were proudly displayed at the 1813 opening of their first London retail shop at 63 Piccadilly. This was transfered to 155 New Bond Street in 1816. Thomas Baxter* joined the factory in 1819 and stayed until his death, also tragically young, in 1821. Among other important services made by Chamberlain were special designs for the Duke of Cumberland (1806), Princess Charlotte* (1816), the East India Company* (1818), and the Nabob of the Carnatic*

Colour Plate 17. ***Chamberlain and Co.*** *A small basket painted with a King Charles spaniel, and a square perfume bottle, both encrusted with a profusion of modelled shells, script mark, c.1840-5, the basket 8¼in. (21cm). The workmanship is superb but the taste at this time can be somewhat questionable. (Colin Harper Collection.)*

(1820). Several orders were made for George IV including a harlequin set comprising 186 pieces (with each piece different) ordered in 1811, and a vast armorial service ordered in 1816.

Humphrey Chamberlain sen. retired in 1827 and his son-in-law, John Lilly* was brought in as a new partner to assist Walter Chamberlain*. Gradually trade became more difficult and the offer to take over the rival Flight, Barr and Barr factory in 1840 led instead to the formation of a joint stock company under the name of Chamberlain and Co.*, with Walter Chamberlain and John Lilly* as senior among many business partners. Disagreement led to the partnership being dissolved in 1844. Walter and John Lilly kept the porcelain factory trading and in 1850 brought in W.H. Kerr* as a new partner. Kerr was left in sole control in 1851 and was joined by R.W. Binns* in 1852.

Because of the heavy competition in Worcester, most products of the Chamberlain factory were marked, either inscribed Chamberlains or Chamberlains Worcester in coloured enamel or gold. From the later 1830s an impressed mark Chamberlains was used in upper case, while the title Chamberlain & Co. was used generally after 1840. Pattern numbers began to be used from the introduction of their own porcelain in 1791. Most pieces were marked with the pattern number in gold and these patterns are simple progressive numbers which had reached around 3100 before a different sequence was attempted in the 1840s.

Chamberlain, Humphrey jun.

Born in 1791, the son of Humphrey Chamberlain sen.* joined his father's firm at an early age and proved himself as a very talented figure painter. His family later told R.W. Binns* that at the age of only nine or ten Humphrey had produced a pen and ink portrait of Garrick which was considered a very extraordinary production. By 1807 he had shown sufficient skill as a china painter to be entrusted with the historical figure centres in a most important dessert service made for the Prince Regent*. In 1813 he worked on the order for Lord Nevill* (*see* Colour Plate 63), including the magnificent pair of grace mugs* painted with 'The Power of Love' now in the Dyson Perrins Museum. Humphrey Chamberlain specialised in copying prints after famous paintings, executed in a most dramatic fashion making full use of contrasting colours and light and shade. Binns wrote that

> One of the boasted beauties of Mr Chamberlain's work was that you could never distinguish the touch nor discover how the effect was produced, hence a powerful magnifying glass was always placed in the hands of strangers in order that they might examine its minute beauties.

Present day painters have confirmed that the reason no one could see his brush strokes was because much of the time he did not use a brush. Instead finely powdered colour was dusted on to oil and delicately shaded to produce the desired effect. Binns felt that his remarkable talent had been wasted on these

Colour Plate 18. ***Charlotte, Princess, Services.*** *A Chamberlain plate from the service made for Princess Charlotte in 1816-7. The panels of* Fancy Birds* *are believed to have been painted by George Davis*. The original cost of each plate was £2. Printed mark, 10in. (25.5cm). (Dyson Perrins Museum.)*

mere copies and gave an account of how, in c.1820, there were frequent discussions between Humphrey Chamberlain and Thomas Baxter* about the artistic merit of the former's painting. Baxter felt Chamberlain's work was wonderful for its manipulative power but for nothing else. Most present day collectors disagree with Baxter and Binns and can only admire the incredible talent of the young Humphrey Chamberlain. His work was justifiably very expensive — for instance the 'British Champion' plate illustrated here was valued at £21 in 1816 when it was sent to the London shop. Humphrey's untimely death in 1824 at the age of thirty-three means that his work is now very scarce. Fortunately, however, many pieces were signed and it is not difficult to recognise his work.

Confusion with his father of the same name makes it difficult to be certain whether Humphrey jun. concentrated purely on painting or else was more actively involved in the running of the company. Most likely it was Humphrey sen. who was involved in the day to day running of the firm along with his other son Walter Chamberlain*, while Humphrey jun. devoted his time to his remarkable painting.

Chamberlain, Humphrey jun. *A remarkable cabinet plate signed 'H. Chamberlain Pinxt', depicting the celebrated boxer Thomas Cribb, inscribed on the reverse 'The British Champion' with a list of his victories. Script marks, 9⅝in. (24.5cm). The Chamberlain records list '1 plate with Painting of Cribb, £21', sent to their London shop on 31 January 1816. (Sotheby's/Kiddell Papers.)*

Chamberlain, Humphrey sen.
Born in Worcester in 1762, Humphrey Chamberlain was apprenticed to his father, also Humphrey, on 30 April 1776 and would have learnt all aspects of the decorating processes while at Davis and Co's* factory. Humphrey is credited with the title of china painter in many apprenticeship indentures although no signed work survives and it is likely that his role in the business was much more managerial than as a practical potter. His wife Anne, whom he married in 1786, was equally important to the company as she acted as clerk and book-keeper and managed the shop. In spite of being five years younger than his brother Robert*, Humphrey was a far more important partner in the porcelain manufactory and when the firm was restructured in 1796 he was allocated one half share while his father and brother Robert received only one quarter share each. Following their father's death in 1798, the two brothers traded as H. and R. Chamberlain and Co. although Humphrey continued to hold a much larger share in the capital, having bought his late father's shares in 1801.

Humphrey and Anne had nine children, among whom were sons Walter Chamberlain* and Humphrey Chamberlain jun.*, both of whom painted at Chamberlain's factory. Humphrey sen. was himself Mayor of Worcester in 1819. He retired from the porcelain factory in 1827 and must have found it difficult to pass on all of his interests to his son. While dependent on market forces, Humphrey would have been saddened to see the way in which standards had declined by the time of the merger in 1840. He died in 1841.

Chamberlain, Robert jun.
Baptised on 29 October 1755, the eldest son of Robert Chamberlain*, who was then an apprentice china painter. In spite of his apprenticeship to his father in February 1775 Robert jun. does not seem to have had anything like as much interest in porcelain manufacture as his younger brother Humphrey Chamberlain*. Although his name appears on indentures alongside his brother and father from 1796 he does not seem to have played an active role, in spite of having been given a one quarter share in the factory by his father and the company having traded as H. and R. Chamberlain and Company. Robert jun. may have been trained and indeed worked as a painter but there is no evidence to support this. It has been shown that he was at one time licensee of the Crown public house in Worcester and he and his wife Mary had nine children although none seems to have been connected with the china factory. Like his brother he seems to have played an active part in civic life and was Mayor of Worcester in 1817. Robert jun. died on 22 September 1832.

Chamberlain, Robert sen.
Although early records are slight and inconclusive, it seems likely that the Robert Chamberlain who founded the porcelain factory was born in Worcester and was baptised on 1 August 1736. This would have made him about fifteen when the Bristol factory was transferred to Worcester and the Worcester porcelain company was in a position to take on apprentices. Robert Chamberlain was apprenticed to Richard Holdship* as a 'pot painter' and we know from Valentine Green* writing in 1796 that he was the first apprentice bound to the Worcester Porcelain Company. Green would have known Chamberlain well and worked alongside him at the porcelain factory. Green tells us that 'The ornamental part of the production of that factory, and the embellishing of the ware, were carried on under the immediate direction of Mr Chamberlain and his son for many years' (*A History of the City and Suburbs of Worcester,* 1796). It is clear from many sources that Chamberlain played a major part in the decoration of Worcester porcelain up until the arrival of John Flight* who recorded in his diary the frightful situation his company found itself in when the Chamberlains took over Flight's old shop in the High Street and set up as china decorators in direct competition. Geoffrey Godden in his *Chamberlain-Worcester Porcelain* and more recently Sonia Parkinson writing in the *Journal of the Northern Ceramics Society* (1991) have provided conclusive evidence that Robert and Humphrey Chamberlain* set up on their own c.1786 and continued to decorate for Flights until c.1788. From this time they entered into an agreement with Thomas Turner* of the Caughley factory* to supply them with white porcelain for decoration. By 1791 the Chamberlains were certainly manufacturing their own porcelain and continued to do so until 1840. Robert Chamberlain was trained as a china painter but no signed pieces survive to give any clues as to his own work. He had chosen to become a Freeman of the City of Worcester on 26 December 1774, which was some time after completing his apprenticeship and when he had already become a senior figure at the Worcester factory. His Freedom entitled him to take on apprentices and he subsequently took on his own sons Robert* and Humphrey* in 1775 and 1776. Curiously, his work at the factory left Robert Chamberlain enough time to act as licensee of the Chequer public house in King Street near to where he was to set up his own porcelain factory.

By 1798 at the time of Robert Chamberlain's death the size of the factory had grown considerably and agents were employed around the country to market the wares. He died following a 'lingering illness' on 19 December 1798 and the works passed to his two sons and other backers to carry on the successful business.

Chamberlain, Walter. *A Chamberlain cabinet cup with a remarkable pineapple finial, painted with a scene from Timon of Athens, script mark, c.1816. This Shakespearian scene differs from the signed work of Humphrey Chamberlain jun.* and it is therefore reasonable to attribute this to Walter. (Dyson Perrins Museum.)*

Chamberlain, Walter

Walter was the son of Humphrey Chamberlain sen.* and his wife Anne. Humphrey, with his father and brother, had left the employment of the Worcester Porcelain Company to set up on their own and Walter would have grown up with a sound knowledge of all aspects of the business. Sadly his dates are not known and as son of the owners of the factory his name does not appear in the wages books. The only record we have of Walter Chamberlain as a painter of Shakespearian* subjects is on three 'Regent' shaped vases sent to London for the opening of the Bond Street shop in 1813, and three other ornaments painted in the same year. Walter's work was not priced as highly as the work of his brother Humphrey jun.*, and it is unlikely that Walter was as talented. Humphrey signed many of his fine Shakespearian pieces but no signed work by Walter is known. It is not unreasonable, however, to ascribe to Walter a secondary and less accomplished hand also painting Shakespearian subjects. The cabinet cup illustrated was ascribed to Walter during the 1860s by R.W. Binns* who knew Walter and had learnt much about the history of the firm from him. A flower painted plaque in the Victoria and Albert Museum is inscribed in pencil 'Walter Chamberlain Esq, China Factory' and if this is indeed by him it suggests that he probably concentrated on the easier subject of flower painting and left figures to his more talented brother.

Walter's main contribution to the firm was as manager of the Worcester factory. He is known to have travelled to France in November 1817 on company business and in the early 1820s was probably helping to run the company, drawing a salary of £100 per year. Humphrey jun.'s death in 1824 left Walter alone to manage the day-to-day activities of the factory, assisted by his uncle Robert* and father Humphrey sen.* who retired probably at the end of 1827. To assist Walter a new partner was needed. John Lilly,* his brother-in-law, joined the firm at this time and remained a close ally throughout the difficult period of the 1840s and the merger with Flight, Barr and Barr (*see* **Chamberlain and Co.**). Walter Chamberlain and John Lilly were the senior shareholders and by 1848 were the only partners remaining. Walter finally retired in 1851, just after their disappointing show at the Great Exhibition*. The company was left in the hands of W.H. Kerr* who was to be joined by R.W. Binns*.

Charlotte, Princess Services

Chamberlains were invited in May 1816 to submit specimens of their porcelain to Warwick House so that Princess Charlotte might choose a service for her forthcoming marriage to Prince Leopold. Two sets were ordered, one for dessert in 'Union Embossed' shape with a drab ground and flowers; the other a dinner service with a light blue ground and lozenge-shaped

Colour Plate 19. **Charlotte, Princess, Services.** *A fine oval dish from the Chamberlain service ordered in 1816, the panels of* Fancy Birds* *believed to be by George Davis*, script mark. (Dyson Perrins Museum).*

Colour Plate 20. **Charlotte, Princess, Services.** *A plate from the breakfast service made by Flight, Barr and Barr for the marriage of Princess Charlotte and Prince Leopold. The flower painting was attributed by Binns* first to Samuel Astles* and later to Henry Stinton*. Printed mark, c.1816, 9in. (23cm). (Dyson Perrins Museum.)*

Colour Plate 21. ***Chestnut Baskets.*** *An elaborate example with pierced cover and stand, the modelled flowers including hot cross bun buds* c.1768-70, 6in. (15cm). These baskets originally accompanied dessert services and were probably intended for cream. (Phillips.)*

panels of *Fancy Birds** around a fruit and flower centre (Colour Plates 18 and 19). The dinner service comprised nearly three hundred pieces including 144 plates each costing £2. The pattern was not apparently a special design but instead a pattern from stock and therefore it is not possible to describe every piece of the design as coming from the royal service. In recognition of the important order, Chamberlains commemorated the marriage itself by producing a special armorial plate (*see* illustration on page 104) and in addition an oil painting was commissioned to mark the occasion.

Although Chamberlain held her Royal Warrant, Princess Charlotte also ordered a breakfast service at the same time from Flight, Barr and Barr, once again choosing a pattern from stock rather than a special commission (Colour Plate 20). The design was a solid apple green ground with panels of colourful flowers and butterflies within a gold gadroon* rim. Binns* ascribed the painting of the service first to Samuel Astles* but later to Henry Stinton*. Sadly the Princess died the following year during childbirth, and so is unlikely to have used any of the three Worcester services herself.

Charlotte, Queen, Pattern

Although initially inspired by Japanese porcelain, the direct origin of Worcester's pattern was Meissen* where the design was made from the 1730s. Exact copies of Meissen were made in Chinese porcelain and Chinese teawares even reproduced the crossed swords mark used at Meissen. It is possible Worcester copied these Chinese copies, but more likely it was Meissen porcelain which served as the prototype for what was to become a very popular pattern at Worcester. The whorl pattern is painted in underglaze blue with added Imari* colours, and while the blue panels remain remarkably constant, a number of variations occur in the coloured portion, including very occasional use of painted European flowers.

The earliest examples of the *Queen Charlotte* pattern appear in the late 1750s with workmen's marks*, although these are rarely seen and most pieces date from c.1765-75 on teawares and very occasional dessert wares. More unusual shapes in the pattern which are known from this period are water bottles*, plain and cabbage leaf moulded mask jugs*, dessert baskets and butter tubs*. Most pieces are marked with the square mark*. *Queen Charlotte* pattern was still in production in the Flight period c.1790-1800, mostly on teawares and some dessert sets, while dessert services* are known from the later Barr, Flight and Barr and Flight, Barr and Barr periods. Coalport produced the pattern but curiously no Chamberlain or Grainger examples have been noted.

The origin of the name is uncertain. Queen Charlotte visited Flight's factory in 1788 together with the King and they placed an order for porcelain. It is said that the *Blue Lily* pattern was renamed *Royal Lily** in honour of a royal order

Charlotte, Princess. *A truly magnificent Chamberlain presentation plate illustrating armorial* decoration at its very best, made for the royal marriage in 1816, 9½ in. (24cm). (Dyson Perrins Museum.)*

placed at this time. Possibly the *Queen Charlotte* pattern, also called in the past *Whorl* pattern or *Catherine Wheel* pattern, was renamed in 1788 to honour the Queen's visit and to celebrate the granting of the Royal Warrant. Sadly, though, there is no evidence surviving to identify the royal order and the true origin of the name is now clouded by history.

Chelsea Ewer Creamboats
The Chamberlain account books include references to two versions of Chelsea ewers on sale c.1790, called 'Low' and 'Tall'. The shape referred to is a creamboat with a lobed body and acanthus moulding around the base. The handles are moulded and serpent-like. The low version is by far the most common and was issued in an extensive range of patterns. The coloured patterns used were mostly standard teaware designs and some Chelsea ewers were sold with tea services after c.1770. The shape is indeed copied from a rare Chelsea version which is closer to the tall Chelsea ewer shape and was made in the Red Anchor period c.1755. The earliest Worcester examples appear to be from the early 1760s although Chelsea ewers mostly date from the 1770s. Caughley made very similar shapes which can be distinguished by thicker potting in the Caughley examples although the Caughley handles are sharper and thinner than Worcester. Chelsea ewer creamboats were made by many other factories and Chamberlain produced their own version c.1793 which was a fairly close copy of the Caughley low Chelsea ewer shape they had sold previously. These were sold with tea sets but did not match the rest of the service very well and the shape was soon discontinued.

Charlotte, Queen. *The portrait of Charlotte is one of Robert Hancock's* most detailed engravings, shown here printed in black on a bell-shaped mug, c.1762, 3⅛ in. (8.5cm). (Dyson Perrins Museum.)*

Charlotte, Queen, Pattern. *An interesting selection of pieces decorated with this popular pattern in Imari* style. The cups and saucers are all Worcester, c.1768-75 with the exception of the teabowl, top right, which is the Chinese porcelain prototype. The Worcester* Blind Earl* *moulded sweetmeat dish in the centre is rarely decorated in this way. (Sotheby's, New York.)*

Chelsea Ewer Creamboats. *A 'low' Chelsea ewer creamboat painted with a simple* convolvulus *pattern in underglaze blue*, crescent mark*, c.1770, 2½in. (6.5cm). (Private Collection.)*

Chelsea Porcelain, Decorated at Worcester
In the Art Gallery reserve collection in Melbourne, Victoria, is a pair of beakers of Chelsea porcelain from the Triangle or early Raised Anchor periods, c.1748-50. They are decorated with the *Red Bull* pattern* printed in black outline and coloured in exactly the same way as the popular Worcester version. There is evidence of a certain amount of spit-out*, appropriate for pieces of white Chelsea decorated several years later.

It would seem reasonable to assume that these were decorated at Worcester c.1754-6 to supply a shape Worcester were unable to provide. The alternative is that the copper plates for printing the *Red Bull* pattern were available to an outside decorator, possibly in Birmingham, who carefully copied Worcester's colouring. Otherwise, other Worcester *Red Bull* pieces may not have been decorated at the factory. If Worcester were prepared to decorate white Chelsea porcelain, it is likely that other porcelain, especially Chinese, could have been decorated at Worcester also.

Chemical Porcelain
The trade name used by George Grainger and Co. for their range of chemical apparatus made for laboratories. Although much of it was porcelain, many shapes were probably in 'Semi China' (*see* **Semi-Porcelain**) as well as coarse pottery. All manner of shapes were made, from filter funnels and capsules to pestles and mortars and photographic dishes for processing negatives (*see* illustration on page 108). Grainger were proud to receive a testimonial from a chemist in Bristol which they published on advertising plaques...

Sir — I have now worked for some months with your Semi Porcelain Ware in my Analytical Laboratory, subjecting it not

Colour Plate 22. ***Clarence, Duke of.*** *A plate from the service made to honour the creation of Prince William as Duke of Clarence and St Andrew, ordered in 1789, marked Flight with a crown and crescent*, 9½in. (24.3cm). (Phillips.)*

only to the ordinary usage of the place, but to very severe trials, with the view of learning the extent of its qualities, and I feel pleasure in certifying that, for Chemical purposes, it is superior to every article of English Manufacture I have hitherto had in use.

William Herepath, Bristol, 1 December 1849

Chequered Tent Pattern
A curious design of flowering trees and bamboo with a bird in flight and a triangular shape in the foreground brightly coloured in green and red. This occurs on strongly fluted teaware shapes, c.1768, and was probably inspired by Meissen rather than Chinese porcelain. Examples have been attributed to the Giles* workshop but there is little evidence on which to base this except for the strange nature of the design.

Chess Tables
Mentioned in the Grainger shape books c.1845, these were flat, circular trays with raised scroll rims, painted with the squares of a chess-board on one side and a decorative flower panel to show on the other side when not in use. An example is known with a pink ground.

Colour Plate 23. ***Clarence, Duke of.*** *A plate from the 'Hope'* service ordered by the Duke of Clarence in 1790 and painted by John Pennington*, marked Flight with a crown and crescent*, 9½ in. (24cm). (Phillips.)*

Colour Plate 24. ***Coffee Pots.*** *Two contrasting shapes. Left: feather moulded* in European style, c.1757, 7⅞ in. (20cm). Right: the* Scarlet Japan* *pattern inspired by Japanese porcelain, c.1770, 8¼ in. (21cm). (Phillips.)*

Chemical Porcelain. *A page from a Grainger catalogue showing part of their range of chemical and laboratory apparatus, mostly introduced during the 1840s; this sheet is dated 1854.*

Chestnut Baskets

These impressive pieces have been known as chestnut baskets since the 19th century although this does not appear to be their original purpose (Colour Plate 21). The 1769 Worcester sale catalogue included several cream basons (*sic*) with pierced covers and plates, such as the 'Two fine oval white and gold cream-basons, pierced covers and plates' which sold for £15.6s. The dessert services in the sale also included 'cream basons', but the covers of these were not pierced and these will be the standard oval dessert tureens now known as sauce tureens. Chestnut baskets are listed in some 18th century records but these were probably round shapes or else possibly open baskets. The fine oval cream basins will probably always be referred to by collectors as chestnut baskets, however.

The shapes are based on silver and have an elaborate moulded honeycomb of florette panels on the outside of the tapering baskets. The covers are pierced with similar arcaded panels of florettes and the stands are usually pierced also. Many baskets are marked with a number, sometimes in Roman numerals, on the underside of the cover and inside the bases of the baskets. These were painted in blue probably before the biscuit firing to ensure the correct match of cover and base. Many have become mixed up but not necessarily later as many parts of baskets never survived the firing and other pieces were switched round when the pieces were decorated. A significant feature of the baskets which were only made c.1768-72 is the flower modelling which grows from the gnarled twig handles. Large flat leaves, complicated flowers and hot cross bun buds* relate to other pieces bearing the 'To' or 'IT' marks which are found on Worcester and Caughley 'chestnut baskets' which can have identical flowers. John Toulouse* probably went to Caughley after leaving Bristol. The flower modelling should always be the same on a matching basket, cover and stand. Very rare examples are known with modelled oak leaves and acorns instead of flowers. Another very rare variant uses a cabbage leaf dish as a stand, the outline of the basket reserved in the centre of the leaf.

Chinese Copies of Worcester Porcelain. *Two blue and white junket dishes*. Left: Worcester; right: a Chinese copy exact in every detail. Both with crescent marks*, c.1765, 9⅞in. (25cm). (Colin Harper Collection.)*

Worcester chestnut baskets are found in a variety of patterns, usually with simple coloured flower painting or else underglaze floral prints and painted birds and foliage. Rare examples have been seen in Japan* style while particularly rich examples have scale blue* grounds with bird panels, the exteriors on the baskets sometimes additionally with yellow grounds*. Some of the finest were decorated in the Giles* workshop with characteristic fruit, flower, bird or figure painting.

Chinese Copies of Worcester Porcelain
The popularity of Worcester's blue and white porcelain, especially in Holland, led to a surprising trade with the Far East in the 1760s and 1770s. Specimens of Worcester and other English porcelains were taken to China and exact copies were then shipped back for sale in Europe. These Chinese copies are so faithful to the originals, even to the use of the crescent mark, that they can cause much confusion. They are, of course, in hard paste porcelain and for this reason specimens are often condemned as Samson, the notorious French forger.

The most frequently seen are copies of junket dishes* with blue painted panels. A relief moulded sauceboat* with embossed flower sprays was also most faithfully copied, along with a Chelsea ewer* creamboat. The *Pine-cone* pattern* on scalloped dessert plates is also known, but the Chinese copies are hand painted instead of transfer printed. With Chinese painted patterns in some cases it is difficult to know which came first. I know of two Chinese coffee cups in *Gazebo* pattern*, a blue and white design which was probably invented at Worcester. The Chinese cups have grooved handles, a form which could only have been copied from Worcester originals. Thus the absurd situation must have arisen of a European dealer selling Chinese copies of a Worcester version of a Chinese design.

Chinese Decoration
While the Bow factory made a speciality of copying Chinese porcelain for much of their early production, Worcester instead preferred to adapt Chinese patterns to their own style and palette (*see* **Chinoiserie**). Apart from the Canton* style, relatively few popular Worcester patterns have exact Chinese prototypes, especially coloured designs although certain blue and white patterns are reasonably faithful copies. Direct copies of Chinese patterns were more usually made at Worcester as replacements for Chinese porcelain sets (*see* **Chinese Porcelain, Replacements for**).

Chinese Family Pattern
The origin of this popular pattern is presumed to be Chinese export porcelain, although no exact Chinese counterpart has been seen. The *Chinese Family* design was made with a transfer printed outline but, unlike *Red Bull** and other coloured-in transfers, it did not appear until c.1765. The pattern was used on the full range of teaware shapes, always in conjunction with a crowfoot border*. A rare hand painted version of the *Chinese Family* print is recorded, also from c.1765 and this possibly just pre-dates the coloured print.

Chinese Marks
In spite of considerable discussion in the past as to their meaning, the variety of Chinese style markings which occur on Worcester porcelain mostly form nothing more than part of the pattern. Most pseudo-Chinese marks are unique to one particular pattern and some of these were probably copied from the original Chinese or Japanese example which inspired

Chinese Family Pattern. *A teapot printed in black outline and coloured in with the popular pattern, c.1765, 5½in. (14cm). (Phillips.)*

Chinese Musicians Pattern. *A large cabbage leaf moulded dish painted in Chinese style within a thick green enamel border, c.1758, 10in. (25.5cm). (Formerly Henry Sandon Collection.)*

Worcester's version. In most cases, however, the symbols used at Worcester are pure imagination on the part of the Worcester painter and cannot be translated into Chinese. Patterns such as *Old Japan Fan* pattern (*see* **Japan Patterns**) and *Old Mosaic** almost always carry the same mark and are certainly not any form of factory code. The workmen's marks* which occur on early blue and white and some coloured pieces in the 1750s can resemble oriental characters and certain larger marks are undoubtedly copied from emblems found on the bottom of some Chinese *Kangxi* porcelain. The disguised numeral* marks from the 1780s, on the other hand, are merely English numbers hidden within doodles. Apart from occurring mostly on Chinese style patterns, the significance of these marks is unknown.

Chinese Musicians Pattern
A popular pattern used on teawares and large leaf-shaped dishes c.1756-8. The origin would appear to be Chinese although the green diaper border is more likely to be a

Colour Plate 25. **Cottages.** *Two Worcester porcelain pastille burners* shaped as rustic cottages, both c.1820-5. Left marked Chamberlains Worcester, 3⅛in. (8cm), right marked Flight Barr and Barr, 6⅝in. (17cm). (Henry Sandon Collection.)*

Colour Plate 26. **Creamboats.** *An early hexagonal creamboat, the delicate modelling left in white. Painted inside with ribboned emblems, c.1753, 4⅜in. (11cm) long. (Phillips.)*

Colour Plate 27. ***Cutlery Handles.*** *An exceptional collection of Worcester cutlery handles. Left to right: scale blue c.1768-70; dry blue enamel c.1770; an important pair with monochrome flowers and rococo panels containing the arms of Stoughton, c.1758-60; Meissen style flowers c.1758; the Cobbe* service (scale blue with insects), c.1770 and c.1785 replacement; scale blue c.1768-70. (Tony Stevenson Collection.)*

Chinese Porcelain, Replacements for. *A Chinese saucer with a Worcester replacement teabowl, painted in Jesuit* style with 'Provender for the Monastry'; and a Worcester teapot pencilled with Diana, exactly matching a Chinese export pattern. Both c.1765-70. Saucer 4¾in. (12cm), teapot 5¾in. (14.8cm). (Sotheby's, New York.)*

Worcester addition. The pattern depicts three separate Chinese ladies, one playing a flute, another seated with a fan, the third standing with a child by her side. This standing mother and child was also used as a separate pattern painted over a transfer printed outline on bottle vases and mustard pots, c.1754.

Chinese Porcelain, Replacements for

While most Worcester patterns in Chinese style were used by the factory for their own services, the factory and James Giles* both claimed to be able to make replacements for foreign china without perceivable difference and in a short space of time. This usually meant copying the original Chinese or Japanese pattern on to Worcester's own shapes but occasionally the special shape of the original was copied, as in the case of the Sebright service*. It is of course likely that a design originally commissioned as a replacement could have appealed to the factory and have been used subsequently on full services of Worcester porcelain. The well-known teapot showing *Potiphar's Wife**, in the Dyson Perrins Museum, and a teapot from the Nina Weil Collection sold by Sotheby's in New York with the subject of Diana in black monochrome are typical of the unusual European subjects which were special productions in China. Worcester would not have had much of a market for such curious designs and these can only have been made as direct replacements. All pieces in Jesuit* style seem to fit into this category, along with other very elaborate patterns with ruby grounds*. Occasionally a service has survived with Worcester replacements remaining with the Chinese originals. Some of these combined Chinese and Worcester sets can be very confusing as in the case of the *Staghunt* pattern*, or one particular form of decoration with so-called scarlet ground*.

Chinese Porcelain, Replacements for. *A large Worcester serving dish painted with the arms of Bourne, exactly copying a known Chinese service, c.1770-5. (Christie's.)*

The painting in the Worcester and Chinese pieces is so exact that the Chinese must also have been decorated in England, by Giles or another London decorator. There is a tendency to assume all copies of strange Chinese patterns were decorated in London, but there is no reason why they were not factory decorated instead.

It should be remembered that copying also worked the other way — *see* **Chinese Copies of Worcester Porcelain.** Also, in the case of the coffee cup illustrated under **Meissen Style,** Worcester made a replacement for a Chinese pattern which in itself was exactly copying Meissen.

Chinoiserie

The term has been applied to virtually every design which is after a Chinese original, although strictly speaking true chinoiserie is much more of a European adaptation. It can best be summed up by the work of Jean Pillement* who created a fantasy world of crazy structures and scenery peopled by Europeans dressed up as Chinamen. The Chinese artists' use of scale and perspective became jumbled as figures dwarf buildings and animals become giants. Illustrations from Pillement's *Livre de Chinois* published in 1758 were well known to Worcester decorators and influenced many transfer printed patterns. Most coloured patterns in early Worcester owe much of their inspiration to Meissen where chinoiserie played a major role earlier in the 18th century. Chinoiserie designs are well represented in Robert Sayer's *The Ladies' Amusement** and it is often claimed that Worcester copied many printed designs from this well-known source book. It is more likely that the subjects were introduced directly to Worcester by Robert Hancock or other engravers, as Hancock signed certain prints after designs of Pillement published by various booksellers. Chinoiserie was an important spirit behind many Regency patterns, especially from Barr, Flight and Barr, although the taste for flamboyant chinoiserie declined in the 19th century.

Chocolate Cups. *A very richly decorated cup and saucer with a scale blue ground and panels of Watteau* figures playing musical instruments, c.1770. The elaborate gilding inside the cup indicates that this example would not originally have had a cover. (Sotheby's/Kiddell Papers.)*

Chocolate Cups

In the early 18th century, especially on the Continent, there was no real distinction between coffee and chocolate cups; the latter were perhaps a little larger but both could have served either purpose. In early English porcelain there is reason to believe that certain larger beakers or big handled cups were for chocolate, and some of the small mugs and tankards made at Worcester in the 1750s could well have been for chocolate also.

The earliest cups which can certainly be thought of as chocolate cups are wide, double ogee in section with fluted rims and can have one or two handles. They came with deep saucer-shaped stands and, I believe, optional covers. This is unproved but so many examples survive today without covers (even in sets while other sets have covers) and many of these have no evidence at all of rubbing to the rim which might have been caused by an ill-fitting cover. This shape seems to have been introduced around 1765, mostly aimed at up-market customers as blue and white examples are very rare. The handles almost always follow the same serpent-scroll shape, which has been unconvincingly described as a swan-neck. In very rare instances the handles are pierced scrolls which must have been difficult to manufacture. The covers always have large flower finials. The shape is unknown after about 1775 or possibly 1780 although Caughley made examples until at least the late 1780s.

Chamberlain's and Flight's factories both made chocolate cups and many references in the Chamberlain archives show that they were sometimes very rich productions indeed. Most were probably just ornamental as they were not sold in sets and cost as much as the richest cabinet cups*.

Chrysanthemum Pattern. *An elegant coffee pot with crisp moulding left white, the simple underglaze blue* borders copying early French porcelain, crescent mark*, c.1760-5. 9in. (23cm). (Dyson Perrins Museum.)*

Chrysanthemum Pattern

A moulded teaware pattern introduced around 1755. The embossed pattern of flowers is inspired by Chinese porcelain although it is likely to follow more directly from a silver prototype. Earlier examples are decorated exclusively in blue with a *lambrequin* border inspired by early French porcelain, the centre usually painted with a single large chrysanthemum flower. This pattern in blue continued until c.1780. Coloured decoration occurs from about 1765. The rarest form is with a yellow ground* although there is doubt about the authenticity of some yellow ground pieces. Pieces also occur with the moulding left plain and with slight decoration to the rim and centre. Sometimes the *Old Worcester Parrot** pattern was used, and other patterns include apple green borders, dry blue or gilded sprig centres and a pattern with a central ladybird. A teapot in the Dyson Perrins Museum is decorated with a coloured-in overglaze landscape print which seems quite out of place on the moulded surface. It is possible, although unlikely, that this decoration was added outside the factory, even by Giles* in London. A small number of knife handles (*see* **Cutlery Handles**) are known with the chrysanthemum moulding left in white and a matching waster was found on the factory site. Unglazed wasters show just how crisp the modelling could be.

Clarence, Duke of, Services
William Henry, Duke of Clarence and later William IV became Flights' most important patron, altering the factory's ailing fortunes by placing orders for two major services. The first was an armorial dessert service (Colour Plate 22) made in 1789 when William Henry was created Duke of Clarence and St. Andrew. This was the first royal armorial service made at Worcester and the design chosen was unconventional, inspired by Sèvres and using a ribbon border in heavily contrasted blue and green colours which produced a stunning effect. Later in 1789 the Duke of Clarence commissioned a new dinner service to be painted with figures in landscapes (Colour Plate 23). John Flight recorded in his diary* for January 1790 how he had sent three sample plates to the Duke, one with gold arabesques, the others with figures of Peace and Plenty and Hope and Patience. Derby had also submitted samples but the Duke, preferring Flight's proposals, chose the Hope and Patience design within a different border and placed an order for a whole dinner service to be ready in one year at a cost of £700. John Pennington* was given the task of executing all the figure panels in sepia monochrome. A deep blue border with brilliant gilding was used to frame his dramatic paintings. Several fine dishes from the service were kept at the factory and entered Binns' museum, and a large part of the service itself was sold by Christie's in the 1970s.

Claret Ground
Undoubtedly the most controversial ground colour used at Worcester as so many pieces exhibit signs of redecoration*. Some pieces seem to be perfectly acceptable, such as the teawares with panels of birds and fruit and certain Giles* decorated baskets and plates. The *Hope-Edwardes** pattern is inconsistent and it may well be that most but not all pieces are redecorated. A tankard of Hope-Edwardes type with a floral wreath enclosing a letter 'E' seems authentic and stylistically confirms that the colour was used late on at Worcester, not introduced before c.1775 and continuing into the 1780s. For this reason the claret ground on a hexagonal creamboat from the late 1750s can only be condemned as a bad fake. A ruby ground* does occur in the 1760s but this is a very different colour. Two principal forms of decoration which occur in panels on claret grounds are now regarded with almost total scepticism. One has panels of Teniers* figures, the other *Fancy Birds** in rich vegetation. A teapot of *Eloping Bride** pattern filled in totally in claret is another case of redecoration taken into the realms of disbelief. Claret ground striped patterns are more problematic. Contemporary descriptions show that claret stripes were used, such as 'a tea and coffee equipage of mazarine blue and gold enriched with claret coloured stripes', but this probably refers to a *Hop Trellis** pattern. One class of Worcester porcelain with flower panels between claret stripes is almost certainly of much later date. Another pattern with alternate claret and turquoise stripes is usually accepted as contemporary, but all pieces seem to exhibit signs of redecoration including green flower festoons having been covered up with new gilding. Great care must be taken, but we have to go on believing that some at least of these wonderful claret ground pieces are fully authentic.

***Claret Ground.** A saucer-dish decorated in the Giles* workshop with distinctive birds and fruit, the claret ground somewhat mottled below tooled gilding, c.1765-70, 7in. (18cm). (Dyson Perrins Museum.)*

Clobbering
A somewhat inappropriate term used to describe a piece of blue and white porcelain which has had additional decoration added in colours and gold to produce a richer effect. It is usually clear that such overpainting has been added but there is great uncertainty over when and where. The original Worcester or Caughley porcelain which has been clobbered was usually decorated with blue painted patterns or some prints from the 1770s. Presumably this plain style was unfasionable a decade or more later when the new style of heavy Chinese landscapes came into popularity. It is believed that china dealers were left with a certain amount of unsaleable stock, including some Chinese blue and white porcelain which could not be offered to buyers unless the patterns were brought up to date. Some time in the 1780s and 1790s this was given to a china painter to add leaf and flower designs or else colour in the patterns, mostly in red, green and gold. It has been suggested that most clobbering was done in Holland where this colouring was used also on Dutch-decorated Chinese porcelain. There remains no evidence at the moment to confirm this possibility, or indeed any others, except to note the existence of two dated pieces. One earlier Worcester blue and white printed mug of c.1760 has had rather coarse clobbered decoration of foliage added. This is dated below the handle in the same colouring 'R.D 1760', a date which, if genuine, suggests that the colouring was added by an outside decorator at the time of making. A Caughley mask jug with blue-printed flowers is recorded where coloured fruit sprays have been painted to fill in and enrich the decoration. In gold

Clobbering. *Two teabowls printed on blue with the* Birds in Branches* *pattern, the example on the left subsequently 'clobbered' with overpainting in red, green and gold, the porcelain c.1780. (Henry Sandon Collection.)*

underneath are the initials 'L.B.K.' and date 1784. In my opinion this is when most clobbering was carried out, but some may well have been added very much later than this. Clobbering, which applies only to blue and white porcelain altered as above, should not be confused with redecoration* where the original pattern, usually in colours, is hidden or removed and replaced with a new, richer form of decoration.

Coasters

A shallow circular dish with straight sides, about 4¾in. (12cm) in diameter was in the Gilbert Bradley Collection, painted in blue with the *Mansfield pattern**, c.1770. The exact purpose of this piece is unknown but it could have served as the stand for a small bottle.

Cobbe, Archbishop, Service

A set of knives and forks with Worcester porcelain handles is reputed to have been made for Charles Cobbe who became Archbishop of Dublin in 1742 and died in 1765. The handles have panels of colourful insects framed in gold on a blue scale ground although the decoration is usually now somewhat worn through use. The known examples seem to range from about 1770 with some in bright blue suggesting a date of at least 1780. It is likely, therefore, that several sets were made, none quite early enough to have been made for Archbishop Cobbe himself. Some replacements are said to have been made by Chamberlain but with unmarked cutlery handles it is impossible to confirm such an attribution. *See also* **Cutlery Handles** and Colour Plate 27.

Coffee Cups and Cans. *A spreading based can of Scratch Cross* type with the* Willow Root *pattern in underglaze blue*, c.1753, together with an early panel-moulded coffee can in coloured enamels, c.1752, both 2½in. (6.5cm). (Formerly Author's Collection.)*

Coffee Cups and Cans. A selection of Worcester coffee cups c.1753-75, forming a very attractive display and understandably popular with collectors. The early ribbed can and octagonal cup on the top shelf, as well as the large 'chocolate cup' in the centre on the bottom, would not originally have had saucers. (Phillips.)

Coffee Cups and Cans
Taller than teabowls and with side handles, these shapes were made by every factory and sold with tea services, even though such sets usually included only a teapot and not a coffee pot. The earliest examples from the Bristol factory c.1750 and made in the first year or so at Worcester are hand-thrown on a wheel and turned and can have plain rolled handles. The typical Worcester single grooved handle was introduced c.1752-3 and was to remain in use on virtually every coffee cup until c.1785-90. It is interesting to note that the price list of the London Warehouse, c.1755-6 (*see* **London Shops**), includes 'Coffee Cups and Cans' at 5s. per dozen and 'ditto ribb'd and Wav'd' at 8s. Cups and saucers are listed separately at 3s. 6d. per dozen, grouped with large teabowls called '¼-pint basons' and 'King's Coffees' at the same price of 3s.6d. These 'King's Coffees' were probably plain coffee cups which were sold with saucers, while the more expensive coffee cups and cans could possibly have been the small spreading-based mug shapes but were more likely the octagonal shapes with ornate handles. The 'wav'd cans' were 'feather moulded*' and the 'ribb'd' were finely reeded examples. These were probably sold without saucers and were instead served on a tray. One small mug with a spreading base is inscribed 'I drink up the liquor, Tho the cup is but small, And heres a good health, To Edmund Wall'. This shows that these mugs which can be the same size as a coffee can, were used instead for spirits.

From the earlier 18th century it was standard in tea services of Chinese and Continental porcelain for the teacups, teabowls and coffee cups to share the same saucer. Only very occasionally were larger saucers also provided. English porcelain factories continued this tradition until at least the middle of the 19th century, on the assumption that customers were not going to drink coffee and tea at the same time. Straight-sided coffee cans were made in the late 1760s and 1770s, usually in blue and white or very simple coloured patterns. These probably did not have saucers. By c.1790 straight-sided coffee cans had become the usual shape provided with most tea services, or else the coffee cups were simply taller versions of the teacup shapes. Coffee cans went out of popularity by c.1815 and throughout the Regency period the can shape was decorated with fine painting as cabinet cups*, sold singly or in pairs and probably not intended for use.

Coffee Pots
Although most tea services also had coffee cups, the inclusion of a coffee pot seems to have been very much of an exception. Examples of coffee pots are known as early as the Bristol period in blue and white and from c.1752-3 at Worcester, and these were of a surprisingly small size. Coffee pots of Scratch Cross class*, c.1753-5, were mostly coloured in Meissen style* and had thickened footrims and very flat covers. Domed covers were introduced c.1756 on feather moulded* coffee pots and gradually the size increased as well. Simon Spero has

Coffee Pots. *A plain thrown shape with the flat cover typical of the mid-1750s, painted with the* Zig Zag Fence *pattern, 7½in. (19cm), together with a reeded shape in early French style, c.1758-60, 9¼in. (23.5cm), both with workmen's marks*. (Sotheby's.)*

Coffee Pots. *An early Chamberlain ribbed coffee pot with an unusual Continental style pouring lip, decorated in underglaze blue* and gold, unmarked, c.1795, 9½in. (24cm). (Private Collection.)*

noted that the shape of the feather moulded coffee pot was derived from a Paul de Lamerie silver coffee pot from the 1730s. It is curious that feather moulded coffee pots are far more frequently encountered than feather moulded teapots, which suggests that the coffee pots were sold on their own rather than as part of a tea service. Coloured examples were only made for a few years but the shape continued in blue and white until c.1780.

Finely reeded coffee pots are less common but also date from the late 1750s. Plain shapes are unusual at this early period although a few are known with European flower painting such as the yellow ground example illustrated in Colour Plate 99, from c.1758. The early handle shape with a long thumb-rest was replaced by a plainer handle with only a slight thumb-rest by c.1765. This became the standard form for the next twenty years and there is very little variation although some covers can be reasonably flat while others are domed. Flower finials were usual after c.1770. Late 18th century coffee pots are very rare in English porcelain. Flight and Chamberlain and Grainger all made examples with spiral fluted or shanked* moulding, and others with reeded or plain bodies, usually with small pouring lips rather than long spouts. No Worcester coffee pots are known after c.1810, even though coffee cups remained part of every tea service. *See* Colour Plates 5 and 24.

Cole, Solomon

A figure painter employed at Flights' factory, Cole is best remembered for his extensive account of life at the factory around 1815-20. This had been told to William Chaffers in the 1870s when Cole was himself in his seventies, and first appeared in Chaffers's *Marks and Monograms*. Solomon Cole was a pupil at Thomas Baxter's* painting school in Edgar Street, Worcester, 1814-16, and according to Cole, he and Thomas Lowe* succeeded Baxter as figure painters at the factory. Cole maintained a high regard for Thomas Baxter and probably adopted many of Baxter's mannerisms. To date no example of Solomon Cole's painting has been recognised.

Coloured Grounds

A visit to the Lady Ludlow collection at Luton Hoo and, to a lesser extent, the Dyson Perrins Museum, leaves any porcelain collector dazzled by the effect of Worcester's coloured grounds when gathered together. Each is discussed in this *Dictionary* separately but it is worth noting here that most are fairly original Worcester inventions rather than direct copies of Meissen, Sèvres and Chelsea. A good yellow* ground was certainly in use by c.1757 and a ruby* ground by c.1765. By 1769 a full range of colours had been introduced for a sale catalogue in May 1769 included mazarine blue and gold; sky blue; pea green; french green*; sea green*; purple; and scarlet* and gold. Some of these are obvious although others are difficult to identify with surviving ground colours. Sky blue was the turquoise* ground while pea green was probably the colour we call apple green* today. Purple could have been ruby or else a scale pink ground. Scarlet* and gold may have been claret but is more likely to have been the deep flame orange colour. Twenty years later this was still used on Caughley porcelain and Chamberlain were selling a pattern called *Scarlet Japan**.

Claret ground* was probably not introduced at Worcester until c.1775, and an overglaze blue enamel ground, when genuine, also occurs on late pieces from c.1780. Certain ground colours were further decorated with finely painted scales, herringbone or cailloute (pebble patterns), while a bright green ground was painted in black to imitate shagreen*. *See also* **Scale Grounds** and **Redecoration.** Unfortunately a great many of the finest coloured ground pieces from the 18th century exhibit signs of redecoration.

By the 1790s a wonderfully rich deep yellow ground had been perfected and was used to great advantage at Flights and Chamberlains. Another popular colour from c.1800 was a rich deep orange or tomato colour which has become known as Barr's Orange*. A very similar colour was used at Chamberlains as well as Graingers. In the 19th century a great many new and perfectly controlled ground colours were introduced, the most successful having been used by Flight, Barr and Barr.

'Compagnie des Indes' Style
A somewhat confusing term used to refer to Worcester's copies of coloured Chinese export porcelain. Several *famille rose** floral patterns were used at Worcester from c.1768 although these were not a major part of the company's production, as Worcester chose not to try to compete with the cheaper end of the Chinese export trade. By the 1780s Worcester was happy to leave these simple patterns to New Hall and other factories in Staffordshire, although Chamberlain made several copies of cheaper Chinese patterns. The East India Company in London, as well as the better known Dutch East India Company (VOC), were responsible for most of the importation of Chinese porcelain and the French term *Compagnie des Indes* is still occasionally used in England and the United States in reference to Chinese porcelain.

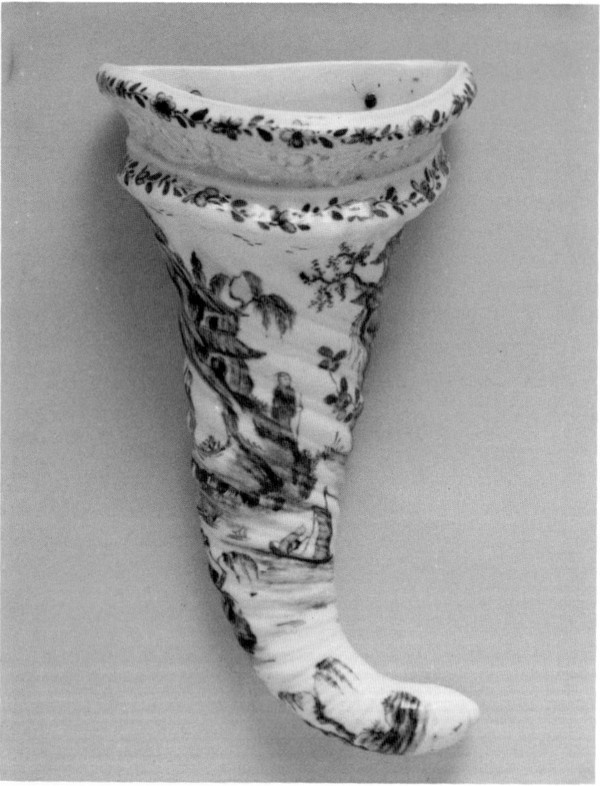

Cornucopias. *The strongly ribbed spiral shape was unsuited to underglaze blue* decoration and consequently painting of this quality is of great rarity. Workman's mark, c.1755, 10in. (25.5cm). (L.O. Branyan Collection.)*

Cornucopias
Two sizes of cornucopias are listed as selling in the London Warehouse c.1755-6 (*see* **London Shops**). These would be of a standard horn shape with spiral moulding and a border of flower heads and leaves below the rim. A rarer version has stronger moulded spiral flutes and a scroll design at the rim. These were made as left- and right-hand examples to sell as matching pairs and, while usually painted in blue, coloured flower painting is occasionally seen. Two other moulded shapes were made, one of which is more correctly described as a wall pocket as it is not horn shape. This has moulded rococo cartouches with a modelled bust of Flora holding a cornucopia. Blue and coloured flower painting is recorded in the moulded panels but examples are extremely rare. The final shape is a

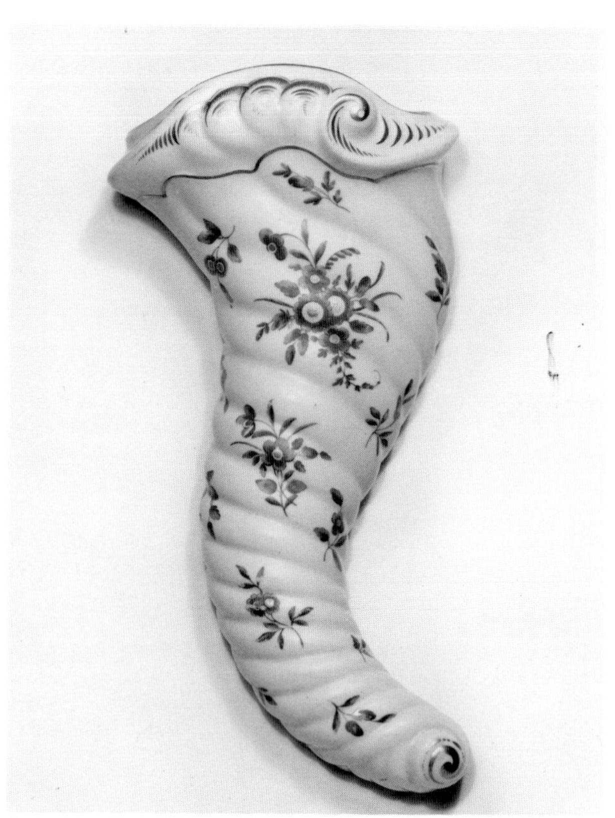

Cornucopias. *A rare form of cornucopia usually found in underglaze blue*, but this example enamelled in green and gold, c.1765-70, 11in. (28cm). (Bonhams.)*

crisply moulded horn with an embossed landscape including a church, a man seated below a tree and various cattle among trees. Flowerheads and scrollwork further ornament this remarkable shape which is usually left white with just a blue-painted border. Fully coloured examples are also known. Cornucopias were popular shapes in Staffordshire earthenware in the 1750s and 1760s but soon went out of popularity. No Worcester examples can be dated after c.1760-5 although large cornucopias are recorded as made by Chamberlain in the 1840s. These were probably free-standing vases rather than vases for hanging.

Corporation of Worcester Jugs
A highly important pair of presentation jugs dated 1757 belongs to the Corporation of the City of Worcester. The jugs are of standard cabbage leaf shape without mask spouts and are painted in colours with the full arms of the city within rococo cartouches flanked by allegorical figures of Commerce and Justice. It is not known why they were made or presented to the city. As the painting appears to be by the same hand as the mug inscribed 'I. Rogers Pinxit 1757', now in the British Museum, the Corporation of Worcester jugs are equally important in attributing the work of I. (or J.) Rogers*.

Cos Lettuce Sauceboats
See **Leaf Sauceboats**

Cottages
Pastille burners* were essential in the town houses and big cities to add perfume to the air and mask the pungent odours of poor sanitation. What is more natural than to model the pastille burner as a rustic cottage (Colour Plate 25) to remind

the city dweller of the countryside? The Staffordshire porcelain industry supplied *cottage orné* pastille burners in enormous variety and Chamberlain joined in the fashion from as early as 1813. Geoffrey Godden's *Chamberlain-Worcester Porcelain* illustrates four different marked Chamberlain models, the largest in white biscuit probably corresponding to the 'Swiss Cottage' sold for £1.11s.6d. in 1829. Strictly speaking, to be a pastille burner the models have to be pierced underneath to allow an up-draught, with the roof lifting off or a separate tray at one side in which to place the pastille cone. The scent would drift from the chimneys or, in one instance, through the pierced gothic windows. Flight, Barr and Barr ventured into the unusual area of ornamental modelling to produce a single large cottage model which combined as a pastille burner and nightlight*, the thin walls and windows allowing a delightful glow to penetrate. Very few of these have survived although a good example is in the Dyson Perrins Museum in Worcester.

Cotterell, Joseph
Solomon Cole* tells us that Joseph Cotterell was employed by Flights to write the factory name and address as well as the subjects of the figures and names of the views on the back of the richest pieces. Some of the long quotations from literature would have been written carefully by Cotterell with a pen and enamel colour. One piece of early Flight porcelain in the Godden Reference Collection has 'J. Cottrill, Decr. 22d 1795' on the base. The spelling differs but if this is the same person then it can be assumed that he painted some of the simple puce and brown sprig patterns while still an apprentice. He was admitted Freeman in 1804.

Cow Models. *A circular tureen printed with underglaze blue* floral sprays, the modelled cow also picked out in blue, crescent mark*, c.1768-70, 8in. (20.5cm) diameter. (Dyson Perrins Museum.)*

Cow Models
The quest for examples of early Worcester figures was encouraged by Charles Dyson Perrins' discovery of a circular cream bowl or tureen bearing standard underglaze blue prints and a modelled cow as the finial. Surely a factory capable of modelling such a knop could also make other animal or figure models? This only known example is still in the Dyson Perrins Museum and dates from c.1768. I have long dreamt of discovering a similar Worcester cow used not as a finial but as a model on its own. This is not a purely fanciful idea as a

Cracked Ice Decoration. *A small plate copying a Chinese* Kangxi *original, the cracked ice and prunus effect particularly well controlled, c.1765, 4½in. (11.5cm). (Private Collection.)*

companion cow model, virtually identical but in reverse, is in the Schreiber Collection in the Victoria and Albert Museum, item 686. In this case, however, it is in Plymouth or Bristol hard paste porcelain. John Toulouse*, who is believed to have been responsible for most of the Worcester figures, went to Bristol c.1771 and introduced many very familiar themes which had originated at Worcester. The flower modelling on the base of the Bristol cow immediately brings to mind the work of John Toulouse and there is no reason to suppose a pair of similar cow models could not have been made at Worcester.

Cracked Ice Decoration
A popular form of decoration in Chinese porcelain developed during the 17th century. The underglaze blue* ground is softened by painting a light wash of cobalt followed by darker veining on top, much in the same manner as blue scale (*see* **Scale Blue**). Worcester used the technique with scattered prunus blossoms as a ground colour for a blue-painted pattern with panels of standing Chinese figures, dating from about 1768-70. This pattern, called 'Cracked Ice Ground', is number I.A.14 in Branyan, French and Sandon. A further pattern, so far known by only a single plate of about 1765, is painted all over solely with cracked ice and prunus, directly copying a Chinese *Kangxi* original.

Creamboats
The factory distinguished between milk jugs and cream ewers in the price list of the London Warehouse (*see* **London Shops**) c.1755-6. Milk jugs were 'round and press'd' while cream ewers were 'ribb'd and pannel'd'. The two principal shapes of creamboats or ewers were either hexagonal ('panel'd') or oval with vertical fluting ('ribb'd'). The hexagonal creamboats have been recorded moulded with a great variety of rococo cartouche panels. Some have a geranium leaf moulded under the lip while others are plain. The handles vary although the most usual is of squared section with a rounded thumb-rest (Colour Plate 26). The shapes originated at Bristol from where marked examples of both basic varieties are known in blue and

Creamboats. *A particularly thinly potted creamboat moulded with overlapping flutes, with a handle more usually found on coffee cans, painted in pale underglaze blue*, c.1753-4, 5⅜in. (13.5cm) long. (Sotheby's.)*

Creamboats. *The* Two Porter Landscape *pattern used on an unusual helmet-shaped creamboat with delicate moulding, workman's mark of an arrow and annulet*, c.1758, 4½in. (11.5cm). (Phillips.)*

white. Worcester continued these types and added a new variety of hexagonal creamboat moulded in relief with Chinese landscapes. One only is marked Wigornia* while several other variations are recorded. One other variety of early creamboat became more oval rather than hexagonal and had a finely moulded basket-weave ground. Most of these creamboat types are limited to the 1750s although a few seem to have continued until c.1765. They were replaced by a standard shape known as a Chelsea ewer* introduced c.1765 in two sizes, and a small rococo shell-moulded shape called a dolphin ewer* was introduced by c.1770. A further plain quatrelobed shape known as a gadroon boat* occurs after c.1775 and is rare in Worcester. All three of these standard later creamboat shapes were also made at other factories, especially at Caughley. Worcester Chelsea ewers continued until c.1790 and were also made by Chamberlain in their early porcelain.

Crescent Marks

Henry Sandon, in his *Worcester Porcelain 1751-1793* (1969), gave a reasonable explanation for the use of the crescent by the Worcester Porcelain Company as a factory mark. The factory occupied the old mansion of the Warmstry* family whose coat of arms included a cross moline between four crescents. These arms were recorded as having been carved in parts of the building. The first use of a crescent by the factory seems to have been as a workman's mark on certain large painted blue and white hexagonal vases and some cabbage leaf jugs, the crescent appearing very large on the bases. The earliest use of a crescent as a form of factory mark is on underglaze blue transfer printed patterns c.1757 or 1758, the mark at this time being round and fat with cross hatching. Painted crescent marks on blue and white pieces can date from c.1760-2 and are usually present after c.1765. Overglaze-decorated pieces which use underglaze blue in the pattern can bear crescent marks from c.1770 until well into the Flight period, c.1792. Transfer printed crescents are very uniform and occasionally contain a letter or a number within the points of the mark, the significance of which is unknown. One rare print used on *Fence* pattern* saucers takes the form of a *Man in the Moon**. A crescent mark in gold occurs on patterns including the Duke of Gloucester service* and the *Quail* pattern*, although why these few should be singled out in this way is a puzzle. Similarly some rare teawares with a powder blue ground and Kakiemon panels are marked with a crescent and a square mark together, the crescent in red enamel.

By the Flight period in the 1780s, the crescent mark, which had been clumsily painted for some time, became smaller and smaller. It was eventually incorporated into a mark with a crown and the word Flight, used on special productions c.1790. The crescent was generally replaced as a mark by the incised 'B'* mark c.1792, although it was possibly used very occasionally after this date.

Crescent Moon Pattern

This is one of the first definitive patterns used in underglaze blue at Worcester and there is naturally considerable variation between different examples. Introduced as early as 1752 or 1753, the pattern occurs on large mugs, jugs, bottles and punch pots as well as on a much smaller scale in the panels of sauceboats. The primary subject is a folded fence linking islands and the pattern can have the addition of a bird flying above or a fisherman in a boat. The crescent-shaped moon is always present but this has no connection with the factory mark of a crescent used later on. Occasionally the pattern was used on the reverse of large items painted with important figure subjects. It is listed by Branyan, French and Sandon as pattern I.B.4.

Cress Dishes

See **Strawberry Dishes**

Crossed Swords Marks

Worcester's version of the crossed swords mark was a copy of that used on Meissen teawares in the 1740s. These particular pieces were painted in underglaze blue with simple European flowers and insects and marked with long crossed swords and a number 9 and dot or a line within the points of the swords. Worcester were asked to make a copy of such cups c.1758 and an example in the Godden Reference Collection bearing this mark is illustrated in Branyan, French and Sandon as pattern I.E.29A. Subsequently, when Worcester produced white teawares intended for decoration in Meissen or European style overglaze, they remembered this particular form of the Meissen mark, complete with a 9 and a dot. This was used from the late 1760s until c.1775, generally on factory decorated pieces although some items bearing this mark can be linked to the Giles* workshop. The mark is always in underglaze blue.

Crossed swords marks are also recorded on some early blue

Custard Cups. *A rare example with a plain loop handle and thick apple green* border hung with coloured flowers, c.1770, 3⅜in. (8.5cm). (Phillips.)*

and white Worcester hexagonal vases with *Fancy Bird** decoration, used in this case probably as a form of workman's mark*. In the 19th century Minton, Derby and Coalport regularly used the crossed swords as a mark and some pieces with this mark, particularly plates with rose painting, have been called Chamberlain, an attribution I now strongly doubt.

Crowfoot Borders
Evidence from the Chamberlain factory records shows that the term 'crowfoot' was used for a simple border pattern of loops in red enamel. The tiny loops usually have a dot at each point but not exclusively so. These red loops or loop and dot borders occur with several Canton style* figure patterns and other designs, c.1765-80, including the *Chinese Family** pattern. They also occur with formal flowers. Sometimes the red crowfoot border is filled in with a gold line. Similar borders were also used at several other factories.

Cup Plates
Small plates, only about 3½in. (9cm), they accompanied tea services and were used in some quarters for standing the teacup on while the tea was drunk from the saucer. Mostly made in England for the American market where this custom was much practised, cup plates were made by Grainger in 'Gloster'* shape c.1840. Certain miniature Chamberlain plates could have served a similar purpose.

Custard Cups
These small, plain ogee-shaped cups with single handles and covers with flower finials date mostly from the 1770s although examples are rare. They follow French porcelain forms popular at Sèvres although it is interesting to note that in France the cups were called *Pot a Juice* and were used to serve an accompaniment to a savoury course rather than a dessert. Examples of Worcester directly copying Sèvres patterns were possibly made as replacements. It is surprising so few Worcester custard cups survive as Caughley and Derby examples from the 1770s and 1780s are fairly common, usually French in inspiration. In the 1820s Chamberlain made custard cups, in sets of, strangely, seven which were sold on a custard stand. Earlier custard cups were sold in 1803 with individual stands as well as covers, although none has survived. A similar shape was probably referred to in the Chamberlain stock list in 1795 as an 'ice cup and cover' as French ice cups* do not usually have covers.

Cutlery Handles
Porcelain handles for knives and forks originated in France in the early 18th century. They were adopted at Meissen by c.1730 and subsequently porcelain handles were made at most European porcelain manufactories. Worcester made only three basic shapes, plain so-called pistol-grip handles and two rare variations embossed with the *Chrysanthemum** pattern and an intricate scroll pattern copied from St Cloud. The earliest Worcester handles in blue and white also copy St Cloud originals but, in keeping with most English handles, the rounded ends of Worcester pistol-grip handles are solid while the French examples are pierced for a silver fixing stud to be attached. Two formal scrollwork patterns were copied at Worcester and these are shown by Branyan, French and Sandon as patterns I.E.43 and I.E.44. These date from c.1757 into the early 1760s. Coloured cutlery handles tended to wear badly during use and are consequently very rare. Quite a number of patterns are recorded, however, including *Dry Blue** flowers and the *Gold Queen's** pattern. The finest surviving Worcester cutlery dates from c.1758 with armorial decoration. Two examples from the set with the arms of Stoughton, c.1758, are illustrated in Colour Plate 27 together with later handles from the celebrated Archbishop Cobbe service* with blue grounds and insect panels. Replacements for this pattern were made in the Flight period and occasional reference is made to knife handles in the Chamberlain account books, although the only examples known to have survived are a few experimental handles from the 1840s made to simulate bone. Later in the 1890s and in the 20th century various Royal Worcester cutlery sets were made.

Daisy Plates

Numerous small Staffordshire factories made daisy plates — small plates with borders of embossed daisy-heads — mostly for children, in the 1820-40 period. Worcester did not make nursery plates in this way but Grainger used similar daisy-head moulding on small dessert plates dating from c.1815. Unglazed wasters from the Grainger factory site show how crisp the modelling of the daisy border was, but finished examples are so thickly covered with glaze that the delicate effect is mostly lost.

Dalhousie, Earl of, Pattern

The origin of this name is unclear, but according to H. Rissik Marshall a dessert service decorated with a version of this pattern was at one time owned by the tenth Earl and Marquis of Dalhousie. The name has become associated with a form of decoration popular at Worcester from c.1775-85. A deep underglaze blue border is gilded with foliage and scrollwork and the central panels of colourful landscapes are framed with fine turquoise and black husk chains. The white ground is painted with festoons or clusters of ripe fruit and scattered insects. Opinions differ as to whether the *Dalhousie* pattern should have flowers or fruit on the white ground, but it is a popular pattern and a great many minor variations exist, both on plain mugs and jugs, dessert services and fluted tea services. When birds are included amongst the fruit on dessert services the pattern is known as *Lord Henry Thynne**. Most examples of *Dalhousie* type are attributed to the early 1770s although the bright colour of the underglaze cobalt borders and blued glaze suggests that most pieces are at least ten years later.

Daisy Plates. *A Grainger dessert plate shown with matching wasters* found on the factory site, marked in orange script Grainger Lee & Co. Worcester, 9in. (23cm). (Private Collection.)*

Dated Pieces

Dated porcelain was made only as a special production as no china shop could sell anything with the previous year's date appearing on it. Lowestoft catered mostly for the local trade and specialised in dated pieces, whereas Worcester, who sold their porcelain through London shops, made reasonably few dated pieces compared with their much larger output. Dr Nigel Cook has researched known examples of dated Worcester and his list was published in 1984 in Simon Spero's *Worcester Porcelain. The Klepser Collection*. Dr Cook listed forty-two dated pieces up until 1780 and a few more can be added since this publication. These rarities are of vital importance in dating other standard products of the factory which have related decoration.

Davis-Flight Period

When Henry Sandon wrote his *Worcester Porcelain 1751-1793* in 1969 he needed to find a way of distinguishing the period between the end of the so-called Dr Wall* Period and the arrival in Worcester of Martin Barr* in 1792. William Davis* had been the senior figure in the affairs of the company until its sale to Thomas Flight in 1783. It remained unclear whether the Davis-Flight Period began in 1772 when the factory was sold to a new partnership, or 1774 when Dr Wall retired, or else 1776 when Dr Wall died. William Davis sold out completely to Thomas Flight in April 1783 and it is therefore more correct to refer to the period from 1772/4 until 1783 as the Davis Period* and from April 1783 until 1792 as the Flight Period (*see* **Flight Factory**).

Davis, George

Also known as 'Doctor Davis', George Davis was an important painter who probably began working at Dr Wall's factory, specialising in *Fancy Birds**. A few pieces of early Flight period, around 1780-5, have been noted with the name 'Davis' hidden amongst the vegetation in the foreground of colourful bird paintings. The presence of a signature suggests that these could have been decorated by Davis as independent

Dalhousie, Earl of, Pattern. *A pair of dessert tureens closely matching a service at one time owned by the 10th Earl of Dalhousie. This popular pattern occurs with very many variations. Crescent marks*, c.1775-80, 7in. (18cm). (Phillips.)*

Dalhousie, Earl of, Pattern. *A coffee cup, teacup and saucer decorated with one of the many versions of this pattern, associated with the name of Dalhousie, crescent marks*, c.1780. (Phillips, Edinburgh.)*

Dated Pieces. *A particularly elaborate mug painted in underglaze blue* for Samuel Sheriff*, with the arms of the Foresters Company and various mottoes of the society, dated 1771, 4¾in. (12cm). Worcester dated pieces are rarely as complicated as this. (Present whereabouts unknown.)*

Davis, George. *An early Chamberlain beaker painted with the unusual addition of a dog beside 'Doctor' Davis' typical* Fancy Birds*, *about 3½in. (9cm). (Sotheby's/Kiddell Papers.)*

work, especially as they tend to exhibit bad signs of misfiring. George Davis seems to have joined Chamberlain's factory early on for his name is frequently mentioned in the Chamberlain archives during the 1790s as a senior person with responsibilities for other men. He is the only artist at this time mentioned by name with many references to 'Davis's Birds' as a form of decoration. Some Caughley porcelain decorated at Chamberlains and many examples of early Chamberlain manufacture are painted with his distinctive colourful birds in landscapes painted in a rather sombre palette which differs noticeably from earlier Flight painting. A teabowl and saucer in the Dyson Perrins Museum is dated 1794 and shows the possible influence of Fidelle Duvivier* who painted at Chamberlains for a short time in 1792. Davis' work was expensive but he seems to have been prolific. His name occurs in the Chamberlain records until 1824 but with several gaps in his employment, periods when he worked for the rival Flight factory or on his own as a decorator in Worcester. Solomon Cole* refers to him as a painter of brilliant coloured birds at Flight's factory around 1815 but at this time he is also believed to have painted the Chamberlain breakfast set for Princess Charlotte (*see* Colour Plates 18 and 19). A mug signed by George Davis as a free-lance piece dated 1818 is illustrated in Geoffrey Godden's *Chamberlain-Worcester Porcelain*, pl.237. Care has to be taken in attributing all *Fancy Birds* to 'Doctor' Davis as Charles Stinton* painted in a similar style for Flight's and there were probably several other junior artists responsible for this most popular decoration.

Davis Period

Whereas William Davis* and John Wall* had headed the partnership trading as the Worcester Porcelain Company, this was sold in January 1772 to a smaller partnership still including Davis and Wall. John Wall retired in 1774, however, leaving William Davis in full charge of the factory assisted by his son and with financial backers. They traded as William Davis and Co.* The Davis Period is therefore from 1774 when John Wall retired until April 1783 when the entire company was sold to Flight*. William Davis was by this time reasonably elderly and the factory was far too set in its ways. The Davis Period saw a decline both in the quality of the factory's products and in the prosperity of the company. It had cost £5,250 in January 1772 but sold for only £3,000 in 1783. (*See* Colour Plate 28).

Davis, William

Born in 1710, William Davis was an apothecary in the city of Worcester. From the Articles for carrying on the Worcester Tonquin Manufacture*, drawn up in June 1751, it is clear that William Davis was to play a very leading role in the porcelain venture. Indeed he and John Wall* are claimed as the inventors, having made 'the discovery of the secret of making the said porcelain'. In return Davis and Wall were rewarded with their shares of £225 each being paid for them by the other subscribers, with further payments once the manufacture had produced a profit. Great pains were taken to protect the secret which they had discovered and Davis and Wall further agreed to continue to:

> discover for the benefitt of themselves and the other subscribers the real true and full art mistery and secret by them hitherto

Davis Period. *During the late 1770s and prior to the arrival of John Flight*, the artistic merits of the factory were frequently questionable. This jug of c.1780-2 is merely adapted from a mug by the addition of a totally inadequate lip, resulting in a shape which is understandably rare. 6in. (15cm). (Geoffrey Godden.)*

> invented and found out with such further improvements and secrets as shall from time to time hereafter be made and found out by them or either of them shall not directly or indirectly discover the art or secret which they now have or hereafter may acquire for the making or improving of the said ware unto any other person or persons whatsoever under the penalty of four thousand pounds each...

William Davis was an apothecary and John Wall a doctor of medicine. Davis owned premises at 33 Broad Street, Worcester, partly used as a laboratory. According to Chambers' *Biographical Illustrations of Worcestershire*, Wall and Davis built a temporary 'kiln' there for their experiments using an iron pot round which the fire was heaped and kept up as near as possible to a furnace heat. They may well have been the inventors as they claimed but it has generally been felt that they were intending all along to make use of the secrets previously discovered at Bristol. Speculation about this early period is discussed in the opening historical review in this *Dictionary*. William Davis had collaborated with Dr Wall on investigating Malvern water as early as 1743 and one of Wall's published cases involving his water treatment was that of a 'Mrs Davis, wife to a very skilful apothecary and chemist in Worcester'.

All the evidence suggests that Davis was equally as important in the venture as Dr Wall and, in view of Wall's retirement in 1774, was overall by far the more important figure. The Giles* ledgers record payments by Giles for porcelain from Mr William Davis and Co. prior to 1774. Davis had acted as manager since the founding of the company and the porcelain tokens* printed at the factory bore his name alone. No surviving records mention John Wall except when he bought the company in 1772 along with William Davis sen., his son also William Davis, Robert Hancock*, Thomas Vernon* and Richard Cook. Hancock left in October 1774 and Dr Wall retired to Bath in the same year. By 1783 the remaining partners were Vernon and the two Davises, still trading as William Davis and Co. Facing difficult times they sold out in April 1783 to their London agent Thomas Flight (*see* **Flight Factory**) for £3,000. William Davis was seventy-three by this time and was probably glad to retire. He died eight years later in 1791.

Davis, William and Company
Although Thomas Vernon* probably owned the majority share in the company following its purchase in 1772, William Davis* had been the manager and was the most influential figure. His name was used for the firm, trading as William Davis and Co., at least by 1772 and possibly earlier. This form continued until the company was bought by Thomas Flight (*see* **Flight Factory**) in 1783.

Déjeuner Sets
A French name for a tea service for two contained on a single tray. With only one cup they should more correctly be called *solitaire* sets and the names *Cabaret* or *Tête-à-Tête* are also used frequently to refer to any tea service on its own matching tray. The earliest Worcester example has depressions in the tray for the somewhat unusual barrel-shaped wares with acorn finials. The only known set of this type is in the Marshall Collection in the Ashmolean Museum, painted with dry blue* flowers reserved on a yellow ground. It dates from about 1778 (*see* page 62). A déjeuner set of c.1785 has been recorded painted with scale blue and *Fancy Birds** and may well date from shortly before the departure of the Chamberlain family. Another set of similar date in *Dragon in Compartments** pattern is illustrated by Henry Sandon in *Flight and Barr Worcester Porcelain* (pl. 24). The shapes are very French, possibly copied from Tournai, and follow the same plan as most cabaret sets in that they do not occur in larger sizes for inclusion with normal tea services. The fine Flight, Barr and Barr cabaret illustrated on page 62 is painted by Thomas Baxter* as a harlequin set with different subjects in each panel. It dates from c.1816 and, while the cup shapes are standard, the main pieces are once again designed expressly for the *déjeuner* set.

All Worcester *déjeuner* sets are rare, particularly Chamberlain, although examples are listed in the order books with a note that the teapots are small. No Grainger sets are known. In the late 1840s a very distinctive *déjeuner* set was made by Chamberlain and Co. using reticulated* shapes with honeycomb piercing directly copied from Sèvres. During the Kerr and Binns period and into the 1860s *déjeuner* sets came back into fashion again and examples are not so hard to find. Curiously, both Chamberlain c.1817 and Flight c.1790 made miniature *déjeuner* sets as toys.

Dentil Gilding
A fine pattern of tiny gold 'tooth'-like dots used as an edging to the rims of a wide variety of designs. The Worcester factory probably copied Sèvres to a certain extent although the use of such a simple motif was widespread in the 18th century. Introduced to Worcester c.1768, fine dentil rims were extensively used until c.1775, primarily on wet blue* grounds and deep underglaze borders. They are most effective on a white ground, however. Patterns such as the Stormont service* and a design of *Fancy Birds** on dessert shapes c.1775 display the skill of the factory's gilders who managed to make every little tooth the same size. In the later 1770s and 1780s dentil rims continued on blue borders and were used with patterns just in gold such as the *Gold Queen's** pattern. Other designs combining underglaze blue with gilding used dentil rims up until c.1788-90 with the advent of mercury gilding*. The Giles* workshop used much larger pointed dentils in bright gold as a very distinctive rim design, and only very

Déjeuner Sets. *A most remarkable set, with unusual shapes of teawares designed to fit on a matching tray, decorated probably in the Giles* workshop in dry blue* enamel on a yellow ground*, c.1775, the tray 12in. (30.5cm). (Sotheby's/Kiddell Papers.)*

Dentil Gilding. *The factory's fine dentil gilding on a tea canister and dessert basket, c.1770-2, contrasts with the larger dentil rim on a Giles* decorated teabowl and saucer of similar date. (Sotheby's, New York.)*

Desk Sets. *A Grainger, Lee and Co. inkstand with matching candlesticks, printed and coloured with a pattern called* Chamberlain *in the Grainger pattern books, c.1815, 10in. (25.5cm) wide. (Sylvia Watkins Collection.)*

Dessert Services. *A pair of Barr, Flight and Barr tureens from the Gordon service*, script marks, c.1810, 6in. (15cm). The pair of small tureens in dessert services are often incorrectly called sauce tureens but originally these would have served sugar and cream. (Phillips, Edinburgh.)*

Dessert Services. *Representative shapes from a Grainger and Co. dessert service in the style of the rococo revival*, the shape known as New Dresden, pattern number* 203x, c.1830-5. (Phillips.)*

occasionally used fine dentils as in the Lord Dudley service*. This is still more pointed or brighter in appearance than the factory's fine rounded dentils. Therefore, when a rim of fine rounded dentils occurs with Giles type decoration, as in the case of many striped patterns, there is a likely chance that redecoration* has taken place.

Desk Sets

These are discussed here under their component parts, inkstands*, inkwells* and pounce pots*. Some desk sets also included a pen tray*, candlesticks* and a pair of spill vases.*

Dessert Centrepieces

While full dessert services* included numerous dishes and plates, it was usual for only one centrepiece to be included. These were normally oval and often very unexciting shapes, similar in many ways to shapes popular in creamware. The largest and most elaborate date from about 1775 and usually have slight basket-weave borders and spreading feet. Barr, Flight and Barr and Flight, Barr and Barr dessert services often included a star-like shape, sometimes with a gadroon rim. Chamberlain favoured a rectangular form raised on four richly gilt dolphins and these were included with the most expensive Regency services. Grainger and later period Chamberlain centrepieces from the 1825-50 period can be particularly impressive shapes matching the spirit of the rest of the service.

Dessert Services

Since the 17th century dessert had become the most important course at dinner in England and gave the host an opportunity to impress. The tradition of ornamental figures made of sugar gave way to porcelain as Meissen, Chelsea, and other factories' figures were placed on the dessert table as decoration. Worcester made few figures but otherwise led the field in England for the manufacture of rich dessert services following the decline of Chelsea.

Early dessert sets consisted mostly of plates with various leaf-shaped dishes and sauceboats rather than tureens. By the mid-1760s, the standard forms of dessert wares were introduced and these continued with little variation until the 1840s. Although components could vary, a typical dessert service would have had plates in multiples of six and dishes in multiples of two. The four standard dish shapes were square, oval, heart, and shell (Colour Plate 29). A set would contain two or four of each of these shapes, sometimes with a larger size of oval dish. The centrepiece was a single, usually oval dish on a high foot. The oval and heart-shaped dishes were lobed and are often referred to as kidney shaped, although this does not seem to be a contemporary name. A service would usually include a pair of oval tureens with covers and stands and optional ladles. These are commonly called sauce tureens today, but it is clear from original records that they were intended to hold sugar and cream. Ice pails* (*see* Colour Plate 54) or ice coolers were included with larger or more expensive

(Opposite) Colour Plate 29. ***Dessert Services.*** *Left: a* Hop Trellis* *pattern shell-shaped dessert dish with bright underglaze blue* and turquoise* caillouté *borders, c.1775, 7⅝in. (19.5cm). Right: a shell-shaped dessert dish decorated with the arms of Bostock* with Rich in pretence, c.1785-90, 7⅝in. (19.5cm). (Phillips.)*

Colour Plate 28. ***Davis Period.*** *Although the pattern originated c.1765-70, the bright colours, especially of the pure cobalt blue, confirm a date of c.1780-5. This service represents a transition with new shapes of cups, milk jug and canister combined with more traditional teaware shapes; crescent marks*. (Phillips.)*

Dinner Services. *Part of a very extensive Grainger, Lee and Co. dinner service decorated with the popular* Blue Ball Japan* *pattern, the tureens combining round and oblong shapes, unmarked except for pattern number* 1472, c.1825. (Sotheby's.)*

services and these kept fruit chilled. They were never intended as wine coolers* although without their covers and liners they could be used as such. The Continental shape of *sceaux* as wine coolers were not usually included in English dessert services.

Because they were upmarket items, the Worcester dessert services tended to be richly decorated with relatively few produced in blue and white. At their most flamboyant in the Regency period, the very richest gilding and coloured marbled grounds* were used to frame armorial or finely painted centres. Such sets were too costly to use and were replaced by a plainer set once the dessert was actually served, the purpose of the richness being merely to impress. Some of the most magnificent sets such as those made for the Marquis of Donegal* or the Earl of Plymouth* were 'harlequin' services, where each piece was different, although united by the same border or style.

The importance of dessert services to the London customers meant that Flight's factory in the 19th century made little else, while Grainger, supplying a cheaper market, produced relatively few dessert wares.

Dinner Services

Worcester generally had great difficulty making dinner wares as flat plates and large tureens and platters presented a problem to their soaprock* body which tended to distort. They were unable to compete with Chinese dinner services and it was not until c.1770 that larger dinner services were attempted in blue-printed floral patterns and occasionally in colours or with rich blue grounds. Tureens and other shapes associated with dinner sets were made as individual items earlier on, *see* **Tureens** and **Plates.** By the Flight and Barr and the Grainger, Lee and Co. periods, and from the outset at Chamberlain's factory, the three Worcester makers were able to make any dinner service shapes required. It was usually left to the customer to specify the shapes but there were standard components which were made for all services. Tureens were normally supplied in multiples of two, such as two soup tureens, four vegetable tureens and two or four sauce tureens. Platters came in up to eight sizes and usually a pair of each size was supplied with four of each of the smaller platters. There would normally be only one large platter with a moulded gravy well or 'tree' and these are known as 'tree dishes'. Also one fish drainer* was usually sufficient and a single large bowl for salad. Optional extra shapes could include covered entrée dishes with separate bases for hot water. Plates usually came in four sizes: dinner plates of roughly 10in. (25cm), dessert plates of 8in. (20cm), side plates of 6½ or 7in. (17 or 18cm) (sometimes called cheese plates or pie plates), and soup plates which are the same size as the dinner plates but deeper. Hot water plates* were sometimes included at Chamberlains. Plates were usually in multiples of twelve and it was not uncommon for large sets to have sixty, seventy-two or even one hundred and forty-four dinner plates.

Disguised Numeral Marks
C.W. Dyson Perrins, the great collector of fine Worcester porcelain, always advocated that these marks were Caughley as, like many collectors in his day, he could not believe that inferior wares could have been made at his beloved factory. He assumed that pieces bearing the disguised numeral mark as well as Flight marks had to have been made at Caughley and decorated at Flights, a suggestion which has been repeated occasionally in recent times. Geoffrey Godden first realised that the marks had to be Worcester when excavations at Caughley failed to yield any of this class of porcelain. Subsequently Henry Sandon's excavations* at Warmstry House* in 1968 confirmed for all to see that the marks were used at Worcester during the 1780s.

The new markings occur on Chinese patterns in the heavy printed styles which became popular on blue-printed Staffordshire earthenware copying cheap Chinese imports. Worcester tried to compete with this end of the trade but its products were far inferior to the Caughley factory and worse than much of the pottery. It has been suggested that the disguised numeral marks were used to protect Worcester's reputation, hoping that their established clients would not realise that these heavy printed patterns were indeed made at Worcester. Generally the disguised numeral marks were used on Chinese style patterns while the crescent* continued on patterns in the European style. The numbers 1 to 9 have been noted and it is not known how these were used within the factory. The likely date range for the marks is c.1782-90.

Dishevelled Birds
A style of bird painting used at the Worcester factory, usually within the panels of scale blue* (Colour Plate 30) or scale yellow* grounds. Colourful, somewhat plump birds are proudly perched in twig-like trees which seem barely able to take their weight. Usually there is a slight landscape behind with a castle tower or a ruin. The *Dishevelled Birds* are not painted with such detail as *Fancy Birds**.

Divergent Tulip. *A cabbage leaf moulded dish, the painted flowers including a typical divergent tulip and a small sprig of heart's-ease found on many Giles* decorated pieces, c.1770, 13in. (33.5cm). (Phillips.)*

Divergent Tulip
A characteristic feature of Giles'* flower painting (*see* Colour Plate 48). The prominent use of a full-blown tulip can be seen in many flower sprays c.1770-5, painted with a sense of freedom which is lacking in Worcester factory flower painting. The petals are spread open and usually shaded in red and yellow. These do not represent the work of a single painter, but instead would have been the work of several artists, in the style of the Giles workshop.

Doctor Wall Period
The most widely used term for the period from 1751 until 1776 is in reality a misnomer, as John Wall was just one of the many partners and in no way senior to William Davis.* Wall and Davis had claimed to have invented the porcelain but were minority shareholders; indeed, William Davis was probably the manager at Worcester rather than Dr Wall. *See instead* **First Period.**

Doe and Rogers
A partnership of two experienced china decorators established at 17 High Street, Worcester, from the 1820s until at least 1835 when George Rogers sen. died. His son and widow continued the partnership. Geoffrey Godden has discovered a previous partnership in London between Enoch Doe*, John Wright and George Rogers* at No. 25 Clerkenwell Close, which was mutually dissolved on 26 December 1807. No china painting from this period has yet been recorded and there is uncertainty whether these were the same Enoch Doe and George Rogers who were partners later at Worcester. More likely these were the previous generation of the two families. Some authors have written that it was William Doe*, not Enoch, who was in partnership with Rogers in the 1820s and while this needs further investigation, an Enoch Doe lived at 17 High Street, the same address as used by Doe and Rogers. Porcelain decorated by Doe and Rogers at Worcester includes Coalport and Daniel shapes as well as Chamberlain. Some unmarked Grainger porcelain has been attributed to Doe and Rogers but without any firm evidence. The partnership specialised in landscape panels on coloured grounds with raised gilding, views of the city of Worcester being particularly favoured. The class of porcelain marked 'New China Works Worcester'* has been suggested by Geoffrey Godden to be the work of Doe and Rogers but there is little evidence to confirm this.

Doe, Enoch
A very talented artist probably born in Worcester around 1795. His early career is uncertain as he would have been too young to have been the same Enoch Doe who completed his apprenticeship with Chamberlains in September 1805 and whose partnership with George Rogers* and John Wright at Clerkenwell in London was dissolved in 1807. Solomon Cole* mentions a painter named Doe as a pupil at Thomas Baxter's china painting school in Edgar Street, 1814-16, and this may have been the son of the other Enoch Doe. The younger Enoch was a most observant pupil, evidenced by a signed plaque on Coalport porcelain painted after an original painting by Thomas Baxter, sold at Phillips in 1990 (Colour Plate 31). Whether this Enoch Doe worked for Flights or Chamberlains is uncertain, but an Enoch Doe made more of a name for himself as an independent painter working in Worcester. Signed landscape painting, again very close in technique to that of Baxter, is always of the highest quality. During the 1820s the partnership existed in Worcester of Messrs Doe and Rogers*. The younger Enoch Doe was in partnership with George Rogers at 17 High Street. Enoch Doe is listed on his own as a landscape painter in an 1835 Worcester directory and exhibited very fine specimen plates with armorials or Shakespearian* scenes at the 1851 Exhibition, one of which is illustrated in Godden's *Chamberlain-Worcester Porcelain* (pl. 243).

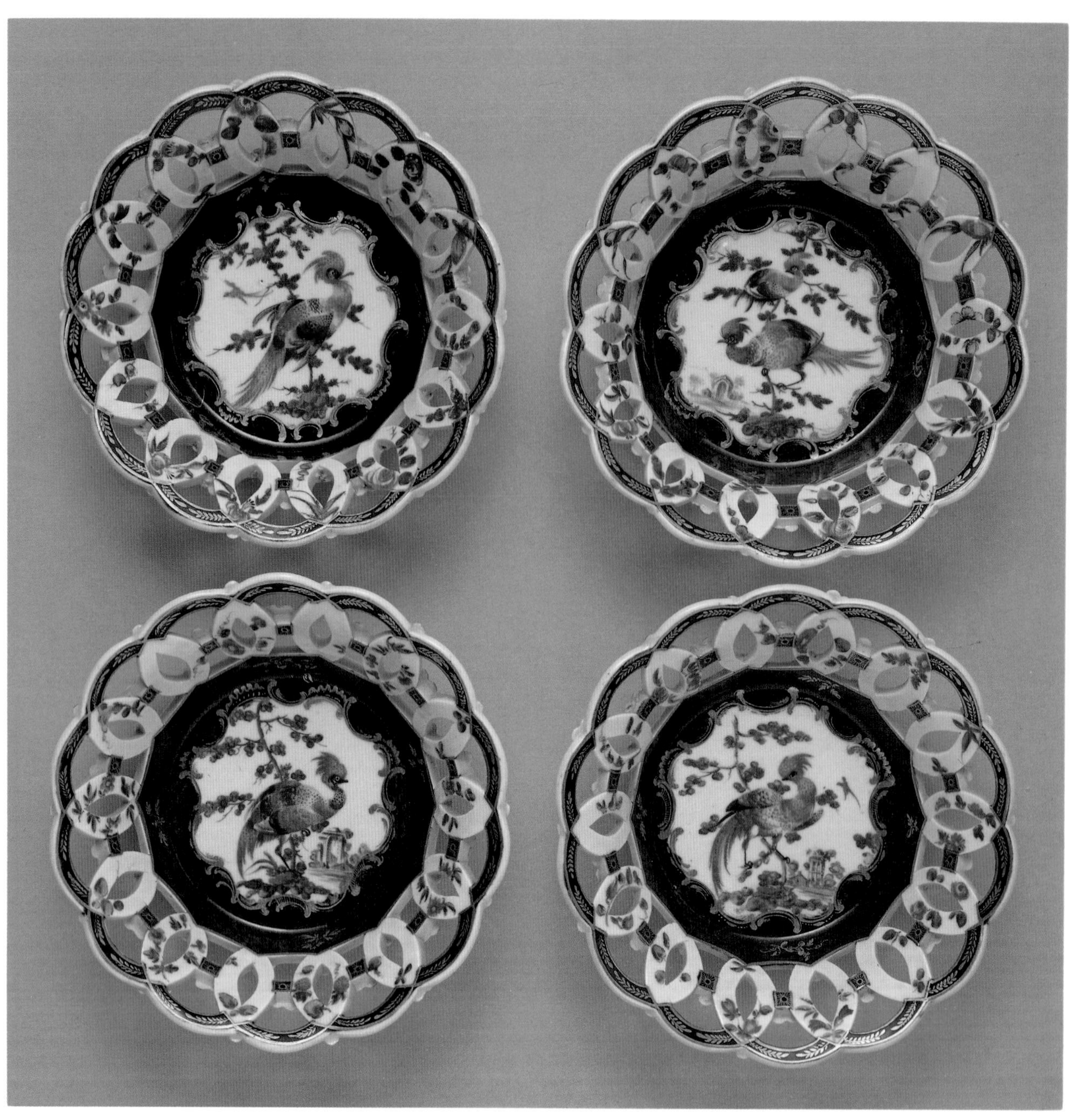

Colour Plate 30. ***Dishevelled Birds.*** *A remarkable set of four small dessert baskets with scale blue* grounds, the bird painting typical of the Worcester factory, square marks*, c.1765-70, 6in. (15.5cm). (Phillips.)*

Colour Plate 31. **Doe, Enoch.** *A plaque of Coalport porcelain decorated at Worcester by Enoch Doe, inscribed on the reverse 'Painted by E. Doe. . . Worcester, From the original painting by T Baxter. In the possession of R. Lawrence Esq.', probably c.1815-20, 13½ x 17in. (34.5 x 43cm). (Phillips.)*

Doe, William
A painter at Flight's factory, admitted as a Freeman 15 May 1815. Solomon Cole* tells us that a painter named Doe was a pupil at Thomas Baxter's china painting school in Edgar Street in 1815 but this was undoubtedly Enoch Doe*. William remained at Flights where he was listed by Cole as having painted 'natural birds, feathers, insects, &c.' From this single entry written many years later it has become accepted that all feather painting at Worcester was by William Doe. No doubt some of the magnificent feather painting on Flight, Barr and Barr is by him, but he would have been too young to have painted the best feathers on Barr, Flight and Barr pieces and there would have been others who painted this same subject. William Doe exhibited at a local Arts Exhibition in 1818 but otherwise little is known of his career. Confusion with other Does working in Worcester has led some authors to write that it was William who was in partnership with George Rogers* in the 1820s as the decorators Doe and Rogers*. We now know that this is clearly not the case, however, and it was Enoch who painted for Doe and Rogers.

Dolphin Ewers
An attractive shape of creamboat* introduced c.1770 and made in two sizes. Based on an earlier silver shape, the crisp modelling shows to best advantage when the creamboat is left white with only a fine gold dentil* rim. The name comes from the motif of two entwined dolphins with tridents embossed below the lip and the handle is in the form of a lamprey eel. Examples of both sizes were made in blue and white, with coloured flowers and with simple gilded patterns. Occasionally a Japan* pattern has been noted. Many other English porcelain factories made dolphin ewers, especially Derby and Caughley who made a virtually identical shape to Worcester.

Donaldson, John. *Leda and the Swan after Boucher, painted on a fine large vase with wet blue* ground, signed with a monogram 'JD', square mark*, c.1765-8, 12½in. (32cm). (Dyson Perrins Museum.)*

Dragon in Compartments Pattern. *An early use of the pattern on one of a pair of large vases of very unusual hexagonal shape, painted in brilliant colours and finely gilded, unmarked, c.1768, 9⅞in. (25cm). (Phillips.)*

Donaldson, John

A well-known miniaturist and figure painter, he was born in Edinburgh in 1739 and by the age of fifteen had already won prestigious awards. He moved to London in 1760 where he painted society portraits and exhibited at the Royal Academy, giving his address as Leicester Fields. He worked at the Chelsea factory from 1761 and painted some magnificent vases after Watteau* and Boucher, some bearing his monogram, but it is unsafe to attribute all such painting on Chelsea to John Donaldson. It is not known when he moved to Worcester but, probably around 1765, he painted large vases with copies of important paintings. About twenty pieces are known including a truly magnificent garniture in the Dyson Perrins Museum where also can be seen an unfinished vase which split after the first firing of colours, showing how Donaldson built up his bright colours. When finished the large panels were framed in intricate gold scrollwork in a style typical of the factory's own decoration — evidence that Donaldson worked at Worcester rather than in London (Colour Plate 32). His stay was only brief but he probably influenced other artists. Paintings of figures in formal chinoiserie* settings in panels on vases* and chocolate cups* have been attributed to John Donaldson and while there are similarities in the colours used, there is insufficient evidence to link these with any certainty. Donaldson has been described as a free-thinker who was later affected by a mental disorder. He died in 1801 but is not known to have painted on porcelain after leaving Worcester.

Donegal, Marquis of

Undoubtedly the most important order received by the newly established Chamberlain factory was for an extensive dessert service which is listed in the factory records for 18 September 1793. Ordered by the 'Rt Honble. Lord & Marquess Donegall' it comprised a 'harlequin' set, each piece having a different border united by the family crest at the top and central coronet with initial 'D' (Colour Plate 33). The cost of the service was an incredible £210.10s.0d. A portion of the service was sold by the Donegal family at Phillips in 1981 and, with the exception of one piece, all was made of Caughley porcelain with decoration carried out at Worcester. Only one dish-stand was made in Chamberlain's own early porcelain. The set originally included four ice pails and eight sugar and cream tureens, as well as sixty plates, and represents the popularity of French styles continuing into the 1790s.

Door Furniture

As Queen Victoria ascended the throne the fashion for more elaborate interior decoration led to an enormous demand for door furniture. Imported French finger plates in porcelain and knobs in millefiori glass competed with examples from most British manufacturers. Binns* tells us of Chamberlain and Co. in his *Century of Potting* that 'at one time the manufactory may be said to have been employed in making door furniture alone'. Grainger likewise devoted an entire pattern book to hundreds of different designs (Colour Plate 34). Both factories in the 1840s made finger plates as well as knobs, 'rosettes' or roses to encircle the knob, and 'escutcheons' to cover the keyholes to prevent draughts. From what Binns tells us, this venture was fairly disastrous for the fortunes of the company and none was made during the subsequent periods. Most examples are unmarked and, as fashions changed in later periods, most of the door furniture used in Victorian houses has been destroyed by modernisation. Virtually the only Worcester porcelain examples known are those that remained at the factory and are now in the Dyson Perrins Museum.

Dragon in Compartments Pattern
The original Chamberlain factory name for a pattern which has become generally known to collectors as *Bengal Tyger* pattern, and also as *Kylin* pattern. These names have become confused with other patterns and so I prefer the name used by Worcester in the 1780s. The origin is Chinese, a *famille verte** pattern from the *Kangxi* period early in the 18th century. Apart from a slight variation in palette, the pattern was copied exactly from the Chinese. It was first used at Worcester c.1765-8 on wide-fluted teawares, and on the normal range of dessert wares from about 1770. A few very fine large hexagonal vases were produced around 1770. Although there is no underglaze blue in the design, pieces frequently carry the square mark. The popularity of the pattern might suggest that Giles'* workshop would have issued their own version but no recognisable London decorated pieces have been noted.

The pattern was rarely used by Flight and even less frequently by Grainger. Instead, it was mainly the Chamberlain factory which continued the design into the 19th century. Initially used on Caughley blanks painted at Chamberlain in the late 1780s, it became pattern 75 on Chamberlain's own porcelain teawares as well as the full range of dinner and dessert shapes. On the most elaborate services the central wheel motif could be replaced by the full coat of arms of the original owner (*see* Colour Plates 54 and 64), or simply the family crest.

Care has to be taken in attributing unmarked examples, as the *Dragon in Compartments* pattern was used by a great many other makers, especially Coalport, around 1800-10. These Coalport pieces have often been mistaken for Worcester and illustrated as such in the past, but the shapes of these examples differ from Chamberlain. Royal Worcester occasionally reused the pattern in the late 19th century and c.1930. A more decorative version was issued in the 1970s. *Dragon in Compartments* should not be confused with *Bishop Sumner**, another direct copy of Chinese *famille verte*.

Dragon Pattern
While many designs include dragons, the name 'Dragon' is really only associated with two blue and white patterns, one painted, the other printed. The earlier version is a direct copy of Chinese porcelain and features a dragon chasing a flaming pearl among clouds. Somewhat stylised, the pattern varies in quality and detail but is usually clear and precise, with part of the dragon's body and further clouds painted on the underside of saucers or inside cups. The pattern seems to have been produced at Worcester from about 1757 until at least 1785. Similar copies of the Chinese pattern were made by other English factories, most notably Bow, and copies are also known in delftware. In addition to copies in blue, the Worcester factory experimented with the *Dragon* pattern painted in underglaze manganese*. This occurs on small circular bowls which probably date from c.1760, although very few seem to have been made.

The second and later version of the pattern, usually referred to as *Blue Dragon*, was developed as a printed pattern at Coalport and introduced at Grainger's factory around 1812-15. Several copper plates of this pattern survive at the factory from the Grainger, Lee and Co. period and the design was re-issued later by Royal Worcester.

Dragon Pattern. *A small plate of unusual shape copying a Chinese original, the blue painting in this case closely capturing the spirit of the Chinese, crescent mark*, c.1765, 4⅜in. (11cm). (Dyson Perrins Museum.)*

Drainers
See **Egg Drainers** and **Fish Drainers**

Drawing Room Flower Pots
Patented by Grainger in the 1830s, these were bucket-shaped jardinières with decorated patterns into which a porous lining was placed. Fresh flowers could be grown outside or in a greenhouse in the porous pots which were then placed in the 'Patent Drawing Room Flower Pots' when they were fully in bloom.

Dry Blue
Blue enamel was a very difficult colour to control when used overglaze. Oxidisation tended to occur, resulting in white mottling and eventually total breakdown. Worcester overcame this by developing a very vibrant bright blue enamel which was applied thickly, even to the extent that it could be tooled on the surface. It never became smooth and can be felt raised above the glaze, with a slightly rough texture. Dry blue does not mix happily alongside other colours, but is most effective when used by itself (Colour Plate 35). Strangely, it was virtually only used for flowers, either in a very formal manner at the factory, or in a much freer and more exciting way at the Giles* workshop (*see* Colour Plate 48). Dry blue was probably not used on its own until c.1768-70.

A mug in the Dyson Perrins Museum is transfer printed* with a portrail of General Wolfe* in dry blue enamel. The

Colour Plate 33. ***Donegal, Marquis of, Service.*** *Just a small portion of the remarkable harlequin dessert service ordered from Chamberlain in 1793, each piece with a different border in French style. The porcelain is all Caughley although Chamberlain had themselves begun to manufacture by this time. (Phillips.)*

(Opposite) Colour Plate 32. ***Donaldson, John.*** *A fine vase painted in the style of Boucher, the elaborate gilding confirming the vase was decorated at the Worcester factory, square mark*, c.1765-68, 12 ⅜in. (31.5cm). (Phillips.)*

Dry Blue. *Worcester's overglaze 'dry blue' enamel is seen at its best on a series of large vases decorated at the factory, c.1768-72. This example has unusual reticulation* around the shoulder and cover, 17½in. (44.5cm). (Dyson Perrins Museum.)*

Dudley, Lord, Service. *A sucrier* matching the service once owned by Lord Dudley, finely decorated in the Giles* workshop, on a powder blue* ground, c.1768, about 4in. (10cm). (Sotheby's/Kiddell Papers.)*

result is most effective and it is surprising that the colour was not used for other overglaze printing. A portrait of the Marquis of Granby* is known printed in black and washed over in dry blue.

A blue overglaze enamel continued in use for blue and gold sprigs into the Flight period and occurs on Caughley porcelain decorated by Chamberlain. The enamel became smoother, however, and 19th century painting in blue monochrome is not thought of as dry blue.

Dry Mustard Pots
See **Mustard Pots**

Dudley, Lord, Service
A tea service painted with Watteauesque* figures seated among rich vegetation, some playing musical instruments. The figures are in fan-shaped panels reserved on a powder blue* ground with smaller circular insect panels. Each panel is framed in very rich tooled gold confirming the attribution of this service to the Giles* workshop. Although dating from about 1768, a set, probably of similar design, was included in the March 1774 sale of Giles' stock, fourth day, lot 84. The service is believed to have belonged at one time to the Earl of Dudley, whose family in the 19th century were great patrons of the Worcester factory.

Dutch Jugs
The name used in the 18th century for cabbage leaf jugs*.

Duvivier, Fidelle
The career of Monsieur Duvivier is one of the most discussed of all the artists who decorated English ceramics. A Huguenot born at Tournai in Belgium in 1740, he received his early training at the Tournai factory where he painted until 1763. His cousin Joseph Duvivier moved to London as a painter at the Chelsea factory and it is likely Fidelle joined him there in 1764. Fidelle Duvivier was at Derby in 1769 when he entered into an agreement with William Duesbury to paint at the Derby factory and his son Peter Joseph was baptised in Derby in March 1771. It is not known when the Duvivier family left Derby and Fidelle is next noted as being in France in 1775. In the Ashmolean Museum in Oxford is a remarkable Worcester teapot painted with children and signed by Duvivier with the date 1772. The bright dog-tooth gilding around the rim is reminiscent of the Giles* workshop and suggests Duvivier was employed in London, probably by Giles for a short time to decorate white Worcester porcelain. Very few examples of Worcester porcelain painted in his most distinctive style are recorded. His travels continued, for he signed pieces during the 1780s while working for the New Hall factory and for Turner in Staffordshire and it is possible he visited Caughley. He also taught drawing at Stone and Newcastle-under-Lyme. Geoffrey Godden presents convincing evidence in his *Chamberlain-Worcester Porcelain* that Fidelle Duvivier was employed at the Chamberlain factory for only two weeks in October 1792 (Colour Plate 36). A tea service of Caughley porcelain, undoubtedly painted by Duvivier, is discussed and illustrated by Godden (pls. 30 and 238-241). Apart from a New Hall service dated 1796 which has been attributed to Duvivier, no other later porcelain painting has been recognised and Fidelle is likely to have returned to teaching. He probably died in Staffordshire in 1817.

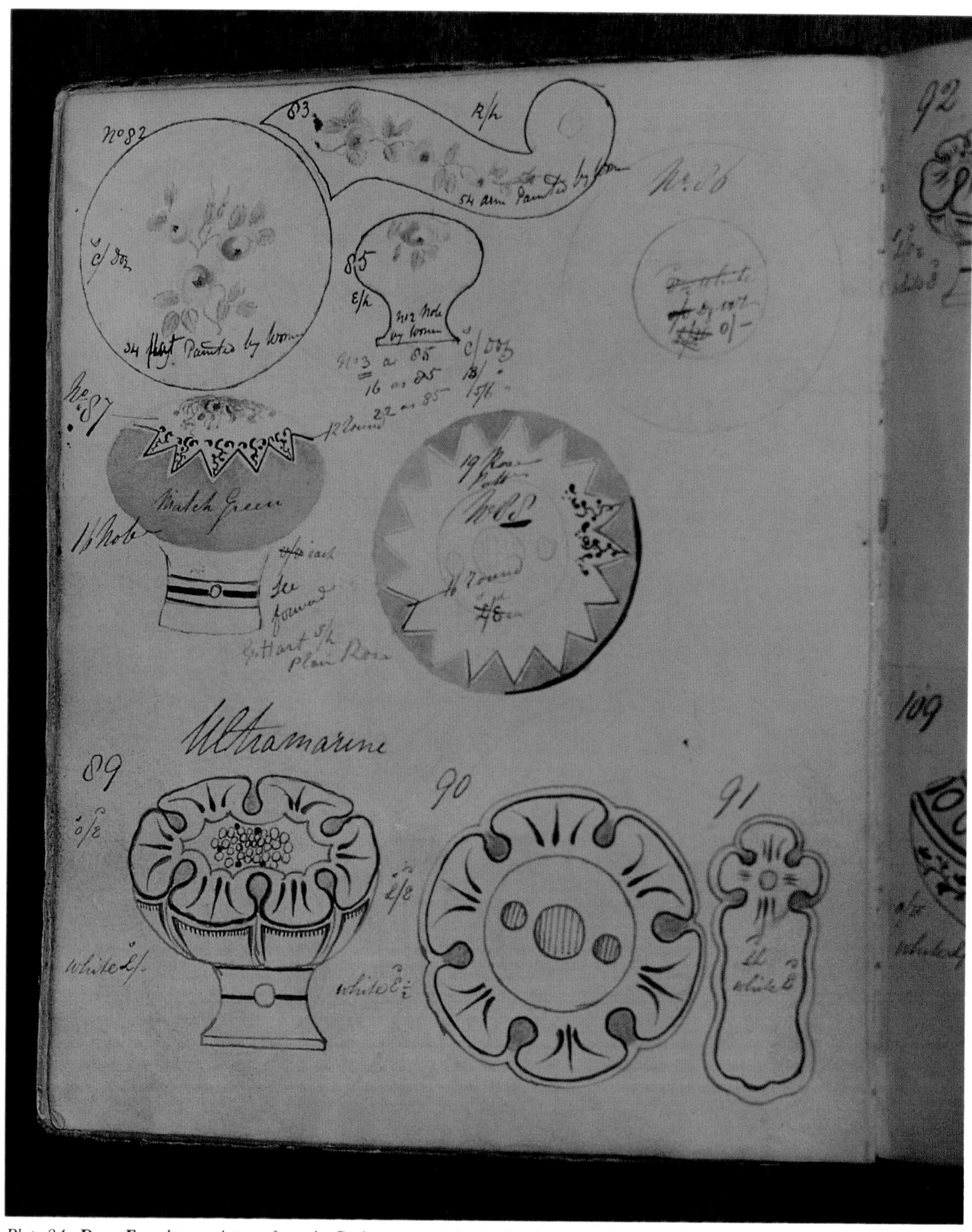

Colour Plate 34. ***Door Furniture.*** *A page from the Grainger pattern books showing part of their extensive range of door knobs and fittings, c.1840. Grainger and Chamberlain were both prolific makers of door furniture. (Worcester Royal Porcelain Company.)*

Colour Plate 35. ***Dry Blue.*** *A very elaborate pot-pourri vase with unusually detailed modelled flowers left plain white, the simple dry blue* decoration considered sufficient colouring, c.1770. (Dyson Perrins Museum.)*

Colour Plate 36. ***Duvivier, Fidelle.*** *A Caughley* spoon tray* decorated by Duvivier in the Chamberlain factory during his brief employment there in October 1792, 6⅝in. (17cm) (Phillips.)*

E

East India Company, The Honourable. *A Flight, Barr and Barr saucer from one of several remarkable services made at Worcester with the full arms of the East India Company. In this case the fine detail on the lion supporters can be attributed to John Bly*, impressed mark*, c.1816, 5in. (12.5cm). (Author's Collection.)*

East India Company, The Honourable

Having supplied Europe with so much Chinese porcelain during the 18th century, the Honourable East India Company had changed direction and by 1815 was vital in shipping the best of English manufacture to the wealthy markets in far away India. Chamberlain and Flight, Barr and Barr were both given orders for the East India Company's own use within a year or two of each other and both put their finest efforts into their productions.

Flight, Barr and Barr used their new gadroon* rim as well as plain shapes and, for them, an uncharacteristic scrolling pink ground border hung with slight rose sprigs, almost suggesting a feeling of the rococo revival*. The lion supporters for the company's arms were in tooled gold with the most marvellous expressions, probably the work of John Bly*. The service was for dinner, dessert and tea although the full extent of the order is unknown. It probably dates from c.1816, and maybe was too costly as for some reason it was to Chamberlain that the East India Company switched its allegiance. It placed with them in 1817 and 1818 the most incredible orders for two services totalling well over 7,000 pieces, for use at the company's headquarters at Fort St. George, Madras.

The 'Dress Service' comprised around 1,500 pieces, each with the full arms of the company within a richly gilded salmon ground border. The other set for everyday use had a plain grey border and smaller armorials using printed outlines. This included 700 of each size plate, one hundred fruit baskets and twenty-four soup tureens with stands. In all the two services included 6,956 separate coats of arms. The total cost for the order was £4,190.4s. The set was finally invoiced in July 1820.

Egg Cups. *An early egg cup of typical rounded shape on a solid spreading foot, painted in underglaze blue*, crescent mark*, c.1765, 2¾in. (7cm). (Dyson Perrins Museum.)*

Egg Cups

The earliest Worcester egg cups appear to date from about 1765 in underglaze blue, the simple floral sprig patterns and borders with little variation. These egg cups are always plain thrown shapes and very occasionally examples are seen with applied prunus sprigs, probably copying Bow, although with decoration in blue instead of plain white. Coloured examples from the 18th century are extremely rare. Early Worcester egg cups tend to be larger than those of most other English factories, suitable for duck rather than hen's eggs. Large plain shapes c.1775 with pierced geometric borders and gold rims have been called egg cups, but an example with a flat cover proves that these are actually vases of some kind. However, a single Worcester egg cup of c.1785 has been seen with a domed cover fitting into a flange and this could have held a small egg (Colour Plate 37).

All three main Worcester factories made egg cups into the

19th century, usually as accompaniments to breakfast services. These normally fitted into egg stands*, the oval platforms with holes for six egg cups. Occasionally Chamberlain made tri-lobed egg stands for three egg cups. The quality of Worcester Regency period egg cups is always outstanding and examples are prized by the great many egg cup collectors.

Egg Drainers. *An early Chamberlain egg drainer, one of a set of six decorated with a crest and cipher, c.1795-1800, 4in. (10cm). Egg drainers are rarely as richly decorated as this. (Phillips.)*

Egg Drainers
Small saucer-shaped objects with side handles and pierced with tiny holes. The argument as to how they were used goes back to the earliest days of porcelain collecting and will probably never be resolved. Contemporary records such as the Chamberlain account books and Wedgwood and other pottery manufacturers' catalogues refer to these either as egg drainers or strainers and the term egg poachers is occasionally used. We do know that they came in sets and were associated with egg cups, as the order for Lord Nelson's* breakfast set in 1802 included '6 Egg cups and Drainers'. Other earlier orders for Caughley examples sold by the Chamberlains include entries such as '36 Egg cups and strainers' or '6 egg stands and drainers, Pleasure Boat [pattern]'. Most likely they were used for *serving* poached eggs since using them to cook an egg or lift it from boiling water is impractical. It is also possible that they were used to separate egg yolks but there would be no need for sets of six at breakfast. Whatever the explanation, Caughley had the virtual monopoly for porcelain examples although some were made by Derby, Lowestoft and at Worcester in Flight's factory around 1790. Worcester egg drainers are surprisingly rare although they have been seen in the *Fisherman and Cormorant** pattern as well as the *Music** and *Royal Lily** patterns. A few coloured and gilded border designs have also been seen. Chamberlain egg drainers in their own porcelain can be more lavishly decorated. The example shown here was one of a set of six decorated with the crest of the original owner and dates from c.1795-1800.

Egg Stands. *A Flight, Barr and Barr egg stand containing six separate egg cups, made as part of a breakfast service*, impressed marks*, c.1815, 8⅝in. (22cm) diameter.*

Egg Stands
More correctly stands for egg cups, these usually take the form of an oval platform on a spreading base with a central ring or scroll handle. Flight and Grainger stands have holes for six egg cups and most Chamberlain examples were similar. Occasionally, however, Chamberlain made triangular stands, c.1800, with only three holes for the egg cups. No egg stands are known before this date.

Eight Horses of Mu Wang Pattern
Initially developed as a design in 17th century transitional Chinese porcelain, the Worcester version appears to have been copied directly from a *Kangxi* period dish from the early 18th century. The pattern has only been seen on a few Worcester dessert dishes dating from c.1775 and it is possible that they were made as straightforward replacements for a Chinese service, especially as no Worcester plates have so far been discovered. The pattern occurs in a virtually identical form on English delftware plates and a teaware pattern featuring a single horse was earlier used at the Vauxhall porcelain factory. The design illustrates a popular story from Chinese mythology. (*See* illustration on page 145.)

Electioneering Wares
Politics has always been very important in the City of Worcester and most of the proprietors of the porcelain factories seem to be heavily involved, as would be expected. It is curious, therefore, that Worcester made relatively few commemorative wares for local elections, while Coalport, for example, made a speciality of such pieces. One explanation could be that many elections in Worcester were not only controversial but also openly corrupt. The Tracy mug* which proclaimed the victory of Robert Tracy in the 1747 Worcester election was not made until several years after he had been declared the winner following much dispute. Likewise, the

Colour Plate 37. **Egg Cups.** *An extraordinary Flight covered egg cup decorated in underglaze blue* and gold, crescent mark*, c.1785-90, 3 ⅛ in. (8cm). (Private Collection.)*

Colour Plate 38. **Embossed Decoration.** *A curious small hexagonal teapot with embossed decoration modelled in a distinctive hand. The decoration is uncharacteristic and suggests the painting could have been added by an outside decorator, c.1756-8. 3 ⅞ in. (9.75cm) high. (Phillips.)*

Eight Horses of Mu Wang Pattern. *A dessert dish finely painted in underglaze blue*, the pattern adapted from a Chinese original, pseudo Chinese mark, c.1775, 4in. (10cm). (Dyson Perrins Museum.)*

Eloping Bride Pattern. *A drawing by Neal French of the complete design from a coffee cup, c.1770.*

election in 1774 led to claims of bribery and a disputed result. A fascinating large mug in the Dyson Perrins Museum is believed to have been made at this time and is painted with clasping hands within a heart-shaped panel and a ribbon inscribed 'In Spite of The Nabob's Gold'. The flowers in dry blue* around the panel confirm Worcester factory decoration. Less controversial was the election of William Gordon in 1807. Chamberlain made a number of jugs inscribed in careful gold calligraphy

> To record the Memorable Triumph of Liberty in the Return of Wm. Gordon, Esq., 17 Feby 1807, by a glorious Majority of 352.

These were sold by Chamberlain in June and July 1807 for one guinea each, made with different initials on the side.

Eloping Bride Pattern

Possibly the best known of all Worcester blue and white patterns, although examples are rarely seen. It was made around 1770, copying a Chinese pattern from the *Kangxi* period some fifty years earlier. Worcester duplicated not only the design, but also the simple Chinese mark and the small size of the teabowls and saucers. The pattern appears to show a Chinaman and lady fleeing on a horse from a row of soldiers. The soldiers could, however, be some sort of attendants, as they are holding a form of parasol. Much discussion has taken place as to the identity of the characters in Chinese folklore, but as yet no convincing answer has been found. While the normal range of teaware shapes was used for this pattern, unusual oval spoon trays* are exceptions. A well known teapot with the *Eloping Bride* pattern on a claret* ground appears to be a later attempt to deceive a collector through redecoration*.

Ely, Marchioness of, Pattern. *A tea canister with the very full landscape background and intricate scroll gilding associated with this pattern, crescent mark*, c.1770, 6½in. (16.5cm). (Phillips.)*

Ely, Marchioness of, Pattern

A popular design found on rich teawares c.1770. The ground is a solid wet blue* and reserves a central circular panel of *Fancy Birds** in particularly elaborate landscapes framed with intricate rococo foliate gilding. The design occurs with far too many variations to be a single service but one tea set of the pattern was sold at Christie's in 1908 as the property of Caroline, Marchioness of Ely. The name Marchioness of Ely pattern should therefore refer only to teawares and related shapes such as butter tubs*, although dessert plates in similar style are sometimes called by the same name.

Embossed Decoration

The process of jollying — pressing clay into a revolving mould — resulted in some very detailed modelling which could be surprisingly crisp on the surface of Worcester porcelain. Patterns and shapes moulded in this way were known as 'embossed' and are best represented in the earlier period by the *Chrysanthemum** or the *Blind Earl** patterns. Chamberlain and Grainger both made full use of the technique after c.1812-5, with the development of bone china and Regent china*. Names such as 'Essex Embossed', 'Dresden Embossed', and 'Wellington Embossed' were used at Grainger for a variety of distinctive patterns which could either be richly decorated or left quite plain. Wasters* from the factory sites show that a great deal of detail was lost when embossed shapes were covered with glaze. *See* Colour Plate 38.

Encaustic Tiles
See **Tiles**

Enniskillen Service

A dish belonging to the Earl of Enniskillen was described by Robert Drane and was probably from a single service decorated in the Giles* workshop c.1770. The design is boldly painted with fruit and leaves in the centre and large fanciful insects around the border in the manner of the wet brush style*. A plate is in the Klepser Collection, *see* Simon Spero's catalogue item 160.

European Figure Decoration. *A high-footed sauceboat, the moulded panels with rare enamelled figures and elegant buildings, the rim edged in brown in Chelsea style, c.1756, 3¾in. (9.5cm) high. (Phillips.)*

European Figure Decoration

Chinese decoration dominated the early years of Worcester and it was only when the factory had become firmly established that it branched out into the purely European styles. European figures were first painted in monochrome on leaf* dishes and in coloured enamels on sauceboats* c.1756. The figures used in the sauceboat panels show little variation and were probably copied from Meissen. This Meissen influence is most noticeable on a sauceboat in the Dyson Perrins Museum painted with figures by a boat. One attractive teaware pattern, also from c.1756, features a lady and gentleman beside a tree with a lake behind and a group of buildings on the right-hand side. The shape of the panel varies considerably but the figure subject is always consistent. This pattern was used on at least four different moulded shapes, with painted flower sprigs on the white grounds.

More individual painting used on large leaf moulded jugs frequently includes figures in the extensive coloured landscapes. The celebrated mug in the British Museum is painted with a gentleman proudly standing in the grounds of an estate and is inscribed 'Lord and Lady Sandys* Health, T.G. 1759'. Painting of this quality is exceptional and far removed from the teaware and sauceboat patterns. Some paintings of ruins, popular in monochrome c.1756-8, include tiny figures in European dress and these are likely to be influenced by Vincennes porcelain.

European Figure Decoration. *A feather moulded* coffee can and a lobed saucer with a modelled border, both with matching decoration enamelled in Meissen* style, c.1756. (Phillips, Oxford.)*

Evans, David

An accomplished flower painter whose early career is surprisingly little documented. He worked at Swansea from about 1815 and probably moved to Worcester following the closure of the Welsh venture in 1819. He joined Graingers as an important painter of flowers and his name appears in the pattern books against several designs similar to the work he had practised at Swansea. Wild flowers were his speciality, painted in a free style unlike any other artist working at Worcester at that time. Three fine plaques are known, depicting vases of flowers and signed by Evans. One is further inscribed on the frame that it was painted by David Evans, Worcester, suggesting he was working as a free-lance artist. William Evans, believed to be David's son, also worked as a decorator at Graingers and writing much later described David Evans as 'the finest wild-flower painter in the trade'. William recorded in the *Pottery Gazette* (quoted by Godden, *Victorian Porcelain*) that his father

> used to give the last touches to the hearts and edges of his flowers with the purest white enamel, like seed pearls, and streaks of light...The pencil used by Evans in this work was a fine, small camel-hair one....Mr. Evans would use only the colours of certain makers and these colours he would travel miles to obtain.

Not all of the flower painting at Graingers is by the same hand, however, and only certain pieces can be attributed to Evans. After leaving Worcester David Evans continued to travel and worked variously at the Coalport, Minton, Copeland and Alcock factories. It is thought he died in 1881.

Evans, David. *A fine plaque signed by David Evans, probably painted in his own time while he was employed at Graingers, c.1820-5, 9⅞in. x 7⅝in. (25 x 19.5cm). (Private Collection.)*

Ewers and Basins. *A large deep basin with shell moulded corners suggesting a use with water. The* Willow Bridge Fisherman *pattern painted in blue indicates that this was used with a ewer or bottle decorated with the same pattern (see* ***Bottles****); c.1765-70, 13in. (33.2cm) wide. (Sotheby's.)*

Ewers and Basins

While bottles* or guglets were more usually made to accompany wash basins in the 18th century, a few graceful ewers were made c.1770-5. These were of plain baluster shape with large rounded lips and high loop handles, usually printed in underglaze blue* or occasionally painted with a Chinese landscape. A few water ewers and basins were sold by Chamberlain at different periods but none is known to have survived. Miniature ewers or jugs and bowls were made as toys* by all three main Worcester factories, mainly in the 1820s.

Excavations on the Factory Sites. *A selection of wasters* found on the Warmstry House* site. Top row from the left: part of a cabinet cup, c.1820; a face handle terminal* (see *page 151), c.1753-4; part of a tub of modelled flowers, c.1770; two spoon handles, c.1765-70; a mask lip, c.1770; middle row: handle of a butter boat, c.1760; a pierced drainer, c.1775; the bowl of a spoon, c.1770; a dolphin ewer creamboat, c.1765-70; bottom row: the lid of a butter cooler, c.1757; a miniature or toy Dutch kettle stand, c.1760; and a three-footed salt, c.1770.*

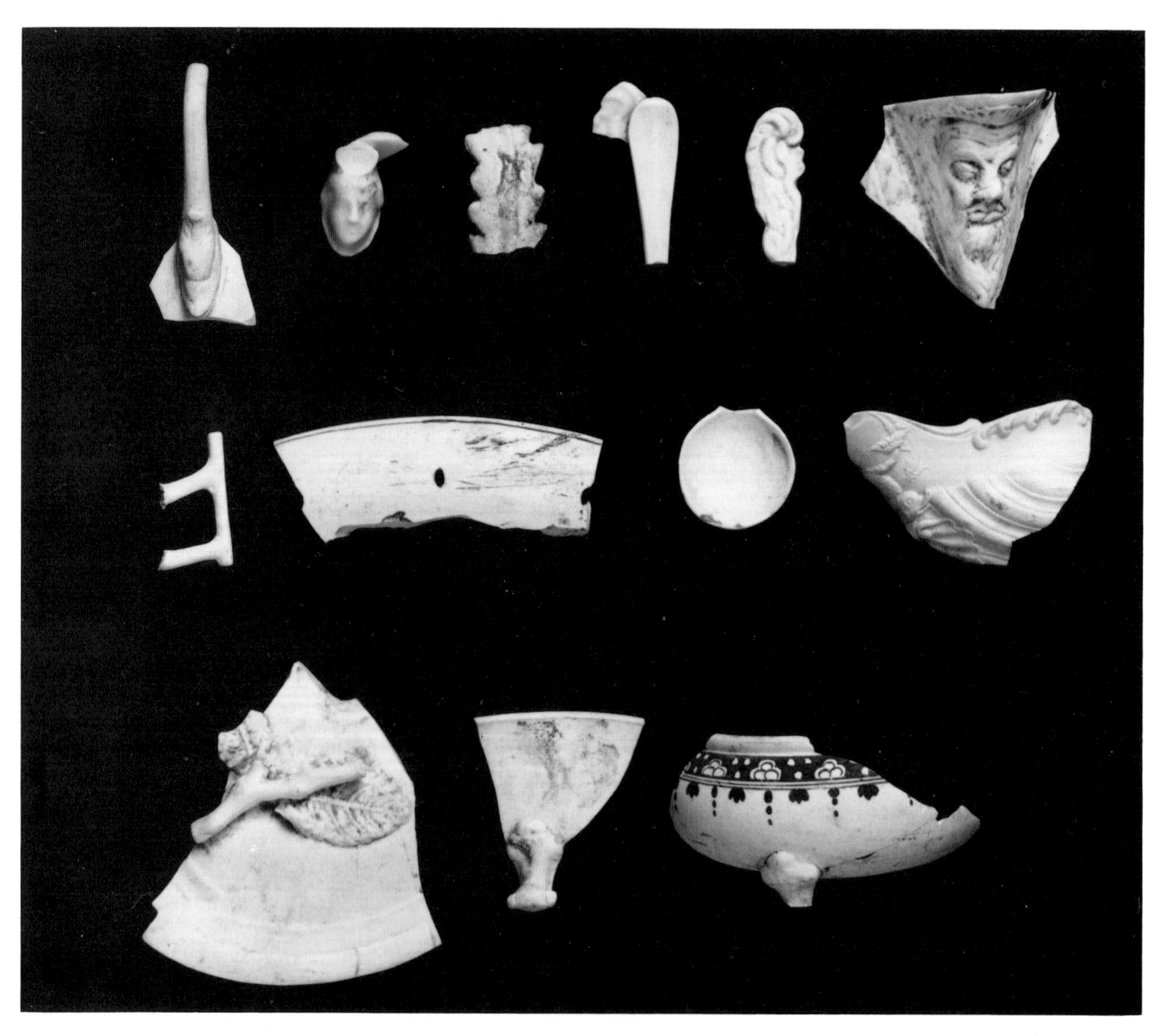

Excavations on the Factory Sites

Archaeology has played a very important part in furthering our knowledge about Worcester porcelain (*see* Colour Plate 1). C.W. Dyson Perrins and Cyril Shingler had both recovered some fragments from the Warmstry House* site, but, incredibly, no detailed investigation was ever carried out while most of the original buildings were still standing. Following their final demolition as recently as the 1960s, the site was partly redeveloped with the construction of the present Worcester Technical College buildings. Fortunately most of the site of the original porcelain works became the college's car park and no deep foundations had disturbed the ground. Henry Sandon had developed his interest in ceramics through archaeology in Worcester. Following his appointment as Curator in 1968 he commenced the first detailed examination of the site, a large trench which took nine months to excavate by hand down to depths of 13ft. (4m). The results of this excavation were reported in Henry Sandon's *Worcester Porcelain 1751-1793*. Probably the most important discoveries were finding fragments which confirmed the entire class of porcelain from the early Flight period was of Worcester rather than Caughley manufacture, and that most of the early shapes at that time known as 'Lunds Bristol' (*see* **Bristol Porcelain**) instead originated at Worcester. Finding part of the mould for a figure led to the discovery of a new Worcester figure*, Cupid at Vulcan's Forge, previously thought to be Longton Hall. The fragments found on the site are pieces which went wrong during manufacture and are known by the term wasters*. Other pieces were factory trials which could never be sold. Factories did not send wasters to be dumped on other porcelain factory sites and, therefore, finding unfinished pieces on the Warmstry House site is conclusive proof that matching finished pieces were made at Worcester.

Seven other excavations have been possible on the Warmstry House site, the most important in 1982 achieving a depth of more than 20ft. (6m) before the water table was reached causing flooding and preventing further digging. The lowest levels produced evidence of the original medieval sandstone wall which formed the boundary of the first factory, and the tidal slipway of the River Severn which can be seen on the 1752 and 1758 engravings of the factory. It was discovered that by about 1770 the Porcelain Company had reclaimed a sizeable area of land from the river by successive dumping of their own waste material. Many of the finds from the excavations are still to be properly examined and published and far more material still lies buried below the surface of the car park.

The site of the Grainger factory has yielded an enormous amount of archaeological material as successive redevelopment of the area has taken place. This has likewise proved invaluable in our researches into Grainger's history. Sadly the Chamberlain site has not yet produced anything other than small, isolated deposits of waste material, as most of the early levels lie under existing buildings such as the large block housing the present factory's mill and even part of the Dyson Perrins Museum (formerly St Peter's School). Hopefully, however, some time in the future a detailed archaeological excavation may be possible to help answer some of the remaining questions concerning the earliest period of Chamberlain production.

Eye Baths. *The two standard shapes of Worcester eye bath, c.1775-80, crescent marks*, 1¾in. (4.5cm) and 2in. (5cm). The example on the right is a particularly rare form. (Dyson Perrins Museum.)*

Eye Baths

Also known as eye cups, these highly collectable items were made by many factories but relatively few survive. Continental examples date from the 1740s but the earliest English eye baths in porcelain are from the 1770s. Worcester examples are very plain in shape and appear to date around 1775-80. They are known with only the simplest decoration in underglaze blue. Caughley made rather more examples and these were retailed by Chamberlain, some with added gilding. It is likely Chamberlain made eye baths as they are mentioned occasionally in the order books, but no surviving example has been seen. Most English eye baths were made of glass.

F

Fable Decoration

A speciality of the Chelsea factory in the 1750s, although not generally used at Worcester until c.1765-8, with the arrival of Jefferyes Hamett O'Neale*. 'The Fox and the Grapes' occurs in monochrome on very rare Worcester dishes of c.1757, however, and also on a curious punch bowl in the Rous Lench Collection which was decorated outside the factory. Otherwise all fable decoration is attributable to the factory and mostly to the hand of O'Neale, c.1768-72. Dessert services were painted with full centres after La Fontaine or Aesop within wet blue grounds with gold scrollwork. Another hand also painted fables with figures and animals in formal landscape vignettes, the exotic foliage more usually seen with fancy birds. These have been attributed to Fidelle Duvivier*, but without any evidence and it seems most unlikely. Chamberlain made a fine fable painted service painted in sepia monochrome with blue and gold borders. Most animal painting from the 19th century is naturalistic, however, and does not depict any actual fables.

Fable Decoration. *An oval dessert dish painted by Jefferyes Hamett O'Neale* with an unidentified fable of a monkey riding on a donkey, square mark*, c.1768, 9½in. (24cm). (Sotheby's/Kiddell Papers.)*

Face Terminal

An extraordinary flight of fancy on the part of the early Worcester factory was to model a human face as ornament for a mug handle. Used on bell-shaped mugs of Scratch Cross* type, c.1753-4, this replaces the simple flourish at the base of a strap handle with a stylised face with pointed chin. A glazed example was found on the factory site excavations* which had not even survived handling in the works without having been knocked off. Inevitably very few have remained intact after use in the 18th century and mugs with this remarkable terminal now rank amongst the greatest rarities.

Fable Decoration. *An early Chamberlain plate with a popular blue and gold border, painted with the fable of the hare and the tortoise in sepia monochrome, part of a service ordered from Chamberlains in July 1795, 8in. (20.5cm). (Bearnes, Torquay.)*

Famille Rose

A palette of colours used on Chinese porcelain primarily in the *Yongzheng* and *Qianlong* periods. The first use of a thick rose pink enamel distinguishes this form of decoration which was copied extensively in Europe. Worcester only occasionally copied *famille rose* exactly, often as a direct replacement for a Chinese service. Instead, up until c.1770 Worcester preferred to use a combination of *famille rose* and *famille verte** adapted to their own factory style of decoration (*see* Colour Plate 60).

Famille Verte

The palette of enamel colours developed in China in the *Kangxi* period using the principal colours of green, blue, yellow, red and purple with limited gilding. After c.1760 Worcester copied some *famille verte* patterns and usually changed these colours noticeably, replacing the purple with a rose pink, for instance. The best known Worcester copies of *famille verte* are the *Bishop Sumner* pattern* and *Dragon in Compartments**, the latter being altered significantly by the addition of bright gilding.

Fan Pattern

The 1769 sale catalogue includes several references to *Old Japan Fan* pattern. This is almost certainly the popular design we now know as Fan pattern. Although originally a Japanese

Face Terminal. *An early bell-shaped mug in underglaze blue*, the handle applied with a mask face as a terminal, shown together with a matching fragment from the factory site excavations*, c.1753-4. (Geoffrey Godden, Chinaman.)*

Fan Pattern. *An unusually small teapot decorated with this distinctive pattern, pseudo Chinese character mark, c.1768-70, 4½in. (11.5cm). (Phillips.)*

design from Arita at the end of the 17th century, Worcester's version is more likely to have copied Meissen. Occasionally, unfinished examples are seen, clearly showing the underglaze blue portion which, after glazing, would have been painted in bright colours and carefully gilded in a very different manner from Giles* gilding found on other *Japan** patterns. The *Fan* pattern does not occur earlier than about 1768, with most examples dating from the early 1770s. Flight and Chamberlain

Fan Pattern. *A chocolate cup* and saucer, a dessert dish and a teabowl* and saucer, all marked with pseudo Chinese characters, c.1768-75. (Phillips.)*

examples are known but uncommon and the pattern was re-used on several occasions by Royal Worcester.

The *Fan* pattern was used on the full range of tea and dessert ware shapes, almost always with its own mock oriental mark. A strange series of round-bottomed bowls in several sizes has been seen only in this pattern, dating from about 1780; their use is unknown. Two large punch pots in *Fan* pattern have a painted fox on the spout with 'Tallio', c.1770. Certain other English factories made the *Fan* pattern, notably Derby and Coalport.

Fancy Birds. *A large dessert centrepiece with osier moulded border, painted with particularly elaborate fancy birds, the treatment of the foliage and the gold dentil* rim confirming a factory attribution, c.1775-8, 11⅞in. (30cm). (Phillips.)*

Fancy Birds

Fantastic imaginary birds in landscapes with bright foliage are referred to today by several names including *Fabulous Birds* or *Dishevelled Birds**. The contemporary name in the 18th century and early 19th was *Fancy Birds,* referring to a form of decoration exemplified by the work of 'Doctor' George Davis* (*see* Colour Plates 18 and 19). The style developed during the 1760s (*see* Colour Plate 47) and its use was widespread by c.1775 (Colour Plate 39). The Chamberlain family introduced the style to their early decorating workshop c.1790 and they also employed Dr Davis to paint some wonderfully full bird painting on Caughley blanks, even though he was associated more closely with Flight's factory. Solomon Cole* wrote that at Flight, Barr and Barr c.1819 they employed George Davis and also Charles Stinton* to paint *Fancy Birds.* Most *Fancy Birds* remain firmly attributed to George Davis, however, even though others are known to have worked in this style. *Fancy Birds,* which probably derive from French porcelain, were also painted by George Davis on his own as a free lance and were copied as well at Graingers.

Feather Moulded Floral Pattern

A popular pattern which remained in production for nearly thirty years as the principal blue and white design used on feather moulded shapes*. The painted sprays actually bear no relationship to the moulded pattern underneath which usually caused the blue to run in parts. By the 1770s and into the 1780s the treatment of the pattern had changed to more stylised and boldly painted flowers in the brighter blue. The pattern is listed in Branyan, French and Sandon as I.E.6.

Feather Moulded Floral Pattern. *A coffee pot shows clearly the complete moulded feathers which give the shape its name. Sadly most examples in underglaze blue* have blurred badly due to the moulded ridges, workman's mark*, c.1760, 8½in. (21.5cm). (Formerly Author's Collection.)*

Feather Moulded Shapes. *A coffee can with simple underglaze border, workman's mark*, c.1754, 2⅛in. (5.5cm). The price list of the London warehouse (*see **London Shops**) *1755-6 included 'coffee cups and cans, ribb'd and Wav'd' selling for 8s. per dozen. (Bearnes Torquay.)*

Feather Painting*. A Flight, Barr and Barr teacup, coffee can and saucer from a full tea service, each piece painted with a border of fine feathers, impressed* 'FBB' mark, c.1820. (Phillips.)*

Feather Moulded Shapes
The undated price list of the London warehouse (*see* **London Shops**), c.1755-6, includes 'coffee cups and cans, ribb'd and Wav'd'. The waved shape is what is now known as feather moulded, a design based on English silver, probably from the 1740s. Only when a coffee pot is encountered does it become apparent that the shape actually represents full peacock feathers inverted (*see* Colour Plate 24). Otherwise the wavy, almost herring-bone effect is rather too stylised. The shape was one of the factory's first, introduced c.1752-3 and seems to have been unique to Worcester. Almost the full range of teaware shapes have been recorded except for spoon trays and teapot stands. The 'Wav'd' coffee cans did not have saucers although teabowls and saucers were being produced shortly afterwards. Frequently found in blue and white, and rarer in colours, the best decoration of birds or flowers dates from c.1756. Blue and white feather moulded floral* pieces continued to be made as late as 1780 although the quality had declined by then.

Feather Painting
A delightful speciality of Flights in particular and also to some extent Chamberlains from c.1805-20. Single bird's feathers were painted with such a high degree of accuracy that it is

Feather Painting*. A Chamberlain dolphin ice pail* painted with very realistic feathers above an orange ground with gold marbling*, unmarked, c.1810, 13¾in. (13cm). (Phillips.)*

Fence Pattern. *A teabowl and saucer of a type made in enormous quantities from 1765-85. This example is unusual only in that it bears a Man in the Moon mark*, c.1765-70. (Author's Collection.)*

Fence Pattern. *An unusual jar, the cover with an acorn finial, printed in blue with this popular pattern, crescent mark*, c.1770, 4½in. (11.5cm) high. (Dyson Perrins Museum.)*

usually possible to identify the exact species of bird. Mostly gamebirds' feathers were singled out, for obvious reasons. The best painting occurs on Barr, Flight and Barr (Colour Plate 40), while Chamberlain painting, although good, is not of a similar standard. Even so it was expensive and the Chamberlain order books contain many references to very costly pieces painted with feathers, such as '1 tea set, different feathers' which sold for 30 gns. in 1813. Solomon Cole* listed the Flight, Barr and Barr artists and recorded that in c.1819 'William Doe painted natural birds, feathers &c.' As a result of this brief statement most feather painting has been attributed to Doe*, while clearly there were other hands capable of this fine execution. Feather painting was revived in the Kerr and Binns period in the 1850s and later by such artists as Robert Rea, Harry Davis and most recently David Peplow.

Feeding Cups
See **Papboats**

Fence Pattern
Undoubtedly the most popular blue and white pattern in the 18th century, although it did not appear until c.1765-8. From that time it was used on a very extensive range of shapes, primarily teawares but including some dessert wares and many more unusual forms such as butter tubs*, spittoons* and mustard pots*. Probably Chinese in origin, *Fence* does not seem to follow exactly any earlier Worcester painted design. Most examples have a carefully painted tramline border. The archaeological excavations* yielded an enormous quantity of the pattern and a statistical analysis of these finds is included in Branyan, French and Sandon, where the pattern is listed as II. B. 9.

Fence pattern was used until the Flight period, c.1790 or possibly c.1795 when blue printing was finally abandoned at the factory. Most examples bear a crescent mark*, often with an additional letter, and one print for a saucer uses the Man in the Moon mark*. The pattern was extensively copied at Caughley, Coalport, Lowestoft and Derby, as well as in pearlware. Often these copies bear crescent marks and collectors are frequently confused. The common occurrence of this pattern in Holland today shows that the factory had a considerable export trade with that country in the 18th century.

Figures. *The Turk's companion, a relatively simple model but usually found with particularly rich decoration, c.1765-70, 5⅛in. (13cm). (Geoffrey Godden.)*

Figures. *The gardener and companion, she in the plain version, he elaborately fitted up as a candlestick* with bocage and a tulip nozzle, on a high scroll base, c.1765-70, 6in. (15cm) and 10⅝in. (27cm). (Sotheby's/Kiddell Papers.)*

Figures. *The canaries, an elaborate model clearly influenced by the popular Bow group of birds in branches, the typical Worcester flowers including hot cross bun buds*, c.1765-70, 6½in. (16.5cm). This example probably originally supported a candle nozzle. (Dyson Perrins Museum.)*

Figures

It is really most extraordinary that a factory as obviously competent as Worcester should have devoted so little time to the manufacture of figures which were, after all, the principal product of the Bow and Derby works. The reason has to be that Worcester's superior body for teawares left them with a virtual monopoly in this area and they did not need to venture into other branches of the trade. Apart from the Bristol Porcelain Manufactory's* single attempt at figure making, the statue of Lu Tung-Pin*, only a single model is ascribed to Worcester before the late 1760s and a mere handful after this date. They are great collectors' rarities today but are far from being a credit to the factory.

The earliest known Worcester figure was ascribed to Longton Hall until Henry Sandon discovered part of the original mould on the factory site and it was recognised by Dr Bernard Watney. Cupid at Vulcan's Forge (Colour Plate 41) is primitive by every standard. It is believed to date from about 1760, or possibly a little earlier, and while it has decorative rococo modelling on the forge itself, the plain base and scant flower modelling is somewhat in the manner of earlier Red Anchor period Chelsea and would have become unfashionable by 1760. Figure making seems to have stopped with this failure, for in a letter from T. Falconer written on 30 August 1766, discovered by C.W. Dyson Perrins, the writer

Figures. *A finely modelled Flight, Barr and Barr figure of a lady in classical dress, in biscuit* porcelain, c.1815, 9½in. (24cm). This appears to be Flight's only venture into figure making and is possibly the work of Thomas Baxter*. (Dyson Perrins Museum.)*

says of Worcester 'they have not yet debased it by making vile attempts at human figures, but stick to the usefull' (*see* Appendix 2).

The next phase of Worcester figure modelling can possibly be attributed to the arrival in Worcester of John Toulouse*. The mark 'T', 'To' or 'IT' which appears on some Worcester figures also occurs on Bow and Bristol and the similarity to the figures from these other two factories is immediately apparent. The following only have been identified as of Worcester manufacture:

A pair of figures of a Turk and his lady companion, he with a long curved sword; on plain mound bases with slight flowers.

A pair of figures of a gardener holding a flower pot and a spade and his female companion with a basket under her arm and holding a nosegay; on plain mound bases with slight flowers as well as high-footed bases with elaborate bocage and supporting candle nozzles.

A pair of figures of a sportsman with a gun and a bird held behind his back, his female companion with a bird and what looks like a powder flask; on shell and scroll moulded mound bases with flowering bocage at either side (Colour Plate 42).

A group of two canaries on a flowering tree of apple blossom which supports a candle nozzle, the base with shell and scroll modelling and a handle at the reverse.

A waster of the arm of a figure was found on the factory site and this does not match any of the above, so there is at least one further model still to be discovered. Also the head and torso of the female gardener was made separately as a tobacco stopper* although only a single example is known. In the *Public Advertiser* announcement of a sale of Worcester porcelain in December 1769, mention is made of figures, although none was actually included in the printed catalogue. A model of a cow* used on the cover of a bowl, c.1768, leads to the question of whether this was made on its own.

Figure production was still continuing at Worcester in 1771 as the diary of Mrs Powys* refers to watching figures being made when she visited the factory in August 1771. Two months later Captain Roche also described Worcester figures in his own diary account of a visit to the factory. John Toulouse probably went to Bristol in 1771 or '72, however, and this seemed to bring an abrupt end to figure making at Worcester. No other figures were made at Warmstry House* except for a single biscuit* statue of a Grecian lady which is believed to date from c.1815. It is marked 'FBB' for Flight, Barr and Barr, consistent with the period Thomas Baxter* was at the factory. Interestingly, it corresponds almost exactly with a simple pen sketch drawn by Baxter ten years earlier in London, and Baxter is known to have modelled portrait medallions* in biscuit porcelain for Flights in 1815. The figure is far from beautiful and was probably not a success.

It was left to the Chamberlains to rediscover figure making at Worcester, even though it is once more an area which was generally avoided. The early Chamberlain records refer to figures of Apollo being made in 1795 and these were made as watch holders* or as pickle stands (*see* **Sweetmeat Stands**). Godden has shown that it is likely John Toulouse was again responsible, referred to by this time as 'Old Toulouse'. A model of a kingfisher (*see* **Toulouse, John**), so far known only in white*, dates from this same period and it is likely a sheep was also made (*see* **Animal Models**). The Apollo figure and kingfishers are known with hot cross bun buds* which help to confirm Toulouse's involvement. Again, in terms of quality these do not begin to compare with Derby or other Staffordshire makers of the same period.

It was not until the late 1810s and 1820s that Chamberlain began to make figures of which they could be justly proud. Issued mostly in biscuit or occasionally fully coloured, these were principally small Cupids, either playing on their own, seated on large chairs or with a dog. Another popular model was a seated classical lady, reading. A series of standing figures from the mid-1820s was based largely on theatrical themes, such as Madame Vestris or Miss Love as the Broom Girl, a milkmaid and a beggar girl, this time all well coloured and on distinctive circular bases. The set of figures of the Rainer family* must rank as the factory's finest venture into the figure market, issued c.1828. Numerous animal models* were also made during the period 1825-30.

Grainger figure production was likewise slow to develop and until the 1830s was restricted to animal models discussed here under that heading. A series of finely modelled Cupids from c.1830 are exemplified by the bower groups* which are nearly as fine as Derby and the equal at least of every other contemporary factory. The Grainger figure of Cupid asleep on a sofa is a charmingly observed study although sadly these models were short lived. Separate figures of Queen Victoria and the Princess Royal maintained the high traditions of Grainger's biscuit figure modelling into the 1840s. In 1845, under the direction of George Grainger, the factory published a series of large figures of young ladies, issued in biscuit and adorned with fine lacework. By this time, however, the standards had declined and Grainger's attention to detail was lost on figures of this scale. They remain clumsy rarities and mark the end of figure making at Graingers.

At the time of the Great Exhibition* in 1851 many of their contemporaries were showing parian* statues while Chamberlain and Co. had nothing to offer in competition, figure-making having been abandoned long since. Fortunately, however, R.W. Binns* was able to redress the balance over the next decade.

Fine Old Japan Pattern

An appropriate description from the Chamberlain factory list for their pattern number 240, which occurs on the full range of tea, dessert and dinner wares as well as on vases and desk sets. The origin of the design is a very close copy of Japanese *Arita* porcelain of c.1700, although by the English Regency period taste had demanded even brighter use of gold. The pattern was possibly used first at Chamberlains, c.1800, although it was also used at Coalport, Spode and other factories including Grainger. A tankard of the pattern marked Grainger & Co. and dated September 1807 is illustrated in Colour Plate 50. When Lord Nelson visited Chamberlains in 1802 he chose an extensive service of *Fine Old Japan* with the addition of his armorials (*see* **Nelson Service**). The border panels of the pattern often include small green birds and occasionally other oriental beasts. In the past it has been claimed that these birds represent Nelson and Lady Hamilton but this is simply nonsense. The pattern does not appear to have been used by Flight and Barr. Recently a number of fakes of the pattern have been made in the Far East and, although unmarked, some of these have been offered for sale as Chamberlain.

Finger Bowls

Worcester finger bowls are simple shapes with straight sides and rounded bases flat on the underneath. The rims can be either plain or wavy and match the circular stands on which they sit to avoid splashes. The shape was made in three sizes and probably copies Meissen originally although Chelsea examples are more frequently seen. Worcester finger bowls were made c.1757-60 and occur in blue and white with standard patterns as well as a special freely-painted bird design. Coloured flower painting in the Meissen style* is recorded and several printed patterns were used, in particular bird prints by Robert Hancock* in the style of C. Fenn. Most of these prints and the painted bird patterns relate to water, for obvious reasons. One other shape of finger bowl with a rounded base and sharply incurving sides was found on the factory site in a level dating from the late 1750s, although no finished example of the shape has yet been seen.

Figures. *A Chamberlain figure standing on a characteristic circular base, impressed mark* Chamberlains, c.1825-30, 8¼in. (21cm). The attention paid to the colouring sets Chamberlain figures well above most contemporary Staffordshire models. (Geoffrey Godden, Chinaman.)*

Finger and Thumb Pattern

The Chamberlain factory records refer to their bright design number 276 as 'India, Thumb and Finger', a very appropriate description in view of the shape of the underglaze blue portion which was heightened in gold. The term India was used for the patterns now known as 'Japan'*, and *Finger and Thumb* is derived from a Japanese design but much adapted to suit English taste. The pattern enjoyed great popularity c.1800-10.

Finger and Thumb Pattern. *One of the most striking Japan* patterns used on a Chamberlain tea service, c.1805, the saucers marked with pattern number* 205. (Phillips.)*

Finger Bowls. *A finger bowl with its stand, painted in blue with the* Cormorant *pattern, workmen's marks*, c.1757-60, the stand 5 ¾ in. (14.5cm) diameter. (Phillips.)*

It is not possible to determine whether Coalport or Chamberlain used the pattern first but both factories produced many tea and dessert services. Grainger examples are known also from c.1810 although I have never seen any Flight and Barr pieces in this pattern. On at least one Chamberlain dessert service an oval panel for a crest is reserved in the pattern, looking quite overwhelmed by the rich foliage.

Firing Supports
See **Kiln Supports**

First Period
A more appropriate name for the early years in the history of the Worcester Porcelain Company than the much used term Doctor Wall Period*. Clear definitions are difficult but the First Period must begin in 1751 on the formation of the company. It ends with the Davis Period* which commenced in 1774 when Dr Wall* sold his shares, even though William Davis* had probably been in sole charge prior to this date. The term First Period Worcester will always remain less than well defined as there are areas of considerable overlap; many pieces made in the late 1770s and 1780s to traditional design

Fish Drainers. *A very rare circular drainer pierced with geometric shapes, printed in underglaze blue* and corresponding with the factory site waster* illustrated under* ***Excavations on the Factory Sites,*** *c.1775, 9½in. (24cm) diameter. (Phillips.)*

are not unreasonably thought of as 'First Period' even though they would have been made after the death of Dr Wall and during the managements of William Davis and Thomas Flight and his sons (*see* **Flight Factory**).

Fish Drainers

From c.1810 most dinner services included a drainer which is roughly oval, flat and pierced with small holes around a central larger hole. It fits inside some large serving dishes and was used to drain juices when serving fish. It has often been argued that it was for draining meat but this can be dispelled by most Chamberlain examples. The second drainer illustrated here is pierced with holes in the pattern of two fish, a feature aparently unique to Chamberlain. The decoration on fish drainers can be as diverse as on dinner services and makes a fascinating area for collecting. The late Robert Hirsch's vast accumulation of drainers became almost legendary in collectors' circles. A few Grainger fish drainers are recorded but as yet no Flight factory examples have been seen.

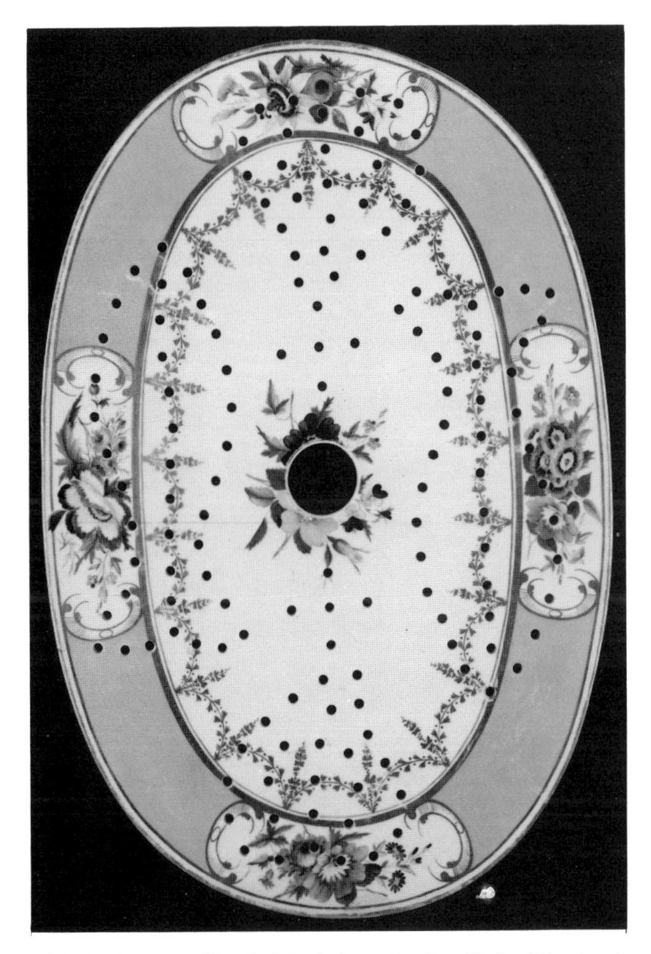

Fish Drainers. *A Chamberlain drainer, the pierced holes following the distinctive outline of two fish, unmarked, c.1820, 14in. (35.5cm). (Robert and Elizabeth Hirsch Collection.)*

Fisherman and Cormorant Pattern

One of the most popular patterns in its day, versions of which were used by many porcelain and pottery manufacturers during the last quarter of the 18th century. The basic origin is Chinese although there is uncertainty whether rare Chinese examples of the version used at Worcester pre-date the English or were themselves copied from an English compilation of earlier Chinese motifs. The pattern we now know as *Fisherman and Cormorant* was introduced c.1775 although collectors will always disagree as to whether Worcester or Caughley were the first to introduce their own popular versions. The fact that there are so many significant differences between the versions used at these two factories suggests that neither was copying each other directly.

In his pioneering work distinguishing Caughley porcelain from Worcester, Geoffrey Godden discussed the *Fisherman and Cormorant* pattern at great length and pointed out the principal differences. At Worcester the standing fisherman is short and holds a long fish, while the seated figure holds a wavy fishing line. Caughley is the opposite with a tall figure holding a short fish and a noticeably straight fishing line (except in very rare instances where the paper print was probably crumpled, distorting the line). Inferior Liverpool porcelain versions seem to copy Caughley rather than Worcester.

For some reason the pattern is known as *Fisherman* by Caughley collectors but *Fisherman and Cormorant* in Worcester. The curious contemporary 18th century name was *Pleasure Boat*. There are numerous references to this (usually shortened to *P Boat*) in the Chamberlain archives where the pattern was clearly one of the most popular. Mostly Chamberlain was selling the Caughley version, either unembellished or with their added gilding to the border. Some entries in the account books make it clear that they sold Worcester porcelain with the pattern also. Indeed, one letter sent by Chamberlain in 1788 to Thomas Turner* at Caughley asks him to send 'no more teas [tea services] P Boat unless they can be sent at the Worcester price 5s.6d.'

Fisherman and Cormorant Pattern. *The very popular* Fisherman *or* Pleasure Boat *pattern used in the centre of a junket dish*, crescent mark*, c.1785, 10¼in. (26cm). The border panels are a very rare series of prints after Jean Pillement*. (Phillips.)*

Flight and Barr. *A déjeuner* set of new French shapes but using the traditional Worcester factory decoration of scale blue* and* Fancy Birds*, *a most successful combination, incised 'B' marks*, c.1795. (Phillips.)*

Flight and Barr. *An important pair of punchbowls* presented to the Corporation of Worcester by Messrs Flight and Barr, painted by John Pennington* with portraits of George III* and Charlotte, the special factory marks dated 1792, 12in. (30.5cm) diameter. (Corporation of Worcester.)*

Colour Plate 39. ***Fancy Birds.*** *A shell-shaped dessert dish, the painting attributable by style and palette to the Worcester factory, c.1775, 8in (20.5cm). (Colin Harper Collection.)*

Flight, Barr and Barr. *A gadroon edged dessert service with a pale green border, continuing classical traditions into the 1830s at a time when public taste had largely changed in favour of the rococo revival*. Impressed marks* and painted names of flower specimens, c.1830. (Sotheby's.)*

By 1790, when Chamberlain were selling both versions, the customer would not have had a difficult choice, as Caughley made a far greater variety of wares in the pattern than Worcester and Caughley by this time was generally superior in quality. In the late 1770s, however, Worcester pieces bearing the *Fisherman and Cormorant* print had been clear and precise. Some very large bowls in particular were a credit to the factory at this time. Mostly Worcester stuck to tea wares, although bowls and a few mugs are known, as well as egg drainers*, egg cups*, asparagus servers*, mustard pots*, creamboats* and sauceboats*. On large shapes such as bowls* or junket dishes* several subsidiary prints were used in addition. Worcester had great difficulty applying the prints to moulded shapes and often examples can be little more than a smudge.

Early examples of the *Fisherman and Cormorant* pattern can bear crescent marks*, although the disguised numeral* is more usual. By the 1790s the pattern seems to have gone out of fashion, at the same time that Flight and Barr gave up blue printing*. Chamberlain seems to have experimented with underglaze blue* printing but there is no reason to believe that any of the *Pleasure Boat* pattern they sold was actually of their own manufacture.

Flight and Barr

Following the death of John Flight* in July 1791, Thomas Flight no longer had any interest in the business. His other sons Bannister and Thomas jun. also showed little interest. The Worcester Porcelain Company therefore remained under the control of Joseph Flight* who had generally only assisted his brother John. A new business partner was needed and Martin Barr* joined to form the partnership of Flight and Barr. James Ross*, the engraver, was asked to engrave a billhead and cards with the new name on 18 June 1792, and on 2 August 1793 Flight and Barr were attempting to sell off cheaply some surplus stock of jewellery, silver and Sheffield plate from their Worcester shop to allow more room for their expanding trade in porcelain. Valentine Green* tells us that in 1795 there had been improvements made in the texture of the ware and he comments very favourably on the quality of the articles made there. The change was towards a much whiter body of so-called hybrid hard paste type. The old crescent and Flight marks were replaced by an incised 'B' mark, presumed to stand for Martin Barr, although why Joseph Flight, whose name appeared on letterheads and over the London shop, should not have had his initials used alongside is a total mystery. Only a handful of pieces are known marked 'F & B' incised.

Flight, Barr and Barr

George Barr* had completed his apprenticeship under his father and became a Freeman of Worcester in 1808, but, unlike his brother Martin jun.*, George did not become a partner until the death of his father, Martin sen.* in November 1813. Joseph Flight* was now the senior partner and his name was followed in the firm's title by the two younger Barrs as Flight, Barr and Barr. Their partnership lasted for twenty-five years of mixed fortunes, during which time some wonderful porcelain was made (Colour Plate 43). Joseph Flight died in 1838 leaving his share of the business to Martin and George Barr. His will took until February 1840 to be proved and Martin and George realised that they could no longer continue in competition with the Chamberlain factory. While technically an amalgamation to form a joint stock company, it is clear from records surviving that the Barrs wished to play little further active role in the business. Consequently the name Chamberlain and Co.* was adopted by the new joint company which began trading in 1840 as the Worcester Royal Porcelain Company. The marks used during the Flight, Barr and Barr period were the full name in script with Worcester and the London address, or else just the initials 'FBB' impressed below a crown.

Flight Factory. *A plate decorated with a meticulously hand painted copy of a Chinese blue and white pattern at a time when transfer printing* in Staffordshire could produce the same effect far more cheaply, c.1785-90, 8½in. (21.5cm). (Author's Collection.)*

Flight Factory

When Thomas Vernon*, William Davis sen.* and William Davis jun. sold the Worcester Porcelain Company on 10 April 1783, the manufactory, all stock, equipment and buildings were bought by Thomas Flight for £3,000, to be paid in instalments over the next year. The works had declined by this time and were very much living on former glory. Thomas Flight had been London agent for the Worcester company for fifteen years but was a businessman, not a potter. He did little to reverse the factory's fortunes and as soon as his sons were old enough to be able to assume responsibility, Thomas passed the running of the firm to them. Joseph Flight* became a Freeman of Worcester in 1784 and John* in 1788. They looked to ways of recovering lost custom and set up a new retail shop at 45 High Street, Worcester, in July 1788. They also tackled the problems of failing kilns and a fraudulent works foreman named Shaw. George III's* visit in August 1788 gave the firm great encouragement followed by the Royal Warrant. Worcester's first Royal Warrant was issued in March 1789 in the name of Joseph and John Flight with no mention of their father Thomas.

Joseph and John followed up the King's recommendation and opened a London shop at 1 Coventry Street, selling principally French porcelain until their own porcelain had been improved. As the result of a suggested treaty to reduce the duty on French imports from 80% to 20%, English manufacturers had prepared for a great influx of French porcelain. Thomas Turner* of Caughley had gone to France in June 1787 and brought back both porcelain and workmen. John Flight paid several visits to France and agreed to take a vast stock of Angoulême porcelain for the London shop. At the same time a new modeller was engaged to produce shapes suitable for a changed London market. It is likely the shanked* shape was introduced in 1788-9 along with many French shapes.

John Flight acted as manager in Worcester coping with the problems caused by the loss of their decorating department to Chamberlain's own business by c.1788. New kilns were built and with Joseph's help a fine painter named John Pennington* was engaged to work on the important Hope service* made for the Duke of Clarence* in 1789. This led to a turn-round in the fortunes of the factory, John Flight having overcome most firing difficulties. The troublesome foreman, Shaw, died and John was able to buy his papers from Shaw's family for ten guineas which was considered a bargain price. The tragic death of John Flight in July 1791 left Thomas in a difficult position. Joseph was incapable of running the business single-handedly and after a year a new partnership was formed involving the business partner of John Flight's father-in-law. By June 1792 they were trading as Flight and Barr*.

Flight, John

Believed to have been born c.1766, John was the son of Thomas Flight who bought the Worcester Porcelain Company in 1783. John Flight was a deeply religious person and kept a diary recording his thoughts and beliefs as well as certain accounts of his work (*see* **Flight, John, Diary of**). There is no record of his early life although he was probably apprenticed to his father. He became Freeman of Worcester on 15 November 1788 and just prior to this he had travelled to Cornwall on behalf of his father, probably to liaise with mine owners and to confirm supplies of clay and soaprock.*

In July 1788 John Flight had come to Worcester to help set up a new retail shop at 45 High Street. He found that the factory was in a very troubled way. The works foreman was defrauding the firm and whole kiln loads of porcelain were regularly failing. John Flight's diary shows that they even considered plans to move the entire porcelain making to Swansea where coal was cheaper.

The King's visit on 9 August 1788 was a great tonic to the company. Their Majesties spent more than two hours viewing the works and left 10 guineas with Mr Flight for the workmen as well as important orders for china. Of even greater importance was the Royal Warrant as well as the King's personal encouragement to John Flight to set up a London retail shop. John made several visits to France to buy Paris porcelain to sell in the London shop. He agreed to stock 50,000 livres of Angoulême porcelain which was fresh to the London market and they had little of their own to sell. John Flight engaged a new modeller to work on French shapes at Worcester aimed at the London market. Following the departure of the Chamberlains, John Flight returned to Worcester in June 1789 to take charge, his father Thomas having apparently given John and Joseph Flight* full control. Chamberlain had taken many of the best workmen as well as taking over Flight's old shop at 33 High Street. John Flight worked closely with his kiln men to develop a new kiln which helped remedy the trouble with sulphuring (spit-out*), but the factory experienced many other problems with their firings. In October 1789 John travelled again to Cornwall to buy shares in a lead mine. Lord Harcourt advised him against returning to France because of the Revolution, although Flights continued to buy Angoulême porcelain.

Colour Plate 40. ***Feather Painting.*** *A pair of Barr, Flight and Barr jardinières with marbled grounds* and very finely painted panels, script marks, c.1805-8, 5in. (12.7cm). (Phillips.)*

The fortunes of the factory were improving and in 1790 John Flight met and married Ann Gillam, daughter of Thomas Gillam who was a prominent merchant in Worcester. John travelled again to France late in 1790 but this was to be his last visit. Tragically he died in July 1791 aged only about twenty-five. He left Ann an income of £2,400 a year. Joseph Flight continued to run the factory and was joined by Martin Barr* who had been the business partner of Ann Flight's father, Thomas Gillam

Flight, John, Diary of

The preservation of John Flight's diary through the family of his brother, Bannister, has provided an enormous amount of important information relating to the Worcester porcelain works during the difficult times in the 1780s. The diary commences in December 1785 and was added to very intermittently until February 1791, five months before Flight's untimely death at the age of twenty-five. The diary is written partly in French and is mostly concerned with John Flight's thoughts about religion and moral philosophy. Yet amongst the pages are accounts of his visits to Cornwall in search of stone and clay; visits to France; and, especially important to ceramic historians, details of the difficulties he encountered in the day to day running of the china factory following the departure of the Chamberlain family. The diary has now been acquired from the family by the Dyson Perrins Museum where it is displayed in its original iron security casket. It is hoped that necessary conservation work can be carried out to further preserve this unique record. The diary is quoted extensively in Henry Sandon's *Flight and Barr Worcester Porcelain,* appendix III.

Flight, Joseph

The second son of Thomas Flight, Joseph was born c.1762. Thomas Flight bought the Worcester Porcelain Company in 1783, presumably for his sons although only two showed any interest in the factory. Joseph was admitted Freeman of the City of Worcester the following year on 27 December 1784 and his brother John Flight* had joined him in the business by 1787. John Flight's diary* shows that Thomas was happy to leave the company in their capable hands, John acting as principal manager while Joseph assisted, both at Worcester

Colour Plate 41. **Figures.** *Cupid at Vulcan's Forge. The only known example of this Worcester figure, shown with the matching master mould for casting part of the forge, found on the factory site, c.1760-5, 6½in (16.5cm). (Dyson Perrins Museum.)*

Colour Plate 42. **Figures.** *A pair of a sportsman and companion, the brilliant colouring and modelled bocage compensating for the generally poor modelling and imperfect potting, c.1770, 7in. (18cm). (Holburne Museum and Study Centre, Bath.)*

Flight, John. *The French influences introduced by John Flight are very apparent in this vase which represents a complete change in style from the wares of the Davis period*; the panel was painted by John Pennington*, crescent mark*, c.1790, 11¼in. (28.5cm). (Phillips.)*

and in London where their shop was opened at 1 Coventry Street. John Flight's death in July 1791 meant that Joseph was left in sole charge. He was joined by Martin Barr* by June 1792 trading as Flight and Barr*, even though Barr was by far the more active partner. Joseph Flight was happy to accept this position until Martin Barr's death in November 1813 when Joseph became the senior partner to Martin Barr's two sons as Flight, Barr and Barr*. Martin Barr jun.* and his brother George* seemed to have lacked any full commitment while at the same time Joseph Flight took a back seat. The result was little new initiative, the factory continuing to make the same styles year after year and falling considerably behind their competitors in terms of fashion if not in quality. Joseph Flight had other interests. Like his father he was Master of the Carpenters' Company and he was an accomplished miniaturist, exhibiting portrait miniatures eight times at the Royal Academy between 1801 and 1806. In 1976 I discovered a rectangular plaque of Flight, Barr and Barr porcelain painted with Hippolytus thrown from his chariot. It is signed 'Joseph Flight November 14th 1818'. The painting is not in the same class as Thomas Baxter's but it is competent enough to lead to speculation about other painting he might have done at his own factory. This plaque is now in the Dyson Perrins Museum. Joseph Flight died in 1838 and, having no wife or children himself, he left his share in the company to Martin Barr jun. and George Barr.

Floral Encrusted Porcelain

The technique of applying porcelain flowers to the surface of wares originated in Meissen in the 1730s and was adopted in China as well as by most European porcelain manufacturing centres. Worcester does not appear to have been interested in the process until much later than other English factories and it was probably only introduced by John Toulouse* in c.1768. Modelled flowers were applied to the handles and covers of baskets and in addition a series of frill vases* were made in the manner of examples previously made at Bow. In the case of Worcester, however, Toulouse used a popular shape of hexagonal large vase and modelled new mask handles and a frill of shell-like leaves around the body. Very finely modelled flower festoons were then applied all over the vases and were either left in white or very brightly coloured. Companion beaker-shaped hexagonal vases were also made along with large baluster vases which were applied with similar masks and flowers but without a 'frill'.

Flower modelling was avoided completely at Flight's factory and only used for basket handles in the early years of Chamberlain. The rococo revival* and a very important interest in Dresden porcelain in the 1830s saw increased demand for English floral encrusted wares. The Coalport, Minton, Rockingham and Derby factories all produced direct copies of Meissen as well as many new shapes with modelled flowers, a style which has become known as 'Coalbrookdale' after the prolific flower modelling at Coalport. Worcester examples are less common but Chamberlain and Grainger both made a wide range of designs in the 1830s. Grainger flower modelling was of the highest quality and represents some of the finest work made in England at this time. Biscuit* baskets of flowers, ornamental ewers and vases, and bower groups* were made, sometimes with the flowers tinted in colours. Often unmarked, it is the delicate quality of the flowers which leads to a positive identification of these Grainger pieces. Chamberlain and later Chamberlain and Co. wares were sometimes applied with somewhat crude flower modelling but these were brightly coloured and can be highly decorative.

Flower Baskets

See Baskets

Flowers

Modelled flowers are unusual in Worcester before the 1760s. A simple closed bud finial was used on teapots and vases c.1760 and this developed into an open flower c.1765. The probable arrival of John Toulouse* from Bow c.1768 saw the introduction of a much more elaborate use of flower modelling on the handles of baskets*, on figures* and on elaborate vases known as frill vases*. Many of the individual flowers themselves are distinctive and serve as a clue to a Worcester origin, even though some are also found on Bristol hard-paste porcelain and Caughley where Toulouse is believed to have worked. Probably the most distinctive feature of Worcester flower modelling is the so-called hot cross bun buds* which are often seen in conjunction with the 'To' or 'IT' mark. Bow had made tubs of modelled flowers and these were introduced to Worcester in the late 1760s in very similar style, the leaves resembling fleshy spikes of a cactus and the tubs moulded with false ring handles. The more elaborate version illustrated is the only example known, just in white porcelain. After c.1772-5 the standard of Worcester flower modelling declined and was almost non-existent at Flight's factory. John Toulouse rejoined Chamberlain in the 1790s and taught their modellers the same style of flowers and hot cross bun buds as had been made twenty years earlier. Later in the 19th century both Chamberlain and Grainger made some very fine modelled baskets of flowers, mostly in biscuit* porcelain (*see* **Baskets**) and others were modelled for brooches.

Footrims
An important clue to the the identification of any 18th century porcelain factory, the shape of the footrim on standard teaware shapes tends to conform rigidly to a set policy within each factory. Thus Lowestoft and Bow have shallow triangular feet and Caughley long square feet. Chaffers, Christian and Pennington all have a tendency to be undercut. There are of course many exceptions with all these makers and the footrim should only ever be used as a clue towards reaching an identification, never as the only method of attributing a piece.

Worcester does seem to have been remarkably consistent in the formation of its footrims in the 18th century. Very small feet are usual in the early 1750s but by c.1755 the standard triangular foot was used on most shapes, sloping gently on both sides of the footrim and flattened at the point. To prevent adhesion to the kiln a glaze-free margin* occurs from c.1760-5. The centres of the bases are flat and occasionally have an incised ring cut into the middle, a feature seen mostly after c.1772 and which also occurs on Caughley and some Liverpool porcelain.

Four Ages of Man
A set of four small Smoky Primitive* prints which were used on sauceboats* and leaf pickle* dishes c.1754-5. The original copper plate was probably engraved by Robert Hancock* after designs by Boitard, and the name L. P. Boitard* occurs in reverse below the print of Old Age.

Freemasons' Arms
An impressive engraving by James Ross* used on cylindrical mugs and cabbage leaf moulded mask jugs, from c.1765-80. The arms of the Freemasons are contained in a rococo cartouche in a landscape with various masonic insignia and three standing figures of freemasons. When space permits the main print is flanked by prints of two obelisks supporting celestial and terrestrial globes. The original copper plate is preserved at Worcester and is signed *J Ross Vigorniensis sculp.* Most examples were printed in black but a jug still belonging to the Worcester Masonic Lodge is printed in underglaze blue.

French Green
One of the ground colours listed in the advertisement for the 1769 London sale of Worcester porcelain which has proved difficult to identify. Probably the factory merely used this as another name for what is now called apple green* which was inspired by Sèvres porcelain. The term French green is used by collectors today for a darker variant of Worcester's overglaze green which occurs only as a border design, c.1770-5. It occasionally was used as a plain band on reeded teawares but more usually is found on dessert wares with

Flowers. *A very finely modelled basket of flowers, probably left in white* to show the quality of the modelling which includes hot cross bun buds*, c.1770, 6¼ in. (16cm). (Phillips.)*

borders of large triangular dentils. The centres have a formal peony-like flower in the same dark green with careful honey gilding* indicating the decoration was carried out at the factory. A rare reticulated plate of the pattern is illustrated under **Reticulated Porcelain.** Some examples of this pattern have been subject to redecoration* with the addition of berried leaf festoons between the French green borders.

Fretted Square Marks
See **Square Marks**

Frill Vases
The curious products of several English porcelain factories, the name frill vase derives from an applied band of shell-like overhangs near to the bases of large, flower-encrusted vases. Bow and Derby frill vases are quite common while Worcester examples are much rarer. Worcester frill vases were produced c.1768-72 and are the work of John Toulouse* who brought the idea from Bow (*see* Colour Plate 85). Subsequently identical modelling was used by Toulouse on hard-paste Bristol porcelain frill vases. Worcester made two principal

Colour Plate 43. **Flight, Barr and Barr.** *The classical elegance of Flight's vase shapes combined with sumptuous paintings of shells, landscapes and literary subjects, yet it is the quality and richness of the gilding which sets these wares apart from those of any other English factory. All marked Flight. Barr and Barr with the exception of the central shell decorated vase which is 11in. (28cm) and marked Barr, Flight and Barr. (Sotheby's.)*

forms, hexagonal vases and covers and smaller hexagonal beaker vases with inner pierced platforms. They are known in full colours or just white and usually include forms of the 'To'* or 'IT' marks associated with Toulouse. The flower modelling is distinctive, usually very fine with hot cross bun buds*.

Fruit Decoration

Considering the importance of fruit growing in local agriculture, it is understandable that fruit decoration played a major part in all periods of the Worcester porcelain industry. 18th century fruit patterns mostly fall into three groups, one of which is discussed here under the heading **Spotted Fruit.** In contrast sliced fruit* seems to be related to the Giles* workshop while a number of underglaze blue transfer prints include fruit sprays. The Duke of Gloucester service* of c.1775 is painted with groups of incredibly lavish fruit, while, at the other extreme, underglaze blue fruit prints were cheap and popular also in the 1770s. Thomas Baxter* painted a series of wonderful cabinet plates for Chamberlain with fruit and vegetable subjects c.1819.

Frill Vases. *One of the rare hexagonal beaker-shaped vases with flower modelling associated with John Toulouse*, complete with inner pierced cover, c.1768-70, 8⅝in. (22cm). (Dyson Perrins Museum.)*

Futteh Ali Shah and Abbas Mirza

Flight, Barr and Barr produced a pair of delicate bat* prints c.1833-5 which were used on oval medallions about 2⅜in. (6cm) high, as well as cabinet cups* and spill vases*. The subjects are sometimes titled 'Futteh Ali Shah, King of Persia' and 'Abbas Mirza, Prince Royal of Persia'. They were copied from prints published by Thomas Dudley and the Worcester versions are usually fully coloured in so that it is difficult to detect any form of printed outline. An uncoloured pair of medallions, however, is in the Dyson Perrins Museum. Futteh Shah died in 1834, the year after the death of the Prince Royal, his favourite son, so the Worcester portraits are probably memorial pieces.

Futteh Ali Shah and Abbas Mirza. *A pair of Flight, Barr and Barr medallions printed in black but uncoloured, together with a cabinet cup in full colours with raised gold, the medallions 2½in. (6.3cm), printed name marks, c.1833-5. (Dyson Perrins Museum.)*

G

Gadroon Boats

Creamboats with plain, slightly lobed bodies and gadroon* moulded rims and feet. Versions were made in several sizes including larger sauceboat sizes, but generally only the smallest creamboats are referred to as gadroon boats. The name derives from references in the Chamberlain archives to Caughley gadroon boats sold by them. Worcester examples are not as crisply moulded as Caughley and rarely as well printed. Curiously, the Caughley gadroon boats usually have an impressed star mark under the footrim, a feature not recorded in Worcester. Worcester sauceboats date from c.1770 although the creamboats date from the 1780s, usually printed in blue or with simple gilded decoration. A somewhat similar shape was made at Liverpool and pearlware examples are also known.

Gadroon Boats. *A small creamboat with gadroon moulded rims, printed in bright blue with the* Obelisk Fisherman *pattern, disguised numeral mark*, c.1785, 4in. (10cm) long. (Godden Reference Collection.)*

Gadroon Rims

Although popular in silver in the mid-18th century, gadroon rims were probably considered too heavy and indelicate for porcelain. Worcester did, however, use a crisply moulded gadroon rim on large, flat dinner plates, c.1775, usually transfer printed* in underglaze blue.* Curiously, tureens to match these are far more frequently seen than the plates, either in blue and white* or full scale blue.* The gadroon moulded tureens from the Duke of Gloucester service* prove that these were sold with plain rimmed plates. A date of 1816 has been suggested for the reintroduction of gadroon rims at Worcester but Flights were certainly using the shape c.1815 when Thomas Baxter* painted the service for Lord Valentia. This remained the most popular shape used by Flight, Barr and Barr, with a particularly sharp gadroon rim which was smart but prone to chipping. Grainger made two distinct versions,

Gadroon Rims. *A Flight, Barr and Barr cabinet plate with a finely painted view of Windermere Lake, Westmorland, the gadroon rim brightly gilded in contrast to the deep blue border, impressed* and printed marks, c.1816, 9½in. (24cm). (Phillips.)*

one with a regular design, including three finely moulded strokes between each large gadroon, the other called 'Full Gadroon', with additional shell-like motifs spaced at intervals around the rim. Grainger gadroon rims date from c.1815-25 (Colour Plate 44). Chamberlain probably introduced their version slightly later but were certainly making gadrooned rims by c.1820. They continued to produce the shape until after the amalgamation with Flight, Barr and Barr and it was also continued into the 1850s by Kerr and Binns.

Gardener Grafting a Tree

An unusual transfer print usually occurring on the reverse of more popular prints such as *The Tea Party** and *The Whitton Anglers**. A lady and gentleman watch as their gardener is attaching a small cutting to a tree stump. The subject appealed to a nation interested in gardening and was frequently depicted in Staffordshire pottery figures. The Worcester print is known only in black, from c.1765-70. (*See* illustration on page 194.)

Gardener Pattern

A blue and white pattern used primarily on mugs but also occurring on teawares, c.1765-70. It depicts a Chinese lady seemingly scolding a kneeling man who is planting or has just picked a flower. The design is always carefully and exactly painted using a dark blue and strong areas of heavy shading

Gardener Pattern. *A drawing by Neal French of the pattern used on a saucer, c.1765-70, 4⅝ in. (11.7cm).*

Gayton, Admiral, Service. *A reeded coffee cup pencilled* in black with gold highlights, the design adapted from the earlier King of Prussia* prints, c.1780, 2⅝ in. (6.8cm). (Author's Collection.)*

which can often be badly blurred. The pattern was probably copied from Chinese porcelain but the original oriental version has not been seen. *The Gardener* is listed by Branyan, French and Sandon as pattern I.A.13.

Gayton, Admiral, Service
This unusual tea service has been traced back through its original owner's family to Admiral Clark Gayton (1720-1787). Gayton had followed an undistinguished naval career until he received the captaincy of the *St George,* under Commodore Moore, seeing action at Martinique and Guadeloupe in 1759. Gayton later commanded the Jamaica Station 1774-8. He rose to Rear-Admiral in 1770 and Vice-Admiral in 1776. Gayton returned to England for the last time in April 1778 and was appointed Admiral in April 1782. He retired to Fareham where he died in 1787. The Worcester service of fluted shapes dates from c.1780, after his return to England. It is interesting as the design is a pencilled* copy of the print used much earlier on the reverse of the popular King of Prussia mugs*. A tea canister and a small number of cups were in the Godden Reference Collection.

Gazebo Pattern. *A particularly fine teapot* painted in a light tone of underglaze blue*, workman's mark*, c.1756, 5⅛ in. (13cm). (Phillips.)*

Gazebo Pattern
One of the more distinctive of the painted Chinese patterns in blue and white Worcester from the mid-to late 1750s. The design features a small hut within diagonal rocks and a figure looking out towards a boat. It was probably copied from an original pattern in Chinese porcelain, but most Chinese versions of the design, especially groove-handled coffee cups, seem to have been copied from Worcester rather than the other way round.

George II
Two portraits of the King were engraved by Robert Hancock,* the most popular being a profile bust after Thomas Worlidge's 1753 painting. This was printed in black on mugs, and very occasionally on jugs, from c.1757 until the King's death in 1760. The prints are usually accompanied by naval and military trophies emblematic of Liberty and on the reverse is usually a print of a sea battle. Occasionally the same portrait was used in the centre of bowls printed to raise funds for The Marine Society founded in 1756. A very much rarer portrait of George II on horseback is known only on vases, dating from c.1758.

George III
During his long reign a number of pieces of Worcester porcelain were made bearing the likeness of the King who played an important role in encouraging both Flight and Chamberlain. Following the royal marriage in 1762 Worcester issued portrait mugs printed with busts of George III and Queen Charlotte* after engravings by James McArdell. These prints in profile are sometimes titled 'K. George ye IIId' and 'Q. Charlotte' although most surviving examples are untitled.

Colour Plate 44. ***Gadroon Rims.*** *A Grainger, Lee and Co. dinner service, the decoration looking towards the rococo revival*, the flower painting very typical of Graingers, pattern number* 1358, c.1825. (Phillips.)*

They are usually in black although puce and underglaze blue versions are known. The same print of the King was reissued by Flight and Barr on a tapering jardinière dating from c.1800 which possibly celebrates the King's return to health. An exceptional pair of mugs in the British Museum are painted in colours with portraits of George and Charlotte, undoubtedly originating from the Giles* workshop, c.1765-70.

George III visited Worcester in 1788 to attend the Music Meeting and he visited Flight's shop and subsequently the factory, spending more than two hours viewing the works. The King left ten guineas for the workmen as well as orders for porcelain, and conferred on the company their first Royal Warrant (*see* **John Flight***). Flights issued a porcelain token* to commemorate this visit, with a portrait of George III on one side. During the same visit to Worcester it is said the King spent much time wandering around the city and came across Chamberlain's new retail shop which was being refurnished. The King and Queen insisted on seeing what was going to be done. Mrs Chamberlain's account of the visit was recounted by R.W. Binns.* The King and Queen

> ascended the stairs, even to the top rooms of the house, picking their steps over wood and shavings and tools, until, having reached the top, and being somewhat fatigued with their wanderings, His Majesty said 'Come, Charlotte, come and sit down for I am rather tired;' whereupon they seated themselves on the top stair of the upper staircase, laughing heartily at the very extraordinary position in which they found themselves.

Flight and Barr presented the Corporation of Worcester with a pair of punchbowls painted with portraits of George and Charlotte (*see* **Flight and Barr**) and also made a number of jugs painted with monochrome portraits of the King, almost certainly by John Pennington* (Colour Plate 45). George III favoured Flights with his own orders rather than Chamberlain. Two royal services were made by Flight and

(Opposite) ***George II and George III.*** *Two fine portraits engraved by Robert Hancock*. Left: George II, signed 'RH Worcester' with an anchor*, c.1757, 5¾in. (14.5cm); right: George III printed in lilac, the reverse with a portrait of Queen Charlotte, c.1762-5, 4¾in. (12cm). (Phillips.)*

Colour Plate 45. ***George III.*** *A Flight and Barr jug painted by John Pennington* with a monochrome portrait of the King, the borders decorated in the French style, mark in gold, c.1792, 6½in. (16.5cm). (Bonhams.)*

Colour Plate 46. ***George III.*** *An ornate Barr, Flight and Barr jug made to accompany the service ordered by George III in 1805, the front bearing the full royal arms, elaborate printed mark, c.1805-10, 5½in (14cm). (Fine Arts Centre, Cheekwood.)*

George III. A large serving dish from the service originally ordered by the King in 1805, this example made as a replacement during the Flight, Barr and Barr period, c.1815-20, impressed mark, 16⅞in. (42.7cm). (Phillips.)*

Barr although sadly no details survive of the extent of the orders. One appears to date from c.1805 and uses an all over Barr's orange* ground with gilding and small reserves of the crowned cipher 'GR'. The other set was first ordered in 1805 with additions made during the Barr, Flight and Barr and Flight, Barr and Barr periods (Colour Plate 46). The full royal arms of George III were placed within a deep blue border gilded with oak wreaths containing Union sprigs and the royal cipher.

George IV Service

On his accession in 1820 the King commissioned a service from Chamberlains although the full extent of the order is not known. A duplicate plate kept by the factory is in the Dyson Perrins Museum and is decorated with the full royal arms within a very bright green border reserving three flower panels. The rim is gadrooned.

Gilders' Marks

The rarity of gilding during the early period of the factory when workmen's marks* were generally used means that gilded marks of any kind are virtually unknown at Worcester. A few numbers or letters have been seen either in gold or coloured enamel on the footrims of early Flight pieces, c.1790, but it was clearly not an established procedure at Worcester. Gilders' marks are often encountered on Caughley porcelain where gilding has been added and it is likely that Chamberlain gilded these pieces. Such markings also occur on Chinese porcelain gilded in England; however, in this case there is no evidence of Chamberlain gilding on Chinese, so other gilders were probably responsible for these. Chamberlains' own porcelain and Grainger wares never have any gilders' marks.

Gilding

The quality and richness of Worcester gilding in the 18th century sets it apart from the other English factories with the possible exception of Chelsea in the Gold Anchor period. English gilding is rare in any factory before the 1760s and Worcester generally avoided its use until c.1765. Before this time gold was used mostly for adding minor details to a pattern, such as the petals of chrysanthemum flowers in *Kakiemon** patterns or to edge costumes and pick out precious objects or butterflies in Chinese figure patterns. For example, one early pattern of c.1754 includes a bird perched in a ring suspended from a standing pole which is gilded and a gold pedestal table supports a vase and bowl behind the main figures, but no other gilding occurs and the rims are left plain. Gilded borders are particularly rare before c.1765 and even gold lines edging the rims are very seldom seen. For this reason it is possible that some of the pieces of *Staghunt* pattern* which have gold borders were decorated outside the factory.

The influence of London in the 1760s brought about a change in direction as richer patterns called for gilding in competition with Chelsea. Chinese porcelain used very little gilding, which tended to be rather pale, so Worcester saw a great opportunity to create a new market for itself. From c.1765-70 the use of gold lines on the rims became usual rather than exceptional and gradually more gilding was used for cartouches to frame decorated panels. The principal influence here was the rococo of Sèvres where fancy gilding was used to frame a panel whereas Meissen had favoured plain gold lines. The Worcester factory developed its own distinctive styles of gilding which can be used for identification. The London style of gilding was totally different in most cases and is one of the easiest ways to differentiate between the Giles workshop and the Worcester factory. Worcester used honey gilding* up until c.1788-90 while there is evidence that the brighter, flatter London gilding meant Giles was using mercury gilding* far earlier. Giles was able to tool gold on the surface by using burnishing techniques while Worcester tended to rely more on the texture of the honey gold itself.

By the 1770s complete patterns just in gold suited the new classical taste. Medallions of husks and flower festoons hang from ribbon bows on fine teawares and some plates and baskets which would have been quite expensive. Some designs such as the *Gold Queen's Pattern** were decorated by Giles as well as the factory, although most gold patterns were only done at Worcester. The factory favoured a rim of very fine dentil gilding* which was used on many patterns in the 1770s and into the 1780s. The Chamberlains had been responsible for overseeing the gilding at Worcester and their departure c.1788 left the Flight factory in severe difficulty, saved only by Mrs Hampton* who had to reintroduce the technology they had lost. Her arrival probably coincided with the change-over to mercury gilding. Early Chamberlain gilding on Caughley porcelain is flat and smooth and still sometimes dull compared with the subsequent gilding on their own porcelain which also was mercury based. During the Regency period the quality of Worcester gilding, especially at Flights but also to some extent at Chamberlains, was outstanding and quite unequalled in England. Flight and Barr introduced raised gilding by c.1814 when it was used to great effect on cabinet plates by Thomas Baxter.* This involved building up the design in thick enamel paste, probably over several firings, before gilding on the top. Coloured enamel jewelling by Ishmael Sherwin* and other gilders completed these wonderful effects. These were of course terribly expensive and cheaper gilded designs were also used. *Vermicelli* gilding* and weed gilding* were used at all three main Worcester factories and Grainger specialised in gold twigging*. Generally the Grainger gold is warmer, with a slight red tint, and usually not as fine as Flights.

Giles, James

The son of a London Huguenot, James Giles was born in 1718 and apprenticed in 1733 to John Arthur, a jeweller at St Martin-in-the-Fields. This is significant, as grounds of finely worked gold were used to wonderful effect on Giles decorated porcelain. James Giles' father, also James, worked as a chinaman and either James sen. or his eldest son, Abraham, was described as a china painter as early as 1729 when Abraham was apprenticed to Philip Margas, a London dealer in Chinese porcelain. A James Giles, probably the father, was recorded as a 'Chinaman at Berwick Street' in the poll list in November/December 1747, indicating he was trading in porcelain.

Curiously, a James Giles took a lease on a tenement in

Giles, James. *Attributing Chinese patterns to the Giles workshop can be difficult, but in this case the flower sprigs in the smaller panels provide strong evidence in favour of London decoration. c.1765-70, 6in. (15cm). (Phillips.)*

Giles, James. *Fruit and flower painting in an unmistakable and very distinctive style which occurs on a great many pieces of Giles decorated porcelain, in this case combined with a scale pink* border, c.1770, 9in. (23cm). (Sotheby's/Kiddell Papers.)*

Worcester in 1745, near where the porcelain works would be established six years later. This was possibly the younger son of the London chinaman. No definite link between Giles and Worcester porcelain is known from this early period, but by 1756 he was sufficiently knowledgeable on the subject to move

Colour Plate 47. ***Giles, James.*** *The London style of* Fancy Bird* *painting first used by Giles on Chinese porcelain and used here on a Worcester tea service of c.1760-5. The gold is softer than later Giles decoration. (Phillips.)*

***Giles, James.** An attractive landscape painting in colours within a border of simple flower sprigs in dark mauve. Similar sprigs occur on many other Giles decorated pieces, c.1770, 9in. (23cm). (Formerly H.R. Marshall Collection, photograph Sotheby's/Kiddell Papers.)*

to Kentish Town where he took over an existing workshop with its own decorating kilns. It is not unreasonable to suppose that Giles was in some way connected with decorating Worcester porcelain prior to this date.

It seems probable that initially only Chinese porcelain was decorated at Kentish Town, with the exception of certain pieces of Bow porcelain under an arrangement with the Bow factory, recorded by Thomas Craft. The Giles family understood the trade in Chinese porcelain and were not alone in painting European subjects on white Chinese blanks imported into London. The earliest Worcester porcelain which is stylistically linkable to Giles appears to be from the early to mid-1760s (Colour Plate 47). The painting is identical to that found on Chinese porcelain painted in London; indeed, some sets are known where both Worcester and Chinese pieces occur within the same service. Giles would have bought from Worcester shapes which he could not obtain elsewhere.

In 1763, Giles is recorded again at 82 Berwick St, Soho, where he continued as a 'china and enamel painter', possibly having taken over his father's business. James Giles claimed in *The Universal Director* to copy 'patterns of any china with the utmost exactness ... either in the European or the Chinese taste'. Worcester became his principal source, and in 1767 a formal agreement was drawn up for the supply of white Worcester porcelain for Giles to decorate. He continued also to act as a retailer as well as a decorator.

While considerable documentation has survived, there are frustrating inconsistencies about Giles which leave many questions unanswered. In December 1767, Giles advertised a new warehouse selling Worcester China in Cockspur St, just a stone's throw from Spring Gardens where the Worcester factory had its own retail outlet. Both establishments continued to advertise, apparently in direct competition. For instance, on 8 January 1768 the *Public Advertiser* announced that 'J. Giles, China & Enamel Painter, Proprietor of the Worcester Porcelaine Warehouse, up one pair of stairs in Cockspur-Street', was selling to the Nobility and Gentry

> a great variety of Articles of the said manufactory ... superior to anything before exhibited to the public on that porcelaine. As the Enamelling Branch is performed in London by the said J Giles, and under his Inspection, this Warehouse will be daily supplied with a variety of new goods, which will be sold as cheap as at the Manufactory, or any Place in Town, with the usual Discount to the Trade: as the Proprietor has a great Variety of white goods by him, Ladies and Gentlemen may depend upon having their Commands executed immediately, and painted to any pattern they shall chuse.

This strangely worded advertisement was followed three weeks later by the Worcester factory's own claim that

> as several of the Nobility and Gentry have lately been disappointed of seeing the large and curious Collection of the Worcester China Manufactory; as some of their ware is advertised at another Room, painted in London, the chief Proprietor and acting Manager has sent some thousand Pounds Worth of the said Ware from their late Warehouse in Aldersgate-Street, to be sold in the same Exhibition Room, where will be sent every week, new variety of the finest goods. Curious Patterns that are wanted will be made in a short Time not to be distinguished from the Original, as the proprietors have engaged the best painters from Chelsea etc. Any Orders will be executed in the highest Taste, and much cheaper than can be afforded by any Painters in London. The said Goods are marked at the Lowest Manufactory Prices in Worcester.

These opposing advertisements were both repeated in subsequent weeks. Several authors have taken Giles' claims at face value to suggest he was virtually the sole 'Enamelling Branch' of the Worcester Manufactory at this time, with only printing, blue and white and simple floral patterns executed at Worcester. Careful reading of the factory's advertisements, however, clearly refutes this and I believe the factory rather regretted having drawn up the agreement to supply Giles with white pieces and thus continued to produce fine goods in direct competition with him. By 1771 the factory had clearly lost patience with Giles and the agreement was terminated. Giles presumably held a large stock of white wares but was forced to find alternative supplies, such as Christian of Liverpool, Turner at Caughley, and Duesbury at Derby. Some Worcester was probably still supplied and it is possible that Giles bought finished Worcester porcelain with simple patterns and redecorated such pieces in a richer style (*see* **Redecoration.**)

By 1776, Giles was in difficulty. He closed his Cockspur St warehouse and sold solely from Berwick St. His remaining stock was sold off at auction on 5 March 1776 followed by a further sale on 6 April after the death of Mr. Higgins, 'Late partner with Mr. Giles, of Cockspur Street, chinaman and enameller'. The porcelain on sale was described as 'of various manufactures'.

There remains, from a period of between twelve and fifteen years, a great quantity of Worcester porcelain decorated in London under the direction of James Giles and distinctly different from the factory's own decoration. Recognising these differences will always be controversial, but certain styles are without question Giles' work. Gerald Coke, in his work *In Search of James Giles*, discusses these differences at great length and it is possible to list here only a few important characteristics (*see* **Aggressive Birds, Divergent Tulip, Watteau Figures** etc.) The flower painting (Colour Plate 48) and gilding styles offer the greatest clues and once studied are really unmistakable, being much freer and less restricted than factory paintings. The wet brush* painting style carries this freedom to its limit and, as the name aptly implies, the painting consists of solid blocks of enamels highlighted with veins and details usually in purple or puce. Rockwork, birds

Giles, James. One of a pair of hexagonal vases painted with extraordinary figures and birds, the gilded patterns on the blue grounds and the flower sprigs in the smaller panels offering the best clues to a Giles attribution, square marks, c.1765-70, 13½in. (34.5cm) high. (Sotheby's/Kiddell Papers.)*

and fruit painting are highly original and can be traced back to Giles decoration on Bow but not really directly back to Chelsea. Giles apparently never decorated Chelsea porcelain and there is no evidence to suggest that any of his artists worked previously at Chelsea.

The most significant clues to a Giles workshop attribution involve the four celebrated Grubbe* plates and two tea canisters which belonged to a descendant of James Giles, Mrs Dora Grubbe. The plates are in the Victoria and Albert Museum and are the starting point of detective work linking certain decorative motifs on the plates to similar motifs on other wares. The flowers, not only large 'divergent tulips' but, more importantly, very distinctive subsidiary sprigs, are the easiest purely Giles motifs to recognise.

Problems in identifying Giles wares stem also from the rivalry with the Worcester factory outlined here. It has been suggested that much of the 1769 sale catalogue lists pieces painted by Giles as well as at the factory. This seems highly unlikely, and I believe the factory was copying the London style of decoration when necessary just as Giles copied the factory's own most popular forms of decoration. Some patterns occur in distinctly varying versions originating from the different decorating establishments. Certain Chinese patterns are now attributable to Giles although it is dangerous to assume a pattern is London decorated just because it is strange.

The position is further complicated by a small group of pieces of Giles decorated porcelain, complete in themselves but to which a somewhat muddy green ground has been crudely added, not necessarily much later. The gilding on these pieces is usually of a very poor standard and yet has direct links with better quality Giles decoration. Possibly these crude decorations and added green grounds are the work of other London decorators trained by Giles, or former Giles workmen completing old stock after 1775. The presence of Fidelle Duvivier's* painting on Giles-related pieces indicates that artists at Giles' workshop came and went, and we know of other outside decorators who worked in London. Much care and a certain amount of scepticism must be exercised as there is still a great deal to learn about decorators of this period. Giles' work should not be confused with the red-line bordered group*, for instance.

Gillyflower Pattern

An old English name adapted from French for a carnation or pink. The pattern derives from French porcelain, principally Chantilly where it enjoyed great popularity in underglaze blue in the 1760s and 1770s. Worcester copied the pattern faithfully and with a certain amount of care on teawares, mugs* and small shapes such as pickle dishes* and asparagus servers.* These range from c.1770-85 as a painted pattern and also as a similar printed version. A companion motif of a narcissus is regularly encountered on larger painted pieces. The variations are discussed by Branyan, French and Sandon, pattern I.E.12. Derby made an identical pattern which was also copied at Caughley and Coalport.

Glaze-free Margins

To prevent glaze running down the inside of footrims and sticking pieces to the kiln during firing, the Worcester factory developed a method of wiping away the glaze from the inside of the feet before firing. This created a glaze-free margin around the inside of the footrim. This feature first occurs on Worcester teawares c.1758-60 and was used on virtually every product of the factory until the Flight period. While usually present on Worcester, these glaze-free margins do occur on Caughley and some Liverpool porcelain, however, and therefore no piece can be attributed solely on the presence of this feature. The glaze free margin is also known as 'pegging' or a pegged foot because of the assumption that it was a wooden peg which was used to wipe away the surplus glaze. It is more likely that some kind of glaze resistant material was painted around the inside angle of the footrim. This would have burnt away in the kiln and left an unobtrusive unglazed band underneath. From c.1770 a narrow yellow or orange line occurs encircling the unglazed margins. It has been suggested that this was caused when the glaze was wiped away by a metal

Gloster Shape. *A Grainger, Lee and Co. tea service of pattern no. 1855 including the rare form of teapot designed to accompany this shape. The Gloster shaped cups and saucers were more often supplied with principal pieces of different shapes. c.1830-5. (Geoffrey Godden.)*

stick instead of a wooden peg, but these marks are too even for this. Instead the fine yellow lines are probably the residue of some form of chemical used at the factory to repel the glaze when the piece was dipped into the glaze. This yellow line has also been seen on Caughley porcelain but is most usual at Worcester. The underside of the flange of Worcester teapot lids and other sizes of lids have similar removal of glaze after c.1765 with some having unglazed rims as early as c.1760.

The old belief that the glaze-free margin around the footrim was caused by glaze 'shrinkage' can be discounted. The presence of a pegged foot can be more clearly seen by drawing a lead pencil around the inside of the footrim, but this should be avoided. Such marks are virtually impossible to erase and can give a false impression of re-firing.

Gloster Shape

The most popular teaware shape made at Graingers in the 1830s was named Gloster (*sic*), presumably after the neighbouring city but always spelt without a letter 'u'. The rims feature undulating beaded sections divided by groups of two flowerheads and scrolls. A very similar shape was made at a number of factories including Derby, Davenport and Copeland and Garrett as well as in France and Russia, so attribution has to be based on an identical handle form and corresponding pattern number. The Grainger pattern books record the Gloster shape between pattern numbers 1791 and 2019 and then from 1x until at least 1314x. The leaf-moulded ring handle designed for the Gloster shape was used on four differently moulded cup shapes, making identification all the more difficult. In addition to the standard teaware shapes cup plates* and a honey pot* have been seen.

Gloucester, Duke of, Service. *This large fluted dish provided the painter with room for a particularly fine spray of fruit including spotted fruit*, gold crescent mark*, c.1770, 9⅞in. (25cm). (Phillips.)*

Gloucester, Duke of, Service

Probably the most lavish pattern occurring on Worcester porcelain in the 1770s (Colour Plate 49), it seems likely that just a single service was made for William Henry, Duke of Gloucester (1743-1805). The shapes used were standard dinner wares of c.1775 including gadroon-edged tureens, several sizes of lobed circular dishes and large rectangular platters. The design incorporates colourful spotted fruit* and border panels of scrollwork enclosing imaginary insects, within a rim of blue enamel and gold flecking. All known pieces are marked with a gold crescent*, confirming not only that this represents a special service but also suggesting that the decoration originated at the Worcester factory rather than in London. The old attribution to Giles* has mostly been discounted and nowadays a factory attribution is generally accepted. The service passed to the Dukes of Cambridge and seventy pieces were sold by their family at Christie's in 1904, along with a Chelsea set made for the Duke of Cambridge in similar style although in far less vibrant colours. A small number of pieces from the Duke of Gloucester service have also been passed to another descendant of George III. As the factory's first documented royal service, the design certainly does them proud, justifying the high prices paid for any specimens offered for sale today.

Goblets

These are uncommon shapes in porcelain, since glass has always been so much better suited for drinking wine. Flight and Barr did make elegant footed goblets to accompany presentation jugs and an example with shells by Samuel Smith* is illustrated in Colour Plate 78. Grainger made large

Gordon Service. *The plate on the right from the Gordon service, painted with a specimen of* Conus generalis, *contrasted with a similar unfinished plate with only the first firing of enamel colours completed, impressed* and printed marks, c.1812, 8¼in. (21cm). (Colin Harper Collection.)*

Grace Mugs. *One of a magnificent pair of early Grainger Grace mugs painted with fox hunting subjects, the gilding particularly rich, script marks Grainger & Co., 4½in. (11.5cm). (Phillips.)*

Grainger and Co. *An important documentary jug with fine gilding, the base inscribed 'Manufactur'd by Messrs Grainger & Co. Worcester May, 1809.' 6½in. (16.5cm). The entire factory had burnt down only the previous month yet clearly they were very much back in business. (Dyson Perrins Museum.)*

goblets as presentation or trophy cups and certain later Chamberlain ornamental chalices have been described as goblets. Generally, however, the items referred to in the Chamberlain records as goblets are more likely to have been of beaker or tumbler* shape.

Gold Crescent Marks

Marks carefully drawn in gold on only a small number of patterns produced c.1770. The Duke of Gloucester service* is a special production well deserving this special attention, the mark helping to confirm the theory that the pattern was decorated at the factory. The *Quail* pattern*, on the other hand, is a straightforward copy of the Japanese or Meissen original. Perhaps the mark was added to unmarked examples to distinguish Worcester's copies from Bow, Meissen, or indeed the Japanese. This theory makes sense in relation to the other two patterns which usually bear a gold crescent mark on dessert wares. The *Bishop Sumner** and *Brocade** patterns are both more or less exact copies of oriental originals although the colouring of each is certainly adapted for the benefit of Worcester's customers. Without the marks they could have been passed off for oriental, but why the factory bothered to mark only a few patterns in this way remains a mystery.

Gold Queen's Pattern

A simple design of gold petal-shaped panels used on plain and fluted shapes c.1770-90. The pattern is discussed under **Queen's Pattern**.

Gordon Service

A remarkable Barr, Flight and Barr dessert service was made c.1812 for the Gordon family and was sold in 1980 by Phillips in Scotland from the estate of a descendant, the Honourable Mrs Jock Leith of Glenkindie Castle, Aberdeenshire. The centres of each piece were painted with shells in the distinctive hand which has been attributed to John Barker* (*see* Colour Plate 76 and page 204). The marbled grounds* were reserved with the family crest within a neo-classical gold border.

Grace Mugs

Large cylindrical mugs of about two quart (2.2 litres) capacity were listed in the Chamberlain records as grace mugs, such as the pair made for Lord Nevill* in 1813, painted by Humphrey Chamberlain jun.* at a cost of £42. Most often painted with game or hunting scenes, grace mugs were also made at Graingers and at Flights. They were used to offer a toast after grace had been said and were passed around among the guests, sometimes several times. Some are also called toast mugs in factory lists. Clearly the original owners wanted to show off to their hunting guests and it is to be hoped that not too many of these impressive pieces of porcelain were shattered during such a celebration.

Grainger and Co.

All of the various partnerships involving Thomas and George Grainger* and their successors, from c.1805 until 1902, have at some time used the name Grainger and Co., either in written documents or as a name mark (Colour Plate 50). Only occasionally is the particular Grainger referred to and it is necessary to examine the style of decoration to determine the period of a Grainger and Co. piece. *See* **Grainger Factory**

Grainger Factory

In 1808 the *History of Worcester* listed the firm of Grainger, Wood and Wilkins in Lowesmoor. This is the earliest surviving reference to the partnership which had been formed by two former Chamberlain employees. After becoming a Freeman of the City of Worcester on 9 September 1805, Thomas Grainger* formed a partnership with John Wood* and Stephen Wilkins*. Their premises were near the canal by St Martin's Gate and Pheasant St. The first porcelain was probably produced in 1806 although the earliest documentary piece is dated 'Sepr 26 1807' (Colour Plate 50). Thomas

Grainger, George jun. *A biscuit* porcelain figure of 'Parisina' from a series of female figures made during the 1840s, the base incised 'Published by George Grainger, Worcester, Sep 14 1845' 11⅜in. (29cm). (Sotheby's, Belgravia.)*

Grainger and John Wood were the senior partners and the name marks 'Grainger Wood & Co.' or 'Grainger & Co.' were used up until 1811. In spite of a serious fire which destroyed the Grainger works on 25 April 1809, the firm was rebuilt and continued to produce porcelain in competition with Flight and Chamberlains. John Wood withdrew on 7 March 1811, and the factory then traded as Thomas Grainger and Co.* In October 1814 the firm became Grainger, Lee and Co.*, with the arrival of James Lee*, the son of John Lee*, an earlier backer of the company. James Lee was probably Thomas Grainger's brother-in-law and he remained at the factory until 1837 when he left Worcester. Thomas Grainger was then the sole proprietor of the factory, now known as Thomas Grainger and Co., until his death on 28 December 1839. His widow, Mary Ann Grainger, eventually sold her interest in the factory to her son, George Grainger*, in 1843. George Grainger was the firm's driving force for the next forty-five years, until his death on 14 July, 1888. The later production and fortunes of the Grainger factory, are discussed by Henry Sandon in Volume 2 of this *Dictionary* and are fully covered in our joint work *Grainger's Worcester Porcelain.*

Grainger, George and Co.
From December 1839, following the death of Thomas Grainger*, and certainly from March 1843 when George was in sole charge of the factory, the firm traded as George Grainger and Co. (Colour Plate 52). Many pieces were marked in this way or impressed with initials 'G G W S P' for George Grainger Worcester Semi Porcelain. George Grainger died in July 1888 and the factory was absorbed by the Worcester Royal Porcelain Company the following year.

Grainger, George jun.
The eldest son of Thomas Grainger*, George was born c.1812 and presumably served an apprenticeship under his father, learning all aspects of the family business. He was admitted Freeman of the City of Worcester on 14 July 1834. During his training, George Grainger painted some porcelain, for pattern 1601 from the mid-1820s is listed as 'Panels of roses, rose centre, brown leaves, by George Grainger'.

Following his father's death in December 1839, George ran the factory with his mother, Mary Grainger, until she sold her interest to him on 30 March 1843. From this date, apart from some sleeping partners, George Grainger was in sole charge of the factory for the rest of his life. His obituary following his death on 14 July 1888 stated that he was the oldest master potter in the country, a somewhat dubious claim. He was, however, responsible for introducing the semi-porcelain* body in 1848 and was proud of his chemical* or laboratory porcelain.

George Grainger's interests included music (he played the flute in the works band), racing greyhounds and, later, horticulture. He sat on the Town Council from 1864 and was elected as a magistrate in 1878, building up a reputation for extreme leniency towards all offenders who were brought before him.

In the year before he died, George Grainger brought his son Frank into full partnership and most probably would have been saddened by the thought that less than a year after his death his son would sell his beloved factory to the rival Worcester Royal Porcelain Company.

Grainger, George sen.
Records survive to show that George Grainger was apprenticed to Samuel Bradley* of Worcester in August 1767. He was possibly the George Grainger baptised at St Swithin's, Worcester, on 21 October 1754 but this would make him only twelve or just thirteen when he began his apprenticeship. He was taught china painting and presumably remained at the Worcester porcelain company until the departure of the Chamberlain family. George Grainger married Sarah Chamberlain, daughter of Robert Chamberlain sen.* on 30 March 1777. As his son, Thomas*, was himself apprenticed to the Chamberlains, it is clear where George Grainger's allegiance belonged. George Grainger is not mentioned in the Chamberlain archives and he died in 1797.

Grainger, Lee and Co.
The Lee in question is James Lee*, son of John Lee*, a previous backer of the firm of Thomas Grainger and Co.* The new partnership of Thomas Grainger* and James Lee commenced on 10 October 1814, although it is just possible that the new name was not fully adopted until 1 January 1817 when Joseph Gillam withdrew from partnership with Thomas Grainger and James Lee, also trading as Thomas Grainger and Co. Certainly from January 1817 until 1837 the firm used the script mark 'Grainger, Lee & Co.' on most of their ornamental production. Using a bone china body of varying

Grainger, Lee and Co. *A small vase following a classical shape, script mark Grainger Lee & Co, c.1820. The delicate flower painting is associated with David Evans* but became a Grainger factory feature and was clearly executed by a number of hands. (Bearnes, Torquay.)*

quality, the firm competed for the lower end of the fine porcelain market in Worcester. Their wares are discussed variously in this work, as well as in *Grainger's Worcester Porcelain.*

Grainger, Thomas and Co.
I believe that the name mark 'Thomas Grainger & Co.' was used between March 1811 and October 1814 and again from 1837, following the departure of James Lee*, up to Thomas Grainger's death on 28 December 1839. Thomas Grainger*

Grainger, Thomas. *An interesting trial mould for a teaware pattern, inscribed into the plaster 'Engraved by Thomas Grainger Sen. March 10th 1818'. (Dyson Perrins Museum.)*

Grainger, Lee and Co. *An elegant vase painted with the view of Worcester from the North-West which features on a great many Grainger pieces. This example is an impressive 23½in. (60cm) tall, script mark, c.1825. (Sotheby's.)*

had been the senior figure during all partnerships and at one point the Chamberlain records refer to Thomas Grainger and Co. in 1826 when the company was officially trading as Grainger, Lee and Co.* The rare mark of 'Thos. Grainger & Co.' should therefore be dated with caution.

Grainger, Thomas
The son of George Grainger sen.* and grandson of Robert Chamberlain sen.*, Thomas Grainger was born in 1783 and baptised on 22 August of that year. He was apprenticed to Robert Chamberlain sen.*, Robert Chamberlain jun.*, and Humphrey Chamberlain* in 1798 and seems to have been highly regarded by his employers, for the Chamberlain account books record him in 1803 as going on business journeys for his uncle. He was admitted Freeman of the City of Worcester on 9 September 1805 and wasted no time in leaving his employment to set up in business on his own, just as the Chamberlains had done. He took into partnership John

Wood*, also a china painter and probably the John Wood who was a figure painter at Chamberlains. They traded as Grainger, Wood and Co.* (or Grainger, Wood and Wilkins) and leased premises in Lowesmoor. I have recently received details of a letter in the Wedgwood archives sent by Thomas Grainger to Josiah Wedgwood in 1821 complaining about Wedgwood asking for payment in advance for a shipment of clay. He wrote:

> I beg to tell you that this is the 17th year I have been a manufacturer of china and until I rec[eive]d your [letter] never was asked for cash before I saw the goods...

This would mean that he began to make porcelain in 1805 but in spite of this claim I feel it is unlikely that any production could possibly have been under way until at least the middle of 1806, except possibly some decoration of Coalport blanks.

Thomas Grainger had served his apprenticeship as a china painter although no signed pieces are known. The only evidence of his skill as a practical potter is a trial mould for a teaware pattern inscribed 'Engraved by Thomas Grainger Sen. March 10 1818'. Thomas Grainger married Mary Anne Lee, probably the sister of James Lee*, his partner from 1814 until 1839. Thomas was always the senior partner in the factory up until his death on 28 December 1839. Mary, his widow, continued his work until March 1843 when she sold her interests to their son, George Grainger jun.*

Grainger, Wood and Co.
The partnership of Thomas Grainger*, John Wood* and various backers traded as Grainger, Wood and Co. from c.1805 until 7 March 1811 when John Wood withdrew. The name mark 'Grainger, Wood & Co.' was used on teawares and some ornamental porcelains during this period. Although Thomas Grainger claimed to have been a manufacturer of china from 1805, it is possible early marked examples are of Coalport porcelain decorated at Worcester. Grainger, Wood and Co. were certainly making their own wares by 1807.

Granby, Marquis of. *A rare version of the engraving by Hancock*, painted over in dry blue* enamel, the colouring and gilding possibly added in the Giles* workshop, c.1765, 3¼in. (8.3cm). (Sotheby's/Kiddell Papers.)*

Granby, Marquis of
The distinctive balding features of General John Manners, Marquis of Granby, occur frequently in English art in line with the enormous popularity of this nation's great military hero. Worcester produced an overglaze print of the Marquis in the early 1760s, although examples are relatively uncommon. The print was copied from Richard Houston's engraving of Sir Joshua Reynolds' portrait published in 1760 following General Manners' victory at Minden in 1759. The engraving on Worcester porcelain is almost certainly the work of Robert Hancock* and is usually found in conjunction with the same subsidiary prints of Fame and Mars as were used with the George II* and King of Prussia* prints. The Marquis of Granby is usually printed in black on cylindrical mugs although bell shapes and lilac prints have been recorded. One exceptional example now in the Dyson Perrins Museum has the print of the Marquis of Granby washed over in blue enamel but it is not possible to say if this was done at the time or very much later.

Granite China
Not a china but in fact an earthenware related to ironstone introduced by Chamberlain and Co.* in the 1840s in an attempt to compete with Staffordshire. It was opaque and somewhat coarse, far inferior to the Regent China* body, but was durable and stood up well to ordinary domestic use. The

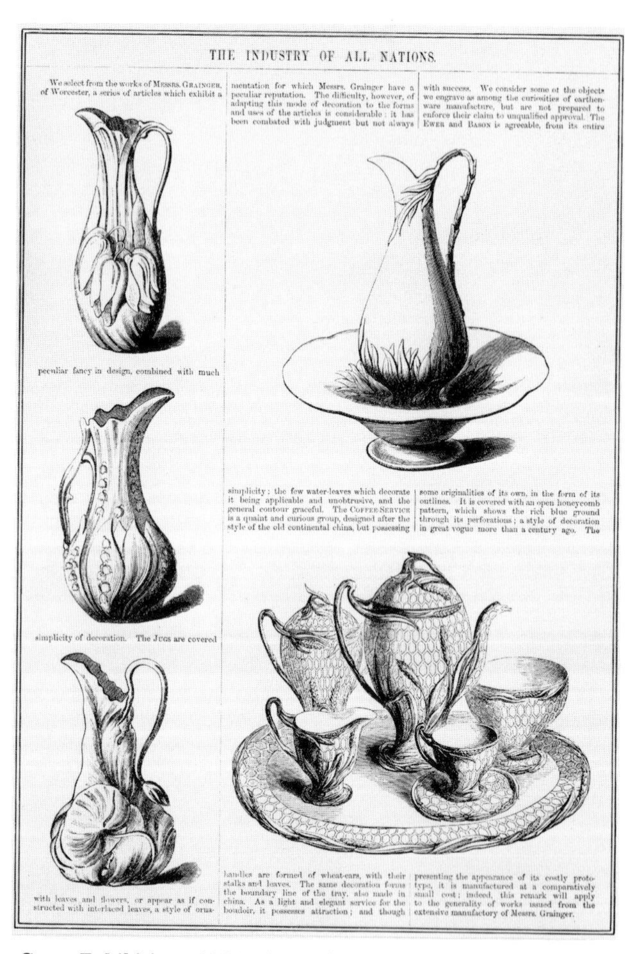

THE INDUSTRY OF ALL NATIONS.

We select from the works of MESSRS. GRAINGER, of Worcester, a series of articles which exhibit a peculiar fancy in design, combined with much simplicity of decoration. The JUGS are covered with leaves and flowers, or appear as if constructed with interlaced leaves, a style of ornamentation for which Messrs. Grainger have a peculiar reputation. The difficulty, however, of adapting this mode of decoration to the forms and uses of the articles is considerable: it has been combated with judgment but not always with success. We consider some of the objects we engrave as among the curiosities of earthenware manufacture, but are not prepared to enforce their claim to unqualified approval. The EWER and BASON is agreeable, from its entire simplicity: the few water-leaves which decorate it being applicable and unobtrusive, and the general contour graceful. The COFFEE-SERVICE is a quaint and curious group, designed after the style of the old continental china, but possessing some originalities of its own, in the form of its outlines. It is covered with an open honeycomb pattern, which shows the rich blue ground through its perforations; a style of decoration in great vogue more than a century ago. The handles are formed of wheat-ears, with their stalks and leaves. The same decoration forms the boundary line of the tray, also made in china. As a light and elegant service for the boudoir, it possesses attraction; and though presenting the appearance of its costly prototype, it is manufactured at a comparatively small cost; indeed, this remark will apply to the generality of works issued from the extensive manufactory of Messrs. Grainger.

Great Exhibition, 1851. *A page from the* Art-Journal Illustrated Catalogue *of the 1851 Exhibition. Grainger's jugs were much admired, although the public failed to share the judge's enthusiasm and examples are rarely seen.*

Colour Plate 48. ***Giles, James.*** *A very fine teapot in the Sèvres* style. The dry blue* flower painting, typical of the Giles workshop, includes a 'divergent tulip'*, crossed swords mark*, c.1770, 5½in. (14cm). (Powerhouse Museum, Sydney.)*

Grubbe Plates and Canisters. *The pair of tea canisters sold in 1952 by Mrs Grubbe, a descendant of James Giles*, c.1770, 5in. (12.5cm). The reverse panels are painted with fruit and flowers. These canisters together with the four 'Grubbe Plates' help to identify other pieces of Worcester porcelain decorated in the Giles workshop. (Sotheby's/Kiddell Papers.)*

fact that few examples have survived tends to confirm that this was a failure. Indeed, most attempts by the Worcester factories over the years to make earthenware were notably unsuccessful. R.W. Binns* was quick to halt production of Granite China when he joined with W.H. Kerr* in 1851.

Great Exhibition, 1851

As R.W. Binns* had arrived at Worcester in 1852 he felt able to speak frankly about the Chamberlain and Co. display the previous year. Binns wrote:

> Had the Great Exhibition taken place at a later period, we have no doubt that a respectable display would have been made, but that great manifestation was a trying ordeal for the Worcester Porcelain Works. With a few creditable specimens of their own manufacture, backed by some of the glories of former years... they passed muster, and received the not very high compliment of 'honourable mention'.

The only new work they had to show was some of their reticulated porcelain* which had itself been copied from Sèvres. Minton, Copeland and others proudly showed parian* and majolica ware. Meanwhile the Worcester Porcelain Company had to resort to showing specimens made thirty-five years earlier, reminding them of 'past triumphs and present deficiencies'.

George Grainger and Co., on the other hand, attracted reasonably complimentary criticism from the judges for their display at the 1851 exhibition, especially for their ingenious leaf and plant moulded jugs made in parian. The *Art-Journal Illustrated Catalogue* of the exhibition devoted a whole page to these wares (*see* page 184), remarking that they were manufactured at comparatively small cost. The judges concluded with the opinion:

> We consider some of the objects we engrave as among the curiosities of earthen-ware manufacture, but are not prepared to enforce their claim to unqualified approval.

Green, Valentine

An engraver who was born in Worcester in 1739 and was apprenticed to Robert Hancock* in 1760. He left Worcester in 1765, however, to pursue his career in London where he became a Fellow of the Society of Artists in 1767. Green was made an associate engraver of the Royal Academy in 1775 and was appointed mezzotinto engraver to George III* and Keeper of the British Institution in 1805. He died in 1813.

Green first published his *Survey of the City of Worcester* in 1764 including engravings mostly by Robert Hancock. This book included a detailed account of the processes used at the factory at that time (*see* Appendix 2). In spite of following his career in London, Valentine Green retained a great fondness for Worcester. In 1795 the first volume of his most impressive book was published. *The History and Antiquities of the City and Suburb of Worcester* contains numerous engravings by James

Ross* and others and includes also an extensive account of Flight and Barr's factory. Strangely the history of the firm is given only the briefest mention by a seemingly vindictive Valentine Green. He wrote:

> The original company confined themselves principally to making blue and white ware: and the very ingenious method of transferring the impressions from copper plates upon the inferior articles, was their invention, and for a long time known only in this manufactory: but the *present* proprietors have engaged in this arduous undertaking with the laudable ambition of not only improving the strength and colour of the ware, but also of giving the most liberal encouragement to ingenious painters in emblematical compositions, and in landscape.

It is unclear whether Green is referring still to printing when he talks about the improvement in the strength and colour of the ware. Possibly he referred to the stipple-engraved bat* prints which may have been introduced at this time. Green mentions that 'The process of printing the common ware, formerly kept a profound secret, is now openly shewn among the other operations of the manufactory.' Green was obviously interested in printing and it is possible that, as a specialist in mezzotints, he provided some of the stipple-engravings used by Flight and Barr for bat printing. Green was certainly a little biased towards the Flight concern as he gave the rival Chamberlain firm only a very slight mention in passing.

Grog
A name sometimes used in china factories for broken china, crushed-up and used in the body or glaze. Grog, having been fired once until vitrified, helps to reduce shrinkage. Dossie's *Handmaid of the Arts* published in 1764 described a porcelain factory near London (probably Bow) where Dossie saw 'eleven mills at work grinding pieces of the Eastern China...' The recipes supplied by Richard Holdship* to Duesbury when he went from Worcester to Derby in 1764 included 'Foreign China' as an important ingredient used in the glaze. This was literally crushed-up broken porcelain which had to be obtained by the factories. Evidence survives that Thomas Turner* bought broken Chinese porcelain at the ports, probably some that had been used as ballast in the East Indiamen. This was used in the Caughley formula in just the same way.

The broken Chinese porcelain found scattered on the Caughley and Worcester factory sites was not there, as has been wrongly supposed in the past, for the painters to copy from. Instead these fragments had fallen from the barrels before shipment to the crushing mills many miles away. Most of the factory's own glazed wasters were probably crushed in this way. My father and I once excavated the site of the Caughley crushing mill and found broken Chinese and Caughley porcelain as well as some Worcester, Chelsea, Bow, Lowestoft, Bristol and Meissen fragments. Two shards had rivet holes drilled in them, showing that the pieces had been acquired from a china mender and had proved too difficult to piece together. The presence of these imported pieces on porcelain factory sites does serve as a warning to all of us archaeologists that a glazed shard is not conclusive proof that matching wares were made on that site.

Grubbe Plates and Canisters
In 1935 Mrs Dora Edgell Grubbe, a direct descendant of James Giles*, presented to the Victoria and Albert Museum a collection of four lobe-edged plates which had been passed down in her family. According to family tradition these had been painted by Giles on the occasion of the marriage of his daughter. The plates were regarded as important pointers to identifying the work of the Giles workshop. Now that a great deal of work has been done to identify Giles characteristics there is no doubt whatever that the Grubbe plates were painted in his London workshop. Two of the plates are painted with figures in landscapes, one in green and black, the other in puce or carmine monochrome. The third plate had a scale ground* border in puce, blue and gold with central coloured sliced fruit* and flower sprigs. These all link closely with other Giles decoration although the fourth Grubbe plate, painted with dead game in a landscape and hanging from border festoons, has no known counterpart. The plates all date from c.1770.

The same Mrs Grubbe sold at Sotheby's in 1952 a pair of tea canisters which had also been in her family. These have a scale blue* ground and panels of children painted in colours. The gilding is elaborately tooled and again these relate to many other examples from the Giles workshop, in particular a part tea service in the collection of Her Majesty the Queen with similar so-called Teniers* figures. One of these canisters is now in the Rissik Marshall Collection at the Ashmolean Museum, Oxford.

Guglets
See **Bottles**

Colour Plate 49. **Gloucester, Duke of, Service.** A particularly fine spray of strawberries on a deep plate possibly for soup, the decoration attributed to the Worcester factory, gold crescent mark*, c.1770, 9in. (23cm). (Sotheby's, Rous Lench Collection.)

Colour Plate 50. **Grainger and Co.** An important early mug in Japan* style, inscribed under the base 'Grainger & Co. Worcester Sepr 26 1807', 5in. (12.75cm). This is the earliest known dated Grainger piece and uses a pattern which was very popular at Chamberlains. (Henry Sandon Collection.)

Colour Plate 51. ***Grainger Factory.*** *A thistle vase, unmarked but corresponding with the Grainger factory shape books, c.1840, 7⅝in. (19.5cm). Grainger specialised in eccentric plant forms such as this. (Formerly Author's Collection.)*

H

Hadley, J.

Extensive research in Worcester city records has failed to discover any information about an artist who signed landscape and flower paintings on Grainger porcelain c.1825. Clearly working as a free lance, J. Hadley's style suggests he trained in Worcester, probably at Graingers, although his name does not occur in any of the factory records. He is unlikely to have been related to the modeller James Hadley.

Hadley, J. *An English porcelain saucer painted with a crest and flower painting similar in style to Chamberlain, signed on the reverse J Hadley, c.1825. (Private Collection.)*

Half-shaded Bells

A decorative motif of a bell flower, one side cross-hatched, the other solid, is used as a border design on many Grainger vases and some teaware patterns from c.1812-25. The same motif was also used on pieces marked 'New China Works Worcester'* c.1820-5 but is rare on any other class of English porcelain.

Hampton, Charlotte

One of the most important figures working for Flights following the departure of the Chamberlain family. John Flight's diary* for 1 June 1789 records how he had been unable to agree with Chamberlain in Worcester and returned to London where he 'agreed with Mrs. Hampton to come down with us & teach us the Gilding & assist us for 3 years'. He goes on to remark that Mrs Hampton arrived on 6 June. On 21 June John Flight, complaining of Chamberlain's rivalry, states '...what we could have done had we not met with Mrs Hampton I cannot tell. I see no possible way by which we could have carried on the business'.

The original agreement drawn up between Charlotte Hampton and John and Joseph Flight has been discovered by Harry Frost. Dated 28 May 1789, it mentions that

> Charlotte Hampton hath long been experienced and conversant in the several arts of gilding china and also in preparing the gold and in firing and burnishing the same.

It is possible that Mrs Hampton had worked for John Flight earlier in London, decorating some of the French porcelain which he imported for his retail shop. The Chamberlains must have taken with them all of the senior gilders leaving no one at the Worcester factory to oversee this important work. Mrs Hampton remained in charge at least until 18 February 1791, when John Flight again wrote in his diary

> On Friday Mrs Hampton was taken very ill, so I was obliged to manage the burning of the (Gold) kiln: Fortunately, by the attention I have paid to this, was able to do it & I hope coud without much difficulty in case we were to loose her, but this I hope will not be the case as she is getting better. It would however, I fear put us to some inconvenience.

Mrs Hampton recovered but Flight tells us how his time had been pretty fully taken up while she had been confined. The diary ends at this point and so we know nothing of her stay at Worcester or her continued importance to the factory.

In a paper to the International Ceramics Fair in 1991 Harry Frost discussed the gilding found on Flight period porcelain and identified a change in the appearance of the gold. The new, brighter, flatter gold he attributes to the arrival in Worcester of Charlotte Hampton in 1789 and this seems a reasonable argument. It is possibly presumptive to refer to the new appearance as 'Hampton Gilding', however, as it is possible that the new gilding was in use at Worcester before 1789, especially as some gold on early Chamberlain porcelain can appear equally bright.

Hampton, Thomas

A Worcester saucer painted with a simple sprig pattern in green was given to the Dyson Perrins Museum by Robert Williams in memory of his mother, the porcelain dealer Winifred Williams. The underside of the saucer is carefully inscribed 'Tho's Hampton pinxt 1771'. Nothing else is known about this painter who probably signed this piece to mark the end of his apprenticeship, as it is the kind of pattern a junior hand would have executed. It is not known if Thomas was related to Charlotte Hampton* who was such an important decorator at Flight's factory.

***Hancock, Robert.** A black printed mug, the subject similar to signed engravings by Hancock after C. Fenn, c.1760, 3⅜in. (8.5cm). (Phillips.)*

Hancock, Robert
The most important engraver connected with English porcelain. He was born c.1730 and apprenticed 28 January 1746 to the Birmingham engraver George Anderson. It has been claimed that Hancock moved to Battersea at the time of the establishment of the enamel manufactory there in 1753 but there is no firm evidence for this. He must have had some London connections, however, as his work is associated with L.P. Boitard* and Simon-François Ravenet. These London artists and engravers greatly influenced the young Hancock as he copied their designs. Hancock's engravings after a Battersea artist, Charles Fenn, also place him in London around the time of the Battersea enamel works, but it is probable Robert Hancock returned to Birmingham to work with transfer printing* on enamel made locally. A few signed prints on enamel confirm his direct involvement with the enamel industry in Birmingham, even though most of the Hancock prints seen on enamel objects date from the period when he was at Worcester. Some prints by Hancock were used on Bow porcelain and factory site excavations indicate that these were printed at the Bow works. One example of the *Tea Party** print signed by Hancock is recorded in puce used on Bow. The dating of this again suggests that it was printed from copper plates engraved while Hancock was at Worcester rather than in London. Some engravings after Gravelot, however, do appear to have been used at Bow earlier than at Worcester.

It is probable that Hancock moved to Worcester in 1756. The following year he signed the engraved view of the Worcester Porcelain Manufactory (*see* **Warmstry House**) showing Mr Holdship's new building, the house Hancock subsequently bought. Richard and Josiah Holdship* were the largest shareholders of the Worcester company and it is likely that the two brothers oversaw the printing department. The famous King of Prussia* mugs are dated 1757 and important in that they are frequently signed with initials 'RH' for Robert Hancock together with an anchor rebus* to denote Holdship. *The Gentleman's Magazine* for December 1757 and *Berrow's Worcester Journal* in 1758 carried correspondence relating to these markings (*see* **Josiah Holdship**) suggesting an uncomfortable alliance existed between Hancock and Josiah Holdship. Only one such mug is known that bears the additional rebus of a hand and a cock, which leaves no doubt as to who was responsible.

The Holdships had probably introduced printing at Worcester and while the 1757 King of Prussia mugs are very fine, uncertainty remains as to where and when the earlier 'Smoky Primitive'* prints were carried out. Some early sauceboats bear prints by Hancock after Charles Fenn, and another designed by L.P. Boitard* includes his name in reverse. These relate to various prints by Hancock published in London in 1754 and others supplied to the London printseller Robert Sayer. The fact that Boitard's name is reversed means that the copper plates used had been engraved for printing on paper, not transfer printing on porcelain which always reversed the design. Either Hancock brought some of these copper plates to Worcester with him c.1756 or else prior to this date he supplied copies of the engravings to Holdship at Worcester at the same time as he supplied the Birmingham enamel works. The sauceboats bearing the Boitard name almost certainly pre-date 1756. Rare use of Hancock prints on Chinese porcelain, probably printed in London, further complicate the issue.

Richard Holdship's departure from Worcester in 1759 probably led to the elimination of the anchor rebus from some earlier copper plates. Hancock became the senior figure responsible for a very large output of designs. Many of his engravings were signed but it must be remembered that Hancock was not the only engraver at the factory. Valentine Green* was apprenticed to Hancock in 1760 and James Ross* in 1765. Thomas Turner* was also a pupil. All would have been trained to work in the same style and signed pieces by Ross bear witness to the skill of Hancock's gifted pupil. Unless a print is signed or can be linked to a signed piece by Hancock it should not be attributed to the master himself.

Robert Hancock purchased in March 1769 the large house previously built by Richard Holdship next to the Worcester factory. When the Worcester company was sold in January 1772 at the end of its lease, Robert Hancock became one of the new partners. In October 1774, however, it was agreed that 'to prevent further dispute' Hancock's share of one sixth was bought out by the remaining partners and he left Worcester shortly afterwards. Thomas Turner had left for Caughley by 1775 and Hancock joined him, possibly not at the Shropshire factory but as manager of the Salopian China Warehouse in Bridgnorth. Hancock's exact connection with Caughley is unclear as, although some of his engraved copper plates were later found at Coalport, none of Hancock's prints has been seen on Caughley porcelain; indeed, only a single overglaze-printed Caughley teapot is known and this was probably printed elsewhere.

Hobson's *Worcester Porcelain* recorded that Hancock lost all his savings (about £6,000) in a bank failure leaving him only with his house in Worcester which was probably let. He returned to Staffordshire and worked on book illustrations. Hancock had supplied engravings for many books including *Survey of the City of Worcester* published in 1764 by his pupil Valentine Green. Hancock exhibited pencil and crayon

Colour Plate 52. **Grainger, George and Co.** *Part of an important dessert and tea service presented by the City of Worcester to the Mayor, Alderman William Lewis, in recognition of his work towards bringing the railway to Worcester. Each piece carries the arms of the city and the centrepiece (top) is painted with the Guildhall, c.1840. (Private Collection.)*

Colour Plate 53. ***Honey Pots.*** *A Chamberlain beehive-shaped honey pot with botanical decoration*, the bees moulded in relief, marked Chamberlains Worcester, c.1815, 5½in. (14cm). (Private Collection.)*

portraits in 1796-8 and he exhibited at the Royal Academy in 1805. It is likely that a number of fine mezzotints formerly attributed to him are in fact the work of his sons. Robert Hancock died at Brislington near Bristol in 1817.

There are many gaps in our knowledge of Hancock's activities still to be filled. Two copper plates surviving at Worcester of the same subject were examined by Cyril Cook and Charles Dyson Perrins and found to be identical, although others have more recently doubted this. Whatever the case, Hancock probably had a method of copying his engravings on copper plates using etching techniques, following the lines of an original very closely. In this way he would have been able to sell the same print to more than one customer at the same time. For example, some of his work from Worcester was published by Robert Sayer in later editions of *The Ladies' Amusement* during the 1770s. By the same token the enamels printed at Birmingham can bear exactly the same subjects as Worcester porcelain, including the full length King of Prussia print dated 1757. More confusing is the connection with James Giles* who bought copper plates from Mr Thomas Turner at Worcester in 1772. Some of Hancock's prints could have been added to Worcester porcelain in London but at present there is no evidence to support this, except possibly the presence of coloured Hancock-type prints on moulded *Chrysanthemum** pattern teawares which are usually left white* and are quite unsuited to this form of decoration.

Hanover, King of, Service

The square dessert dish illustrated on page 195, when sold at Phillips, retained an old paper label on the back saying that it was part of a service made for the King of Hanover. A large part of a matching dinner service is in the collection of Her Majesty Queen Elizabeth the Queen Mother and corresponds to several orders in the Chamberlain archives c.1796, including a dessert service made for the Prince of Orange at Hampton Court. This popular design with border no. 66 includes full figure centres, the classical subjects being in the manner of John Wood*. Strangely, the royal service, said to

Hancock, Robert. *Two prints of waterfowl, subjects much favoured by Hancock, on a finger bowl and stand, c.1758; together with a tea canister of the* Gardener Grafting a Tree* *pattern attributed to Hancock, c.1765-70. (Phillips.)*

have been presented to the King of Hanover, is not listed in the Chamberlain order books. The factory usually wrote out such an important order most carefully and it is possible that the set was ordered through a china dealer. The King of Hanover was in fact a title rarely used by George III.*

Harvest Bug Pattern
See **Astley Pattern**

Hatherell, Anna
A Chamberlain toy* mug has been recorded, unmarked except for the name 'Anna Hatherell Sept. 1823' in red script on the base. It is well painted with roses and doves with the inscription 'L'Amitie'. This will be the work of an independent, probably amateur artist who may have received instruction in china painting at the Chamberlain factory.

Hayton, C.
The name C. Hayton appears under the base of Chamberlain porcelain painted in a style similar to the factory's own products. The archives show that Mr and Mrs C Hayton of Moreton not only bought white porcelain* but had some sort of arrangement between 1821 and 1825 for Chamberlain to fire the decoration and add gilding.* This unique partnership between maker and decorator produced some rich porcelain although the landscape views, principally country houses, have an amateur feel alongside better Worcester painting. Hayton's signed work also occurs on Staffordshire porcelain.

Hibiscus Pattern
See **Honeysuckle Pattern**

Holdship, Josiah
The younger brother of Richard Holdship*, Josiah was listed as a maltster when he signed the 1751 Articles for Carrying on the Worcester Tonquin Manufacture*, having bought a share worth £450. Richard Holdship was the principal backer of the company, particularly when the Bristol porcelain company was purchased in 1752. Josiah was involved with his brother who sold him a half share in his soaprock* licence for £700 on 25 March 1752. Josiah was also joint purchaser of Warmstry House* when the Holdships bought the freehold for £600 in 1759, presumably as Richard by this time was considerably overstretched financially. Josiah does not seem to have been affected by his brother's bankruptcy in 1761, and instead was responsible for petitioning against his brother in favour of Richard Holdship's wife Betty, suggesting considerable acrimony existed between the two brothers. Josiah remained in Worcester, most likely still connected with the factory.

Josiah Holdship was involved with his brother in the development of transfer printing* although it is very uncertain in what capacity. It is worth quoting again the celebrated verse by 'Cynthio' which appeared in *The Gentleman's Magazine* on 20 December 1757. These words were written 'on seeing an arm'd bust of the King of Prussia curiously imprinted on a porcelain cup of the Worcester manufacture... inscribed to Mr Josiah Holdship':

Hanover, King of, Service. *Two nymphs adorning satyr, after Angelica Kauffman, on a Chamberlain square dessert dish bearing an old label claiming this to be from a service given by George IV to the King of Hanover. The same subject also occurs on Caughley* porcelain decorated at Chamberlains, unmarked, c.1796, 8⅞in. (22.5cm). (Phillips.)*

Hayton, C. *A pair of chocolate cups painted with views of country houses, signed C Hayton, c.1820-5, 4⅛in. (10.5cm). The porcelain in this case is Staffordshire although Hayton arranged for some of his painting to be fired by Chamberlains. (Phillips.)*

Colour Plate 54. ***Ice Pails.*** *A Chamberlain dolphin ice pail with cover and liner, the* Dragon in Compartments* *pattern reserving the arms of Incledon quartering Newton, unmarked, c.1805, 13¾ in. (35cm). (Phillips.)*

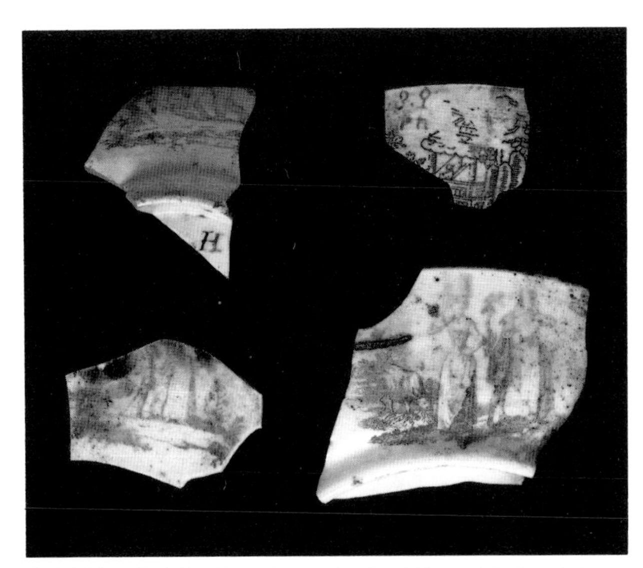

Holdship, Josiah. *Four fragments of printing trials found during excavations* on the Warmstry House* site and possibly connected in some way with Josiah Holdship. Top left: Venus and Cupid, in black signed 'IH'** (see *the mug illustrated under* **Blue Printing**)*; right:* Man in the Pavilion* *pattern, an underglaze trial inscribed with a code including 'i.h.'; bottom left: the rare pattern which Cook called 'Milkmaid and Page Number 1': right:* The Milkmaids* *print also in black.*

> What praise, ingenious Holdship! is thy due,
> Who first on porcelain the fair portrait drew!
> Who first alone to full perfection brought,
> The curious art, by rival numbers sought!

A different version of the verse was reproduced the following month in *Berrow's Worcester Journal*, by another anonymous writer signing as 'Philomath':

> What praise is thine, ingenious Holdship! who
> On the fair porcelain, the portrait drew?
> To thee, who first, in thy judicious mind,
> A perfect model of the art designed;
> An art which, long by curious artists sought,
> By thee alone to great perfection's brought.

A further two lines are added '*Extempore* on the compliment of imprinting the King of Prussia's bust being ascribed to Mr Josiah Holdship':

> Hancock, my friend, don't *grieve*, tho Holdship has the praise,
> 'Tis yours to execute, 'tis his to wear the bays.

Cynthio's verse gave Josiah Holdship the credit for the first printing on porcelain and for bringing this to perfection. Philomath has curiously changed this so that Holdship is just credited with perfecting the art, not of inventing it. Hancock* quite rightly is given credit for engraving the King of Prussia print concerned, but printing had been carried out at Worcester before Hancock arrived.

Forgetting for the moment claims for early printing on porcelain at Battersea or Birmingham, the question remains who invented transfer printing on Worcester porcelain, Richard or Josiah Holdship, or both together. The anchor rebus* probably refers just to Richard, who used it as his own mark at Derby. The rare double anchor rebus has to relate to them both but was used on only a single *Milkmaids** print, the second anchor apparently having been added subsequently to the copper plate. A new clue could lie in a letter from Martin Barr* to Ralph Wedgwood, and I am grateful to Gaye Blake-Roberts at the Wedgwood Museum for bringing it to my attention. It was sent to Ra: Wedgwood, Hill, Burslem, dated Worcester 14 June 1796. Barr is writing about patents for a form of printing and the need for secrecy. The letter is frustratingly cryptic except on one point...

> Remember, pray remember that that worthy *honest* man Josiah Holdship who first invented *printing* at Wor'r lost — mainly for want of *prudent care* upwards of thirteen thousand pounds which he was possessed of when he found out that art...

A small number of early trials for overglaze transfer prints were found during factory site excavations and are illustrated here. The engravings are probably by Robert Hancock but one experimental saucer fragment bearing on the under-rim a portion of a very rare print of Venus and Cupid is marked with a clear painted monogram 'IH'.* This could well be the signature of Josiah Holdship. The Venus and Cupid print (Cook, item 113) has only been recorded on the side of mugs with Queen Charlotte after an engraving dated 1762. The mugs therefore date after Richard Holdship had left Worcester. In the same illustration is a trial waster of an underglaze print of *Man in the Pavilion* pattern*, inscribed with code symbols including the letters 'i.h.' Could these also in some way be related to Josiah Holdship?

Josiah Holdship was still connected with Worcester in 1766 as this date appears on a unique sundial* painted with his name and now in the Dyson Perrins Museum. R.W. Binns noted that Josiah was a subscriber to the Worcester Infirmary in 1767 and that on his death in 1784 he bequeathed £100 to it. In fact Toppin showed that Josiah died on 7 January 1783, aged seventy-one. His will had been witnessed in May 1782 by William Davis* of the china factory, suggesting that Holdship had remained involved in some way. Josiah was unmarried and left £500 to his brother Richard as well as £50 each to Richard's five children. One of these was named Josiah, like his uncle, and was also involved in the china business. A letter from Martin Barr to Thomas Byerley at the Wedgwood Etruria works, dated 3 September 1798, includes the following:

> Mr Jos: Holdship who I understand is well known to you, called upon me today and showed me the enclosed stone, not as an article likely to be useful to me, but as what he apprehends will be of consequence in the Staffs manufactory... Mr Holdship is the principal speculator in the Cobalt mine concerning which there is so much expectation- so much so- that some persons from your county have endeavoured to supplant him by offering the Lords a large sum to be imployed in the concern. H...is being pressed for a decision concerning taking the lease of the cobalt mine....

Let us hope that the younger Josiah Holdship was more successful in his ventures than his father Richard had been forty years earlier.

Holdship, Richard

Richard Holdship was a successful and wealthy glover in the city of Worcester. He was a Quaker, born 1 May 1709. His involvement with the early years of the Worcester factory was not merely as a financial backer. Instead he was one of the most important single contributors. It was Holdship who took out a lease on Warmstry House* on 16 May 1751 on behalf of the future partners in the porcelain company. He leased the site from William Evett, another glover, for twenty-one years at a yearly rent of £30. The following month Richard Holdship paid one of the largest shares of £562.10s in the new company. The Articles for Carrying on the Worcester Tonquin Manufacture* confirm that Holdship had leased 'a certain house situate in the Parish of St Alban' commencing from the following month. Documents relating to Richard Holdship's bankruptcy ten years later help to fill in some of the details of

Holdship, Richard. *A dessert basket printed in black with the* Milkmaids* *pattern, signed with a reversed 'RH'* cipher and two anchors crossed. The double anchor rebus*, believed to refer to the two Holdship brothers, occurs only in conjunction with this print, c.1758, 7⅞in. (20cm). (Phillips.)*

this early period. Holdship had bought the 'stock, utensils and effects and the process of the said Bristol Manufactory' on behalf of the other Worcester partners on 21 February 1752. It has been suggested that because he was a Quaker he was able to strike a better deal for the Worcester partners but this is probably just speculation. Holdship himself had bought personally Benjamin Lund's* lease on the soaprock* mine called Kinance at Mullion on 6 February 1752. Richard Holdship agreed to sell to the other partners at least twenty tons of soaprock at £18 per ton as from the previous Christmas (25 December 1751). This was a way of compensating Holdship for the £1,700 of his own money he spent on purchasing the Bristol concern and the soaprock licence. On 25 March 1752 Richard Holdship assigned a half share in the soaprock mines to his brother Josiah* for £700.

In 1756 Richard Holdship bought some houses to the south of Warmstry House and erected a large and elegant mansion in their place. Robert Hancock's* engraving of the Worcester Porcelain Manufactory in 1757, illustrated under **Warmstry House,** shows 'Mr Holdship's new building' alongside. This 'large commodious dwelling house' possibly proved too expensive as Holdship's business interests fell apart. He bought the freehold of Warmstry House itself for £600 in 1759 but had to take his brother Josiah in as joint owner. Richard Holdship is believed to have left Worcester in 1759. By May 1760 he was bankrupt and the petition for his bankruptcy on 1 April 1761 was discovered by Aubrey Toppin, giving us considerable information about Holdship's business activities. It seems that to raise the capital to buy the Bristol factory and soaprock mines he had persuaded his wife Betty to sell some land she had inherited, for £1,500. In return Richard Holdship was supposed to pay £100 per year for twenty years into a trust for his wife, but had failed to do this. The bankruptcy court ordered this paid from the sale of soaprock to the Worcester company. Holdship sold his shares in the Worcester company to David Henry of London for a nominal 5s.

While at Worcester both of the Holdship brothers had been connected with the development of transfer printing. The anchor rebus* was undoubtedly used by Richard Holdship and a rare double anchor relates to Richard and Josiah together. The controversy over who should be credited with the discovery of printing at Worcester is discussed here under **Josiah Holdship.** The Holdships were most probably responsible for developing and carrying out the printing process while Robert Hancock* provided the engraved and etched plates. Richard Holdship was a competent engraver himself but certainly not in the same class as Hancock.

Holdship's work between leaving Worcester in 1759 and entering into an agreement with Duesbury and Heath at Derby in 1764 is unclear. A Derby mug printed with George III* and Charlotte* includes the mark 'Derby' together with Holdship's anchor. This is titled on a ribbon 'Crown'd Sept 22nd 1761' which can be taken to mean Holdship was at Derby by this date, although the inscription could be merely a commemoration and Holdship could have re-used old plates. An investigation of the similarity between Derby and Bow transfer prints, especially in blue, could provide a link and may fill the gap in our knowledge of Holdship's career. In his agreement with Duesbury, quoted by Jewitt in his *Ceramic Art of Great Britain*, Holdship is described as 'of the City of Worcester, china maker'. He agreed in return for £100 and £30 per year to provide in writing the 'process now pursued by him the said Richard Holdship, in the making of china or porcelain ware, agreeable to the proofs already made [by him] at the china manufactory of the said John Heath and William Duesbury in Derby'. He also agreed to supply them with as much soaprock as they needed, so Holdship had retained a licence to mine this stone. He was to print for Duesbury and Heath any porcelain which they wished to have printed and, although he remained at Derby until at least 1769, the quality of Holdship's printing was not always to the liking of Mr Duesbury. The recipes for making the porcelain as supplied to Derby were handed down to a descendant by Richard's brother, Josiah Holdship. These are reproduced by Binns and Hobson and show that Richard Holdship did indeed have an understanding of the formulae for making soaprock porcelain, even if Derby chose not to proceed with this.

Derby prints attributable to Richard Holdship include versions of Worcester's *La Dame Chinoise* and *L'Oiseau Chinois* (also found on Bow) and Hancock's *Rural Gambols* which at Derby were titled on the print itself 'Summer Amusements'. Some of these occur on Derbyshire creamware although it is uncertain where they were printed. The poor quality of these signed engravings compared to Worcester printing suggests that Richard Holdship did not do any engraving himself while at Worcester.

It is possible that Richard Holdship went to Caughley as his youngest daughter, Sophia, died unmarried at Coalport in 1836. Richard had five children, one of whom was named Josiah and followed his father's interests in clay and cobalt mining for the pottery trade. Richard Holdship died on 19 August 1785, aged seventy-six.

Honey Gilding

To make the gold metal suitable for ceramic decoration it is usually reduced to a sulphate resinate and suspended in a medium which will allow it to flow and then burn away in the kiln leaving the pure gold particles on the surface. In the 18th century the gold at Worcester was mixed with a form of honey which produced a thick gilding with a grainy texture. This can usually be felt proud of the surface and lacks the brilliance of London gilding which probably used oxide of mercury. At

Honey Gilding. *A coffee cup decorated at Worcester with a wet blue* ground and panels of animals, the gold scrollwork typical of the factory's slightly textured honey gilding, square mark*, c.1770, 2½in. (6.4cm). (Jill Gosling Antiques.)*

Sèvres crushed garlic was used as a medium and produced a somewhat similar effect to Worcester's honey gold. The Worcester factory changed over to mercury gilding* c.1788. *See also* **Gilding.**

Honey Pots
The earliest Worcester honey pots date from around 1790 and can be distinguished from butter pots by their domed covers and usually, but not always, by a hole for a spoon. I know of a single early Flight example with a plain coloured border, and several are known from c.1810 with domed lids on cylindrical bodies and fixed stands. Any Flight honey pot is a great rarity although Chamberlain rather more regularly included examples with breakfast services*. The service for Lord Nelson* ordered in 1802 included '2 large hives', an appropriate name as the model even included a number of realistic embossed bees. An example from a botanical service is illustrated in Colour Plate 53. The fashion for realistic beehive honey pots does not seem to have continued after the 1820s. The only Grainger honey pot known to me is in 'Gloster'* shape from c.1840 and this is of stylised domed shape modelled to match the rest of the breakfast service.

Honeysuckle Pattern
A simple pattern in Chinese *famille rose** style used early on at Worcester from c.1752-3 and continuing in a less freely painted version into the early 1760s. The design features an elaborate flower spray which is not strictly honeysuckle, nor is it hibiscus, the alternative name for the pattern used in the United States. A smaller spray of daisy- or chrysanthemum-like flowers is used to balance the design along with a ribboned emblem* and occasionally insects. The pattern was used on plain teaware shapes, larger bowls, and also several dry mustard pots* have been seen in the design, usually with a bird painted on the cover (illustrated on page 242).

Honeysuckle Pattern. *A teabowl and saucer painted in* famille rose* *enamels, c.1760. By this time the pattern had become more formal than examples from the early 1750s. (Sotheby's, New York.)*

Hope-Edwardes Pattern
A rich pattern of painted fruit within a shaped claret border heightened with tooled gold flowers and scrolls (*see* illustration on page 201). The name derives from a service said to have been made for Sir Thomas Edwardes, sold by his descendants who had assumed the name Hope-Edwardes in 1854. The pattern was painted in the Giles* workshop on a full range of dessert shapes and is also found on teawares in a distinctly different palette. Gerald Coke, in *In Search of James Giles*, identified the latter as the factory's own version, probably painted after the demise of Giles. Simon Spero, in his catalogue of the Klepser Collection, repeats this theory and relates the decoration on the Hope-Edwardes teawares to the Duke of Gloucester service*, now believed to be factory decoration. I find the comparison between these two designs much less apparent, however, and have to admit grave reservations about any teawares in the pattern. Many pieces show evidence of redecoration*, especially signs of the Queen's pattern* having been removed before repainting. Similar fruit painting and especially small flower sprigs in distinctive colours occur on other patterns generally condemned now as redecorated. I will avoid being dogmatic on what is after all a very controversial area, but instead I would advocate caution as, if these wares are redecorated, then this would probably have been at a very much later date.

Hope Service
The popular name for the Duke of Clarence service* ordered in 1791, with subjects of 'Hope and Patience' by John Pennington.* *See* Colour Plate 23.

Hopkins, Worcester
This very rare mark of an independent decorator occurs on two pieces of porcelain known to me. One is a tapering beaker of probable Flight manufacture gilded with a formal border and cipher within a wreath. This is marked in gold 'Hobkins [sic] Worcester'. In 1953 Cyril Shingler, then Curator of the Dyson Perrins Museum, recorded the cover of a sucrier which had been shown to him. This was oblong with a moulded finial which is not known to have been used at Worcester. This had simple gold sprigs and was marked in gold underneath 'Hopkins Worcester'. The mark could relate to a retailer but is much more likely to be a gilder working c.1805-10. An identical gilded pattern was used at Graingers.

(Opposite). Colour Plate 55. ***Japanese Porcelain, Replacements for.*** *A Worcester scalloped-edged dessert plate alongside an earlier Japanese coloured Arita porcelain dish from the same service. A number of replacement plates were apparently ordered from the Worcester factory, c.1765-70. (Private Collection.)*

(Opposite). Colour Plate 56. ***Japan Style.*** *A Flight and Barr combined dessert and tea service decorated with one of their most splendid and costly Japan patterns. The ice pail* is a most unusual form. Incised 'B' marks*, c.1800-3. The cup with a scroll handle is a Flight, Barr and Barr replacement. (Phillips.)*

Hope-Edwardes Pattern. *A milk jug decorated with colourful fruit in a manner which differs from Giles* fruit painting. Opinions are divided as to where and when such pieces were decorated, 4½in. (11.5cm). (Kenneth Klepser Collection.)*

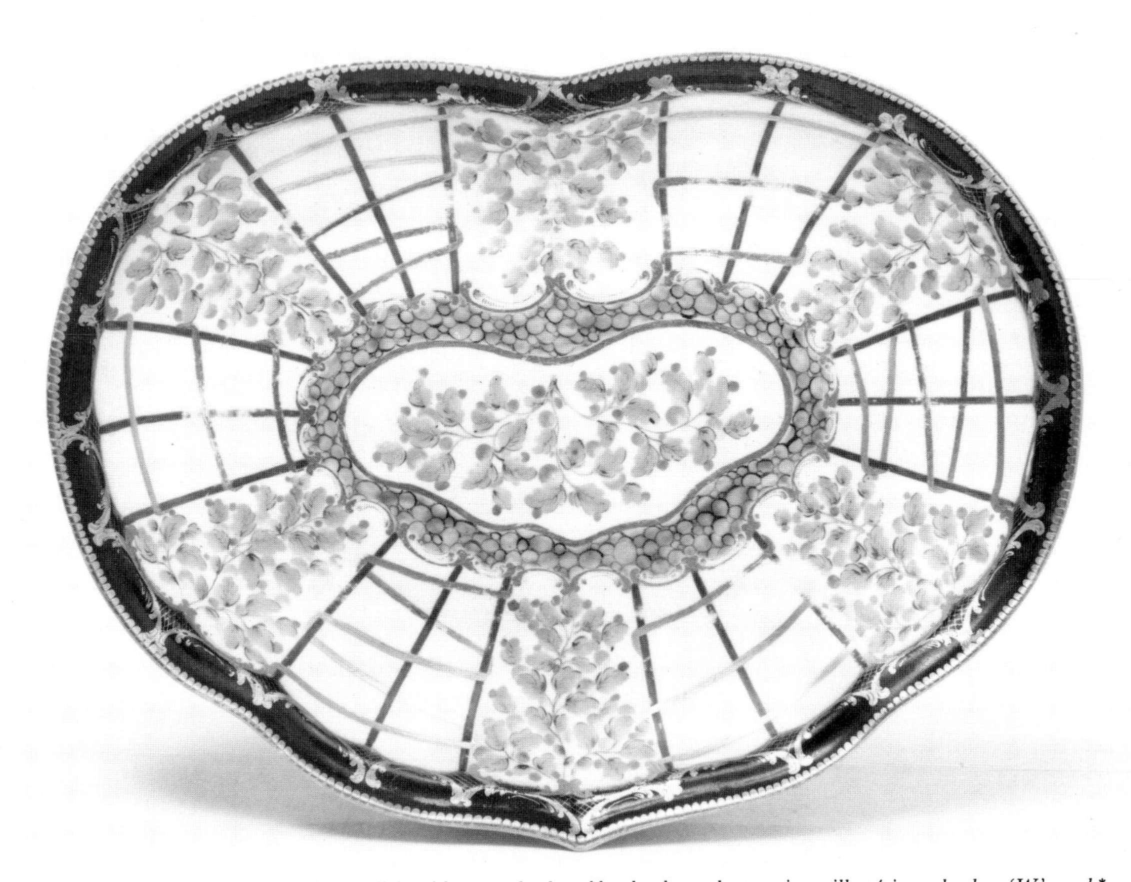

Hop Trellis Patterns. *A heart-shaped dessert dish with an underglaze blue border and turquoise caillouté inner border, 'W' mark*, c.1775, 10½in. (26.5cm). The many hop trellis type patterns are influenced by Sèvres* and, in spite of their popular name, are certainly not intended to represent hops. (Phillips.)*

Hop Trellis Patterns

The influence of Sèvres in the mid-1760s led to a spate of very decorative patterns in the French style. These depict garlands of green leaves dotted with red berries (Colour Plate 29). While it is clear that the designs are not meant to be representations of hop bines, the name has been associated with these patterns since the 19th century, in view of the importance of hop growing in Worcestershire.

Certain colour combinations are encountered more often than others, and the individual quality can vary greatly. The most popular borders are in a rich turquoise* ground with fine black scale patterns and a border in deep underglaze blue (*see* illustration on page 201). Occasionally an overglaze dark blue was used for the border and this could be one of the Giles* versions which are very difficult to distinguish. Only very rarely has an exact parallel been encountered in Sèvres for any of the Worcester versions which mostly date from c.1770-80. Some are clearly later, however, even into the Flight period in the 1790s. Flight, Barr and Barr, and later Chamberlain and Royal Worcester replacements are known, as well as several versions copied at Derby.

Some care has to be taken as certain hop trellis type patterns show evidence of re-firing. Simple patterns such as a popular turquoise and white chain border or French green* dog tooth borders have had coloured trellis and berried garlands added to link the existing outer and inner border designs. These additions seem to be of much later date and were therefore done to deceive.

Hors d'Oeuvres sets. *A rare complete set of seven dishes painted in underglaze blue*. Notice the two different shapes of fan-shaped dishes which usually occur together in the same sets. The central star-shaped dish is particularly rare, workmen's marks*, c.1758-60, about 8½ in. (22cm) diameter. (Present whereabouts unknown.)*

Horner of Mells

The name given to a pattern of fruit and flower sprigs painted in a distinctive palette of two tones of green outlined in purple. The painting is in the unmistakable style of the Giles* workshop and is usually found on dessert wares although rare teawares and pierced baskets are known. A service of the pattern belonged to Sir John Horner of Mells who is believed to have been the original 'Little Jack Horner' of nursery rhyme fame.

Hors d'Oeuvres Sets

While single fan-shaped dishes are frequently seen, a complete set of blue and white hors d'oeuvres dishes is a very great rarity. Made from c.1758-65, they occur in only a single pattern for the side dishes and a different but related design for the star-shaped centres. The patterns are listed in Branyan, French and Sandon as I.D.24 and I.C.9 where they illustrate a matching factory waster. The shapes were thinly cast and probably difficult to make, consequently none is known from any other English porcelain factory although related shapes are known in creamware and pearlware.

Hot Cross Bun Buds. *A waster* from a tureen cover, c.1770, found during factory site excavations*, photographed alongside an early Chamberlain dessert basket, c.1795. Despite the time difference the flower modelling, including hot cross bun buds, is closely related and is probably the work of John Toulouse*. (Photograph Chris Halton.)*

Hot Cross Bun Buds

A distinctive feature of Worcester flower modelling from c.1768-72 is the presence of small buds made of balls of clay, each cut with a cross or three-pointed star. They reminded early collectors of the popular cakes eaten at Easter time. These buds occur among the flowers on dessert baskets, chestnut baskets* (*see* Colour Plate 21) and elaborate frill vases* (*see* Colour Plate 85), pieces which very occasionally are marked with the 'To'*, 'T' or 'IT' marks. C.W. Dyson Perrins and other collectors realised that the same buds appear on some figures* and began a series of investigations which led to the identification of most of the Worcester figures. It was also realised that similar 'To' marks and flowers occur on Champion Bristol and Caughley porcelain. Two white* models of kingfishers were found to have similar hot cross bun buds and at the time were also attributed to early Worcester. Geoffrey Godden's research has since correctly identified these kingfishers as Chamberlain, c.1790-2 and he has recorded identical flowers and buds on some early Chamberlain dessert baskets. The hot cross bun buds were one of the vital links in the detective work which has now re-identified the modeller called 'Tebo' as John Toulouse*.

Hundred Antiques Pattern. *A circular dessert dish or possibly a junket* dish, carefully painted in bright blue, pseudo Chinese mark, c.1775, 10¼in. (26cm). (Sotheby's.)*

Huntley, Marchioness of, Pattern. *A shell-shaped dessert dish with apple green* borders and spiralling flower festoons, c.1770, 7½in. (19cm). (Sotheby's/Kiddell Papers.)*

Hot Water Plates and Dishes
Larger dinner services from the Chamberlain factory sometimes included hot water plates which were the same size as a normal dinner plate but contained a compartment for hot water underneath, filled from a small pouring lip. The lip was sealed with a cork during use and the hot water helped to keep the meal hot. Also called water plates in the Chamberlain records, they were expensive and are consequently rare today. The service made for the Nabob of the Carnatic* in 1820 contained many dozens of these shapes as well as hot water dishes in several sizes. These were large serving dishes which fitted into oval troughs filled with hot water and a domed cover was placed over the food. These were first made in the 1790s and are also great rarities. Flight and Grainger are not known to have made any hot water plates.

Houses
See **Cottages**

Hundred Antiques Pattern
A direct copy in underglaze blue of a Chinese porcelain pattern used on dessert ware from c.1768-85. The design uses a variety of Buddhist symbols and 'Precious Objects' frequently encountered in Chinese porcelain although the exact prototype is very rarely seen. A Chinese plate in the Victoria and Albert Museum from the *Qianlong* period is painted with a design which is very close to the Worcester pattern. When copied at Worcester the pattern always included a distinctive mark, loosely based on a Chinese character mark but with no apparent meaning, even though some sort of date code has been suggested. The pattern is listed by Branyan, French and Sandon as I.F.2.

Hunting Pattern
See **Staghunt Pattern**

Huntley, Marchioness of, Pattern
Worcester's distinctive apple green* ground used as a thick rococo border edged with gold scrollwork and hung with spiralling festoons of coloured flowers. It was decorated at the Worcester factory c.1770 on the full range of dessert wares including baskets* and ice pails*. The pattern is named after the second wife of the tenth marquis who sold a service of the pattern in 1882. It was clearly a popular design, however, and many such services must have been made. Several Flight, Barr and Barr replacement pieces have been seen bearing impressed marks*.

I

'I H' Marks

When Neal French examined the different forms of workmen's marks* following the major factory site excavations* he realised that they form distinct groups. The largest group by far is the 'I H' group and in the revised edition of *Worcester Blue and White Porcelain* (Branyan, French and Sandon, 1990) he has drawn about twenty different marks which could in some way be interpreted as an 'I H' monogram. These were painted by different hands on different patterns, possibly to refer to a particular department or supervisor, but we can only speculate as to the meaning. They are not factory marks in the true sense. An underglaze transfer-printed 'trial' waster for a Chinese style pattern found on the factory site includes the initials 'I H' as some kind of code and this is illustrated here on page 197. The initials could, of course, relate to Josiah Holdship*, a senior partner in the company who is known to have had interests in cobalt mines. He also claimed to have invented printing on porcelain and the 'I H' marked printed waster is clearly an experimental trial for early blue printing. There is absolutely no reason to link the Worcester workmen's marks with the moulded initials 'I H' which occur on certain Lowestoft embossed patterns in the early 1760s.

Ice Coolers

See **Ice Pails**

Ice Cups

Probably used for an ice cream or sorbet, these small bell-shaped cups with scroll handles originated at Sèvres and were served on a flat tray holding six or more cups. The only two Worcester examples known to me were included with identical Sèvres cups in a dinner service of 18th century Sèvres *Feuilles de Choux* pattern sold at Phillips in 1981. The Sèvres set carried date letters ranging from 1767 to 1778, which suggests the Worcester replacements were later, probably c.1778-80. Worcester rarely made such careful copies of shapes as replacements, but in this case the Worcester copies could hardly be distinguished from the originals. The Derby factory was willing to replace almost any shape and several sets of similar shaped Derby ice cups are known from c.1790. A similar shape was also made at Caughley and has in the past been incorrectly called an egg cup.* The Chamberlain stocklist for 1795 includes '2 dozen of ice cup and covers 16s.' but these will be the shape we now know as custard cups.*

Ice Cups. *A Worcester ice cup made as an exact replacement for a Sèvres* ice cup or* tasse à glace *with overglaze blue* feuilles de choux *decoration, c.1778-80, 2½in. (6.5cm). (Phillips.)*

Ice Pails. *One of a pair of Barr, Flight and Barr ice pails from the Gordon* service, the finely painted shell panels painted by a hand attributed to John Barker*. This example with satyr mask handles is complete with its original liner, full script marks, c.1812, about 11½in. (29cm) high overall. (Phillips, Edinburgh.)*

Ice Pails. *A magnificent pair of Grainger, Lee and Co. ice pails of full gadroon shape, painted with named views of Lynmouth and Linton, Devonshire, and Rue Castiglione, script marks, c.1820, 14½in.(37cm). Grainger ice pails are particularly rare. (Phillips.)*

Ice Pails

Larger dessert services were always supplied with a pair of ice pails and it has to be remembered that these services were for fruit. The purpose was to serve cool fruit and possibly ice cream and the pails work by filling the bodies with crushed ice or iced water and placing the fruit in the bowl-shaped liner. The sunken centres of ice pail covers were also originally intended to be filled with ice for additional refrigeration but many shapes became too intricate and the rim of the cover is often purely ornamental. Ice pails should not be confused with wine coolers*, as wine was never placed in the liner of an ice pail, even though it is possible that the bases of ice pails alone could be used as wine coolers.

The earliest Worcester ice pails are great rarities which seem to date from c.1776-80 although there has been a tendency to attribute such pieces to 1770 or earlier. The shape at this time copied Sèvres with 'U' shaped bodies and heart-shaped scroll finials set into the centres of the covers. The handles are usually slender square loops although scallop shell handles have also been seen. Examples are known with rich blue grounds and bird decoration as well as more simple coloured flowers and in underglaze blue with the *Gillyflower** pattern. The same shape was also made at Caughley.

Flight and Barr and later Flight factory ice pails tend to be more varied than Chamberlains (*see* Colour Plate 56), and it almost seems intentional that they should serve as vases when not in use, the decoration being always of the highest quality. The classical campana vase shapes came with plain or ram's head handles and were raised on square plinths. Others were more squat with scroll handles or with twisted handles based on the Warwick vase.*

Chamberlain started by introducing a fairly plain shaped ice pail c.1792, decorated with stiff leaf moulding around the base. I have seen a most elegant pair of these in *Dragon in Compartments** pattern. By 1800 the dolphin ice pail had become standard, with a pierced cover, mermaid handles and supported on three gilded dolphin feet, which look magnificent even though they presented the decorator with a difficult task of fitting in painted panels between the dolphin's tails (Colour Plate 54). From at least 1813 the dolphin shape was replaced by one of two ice pail shapes Chamberlain made that copied the Warwick vase. As the ice pails had to match dessert services the sides of the Warwick vases were left plain with only the applied vine borders. A more faithful copy of the famous vase was made as a wine cooler complete with modelled heads. Other factories joined in the fashion to make Warwick vase ice pails and it is fortunate that Worcester examples are invariably marked.

Grainger made relatively few dessert services and ice pails are very rare. One plain shape on bun feet from c.1815 is marked 'Grainger 'Ice Box, Worcester' inside the lid. Grainger's elaborate 'Full Gadroon' dessert services c.1820 occasionally included impressive ice pails of vase shape with lion mask handles. The Grainger body at this time does not

Imari. *A direct copy of a Japanese Imari pattern on a Worcester plate, using an overglaze blue enamel which suggests outside decoration, possibly in the Giles* workshop, c.1770, 9in. (23cm). (Phillips.)*

seem to have stood up to use very well, however, and the cold probably caused the ice pails to crack. Certainly every Grainger ice pail I have seen has been very badly cracked.

Ice pails went out of fashion by the late 1820s and only very occasional references to them are made after this date.

Imari

A style of decoration based on a type of early Japanese porcelain, decorated primarily in red, blue and gold. The name Imari derives from the port where it is believed the wares originated but the Japanese porcelain was actually made at Arita and often shipped via Chinese trading ports. The Chinese copied the Japanese designs in the Imari style for shipment to Europe and when these arrived there was considerable confusion. Meissen, other German, Dutch and English copies were made, variously described as Imari or Japan. The terminology remains confused. Some collectors believe that Imari patterns should only include underglaze blue, red and/or orange enamel and gold. Technically this is probably correct. Many other patterns have green and purple included also, as well as, occasionally, yellow, colours unknown in the original Arita porcelain. These were known in England as *Japan** patterns. Original 18th century Worcester records do not use the term Imari but group all Japanese designs together under the name Japan. Several of these are in fact purely Imari in their palette, however, such as the *Queen*

Imari. *A combined dinner and dessert service decorated with Chamberlain's most popular Imari pattern, coloured in red and gold over a printed outline, red script and printed marks, c.1820. (Phillips.)*

Inkstands. *An unusual Grainger rectangular inkstand in Continental style with stripes in deep ultramarine and gold, marked G Grainger, Royal Porcelain Works, Worcester, c.1840, 11¼in. (28.5cm). (Private Collection.)*

*Charlotte** pattern and a rare design featuring four carp among waves. Other very rare Imari designs are recorded, probably as direct replacements for Japanese services. A series of large lobed plates c.1770 were decorated with a complicated floral design in overglaze blue enamel, red and gold and these have been attributed to Giles.* In the later Regency period more colours were preferred and the bright patterns made by Flight and Chamberlain should be more correctly termed Japan.

Immortelle Pattern
A blue and white pattern with a direct Continental origin. First used at Meissen c.1730, the pattern on finely ribbed teawares was copied by several lesser German factories and became famous at the Copenhagen factory. Worcester copied the shape in the early 1760s and introduced the blue pattern about a decade later. Most examples seen are from the 1780s, however, and as many sets now turn up in Holland it is likely that the pattern in Continental taste was intended from the outset for export. The name derives from a small alpine flower and the pattern is listed as I.F.10 in Branyan, French and Sandon.

Impressed Marks
Marks pressed or stamped into the wet clay occur first at the start of the Barr, Flight and Barr period c.1804, when the initials 'BFB' were impressed below a crown. Very occasionally the crown was impressed by itself. The letters were changed to 'FBB' at the commencement of the Flight, Barr and Barr period in 1813 and this mark continued until 1840. The Chamberlain factory used their name impressed only during the last phase of the factory after 1840, stamping their wares either with 'Chamberlain & Co' or 'Chamberlains' in upper case. Grainger only used impressed marks on animal models* and some figures* during the Grainger, Lee and Co. period, the mark having been adapted in c.1837 by removing Lee's name from the stamp to make it Grainger & Co. The mark of the modeller or repairer believed to be John Toulouse* is often impressed, *see* **'To' mark.**

Indian Style
It seems likely that contemporary references to India or Indian style describe patterns inspired by Chinese *famille rose.** Generally speaking, by the early 19th century the term Nankin was used for blue and white patterns and Japan* or Imari* for copies of Japanese. These porcelains had all been brought to England by the East India Company and there was considerable uncertainty in most people's minds as to just where India was. The best known Indian pattern, Indian Tree which enjoyed widespread popularity, was not apparently used at Worcester. Instead, Worcester's most popular India design was *Old India** used at Graingers c.1812-25, an adapted Chinese pattern printed in blue and coloured in a pale *famille rose* palette.

Inkstands
Elaborate desk items with more than one inkwell* tend to be referred to as inkstands, although there are no hard and fast guidelines to the use of the term. Barr, Flight and Barr and Flight, Barr and Barr produced simple shapes with only two covered wells and very rarely a pounce pot* replacing one of the wells. Classical heads or snake handles added ornament but the main decoration was painted on the front panels. Chamberlain produced more elaborate shapes with three covered wells or one pounce pot and often a pen tray included along the front. The 'fine new ink' listed in the Marquis of Abergavenny (*see* **Nevill, Lord,** and Colour Plate 63) order in 1814 included the full crest of the marquis modelled as a cover, and other crests have been noted used in the same way. Later Chamberlain inkstands follow the styles of the time in revived rococo*, some with modelled flowers. Grainger examples are very rare and also very individual, although loosely based on Derby porcelain. Novelty inkstands were introduced during the Chamberlain and Co period, including a hunting design with a stag trophy, and the extraordinary King John's Tomb* inkstand which continued into the Kerr and Binns period.

Inkwells
Rarities from any factory in the 18th century, Worcester produced few inkwells before about 1810. Early shapes have a very individual hand-thrown feel and follow a basic drum shape with a central well surrounded by quill holes. Examples are decorated mostly in blue with standard patterns. Some examples have a detachable central well, such as a blue and white inkwell in the Dyson Perrins Museum, which is inscribed 'WPC', presumably for Worcester Porcelain Company. Very occasionally coloured ground or rich scale blue decoration has been noted on inkwells, c.1768-75.

The French shape of drum inkwell with side handle and pouches for pounce was introduced at Coalport and elsewhere around 1795 and adapted by Barr, Flight and Barr. Care must be taken in attributing unmarked examples, as many have in the past been incorrectly identified as Worcester. Certain shapes became standard during the Regency period. Chamberlain favoured a plain circular drum inkwell with central conical well and three evenly spaced quill holes; this form was produced from about 1805 until the 1840s. Flight and Barr made a more waisted version which is rather less common. Both factories produced elaborate covered inkwells with handles in a number of forms as well as multiple inkwells, discussed here under **Inkstands**. Single Grainger inkwells are not recorded although they did make several interesting patented inkwells with metal fittings, dating from the 1840s.

J

Jabberwocky Pattern

The image of Lewis Carroll's fantasy verse is aptly conjured up by this pattern which was loosely based on Japanese *Kakiemon**. The dragon-like bird and rich foliage owes much of its inspiration to Meissen, however. It was used primarily on wide-fluted teawares c.1768-70, the border of turquoise rococo and diaper panels adding a distinctive frame to the design. The 1769 sale catalogue of Worcester porcelain at Christie's included a set of 'fine old rich dragon pattern, bleu celeste borders', clearly a description of this design which was decorated at the factory. Giles* made a version of the pattern, more often on dessert wares, and some lobed dinner plates of factory decoration appear to date as late as c.1780.

Japanese Porcelain, Replacements for

The Worcester factory and Giles* both copied a great deal of oriental porcelain, for full production and as replacements for existing services. Most direct copies were Chinese (*see* **Chinese Porcelain, Replacements for**), but some instances are known where Japanese prototypes were copied also. Trade with Japan had been suspended since the early 18th century and all Japanese services in use in England would have pre-dated this. By the middle of the century early *Imari** and *Kakiemon** wares had been collectable and highly prized, with owners unable to obtain replacements from Japan. Colour Plate 55 shows a Japanese *Arita* dish, c.1700, together with a Worcester plate of c.1765-70. These have remained together as part of a set with a number of Worcester additions, in this case on standard Worcester shapes. Some of the more unusual *Imari* patterns made at Worcester could well have been made as replacements rather than just as copies for sale.

Japan Style

The various 18th century sales catalogues for Worcester porcelain as well as the Chamberlain account books show that the term 'Japan' was used for any pattern in the style of Japanese porcelain. These ranged from direct copies of *Arita* and *Kakiemon**, others in Imari* palette, and certain of Worcester's purely fanciful adaptations partly inspired by Meissen. Names such as *Fine Old Japan Star, Old Rich Mosaic Japan, Old Japan Fan* and *Scarlet Japan* pattern conjure up exact designs well known to collectors today, popular from c.1770. Chamberlain pattern 240, used for the Nelson service* was called *Fine Old Japan* pattern and does indeed derive from a much earlier Japanese *Arita* design. In an attempt at some sort of classification I prefer the term Imari for any design purely in blue, red and/or orange and gold: the name Japan I use for patterns including any other colours (Colour Plate 56). Pure copies of *Kakiemon** do not really count as Japan patterns and I prefer also to use the term 'Rich Kakiemon'* for Worcester's

Jabberwocky Pattern. *A part tea service decorated with the popular pattern in* Rich Kakiemon* *style, the border in bright turquoise, c.1765-70. (Phillips.)*

Japan Style. *A Chamberlain 'Regent' vase decorated with their popular* Fine Old Japan *pattern which is rarely seen on ornamental wares, script mark and pattern number* 240, 10⅝in. (27cm). (Phillips.)*

Japan Style. *A Flight and Barr armorial* plate, the elaborate coat of arms almost smothered by the richness of the border decoration. Close examination reveals three birds and banded hedges within the border, incised 'B' mark, c.1800, 9¼in. (23.5cm). (Bonhams.)*

Jars and Covers. *A pair of ornamental covered jars of uncertain use, decorated in the Giles* workshop with characteristic bird and floral painting, square marks*, c.1770-5, 4in. (10cm) high. (Sotheby's, New York.)*

adaptations such as the *Phoenix** or *Jabberwocky** patterns.

The situation is further confused by contemporary descriptions such as India, as in the case of the *Finger and Thumb** pattern which is listed in Chamberlain as 'India Thumb and Finger'. I fear therefore that it will never be possible to categorise satisfactorily the vast number of very different oriental inspired patterns made at Worcester.

Jars and Covers

References to jars in the 1769 Worcester sale catalogue probably relate to vases, used for ornament rather than storage. However, there are some covered vessels made at Worcester which are of uncertain use but must have been functional in some way. The pot with a domed cover and acorn finial, illustrated under **Fence Pattern**, is too tall probably to be a sucrier and has not been seen as part of any existing set. The pair of scale blue ground jars illustrated on page 209 were sold in 1990 as sugar bowls but the fact that they occurred as a matching pair tends to refute this. Instead the covers have applied rings which meant that they could be reversed to form saucer-like stands. The very rich decoration, typical of the Giles* workshop c.1770, suggests that these were largely ornamental. No other examples have apparently been recorded.

Jardinières. *A rare shape of jardinière and matching saucer-shaped stand, painted with a loose style of flower painting probably decorated at the Worcester factory, c.1775, 4in. (10cm). (Phillips.)*

Jardinières. *A large octagonal jardinière painted in underglaze blue* with an adaptation of a Japanese design, crescent mark*, c.1760-5, 10⅞in. (27.5cm). Originally this would have rested on a matching stand. (Zorensky Collection.)*

Jardinières

While the French terms *jardinière* and *cache pot* are commonly used today, the Chamberlain factory preferred the name root pot for open plant pots on separate stands. The pots themselves have a drainage hole in the base and would have been used for bulbs rather than for cut flowers. Massive octagonal jardinières on shallow stands were made in the 1760s in a blue and white pattern of *Fancy Birds** copying *Kakiemon** originally. Very few are known today and considering how badly the example in the Rous Lench

Jardinières. *One of a pair of Flight and Barr jardinières on fixed, spreading feet, painted in monochrome probably by John Pennington*, incised 'B' marks* and painted titles, c.1795, 5½in. (14cm). (Phillips.)*

Jesuit Style. Although not a biblical subject, the term Jesuit is still used by Worcester collectors to refer to all pencilled figure subjects in the style of Chinese export porcelain. In this case the original Chinese design copied a print representing 'Water from the Elements' and the Worcester teabowl and saucer is probably a straightforward replacement, c.1765. (Dyson Perrins Museum.)*

Collection had distorted and blurred in the kiln, it is little wonder. In a smaller size, a plain 'U' shape of jardinière is known from only three examples dating from the 1770s.

The shapes enjoyed great popularity at the begining of the 19th century, however, and tapering jardinières were made by most English factories. Curiously, while Flight and Barr made many vases of the same shape as a jardinière in a single piece, complete with false-ring handles (*see* Colour Plates 40 and 58), they do not appear to have made any examples in two parts. Instead it was left to Chamberlain to compete with the vast output of Coalport jardinières, often decorated in London and frequently incorrectly attributed to Worcester. Chamberlain made a plain bucket shape from c.1800 with false-ring handles which could also have been bought with a pierced cover. A slightly later version has sea-monster handles and can sometimes be raised on paw feet. The fashion for two-part jardinières generally declined after the 1810s. No Grainger examples are recorded although wasters* of plain bucket shapes were found on the Grainger site and it is probable that unmarked examples are now indistinguishable from Coalport.

Jesuit Style

Amongst the earliest purely European designs commissioned from the Chinese for export were copies of prints from illustrated Bibles. The source prints were usually only in black and so were carefully copied in black with a technique called *grisailles* in France and *Schwarzelot* in Germany. In England, the term pencilled decoration* is used by collectors. Many so-called Jesuit designs were copied in Holland, often on white Chinese porcelain. Worcester replacements for Chinese patterns pencilled in black are usually called Jesuit even though these are usually classical or allegorical rather than biblical. The pattern illustrated here derives originally from a well-known print of 'Water from the Elements'.

Jet Enamels

The contemporary name used by the Worcester factory to refer to black overglaze transfer prints.* Once perfected by the late 1750s, these wares were not regarded as in any way inferior to fine painting.

Jewellery

See **Brooches** and **Beads**. The Chamberlain account books contain many other references to jewellery and these are listed by Geoffrey Godden in *Chamberlain-Worcester Porcelain*, p.255. These include necklaces, earrings, bracelets, slides and pin heads (for hat-pins). All would have been mounted using specially designed porcelain sections. Unfortunately no examples have been recognised.

Jewelling
A form of decoration introduced at Barr, Flight and Barr's factory c.1815. The first use of jewelling occurs on portrait medallions and other pieces associated with Thomas Baxter* and it is possible it was Baxter who introduced the technique to Worcester. It was a particularly skilful craft to apply just the correct amount of thick enamel paste to the porcelain. The secret was to leave a raised point in the middle of each 'jewel' so that in the kiln the enamel would melt into the proper shape. Solomon Cole* wrote that at Flights in c.1819 Ishmael Sherwin* decorated 'the rich pieces with gems &c., and attended principally to the embossed gold'.

With the exception of simple white enamel dots on deep blue grounds, the technique was not used at the other Worcester factories except for a few rare attempts by Chamberlain to copy Flight c.1818-20. This probably proved too costly and the technique was not continued. Later after the amalgamation with Flights in the late 1840s, jewelled borders were used on pieces of Chamberlain and Co. reticulated porcelain*.

Jugs
During the century covered by this book the variety of jugs produced in Worcester porcelain is too wide to mention. Certain shapes are discussed separately, however; *see* **Mask Jugs, Sparrow Beak Jugs, Presentation Jugs, Milk Jugs, and Cabbage Leaf Jugs.**

Junket Dishes
The origin of the name is unknown along with the exact purpose of these popular Worcester dishes. Junket is a preparation made from soured cream and curds, sweetened and flavoured, and traditionally needs a textured surface to help it set. The Worcester junket dishes could serve this purpose but it would seem peculiar to cover up some of the richest decoration in this way. Also, some are hardly moulded at all and would have given little adhesion to the junket. Blue-printed examples are often printed with salad vegetables on the underside and so it is possible that junket dishes were in fact used for serving salad. While an attractive idea, most salad bowls of slightly later date are deeper with decoration on the outside. The term junket has been used for merrymaking and feasting and it may just be that these were used at some sort of banquet.

The earliest Worcester junket dishes are crisply moulded with a basket-weave ground and reserved with three border panels. These are usually found in underglaze blue or with flower panels reserved on a strong yellow ground.* They date from the late 1750s until c.1765. The most popular shape of dish was in use by c.1765 until c.1780. This has six scallop shells moulded around the border on a scroll-moulded ground.

Junket Dishes. *The spiral shell moulding conveys a very rococo feeling to this junket dish with scale blue* borders and particularly fancy insects, decorated at the factory, square mark*, c.1770, 10¼ in. (26cm). (Phillips, Edinburgh.)*

Different forms of large flowerheads are moulded in the centres. In later examples all six scallops are plain but earlier ones have alternate fluted and plain scallops. These are usually found in blue and white and were possibly inspired by Sèvres. Other mouldings have scroll cartouche panels on a ground of basket weave, while a different sort has radiating scale moulding, again suggesting the texture of a shell. Plainer shapes with broad moulded flutes were also made.

The patterns used in the panels of blue and white junket dishes are only found on these shapes and some are listed in Branyan, French and Sandon as patterns I.B.31A, I.E.35 and I.E.35A. Other designs have been more recently discovered such as the *chinoiserie** patterns after Pillement* illustrated with the *Fisherman and Cormorant** pattern. Some rare coloured decoration of *Fancy Birds** and fruit on junket dishes can be associated with the Giles* workshop. A great many fragments of junket dishes were found on the factory site, suggesting that they were difficult to control in the kilns.

K

Kakiemon. *An unusual early fluted bowl, the very oriental shape well suited to this copy of* Kakiemon *flowering chrysanthemums, scratch cross* or T mark incised, c.1752-3, 4½in. (11.3cm). (Phillips.)*

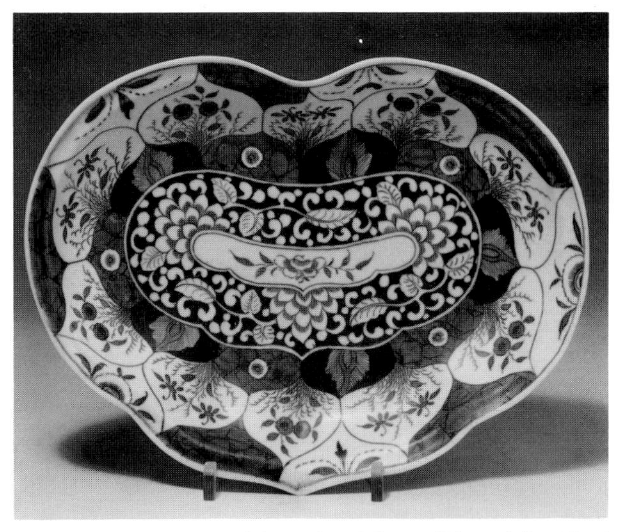

Kangxi Lotus Pattern. *A heart-shaped dessert dish carefully painted in underglaze blue*, with a copy of an earlier Chinese design, mark of an oriental emblem, c.1770-5. 10¼in. (26cm). (Phillips.)*

Kakiemon

Only a limited amount of *Kakiemon* porcelain found its way to Europe from Japan early in the 18th century and it was greatly prized by collectors at the time. Augustus the Strong of Saxony built up a vast oriental porcelain collection and founded his own porcelain factory at Meissen to copy exactly every *Kakiemon* design which he treasured above all else. It was made very much in the Japanese own taste, quite unlike the gaudy Imari* patterns which were intended for export. Traditionally *Kakiemon* porcelain is associated with a single Japanese family of potters and painters but was made in sufficient quantity to suggest this is very unlikely. None was probably exported to Europe after the 1730s and all English copies are much later. The question remains, did the English factories copy Japanese or Meissen originals?

Chelsea were the principal makers of English *Kakiemon* and they were influenced by Meissen far more than the Orient. Bow also made certain Japanese designs in reasonable quantity, especially the *Quail** pattern. Worcester, on the other hand, does not seem to have made many exact copies of *Kakiemon*. The *Joshua Reynolds* pattern* must count as one but Worcester mostly placed this within their own deep blue borders. Worcester's various *Quail* patterns possibly copied Bow and are usually inferior in execution, probably because they date from the late 1760s and 1770s, far later than Chelsea or Bow *Quail* patterns. Worcester did, however, succeed in the case of the *Yellow Tiger** pattern which manages to capture the spirit of the Japanese original. Their *Banded Hedge** pattern also follows Japan quite closely, even though the shapes on which it appears are totally English. Chamberlain and Flight occasionally used these old *Kakiemon* patterns used previously at Worcester but these generally became debased by the 19th century. Mostly, however, Worcester chose to adapt *Kakiemon* designs to their own style; *see* **Rich Kakiemon.**

Kangxi Lotus Pattern

A fairly exact copy of an early 18th century Chinese blue and white design used on Worcester dessert services from c.1770, continuing into the 1780s, the later examples painted with less care and in somewhat brighter blue. The complicated pattern comprises a variety of petal-shaped panels including cracked ice*, and examples are always marked with a ribbon-tied emblem as part of the design on the underside, copied also from the Chinese original.

Kempthorne Pattern

A direct copy of Japanese porcelain, the story of the *Kempthorne* pattern was told to R.W. Binns* and appeared in his *Century of Potting*. According to family tradition, John Thorneloe*, one of the original partners in the Worcester Porcelain Company, travelled to Mullion in Cornwall in search of soaprock* near the mines at Gew Graze. There being no accommodation at the local inn, he was invited to stay with Renatus Kempthorne, a local gentleman who would accept no payment for several weeks' lodging. In return Thorneloe is said to have had made a special service using the soaprock and sent this to Kempthorne. Binns illustrated a saucer from the Kempthorne family service which was a well-known pattern from c.1768-70. This was made some years later than the suggested expedition to Cornwall, but, even so, the story is appealing

Kent, Duchess of, Service. *A teacup and saucer exactly matching the Duchess of Kent service in decoration but of conventional shape instead of the distinctive beaker-shaped teabowls usually encountered. This probably represents another separate service, therefore. Crescent mark* on saucer, c.1770-5. (Phillips.)*

and probably was based on a certain number of facts. The pattern is in underglaze blue and Japan colours with gilding, and is also known in a version belonging to the red line bordered group*. Giles* probably made the same pattern using overglaze blue enamel instead of underglaze. A totally different pattern of chrysanthemum and prunus sprigs in similar colours to *Kempthorne* occurs on teawares and vases of similar date and is often confused with *Kempthorne*, even though this other pattern does not have a border.

Kent, Duchess of, Service

The unusual shapes and distinctive panels associated with this pattern suggest that it may well have been a special order for a royal customer. A service of the pattern is believed to have belonged to the Duchess of Kent, mother of Queen Victoria, although at least two teapots are known, suggesting more than one set was made. The bird painting is typical of the Worcester factory c.1770 although the shapes suggest a date c.1775 is more likely. The oval or kidney-shaped panels are unusual at this time and the wet blue* ground is usually poorly controlled. The shapes used include shallow beaker-shaped teabowls without feet, tall baluster teapots and tapering cylindrical tea canisters. Teacups of conventional shape are known in the pattern and these will probably be from another service with no royal connection.

Kerr, W.H.

A china dealer from Dublin who joined the ailing firm of Chamberlain and Co. in 1850 following the retirement of John Lilly.* The Irish market had always been important to the Worcester factories and Walter Chamberlain* looked to Kerr to provide new direction in view of his understanding of the market place. The factory's failure to raise much acclaim at all at the Great Exhibition* finally led Walter Chamberlain to retire, leaving Kerr in sole charge of a company in need of salvation. He knew he could not achieve this single-handedly and, although the firm traded for a short while as W.H. Kerr and Co., he invited Richard William Binns* to join him in 1852. The firm of Kerr and Binns operated for ten years until Kerr retired in 1862. Some porcelain marked with the name of Kerr, Dublin, would have been made for sale through his retail business and is rarely of Worcester origin.

Kew Service

A fluted tea service of c.1775-80 is decorated with a deep blue and gold border and the *Marriage** pattern of coloured flowers concealing a bow, arrow and lover's knot. Each piece is further painted with a neo-classical urn-shaped vase with the word 'KEW' superimposed. No records remain to confirm the origins of the set, but Kew was famous for the royal residence of Kew House where, following the death of the Dowager Princess of Wales in 1772, King George III* stayed on many occasions, principally to recover from bouts of sickness and madness. It is possible that the King used the Worcester set while convalescing. Several other patterns were made in the 1770s and 1780s featuring a classical vase and blue borders. These are sometimes referred to as *Kew* pattern but without an inscription on the urn this is incorrect. Examples of the Kew service are in the collection of Her Majesty the Queen.

Kiln Supports
The methods employed by different factories to overcome the problems of firing produce some of the most important clues to identification. Worcester managed to avoid the need for spurs or stilts as were used at Chelsea, Lowestoft and elsewhere. Instead, they fired the wares on crushed calcined flint which acted as a buffer and prevented pieces from sticking to the kiln shelf. Kiln rings, circles of clay the same size as the rim of a cup or bowl, were used during firing to help the wares retain their shape and the flint successfully prevented any fusion. Very few wasters on the factory site had fused with their firing supports. Some 'spurs', long pegs of fired clay, were found in a level dating from the 1770s but were probably used for specific shapes such as aparagus servers* which were glazed all over. During the Flight, Barr and Barr period stilts were sometimes used to stack plates in the kiln, but evidence of these on Worcester plates is generally very difficult to recognise.

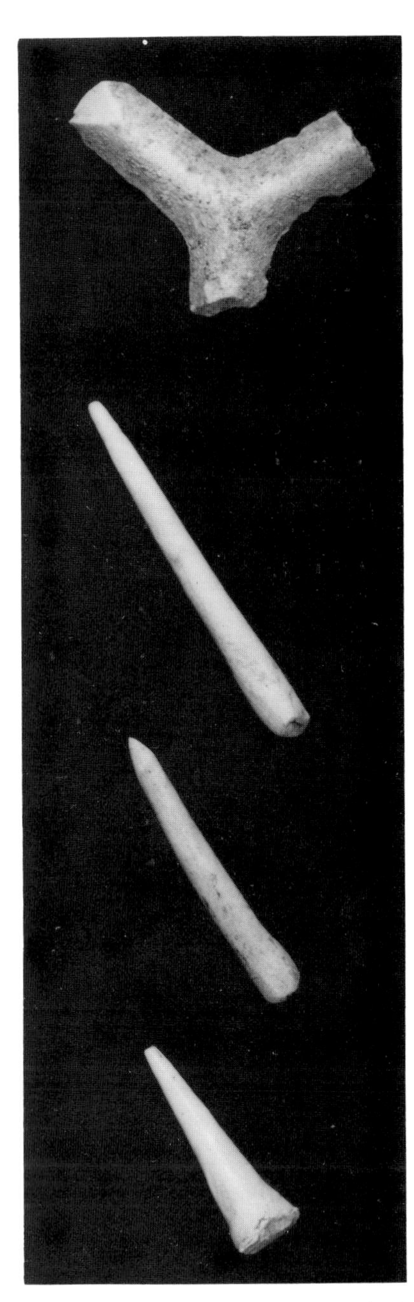

Kiln Supports. *Three 'spurs' and the centre of a tripod kiln support, found in various levels during excavations* on the Warmstry House* site. The spurs were pushed through holes in a saggar (fireproof clay box) and porcelain vessels rested on the spurs.*

King John's Tomb Inkstand
The medieval tomb of England's King John in Worcester Cathedral has long been one of the most important tourist attractions in the city. The King was buried between the two local saints, Oswald and Wulstan, in the hope of slipping into heaven disguised as a monk. His tomb was carved with his effigy flanked by images of the saints. This was modelled by Chamberlain and Co. c.1840-2 and is typical of the lack of taste which epitomised the late Chamberlain wares, for if you lift the lid off the poor old King's tomb you find inkwells* and a pen tray inside. The tomb was issued in full bright colours or else in a creamy vellum finish. An elaborate inscription was printed inside the lid.

Knife Handles
See **Cutlery Handles**

Knife Rests
No finished examples have been recorded but Geoffrey Godden has shown from the order books that Chamberlain were selling porcelain knife rests in 1817 and 1822. In 1844 'Asparagus knife rests' are recorded and these will be similar to well-known Continental porcelain models of single spears of asparagus. Strangely, no Grainger knife rests are recorded in factory archives.

Kylin Pattern
See **Dragon in Compartments Pattern**

L

La Cascade

An interesting early transfer print* which was based on a painting by Watteau* now in the Wallace Collection. It depicts a lady and gentleman walking beside an elaborate fountain and occurs in several versions on teawares from c.1755-60. Differences in some of these versions suggest that they were not all printed at Worcester. One version is signed 'R Hancock Fecit', either in black or red. Other examples may have been printed in Birmingham* where the print was used on enamels, while other pieces were probably printed in Liverpool* by Sadler. Versions of *La Cascade* occur on Liverpool porcelain also printed by Sadler.

Ladies' Amusement, The

The London printseller Robert Sayer had the idea to reuse a large number of odd engravings in a single major publication which could be used as a source book of designs. *The Ladies' Amusement, or the Whole Art of Japanning Made Easy*, was actually intended for ladies to cut up and use the prints to decorate japanned metal trays and such objects below a special varnish. A note in the introduction suggests that the book would also be useful for porcelain decorators. The first edition of *The Ladies' Amusement* was published in 1760, followed by a slightly enlarged edition two years later and a third edition c.1775 which contained many additional prints by Robert Hancock.* All editions contained mostly flower or bird prints as well as numerous chinoiserie* subjects after Jean Pillement*. These were undoubtedly used by several English porcelain and pottery manufacturers for inspiration, not only at the time but even as late as the 1820s.

Many prints in *The Ladies' Amusement* are by Robert Hancock. He would have sold these engraved copper plates to Robert Sayer and probably kept copies, for the same subjects were used, normally in reverse, on London and Staffordshire enamel and on Worcester porcelain. It is wrong, therefore, to assume that a design such as the *Parrot Pecking Fruit**, which occurs on page 74, was copied on to Worcester porcelain from the book. It is far more likely that Sayer acquired the same engravings as the Worcester factory. Two original volumes of *The Ladies' Amusement* were bought by C.W. Dyson Perrins and are preserved at the Worcester factory where some of the Pillement designs were copied in the 1930s. A reprint was published by The Ceramic Book Co. in the 1960s.

Ladles

Most dessert tureens have a hole reserved in the cover for a ladle but the ladle was not necessarily made of matching porcelain. Contemporary sale catalogues list some dessert tureens with covers, stands and spoons while in other cases no spoons are listed. Most ladles from the 1770s have plain circular bowls and plain curved handles, although some are recorded with more graceful wavy bowls and moulded scroll handles. Flight made some ladles in the 1790s with shell moulding and Chamberlain made plain ladles with their earliest dessert services. Generally, however, ladles were not made in the 19th century. Large ladles suitable for a soup tureen are very rare in porcelain and only a few are known in Worcester blue and white, c.1770.

Ladles. *A rare large ladle with a moulded terminal in French style, painted in underglaze blue* with a border found on blue-printed dinner services*, unmarked, c.1770, 8in. (20.5cm). (Dyson Perrins Museum.)*

Lady at the Loom Pattern
See **Spinning Maiden Pattern**

L'Amitie Pattern

One of the earliest patterns that was used by Chamberlain on their own porcelain and on Caughley porcelain decorated at Worcester, c.1789-92. The order books contain numerous references to the pattern by name, spelt in various ways, or else referred to by the name *Doves*. The pattern was used on Caughley teawares of various shapes including shanked*, as well as on finely ribbed shapes continued in Chamberlain's own porcelain. The origin is probably French and examples are known with several different leaf and ribbon borders. The panels are always consistent, however, with doves and the name *L'Amitie* inscribed on a ribbon. Occasionally the doves were used without the ribbon as on this presentation mug on Caughley porcelain ordered in 1791 by a Worcester chemist, listed in the order books as '1 ½-pint mug with doves lett'd F'. The pattern was discontinued by c.1795 but the *L'Amitie* and doves motif was used by at least one outside decorator on a Chamberlain miniature or 'toy' mug signed 'Anna Hatherell, Sept. 1823'.*

L'Amitie Pattern. A Caughley mug decorated at Chamberlains in 1791 for Edward Pritchett of Worcester, listed in the order books as '1 ½-pint mug with doves, lett'd F'. The L'Amitie *doves usually form part of a teaware pattern but were occasionally used on their own, 3½in (9cm). (Formerly Author's Collection.)*

L'Amour
One of the most popular of Robert Hancock's prints, *L'Amour* was used extensively on Worcester teawares from c.1757. It is believed to have been copied from a design by C.N. Cochin of c.1745 but very many versions exist and there may be an even earlier prototype. The main subject depicts a gallant seated on the edge of a bench kissing the hand of an elegant lady by his side, while a maid stands behind looking slightly bewildered. Most examples include a fountain, a dog and a garden roller, but these are sometimes omitted. The print was usually in black although lilac examples are known, as well as several coloured-in versions. The 1769 Worcester sale catalogue included teawares 'Jet, enamel'd *le amour*'. The pattern is known signed by Hancock with the anchor rebus* and also occurs on Bow porcelain and enamel. Much later copies were made in Staffordshire.

La Pêche and La Promenade Chinoise
Two prints which always occur together and therefore can be regarded as a single pattern. The designs were first published in *Livres de Chinoise*, an important source book of Chinese designs by Jean Pillement*, engraved by P.C. Canot in 1758. The form used on Worcester porcelain also occurs in Robert Sayer's *The Ladies' Amusement** but it is dangerous to assume that this served as the origin of Worcester's design. It is more likely that Robert Hancock* supplied a copy of his copper plate to Robert Sayer. The engraving was intended to be used in underglaze blue and therefore lacks the usual subtlety of Robert Hancock's hand. The prints were used from the outset

La Pêche and La Promenade Chinoise. *The reverse of a large grace mug* printed in blue with* La Promenade Chinoise, *the design probably originally adapted by Robert Hancock* after Pillement*, crescent mark*, c.1775-80, 5¾in. (14.5cm). (Dyson Perrins Museum.)*

at Caughley and it may well be that Thomas Turner* played some part in their execution. Worcester mugs printed with the two designs were made from c.1770-5 until c.1785, contemporary with the Caughley mugs. The prints are listed by Cook as items 81 and 88 and by Branyan, French and Sandon as II.A.10. A crude copy has been seen in pearlware and *La Pêche* also occurs on English delftware plates, probably copied in this case from *The Ladies' Amusement*.

Landslip Pattern. *A saucer painted in very dark blue with this curious pattern inspired by Chinese porcelain, workman's mark*, c.1758, 4¾in. (12cm). (Dyson Perrins Museum.)*

Landslip Pattern
A carefully painted blue and white pattern inspired by, but probably not copied directly from, Chinese porcelain. The design features a landscape with chrysanthemums and a

willow tree and includes the distinctive feature of a pavilion on a rocky outcrop appearing as if it is sliding dramatically downhill. The pattern, number I.D.21 in Branyan, French and Sandon, was used on teawares from c.1755 for about ten years.

Lea and Perrins

The famous Worcester sauce manufacturers began as chemists. The partnership in Malvern of Lea, Perrins and Burrows commissioned Grainger to make pots for selling 'Muroma', their speciality hair restorer invented by Dr Gully. These date from the 1850s. Lea and Perrins Worcestershire Sauce was already famous by 1851. For their stand at the Great Exhibition* the company commissioned a massive display vase from Chamberlain & Co., using an earlier Flight, Barr and Barr shape. This vase, painted with hanging game, is at present on loan to the Dyson Perrins Museum, named after Charles Dyson Perrins whose fortune was founded on the the success of the sauce. The Lea family of Lea and Perrins has no connection with the Lee family (spelt differently) of Grainger, Lee and Co.

Leaf Dishes. *An early fig leaf dish with very crisply moulded veins and a reserved unrolled scroll panel, painted in red-brown monochrome with a European figure and ruins, the rim edged in green, c.1755-6, 7½in. (19cm). (Phillips.)*

Leaf Dishes. *An early form of vine leaf dish, usually encountered with naturalistic green shading but here painted in colours with a copy of an engraving, against a rare plain white ground, c.1757, 6½in. (16.5cm). (Sotheby's/Kiddell Papers.)*

Leaf Dishes. *The standard shape of Worcester's cabbage leaf dish used for dessert, the shape copied from Meissen* and in this case the decoration also based on Meissen's* deutsche Blumen, *c.1758-60, 13¾in. (35cm). (Phillips.)*

Leaf Dishes

Dishes modelled in the shape of leaves served various purposes but principally small leaves were for pickle (*see* **Pickle Dishes**). Larger leaves were mostly issued as part of a dessert service* although they have generally become separated over the years. The 1769 Worcester sale catalogue included:

> A Dessert Service of the fine white and gold, containing two round scollopt compoteers, four deep ditto, one oval ditto, four cabbage leaves, four vine ditto, two oval cream basons, covers and plates, two ditto pierced baskets and stands and 24 plates.

All this sold for £3.6s. These two standard shapes of leaves are well known to collectors today. The 'Cabbage Leaves' are shaped as two overlapping leaves with stalks crossing over to form a handle at one end. These were made in at least three sizes and can be decorated in a wide variety of styles. The same shape was used as a stand for a basket with a moulded quatrelobed centre, but these are great rarities. The dishes called 'Vine Leaves' are less frequently seen but were still made in a variety of patterns, both blue and white and richly coloured. They have a looping twig handle at the side.

Earlier leaf dishes were possibly intended as stands for leaf sauceboats* but there is no evidence for this. The cauliflower tureens* were sold with matching leaf dishes as stands, but these single heavily veined leaves are nowadays much more common than the tureens, suggesting that the leaf dishes were also sold by themselves. The 'Vine Leaves' listed c.1755-56 on

Leaf Dishes. A Grainger Lee and Co. dessert dish, the shape harking back to an earlier period, decorated with the Old India* *pattern with additional* famille rose*, *blue printed mark, pattern number* 1418, c.1818-20, 7in. (18cm). (Private Collection.)*

Leaf Sauceboats. A very rare variation on the popular leaf-shaped sauceboat, the main body left plain except for very fine grooves and a leafy rim, c.1755, 8⅝in. (22cm). (Bonhams.)

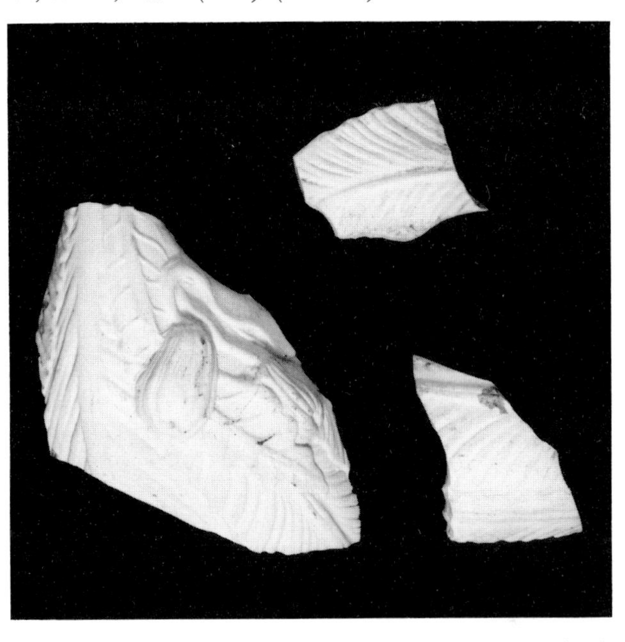

Leaf Sauceboats. Biscuit wasters* from the factory site excavations* exactly corresponding with the popular sauceboats. These occurred in only a single level dating from c.1755 and indicate a very short but intense period of production.*

sale in the London Warehouse (*see* **London Shops**) came in two sizes at 4s. and 8s. per dozen and these will have been pickle dishes and the slightly larger dishes for sweetmeats. 'Fig Leaves' sold for 4s. and 12s. per dozen, the small size being used for pickle while the larger dishes were probably for dessert. Most examples of the larger fig leaf dishes from c.1755-60 are in colours with green shaded edges, while others were painted in blue with Chinese style rocks and peonies. The modelled veining is so detailed that it is likely a real leaf was used, at least to assist in the initial mould-making. A rare variant is moulded with an unrolled Chinese scroll panel in the centre of the leaf which is usually painted with a European subject in monochrome.

H. Rissik Marshall, *Coloured Worcester Porcelain*, item 1055, illustrates a curious pointed leaf-shaped dish which has a flowerhead terminal from which projects a short cylindrical peg. Examples are known from the Bow factory where a set of such leaves fitted into a central stand. Only this one single Worcester leaf dish has been recorded, painted with coloured flowers in the style of the early 1760s. The Worcester shape is not as narrow as the Bow examples.

Grainger made a leaf-shaped dish to accompany dessert services c.1815-20. An example in the popular *Old India** pattern is illustrated here. Leaf dishes seem to have gone out of fashion after the 1780s and the Flight and Chamberlain factories did not, apparently, make any.

Leaf Sauceboats

Attractive pairs of sauceboats in the form of cos lettuces were copied from Meissen and made in considerable numbers, c.1755-7. The curled stalks of the lettuce form the handles and left-hand and right-hand examples were made. They come in two sizes and 'Leaf sauce-boats Enamel'd' were sold by the London Warehouse (*see* **London Shops**) c.1755-6 at 3s. and 3s.6d. per dozen. They were made for only a short period, probably less than three years, and the form of enamelling varies very little. During this time, however, it is clear from the examples surviving that great numbers must have been made. In spite of this, only one small dumping of wasters was found during all the factory site excavations*, thus confirming a Worcester origin for the shapes. Evidently it did not matter if examples were distorted or blemished in the kiln as such imperfections were easily lost in the decoration. The flower and insect painting on the leaf sauceboats is surprisingly rare on any other Worcester shape. Examples frequently carry workmen's marks* in black or brown enamel and are edged with brown line rims in Meissen style.* Very few blue and white examples of the larger size are known and they are even rarer just in white. One variation of the shape is known from a single white example and this is moulded with formal scale fluting instead of lettuce leaves. Another variation is almost as rare and has moulded rococo cartouche panels on a plain ground. This has been recorded with coloured European figures in the panels and also with the *Staghunt** pattern. Leaf sauceboats were made by many other English factories but not in quite the same form as at Worcester.

***Leaf Sauceboats.** From the numbers surviving today, Worcester leaf sauceboats must have been made in enormous quantities. Most are carefully painted with coloured flowers in Meissen style* and have a brown rim; workman's mark* in black, c.1755, 7½in. (19cm). (Phillips.)*

***Lee, James.** A Grainger, Lee and Co. trio with the rare moulding called by the factory 'Lee's Embossed', in this case with a rose pink ground, c.1835. (Henry Sandon Collection.)*

Lee, James

According to Geoffrey Godden's *Encyclopaedia of British Porcelain Manufacturers*, the partnership between Thomas Grainger*, John Lee*, James Pardoe and Benjamin Crane was dissolved on 10 October 1814 in favour of a new partnership between Thomas Grainger and James Lee, the son of the said John Lee. They traded as Grainger, Lee and Co.* Like his father, James Lee was a financial backer, but was also possibly involved with production, as one shape c.1826 was called 'Mr. Lee's shape' or 'Lee's Embossed'. In 1818 James Lee lived in Pheasant Street, next to the factory. He and his wife Rachel moved from Worcester in 1837, although he kept a small business interest in the company until at least 1853.

Lee, John

Much confusion in the past between James Lee* and his father, John, has led to inaccurate accounts of John being in partnership with Thomas Grainger* as Grainger, Lee and Co.* Instead, John Lee was himself a minor partner in the firm of Thomas Grainger and Co.* from 12 March 1811 until October 1814, when he passed his interests over to his son. There is some doubt that this John Lee was the same as John Lee, glover of Lowesmoor, whose daughter Mary Anne Lee married Thomas Grainger in August 1809. John Lee was a financial backer of the factory and not directly involved in porcelain production.

Les Garçons Chinois

While very much in the manner of Jean Pillement*, the origin of this very rococo design is unknown. The print in black enamel was used from c.1755 on plain or feather-moulded teawares, very rare onion-shaped vases and on only two known underglaze blue small mugs. Occasionally the overglaze black version is seen with colouring-in and a subsidiary design of flowering plants and vases was sometimes used. The complete pattern shows one Chinese boy sawing through the scroll on which his companion is sitting, but on

Les Garçons Chinois. A 'pull' from the original engraved copper plate preserved at the Worcester factory. The pattern is a curious mixture of chinoiserie with a European landscape behind.*

shallow pieces there is not room and the pattern was adapted by placing the second boy on a scroll on the far right of the print. Illustrated is a 'pull' from an original copper plate of the design which survives at Worcester.

Letter Racks
See **Card Trays**

Lewis, George
All that is known about George Lewis is the inscription on his monument in St Alban's Church in Worcester, commemorating

> George Lewis, who departed this life the 29th day of September 1790, aged 51. He was conductor of the printing business of the porcelain Manufactory in the city upwards of thirty years, in which capacity his indefatigable attention and integrity was worthy of imitation.

Lewis may well have joined the printing department before 1760 but at only twenty-one years old he will have been very much junior to Robert Hancock* and the Holdship* brothers. Valentine Green*, James Ross* and Thomas Turner* were probably all senior to him, but they all left the factory and it was in his later years that Lewis rose to the position his monument proclaimed. John Flight* wrote in his diary* in February 1791:

> Soon after Shaw, Lewis died. He managed the printing. This was a sudden event, but also instead of being an injury, was the contrary, as we carry on that at less expense.

Lilly, John
A businessman and property owner from Somerset who was brought in as a partner in the firm of Chamberlain and Co. in 1827 on the retirement of Humphrey Chamberlain sen.* John Lilly had, according to R.W. Binns*, married one of Humphrey Chamberlain's daughters. Lilly became the largest shareholder when the company was re-established in 1840 following the merger with Flight, Barr and Barr (*see* **Chamberlain and Co**). This difficult period in the 1840s saw most other partners withdraw and the company was dissolved in 1844. Walter Chamberlain* and John Lilly retained control

***Lithophanes.** A Grainger, Lee and Co. nightlight* shaped as a sentry box, the front lithophane panel depicting a soldier confronting Napoleon, script mark, c.1830-5, 6½in. (16.5cm). (Neales, Nottingham.)*

of the former Chamberlain porcelain factory in Diglis and the shop in the High Street. John Lilly was not a practical potter in any way. On his retirement in 1850 his son Frederick took his share, but he too soon withdrew, leaving W.H. Kerr to run the company.

Limehouse Porcelain Manufactory
The only direct link we have between Limehouse and Worcester is Dr Richard Pocock's* statement that the Bristol manufactory had been 'lately established here by one of the principal manufacturers at Limehouse which failed'. Joseph Wilson and Company were responsible for porcelain making at Limehouse between 1746 and 1748 and while it is known that Wilson himself went to Newcastle-under-Lyme, there is as yet no evidence to identify this other 'principal manufacturer' who moved to Bristol. It is most likely this was Benjamin Lund* although Robert Podmore* is another possible candidate.

The site of the Limehouse factory was excavated in 1990 and it was possible to identify the porcelain made there as the class of wares previously attributed to William Reid. The Limehouse porcelain body contained soaprock* which was the significant ingredient in Bristol porcelain, and there are certain obvious links between some of the Limehouse and Bristol products. Scallop shell pickle dishes* painted with bamboo were made at both factories and some Limehouse painting is very close to that of the 'Three Dot Painter'* type used at Bristol. The formula and firing conditions must have been modified by Benjamin Lund as the Bristol and Limehouse porcelains appear noticeably different.

Liverpool Decoration. *A small mug printed in black with a portrait of Queen Charlotte*, the style typical of Sadler's printing workshops in Liverpool, c.1765, about 3½in. (9cm). (Wallace Elliot Collection, photograph Sotheby's/Kiddell Papers.)*

Lithophanes

Thin, flat slabs of porcelain which present a three-dimensional image when a light is shone through. It is believed that Grainger, Lee and Co.* bought the British patent to make lithophanes taken out by Robert Griffith Jones of Middlesex in 1828. Jones had learnt the technique in France and the hard paste porcelain of the Continent was much better suited to survive the difficult firing. At least two moulds for lithophanes survived at Worcester. One shows a lady undressing and struggling with her corsets, the other is a portrait of a gentleman who might be William IV, but until a cast can be taken from the mould and fired in porcelain it remains very difficult to tell. The example illustrated on page 221, depicting Napoleon, is the only marked Grainger lithophane so far recorded. It is made as part of a nightlight in the form of a sentry box. Grainger also made a nightlight* with an angel which is in a similar technique to lithophanes. Chamberlain sold '5 Transparencies, biscuit, Our Saviour' in 1842 and these were probably their own attempt at lithophanes. The name 'Berlin Transparencies', after the two principal Berlin factories where the finest examples were made, had been used to describe lithophanes.

Liverpool Decoration

From the time of Robert Podmore's* defection from Worcester to Liverpool in June 1755 there would have been serious rivalry between the two centres of manufacture. It seems very surprising, therefore, that white Worcester porcelain should have been sent to Liverpool for transfer printing* when Worcester were themselves market leaders in printed porcelain. John Sadler had developed his technique for printing on delftware tiles and seems largely to have printed on earthenwares. Certain porcelain pieces bearing his prints are known, mostly on Chaffers and other Liverpool makers. Some printing by Sadler does occur on Worcester porcelain, however, and was discussed by Dr Knowles Boney in *Apollo* in March and April 1961. A Masonic print is signed 'Sadler Enm. Livpl.'.

A mug of the King of Prussia* which must be more or less contemporary with the Hancock* print used at Worcester, is titled on the print 'Gilbody maker, Evans Sct'. This print is recorded both on Worcester and on Gilbody's own Liverpool porcelain. It is unclear if this was printed at Samuel Gilbody's own china factory in Liverpool or under licence to Gilbody by Sadler. It is possible, of course, that Podmore took a supply of white porcelain with him when he defected and sold this to Sadler.

I know of one coffee pot and a cup and saucer of undoubted Worcester porcelain c.1765-70 painted with coloured floral sprays including roses and tulips in an identical manner to that used on Christian and early Pennington Liverpool porcelain. The borders in red enamel belong typically to this Liverpool group. It is of course possible that Worcester copied Liverpool to make an exact replacement, but I feel from the painting style that the decoration was probably carried out in Liverpool.

London Shape

This most popular of all teaware shapes was produced by virtually every English and Welsh porcelain factory. The name 'London' was given to the shape by the Spode factory and has since been used to refer to the different versions of all factories. Flights remained traditional and never seem to have made a London shaped teapot although they did introduce London shaped cups and saucers to accompany oval teapots (*see* Colour Plate 57). The form was used extensively by Grainger from c.1812 or 1813, and at Chamberlains also from c.1813. Grainger used two very different versions, one thinly potted with very elegant handles, the other particularly thick and clumsy. The latter was used in addition with three distinct embossed patterns. Chamberlain's version has a very sharply pinched shoulder and can have either a flat finial or a moulded scrollwork loop. This was discontinued by c.1820 although Grainger probably continued their London shape well into the 1820s.

London Shops

The Worcester factories were well aware of the importance of a presence in London where the most important retail trade was carried out. Fine porcelain could be sold there for much higher prices than in Worcester itself. The first shop opened by the factory was called 'The Worcester Porcelain Warehouse' and was mentioned in an advertisement in *The Public Advertiser,* 1 March 1754:

> **For SALE by the CANDLE,** At the Royal Exchange Coffee-house, Threadneedle-Street, *On Friday the 15th Inst. at Five in the Afternoon,* **ABOUT 40,000 Pieces of China Ware of** the Worcester Manufactory; the Commodity will speak for itself. They will be shewn at London House in Aldersgate-Street. Timely Notice will be given when, the Bills of Sale delivered, by **CHARLES MARGAS,** Swor-Broker, *in St. Thomas Apostles, Queen Street, Cheapside*

The following year a further sale was announced, this time in the *General Evening Post*, 9-12 August 1755:

> *For Sale by the CANDLE.* At the Royal-Exchange Coffee-House in Threadneedle-Street, London, on the 17th, 18th and 19th of September next ensuing, at Five o'Clock in the Afternoon, A Large Assortment of the **WORCESTER CHINA-WARE**. This early Advertisement is given that Country Traders may have timely Notice to give their Orders to those whom they deal with in London, as the Proprietors of this Manufactory do not send Riders to vend their Ware by Pattern or Description, making London their only Mart of Sale, where their Goods will be shewn open at London-House in Aldersgate-Street. N.B. Sold among the Trade only.

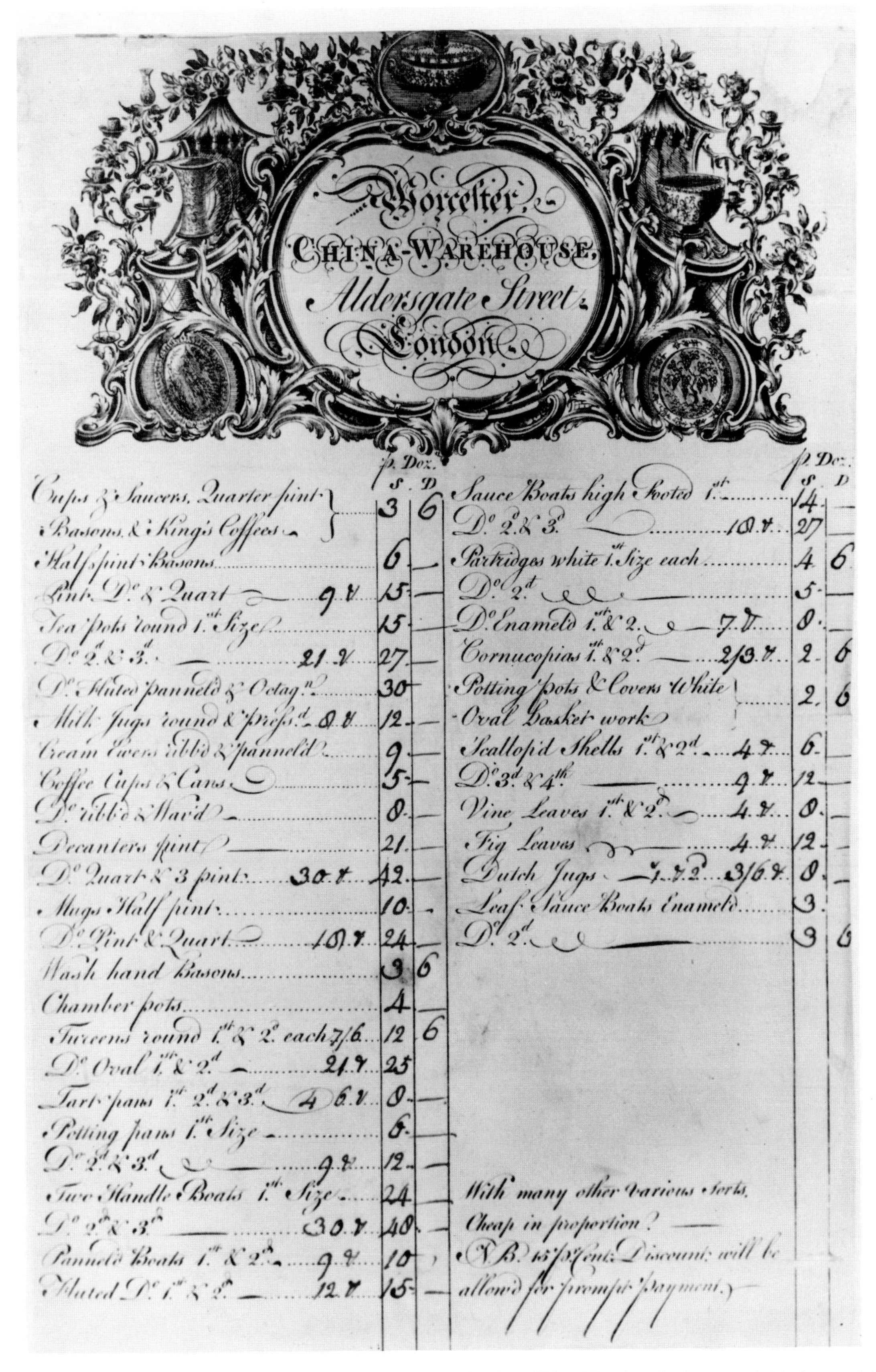

Worcester China-Warehouse, Aldersgate Street, London.

	p. Doz. s	d
Cups & Saucers, Quarter pint Basons, & King's Coffees	3	6
Half pint Basons	6	—
Pint Do & Quart — 9 d	15	—
Tea pots round 1st Size	15	—
Do 2d & 3d — 21 d	27	—
Do Fluted panneld & Octagn	30	—
Milk Jugs round & Press'd — 8 d	12	—
Cream Ewers ribb'd & panneld	9	—
Coffee Cups & Cans	5	—
Do ribb'd & Wav'd	8	—
Decanters pint	21	—
Do Quart & 3 pints — 30 d	42	—
Mugs Half pint	10	—
Do Pint & Quart — 18 d	24	—
Wash hand Basons	3	6
Chamber pots	4	—
Tureens round 1st & 2d each 7/6	12	6
Do Oval 1st & 2d — 21 d	25	
Tart pans 1st 2d & 3d — 4 6 d	8	—
Potting pans 1st Size	6	—
Do 2d & 3d — 9 d	12	—
Two Handle Boats 1st Size	24	
Do 2d & 3d — 30 d	40	—
Panneld Boats 1st & 2d — 9 d	10	—
Fluted Do 1st & 2d — 12 d	15	—

	p. Doz. s	d
Sauce Boats high footed 1st	14	—
Do 2d & 3d — 18 d	27	—
Partridges white 1st Size each	4	6
Do 2d	5	—
Do Enameld 1st & 2 — 7 d	8	—
Cornucopias 1st & 2d — 2/3 d	2	6
Potting pots & Covers White Oval Basket work	2	6
Scallop'd Shells 1st & 2d — 4 d	6	—
Do 3d & 4th — 9 d	12	—
Vine Leaves 1st & 2d — 4 d	8	—
Fig Leaves — 4 d	12	—
Dutch Jugs — 1 & 2 — 3/6 d	8	—
Leaf Sauce Boats Enameld	3	—
Do 2d	3	6

With many other various sorts, Cheap in proportion.

N.B. 15 p Cent Discount will be allowed for prompt Payment.

London Shops. *An early price list of the Worcester China Warehouse in London which, although undated, was probably drawn up in 1755 or 1756. The prices listed are wholesale and are mostly per dozen. This list provides virtually the only contemporary descriptions of most of these Worcester shapes and is therefore of the utmost importance in researching the factory's wares. (Dyson Perrins Museum.)*

***Long Eliza Figure.** A remarkable garniture of vases, the slender shapes ideally suited to the tall Chinese figures known as Long Elizas, in this case enamelled in* famille rose*, *c.1753, central vase 9⅞in. (25cm). Originally these would have had pointed finials. (Phillips.)*

This sale was in fact postponed until 8-10 October 'on account of the large Quantity of Goods which could not be got ready so soon'. Advertisements for the new sale listed:

> About 300 lots of WORCESTER CHINA-WARE, lotted for Traders. The said goods will be on Shew, in the Worcester-China Ware-House in London-House, in Aldersgate-Street the 6th and 7th; and such Lots as shall remain unsold will be shewn till the Time of Sale on the succeeding Days of Sale.

Presumably the warehouse was only selling by auction at this time but by 1756 it carried a general stock for sale. Notice of this appeared in *The Public Advertiser* on 4 March 1756:

> The Proprietors of the Worcester China Manufacture for the better accommodation of merchants and traders have opened a warehouse at London House, Aldersgate Street, London, where they may be supplied every day, between the hours of nine in the morning and three in the afternoon, with assortment of goods wholesale on the most reasonable terms. Orders are likewise taken and executed with dispatch for home and foreign trade.

A price list for this warehouse is reproduced here and although undated must have been drawn up right at the beginning in 1755 or 1756. The name of the original manager is not known but by 1762 or 1763 John Spurling* was listed as 'Proprietor of Worcester China Manufactory, London-house, Aldersgate-street'. The warehouse continued until 1767 when the factory began to use a large Exhibition Room in Spring Gardens, Charing Cross, claiming in January 1768 that the chief proprietor of the Worcester manufactory had 'sent some thousand pounds worth of the said ware from their late Warehouse in Aldersgate-Street to be sold in the same Exhibition Room...'. The Exhibition Room in Spring Gardens also sold Chelsea porcelain at the same time and was in direct competition with James Giles* who, according to his own advertisements, was

> Proprietor of the Worcester Porcelaine Warehouse, up one Pair of Stairs in Cockspur Street, facing the Lower End of the Haymarket.

Here Giles probably sold only Worcester porcelain he had decorated himself or had bought openly in sales. The factory again advertised in April 1768 their 'Worcester China Warehouse, removed from Aldersgate-Street, to number 12 in Gough Square, Fleet Street'. John Spurling is again listed as manager in 1770, but the business was clearly failing. Subsequently various stock from both the Worcester factory and Giles warehouses was disposed of by auction, leaving Worcester with no London presence until Joseph and John Flight*, encouraged by the visit to Worcester of George III*, and on the direct advice of the King, opened showrooms at 1 Coventry Street in 1788. They stocked the shop with Worcester porcelain as well as large quantities of French porcelain from the Angoulême manufactory. It is probable that they sold more Paris porcelain than their own between 1788 and 1791. The London shop was managed by Joseph Flight while Martin Barr* became responsible after 1792 for the running of the retail shop in Worcester. The name change from Flight and Barr to Barr, Flight and Barr did not occur at the same time as far as Worcester and London was concerned. The curious mark

Flight and Barr, Coventry Street, London/
Barr, Flight and Barr Worcester

indicates that the retail business was continuing along different directions and the London shop remained free to sell foreign china as well as glass and other goods.

Chamberlain did not have their own London showrooms until 1813 with the opening of their shop at 63 Piccadilly. These were followed by a new shop at 155 New Bond Street opened in July 1816. On the amalgamation of the Flight and Chamberlain factories in 1840 their respective shops continued under the name Chamberlain and Co.* 1 Coventry Street was sold in December 1844 and 155 New Bond Street in December the following year. This latter shop was taken over by the china dealers W., P. and G. Phillips who used their own name with 'Late Chamberlain' for several years. This mark causes confusion as it was used on wares made for Phillips by several other manufacturers, but not by Chamberlain and Co. themselves.

Long Eliza Figures

The popular name 'Long Eliza' is believed to be an English corruption of the Dutch *lange lijzen* (tall lady) although it is not known when the term was first used by porcelain collectors. Branyan, French and Sandon refer to just a single pattern (I.A.4) by the name *Lange Lijzen*, but in terms of Worcester porcelain it is more correct to call any elongated Chinese figure a 'Long Eliza'. They feature in many patterns, in blue and white as early as the 1740s at Limehouse* and Bristol*, and at Worcester in colours and blue from at least 1752 (Colour Plate 14).

Loop and Dot Borders
See **Crowfoot Borders**

Lord Stormont
See **Stormont Service**

Loving Cups

The earliest written reference to such a shape is in December 1809 when Chamberlain sold a 'Mug, two-handles, with yellow ground and gold border. Caricature arms on one side, Jesus College on the other £1.11s.6d'. The term loving cup would seem to be a later Victorian idea. The earliest surviving Worcester examples are Flight and Barr, c.1800, and the example in the Dyson Perrins Museum painted with a border of hops indicates clearly that it was intended for beer. It is cylindrical with two delicate scroll handles. A single Grainger two-handled mug is known from the 1820s, rounded at the base and with gnarled *tau*-shaped handles associated with Grainger, Lee and Co. From about 1840 Grainger made the first of a long tradition of presentation cups for the Worcester Rowing Club and Worcester Regatta, although these usually have only a single handle and loving cups are rare before the 1860s.

Lowdin's Glass House

The site of the Bristol Porcelain Manufactory* was formerly a glass works which had been owned by William Lowdin. The lease was auctioned in June 1745 and part of the premises in Redcliffe, Bristol, were occupied by William Miller* and Benjamin Lund*. Dr. Pocock* wrote in 1750 that the porcelain manufactory was at 'Lowdn's Glass House'. William Lowdin had no connection with the making of porcelain either at Bristol or at Worcester, although some early authors and collectors referred to wares as Lowdin's.

Lowe, Thomas

A figure painter at Flight's factory mentioned by Solomon Cole* as having been a pupil at Thomas Baxter's* china painting school and who went on to 'higher branches of their art afterwards'. When Baxter wrote in July 1819 to a friend in London he referred to painting at Flight, Barr and Barr: '...their figure painting is now done by a pupil of mine named Lowe'. A Thomas Lowe was admitted Freeman of Worcester 14 July 1826, a surprisingly late date which suggests that there may have been another painter of the same name. No signed pieces are known from this period and inevitably most of Lowe's work is masquerading now as by Thomas Baxter. In 1971 Sotheby's sold a plaque of a young woman's portrait signed T. Lowe 1834. It is not known if Lowe was still at Flight's factory at this time. In 1845 Thomas Lowe exhibited a portrait at the Royal Academy giving his address as London.

Lu Tung-Pin

The only recorded early Bristol porcelain figure is a copy of a Chinese statue of one of the eight Immortals identified as *Lu Tung-Pin*. He lived from c.755 AD to 805 and owned a magic sword with which he performed great feats. He is usually shown dressed as a scholar and holding a fly-whisk.

At least nine Bristol examples are known, all from the same mould. Embossed from the mould on the back of each is the place name 'Bristoll' and date 1750. This date seems consistent with the porcelain and it is unlikely that any of these figures were made from the same mould later at Worcester, even though the appearance of the body and glaze can vary between examples. All are white in imitation of Chinese *blanc de chine* porcelain, although some of the bases have been mottled in manganese* underglaze.

Lund, Benjamin

A Bristol copper merchant, he was the son of Benjamin Lund, a carpenter from Hammersmith, West London. He was in Bristol by 1728 when he took out a patent for manufacturing copper, and extracting silver from copper in partnership with a London physicist. In October 1738 Lund built a brass manufactory beside the River Avon in Bristol but was bankrupt by December 1741. Lund had several business dealings in London including some sort of involvement with Edward Heylyn of the Bow factory, who was also a copper merchant.

While searching for copper ore in Cornwall, Lund may have become aware of soaprock* and its use in porcelain production. Soaprock was used at Limehouse and it is possible that Benjamin Lund was the gentleman referred to by Dr. Pocock* as 'one of the principal manufacturers at Limehouse which failed'.

Lund was in partnership with William Miller*, a Bristol banker who presumably provided the funding while Lund experimented in perfecting the soaprock formula. On 7 March 1749, Lund was granted a licence to mine soaprock at Gew Graze near the Lizard. He sold these rights to Richard Holdship* of Worcester in February 1752. The Bristol factory was transferred in full to Worcester and Benjamin Lund was referred to in a bankruptcy document dated 23 February 1753 as a 'china maker now of the City of Worcester'. Nothing is known of Lund's later career. He had married but his wife died in December 1749. Three of his sons died in infancy and the fourth also at a fairly young age. Benjamin Lund returned to Bristol where he died on 1 January 1768, his will proved on 25 February of that year. *See also* **Bristol Porcelain Manufactory** and **Soaprock**.

Lyes, John
The original partnership deeds of the Worcester Tonquin Manufacture* list Robert Podmore* and John Lyes as very important figures. Podmore left by 1755 and entered into an agreement with Chaffers at Liverpool. Unfortunately no information survives to record the fate of John Lyes who probably left the Worcester factory at the same time.

Lyttelton Vase
The massive size, early date and unique decoration make this vase one of the most remarkable pieces of early Worcester surviving. At present part of a loan collection at Bristol City Museum and Art Gallery, the vase was formerly in the collection of the Honourable Anthony Lyttelton who acquired it from H. Rissik Marshall. Painted in underglaze blue, the vase depicts chinoiserie* figures and riverscapes between bands of diaper patterns. It stands 22½in. (57cm) high and dates from c.1753. The vase has suffered considerably in the kiln, to the extent that a large part of the painting remains completely unglazed.

Lyttelton Vase. *The powerful shape combines with very careful underglaze painting to make a truly remarkable piece of early Worcester porcelain, workman's mark* of a cross, c.1753, 22½in. (57cm). (Private Collection on loan to the City of Bristol Museum and Art Gallery.)*

M

Magician Pattern

Frequently confused with the earlier *Beckoning Chinaman** pattern, the *Magician* pattern does also include a standing Chinaman raising one hand into the air. Instead of calling to a flock of birds, however, he appears to have conjured up a vase of flowers on a table to the amazement of two ladies who sit watching him. The design is probably copied directly from Chinese porcelain but, as the two ladies are identical to the attendants in the *Pu-Tai** pattern, it is possible the factory adapted the design for themselves. The *Magician* pattern occurs with a crowfoot* border and was used c.1765, mostly on leaf dishes.

***Magician Pattern.** A cabbage leaf dish painted in* famille rose* *colours, with a gilded crowfoot* border, c.1765, 10¼in. (26cm). (Phillips.)*

Man in the Moon Mark

One engraved copper plate for a transfer printed saucer was altered, probably as some kind of joke, but one which was allowed to continue by the factory proprietors. Instead of the usual hatched crescent mark, a face was engraved within the crescent to form a man in the moon. The engraved plate in question was for a small sized saucer of *Fence* pattern* and I have seen nine of these saucers, ranging in date from 1770-80. All are clearly from the same copper plate and it is interesting to see how the engraving was touched up and strengthened with new cutting as the engraved details became worn. Many old texts incorrectly show this mark as a painted open crescent pointing to the right, but the illustration here, photographed from a factory site waster, shows the correct version.

Man in the Pavilion Pattern

An important pattern in terms of the factory's success as this was probably their first underglaze blue printed design. The simple Chinese pattern, featuring a figure in a gazebo looking out towards a sampan on a lake, was usually complete in itself and only very rarely finished off with a border of any kind. The engraving style was designed with blue and white in mind, using deeply cut lines which gave a sharp definition to the print. The *Man in the Pavilion* pattern was in use by at least 1757 and was probably the first pattern to be marked with a crescent mark*. A significant trial waster of a portion of the pattern was found on the factory site and is illustrated under **'I H' Marks**. The pattern, number II.B.1 in Branyan, French and Sandon, was used only on teawares and did not continue into the 1760s.

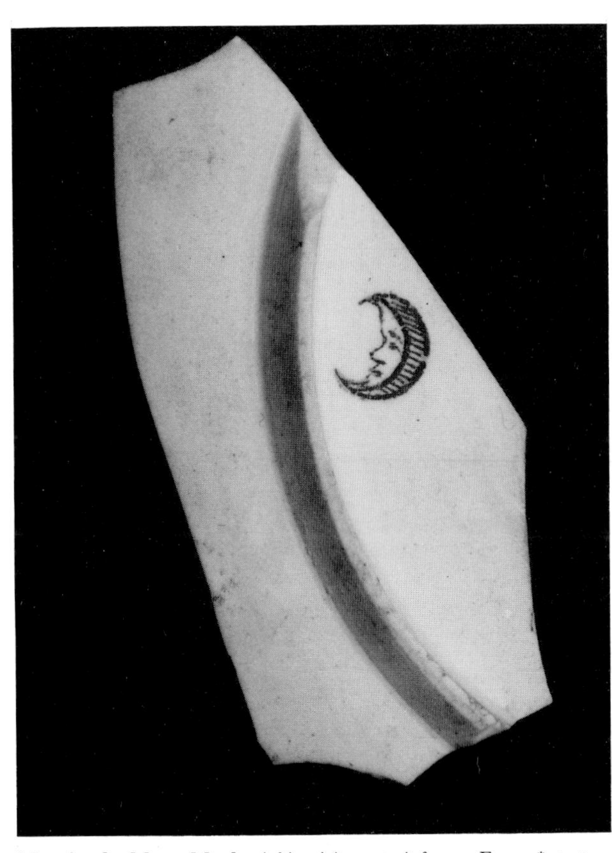

***Man in the Moon Mark.** A biscuit* waster* from a* Fence* *pattern saucer found during factory site excavations*, c.1770.*

Mandarin Style

See **Canton style**

Manganese Decoration

While cobalt blue was the only colour which could be successfully applied underneath the glaze in the 18th century, the Worcester factory did experiment with manganese which produced an aubergine or purple colour. Delftware potters

***Mansfield Pattern.** A large teapot* or punch pot* with an unusual form of handle and spout, the very formal style of painting indicating a late date, crescent mark*, c.1780. (Dyson Perrins Museum.)*

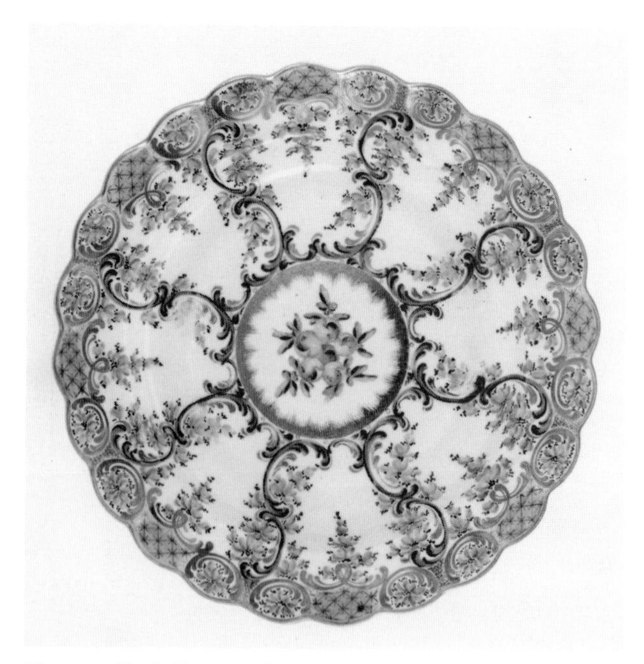

***Manvers, Earl, Pattern.** A scallop-edged dessert plate decorated at the Worcester factory in the style of Sèvres*, the centre with a small spray of spotted fruit*, c.1770-5, 8½in. (21.6cm). (Sotheby's.)*

had little difficulty using the colour, particularly at Bristol. It is understandable, therefore, that the Bristol Porcelain Factory should have used manganese. A small number of pickle dishes, a creamboat and the bases on some of the Lu Tung-Pin* figures are decorated in manganese but are far from successful. Worcester experimented with underglaze manganese and painted the *Dragon** pattern on small circular bowls, probably dating from c.1760. The very few that survive are badly smudged, even though a matching unglazed biscuit waster from the factory site painted in manganese is perfectly clear and detailed.

Mansfield Pattern

Although I have been told about a Chinese example of this pattern I have never seen an actual prototype. Indeed, the border seems to owe its origin more to French St Cloud porcelain than to pure Chinese. The pattern proved to be the most popular blue and white painted design made at Worcester, in production continuously from c.1757 until at least 1780. One reason for its apparent popularity is that it is reasonably straightforward to paint, requiring little skill on the part of the painter. *Mansfield* was used on all teaware shapes and some other shapes such as mustard pots*, butter tubs* and punch pots*. It even inspired a simple printed version for use in panels on potted meat pots (potting pans*) and suchlike. Most English factories copied the pattern and it has been seen in creamware, pearlware and even delftware. The name has become very well known to collectors and it is easy to forget that it was called *Mansfield* only as recently as the 1930s when the pattern was reintroduced by Royal Worcester.

Manvers, Earl Pattern

A distinctive pattern used on dessert wares, c.1770-5. The design is related to other hop trellis* type patterns with berried leaf garlands encircling rococo scrolls which link the puce diaper-panelled border to a central panel of fruit. A service of the pattern is believed to have been owned by Charles Meadows, later Duke of Kingston, who became Earl Manvers in 1806. Enough examples survive to suggest that several dessert sets of this pattern were made, not only for Earl Manvers. A pattern used on teawares with a puce herringbone border is frequently confused with *Earl Manvers* on account of similar colouring, but the Manvers pattern itself has only been recorded on dessert shapes and baskets. The *Earl Manvers* pattern was reproduced by Royal Worcester in the early 1900s.

Marbled Grounds

With the advent of neo-classicism came a renewed interest in ancient marble. In the 18th century a synthetic stone from Italy called *scagliola* imitated exotic marbles for fireplaces and columns in British stately homes, while Wedgwood further encouraged the taste with his 'porphry' and 'variegated' vases in glazed earthenware. Flight and Barr saw great potential in imitating the patterns of *scagliola* as backgrounds reserved with more decorative panels. By 1800 they were producing very clever copies of veined marbles and conglomerates, while their finest work was produced in the Barr, Flight and Barr period c.1810 (Colour Plate 58). The effect was most successful when used to frame dramatic panels of shells or feathers (*see* Colour Plate 40), although many other subjects were used with marble grounds. A plate in the Dyson Perrins Museum uses a blue and gold veined marble as a ground for a gilded classical figure, with an incredibly stunning result (Colour Plate 62). Chamberlain used gilding on their marbled grounds rather more frequently than Flights and their veined marble effects tend to be stronger and less subtle. One most dramatic ground imitates a conglomerate of brightly coloured stones, which almost dazzles the viewer and distracts rather than frames the Shakespearian panels. Grainger used marbled grounds very rarely and the effect is generally unsuccessful. Occasionally marbled grounds were used at other factories but nowhere near as frequently or as well as at Worcester. The fashion for marbling did not suit the revival of rococo and was virtually discontinued by c.1820.

*(Opposite) **Marbled Grounds.** The colourful ground imitating conglomerate marble is almost overpowering on these Chamberlain 'Regent' shaped vases painted with Shakespearian* subjects by Humphrey Chamberlain*, script marks, c.1815, 9⅞in. (25cm). (Phillips.)*

Manvers, Earl, Pattern. *A dessert dish decorated with a pattern which is related to and often confused with the Earl Manvers pattern. In this case the puce herringbone band forms an inner border, while the Manvers pattern has puce diaper panels around the outside, c.1772-5, 10in. (25.5cm). (Phillips.)*

Marriage Pattern. *A fluted teacup, coffee cup and saucer with bright underglaze blue* borders, the flower paintings incorporating bows, arrows and lover's knots, crescent marks*, c.1780. (Phillips.)*

Marriage Pattern

The typical formal coloured flower sprays used on fluted teaware patterns in the late 1770s can sometimes have additional motifs hidden in the groupings. These comprise a bow, an arrow and a lover's knot and occur in conjunction with deep blue and gilded borders. This was certainly not a single marriage service as many different border designs exist. While the centre panels are normally fairly plain, more elaborate versions occur on dessert wares, some including landscape or bird paintings in the central panels. A large dessert dish in the Godden Reference Collection is painted with a cow and two goats in a landscape within three 'Marriage' sprays and the celebrated Kew* service also used the bow, arrow and knot motifs. Dessert dishes of this type are similar to the *Lord Henry Thynne** pattern and all seem to date around 1780, some possibly as late as 1785. The name *Royal Marriage* pattern is occasionally used but there would appear to be no justification for this, except possibly in the case of the Kew service.

Mask Jugs

The mask-spouted jugs with cabbage leaf moulding, called in the 18th century Dutch jugs, are discussed here under cabbage leaf jugs*. Some jugs with the same moulded sleepy bearded man on the lip were made with a plain baluster- or pear-shaped body and loop handle. These can date from the early 1760s but most are later, from the 1770s and 1780s. These plain mask jugs are principally found in blue and white although some rich coloured ground and blue bordered painted patterns were occasionally used. Caughley made a similar shape but with differing details in the mask. Much earlier, c.1753-55, the factory made small milk jugs* and slightly larger half-pint and pint (quarter and half litre) jugs with mask lips. The smaller jugs have a female with wavy hair below a plain rounded lip-rim, while the others use a bearded man but with very different features from the later model. These early mask jugs are great rarities.

Match Pots

Small vases, also known as luminaries, but generally referred to today as spill vases*.

May Day. *A cabbage leaf moulded mask jug with a coloured-in version of the* May Day *print, c.1765, 9in. (23cm). (Dyson Perrins Museum.)*

Maw's Tile Works

Following the failure of the company in 1850, Chamberlain and Co. abandoned tile production on the Warmstry House* site to a new company who traded as Maw and Co. They produced encaustic tiles in the same manner as Chamberlain until c.1853 when the works were transferred to new premises at Benthall in Shropshire, across the river from Coalport and Ironbridge. The firm prospered to become one of the largest tile works in the world. Early Maw's tiles marked with the Worcester name are very rarely seen.

May Day

A popular overglaze print engraved probably by Hancock* after a painting by Francis Hayman which had been commissioned to decorate a box at Vauxhall Gardens. The curious subject depicts a traditional entertainment which was explained in Smith's *Book for a Rainy Day,* pp 14-16:

> The gaiety during the merry month of May was to me most delightful; my feet, though I knew nothing of the positions, kept pace with those of the blooming milkmaids who danced round their garlands of massive plate, hired from the silversmiths to the amount of several hundreds of pounds for the purpose of placing round an obelisk covered with silk fixed upon a chairman's horse. The most showy flowers of the season were arranged to fill up the openings between the dishes, plates, butterboats, cream-jugs and tankards. This obelisk was

***Meissen Style.** A mug of Scratch Cross class* painted in the style and palette of Meissen's* indianische Blumen, *c.1754, 4in. (10cm). (Private Collection.)*

***Meissen Style.** A coffee cup painted in colours with a pattern developed initially at Meissen c.1730. In this case Worcester have probably made a replacement for a Chinese service copying the Meissen original, c.1765-70, 2⅛in. (5.5cm). (Phillips.)*

> carried by two chairmen in gold laced hats, six or more handsome milkmaids in pink and blue gowns... A smart, slender figure of a fiddler, commonly wearing a sky blue coat, with his hat profusely covered with ribands, attended; and the master of the group was accompanied by a constable to protect the plate from too close a pressure of the crowd when the maids danced before the doors of his customers.

May Day was used on mugs and leaf moulded mask jugs from c.1765-75, as well as very occasional teawares. It is usually printed in black, although fully coloured versions are known.

***Meissen Style.** A plate probably made as a direct replacement for a Meissen original of c.1735, the Worcester copy c.1770, 9in. (23cm). Probably decorated at the factory rather than in the Giles* workshop. (Dyson Perrins Museum.)*

Meissen Style

The bankruptcy papers relating to Richard Holdship* mentioned that the Worcester Porcelain Manufactory had been established in 1751 to imitate Dresden Ware whereas the Bristol factory was imitating East India China Ware. 'Dresden' was the popular name for Meissen when sold in England. Most of the earliest Worcester productions were undoubtedly oriental in flavour but, while Bow, for example, made direct copies of everything Chinese, Worcester avoided this. Instead their shapes were taken from English silver and German porcelain and the decoration seemed to combine pure *famille rose** with the kind of foliate ornament used at Meissen. This colourful formal style, called *indianische Blumen* at Meissen, was little known in England and therefore refreshingly original. By adding elements of *famille rose* Worcester managed to tone down the harshness of the Meissen patterns and created their own unique style which continued into the 1760s and beyond (*see* Colour Plate 81).

In addition to these adaptations, Worcester also made direct copies of Meissen decoration popular at the time but difficult to obtain in England. Many ornamental shapes, particularly leaf-shaped dishes, leaf sauceboats and vases, were copied from Meissen. The garnitures of baluster and beaker shaped vases from c.1756-60 (Colour Plate 59) with flowers or *Mobbing Birds** closely copied Meissen in spirit if not in actual palette. Some coloured flower painting was clearly copied directly from the *deutsche Blumen* of Meissen. The blue and white teacup illustrated as I.E. 29A in Branyan, French and Sandon is important as this was made c.1758 as an exact copy of Meissen from about twenty years earlier. The mark used on the Meissen original — crossed swords with a workman's mark of a numeral 9 and a dash — was copied exactly and was subsequently regarded by the factory as their own 'Meissen' mark. This mark was used on Worcester teaware shapes in Continental style from c.1765-72, often but not exclusively decorated outside the factory.

Many copies of Japanese *Kakiemon** designs made at Worcester were likely to have been copied from Meissen rather than directly from Japanese porcelain. On the other hand, the curious coffee cup illustrated which bears a Meissen design from c.1730, was probably made as a replacement for a Chinese service copying Meissen. The influence of the great Meissen factory was so widespread that many of its patterns became universal. *Immortelle**, for instance, painted in blue in the 1770s, was made all over Europe at the same time. At Worcester, however, there was a gradual change during the 1760s and 1770s when French porcelain from Sèvres became a far more important influence.

Mercury Gilding
The use of mercurial oxide as a medium to enable the gold to flow replaced honey gilding* at Flights factory c.1788-90. This was probably due to Charlotte Hampton* who was brought in to teach the factory hands how to do fine gilding following the departure of the Chamberlains. Mercury gilding was probably used in London by Giles* from c.1765-70, accounting for the much brighter and smoother appearance of Giles decorated gilding. The gilding used at Chamberlains from the 1790s onwards is a particularly bright form of mercury gilding, while Grainger used mercury from the time Thomas Grainger* left the Chamberlain factory c.1805.

Milk Jugs. *The moulded leaf scrolls on the lip of this otherwise plain milk jug are certainly flamboyant compared with the normal sparrow beak* lip. This example is painted with the rare* High Island *pattern, unmarked, c.1753-4, 3in. (7.5cm). (John Broad Collection.)*

Milk Jugs
While it is usual for small early Worcester jugs to be called cream jugs, the London Warehouse c.1755-6 were selling 'Milk jugs, round and press'd' at 8s. and 12s. per dozen while 'Cream ewers' (what we now call creamboats*) were listed separately and quite a different shape. The two main forms of these early milk jugs are plain pear shapes which were thrown and turned, and press-moulded baluster shapes with vertical flutes. The plain milk jugs usually have 'sparrow-beak'* lips although rare examples can have a moulded female mask lip (*see* **Mask Jugs**). Slightly later versions with plain bodies and grooved handles can have a leaf moulded below the lip. The pressed shapes have the same moulded double scroll handle as was used on panel-moulded coffee cups. These are usually painted in colours but by c.1756-7 a strap-fluted* version was introduced with reserved rococo cartouche panels which were more suitable for blue and white.

By the 1760s the standard form of sparrow beak milk jug was included with every tea service. Earlier examples are squat and they gradually became more ovoid by the 1770s. The handles are usually single grooved loops but on some slightly larger ovoid milk jugs the handles were moulded with a round section. These larger sparrow beak jugs usually came with matching covers while the smaller jugs with flared rims were complete in themselves. The shape continued unchanged into the Flight period and only very rarely was there any variation, such as the occasional inclusion of a tall Chelsea ewer* as a milk jug in some tea services. In the late 18th and 19th centuries the milk jugs tended to match the rest of the tea service and these jugs gradually became larger.

Milkmaids Pattern
A common inclusion in many rural scenes of the day, milkmaids were incorporated into many early Worcester prints. The principal version which goes under the name of *The Milkmaids* was listed by Cook in *The Life and Work of Robert Hancock* as item 73 and occurs printed in black or lilac from c.1765 until c.1775. It was subsequently adapted as an underglaze blue print and used on teawares during the 1780s. The origin of the print is not known although different versions were published by booksellers in the 18th century. Earlier Worcester examples are often signed by Robert Hancock*, in full or with his initials, while one particular version includes the crossed anchor rebus* believed to relate to the two Holdship* brothers. The underglaze version differs in several respects from the earlier *Milkmaids* print and has its own border pattern. Caughley did not copy this particular print and so the *Milkmaids* tea services sold by Chamberlain in 1788 with their added gold details will be of Flight manufacture. A full tea service sold then for a reasonable 6s., in order to compete with cheaper competition.

Miller, William
A grocer and banker from Bristol, born in 1698, he was involved in property and shipping and owned a 'counting House' in St Johns, Bristol. Miller was in partnership with Benjamin Lund* but probably provided only funding, for he had no practical abilities as a potter. When the rights to the Bristol Porcelain Manufactory* were transferred to Richard Holdship* in February 1752, Miller and Lund were prohibited from continuing to produce porcelain and from disclosing the secret process to anyone else. William Miller died in Bristol on 26 January 1781, aged eighty-two.

Miniature Porcelain
See **Toys**

Mobbing Birds
A very distinctive pattern showing birds in a tree. The principal birds are a cheeky finch chirping at an owl which seems to be hooting in surprise, while a pheasant-like bird takes no notice and continues to preen its feathers. In larger examples it is usual to find two or three additional birds in the same tree, while smaller vases sometimes omit the owl

Colour Plate 57. ***London Shape.*** *A Flight, Barr and Barr teacup and saucer decorated with a rich Japan pattern, the centre replaced with the gilt initial 'G' as a special order, impressed mark*, c.1815. (Fine Arts Centre, Cheekwood.)*

Mobbing Birds. *A vase copying Meissen* both in shape and style of decoration, illustrating the full version of the* Mobbing Birds *pattern painted in colours. Few examples include so much detail in the design; c.1757, 8½in. (21.5cm). (Kenneth Klepser Collection.)*

Mobbing Birds. *A vase of similar shape to the previous example but clearly by a different hand, exhibiting far less skill but stronger outlines, c.1757-8, 6½in. (16.5cm). (Phillips.)*

altogether. Another variation has the owl on a lower branch and the mobbing finch can be on the left- or right-hand side of the tree. The origin of the design was shown by Hugh Tait, *Connoisseur,* April 1963, to be taken from a combination of bird drawings by C. Fenn, some published as prints in *The Ladies' Amusement** and elsewhere, including some engraved by Robert Hancock*. The pattern was used on baluster vases, painted either in colours, black monochrome or underglaze blue. A small number of plates are also recorded. The painting of this pattern on Worcester has been attributed to James Rogers (*see* **Rogers, I.**) but, while some will undoubtedly be by him, others are clearly by different hands. One version of *The Mobbing Birds* was later, c.1770, copied as an engraved pattern for underglaze blue (*see* **Birds in Branches Pattern**).

Monkey's Head Finial

Occasionally the handles of large sized sauceboats* were applied with a finial or thumbrest in the form of a monkey's head although this has sometimes been described as a dog's head. Looking somewhat oriental, the origin is probably English silver where decorative finials were often used on rococo sauceboats in the 1740s. The Worcester boats date

Monochrome Painting. *A simple mug reflecting the spirit of the rococo*, the ruins painted in puce, c.1757, 3⅜in. (8.5cm). (Phillips.)*

Muffin Dishes. *A Chamberlain muffin dish from a breakfast service painted with* Fancy Birds* *probably by George Davis*, reserved on a pale blue ground, printed mark with Piccadilly address, c.1816. (Phillips.)*

from c.1754-5 and occur in blue and white although more usually are coloured. Two-handled sauceboats* were also sometimes made with monkey's head finials, again only on the largest sizes (for illustration *see* **Two-handled Sauceboats**).

Monochrome Painting
Whereas pencilled decoration* was usually executed in black monochrome, a much more subtle form of monochrome painting was popular in the 1750s, principally in puce or tones of lilac. The inspiration was probably Meissen although the rococo* feel of the designs suggests Vincennes could also have been influential. Chinese figure patterns are closer in style to Chinese originals and occur on teawares c.1754-60. European landscapes are very romanticised with outsized ruins and small figures included amongst delicate shading. Some fairly dramatic monochrome painting was used within the confines of panels on leaf dishes and very occasionally in sauceboat panels, while a series of armorial decoration reserved coloured rococo shields against backgrounds of delicate puce landscapes. The fashion for monochrome did not continue into the 1760s except for some rare bird painting.

There was a considerable revival in monochrome painting along with neo-classical* styles during the 1780s. The Duke of Clarence* chose sepia monochrome for John Pennington's figure subjects in the Hope service* and this was probably influential in encouraging the factory to copy the French styles of monochrome landscape and figure painting popular during the 1790s. Chamberlain found the sepia colour was also popular for views of landscapes and country houses, painted in panels on various tea services and some dessert wares, as well as fables and countless views of Worcester. Grainger also painted popular views in black or sepia up until c.1810, when colour mostly returned to favour once again.

Moss Fibre Pattern
A distinctive printed pattern used by Grainger from c.1835. The design of a close leafy webbing could be adapted easily for any shape, and was therefore inexpensive. Mostly printed underglaze in grey or very bright blue, the pattern could also be heightened with gold flecks or twigging*. The pattern usually has its own printed mark and was occasionally used as a background with reserved painted panels. *Moss Fibre* continued into the 20th century.

Mother and Child Pattern
A popular teaware pattern printed in underglaze blue c.1775-85. The Chinese lady is seated by fanciful vases while the standing child looks up either at a butterfly or flowers. The pattern is pure chinoiserie* and was made in a virtually identical form at Caughley, distinguished by differences in the group of vases on the reverse. The Caughley version was sold by the Chamberlains as retailers under the name *Image* pattern. Worcester's version is listed by Branyan, French and Sandon as II.A.13.

Colour Plate 58. **Marbled Grounds.** *A Barr, Flight and Barr jardinière* beautifully painted with a bird panel, the simulated marble ground painted with extraordinary care, script mark, c.1805-8, 6¼ in. (16cm). (Private Collection.)*

Colour Plate 59. **Meissen Style.** *A complete garniture of five vases, the shape and decoration all copied from Meissen although adapted to suit Worcester's palette, c.1758, 8½ in. (21.5cm) and 6⅛ in. (15.5cm). (Phillips.)*

Colour Plate 60. **Mugs.** *A small mug with panel moulding usually found on coffee cans*, the simple decoration in Worcester's adaptation of* famille rose*, *c.1752-3, 3⅛in. (8cm). (Phillips.)*

Colour Plate 61. **Mugs.** *A cylindrical mug painted with care to depict actual flower specimens, unusual at this period, c.1760-5, 6in. (15cm). (Phillips.)*

Moulds

In the reserve collection at the Dyson Perrins Museum are a number of moulds which survive from the 18th century. Most are in a fired clay which was called 'pitcher' and were used as master or block moulds from which the working moulds were made. Their history is unknown and not all appear to be Worcester, as they include designs known only from Derby and Chelsea-Derby porcelain. The most important specimens are the moulds for two massive rococo tureens, like the blue and white ones which have survived but differing in their applied ornament. More simple moulds for feather-moulded* and *Chrysanthemum** pattern cups show instantly just how much detail was lost when the sharp castings were covered with glaze.

One interesting Grainger mould also survived and was left unfinished. The unfired clay is incised 'Engraved by Thomas Grainger Senr. March 10 1818', showing the unexpected skill of the owner of the factory. Moulds are very difficult things to store. When working moulds become worn out they are dumped and master moulds were usually broken when no longer needed. A few fragments of pitcher master moulds were found during the factory site excavations*, but, sadly, any plaster working moulds had crumbled in the damp ground and were unrecognisable.

Mugs. *A so-called bell-shaped mug of Scratch Cross class* with characteristic heavy handle, painted with a combination of Meissen and Chinese styles typical of Worcester c.1754, 3½in. (9cm). (Sotheby's/Kiddell Papers.)*

Muffin Dishes

Shallow circular dishes with covers, muffin dishes or 'muffineers' were part of some breakfast services* and date from the end of the 18th century although early examples are very rare. A Chamberlain muffin dish painted with *Fancy Birds** in a very similar style to the Princess Charlotte service*, c.1816, is illustrated on page 235. Flight, Barr and Barr examples are known but no early Worcester or Grainger muffin dishes have been seen. Kerr and Binns and Royal Worcester examples are much more common as the fashion for muffins swept Britain in the Victorian period.

Mugs

Apart from sauceboats*, mugs are virtually the only shapes regularly encountered from the earliest years of the Bristol and Worcester factories and remained a staple product for most of the next century. There is a great deal of speculation as to their use and there remain more questions than answers. It was probably up to the original owner to decide what liquor should be drunk from different sized mugs. It is significant that the

Mugs. *A set of three mugs surviving in their original graduated set. Many Worcester mugs were probably sold in this way although few have remained together. These examples all depict George II* along with various nautical subjects printed in black, c.1758-60. (Phillips, Edinburgh.)*

Muscat, Imaum of, Service. The Prince Regent *entering Muscat Cove, a fine coloured-in print within a bright green border, a plate from the service given to the Imaum by William IV* in 1836, impressed marks*, 10⅝in. (27cm). (Dyson Perrins Museum.)*

earliest records which survive, from the London Warehouse (c.1756) as well as the Chamberlain archives, refer to mugs by their size rather than their intended contents. Where a coffee can* ends and a small mug (Colour Plate 60) begins is pure speculation, as one very small mug of c.1760 in the Dyson Perrins Collection is inscribed 'I drink up the liquor/ Tho the cup is but small/ And heres a good health/ To Edmund Wall'. While it is reasonable to assume large mugs were for cider or beer, a pair of Chamberlain mugs of four-pint (2.2 litres) capacity are painted with a border of fruiting vine. These are called 'grace mugs' and were used for a special toast between courses at dinner, being passed around among the guests. Considering the enormous cost of some of the richest Chamberlain grace mugs*, the hosts would have been wise to dilute the contents as a riotous evening moved on.

The earliest Worcester mugs follow Bristol shapes but with far less of a pronounced spreading base. Known as 'Scratch Cross*' type, they usually have a single grooved strap handle and date from 1752 to c.1757. The Tracy mug* is typical of the shape from this early period. Baluster mugs are generally referred to in Worcester porcelain as bell shape, even though they are far too narrow at the rim to resemble an inverted bell. This shape was introduced probably as early as 1752 or 1753, initially on a rounded foot rim and subsequently made with only the slightest foot. So called bell-shaped mugs continued throughout the 1760s but very rarely after c.1770. Instead cylindrical mugs (Colour Plate 61), which developed from the spreading base shape, became the standard from about 1765. Examples usually have a double grooved plain loop handle and range in size from a small coffee can to a quart.

There was little distinction during use between a mug with one handle and one with two, but single-handled mugs often came in pairs or even graduated sets of three, while two-handled mugs, called loving cups*, were usually sold separately.

During the early period of the factory mugs are far more common in blue and white than in colours. Over the period covered by this *Dictionary* there is surprisingly little variety in the shapes manufactured as each factory had its own distinctive handle forms which were applied to plain thrown and turned shapes. Grainger tended to make a far higher proportion of mugs than either Flight or Chamberlain, but all of these factories made far less than Coalport, which suggests that the lower classes tended to use rather more mugs and fewer tea services. A great many mugs were never intended for use, however, and these are discussed under presentation mugs*.

Muscat, Imaum of, Service

R.W. Binns gave a full account of this important commission in his *Century of Potting*, recording the last royal service made by the struggling Flight, Barr and Barr factory in 1836. The Imaum of Muscat had presented William IV with a small battleship filled with luxury goods. In return William IV arranged for a little used royal yacht to be restored with costly gilding and painting. This was re-named *The Prince Regent* and sent to the Imaum together with very English gifts. The King ordered from Worcester a dinner service, each piece showing the yacht entering Muscat Cove. The green border included the Imaum's crest and the whole set was completed for dispatch in 1837. Because it had to be made quickly, Flights engraved a fine outline print which was hand coloured to give the appearance of a painting on each piece. This can hardly be detected, but the original engraved copper printing plate survives at the factory to this day. According to Binns, the Imaum had expected a modern steamship instead of an out-of-date yacht, and was even more upset when he discovered that his own gift, the teak ship *The Imaum*, was put to use merely as a store-ship in the West Indies until it rotted. Hopefully the Worcester dinner service was put to better use, especially as it was extremely elegant, albeit old-fashioned for 1837.

Music Pattern

The origin of this curious design is probably Chinese as the lines resemble stylised characters found on provincial late *Ming* blue and white porcelain. *Music* was one of the last blue painted patterns introduced at Flight's factory c.1785 and continued into the Barr, Flight and Barr period. The pattern usually has gilding on the border and brown enamel rims and is often encountered with reserved panels of crests or initials. It is hard to believe the pattern is painted rather than printed as the lines of 'music' are incredibly even. It must therefore have been a costly pattern and is understandably rarer than the *Royal Lily* pattern* used at the same time.

Mustard Pots

As mustard was served in two ways, very different cruets were required. The basic shapes had developed in English silver and were adopted by Worcester very early on, certainly by 1753. Dry mustard pots were used to serve mustard in powder form. They are always of plain baluster shape with a high domed cover and pointed finial. The feet can be either domed or waisted. Early examples are mostly painted in colours in Chinese style, with patterns such as *Strutting Birds** and *Honeysuckle** (*see* illustration on page 242), or else painted with Long Eliza*-type figures. The paste is usually very creamy and the undersides are fully glazed. Rare blue and white versions are known painted with birds or flowers, as well as with the *Prunus Root** and the *Mansfield** patterns on later examples c.1760-5. Dry mustard pots were not apparently made at Worcester after 1765 although they were made at Caughley in the later 1770s. One other early Worcester object which is pear-shaped with an inward-sloping shoulder could

Colour Plate 62. ***Neo-Classical Style.*** *A most extraordinary Barr, Flight and Barr plate with a classical figure in bronze and gold on a ground simulating lapis lazuli, the border with exquisite gilding, c.1810, 8in. (20.5cm). (Dyson Perrins Museum.)*

Colour Plate 63. ***Nevill, Lord, Marquis of Abergavenny.*** *An important Chamberlain inkstand* corresponding with the 'New Long Ink Rich fawn and figures', included in the order placed by Lord Nevill in June 1813, at a cost of fifteen guineas, script mark, 8⅝in. (22cm) wide. The painting is by Humphrey Chamberlain jun.* (Phillips.)*

Colour Plate 64. ***Parker, Thomas, Service.*** *An impressive early Chamberlain soup tureen*, the* Dragon in Compartments* *pattern reserving the arms of Thomas and Elizabeth Parker, made for their marriage in 1796, unmarked, 11⅜in. (29cm) high. (Phillips.)*

have been a dry mustard pot but only a single example has been seen lacking its cover and it is difficult to tell what form this would have taken. This dates from c.1753.

Wet mustard was served with a stick or spoon and called for a wider container with a handle. Worcester's early shape was a cylindrical drum with sloping shoulder and short neck. The handle is the square shape with rounded thumb-rest that was used on many creamboats at the same time c.1753-5. The covers on these early wet mustard pots have pointed finials and do not have a hole in the rim for the spoon to protrude. Once again these are mostly known in colours with Chinese figures, or with coloured-in transfer prints of figures or the *Red Bull* pattern*. The shape was modified in the 1760s to take a spoon and became larger. The handle was a moulded double-scroll as used on chocolate cups and while the finial can be pointed it is most usual to find examples with flower knops. The decoration is mostly restricted to the same popular blue and white patterns as dry mustard pots — *Mansfield** and *Prunus Root**, as well as blue-printed *Fence** and *Three Flowers** patterns. Wet mustard pots were made in two sizes and both continued into the 1780s. Later examples in *Fisherman and Cormorant** pattern have a button finial instead of a flower. (*See* illustration on page 242.)

Porcelain spoons were made with curved handles to fit into the wet mustard pots, while the moulded flat 'salt spoons' are regularly found with Worcester and Caughley mustard pots and must have been sold with them originally; *see* **Spoons.**

***Mustard Pots.** A dry mustard pot with typical high domed cover, painted in enamel colours with the* Honeysuckle* *pattern, the cover with an additional bird, c.1752-3, 5in. (12.5cm). (Phillips.)*

***Mustard Pots.** A very unusual early form of dry mustard pot with simple Chinese decoration in colours. The original domed cover is missing, c.1752, 3½in. (9cm). (Phillips.)*

***Mustard Pots.** A wet mustard pot with a moulded scroll handle popular c.1765-70, printed in blue with the* Fence* *pattern, crescent mark*, 4in. (10cm); together with a spoon probably intended for salt rather than mustard, also c.1770. (Phillips.)*

N

Nelson Service

During his exhaustive tour of England in 1802 Lord Nelson visited Worcester on 26/27 August. The local newspaper account described his visit to Chamberlain's factory where over the door had been thrown

> a triumphal arch of laurel, ornamented with an elegant blue flag, with an appropriate inscription thereon. For more than an hour his Lordship viewed with the minutest attention every department of this highly improved work, so much the object of general curiosity; and on inspection of the superb assortment of china at the shop in High Street, honoured Messrs Chamberlain by declaring that, although possessed of the finest porcelain the courts of Dresden and Naples could afford, he had seen none equal to the productions of their manufactory, in testimony of which he left a very large order for china, to be decorated with his arms, insignia &c...

The Freedom of the City was presented to Nelson in a Chamberlain vase and all of the city was excited by his visit. One painter at Chamberlains, James Plant, later in life told R.W. Binns* how the work-force were all expecting to see this great hero and instead were met by

> a very battered looking gentleman...he had lost an arm and an eye....Leaning on his left and only arm was the beautiful Lady Hamilton, evidently pleased at the interest excited by her companion; and then, amongst the general company following after, came a very infirm old gentleman — this was Sir William Hamilton.

The Hamiltons ordered some porcelain also, but it was the order for Nelson which was so important to the factory. The order books survive and list a breakfast service of 148 pieces, as well as a complete dinner and dessert service and other

***Nelson Service.** A Chamberlain serving dish from the breakfast* service ordered by Nelson in 1802, the standard* Fine Old Japan* *pattern bearing the Admiral's crests in the border panels, marked Chamberlains Worcester 240, 10in. (25.5cm). (Royal Ontario Museum, Toronto.)*

Colour Plate 65. ***Plates.*** *An unusual design in the style of Chinese* famille verte* *but combined with flowers derived from Meissen*. The style suggests an early date but the paste and glaze indicate a date of c.1765, 8⅝in. (22cm). (The Fine Arts Centre, Cheekwood.)*

ornaments. The Admiral chose the factory's most popular rich *Fine Old Japan** pattern number 240. The teapots and dinner wares were to have the full armorials while all other pieces had just crests incorporated into the border panels.

The service was not invoiced for payment it seems until January 1806, after Nelson's death at Trafalgar. Only the breakfast service had been finished (after two and a half years!) and the dinner and dessert services were not produced. Neither, apparently, were the other rich ornaments. A few sample plates from the dessert service have survived, however (Colour Plate 66 right). The breakfast service, called the 'Horatia' set in the list of Nelson's effects, passed to Lady Hamilton and was subsequently sold to offset her numerous debts. Representative pieces are on display in the National Maritime Museum and the Dyson Perrins Museum. See also my article 'Nelson's China' in *Antique Dealer and Collectors Guide*, March 1989.

Neo-classical Style

A 19th century term for what was called in the 18th century the True style or Greek style. While normally thought of as occurring in the last quarter of the 18th century, the style has its origins earlier with the establishment of the British Museum in 1753. Sir William Hamilton, more than anyone else, was responsible for the renewed popularity of classical styles. The collection of Greek vases which he had formed in Naples was brought to England in 1771 and sold to the British Museum for £8,400. He had previously spent £6,000 publishing a catalogue of the designs on his vases which appeared in 1766. This had a very great influence on public taste and was used by Robert Adam and Josiah Wedgwood who worked to create a completely new market, both in London and the stately homes of the gentry. Neo-classicism was basically a revolt against the frivolity of the rococo and the overall feeling of the time was best summed up by the paintings of David.

Worcester porcelain had been so heavily dominated by the rococo style that it took a while to adapt to change. Wedgwood surged ahead taking a vital part of their custom. James Giles* noticed what was happening and introduced a pattern of painted stone vases within borders of palmettes, c.1772-5. The factory imitated this and began to use formal shapes and

Colour Plate 66. ***Plates.*** *Left: a Flight, Barr and Barr dessert plate made for the Prince Regent* in 1815, the raised gold border of exceptional quality, printed mark, 9½ in. (24cm). Right: a sample plate from the proposed dessert service ordered by Nelson* from Chamberlain in 1802. The border is Chamberlain's popular pattern 240. (Phillips.)*

Neo-Classical Style. *An early use of purely classical styles on a pair of dessert baskets decorated in the Giles* workshop, c.1772-5. A dessert* service exactly corresponding with this pattern was included in the Giles sale catalogue of 1774. (Phillips.)*

Neo-Classical Style. *A Barr, Flight and Barr pot and cover based on the shape of an ancient oil lamp with a gilded sphinx finial, painted with different gamebirds' feathers, script mark, c.1810-3, 4⅜in. (11cm). (Formerly Henry Sandon Collection.)*

panels again, although the series of transfer printed scenes of ruins continued to have rococo undertones, especially in the borders. It was the influx of French porcelain into London in the late 1780s following a relaxation on duty which forced the factory to compete. John Flight went to France and saw the new styles, and subsequently the factory altered its direction to become the most important neo-classical porcelain manufacture in England. They became trend-setters, creating new styles with their use of marbled grounds* and bat-printed* classical figures. Chamberlain started straight into the neo-classical period and followed Flights along very similar lines. The Worcester factories felt so at home now in the classical styles (Colour Plate 62) that they did not know when to let go, allowing Coalport and Staffordshire to lead the way once again when the rococo revival* occurred during the 1820s.

Nevill, Lord, Marquis of Abergavenny

One of the most important single orders given to the Chamberlain factory was placed by Lord Nevill in June 1813 with a note that it was to be ready in four months. The order comprised complete dinner, dessert and breakfast services, all in a rich 'Japan' pattern and bearing the arms and crests of the Marquis of Abergavenny. While these services were impressive enough, the order also included a series of vases, chocolate cups, mugs and an inkstand, to be decorated with rich salmon pink and gold grounds and painted panels by Humphrey Chamberlain*. The finished items were eventually sent to Lord Nevill on 21 July 1814. The 'Regent'-shaped vase was painted with a subject from Shakespeare's Henry VIII while the pair of grace mugs* were painted with 'The Power of Love' and 'Bacchante'. These mugs are now in the Dyson Perrins Museum and it is well worth a visit just to see these and thus understand why they cost an incredible £42 when they were ordered. The 'New Long Ink, Rich fawn and figures' (Colour Plate 63) was sold at Phillips in 1990 and its discovery explained the charge in Lord Nevill's order for the modelling of crests. The central cover of the inkwell is in the form of the Abergavenny family crest of a bull and it is likely the same crest was used on the covers of the tureens and ice pails in the services. Lord Nevill's order remains the Chamberlain factory's greatest accomplishment as the quality and sheer richness were never to be achieved again.

New China Works, Worcester

A range of finely decorated vases and a small number of teawares are marked with the painted name 'New China Works, Worcester'. Stylistically these date to the 1820s and have been attributed in the past to Grainger as it was assumed Grainger was the 'new' factory while Chamberlain and Flight were older. Grainger was established by at least 1806, however, and not only were they no longer 'new' in 1820 but

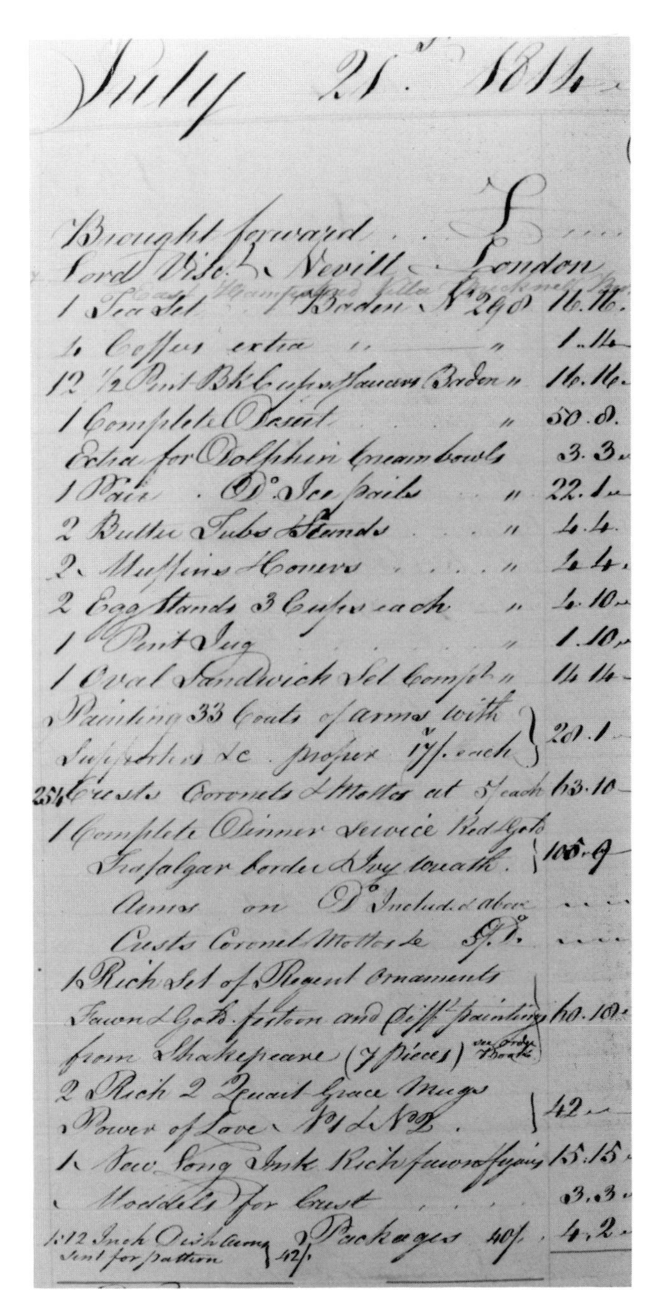

July 2[illegible]. 1814

Brought forward . . . £

Lord Visc. Nevill London

1 Tea Set Border No 298 16.16.

4 Coffees extra 1.14

12 ½ Pint BK Cups & Saucers Border 16.16

1 Complete Desert 50.8

Extra for Dolphin Cream bowls 3.3

1 Pair Do Ice pails 22.1

2 Butter Tubs Stands 4.4

2 Muffins Covers 4.4

2 Egg Stands 3 Cups each 4.10

1 Pint Jug 1.10

1 Oval Sandwich Set Compt 14.14

Painting 33 Coats of arms with Supporters &c proper 17/ each 28.1

254 Crests Coronets & Mottos at 5/ each 63.10

1 Complete Dinner Service Red & Gold Trafalgar border & Key wreath 105.9

Arms on Do Included above

Crests Coronets Mottos &c Do

1 Rich Set of Regent Ornaments Fawn & Gold festoon and diff. painting from Shakespeare (7 Pieces) 60.10

2 Rich 2 Quart Grace Mugs Power of Love No 1 & No 2 42

1 New Long Ink Rich fawn & figure 15.15

Modells for Crest 3.3

1:12 Inch Dish Arms sent for pattern 42/ Packages 40/ 4.2

Nevill, Lord, Marquis of Abergavenny. *A page from the Chamberlain invoice books for July 28 1814, listing the important services and ornaments ordered by Lord Nevill. Entries include 17s. for each full coat of arms, 5s. for each crest and three guineas for modelling the bull's head crest used to surmount the inkstand (see Colour Plate 63). (Worcester Royal Porcelain Company.)*

they were marking their wares Grainger, Lee and Co.* by this time. The vase shapes marked New China Works are significant in that none is the same as any known marked Grainger or Chamberlain. The porcelain body is a bone china and quite different from Chamberlain's porcelain, although the painting of flowers on New China Works pieces is very similar to Chamberlain and it is reasonable to assume from this that the decorator had previously worked at Chamberlains. However, the gilding on New China Works vases often includes half-shaded bells* in a very similar manner to gilding on Grainger porcelain.

New China Works, Worcester. *An English porcelain vase decorated at Worcester, the bird painting by a follower of George Davis*, the gilding including half-shaded bells*, a motif frequently occurring on Grainger porcelain, marked in red 'New China Works, Worcester', c.1820. (Sotheby's.) manner to gilding on Grainger porcelain.*

Almost certainly the porcelain bearing the mark 'New China Works' Worcester, was made in Staffordshire or possibly Shropshire and only decorated at Worcester. Geoffrey Godden has suggested that the New China Works was Messrs Doe and Rogers* who were in partnership from the 1820s. Apart from the similar date and the fact that Doe and Rogers had both worked at Chamberlains, there is as yet no other evidence to confirm his attribution.

Nightlights

Although the cottages* were principally intended as pastille burners*, when thin enough some could also have produced a warm glow from the burning cone placed inside and this would have shone gently through the windows. Grainger made at least two forms of nightlight with lithophane panels (*see* **Lithophanes**).

Norris, Conningsby
Apprenticed as a painter at Grainger, Lee and Co.* in 1826, Norris proved himself to be a competent flower and landscape painter. By 1841 he had set himself up as a dealer in china, glass and earthenware and also carried out gilding and enamelling. Lascelles & Co.'s 1851 *Directory and Gazetteer* lists him as 'C. Norris, 55 Tything, Worcester. Manufacturer of Burnished Gold China Tea and Breakfast Sets, Desserts, Ornaments etc. Matchings executed on the Premises, at the shortest notice'. He was not a manufacturer of porcelain but a decorator, buying blanks from Staffordshire and Coalport. He married Mary Anne Grainger and a series of family presentation mugs painted by Norris are in the Dyson Perrins Museum. In spite of this family connection, however, none of these is of Grainger porcelain. Conningsby Norris had two sons, Conningsby jun. and Henry, and both were listed in the 1861 Census as china painters. Geoffrey Godden has suggested that the 'Worcester'-marked* class of porcelain could be the work of Conningsby Norris, an attractive idea as yet unproven.

Norris, Conningsby. *An English mug, the porcelain probably Coalport, painted at Worcester by Conningsby Norris with the Battle of Waterloo, signed and inscribed underneath and given to the Dyson Perrins Museum by a descendant of the artist. (Dyson Perrins Museum.)*

Old India Pattern
The most popular pattern made by Grainger, Lee and Co.* from c.1815-25. It copies a Chinese *famille rose** design and was printed in underglaze blue with simple hand-colouring. Occasionally the pattern has additional overpainting of coloured thorns and blossom. It was used on plain as well as gadroon-edged dessert and dinner services and occasionally on ornamental shapes including rare massive vases with eagle finials. A similar pattern was made by Spode and Copeland and it also occurs on Staffordshire ironstone. Grainger, Lee and Co. examples are usually, but not always, marked in blue script and can have several pattern numbers depending on the shape and method of colouring-in. The most usual number on plain teawares is 660. The name *Old India* is inscribed on some copper plates used for this pattern but does not appear on any pieces.

Old Mosaic Pattern
The 1769 Worcester Porcelain sale catalogue includes an 'Old rich Mosaic japan pattern'. This term has since been used by collectors to refer to a specific pattern in Japanese style

Old India Pattern. *A Grainger, Lee and Co. dessert tureen with distinctive swan feet, decorated with the popular pattern in underglaze blue**, famille rose* *colours and gold, printed mark, c.1815-20, 5¾in. (14.5cm). (Henry Sandon Collection.)*

(Below) ***Old Mosaic Pattern.*** *A dessert dish and a chocolate cup and saucer, the pattern in underglaze blue* and full Japan colours, pseudo oriental character marks, c.1768-70. (Phillips.)*

Old Worcester Parrot Pattern. *A spoon tray of* Chrysanthemum* *moulding, the parrot pattern in thick* famille rose* *enamels, the ground filled in in yellow, c.1765, 6¼in. (16cm). (Dyson Perrins Museum.)*

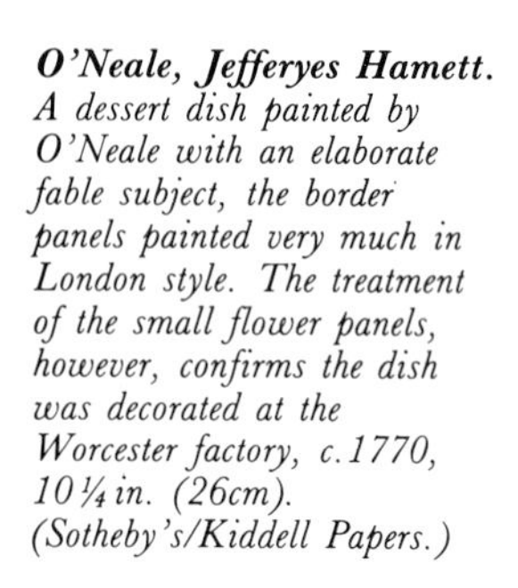

O'Neale, Jefferyes Hamett. *A dessert dish painted by O'Neale with an elaborate fable subject, the border panels painted very much in London style. The treatment of the small flower panels, however, confirms the dish was decorated at the Worcester factory, c.1770, 10¼in. (26cm). (Sotheby's/Kiddell Papers.)*

although several designs from the period could match this description. *Old Mosaic* uses underglaze blue, bright colours and gold and includes eight different formal panels broken up by Japanese crests or *mons* around a central panel with a twisted prunus wreath. The pattern was used both on teawares and dessert services c.1768-72 and can look magnificent on chestnut baskets* and tureens*. The pattern usually has its own mark of pseudo Chinese characters.

Old Worcester Parrot Pattern
The name given in the 20th century when Royal Worcester reissued a pattern which had been popular in the late 1760s. A copy of a Chinese *famille rose** design, it was used on moulded teawares, usually finely ribbed but occasionally with the *Chrysanthemum** pattern moulded in relief. The design features a small green parrot in a circular floral wreath intended to fit in the centre of a moulded saucer, the matching outer border with formal foliage. Some teawares with the *Old Worcester Parrot* pattern have the *Chrysanthemum* moulding enamelled in a yellow ground, but, as the pattern is normally on a white ground, these have been treated as suspicious. The outer border varies from the usual design, however, in the case of these yellow ground pieces and it was probably just a special order for a single service. The pattern is often referred to as *Pecking Parrot* or *Parrot Pecking Fruit**, but these names are more appropriate to the transfer-printed patterns and I prefer the name used by C.W. Dyson Perrins who influenced the reintroduction of the pattern.

O'Neale, Jefferyes Hamett
Like John Donaldson*, O'Neale was an Irish artist and miniaturist of note, born c.1734 and known to have exhibited miniatures at the Society for the Encouragement of the Arts from 1762 to 1766. Before this he painted at the Chelsea porcelain factory, principally landscapes in monochrome and fable subjects although many pieces which have been attributed to O'Neale are now ascribed to other hands. In 1765 he was working at 'The China Shop, Oxford Road, London'. Major Tapp, in his important monograph on this artist, records that by April 1768 J.H. O'Neale was in Worcester, living in the house of Mr Parson, a watchmaker in the High Street, before returning to London in March 1770. O'Neale subsequently did some work for William Duesbury and also Josiah Wedgwood. He died in 1801.

His work at Worcester is remarkable, not only because signed examples make it possible to identify pieces, but also for the quality and originality of his painting. Not every fable painting is by O'Neale, but full landscape scenes with great character are certainly linked to him. The massive sets of vases such as the garnitures in the Dyson Perrins Museum and elsewhere are testament to his skill. One particularly fine set of three vases, all signed 'ONeale pinx' or 'ON invt &c', were given by Samuel Vaughan to George Washington in 1786. They had been bought by Vaughan in 1770 and are still in Washington's Mount Vernon home. One side of each vase depicts tigers, lions or leopards while the panels on the reverse show extensive landscapes including small waterfalls. The many scallop-edged dessert plates with deep blue grounds and fable centres dating from 1768 to 1770 are not signed but still would have been painted at the Worcester factory and not in London.

Ornaments
The term generally used at Chamberlain's factory to refer to bough pots*.

O'Neale, Jefferyes Hamett. *A magnificent baluster vase painted with leopards, the reverse with a panel of classical figures, reserved on a wet blue* ground, square mark*, c.1770, 10⅜in. (26.5cm). (Dyson Perrins Museum.)*

Oude, Nabob of, Service
Two different services were made by Flight, Barr and Barr c.1815 featuring the imposing emblem of the Nabob, supported by two tigers holding flags. One service bears the design in the centre within a wonderfully rich gilded border of the finest quality (*see* illustration on page 252). The other service incorporates the emblem into the gilded borders against a white ground. The centres of the plates in this case are each painted by Thomas Baxter* with a different dancing maiden in a Grecian landscape. Such subjects were a proven speciality of Thomas Baxter and this set would possibly be regarded as among his finest works. Sadly, only a single plate has survived in the factory's own collection.

Oude, Nabob of, Service. *The dramatic coat of arms with tiger supporters within a deep underglaze blue* ground, the service made by Flight, Barr and Barr, elaborate mark incorporating the royal arms, c.1815, 9½in. (24cm). (Dyson Perrins Museum.)*

Outside Decoration

While it seems natural for makers of a successful porcelain body to protect their interests, many factories have been happy to supply white ware to outside decorators. The different Worcester factories entered into various agreements with a number of china painters and it is always difficult to decide to what extent the Worcester companies were involved in controlling and commissioning the end products. The fact that some decorators resorted to redecoration* of Worcester porcelain indicates that not everyone was given access to white porcelain. The independent decorators in Worcester itself were generally prevented from obtaining white Worcester porcelain and obtained their blank pieces from Coalport and Staffordshire. *See* the various entries for **Thomas Baxter, Doe and Rogers, James Giles, J. Hadley, C. Hayton, Liverpool Decoration, New China Works, Conningsby Norris, John Powell** and **George Sparks**.

Outside Decoration. *A mug of early Coalport porcelain, painted with elaborate panels of flowers and a view of Worcester from the North West, c.1800, about 3½in. (9cm). The painting has a somewhat amateur feel which suggests the work of an independent decorator. (Phillips.)*

P

Painters' Marks
See **Workmen's Marks**

Pap Boats
A shape well known in silver, metal and English pottery but exceedingly rare in porcelain. The only Worcester example recorded, sold at Bonhams in 1982, is of plain pear shape without a foot, making the pap boat easy to hold and offer to an invalid. The decoration consists of typical factory flowers within a gold dentil rim and the centre is gilded with the cipher 'JW'. It is interesting to speculate that the date of this piece, c.1775, coincides with John Wall's retirement to Bath where he went to benefit from the spa until his death there in 1776. This pap boat with the initials 'JW' could possibly have been made for the ailing doctor himself.

Parian
Chamberlain and Co. were the only major porcelain factory not exhibiting parian at the Great Exhibition* in 1851. A fine quality porcelain with a high felspar content, parian did not need glaze to keep it clean. It was therefore ideally suited for making copies of sculpture and became the principal product of the Minton and Copeland factories. It was left to W.H. Kerr* to introduce parian after 1852. George Grainger jun.* had made parian earlier, from c.1845, although biscuit* porcelain continued to be made. Initially Grainger used the parian body for making modelled flower brooches which were also glazed. The factory called this new material 'Cryolite' and later used it very successfully for reticulated* porcelain. At the 1851 exhibition Graingers received much critical acclaim for a variety of vessels in the form of flowers, leaves and plants, many of which were made in parian.

Parker, Thomas Service
A very impressive dinner service was made by Chamberlains for Thomas John Parker on the occasion of his marriage to Elizabeth Palmer which took place on 24 October 1796. Parker was merely a tenant at Canbury House, Kingston, Surrey and he married into a much wealthier family with interests in the West Indies. Elizabeth Palmer resided at Whitton Place in Middlesex, a house often depicted on Chamberlain porcelain. The service was possibly a gift from her family. The pattern chosen was *Dragon in Compartments**, the splendid design incorporating the full family armorial into every piece (Colour Plate 64). Sixty-two pieces remaining from the service were sold by Phillips in London in June 1991. (*See* illustration on page 254.)

Pap Boats. *Two views of the only Worcester pap boat so far recorded, the coloured flower decoration suggesting a date c.1775, the initials 'JW' as a mirrored cipher gilded in the base, 4in. (10cm). (Bonhams.)*

Parker, Thomas, Service. *A large Chamberlain serving dish with moulded gravy well, the popular* Dragon in Compartments* *reserving the full armorial centre, c.1796, 21½in. (55cm). (Phillips.)*

Parrot Pecking Fruit Patterns
In fact three very different versions of the *Parrot Pecking Fruit* were made at Worcester, listed by Cook in *The Life and Work of Robert Hancock* as items 78-80. Examples in blue and white of two of these are listed by Branyan, French and Sandon as patterns II.B.22 and II.B.23. The earliest version (Cook's third) is only known on a few bell-shaped mugs and a vase and shows the parrot on a branch above fruit on the ground. This version occurs on enamels and the copper plate for porcelain was possibly sold to Worcester while Hancock* was still in London, as surviving Worcester examples are on shapes suggesting a date before Hancock came to Worcester c.1756.

The second version is a much finer print, known on a few blue and white mugs and many more printed in overglaze black, the bird perching on a branch and curving to reach a spray of berries. There is a common misconception that this print was copied from *The Ladies' Amusement**. A signed print of the subject by Robert Hancock was indeed included by Robert Sayer but Hancock also signed the Worcester prints. He did not need to copy his own work and instead, by a method of duplicating his plates, he supplied the same subject to the London bookseller as was used at Worcester and this version was also used on Staffordshire enamel. In some Worcester examples made c.1760, the signature 'Rt. Hancock fecit' is hidden along the lower branch of the tree.

The final version was not introduced until c.1770 and was designed for underglaze printing, the lines deeply engraved with less detail. Once again the fruit is on the ground and small subsidiary prints of berries, sprigs and butterflies are spaced around the remainder of the piece to be decorated. This version was copied exactly at Caughley though usually with less intricate cross-hatched shading. Worcester examples marked Flight are known and the print was probably continued until c.1788.

Partridge Tureens
The reference in the price list of the London Warehouse, c.1755-6 to 'Partridges white 1st and 2nd [size]' and 'Ditto Enamel'd 1st and 2nd' confirms the early date for these delightful objects. The main difference between the sizes is in the form of the basket base which can include a border of straw-like vegetation mixed with feathers and some bases have additional feathers moulded among the basketwork and a curious lip-like depression for a ladle. Most examples surviving today are fully coloured although they are known just in white. Some with gold dentil rims suggest that the shapes continued until at least 1770, although most will in fact date from the 1750s. They came as pairs initially, always a left-hand and a right-hand example, and sometimes they can have an incised or painted number or some other sign to enable the finished tureens to be matched with the correct covers. The example in the Dyson Perrins Museum was immortalised in the 1960s in a publicity film for Royal Worcester called *The Partridge Tureen*, set in 'Swinging' London.

Parrot Pecking Fruit Patterns. *The signature 'Rt. Hancock fecit' appears hidden on the lower branch of the print on this bell-shaped mug of c.1760, 5⅛ in. (13cm). (Dyson Perrins Museum.)*

Partridge Tureens. *One of a matching pair of 'Partridges Enamel'd', described in the price list of the London Warehouse, c.1755-6 as selling for 7s. each. A slightly larger version was also made; c.1755-7, 7½in. (19cm) long. (Phillips.)*

Pastille Burners
French pastilles were used extensively in England and were frequently of cone shape. It is natural, therefore, that the standard French porcelain conical pastille burner was copied by most English manufacturers. Flight examples have been reported but are very rare, and Chamberlain examples, while slightly more usual, are still hard to come by. All have a gold flame as a finial and are raised on bun feet to allow an up-draught. Many pastille burners shaped as cottages* (*see* Colour Plate 25) were made by Chamberlain and a single model is known from Flight's factory. Rare models from Chamberlain are probably based on Wedgwood models, supported by dolphins or by mermaids, while Flight made more classical vase shapes as pastille burners. Grainger made an 'ornamental incense burner' around 1830 but there is no record of what form it took. They also made in the 1840s two sorts of nightlight — one embossed with a white angel, the other with a lithophane* panel — which would have glowed reassuringly at night. Both could have doubled as pastille burners.

Pattern Books
Most porcelain factories kept remarkably detailed records of their patterns drawn out in books which relate to the pattern numbers* painted on some of the wares. The purpose of these books was to allow the factory to make replacements at a later date and fulfil orders from china dealers who found the numbers easier than descriptions. The original Worcester factory and its successors up until Flight, Barr and Barr were the only major English factory in the 19th century not to use any sort of pattern numbering, although they possibly kept sheets of designs. Chamberlain kept a written list of all of their patterns which has survived but without drawn illustrations. They probably used more detailed pattern books which are now lost. Fortunately the Grainger pattern books survive as an almost complete record of their patterns from book number 2, c.1812, although the first pattern book is sadly lost. These beautifully illustrated books (*see* illustration on page 256) are preserved in the Pattern Room of the present Worcester factory where their own pattern records are also kept for the future.

Pattern Numbers
From the mid-1780s the tradition developed of giving numbers to patterns within porcelain factories. These related to pattern books* and enabled a retailer to reorder stock. Each factory had its own numbering system and pattern numbers can therefore be invaluable in identifying the wares of a particular maker. Flight's factory was exceptional in that it never used any pattern numbers. Chamberlain used a straightforward numerical sequence starting at 1 in c.1791-2 when they began to manufacture their own porcelain. The sequence reached the 800s c.1820, 1100s c.1825, 1300s c.1830 and 1600s c.1840.

Grainger pattern numbers are confusing as they initially seem to have used two different pattern books and two different numerical sequences. The first sequence probably ran from 1 c.1805 up to at least 972 (possibly c.1810). Then the second sequence began, probably at 1 again, c.1810 and reached 391 by c.1812. Numbers 900 to 1292 are omitted from this second sequence which reached the 1600s c.1825 and stopped at pattern 2019 c.1829. A new sequence using a letter X suffix was then introduced. Pattern 1x dates from c.1829-30 and this sequence reached 2008x c.1843-4. This was then followed by a new sequence of fractional numbers beneath a 2, 2/1, 2/2 and so on, into the 1860s.

Patty Pans
See **Tart Pans**

Pavilion Pattern
A direct copy of an early Japanese *Arita* design in underglaze blue, bright colours and gold. The pattern features a main panel with a pavilion at one side and a flowering prunus tree,

Pattern Books. *A page from the Grainger factory pattern books together with a Malvern-shaped teacup and saucer corresponding with pattern number* 1866x. The book attributes the gilding on this pattern to Parry, c.1840. (Cup and saucer Private Collection.)*

while the border includes varied flowers and clouds divided by blue bands reserved with *mons* or family crests. Worcester's copy was used on the full range of dessert and dinner wares c.1770, including pierced baskets, gadroon-edged tureens, splendid chestnut baskets* and drum-shaped butter tubs*.

Peacock Scale Grounds
See **Scale Grounds**

Pecking Parrot Pattern
See **Parrot Pecking Fruit Patterns** and **Old Worcester Parrot Pattern**

Pedestals
Separate pedestals or plinths for vases or figures were popular at some factories but as Worcester were not figure makers they saw little market for such objects. A very rare Worcester square plinth was in the Rous Lench Collection, painted with formal coloured flowers in the manner of the 1770s. This was, curiously, very badly misfired, indicating that Worcester had

Pedestals. *Although the formal coloured flower painting is typical of the Worcester factory, the badly controlled firing on this pedestal is very uncharacteristic, c.1772, 3½in. (9cm). (Rous Lench Collection.)*

***Pedestal Cups.** A curious cup of uncertain use, with very rich decoration of the* Hop Trellis* *pattern in Sèvres* style, the borders in underglaze blue* and turquoise* caillouté, *crescent mark*, c.1780-5, 3½in. (8.8cm). (Rous Lench Collection.)*

***Pencilled Decoration.** A large milk jug with a sparrow beak lip, pencilled in black with the* Boy on a Buffalo* *pattern, c.1755, about 6in. (15cm). (Wintertons, Lichfield.)*

***Pencilled Decoration.** A large bowl, the design pencilled in black and with additional light washes of enamel colours, c.1754, 7⅜in. (18.75cm). (Sotheby's, New York.)*

difficulty making the shape and this one example was probably only finished with colouring as a last resort. Chamberlain made a strongly waisted square pedestal embossed with rams' heads and husk festoons, c.1793-5, and these are equally rare.

Pedestal Cups
Single handled cups of bell shape on tall spreading feet were probably made as replacements for a French service. The shape has only been seen in white with a gold dentil* rim, and in a rich *Hop Trellis** type pattern, the bright colour of the blue border suggesting a date c.1780-5. These cups have been described as duck eggcups but this seems unlikely in view of the applied handle. Most probably they served the same purpose as ice cups*, for a sorbet or type of custard.

Pegged Footrims
See **Glaze-free Margins**

Pen Trays
Part of elaborate desk sets, pen trays were often incorporated into the sides of inkstands but many were made as single objects, long and pointed and usually raised on ball or paw feet. Although mentioned in the Chamberlain records from as early as 1805, the few that are known date from the 1830s and 1840s. From pattern book entries again we know that Grainger made several different models but as yet no marked Grainger pen tray has been seen. Flight pen trays are more likely to have been marked and so more examples are recognised, usually from the Flight, Barr and Barr period in the 1830s. Earlier Barr, Flight and Barr desk sets from c.1810 sometimes included a very elegant canoe shaped pen tray, often decorated with wonderful painted panels.

Pencilled Decoration
Pencilled patterns were painted in a single colour in a style which resembled the shading of an engraving. The technique originated in China where engravings were exactly copied in black enamel for export (*see* **Jesuit Style**). The term is nowadays used somewhat loosely by Worcester collectors to include all patterns painted in monochrome, even those with shaded washes of colour rather than the fine line drawings achieved with a small pointed brush called a 'pencil'. All of the actual 'pencilled' designs used at Worcester were painted in black and are Chinese in inspiration, the best known being the *Boy on a Buffalo* pattern* popular c.1756. Another design of a Chinaman holding a parasol by a fence occurs either just in black or else fully coloured-in. The bowl illustrated here bears a particularly elaborate design which is pure chinoiserie.*

Pennington, John. *A Flight and Barr cylindrical mug painted in brown monochrome with a particularly attractive panel, marked 'Flight & Barr Worcester, Manufacturers to their Majesties', c.1795, 4 ⅜in. (11cm). (Phillips.)*

Another popular chinoiserie pattern from c.1756-8, with two figures by a vase and a two-storey building behind, has been recorded painted in various puce or purple colours. This design, like many paintings of European ruins and other landscapes in these same monochrome colours, is shaded with delicate washes of enamel and is not strictly pencilling.

Pennington, John

Born into a family of porcelain makers in Liverpool, John Pennington was probably the son of James Pennington who ran the pottery at Worksworth. A John Pennington was born at Worksworth in 1774, but would have been too young to have been the painter who worked for Josiah Wedgwood in his London decorating establishment in 1784. John Flight's diary* for 12 July 1789 records:

> My brother has exten'd into an agreement with Pennington, a very clever painter in London. We heard he was eng'd to Chamberlain & this made us first wish to have him. C. had applied to him but he preferred our offer. I expect him on Tuesday.

Pennington seems to have been the first real artist taken on by Flights following the departure of the Chamberlains and his importance to the factory at this time cannot be stressed too strongly. A masterful draftsman, he excelled in the medium of monochrome painting and managed the difficult task of painting original figure subjects perfectly adapted to the shape of the panels on the richest Flight porcelain. The pair of punchbowls presented to the Corporation of Worcester in

Peony Boxes. *A very rare box probably intended as a bonbonnière, naturalistically modelled and coloured, the interior with moulded notches to ensure a perfect fit, c.1768, 3⅛in. (8cm.) (Sotheby's) This box is no longer thought to be Worcester. It is probably early Coalport. (John Sandon, 1996).*

November 1792 bear portraits of the King and Queen by Pennington which are wonderfully naïve but probably true to life (*see also* Colour Plate 45). His best known work is the so-called 'Hope service'* made in 1792 for the Duke of Clarence, each piece with a female portrait representing 'Hope and Patience' (*see* Colour Plate 23).

R.W. Binns* wrote in the 1860s:

> John Pennington was employed by the firm, who always had a high respect for him, for the long period of more than half a century. He was a man of considerable ability, and had a strong love for the art he professed. He was diffident and modest to a great degree, and totally unfitted to make his way in a busy world, or to advance his interests in the higher circles of society.

This modest man never signed his work, and while his earlier monochrome painting is easy to recognise, nothing is attributed to Pennington after 1800 even though he painted for a further forty years. Solomon Cole* recorded him as a painter of rustic figures. It is likely that the figure subjects on the Earl of Plymouth service* are Pennington's work. It is believed that John Pennington's son worked at Grainger's factory.

Peony Boxes

A small circular bonbonnière (*see* **Snuff Boxes** and **Bonbonnières**) or possibly a trinket box was made c.1768, probably copied from either a Chelsea or Meissen original. The box takes the form of a whole peony or rose flower with moulded sepals and stalk on the underside. The petals are coloured, primarily in red and yellow enamels. These very rare boxes would not have been mounted and instead have moulded notches inside the lids which are designed to fit into the bases. Distortion during firing, however, can result in a very ill-fitting lid. This venture by the Worcester factory into the area of *gallantryware* does not seem to have been successful and very few examples are known.

Peony Pattern

A simple blue and white pattern inspired by Chinese, which proved popular from c.1765-75. Two versions were made, one on plain teaware shapes and larger bowls, the other on unusual

Pickle Dishes. A collection of Worcester scallop shell shaped pickle dishes ranging in size from 3⅛ in. to 6in. (8cm to 15cm), all painted with the Two Peony Rock Bird *pattern, workmen's marks*, c.1755-60. (Colin Harper Collection.)*

teaware shapes with scalloped rims. These are listed by Branyan, French and Sandon as patterns I.E.7 and I.E.9. The Peony pattern never achieved the same level of popularity as the *Mansfield** pattern produced at the same time, even though it would have been similar in price. The border designed for this pattern in dark blue with reserved bubbles was also used in conjunction with coloured Chinese figure and flower patterns. It should be remembered that many other Worcester patterns include peonies in their designs, and a printed copy was also used on potted meat pots.

Perfume Bottles
See **Scent Bottles**

Phoenix Pattern
A very intricate *Rich Kakiemon** pattern made at Worcester c.1768. The design probably originated at Worcester although it incorporates many Japanese and Meissen motifs. The birds are perched among very exotic foliage rather than fire but in view of the flame colouring the modern name is appropriate. Gerald Coke, *In Search of James Giles*, believes that two different variations of the design represent Giles' and the factory's own versions of the pattern, but apart from a more complex arrangement of the principal features there is little to distinguish these two. The quality of workmanship in all examples of this pattern means that they would have come from very costly dessert services, worth far less today in real terms than they would have cost their original owners.

Pickle Dishes
One of the most popular shapes of all in English porcelain and amongst the most collectable today. Pickles were essential in the 18th century to disguise the taste of stale food and certain pickles or sweetmeats made of the finest oriental spices were very expensive. They deserved to be served on fine porcelain and dishes in the shape of scallop shells were imported from China to replace the real shells used previously. Leaf-shaped dishes probably originated in Germany and were introduced into England during the 1740s. The Limehouse factory* specialised in scallop shells and leaves and it is understandable that the Bristol Porcelain* Company would continue these shapes, although examples attributable to Bristol are surprisingly rare.

A pointed leaf shape was introduced from the outset at Worcester in 1752 following a mould used at Bristol and these shapes occur mostly in blue and white with a few coloured examples. The earliest leaves are painted with a pointing Long Eliza*-type figure, painted by a hand who had also painted at Bristol. Subsequently, by 1754, a standard pattern was used on all blue and white leaf and scallop pickle dishes painted either in pale or dark blue. This design is known as the *Two Peony Rock Bird* pattern, item I.C.10 in Branyan, French and Sandon. The coloured scallop shells pre-date blue and white examples, probably because at first it was difficult to control the blue on such a strongly ribbed shape. Most coloured scallop shells have simple sprig patterns and panelled borders, while rare versions are painted with birds or the *Banded Hedge* pattern*. Large scallop shells, between 4¾in. and 6in. (12cm and 15cm) wide, are usually slightly later, c.1755-7. The price list of the London Warehouse (*see* **London Shops**), c.1755-6, listed four sizes of 'Scallop'd Shells' for between 4s. and 12s. per dozen. The pointed leaf was possibly the small fig leaf priced at 4s. per dozen. Vine leaves were either 4s. or 8s. per dozen and this represents the new shape, very rare in the large size c.1755, but vast numbers of the small pickle dishes were made over the next twenty years, replacing the scallops and pointed leaves. Virtually all vine leaves are in blue and white with the same pattern of painted grapes and flower sprigs (the *Pickle Leaf Vine** pattern, I.E.42). Occasionally painted daisies or the *Gillyflower** pattern are seen on vine leaf pickle dishes and very rare prints of rocks and bamboo, the *Plantation* pattern, and a spray of fruit are recorded. Coloured decoration did not stand up well to use with the acids in pickle and consequently very few are known. A few are known with European flowers c.1758 and others with formal flower painting c.1765-8. Some vine leaves with just gold decoration are known from the 1770s.

Slightly deeper shell dishes are illustrated as sweetmeat shells* although when some shells were joined together as centrepieces they were called by Chamberlain 'Pickle Stands' (*see* **Sweetmeat Stands**). Small triangular dishes on modelled bases are usually thought of as salts*, although these also could have contained pickle.

Pickle Leaf Vine Pattern
By far the most common decoration used on Worcester leaf-shaped pickle dishes*, introduced c.1757 and continuing with virtually no variation until the 1770s. Painted in blue with a simple feathered rim, the vine decoration in the centre as well as the shape reminds us that recipes for pickle often included dried grapes as well as actual vine leaves. Listed by Branyan, French and Sandon as pattern I.E.42.

Pickle Stands
See **Sweetmeat Stands**

Picturesque Style
The search by artists for beauty in landscape led to the theories of the picturesque. If nature itself was not sufficient, then scenery had to be rearranged in a formal way to create perfect compositions. It was considered perfectly acceptable to take from nature just the best images and leave out any parts which were inappropriate to the painting. Supporters of picturesque ideals believed that a conventional landscape must be framed by trees and rocks, with elements such as ruined buildings, animals, rustic figures and travellers placed carefully in compositions to give the correct contrast between the rough and the smooth. Inspiration came from Claude Lorraine's views of Italy and watercolourists such as Thomas Girtin and Paul Sandby became the greatest exponents of the picturesque in England. By the end of the 18th century the influence of picturesque had spread to English porcelain factories — none more so than Flight and Barr.

Samuel Smith* and Thomas Rogers* were between them responsible for probably the finest landscape painting seen on English porcelain. Their skill was to use contrasts of light and dark; soft, subtle shading of distance and sky framed with dark, dramatic rocks or haunting trees. Thomas Baxter* used more stippled painting rather than gentle shading to produce similar effects, seen at his best in his painting of the gateway of Carisbrooke Castle on a wine cooler in the Dyson Perrins Museum. Here the figures with their dog add interest to the foreground while the ruined arch in the middle distance leads the viewer through to the dramatic castle shaping the background. This is pure picturesque.

Sadly Flight's landscape painting declined after Baxter's departure, as they concentrated on increased production of trinkets, the views becoming commercial and losing imagination. By the Chamberlain and Co. period the landscape paintings were little more than picture postcards, accurate but in terms of artistic composition far removed from the triumphs of Barr, Flight and Barr.

Pierced Porcelain
See **Reticulated Porcelain**

Pillement, Jean
A French painter and designer who excelled in chinoiserie*. He lived in London in the 1750s and was probably known to Robert Hancock* who engraved many subjects copying, or in the style of, Pillement's designs. Jean Pillement is best represented by his *Livre de Chinois*, a book of original designs engraved by P.C. Canot, published in London 2 January 1758. Some of the large illustrations in this were copied at Worcester. More important are Pillement's numerous contributions to *The Ladies' Amusement**, some of which were also engraved by Hancock. Jean Pillement did not design for Worcester porcelain and his influence is therefore only indirect.

Picturesque Style. *A Barr, Flight and Barr coffee can and saucer, the landscape panels using dramatic lighting effects to emphasise the scale of the somewhat imaginary ruins, printed marks, c.1805-8. (Sotheby's.)*

Picturesque Style. *A Flight, Barr and Barr cabinet plate, probably painted by Thomas Baxter*, with a view of the 'East End of Wells Cathedral, Somersetshire', impressed* and printed marks, c.1814, 9½in. (24cm). The exact positioning of the subject has been altered to make a more pleasing composition, complete with weir, rustic figures and sheep. (Phillips.)*

Pillement, Jean. *A blue and white octagonal saucer painted with a simple chinoiserie* pattern based on Pillement's design entitled 'Romantic Rocks' used in* The Ladies Amusement*, *workman's mark*, c.1755, 4½in. (11.5cm). (Dyson Perrins Museum.)*

Pine-cone Pattern. *A very elaborate dessert centrepiece with a reticulated* rim, printed in blue with the* Pine-Cone *pattern within a hand-painted border, crescent mark*, c.1775, 12⅜in. (31.5cm). (Colin Harper Collection.)*

Pine-cone Pattern

By c.1765 the Worcester factory had improved its production of flatware — plates and dishes — to the extent that they could begin to manufacture inexpensive but fine quality blue-printed dinner services. They had to compete with similarly inexpensive Chinese blue and white services (known as Nankin ware) as well as with Staffordshire creamware, which by this time was starting to enter the London market. Worcester used a single pattern on all dinner and dessert ware shapes to allow china dealers to make up complete services with additional shapes such as tureens, baskets and bottles. The primary spray used in the *Pine-cone* pattern features a peony between two pine-cones and a pomegranate. This is usually placed within a painted lambrequin or scrollwork border in earlier French style, as Worcester seemed unable to print a border on moulded edges at all successfully. Occasionally isolated printed sprays were used for the borders and on larger shapes other additional printed flower and fruit sprays were used. For this reason the *Pine-cone* print is included in a group of related prints by Branyan, French and Sandon, pattern II.C.11. Very similar versions of the *Pine-cone* pattern on copies of Worcester's shapes were made at Caughley and Lowestoft c.1775-80. Much later the Staffordshire firm of Booths made faithful copies in pottery while Coalport made bone china copies c.1850 which were marked with a copy also of Worcester's crescent mark. The pattern was reintroduced by Royal Worcester in the 1920s and is still used today on ovenware under the name *Rhapsody*.

Pink Scale Grounds

See **Scale Pink Ground**

Pitt, William. *A large cylindrical mug with a finely engraved portrait of William Pitt the Elder, flanked by figures of Fame and Minerva, c.1762, 5¾in. (14.7cm). Pitt was an enormously popular leader and was behind many important foreign victories and treaties. (Phillips.)*

Pipe Bowls
Only a single example is known from the late 1760s and although I have not examined this there is no reason to think it is not Worcester porcelain. The pipe is roughly 'U' shape and the bowl is painted with coloured flowers. A moulded and brightly painted fish head holds the beginning of the stem which would not have been porcelain. Chamberlain was selling pipe heads and pipe bowls in the 1820s and early 1830s although none has been recognised.

Pitman, John
Solomon Cole* told in his account of artists at Flights factory that John Pitman was one of Thomas Baxter's* pupils at his china painting school in Edgar Street in 1814, listing his subject as animals. It is likely that Pitman remained with Flight, Barr and Barr and he was still residing in Worcester in 1841 when he was recorded as an animal painter living in the Tything. He had exhibited paintings of animals and game at the Worcestershire Society of Arts in 1818 and at the Royal Academy and in other London exhibitions between 1820 and 1827. John Pitman is the only artist known to have specialised in these subjects at Flights' factory but no signed pieces are known and therefore nothing can be firmly attributed.

Pitt, William
Two very different portraits of William Pitt the Elder were printed in black on Worcester mugs, c.1760-5. The most usual depicts the statesman half-length above a simple laurel wreath, flanked by representations of Fame. The delicate shading suggests Robert Hancock* was responsible. The second version shows a bust of Pitt raised on a pedestal and this is very different from other Worcester portrait prints. It is most likely that this rare version was printed in Liverpool. Portraits of politicians are great rarities in English ceramics from this period and these finely printed Worcester mugs are understandably much sought after.

Plaques
Richard William Binns* never approved of plaques as he felt they were taking porcelain too far into the realm of artists and retained little of the tradition of ceramic craftsmanship. There is no doubt that plaques were non-functional but they must still rank as some of the ultimate achievements of any factory which prided itself in fine painted decoration. Some dishes and trays were treated in the same way as plaques but here the term is restricted to totally flat panels.

Oval plaques transfer printed with a portrait of the King of Prussia are known from the late 1750s. These are signed by Robert Hancock* and, while they have been described in the past as adapted from the centres of oval baskets, in reality these were made from the outset to be framed as wall plaques. Examples are very rare and no painted plaques are recorded until much later.

Chamberlain were selling 'pictures, china views of Worcester' and similar 'tablets' in 1795. These were probably oval plaques with moulded rims and examples from this period are known painted with views of Worcester in sepia monochrome. No further plaques from Chamberlain's factory are known until the 1840s when a series with moulded frames was produced. They have a very American looking eagle moulded at the base and examples were painted with views of America in 1845. Views of Malvern are more usual.

Flight and Barr seem to have used the mould for a teapot-stand for a special wall plaque bearing James Ross'* view of their factory. This emphasises the difficulty all factories had in producing flat slabs. Worcester's soaprock body was totally unsuitable and plaques always distorted. Flight, Barr and Barr wanted to make plaques and overcame the problem by firing large plaques and cutting them out after the biscuit firing with pincers to produce the largest possible flat rectangular area. Virtually all Flight plaques have incredibly crude and unsightly nibbled edges but this did not matter at the time as the edges were always covered by the frame. The cut-out flat areas did not always include the impressed mark and the nibbled edges are often the only clue to their Worcester origin.

Signed plaques are very rare. A single example by Joseph Flight* is in the Dyson Perrins Museum and several truly magnificent flower pieces are known by Samuel Astles*. These are reasonably sized, but when Enoch Doe* wanted to paint the large plaque illustrated in Colour Plate 31, he had to buy the blank in from Coalport. With the exception of those by Astles, most plaques recorded as being the work of Flight, Chamberlain or Grainger artists will be on Coalport or other factory's blanks. A cabinet set with shell-painted plaques has been described as containing plaques of Flight porcelain but I suspect that this is just an assumption and may not actually be correct. A smaller shell-painted panel with a beaded frame and another with a classical scene by Thomas Baxter are, on the other hand, undoubtedly Flight, Barr and Barr from about 1816.

***Plaques.** A pair of Chamberlain and Co. plaques, the moulded frames including an eagle with wings outstretched, painted with views of Malvern Abbey and Dover Castle, printed marks, c.1840-5, 8in. (20.5cm) wide. (Phillips.)*

***Plaques.** A Grainger, Lee and Co. plaque with a richly gilded gadroon-moulded frame, painted with an unusually detailed version of this popular view of Worcester, red script mark, c.1835, 10⅞in. (27.5cm). (Christie's.)*

Some marked Grainger, Lee and Co. plaques with views of Malvern and Bath are certainly of Worcester manufacture although the signed plaques by David Evans* were probably only decorated while he was at Worcester. A small number of very fine Grainger plaques from the 1820s have heavily gilded gadroon frames, but others with leaf-moulded and scroll-moulded rectangular frames are never marked and are more likely to be the work of other Worcester decorators. Marked Doe and Rogers* plaques are recorded.

Plates

The Chinese were so successful at making plates that English factories had great difficulty in trying to compete. Bow had introduced plates c.1752 or possibly slightly earlier, but they tended to be thick and clumsy. Chelsea's copies of Meissen usually show signs of great difficulties in firing. Evidence from the Worcester factory site indicates that they were attempting to make plates in the very earliest phase of production at Worcester, but if any did survive the firing they would have been much thicker even than Bow and could hardly have sold well. The earliest plates known today date from c.1753-4 and follow the Chinese shape with a flat, plain rim and hollowed out, turned base. The Tynedale plate* is a remarkable example, although most enamelled plates are surprisingly crude in their decoration. A small number of early blue and white plates are known, the patterns including Long Eliza* figures, birds, and a particularly fine copy of a Chinese *Boys at Play* design. This shape of plate was revived in the late 1760s for direct copies of Chinese patterns.

The influence of Meissen led to the production of a lobed-edged plate, c.1757, painted with *Mobbing Birds** (*see* illustration on page 264). This was adapted slightly into the standard twelve-lobed plate of the 1760s and 1770s. The quality of potting and firing control by this time meant that Worcester's plates were far superior to those of any other English factory (Colour Plate 65).

The scalloped border on dessert plates was probably first introduced c.1765 and continued into the 19th century. The varieties of plate shapes after 1790 are too numerous to discuss here, although generally the range of shapes among dessert wares was greater than with dinner wares. Most plates were parts of services (Colour Plate 66) but occasionally they were sold separately as table plates or cabinet plates. Some of these were incredibly costly, such as the 'Tragic Muse' plate by Thomas Baxter* (fifty guineas in 1816) and plates by Humphrey Chamberlain* (Madonna and Child £42 in 1814 and the British Champion plate £21 in 1816).

Most tea services included two bread and butter or cake plates, although side plates or tea plates were not usual before the 1860s. Some smaller plates were included in earlier breakfast services* and very small plates were made as cup plates*.

Pleat Moulding
See **Strap Fluted Moulding**

Plates. *The earliest use at Worcester of this twelve lobed plate shape occurs c.1757, enamelled with the* Mobbing Birds* *design; the flower sprigs around the border are further evidence of the Meissen* influence; c.1757, 9½in. (24cm). (Formerly Author's Collection.)*

Plymouth, Earl of, Service
Having survived in its entirety, this remarkable dessert service is regarded as the finest set of Barr, Flight and Barr porcelain in existence. Sadly no records remain of the original order which must date from c.1808. The service is 'harlequin' in that it is painted with different centres, united by intricate gold borders. Each piece is surmounted with the full armorial of the Earl of Plymouth. The central subjects comprise English landscapes, flowers, shells, larger armorials, views in India and the Middle East and figures in costumes of different lands. (The Earl's family had many connections with India, partly through Lord Clive.) The ice pails are both painted with different views of the City of Worcester. No artist can be attributed with certainty, although the costume figures are probably by John Pennington* and the shells are by the hand which I have suggested could be John Barker*. The whole service must have been one of the most costly produced by the factory at any period. In addition, a further service was subsequently made by Flight, Barr and Barr, with deep blue ground and panels of flowers and flies which R.W. Binns* attributed to Samuel Astles*. The crest and coronet of the Earl of Plymouth were placed in the centre of each piece.

Pocock, Richard
Dr Richard Pocock (1704-1765) was a traveller and writer who became bishop of Ossory and Meath. During the year 1750 he journeyed extensively around England and wrote a detailed account in letters to his mother. These were acquired by the British Museum and an edited version was later published. The original manuscript needs to be followed for Dr Pocock's true account of his visit in November 1750 to the Bristol china works:

> I went to see a manufacture lately established here by one of the principal manufacturers at Limehouse which failed. It is at a Glasshouse and is called Lowdn's Glasshouse.

He goes on to describe two sorts of ware made there and mentions 'beautiful white china sauce boats adorned with reliefs of festoons, which sell for sixteen shillings a pair.' In an earlier letter written on 13 October 1750 Dr Pocock tells of a visit to a soaprock* mine and how the Bristol Porcelain* Company paid £5 per ton, far more than for ordinary clays.

Podmore, Robert
The important role played by Robert Podmore and his partner John Lyes* is evident from the original Articles for carrying on the Worcester Tonquin Manufacture* drawn up in June 1751. The twentieth section reads:

> For the encouragement of Robert Podmore and John Lyes workmen who have for some time been employed by the inventors in the said Manufacture it is provided and agreed that over and above their usual wages the said Robert Podmore and John Lyes shall after ten pounds per cent per annum profitt shall be made of the said manufacture be allowed such a gratuity out of the further profitts thereof as the majority in value of the subscribers shall determine not less than half one share of the profitt of the said original stock the better to engage their fidelity to keep such part of the secret as may be intrusted to them and therefore it is further provided that in case the said Robert Podmore and John Lyes or either of them shall by any method way or means disclose any part of the secret wherewith they shall be so intrusted or desert the service of the said subscribers that then the said Robert Podmore and John Lyes shall forfeit be liable and accountable to pay back unto the treasurer for the use of the said subscribers so much money as they shall have before received by such gratuity.

If John Wall* and William Davis* had indeed invented the process of manufacture, why were they so worried about preserving the fidelity of Podmore and Lyes? It has been suggested that because Podmore and Lyes had 'for some time been employed by the inventors', this indicates that they had been paid by Wall and Davis while working previously at the Bristol Porcelain Manufactory* and even before that at Limehouse*. There is no evidence to place Podmore at Bristol, save for his interest in soaprock*, and he may simply have worked with William Davis in his laboratory at 33 Broad Street. It is likely that in June 1751, when the agreement was drawn up, Wall, Davis and the other partners believed in their own invention and had no connections with Bristol. It has been suggested that the mark of a letter 'P' incised into the bases of some moulded Bristol pieces could possibly stand for Podmore, but this seems far-fetched.

The partners in the Worcester concern evidently did not completely trust Podmore and Lyes. Article 22 stated that in addition to the clerk of the works appointed to be outward door keeper at the manufactory, there was to be an inner door with a different lock, the key to be kept by Robert Podmore and John Lyes so that they and the clerks may be checks upon each other. Perhaps Podmore had previously cheated on his past employers in favour of the Worcester company and they knew he was not above double-crossing them either. This is pure speculation, but events suggest this view is not unreasonable for, just four years later, on 14 June 1755, Richard Chaffers and Philip Christian, porcelain makers of Liverpool, signed an agreement with Robert Podmore.

Chaffers and Christian were to allow Podmore a guinea a week as manager as well as one-twelfth share of the net profits. He was to reveal to them the secret 'of making earthenware in

***Porringers.** An early form of two-handled porringer with a large flower finial, painted in underglaze blue* with birds carefully copying an engraving, workman's mark*, c.1757, 8¼in. (21cm) wide. (Private Collection.)*

***Porringers.** This Flight, Barr and Barr porringer originally formed part of an extensive breakfast service; impressed FBB mark, c.1814, 6½in. (17cm) high. The* Quail* *pattern is derived from much earlier Worcester porcelain. (Phillips.)*

imitation of or to resemble china ware'. Chaffers early porcelain was of a phosphatic type which did not contain soaprock. Armed with the secret, Chaffers travelled to Cornwall in the summer of 1756 to confirm a regular supply from Mullion. A letter to Richard Chaffers from his agent at Mullion, Gauregan Tippit, sent his compliments also to Mr Podmore. This suggests that either Tippit had met Podmore the previous month with Chaffers or else knew of him from his earlier career obtaining soaprock for Worcester. With access to Podmore's knowledge it is little wonder that Chaffers early soaprock paste resembles Worcester porcelain very closely indeed.

As they feared all along, the Worcester partners had lost the monopoly of making soaprock porcelain which they had taken such pains to protect. There is no evidence that they pursued Podmore for the penalty fines owed to them. Nor is there evidence that Podmore's departure in 1755 was connected with any of the changes in the appearance of Worcester's own porcelain body which occurred in the middle 1750s.

Porringers

Circular bowls with distinctive flat side handles are generally referred to as porringers, although their precise use is uncertain. The bowls which date from c.1758-60 are generally about 5in.-6in. (13cm-15cm) diameter and have either one or two flat shell-like moulded handles applied to the middle of the sides. Two-handled examples have been recorded with covers although it is possible some were sold without lids. No matching stands of any kind have been recorded. Examples in blue and white or colours always carry European style decoration. These are further discussed under **Broth Bowls.**

Portrait Medallions

During Thomas Baxter's* stay at Worcester from 1814-16 he is known to have modelled at least four circular portrait medallions which were made in biscuit* porcelain. The borders are mostly decorated with coloured jewelling on deep blue glazed bands, although one has been noted with classical motifs on a salmon-pink ground. The subjects recorded are a self-portrait of Thomas Baxter aged thirty-three, dated 1814,

or 1815); and the Duke of Wellington (presumably a souvenir of Waterloo). Most are signed on the reverse with the cipher 'TB' for Thomas Baxter himself. The absence of a factory mark suggests these were not Flight factory productions but made instead by Baxter in his own time. Very few examples have survived. Flight, Barr and Barr also issued printed and coloured oval medallions of Futteh Ali Shah and Abbas Mirza* which were issued c.1833-5.

Potiphar's Wife Teapot
The single known example of a most remarkable pattern is on a teapot in the Dyson Perrins Museum. Apparently copying a Chinese export pattern, it is likely to have been made as a replacement for a mid-18th century Chinese service. The subject is Joseph fleeing from the seductive advances of Potiphar's wife and is typical of the curious Chinese interpretations of biblical stories. Opinions have been divided as to whether this is factory decorated or the work of Giles*, but the gilding on the handle suggests the former to be the most likely. The date is probably c.1770.

Potted Meat Pots
See **Potting Pans**

Potting Pans
The price list of the London Warehouse (*see* **London Shops**), c.1755-6, includes potting pans in three sizes priced at 6s., 9s., and 12s. per dozen. These are the oval tubs with tapering sides generally referred to today as potted meat pots or occasionally incorrectly called butter tubs*. The shape dates from as early as 1752 with moulded flutes and strongly embossed rococo cartouche panels. Early examples are known only in colours, with simple Chinese riverscapes. Later examples c.1756 are known with European figures. Blue and white potting pans are not known before c.1757-8. Various moulded or plain backgrounds are known and all have reserved rococo panels and plain thickened rims which probably enabled a cloth or parchment cover to be tied on. Early underglaze transfer prints were used c.1758-60, and other floral prints were popular during the 1760s. Occasionally examples from c.1765 occur with matching oval covers and stands. This seems to be an adaptation of the shape, possibly for a different use as a tureen. Earlier potting pans do not appear to have had covers or stands and instead have decoration inside the bases of the pots.

Some tart pans*, which are generally shallow and circular, are known from the late 1750s and 1760s in a larger size than usual and quite deep, with slightly tapering sides or, rarely, totally straight sides. Usually painted with the *Mansfield** pattern, these were possibly intended to be used in the same way as potting pans.

Potting Pans. *An oval potting pan with moulded rococo* panels, printed in blue with flowers, crescent mark, c.1765, 5⅜in. (13.5cm). In this case the pan has a matching cover although most pans of this shape were probably originally sold without covers. (Dyson Perrins Museum.)*

Pounce Pots
Pounce was a form of sand used to dry ink on a letter, sprinkled from a small container with a pierced top. Pounce pots were filled through the top by crushing a lump of sand into the recess and so do not have a filling hole in the base. Worcester pounce pots are great rarities and only two are recorded. The one illustrated is from the Klepser Collection and dates from c.1760, painted in colours with a somewhat formal flower spray. The other example is a blue and white pounce pot from c.1770 which is larger and of flared shape. Other pounce pots have in the past been attributed to Worcester but these odd spindle shapes seem to have been restricted to Caughley.

Pounce Pots. *A very plain simple shape decorated in Meissen style*, c.1760, 2in. (5.2cm) diameter. The top is slightly recessed to allow filling through the pierced holes. (Kenneth Klepser Collection.)*

Later Flight and Chamberlain inkstands* usually came with a pounce pot as an integral part and not sold as a single item. When separated from their inkstands they look noticeably incomplete.

Powder Blue. *A teapot with its matching stand, the fan-shaped reserves unusually painted in* Kakiemon* *style with smaller panels of chrysanthemum* mons, *unmarked, c.1765, 5½in. (14cm). (Phillips.)*

Powder Blue. *This cabbage leaf dish is an unusually large example of powder blue which was generally difficult to control on a moulded surface. The flowers and insects were decorated at the Worcester factory; unmarked, c.1765-8, 10in. (25.5cm). (Phillips.)*

Powder Blue

A Chinese invention which was used successfully in England on delftware (tin-glazed earthenware) and on porcelain at Bow during the 1750s. The process was introduced at Worcester c.1760. In order to break up the effect of a solid wet blue* ground it was discovered that cobalt oxide could be applied to the unglazed surface of a vessel in the form of a powder, blown on through a tube with a gauze at one end. The fine powder would adhere to some kind of oil painted on the porcelain, leaving finely shaped reserves. Powder blue is finely mottled and usually well controlled although it could sometimes dribble and smudge. Initially the reserved panels were painted only in blue with Chinese fishing scenes, from c.1760. By c.1765-8 the powder blue ground was used with enamelled decoration in the fan-shaped panels, usually in *Rich Kakiemon** style or with *Fancy Birds** and occasionally flowers. Armorial decoration is also recorded. Giles* decorated some powder blue teawares with Watteau figures* for the Earl of Dudley* service and also with panels of *Aggressive Birds**. Powder blue is uncommon after c.1770-2.

Powell, John

John Powell appears in the Chamberlain wages book as a painter between 1792 and 1802. During this time he bought some white porcelain for decorating in his own time. In pursuit of a career as an independent china painter, Powell appears to have moved to London at the end of 1802, setting up at 91 Wigmore Street. As a decorator Powell mostly bought French porcelain blanks but his name and address occurs also on Coalport as well as Swansea porcelain. He seems to have specialised in flower and figure painting and was an accomplished gilder. The Chamberlain archives record numerous sales of white porcelain to Powell although as yet no examples of his signed work have been identified on Chamberlain shapes.

Powys, Mrs Philip Lybbe

A little known traveller whose diary was published by Longmans in 1899. She lived at Hardwick House and between 1756 and 1808 travelled extensively, recording her experiences. On 28 August 1771 she visited Worcester and

***Precipice Pattern.** A large bowl boldly painted in dark underglaze blue*, crescent mark*, c.1770, 8½in. (21.5cm). (Dyson Perrins Museum.)*

although she was unimpressed by the cathedral she described the China Manufactory as:

> ...'tis more worth seeing than anything I hardly ever did see... They employ 160 persons, a vast number of them very little boys.

Her account of the processes is quoted in Appendix 2 and is memorable for the description of making figures ....'these are done in moulds; separate moulds for the limbs and stuck on with a kind of paste'.

Precipice Pattern

A pattern used only on blue and white bowls from about 7in. to 8½in. (18cm to 22cm) diameter. The design is probably copied from a Chinese original although no exact prototype has been seen. The primary feature of the pattern is a precarious rocky outcrop supporting two pavilions and, while unexacting to paint, the pattern conveys a much greater sense of spirit than most of the formal Chinese landscapes copied at Worcester. Branyan, French and Sandon list the pattern as I.D.7 and give it a date range of 1765-75, although workmen's marks* on several examples indicate it must have been introduced as early as c.1760. It is uncertain how bowls of this size were originally used.

***Presentation Jugs.** The celebrated Cottrill jug made by Barr, Flight and Barr. This was presented to Robert Cottrill by Lord Deerhurst, eldest son of the Earl of Coventry, who used to stay with Cottrill while the two friends hunted with the Worcestershire hunt, c.1810. (Private Collection.)*

Presentation Jugs

While mugs were the favoured shape of presentation pieces, a few special jugs were also made, particularly by the Chamberlain and Grainger factories. Mostly these took the form of jugs with the cipher or crest of the original owner or recipient under the lip. A few early Flight examples are recorded and there are many references in the Chamberlain account books to Caughley jugs decorated with initials to special order.

Undoubtedly the most impressive pieces made in the first decade of the factory at Worcester are the cabbage leaf* moulded jugs, with or without mask lips, painted with extensive landscapes and often reserving the full armorial of the original owner. The jugs made for the Corporation of Worcester* with the arms of the city are the most important pieces of this type as these are dated 1757 and can safely be attributed to I. Rogers*. A few cabbage leaf mask jugs are known with the Freemasons'* arms on the front and these were likely to have been presented to Lodges even though they were printed and not made to any special order.

Flight jugs made after the visit of George III* in 1788 with portraits of the king are not necessarily royal presentation pieces. Only occasionally can a special jug be traced to its original owner, such as the pair of early Chamberlain jugs with portraits of Colonel and Mrs Hawley, still owned by the family, and the celebrated Cottrill jug presented to Robert Cottrill by Lord Deerhurst in memory of their fox-hunting together. Grainger made some really splendid jugs and specialised in very intricate gold ciphers. A selection is illustrated by Henry and John Sandon, *Grainger's Worcester Porcelain*, pp.94-7.

Presentation Mugs

There is a certain amount of evidence to suggest that many 18th century and Regency presentation mugs were sold as parts of sets which included a jug and two mugs, although smaller mugs were replaced by goblets or beakers for this purpose around 1790. A natural shape to use for a special production, the earlier trend for only marriage and commemorative mugs from the 1770s gave way to a popular demand for all manner of special production mugs from the 19th century. Armorial productions are the earliest presentation pieces, followed by mugs with ciphers and initials during the 1770s. The earliest Chamberlain order books contain numerous orders for Caughley mugs with added initials decorated by Chamberlain c.1788-90.

As all factories developed and moved towards mass production, Flight and Chamberlain sold more stock through their London shops and relied less on the local market which demanded special one-off productions. Grainger, therefore, who made more for the commercial, cheaper end of the trade, were asked for rather more pieces with individual initials and inscriptions. The independent Worcester decorators also tended to seize any opportunity to make presentation pieces for the local market. Flight and Chamberlain were happy to leave this unproductive market to the others, even though they may have benefited from local sales to a certain extent.

Prince Regent Services

The Prince of Wales (appointed Prince Regent in 1811, later George IV*) was a great lover of porcelain. During his visit to Worcester in 1807 he made a point of inspecting the two major porcelain factories and honoured both Chamberlains and Barr, Flight and Barr with his Royal Warrant. The Prince had previously placed orders for services from Flight's London showrooms and continued to patronise the factory for many years. In the Dyson Perrins Museum are sample pieces from seven different services made for the Prince of Wales between c.1805 and 1815. These were kept back by the factory as duplicates of sets which still remain in the Royal Household. The Prince's taste was known to be flamboyant and he chose the richest Japan patterns imaginable for two of his services, the centres replaced with the full royal arms or just the Prince's crests and garter. The remaining sets followed more traditional styles, mostly with deep blue borders ornamented with remarkable raised gold (Colour Plate 66, left). One breakfast service was painted with a band of flowers by Samuel Astles*. Another tea service featured a rich Barr's Orange* ground with gilding and the full royal arms in reserved panels.

Prince Regent Services. *A Caughley chocolate cup and saucer decorated by Chamberlain with the badge of the Prince Regent. Sadly this service is not recorded in the Chamberlain archives, c.1790-3. (Phillips.)*

Amongst the earliest Chamberlain productions using Caughley porcelain was a pattern called *Princes Feathers*. The emblem of the three ostrich plumes, with or without the motto *Ich Dien*, was used in several designs, not necessarily for the Prince himself. Similar *Princes Feathers* were used by Flight and Barr c.1790. Specimens of a tea service and a large cabbage leaf mask jug are known with the crest and garter of the Prince of Wales in deep blue with wonderful gilding. These date from c.1785-90 and are also of Caughley porcelain decorated at Worcester. In 1807 the Prince ordered from Chamberlain full dinner, dessert, tea and breakfast services. These were to be harlequin services, with every piece of a different pattern. The Prince wanted the richest Japan patterns on every piece. The dessert service alone comprised one hundred and ninety pieces, including ninety-six plates costing an incredible three guineas each. It is understandable that this set was not completed until July 1811, with the dinner and breakfast services not invoiced until 1816. By this time the order had been updated as the breakfast set included twelve plates with views of Waterloo costing 73s.6d. each. The total cost of Chamberlain porcelain supplied to the Prince between 1811 and 1816 was £4,047.19s.

In February 1813 the factory delivered to the Prince a set of three vases which had been painted with historical subjects by the young Humphrey Chamberlain jun.* Humphrey's skill

Prunus Root Pattern. *A wet mustard pot* painted with a formal version of the pattern in dark blue, crescent mark*, c.1765, 3¾ in. (9.5cm). (Sotheby's.)*

Prussia, King of. *A Worcester transfer printed* mug of a type made in enormous quantities during the late 1750s when Frederick the Great was at the height of his popularity in England. Like most examples this is signed 'RH Worcester' with an anchor* and dated 1757, 4⅛ in. (10.5cm). (Phillips, Oxford.)*

as a painter had been mentioned to the Prince previously and he had particularly requested his work to be included in the royal order. These vases alone cost £105. A dessert service now in Los Angeles County Museum, painted with different theatrical subjects, was possibly also made for the Prince of Wales, and is discussed here under *Shakespearian Subjects**. On the Prince's accession in 1820 Chamberlains were asked to make an armorial service for him (*see* **George IV Service**).

Prunus Root Pattern

Although I have been searching for many years, I have not come across a Chinese prototype for this pattern which is almost certainly copied exactly from oriental porcelain. One of the first blue and white patterns introduced at Worcester, probably by 1753, *Prunus Root* was to enjoy enormous popularity for about thirty years, during which time it remained remarkably consistent in its composition. Having copied it on porcelain myself I know how simple the design is to execute and it could be adapted easily to different teaware shapes. It occurs on plain as well as fluted shapes and on bowls and mustard pots as well as a range of mugs. Miniature or toy* services of the pattern were made from c.1758-65, superbly potted and quite delightful. One of the rare examples of the pattern painted in overglaze red enamel, on a fluted teabowl and saucer c.1756, is illustrated in Colour Plate 87 (right).

Prussia, King of

Frederick the Great was Britain's ally during the wars with France and became a national hero. His likeness was clearly in considerable demand at a time when transfer printing* was just coming into its own as a medium for mass production of commemorative pieces. Judging from the numbers surviving, the printed portrait mugs must have accounted for a very considerable part of the factory's output in 1757, bringing fame to the factory and the inventors of the printing process.

Three principal portraits of Frederick are known, all usually signed 'R H Worcester', often with the anchor rebus* of Holdship* alongside. The finest portrait shows the King standing full length on the battlefield pointing towards the conflict in the distance. The scene was taken from Richard Houston's engraving after the painting by Antoine Pesne and Worcester's version is dated 1757. This has been noted on Worcester vases, oval plaques* and a saucer-dish, as well as an identical English enamel plaque in the Schreiber Collection.

The most frequently seen print was used on cylindrical and bell-shaped mugs as well as a single enamel box, and shows the same portrait after Pesne but half-length above a scroll. The King points towards a group of flags and military trophies, the reverse with a winged figure of Fame blowing her trumpet. The names on the flags vary and were shown by the writer Thomas Carlyle to be far from accurate, though it is unlikely that most of the British public would have noticed. Virtually all examples are signed below the prints 'R H Worcester', with an anchor and 1757. The same signature occurs on the third version which shows just a head and shoulder portrait of the King within a ribbon scroll titled 'The KING of PRUSSIA &c.'. This occurs on mugs and teawares with occasionally the hidden signature 'R Hancock fecit Worcester'.

The King of Prussia mugs were discussed in *The Gentleman's Magazine* in December 1757, with credit given for the work and the invention of printing on porcelain to Josiah Holdship*. *Berrow's Worcester Journal* followed this up with an amended account and a note:

> Hancock, my friend, don't *grieve*, tho Holdship has the praise,
> 'Tis yours to execute, 'tis his to wear the bays.

The prints are, however, signed 'R H Worcester' which has been taken to refer to Richard rather than Josiah Holdship.

***Punch Pots.** An exceptionally large teapot probably intended for use with punch, painted in light underglaze blue* with the* Zig-Zag Fence *pattern, workman's mark*, c.1756, 7⅞in. (20cm). (Gilbert Bradley Collection.)*

***Pu Tai Pattern.** A teapot painted with a copy of a Chinese* famille rose* *pattern, the crowfoot border* in red and gold, c.1765, 5⅜in. (13.5cm). (Sotheby's.)*

The anchor, therefore, is probably Josiah's rebus while the 'R H' is possibly Richard or more likely Hancock* himself. The enamel plaque and box were possibly printed at Worcester but it is more likely that, through a method of reproducing his plates by means of etching, Hancock sold the same engravings to a Birmingham enameller for printing there.

A coloured saucer of the King of Prussia in the Marshall Collection was thought to be a fine coloured-in print, but close examination shows this to be a finely hand-painted copy and it therefore has to be treated with suspicion.

Punch Bowls
See **Bowls**

Punch Pots
The question of when a large teapot becomes a punch pot will never be satisfactorily answered. In pottery some large globular pots are known with the word 'Punch' painted on them, while others of similar size are decorated with scenes of tea parties. One clue could lie in the presence or absence of straining holes inside the base of the spout but it is difficult to be sure of the significance of this. Two massive globular pots are recorded in Worcester decorated with the *Fan** pattern. At the base of both spouts is painted a running fox with the legend 'Tally Ho'. It is much more credible that the vessels served strong liquor at a hunt meeting rather than tea. Punch pots, or punch kettles as they are sometimes called, always take the form of a scaled-up version of a normal Worcester teapot. The spouts can be more flared at the ends, however, and occasionally the shape of handle found on a coffee pot was used instead of a plain loop handle. Finials are normally pointed whereas flowers are more usual on teapots after c.1765.

Most examples recorded are in blue and white. Early painted peonies, rocks and fences were used c.1756-8 and in the late 1760s and 1770s *Mansfield** or *Rock Strata Island** were the usual patterns, along with various floral prints. Coloured flowers are very rare on punch pots and none has been recorded with coloured grounds.

Pu-Tai Pattern
An uncommon pattern copied from Chinese porcelain which was painted in colours c.1765-8. The corpulent monk *Pu-Tai* is seated on the ground beside what appears to be a conical pile of rocks, while two elegant lady attendants sit watching him. The pattern usually has a crowfoot* border. It occurs primarily on teawares as well as leaf dishes and cabbage-leaf moulded jugs. An identical design of seated ladies also occurs in the *Magician** pattern. Pu Tai lived in the Tang dynasty in China. The eighteenth Lohan, he is regarded as one of the manifestations of Maitreya, the Buddha of the Future.

Q

Quail Pattern

There are in fact several very different patterns featuring quails after oriental originals and all have become known to Worcester collectors by the name of *Quail* or *Two Quail* pattern. One occurs only in blue, others are in *Rich Kakiemon**, while another is pencilled and lightly coloured after Chinese.

The *Blue Quail* pattern was used on teawares and is always in a very bright blue typical of c.1770-80. The pattern is very simply painted and yet highly effective. It is listed as *The Two Quails* by Branyan, French and Sandon, pattern I.C.15.

The *Kakiemon Quail* pattern was used by very many factories in Germany, France and England. Direct Worcester copies of the Japanese are very rare and always early, dating from the late 1750s. Gradually the factory converted the design more and more into their *Rich Kakiemon* style so that its origin becomes virtually unrecognisable. Some examples c.1768 can be of very fine quality, using virtually an Imari* palate with gilded highlights. Other versions from the 1770s and into the early 1780s have turquoise panelled borders and can at times be very sketchy and clumsy. Some of these *Rich Kakiemon Quail* patterns have been credited to the Giles* workshop but such attributions are very difficult to confirm. The occasional use of a gold crescent mark verifies a factory attribution for these pieces at least. Giles can reasonably be said to have executed one very different pattern with two quails drawn in black and lightly coloured in red and gold, used both on plain and on scalloped teawares, c.1770. Chamberlain and Flight, Barr and Barr both used versions of earlier Worcester *Quail* patterns in *Rich Kakiemon* style.

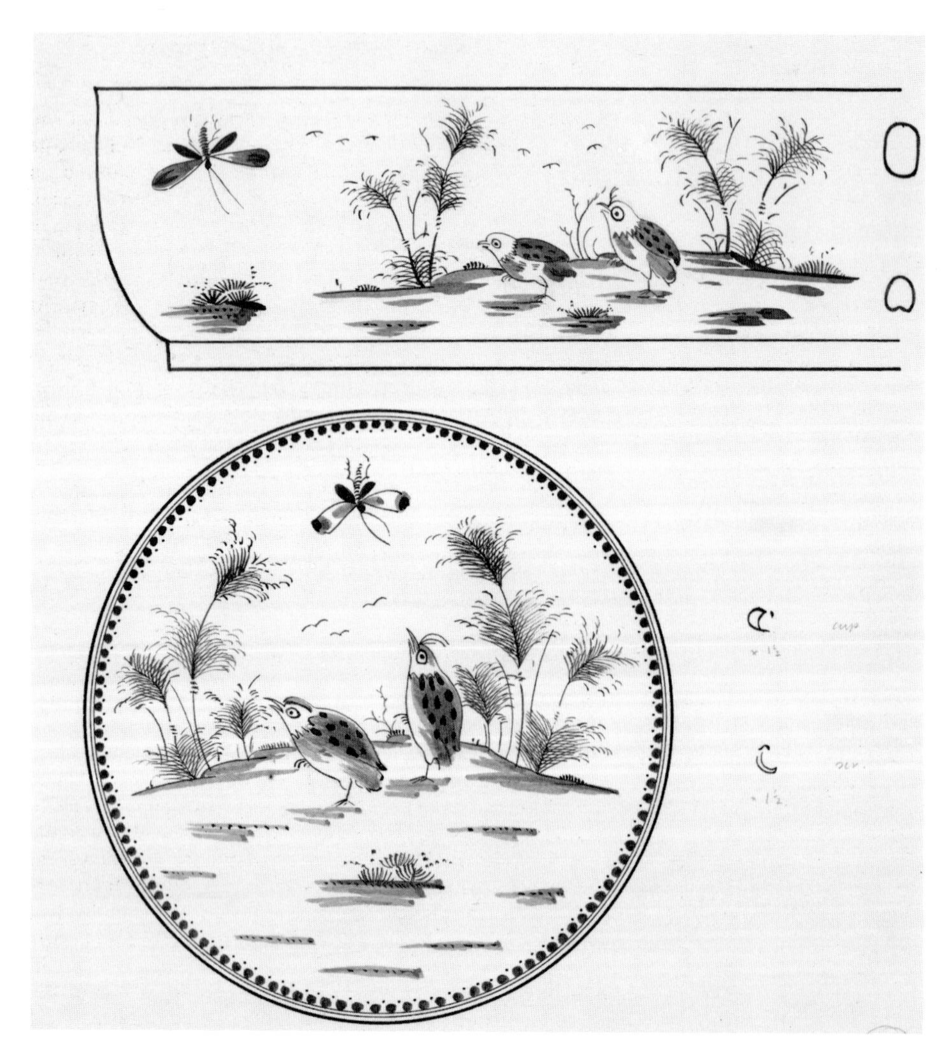

Quail Pattern. *The underglaze blue* version of the* Quail *pattern as used on a coffee cup and saucer, c.1770-5; the drawings by Neal French.*

Quail Pattern. *A teapot of remarkable shape, the 'crabstock' finial and twisted handle both following pottery forms, this particular version of the* Quail *pattern painted with reasonable care, red crescent mark*, c.1770-5, 4⅜in. (11cm) high. (Rous Lench Collection.)*

Queen's Pattern

One of the most confusing of all named Worcester patterns, the origins of which remain obscure. The earliest reference to the name is in the 1769 Christie's sale catalogue which contained many sets described as *Queen's* pattern, at a cost which indicates that they were fairly rich. R.L. Hobson, *Worcester Porcelain*, believed that this referred to the pattern now known as *Queen Charlotte (see* **Charlotte, Queen, Pattern**). This is unlikely as the date is too early, long before Queen Charlotte visited the factory in 1788 and ordered a set of the pattern. Henry Sandon and H. Rissik Marshall, in their *Worcester Porcelain* books, both use the name *Queen's pattern* for a simple design of petal-shaped panels drawn just in gold. This usage of the name has become widespread but this is certainly not the pattern called *Queen's* in 1769. I have been unable to discover when the gilded petal pattern was first given the name *Queen's*, but as this is now in common usage I suggest that this should be called *Gold Queen's* pattern to distinguish it from the pattern Chamberlain called *Rich Queen* or *Best Queen.* This was their pattern number 78 and features panels of Japan foliage between four deep underglaze blue bands reserved with *mons* and gilt with diaper. The full factory description was 'Best Queen mosaic, blue and gold with india work' and this was used on a range of expensive services and ornaments. *See* Colour Plate 2.

The Chamberlain *Best Queen* pattern is directly derived from a popular pattern used at Worcester from c.1768 until at least 1780. If the Chamberlain family brought the pattern with them in the 1780s then it is likely that they just continued to use the name that they had always used. This logical explanation identifies the *Queen's* pattern from the 1769 catalogue and leaves us to sort out the modern use of the name. For the purpose of this *Dictionary* I have used *Gold Queen's* for the gold petal pattern and *Rich Queen's* for the pattern with blue bands and Japan panels.

Queen's Pattern. *A fluted teapot of the pattern known as* Rich Queen's *with panels of banded hedges and chrysanthemums between deep blue bands, square mark*, c.1768-70. This is a particularly fine example of a pattern which can vary considerably in quality. (Phillips.)*

Queen's Pattern. *A fluted coffee cup and saucer decorated with a plainer version of the* Rich Queen's *pattern, square mark*, c.1770. (Phillips, Edinburgh.)*

Gold Queen's pattern was used from c.1770 until c.1790. It can have a variety of gilded borders and also can occur on pieces with blue and gold borders. The pattern was used on Caughley porcelain decorated by Chamberlain and a very rare underglaze blue version occurs c.1770. Many examples of the *Gold Queen's* pattern have been the subject of redecoration* and are discussed in that section.

R

Rainer Family
This family of minstrels from the Ziller Valley in the Tyrol visited England in 1827 and caused a sensation with their Tyrolean dancing and yodelling. The four Rainer brothers and their sister Marie were given the honour of an invitation to perform before the King and there was almost a scandal at court when Marie rushed up and kissed George IV in a passionate embrace instead of the customary kiss on his hand. Unaffected by this, the King was so enchanted by their act that he gave them a present of some old regalia and Prince of Wales ostrich plumes which had been left over from his coronation. The Rainers proudly wore these in their hats and on their belts and were depicted in this fashion in a lithograph published in 1827 by E. Wilson. This was carefully copied by the Chamberlains who quickly brought out a set of five figures of the Rainers to be on sale the following year. To reduce costs they used the same mould for each brother, just changing the positioning of the arms according to the lithograph. As a result the set only cost £2.10s. and remained in production for a few years. A rare surviving complete set is in the Dyson Perrins Museum along with a copy of the lithograph.

Red Anchor Marks
See **Anchor Marks**

Red Bull Pattern
An early Worcester pattern produced by means of a transfer printed* outline. The origin is an uncommon Chinese *famille rose** pattern from the *Yongzheng* period which was faithfully reproduced in a coloured-in black print first used c.1754. This corresponds in date with the earliest use of printing at Worcester and occurs mostly on teawares as well as 'scratch cross'* type mugs*, mustard pots*, leaf dishes* and finger bowls*; also delightful flared hexagonal bowls. Most examples

Rainer Family. *A Chamberlain figure of one of the Rainer brothers proudly wearing the Prince of Wales plumes presented by George IV, c.1828, 6in. (15cm). (Godden Reference Collection.)*

Red Bull Pattern. *An early teapot of rare lobed shape, transfer printed* in black and coloured-in, with a painted green diaper border, c.1754, 5in. (12.75cm). (Dyson Perrins Museum.)*

date from c.1754-6, although the pattern seems to have been reintroduced c.1762-5 on teawares, coloured with less care and delicacy.

A single fragment of the pattern, fully coloured, was found amongst a deposit of biscuit and glazed First Period* wasters* in the grounds of the King's School in Diglis, Worcester, in 1973. The wasters were possibly provided by the factory for some sort of drainage project c.1765 but this does suggest the pattern was decorated at the factory at least on its reintroduction. There would seem little doubt about the origin of earlier pieces except for a pair of beakers in Melbourne Art Gallery, Victoria. These are Chelsea, from the triangle period, and are decorated with the *Red Bull* pattern printed and coloured in exactly the same way as the Worcester pieces. The beakers would have been white and must therefore have been decorated at Worcester, c.1754. If this seems hard to credit, the alternative is that the pieces bearing the *Red Bull* pattern with identical colouring would all be the work of an outside decorator. The former explanation is much more likely, and throws open the whole question of other porcelain, including Chinese, having been decorated at the Worcester factory. One teapot of the *Red Bull* pattern, entirely hand painted c.1760, would appear to be a completely separate replacement for a *Yongzheng* original.

Red Crabs Pattern. *A very unusual moulded bowl showing the reverse design used with this pattern, a dragon swooping through clouds, c.1754, 2⅜in. (6cm) diameter. (Phillips.)*

Red Crabs Pattern

A pattern inspired by Japanese *Kakiemon** but adapted by Worcester into their own richer style of Japan patterns. A most extraordinary dragon is partly concealed by clouds while two red crabs appear to take no notice. The border design was used on several rich Japan patterns, mostly during the 1760s. The *Red Crabs* pattern itself ranges from c.1754-65, on wide-fluted teawares and occasionally other shapes such as a cabbage leaf moulded jug and a rare early lobed bowl. An exceptional service of *Red Crabs* pattern has been recorded with an additional armorial included amongst the design.

Red Line Bordered Group

A large group of blue ground Worcester wares from c.1763-1775 are decorated in an uncharacteristic style which seems to relate to an independent decorator who bought faulty seconds from the factory and added copies of *Kakiemon** and other patterns. The most distinctive feature of this class is the absence of gilding and the use of narrow red lines in place of gold around the rims and edging panels. Most blue ground patterns were decorated in this manner, especially the *Rich Queen's Pattern** using wide vertical blue stripes reserved with small circles, with the blue frequently misfired badly. The *Kakiemon* palette used by the decorator is limited to a slightly muddy red, strong egg-yolk yellow, black and green (Colour Plate 67), with slightly more colours used when copying the factory's own formal flower painting. These European floral painted pieces can sometimes have a narrow gold rim, but this is exceptional and the panels are still edged in red, if at all. Some Chinese designs incorporating underglaze blue, such as the *Kempthorne** pattern, have been completed by the same decorator using the distinctive palette. It may not have been

Red Line Bordered Group. *A cabbage leaf mask jug painted in the distinctive style of this group, contrasted with a teapot decorated at the factory and finished off with gilding, both with square marks*, the porcelain c.1770, the jug 8in. (20.5cm). (Phillips.)*

worth while sending the faulty blue ground blanks to London for decoration and it is possible that the work was carried out near to the Worcester factory. Certainly the work had the factory's blessing and it is significant that related decoration occurs only on pieces which have underglaze blue grounds incomplete in themselves. For this reason, the red line group should not be confused with clobbering*.

The colour of the underglaze ground varies to suggest a date range from before 1765 until at least 1775, by which time the blue had changed to a brighter, purer tone (*see* **Underglaze Blue**). The style of enamelling varies very little, however, which indicates that it was likely to have been executed at more or less the same time. From this it may be deduced that the factory had built up a stock of unsaleable, faulty blue ground wares and kept them in a storeroom. This was then disposed of in one go, possibly in 1772-75 when the factory was sold and Dr. Wall retired. By this time the stock would have become mostly old-fashioned shapes and would not have justified expensive decoration.

A few similar blue scale or deep blue ground pieces are painted with very crude landscapes, usually in a simple colour, again without the use of gold and exhibiting firing imperfections in the blue portion. These pieces have been linked to the Giles* workshop but the absence of gold and of any quality whatsoever must cast doubt on this attribution.

Red Overpainting

Most *Imari** patterns were designed to be painted partly in underglaze blue and completed in red and gold. In many instances, however, English porcelain factories took blue and white patterns, complete in themselves, and added red enamel to produce a richer effect. Liverpool examples are reasonably common and Lowestoft also produced several patterns decorated in this way. Worcester clearly found the technique created an unsuccessful crowded effect and as far as we know it only occurs on a single pattern, known as *Question Mark Island.* The blue and white version is listed by Branyan, French and Sandon as I.B.3, used on teawares and mugs c.1754-6. Most of the mugs surviving in this pattern have been overpainted in red, exactly following the design. It had been assumed that this was clobbering*, the red added at a later date to help sell old stock, but instead we discovered a fragment from a mug with red overpainting already present, among 1750s levels on the factory site excavations. Why only this one pattern was singled out for decoration in this way is a mystery. The rarity of examples today is perfectly understandable as the completed effect can hardly have been popular at the time.

Red Overpainting. *A mug of Scratch Cross class* painted in underglaze blue with the* Question Mark Island *pattern, with contemporary red overpainting, workman's mark*, c.1754-6, 3⅝ in. (9.3cm). (Phillips.)*

Redecoration

There has been more controversy over redecoration than any other aspect of Worcester porcelain; indeed, collectors have disagreed on the subject for more than a century. The essential question is where does outside decoration end and redecoration begin? In the simplest view, if a piece was considered finished by the manufacturer and sold as such, and was subsequently altered or added to by somebody else, this constitutes redecoration. A piece sold in an unfinished state to be completed by an outside decorator, with the factory's approval, has not been redecorated. In the 18th century white Worcester porcelain was prized as the best English porcelain for decorating. In the entry under James Giles*, the rivalry between the Worcester factory and Giles is discussed. Even Giles was probably unable to obtain all the white porcelain he needed and bought Caughley, Liverpool and Derby wares as well. Giles claimed to carry a large stock of white Worcester porcelain but this must have run out at some time and it is possible that he could then have used some of the simply decorated Worcester wares, either from his own stock or bought from the Worcester salerooms. Patterns in white with only a gold dentil rim would have been readily available and Giles' enamel decoration on these would not necessarily have affected the appearance of the original gilding. In this case, the Giles decoration would have been more or less contemporary with the porcelain and would show no evidence of refiring. I hardly consider this to be redecoration.

But what about a more complicated gold and white pattern? Take, for example, the *Gold Queen's* pattern, or one of the many designs of gold flower festoons hanging from ribbons. If the panels of the *Queen's** pattern were filled in with colours, or a coloured ground and insects were painted within the gold festoons, would this be redecoration? In the case of Meissen porcelain such additions are called *Hausmalerei* and are greatly prized. With Worcester porcelain this would be acceptable only if the additions were contemporary with the making of the porcelain. If the embellishment is of a much later date, then it is certainly redecoration.

Taking these case studies a stage further, what if Giles found a way of removing a gold pattern altogether, leaving a plain white surface ready for decoration? It would still be possible, under close scrutiny, to detect evidence of the original gilding, but Giles' customers would probably have been unaware of it and not unduly bothered had they discovered it. This is certainly redecoration, but is it acceptable to collectors? Again, the problem comes down to whether one believes the decoration to be contemporary or later.

In truth, very little actual redecoration can, beyond reasonable doubt, be considered contemporary. Over recent years I have become more and more sceptical, a view shared by many dealers and museum directors who have transferred prized pieces from display cases to storeroom shelves. One of

***Redecoration.** Group I. The addition of a claret ground* to an* Eloping Bride* *pattern teapot has produced an appalling effect which spoils a rare piece of blue and white. (Sotheby's/Kiddell Papers.)*

In truth, very little actual redecoration can, beyond reasonable doubt, be considered contemporary. Over recent years I have become more and more sceptical, a view shared by many dealers and museum directors who have transferred prized pieces from display cases to storeroom shelves. One of the patterns I feel unhappy with is a design of alternate claret and turquoise stripes. This pattern, always attributed to Giles, covers up either gold or, more usually, green enamel flower festoons which become tooled gold festoons in the finished decoration. One giveaway on teapot or jug covers is the use of green enamel on the finial which matched the original green festoons. Other striped patterns are even less believable, especially in overglaze royal blue* enamel, as these show far more evidence of refiring (*see Group VIe*).

The most important clues to the presence of redecoration are signs of re-firing. After a long period of exposure to the atmosphere, Worcester porcelain absorbed moisture and dirt through areas unprotected by glaze. This normally meant the footrim, patches on the rim where the glaze was particularly thin, and any chips or cracks. When a piece was submitted to a later kiln firing, the absorbed dirt burst out in the form of black specks or, in extreme cases, a solid black coating of the affected area. Re-grinding of the footrim and polishing of the rim removes some of this tell-tale blackening but the remedy leaves its own signs. It is important to remember that clobbering* (blue and white porcelain with colour added a few years later) rarely shows signs of blackening. Such evidence is usually the result of a century or more's exposure to the air.

Other clues to look out for are signs of any previous decoration having been removed. Gilded patterns or simple coloured flower sprigs were removed in two ways. A wash of acid would literally eat them away, although a fine 'ghost' usually remained, visible if caught in the right light. The alternative was to use grinding and polishing for removing the decoration. However, even the most skilful work would always leave a faceted surface where the glaze was worn and this was prone to bubbling in the re-firing.

I have divided the principal forms of redecoration into a number of distinct groups.

GROUP I

The simplest form of redecoration is the addition of an all-over coloured ground, especially yellow*. As an experiment, my father added yellow enamel to some plain white wasters from the factory site and they fired perfectly. Modern low-temperature colours left no evidence of re-firing on the wasters, even after two hundred years in the ground. Many valuable pieces of Worcester porcelain have all-over yellow grounds, especially Giles teawares. My criterion for doubt is when a pattern which is well known on a white ground suddenly occurs on yellow. The *Quail** pattern in *Rich Kakiemon**, for instance, or Chinese figures in *famille rose*. In my opinion, such pieces are fakes. Flowers were painted on a yellow background in the late 1750s (*see* Colour Plate 99) but, significantly, most examples have borders of puce rococo scrollwork. Any piece with factory painted flowers on a solid yellow ground without puce borders must be regarded with

***Redecoration.** Group III. Take away all of the colours and gold chequer pattern and you will be left with just the* Gold Queen's *pattern* with factory-decorated dentil* rim. (Phillips.)*

suspicion. Giles flowers are more acceptable but it is important to keep an open mind. Dry blue* flowers occur on yellow grounds and my instincts immediately doubt these, even though the remarkable cabaret set in the Ashmolean Museum is probably genuine. Claret* grounds added to flower painted plates, and the *Eloping Bride** blue and white teapot with a claret ground, illustrated on page 277, are almost too absurd to mention, yet in the past these have commanded high prices.

GROUP II

Added coloured grounds reserving decoration in panels. In normal cases, the panel was always drawn first and the subject matter filled in to fit. Adding a ground created two problems. The panel was not always a regular shape and sprays and insects were often scattered randomly. 'Contour panels', where the shape follows the contour, or outline, of the subject, are always suspect. Some examples look absurd, such as a green ground fitted around birds in trees (not necessarily added much later, however). Yellow grounds occur on mugs and jugs with *Fancy Birds** in trees, where the panels are oval with little cut-out corners conveniently fitting around parts of the tree which overhang. On original coloured grounds, small sprigs occur in evenly spaced small panels. When these occur at random there must be doubt, just as when the colour goes over the top of small sprigs. The usual redecorator's trick was to put gold over the sprigs or insects, and it is often possible to see the original colour underneath, especially when the gold is worn.

GROUP III

Here a popular simple gilded pattern is left untouched and further decoration is added around it. The primary example of this is the *Gold Queen's* pattern, which virtually forms a group by itself. Very attractive diaper patterns and coloured flowers fill the petal-shaped panels, but the style reflects the richness of the London studios whereas the dentil rim* is typical of the factory style of gilding. Dentil rims provide very useful clues here. One sucrier is known with a yellow ground and berried, leafy garlands, but hiding under such richness is the good old *Gold Queen's* pattern. A pattern with gold flower festoons hanging from ribbon bows often has a pale turquoise ground added below and coloured insects painted above. This tends to appear very unbalanced.

GROUP IV

Simple patterns in enamel colours which have further decoration added to them. Various border patterns were relatively elegant and used on otherwise white porcelain. Such a pattern is illustrated here in Colour Plate 91, with reserved white chain on a turquoise band. Borders such as this can occur with *Hop Trellis** type patterns linking the shoulder and basal borders, in very bright colours but otherwise quite convincing. A pattern with so-called French green* borders of large triangular dentils has had garlands of berried foliage added and is again very convincing. The garlands are the same as on the yellow-ground *Gold Queen's* pattern sucrier discussed in the

***Redecoration.** Group IV. This tea canister originally matched the coffee cup shown in Colour Plate 91 with just a turquoise chain border. The* Hop Trellis* *type pattern has been added, 6⅛ in. (15.5cm). (Bonhams.)*

Redecoration. *Group V. The black husk festoons originally hung between flower sprigs on this tall mug of c.1775. Instead the flowers have been replaced by rich fruit and a distinctive landscape. 6½in. (16.5cm). (Formerly Drane and Wallace Elliot Collections, photograph Sotheby's/Kiddell Papers.)*

Redecoration. *Group V. The genuine Worcester factory-painted flowers around the panel together with perfectly correct fruit, insects and gilding led many respected authorities to believe this mug depicted Doctor Wall* himself. The yellow ground, unbelievably early date and totally unconvincing silhouette (which is too big for the panel) caused others to cast doubt and eventually condemn the piece. (Wallace Elliot, Drane and Lady Ludlow Collections, photograph Sotheby's/Kiddell Papers.)*

previous group. In the case of the spoon tray illustrated in Colour Plate 68, the original pattern of a simple floral border and central ladybird has been 'improved' by the addition of a parrot, clearly influenced by Hancock's *Parrot Pecking Fruit** pattern, very cleverly added around the ladybird — one of the most ingenious examples of redecoration I have seen.

GROUP V

Here only part of the original decoration is removed and the remainder added to. A popular pattern of black husk festoons had the scattered coloured flower sprigs removed and replaced with a landscape on a well-known mug from the Drane Collection. Similar landscapes occur on teawares of the *Rich Queen's** pattern, where the *Kakiemon* panels were ground away leaving the underglaze blue ground unharmed. The landscapes tend to have a rather matt appearance on the ground-away glaze, but rich gilding sits comfortably on the deep blue ground (*see also Group VIb*). Possibly the best known redecorated piece belongs to Group V. A large grace mug* was decorated c.1770 with shaped panels of gold and blue enamel scrollwork containing fruit and insects. On the front a floral wreath contained a gold cipher. This fine example was later spoilt by the addition of a silhouette of none other than Dr Wall himself, initialled for easy identification and dated 1759. A yellow ground was added for good measure. This mug was highly prized by the great collector Wallace Elliot and was later sold to Lady Ludlow, so the forger probably benefited quite nicely from this piece also.

GROUP VI

Here no original decoration remains visible. I have subdivided this extensive group into smaller groups, attributable to the same hands.

GROUP VIa

The work of a decorator who specialised in redecorating pieces with original underglaze blue. He used a very thick turquoise enamel to obliterate the blue borders or else left the borders in blue and gold but covered any intruding parts. This redecoration is seen on Caughley as often as on Worcester and can be reasonably ingenious, as when an underglaze blue flowerhead becomes a plum in the finished fruit decoration. The speciality of this decorator was ripe fruit, sometimes spotted*, with bold but clumsy insects. Flowers are also seen with similar insects.

Redecoration. *Group VIa. The thick turquoise enamel border on this teapot smothers the original underglaze blue* cellular border. All the fruit and gilding are also added. (Dyson Perrins Museum.)*

Redecoration.
Group VIb. Originally this cup and saucer was decorated with the Rich Queen's* *pattern with* Kakiemon* *panels. These have been replaced by landscapes and fruit. The fine gilding is exactly the same pattern as used on Group VIc. (Sotheby's.)*

Redecoration.
Group VIb. A fine dish exhibiting most of the hallmarks of this particular decorator, in this case using a pale 'sea green' ground. The glaze is thin, indicating original decoration has been ground away. 11¼ in. (28.5cm). (Dyson Perrins Museum.)*

Redecoration. *Group VId. Although reminiscent of Giles'* figure painting, the treatment of the foliage is similar to the landscape painting found with Group VIb. In this case the gold has worn off the added claret* ground, although the original factory gold dentil* rim remains. (Sotheby's.)*

GROUP VIb

Landscape painting is unusual in redecorated Worcester but it is represented by a distinctive hand which is relatively easy to recognise. Examples of the *Rich Queen's** pattern were doctored by the removal of the *Kakiemon* panels (*see* Colour Plate 84). Instead heavy landscape painting filled the panels, with insects in the smaller panels and fruit in the centre of a bowl or saucer dish. Identical fruit and landscapes are seen on the mug and the dish illustrated here. The fruit painting is unique to this class and the method of painting the foliage also. Thick green and slate- or grey-green enamel was painted on the trees and then stabbed at with a point to incise the effect of leaves. The usual method used at the Worcester factory was to paint with green washes and then use a darker pigment to paint the texture of the foliage. I have seen three separate pieces with these redecorated landscapes which all include a building with a round tower with a row of dark dots representing windows.

GROUP VIc

A class of fluted teawares with simple decoration removed. This is replaced by claret stripes which alternate with festoons of coloured flowers. The claret is gilded with tooled gold foliate scrollwork including an upside-down heart-shaped double scroll below a reserved circular panel. This identical gold pattern was used on the deep blue between the landscapes of Group VIb, indicating that these are by the same decorator.

GROUP VId

Claret used as a solid ground colour. This usually takes the form of a claret ground reserving rococo mirror-shaped panels of Watteau* style figures amongst vegetation and generally occurs on dessert wares although teabowls and saucers are known. The gold is finely tooled foliate scrollwork but has usually flaked off badly. Another design on dessert wares includes panels of *Dishevelled Birds** and again fine tooled gilding on the ground. It is difficult to bring examples together to compare but I believe there is a significant similarity between the flower painting used in the centre of these bird dishes, in the smaller panels amongst the Watteau figures, and most examples of the *Hope-Edwardes** pattern. The palette is

Redecoration. *Group VIe. Alternate claret and turquoise stripes used to obliterate underlying flower festoons, the thick gold used to hide evidence of the flowers showing through. (Phillips.)*

Redecoration. *Group VIe. The royal blue enamel stripes used on this pattern are convincing enough but close examination reveals evidence of a previous pattern having been removed. The flower painting relates to several other redecorated groups. (Phillips.)*

the same, including a very flat almost matt texture. The leaves are painted with different shades of green colour blended much more delicately and smoothly than the usual Giles leaves which tend to have dark veining on a simple wash of green. The distinctive flower painting suggests to me that this claret group (VId), including the *Hope-Edwardes* pattern, is also closely related to Groups VIb and VIc.

GROUP VIe

Striped patterns. There are three basic types which I have classed here as a single group although they are not necessarily related. Alternate claret and turquoise stripes were decorated on fluted teawares on top of existing green or gold festoons (*see* illustration on page 281). Fine tooled gold disguised all traces of the original flowers. Although not always obvious, all examples I have seen display signs of redecoration. Many authorities accept this as original 18th century decoration, but I find this impossible to believe, a view shared by Dr Mackenna when he wrote about redecoration in the 1950s. A pattern of royal blue* overglaze enamel stripes with reserved fan-shaped panels of exotic birds sometimes (although not always) shows heavy signs of refiring. Close similarity with Giles painting leaves the origin of this pattern uncertain. Another version which uses royal blue stripes alternating with tooled gold foliate stripes is, on the other hand, always found in conjunction with evidence of previous decoration having been removed. Sometimes this design has flowers painted in the centre and these once again relate to Groups VIc and VId.

GROUP VIf

A pattern of scale pink* borders used with Teniers figures* occurs on teawares and a cylindrical mug, all clearly by the same hand which is not known exactly on any other Worcester. The Teniers figures are very different from those used on the service in the Royal Collection, for example. Identical decoration occurs on porcelain from Worcester, Caughley and an unidentified Staffordshire factory. Certainly the work of an outside decorator, therefore, there now exists considerable doubt about this once prized form of decoration. A sparrow beak jug with scale pink border in the Dyson Perrins Museum is inscribed 'Henry Cook 1761', but this was originally decorated with a simple puce and gold pattern.

GROUP VIg

Apple green* grounds with bird panels. The faking of Worcester's thick apple green is the most difficult of all to detect as the redecorator responsible managed to match the factory's own ground colour exactly. Some pieces show evidence of previous decoration having been removed, but mostly it is only through heavy blackening of the feet and rims that it is possible to tell anything is amiss. A few years ago a sale at Christie's in London included a collection of about fifteen pieces of Worcester apple green, all of which were redecorated. They were catalogued as such although sadly no provenance was given. These gave an opportunity to examine the *Fancy Bird** painting which tended to be a little stiff and featured a very prominent dry blue* enamel as well as heavy black outlining. The gilding around the apple green is not distinguishable from original factory decoration. In many cases, however, a tendency to add a very elaborate gold border around the rims or footrims where there would not normally be a border can indicate that an apple green piece has been redecorated. I suspect these borders were added to hide evidence of where blackening of the rims or feet had been ground away.

Another significant factor is the presence of some typical 'Worcester' apple green decoration on Caughley porcelain. Looking at all the evidence, it is hard to accept any single examples of apple green grounds with bird panels as genuine — a sweeping statement but I am not alone in holding this view. Some vases are recorded with apple green grounds, supposedly dating from c.1770, fitted around flower painting which has to belong to the late 1750s. Close examination shows the painting to be covered by the ground in some places. These were clearly original vases with flowers on a white ground, to which the green ground and gilding were added later. Another well-known although rare pattern has a green ground and panels of fruit studies placed on backgrounds. All examples I have handled show evidence of re-firing and the fruit painting relates to other pieces with totally suspicious yellow grounds. The fluted shapes on which this decoration occurs are also later in date than the style should suggest.

* * *

We finally arrive at the question of who was responsible. A lot of redecoration has been credited to the Giles workshop, but in only very few instances do I feel this is justified. Only pieces which exactly match Giles' mannerisms can be attributed in this way, not pieces merely in the London style. What about any other contenders? Chamberlain began as a decorator of Worcester and Caughley porcelain and may have been left with some previous stock from their retailing business. A Caughley cabbage leaf jug is known where the blue printed flowers are obliterated by coloured bouquets, fancy birds and the *Dragon in Compartments** pattern. The 'S' mark of Caughley has become the 'S' in the middle of the painted 'WORCESTER' name mark. Chamberlain used the *Dragon in Compartments* pattern a great deal but more evidence is needed.

The fruit used by the decorator of Group VIa is very similar to fruit sprays painted among blue-printed flowers on a

Caughley jug which is dated in gold underneath 'LBK 1784'. I find it tempting to believe that Group VIa was decorated as early as 1784 but other evidence is conflicting, especially underlying Caughley patterns which suggest dates nearer 1790 for the original wares, and heavy signs sometimes of refiring.

The legendary exploits of Randall and others at Madeley in the 1820s and 1830s probably accounted for a large quantity of Sèvres porcelain redecorated in England. The Sèvres porcelain often had turquoise grounds added but there is no similarity to redecorated Worcester porcelain. R.W. Binns* mentioned that, following the merger between Flight, Barr and Barr and Chamberlains in 1840, a large amount of white undecorated old stock had been sold off. Some of this, according to Binns, had been used by fakers. Binns wrote this in the 1860s, so he would have known about these deceptions from his own recent experience. Our own excavations on the Worcester factory site found evidence of this old stock having been disposed of during the 1840s. Amongst Chamberlain and Co. levels we found hundreds of 18th century odd teapot covers thrown away as unsaleable. Old white porcelain would have had some sale value and would not have been dumped in this way.

In 1899 the keen collector of Worcester porcelain Robert Drane put some of his pieces on exhibition at Cardiff Museum. He made a point of showing two pieces which had deceived him, stating that they had been fraudulently decorated only 'a few years ago'. He warned visitors to the exhibition to be on their guard against this, but poor Mr Drane seldom recognised what seems obvious to us today. His collection was found to contain a great many fakes when it was sold off after his death, likewise the Wallace Elliot and Lady Ludlow Collections which were being formed at the same time around the turn of the century. R.L. Hobson warned of 'that most insidious of all falsifications' when he discussed redecorated pieces in his *Worcester Porcelain* published in 1910. Hobson's book in fact illustrated virtually every class of redecoration listed above, indicating that all were made prior to 1910 at least.

Dr F. Severne Mackenna made a most fascinating statement in his *Worcester Porcelain* in 1950. He wrote:

> The names of these persons [who redecorated Worcester] are not usually known to the collecting world but in one picturesque instance there is an exception. This concerns an Italian, named Cavallo, who was chef to the Marchese d'Azeglio, and who attained a very considerable reputation as a redecorator of old Worcester; in fact the term *Cavallo's Worcester* is still occasionally heard. He specialised, I believe, in the most sumptuous grounds and fruit painting, combined with extremely elaborate gilding.

To collaborate this account I came across a letter sent to C.W. Dyson Perrins by G. Croft Lyons in August 1917, referring to a review that Croft Lyons had written of Hobson's book in 1910. Lyons had mentioned a man responsible for redecoration and he told Perrins: 'His name was Cavalli'. Lyons complained that Hobson had failed to mention the best known of those responsible for redecoration. According to Lyons:

> Cavalli worked around 1850-1860 and gained a considerable notoriety as a redecorator of Worcester porcelain. He is supposed to have been a chef but must have been a good artist and specimens of his work are to be found in many collections... A well known dealer still alive [in 1917] told me he was acquainted with Cavalli in former days and Mrs Sidney, since dead, knew about him also.

I believe that Groups VIb, c and d are by the same painter or workshop, and other examples of redecoration such as group VIg are possibly also related. These could be by Mr Cavallo, in which case he did indeed possess a great talent to mimic 18th century decoration.

One final warning has to be given. Now that some modern ceramic colours need much lower temperatures, there is no doubt that redecoration has been revived by unscrupulous painters. Mostly their attention is directed towards later Royal Worcester wares, but I am aware of a series of Barr, Flight and Barr plates which acquired shell painting probably between 1986 and 1988. Also it is suspected that certain Derby pieces have had expensive coloured grounds added in recent years. All collectors need to exercise the greatest possible care.

Regent China

The Prince of Wales had visited Chamberlain's factory in 1807 and granted them the title 'Porcelain Manufacturers to His Royal Highness the Prince of Wales'. When the factory subsequently needed a name for a new porcelain body introduced in 1811, they chose Regent China, partly to commemorate the honour bestowed upon them by the Prince but more importantly to help sell their new product. They claimed to have developed the body especially for a service made for the Prince, but this seems highly unlikely. Regent China was particularly white and glasslike but difficult to make and prone to a crazing of the glaze. It was probably altered soon afterwards until in most respects it differed very little from their usual porcelain body which was improved at about the same time. A factory mark using the name 'Chamberlains Regent China' was used over a considerable period and seems also to have been used on richer examples of their standard porcelain.

Religious Tracts

A small number of Worcester pieces from c.1770 are known where in addition to standard enamelled patterns there is an inscription in red around either the inner or outer border. These take the form of biblical quotations and are always clumsily written and seem quite out of place, especially in conjunction with Chinese figures. It is likely that these tracts were added to existing patterns by an outside decorator for a specific market. There is no evidence of refiring to suggest that these inscriptions were added at a later date. A very rare Jesuit* pattern has been recorded with a black pencilled subject above the appropriate reference from the Bible, but this is known only on a single saucer c.1780, probably made as a replacement for a Dutch-decorated Chinese service.

Reticulated Porcelain

The term used in the 19th century to describe pierced porcelain. Piercing, cut out while the clay was still wet, was practised by the Chinese and occurs in early English pottery. English porcelain was unsuited for fine pierced work and initially only openwork baskets were pierced. Some used a moulded pattern of trellis to guide the reticulator, while on plain sided baskets a compass was used to draw out the pattern of overlapping circles which were then cut out using a sharp pointed metal tool. Pierced creamware from Leeds and elsewhere in the 1770s inspired Worcester to copy the technique on rare dessert plates and a few vases c.1775. Small geometric shapes were punched through the thin clay while it was still in a soft 'cheese-hard' state. Curiously, most examples of this difficult and presumably expensive technique seem to have been decorated with only cheaper blue prints or simple green borders.

Chamberlain reintroduced reticulation in the 1840s and it was used for a series of cleverly constructed double-walled vessels which were well admired at the time. A range of

Reticulated Porcelain. *A dessert plate with an intricate border punched with geometric shapes in the manner of English cream-coloured earthenware, the simple enamelling in French green* and gold, c.1775, 8in. (20.5cm). (Phillips.)*

Reynolds, Sir Joshua, Pattern. *A lobed plate painted with the* Kakiemon* *design in bright enamels within a brown rim, possibly in this case copied from Meissen*, c.1765-70, 9in. (23cm). (Phillips.)*

teawares, covered cups and communion chalices, as well as rosewater and holy water bottles, were made with an outer wall of pierced honeycomb or gothic tracery. These were brightly coloured with raised gold and jewelling*, some with additional painted scenes and biblical tracts. The praise the factory received for these in the *Art Union* magazine in 1846 and at the Great Exhibition* in 1851 was somewhat unjustified as the designs were in fact direct copies of rather better made Sèvres porcelain from the same period. A full set of Chamberlain reticulated porcelain was to be given to the popular singer Jenny Lind when she visited Worcester in 1849, but she declined the offer as she wanted to give her services purely for charity.

From Chamberlain and Co.'s first efforts, the technique of reticulation was subsequently developed by George Grainger and Co.* At the Great Exhibition in 1851 they showed a coffee set embossed with wheat ears and stalks on a ground pierced with honeycomb. The interior was solid and the double-walled effect shaded inside in rich blue. Later in the 19th century Grainger and Royal Worcester both achieved some incredible results in the art of reticulation.

Reynolds, Sir Joshua, Pattern

A direct copy of Japanese *Kakiemon** porcelain which was made by Worcester in three distinct versions. The design of a long-tailed bird on a rock includes brilliant turquoise and yellow enamels. It occurs on a white ground on lobed plates and wide-fluted teawares mostly c.1765, although some versions appear to be much earlier. By c.1770 the same design was used in central panels on a wet blue* ground as well as in panels divided by deep underglaze blue bands. No Flight versions are known although Chamberlain used the exact design on a white ground on spiral-fluted teawares c.1795-1800. The connection between the pattern and Sir Joshua Reynolds is lost in the folklore of collecting.

'R H' Mark

The confusion caused by these initials was evident in the 18th century when *The Gentleman's Magazine* published in 1757 a satirical verse criticising the praise afforded to Josiah Holdship* when Robert Hancock* had executed the engraving of the King of Prussia* mugs. The 'R H' mark occurs not under the base as a factory mark, but as a form of signature on overglaze transfer prints, usually in conjunction with the name Worcester. The fact that similar initials occur on transfer printed Bow porcelain and Birmingham enamel tends to confirm the view that the 'R H' in question was Robert Hancock. Occasionally the rebus of an anchor* is found alongside the 'R H' and it is generally assumed that the anchor relates to Richard Holdship while the 'R H' refers to Hancock.

Ribboned Emblems

Simple motifs copied from Chinese which appear on early Worcester either as part of a pattern or more usually as decoration inside the rims of sauceboats and creamboats (*see* **Wigornia Creamboat**). These symbols have various meanings in Chinese and Buddhist art but were certainly not understood by the painters at Worcester. The emblems on sauceboats date from c.1752-5 and one motif appears in the Honeysuckle* pattern at this time. The Hundred Antiques* pattern uses many ribboned emblems, both on the front and reverse of the design popular in the 1770s.

Rice Bowls

Rare circular bowls with flanged rims to support domed covers. The covers are elaborately reticulated* with patterns of geometric shapes and have very elaborate flower finials. There is always an opening in the rim of the cover to take a spoon. Examples occur in either the *Fence** or *Three Flowers**

Rice Bowls. *The border painted around the rim and cover is normally associated only with the* Pine-cone* *pattern but it always occurs on these curious bowls, either with the* Three Flowers* *pattern or, in this case, the* Fence* *pattern print, crescent mark*, c.1770, 5½in. (14cm) high. (Dyson Perrins Museum.)*

pattern printed in blue and with ornate painted scroll borders. They date from c.1775. The origin of the name rice bowl probably derives from the pierced pattern rather than the original purpose of these bowls which remains uncertain.

Rice Spoons
While we have become familiar with this shape from Chinese rice spoons of this century, the exact purpose of the early Worcester pieces is uncertain. The plain shape and flat handle made them difficult to use except as a small ladle, although they have sometimes been described as caddy spoons. They seem to have been produced exclusively in blue and white and virtually all examples from c.1770-80 are decorated with the Maltese cross floral pattern. A small number have been noted with the *Gilliflower** pattern painted in blue and, apart from a clobbered* specimen, I know of none in polychrome. Examples are between 5⅛in. and 5½in. (13cm and 14cm) long with a variety of flowerheads used as the terminal. Sometimes the flower terminals are painted to resemble a face. Larger examples from about 1785 are printed with the *Fisherman** pattern and have additional moulded leaf motifs underneath the flower terminal. The same shape is known with a pierced bowl, probably for use as a sifter spoon*.

Rice Spoons. *Most Worcester rice spoons are painted with this* Maltese Cross Flower *pattern. In this example the flowerhead terminal is painted with a simple face, c.1775, 5½in. (14cm). (Dyson Perrins Museum.)*

Rich Kakiemon
During the 1760s the Worcester factory developed its own virtually unique form of decoration which owed its origins to a combination of Japanese *Kakiemon** porcelain and the *indianische Blumen* of Meissen (*see* Colour Plate 75). Using basic *Kakiemon* designs and colours, the Worcester painters produced much more elaborate and intricate versions, completely different in spirit. Dragons, phoenix and ho-ho birds were placed among fanciful chrysanthemums, bamboo and other exotic vegetation in imaginary compositions with minimal landscape in the background. The use of gold for details and highlights completed the effect which was copied elsewhere but never surpassed in quality or imagination. The factory used the name Japan* for these designs as well as other more direct copies of Japanese porcelain, yet Worcester deserves all the credit themselves for what were possibly their most flamboyant creations in the 18th century. The large panels on hexagonal vases offered the best scope for originality on the part of the decorators, while at the other extreme teaware patterns such as *Rich Queen's** pattern and *Jabberwocky** enjoyed enormous popularity. Intricacy of the magnitude of the *Phoenix** pattern on commercial dessert services could hardly have been economical, and we should be thankful that at least some patrons could afford such patterns. Chamberlain produced their own version of the *Rich Queen's* pattern and other fanciful *Rich Kakiemon* patterns were attempted by Barr, Flight and Barr, using even brighter colours and gold. (*See* illustration on page 286.)

Rich Kakiemon. *Worcester's decoration at its most opulent, creating a fantasy world of crazy birds and imaginary vegetation which, despite its many influences, is purely a Worcester invention; used here on a scale blue* ground, square marks*, c.1768, 15⅜in. (39cm). (Sotheby's/ Kiddell Papers.)*

Rich Queen's Pattern
A design of 'Japan' foliate panels between four deep blue bands with gilding and reserved *mons*. Introduced c.1765, it was continued by Chamberlain until at least 1815 as pattern number 78. The pattern is fully discussed here under *Queen's Pattern*.

Rickhuss, J.
An important figure connected with both the making and decorating at Graingers. The name J. Rickhuss (also spelt Rickus and Ruckus) occurs against several patterns in the 1820s pattern books, usually in connection with particular colours which he possibly developed. Certain patterns are described as 'in Ruckus's book' while pattern 1344 is 'done by Boys in Rickhuss's room'. The term 'Rickhuss's China' is used in the Ornamental Shape Books where one shape is called 'Rickus's violet basket'. A John Rickhuss, aged fifty-nine, is listed in the 1861 census in Staffordshire as a 'master china and parian manufacturer', and he had probably been in partnerships in Staffordshire from at least 1855. It is possible this is the same J. Rickhuss as he is not mentioned in later Grainger records.

Rock Strata Pattern
One of the few popular Worcester underglaze blue patterns where the design is copied exactly from Chinese porcelain. The simple riverscape includes an island where the ground appears to be shown in section revealing layers of strata in the rock. A sampan is moored to one side and because of this the pattern has also been referred to by the name *Island Sampan,* particularly the Caughley version which copied Worcester exactly. Lowestoft also made a printed version. The Worcester pattern, used on teawares and occasional large bowls, was made from c.1770-80 and is listed by Branyan, French and Sandon as the *Rock Strata Island* pattern, number I.D.8. (*See* illustration on page 287.)

Rococo Revival
The revival of rococo, otherwise called neo-rococo, made its appearance in the frivolity of the 1820s but was not firmly established until after 1830. Basically it was a reaction against what had gone before but, as with any style change, elements of the neo-classical* style remained. Initially classical vase shapes were merely given new ornate handles, then gradually the full eccentricities of the 18th century were copied and taken to their absolute limit. Generally, though, the rococo revival saw more of a sense of symmetry than the original. Rockingham, Coalport and Minton were the most significant porcelain factories to use the revived rococo style. This is understandable as classical shapes had played far less of a role in Staffordshire than at Worcester where the classical style dominated everything.

Flight, Barr and Barr seemed determined to resist any attempts to abandon neo-classicism, clinging instead to outdated themes throughout the 1830s with the inevitable consequence of near bankruptcy. The Chamberlain factory likewise retained most of its classical shapes and designs during the 1830s and made only a few attempts to follow fashion. A few flower-encrusted pieces were made in the Meissen style, c.1830-5, probably copying Coalport, along with scroll handles for gadroon* edged dessert services, but rococo was not fully re-established at the factory until after 1840 under the new management. With marketing advice from Fleming St John*, Chamberlain and Co. made purely rococo card trays* and other flower-encrusted vases and desk sets. Modelled shells were used extensively to produce impressive but somewhat vulgar effects. But Worcester had once more left it too late, for by the late 1840s rococo was again out of date. Instead the public cried out for High Victorian designs in the form of Gothic, classical or Italian Renaissance shapes. It was left to Kerr and Binns to reverse the fortunes of the company and help Worcester catch up with its competitors.

Meanwhile the Grainger factory followed a totally different

Rock Strata Pattern. *A bowl painted with this very formal blue and white pattern copying Chinese porcelain, crescent mark*, c.1770, 7½in. (19cm). (Dyson Perrins Museum.)*

course. Never dominated by classical styles, by 1830 they were making all manner of exciting rococo forms including flower encrusted ewers and figure groups. Some of their vases, such as the scroll-moulded example illustrated here, were just what the neo-rococo movement stood for. Their shop in Worcester must have been a far livelier place during the 1830s than those of their two Worcester rivals.

Rococo Style

The spirit of rococo developed as a reaction against the heavy classicism and religious architecture which epitomised baroque. Rococo brought a new freedom which spread from Paris into Germany and England during the first half of the 18th century. The name rococo was first used in 1796 to criticise the French styles, a pun on *rocailles* and the use of shells. Rococo was concerned with beauty without symmetry, as found in sea shells. Hogarth's *Analysis of Beauty* in 1753 stressed the beauty of undulating lines, while in France Watteau* and Boucher were regarded as great masters as frivolity became the order of the day. In London the Academy in St Martin's Lane became a meeting place for artists, designers and craftsmen, among them Nicholas Sprimont, the silversmith whose Chelsea porcelain factory made full use of the rococo. Other silversmiths, in particular Paul de Lamerie, were to have greater influence over Worcester porcelain designs.

Worcester was initially inspired by silver shapes of the 1730s and 1740s, all somewhat rococo but never daring enough to break away totally from symmetry. Their greatest achievements in rococo were the great tureens* with dolphin finials and embossed flowering scrollwork, c.1755, and the wine cistern* with handles which combine figures with scrolling forms (Colour Plate 96). On a smaller scale exciting teapots had asymmetric panels placed on strap-fluted grounds and with only the very simple *Staghunt** pattern used to allow the shape to speak for itself (Colour Plate 69). Painted patterns in soft puce monochrome, especially European ruins and some chinoiserie* in the 1750s are pure rococo and in complete

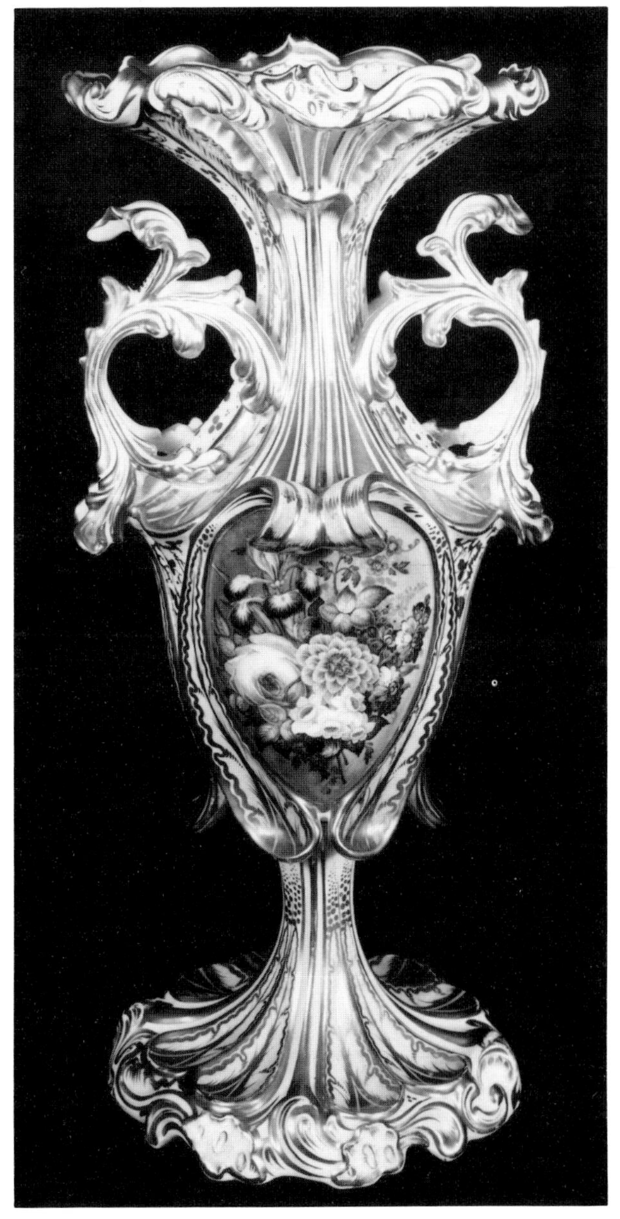

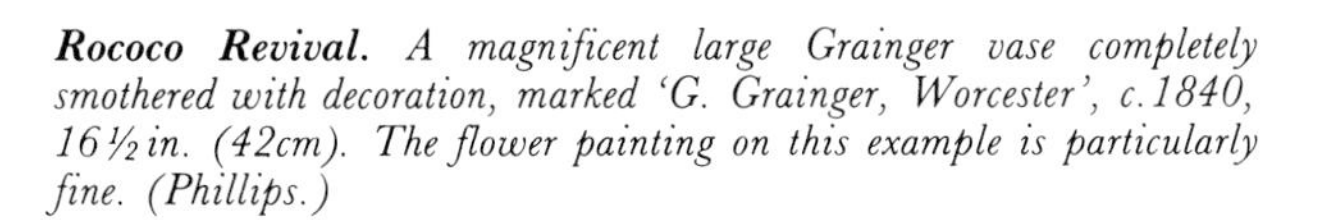

Rococo Revival. *A magnificent large Grainger vase completely smothered with decoration, marked 'G. Grainger, Worcester', c.1840, 16½in. (42cm). The flower painting on this example is particularly fine. (Phillips.)*

contrast to the harder carmine monochrome painting by Giles* fifteen years later. Mostly during the 1760s and 1770s Worcester chose to make commercial use of rococo. Borders of apple green* and scale grounds*, and especially the so-called mirror-shaped panels on scale blue grounds, were framed with token rococo scrollwork with little of the freedom seen in the earlier Meissen originals which they copied. By the late 1780s the rococo taste was seriously out of date. Worcester clung on to the rococo tradition almost to their own extinction while Wedgwood moved ahead in the new classical styles. *See* **Neo-classical Style**.

Rodney, Lord, Pattern
A pattern of finely painted *Fancy Birds** in extensive landscapes, used on dessert wares within deep underglaze blue* borders. The name derives from one particular service

Rococo Style. *An early teapot using very flamboyant rococo* moulding, although this is partly swamped by the decoration in enamel colours, which was possibly added slightly later; c.1754, 4½in. (11.5cm). (Kenneth Klepser Collection.)*

Rodney, Lord, Pattern. *A large dessert centrepiece on a spreading foot, painted with particularly elaborate* Fancy Birds* *within a deep underglaze blue* border, crescent mark*, c.1775-80, 11½in. (29cm). (Phillips.)*

Colour Plate 67. ***Red Line Bordered Group.*** *A teapot which suffered a serious blemish in the glaze kiln and was therefore discarded with only the blue portion completed. The subsequent decoration is in the distinctive red, yellow and green palette, square mark, c.1775. (Private collection.)*

which was passed down in the family of the celebrated British admiral, but clearly a great many other services were made in similar style. The gilded patterns used on the blue borders vary considerably. The pattern occurs c.1780-5 when Lord Rodney was at the height of his popularity, but actually later than the date usually ascribed to pieces by collectors of Worcester porcelain. The bird painting is of exceptional quality and will have been carried out under the direction of the Chamberlain family, although a number of painters will have been involved. The name of Lord Rodney has also been associated with a similar pattern on fluted teawares, although the service originally sold by his descendants is believed to have been for dessert.

Rogers, George

The son of a china decorator and dealer, George Rogers jun. was born in about 1805 and apprenticed at Chamberlains where his father, also George Rogers, worked as a decorator specialising in armorials. Godden has shown that a George Rogers was in partnership with Enoch Doe* and John Wright in London from 1805 until 1807 and these were probably the two fathers of the Doe and Rogers who set up as independent china painters in Worcester during the 1820s. A George Rogers, either father or son, was buying white ware from Chamberlain in 1822. The mark 'G. Rogers No 93 High Street' probably relates to the father on his own while the Doe and Rogers partnership was established by George Rogers sen. and continued at 17 High Street by his son after the death of the father in 1835. Enoch Doe was an accomplished painter but it is not known what part either of the George Rogers played in the business. Rogers jun. became a stained glass painter and died in 1877.

Rogers, I. *Close comparison shows that this cabbage leaf moulded jug is painted by the same hand as the signed I. Rogers mug in the British Museum (Colour Plate 70), although several other painters worked in a similar style, c.1757, 7⅞in. (20cm). (Phillips.)*

Rogers, I.
The discovery of a signed mug led to the identification of a very important painter working at Worcester in the 1750s. This piece (Colour Plate 70), now in the British Museum, is painted with birds in a landscape and inscribed under the base 'I. Rogers Pinxit 1757'. The only other documentary evidence we have is that a James Rogers was working in London in 1765 as an 'Engraver and Enameller' at Dobson China Shop in St Martin's Court. He exhibited a ring engraved with The Lord's Prayer 'in less compass than a silver penny' at the Free Society of Artists in 1765. It was assumed by Hugh Tait in his important paper 'James Rogers', published in *The Connoisseur* in April 1963, that this London enameller was the same as the Worcester I. Rogers. Ideally more evidence is needed to confirm this assumption and it is safer to refer to the Worcester painter merely by his initial I. (or J.) Rogers.

There have been a lot of other assumptions concerning this artist and his work. The signed mug is by the same hand as the Corporation of Worcester jugs*, also dated 1757, and this hand clearly painted many other fine landscapes at the Worcester factory. Some of the *Mobbing Birds** pattern vases are by the same hand, but not all. When we gathered pieces for a major exhibition in Worcester, the British Museum kindly loaned its signed mug and Worcester Corporation loaned their jugs. My father, Henry Sandon, borrowed other *Mobbing Birds* vases to show alongside the museum's own examples. Painters at the factory estimated that there were at least three very different hands responsible for these pieces, although the palette used seems to have been a standard factory palette of colours in use at the time. Only a few of the pieces linked to the I. Rogers mug included flowers other than simple ornament around a cartouche or sprigs on a cover. The vases with flower bouquets were also felt to be by a number of hands. Yet, because this characteristic style of Worcester factory flower painting occurs on pieces with *Mobbing Birds,* collectors have assumed any bird and flower painting in European style from c.1756-62 or so is by I. Rogers or in the manner of this named painter. There is much too little evidence and what there is is conflicting, so great care should be taken and only pieces which are painted with identical foliage and shading to the signed mug should be attributed to I. Rogers.

The style of painting does not continue after c.1762 or so and it is quite possible I. Rogers did leave to become an independent enameller in London. The James Rogers listed in 1765 was also an engraver but there is no evidence to suggest that he had any connection with later Worcester printed copies of *Mobbing Birds* issued as an underglaze blue pattern in the 1770s.

Rogers, James
See **Rogers, I.**

Rogers, Thomas
A painter at Flight's factory, Thomas Rogers was admitted Freeman of Worcester on 2 October 1797 as apprentice of Joseph and John Flight.* Solomon Cole* listed him as a painter of landscapes c.1819 but little else is known of his career. A Thomas Rogers is mentioned in the Chamberlain wages lists as a landscape painter between July 1796 and June 1806 but this may be another artist with the same quite common name. Two vases and a plate with finely painted landscapes in the Dyson Perrins Museum were recorded in Binns'* catalogue as by Rogers. One includes the crest of the Duke of Gloucester in the elaborate border. The quality is very fine and the painting makes good use of fine stippling and gentle washes of colour. Unfortunately no signed pieces can confirm Binns' attribution.

Root Pots
See **Jardinières**

Rose-water Sprinklers
Small objects shaped like watering cans were not intended purely as miniatures or toys but were used to sprinkle scented water to perfume clothes and linen or generally to perfume a room. They were made by Flight, Barr and Barr from c.1820 in the shape of an urn-like vase with a bird-head spout, with a pointed stopper, and also as a slightly taller ovoid ewer with a finely pierced lip. Chamberlain produced similar watering pots, some encrusted with modelled flowers. A Coalport or similar watering can shape has been seen decorated and marked by Doe and Rogers*. (*See* illustration on page 291.)

Ross, James
A skilful engraver who was apprenticed at the Worcester factory under Robert Hancock*. Ross was born in 1745 and so would have been about twenty when he commenced his apprenticeship in 1765. He followed on from Hancock's other apprentice Valentine Green* who had been bound in 1760 but left Worcester in 1765. On completion of his apprenticeship James Ross probably worked in some form of free-lance capacity, as several of his prints used at Worcester are signed

Rose-Water Sprinklers. *A Flight, Barr and Barr sprinkler with its original pointed stopper still surviving, decorated with a matt blue ground, script mark, c.1825-30, 4in. (10cm). (Phillips.)*

Ross, James. *A cabbage leaf mask jug printed in black with a subject taken from Robert Sayer's* Figures and Conversations, *after Vernet, the print signed by James Ross, c.1772-5, 7in. (18cm). (Wallace Elliot Collection, photograph Sotheby's/Kiddell Papers.)*

with Ross' own name. These include the well-known 'Arms of the Grand Lodge of England' which is signed *J Ross Vigorniensis sculp.* This was used on mugs and cabbage leaf jugs and it is appropriate that a blue and white version is still kept in the Freemasons' Lodge at Worcester. Norman Stretton, in *The Connoisseur,* July 1977, drew attention to a series of fine prints of figure subjects after Vernet which were copied on to Worcester porcelain by James Ross. These were taken from a design book published by Robert Sayer in 1771 and titled *A Collection of Figures and Conversations.* One other signed mug depicting a view of Worcester Old Bridge was in the Merton Thoms collection. Hobson recorded this as dated 1779, although when it was sold at Christie's in 1910 the date 1799 was given. If this is correct then the mug will have been Flight and Barr, engraved for them by Ross as a free lance.

Ross etched a view of Birmingham for Robert Hancock in 1785 along with other prints for him. He also engraved some fine illustrations for Nash's *History and Antiquities of Worcester* published in 1781. We are fortunate that James Ross' account books as well as one of his diaries have survived in his family as these give an enormous insight into his work as an independent engraver. Much of his time was taken up engraving trade cards and bill-heads for local tradesmen. His own trade card states that he would carry out 'Engraving in General, Drawings of Gentlemen's Seats, etc.' He engraved silver with crests and ciphers and carried out a considerable amount of this work for Joseph Flight* to sell in the company's London shop. Ross' account records also show that between 1792 and 1813 he engraved printing plates for Martin Barr* showing the factory, as well as several bill-heads which had to be altered with each name change. He also engraved the 'Label Plate for transferring names on china' which was used for the factory mark on Barr, Flight and Barr and Flight, Barr and Barr wares. The dates when Ross was asked to alter these name plates and bill-heads give useful clues to the changes in the names of the different partnerships. It is interesting to note that the plates supplied by Ross to Martin Barr were only for publicity purposes and were not for transfer printing on porcelain. The factory had seemingly given up printing and only reintroduced bat printing* during the Flight, Barr and Barr period c.1808. James Ross died in Worcester in 1821.

Royal Blue Ground

Unlike the *bleu de Roi* of Sèvres, the name in Worcester has become associated with an overglaze blue enamel ground as opposed to underglaze blue. Some examples of *Hop Trellis** type patterns have overglaze borders and these may have been outside decorated. Apart from these, most examples of royal blue appear now to be highly suspect. Fluted teawares with alternate blue enamel and white striped grounds with fine gilding are clearly redecorated. A quite separate class with blue and white stripes and reserved fan-shaped panels of *Aggressive Birds** seem so close to the hand of a Giles* artist to make these, at least, perfectly acceptable, were it not for the presence of heavily blackened footrims on many but not all examples (*see* **Redecoration**). A series of dessert plates, including two in the Klepser Collection, have shaped royal blue borders and colourful exotic bird centres. All examples I have seen have been extensively re-ground on the undersides and footrims to remove signs of burning during much later redecoration.

Because of the bright colour of the narrow blue borders on many of the *Lord Henry Thynne** and related patterns, these

Colour Plate 68. ***Redecoration.*** *Originally this* Blind Earl* *spoon tray* was decorated with only a floral border and central ladybird. The parrot has been added at a later date along with the gilded border. 6in. (15cm). (Private Collection.)*

Colour Plate 70. ***Rogers I.*** *This important mug is painted with birds and signed underneath 'I. Rogers Pinxit 1757', 3⅜in. (8.5cm). Many pieces have been ascribed to Rogers on the strength of this although there were other painters who worked in a similar style. (British Museum.)*

Colour Plate 69. ***Rococo Style.*** *A remarkable combination of an English rococo silver form with Chinese* famille rose* *decoration of the* Staghunt* *pattern, the ground moulded with an early form of strap fluting*, c.1752-3, 5⅛ in. (13cm). (Phillips.)*

Royal Lily Pattern. *A teapot-stand painted with the* Royal Lily *pattern in bright underglaze blue*, the borders gilded and with brown enamel rim, crescent mark*, c.1785-90, 5⅜in. (13.5cm). (Dyson Perrins Museum.)*

have frequently been presumed to be in overglaze blue. In fact the bright colour is due to a late date, normally c.1780, and the borders are therefore underglaze blue, not royal blue.

Royal Lily Pattern

When King George III* and Queen Charlotte* visited the factory of Joseph and John Flight* in 1788 they ordered an 'extensive assortment' of Worcester porcelain from the shop in High Street. R.W. Binns* recorded that this included a breakfast service of the *Blue Lily* pattern which was thereafter to be named the *Royal Lily* pattern. The design was copied from Chinese porcelain and was painstakingly painted in blue with added gold borders and red-brown enamel rims. Worcester probably introduced the pattern c.1780 and continued to produce large amounts throughout the life of the Flight factory up until the 1840s. Chamberlain sold Caughley's identical version of the pattern and then commenced making their own copies of the pattern in the 1790s. Every shape of useful ware was seemingly made in the pattern which sometimes includes an additional owner's crest or initial cipher. Chamberlain referred to the design as 'Lily' pattern as well as 'Royal Lily' after 1789 even though it was their rivals who had received the royal commission from the King. Some authors have used the name 'Queen Charlotte' in view of the 1788 order but this is incorrect and the *Queen Charlotte** pattern refers to a very different Imari* whorl design. Although Binns wrote that the pattern 'has little merit beyond that which is peculiar to many Eastern designs', *Royal Lily* was enormously popular in the 1870s and 1880s for extensive dinner services and other shapes in the Japanesque manner promoted so keenly by Mr Binns. It continued as a popular design until the 1960s.

Royal Mariage Pattern
See **Marriage Pattern**

Royal Services

The two great Worcester factories of Flight and Chamberlain were honoured with several Royal Warrants and produced many of their finest services for members of the royal family. These are discussed here under **Princess Charlotte, Duke of Clarence, George III, George IV, Duke of Gloucester, Prince Regent,** and **William IV**.

Ruby Ground

A rare and very distinctive ground colour used at Worcester c.1765-8. The term 'ruby' has been used to describe various different ground colours from claret to plum and lilac. This has caused much confusion, especially as considerable doubt exists over the authenticity of certain extraordinary colours. I prefer to use the term ruby in the same sense as on Chinese ruby-ground porcelain from the *Yongzheng* period, as the Worcester copies are decorated in an oriental manner. Indeed, a teapot in the Dyson Perrins Museum is an exact copy of a Chinese design and was probably made as a replacement, especially as this piece is the only Worcester example known. A bell-shaped mug uses the same ground with a panel of rich Kakiemon-inspired vegetation. Both pieces date from c.1765-8 and, in view of the uneven texture of the ground, probably proved too difficult to be continued as a regular production.

Ruins

The idea of classical symmetry in architecture breaking down into asymmetry in decay appealed to the spirit of rococo*. Mock ruins were built into the grounds of English country estates and early English monastic ruins were preserved for their beauty. Subsequently, with the development of the picturesque* movement in art, these ruins developed a new kind of appreciation.

Worcester painters discovered the beauty of ruins in some of their most successful rococo decoration, painted in monochrome c.1755-8. This style possibly represents Worcester's

Ruins. *A saucer-dish with fanciful ruins transfer printed* in purple and fully coloured, the border with a bright yellow ground*, c.1770-5, 7½in. (19.3cm). The colouring was possibly added in the Giles* workshop. (Phillips.)*

Rustic Figures. *A pair of Flight, Barr and Barr spill vases* painted with 'The Cottage Girl' and 'The Task', 4⅛ in. (10.5cm); and a cup and saucer with 'The Peasant Girl', all on turquoise grounds*, possibly painted by John Pennington*, script marks, c.1820. (Phillips.)*

own invention and was used on plain shapes without borders, producing a very subtle effect. Prints of ruins were very popular at this time and Robert Hancock* introduced to Worcester a number of engraved plates which had probably been used previously by London booksellers. These remained popular as styles changed from rococo to neo-classical*, and the same black prints were used by Flight in the 1790s.

Gothic ruins suited the ideas of the picturesque movement and abbeys and castles across Britain feature, principally at Flights' factory, from c.1800 until the 1830s. Sketches preserved in the family of Samuel Smith* show his great skills in this area and Thomas Baxter* and Thomas Rogers* were also fine exponents.

Rustic Figures

Peasant figures on Worcester pieces decorated by Giles* c.1770 were copied from Meissen (*see* **Teniers Figure Subjects**), but a much more English form of decoration developed early in the 19th century. Very much part of the picturesque* movement in English art was the fashion for rustic figures in landscape compositions. Flight and Barr were very interested in this style and frequently included farmers, gypsy girls and shepherd boys in simple landscape vignettes, many possibly by John Pennington*. Thomas Baxter* is unlikely to have had any more than a very slight influence here, although some bat prints* of rustic farm labourers could have been based on his designs. These were used into the Barr, Flight and Barr period.

Colour Plate 71. ***Sandwich Sets.*** *A complete Chamberlain sandwich set of four covered dishes around a central tureen, decorated with red kylin and other fanciful beasts on an open scale blue ground, marked 'Chamberlains Worcester', c.1810. (Private Collection.)*

Colour Plate 72. ***Scale Blue.*** *A range of large dinner and dessert dishes illustrating the different tones of scale blue in use c.1765-75, the flower painting and gilding all typical of the Worcester factory, square marks*. (Phillips.)*

Colour Plate 73. ***Scale Pink Grounds.*** *A well-known mug from the Dyson Perrins Collection painted with a boy in Teniers* style, 4 ¾ in. (12cm). In the past this has been attributed to the Giles* workshop but recent thinking suggests that it has been redecorated*. (Dyson Perrins Museum.)*

Colour Plate 75. ***Shagreen Ground.*** *An elegant lobed vase of very early shape, reissued c.1765, with* Rich Kakiemon* *decoration reserved on a rare ground simulating shagreen, 9½ in. (24.5cm). (Phillips.)*

Colour Plate 74. ***Scratch Cross Class.*** *A small mug with spreading base, carefully enamelled with a chinoiserie* subject usually found in monochrome*, c.1755, 2½ in. (6.2cm). (Phillips.)*

S

Sadler Printing
See **Liverpool Decoration**

Saffer Pots
See **Spittoons**

St George and the Dragon Pattern
A blue and white design used only on cylindrical mugs, all of which are dated 1776. Of the four examples known to have survived, three are further inscribed with the name Ann Dunn, and place name Birmingham. So far it has not been possible to trace any tavern or hotel named the George and Dragon in Birmingham at this time, although it seems reasonable to assume that Ann Dunn was the proprietor of such an establishment. The painting style is reminiscent of Chinese export porcelain and it is possible that Worcester copied a Chinese mug, maybe also made for Ann Dunn, although this can only be conjecture.

St John, Fleming
A Worcester businessman who became a senior partner in the Joint Stock Company of Chamberlain and Co.*, formed 13 April 1840, owning £5,000 worth of shares. Fleming St John was appointed Treasurer and Secretary of the company for a salary of £200, increased to £300 the following year. In January 1844 the company assets were divided, St John taking a share in the London retail shop and the tile works. An extraordinary Chamberlain and Co. jug in the Dyson Perrins Museum is painted with a stained glass window and includes the name of F. St John as one of the saints. Sadly he was unable to provide salvation for the ailing company.

Salts
The difficulty in distinguishing between sweetmeat dishes and salts has caused much confusion, especially concerning single shell-moulded examples. The only certain salts made at Worcester are very great rarities indeed and are known in two forms. One is a plain rounded body supported by three small scroll feet, a shape better known in English enamel or glass from the same period, around 1770. Worcester examples are recorded in apple green ground with fruit and also in scale blue, while a single blue and white specimen with a 'bubble' border is known, exactly matching a factory site waster (*see* page 148). A more elaborate moulded three-footed salt was discovered by Simon Spero in 1990 and displayed in his exhibition of Fine English Porcelain in that year. Again it follows a silver shape but was adapted at Worcester. This example is in plain white and remains the only one recorded. Chamberlain made salts with stands in 1800 and double salts in 1819, but none has been identified.

Sandwich Sets
Popular shapes of c.1800, sets of covered dishes were made by many factories although Worcester examples are considerable

St George and the Dragon Pattern. *A most amusing decoration in underglaze blue* on a mug dated 1776 below the handle, crescent mark, 4½ in. (11.5cm). (Dyson Perrins Museum.)*

rarities, Staffordshire pottery sets being much more usual today. They comprise four fan-shaped dishes with covers which fit around a central oval covered dish on a higher foot (Colour Plate 71). This central dish was usually sold complete in itself but could have been supplied with a platform inside to hold either eggs or egg cups. Sets complete with their egg stands are well known in Spode and elsewhere but no Worcester egg centrepieces have survived. Sandwich sets were originally supplied with oval or circular mahogany trays with carrying handles at each end and were called sandwich services in the early 19th century although today they are frequently known as supper sets. The few Chamberlain and Flight and Barr sets I have seen have nearly all been in fairly plain patterns, but an exception is a Chamberlain set offered for sale in New York several years ago and painted with panels of game birds on a rich marbled ground. The sets were usually supplied with twelve or twenty-four matching plates, roughly the size of a dessert plate.

Sandys, Lord and Lady Mug
One of the most remarkable documentary pieces is a Worcester bell-shaped mug in the Frank Lloyd Collection in the British Museum. It is painted with a portrait of a gentleman with his dog in front of a lake within a puce rococo scroll. Underneath the base is the inscription 'Lord and Lady Sandys' health, T*G* 1759'. Samuel Sandys had served as MP for Worcester from 1718-43 and was a prominent politician, serving as a Privy Councillor and Chancellor of the Exchequer. He became Baron Sandys of Ombersley in 1743 and served as Treasurer of the Chamber and ultimately Speaker of the House of Lords in 1756. His connection with Worcester porcelain was only indirect. Following the death of John Wall's* father in 1734, Samuel Sandys became one of John Wall's guardians, even though Wall was twenty-six at the time. In 1740 Dr John Wall married Catherine Sandys who was the daughter of Lord Sandys' uncle, Martin Sandys, Town Clerk of Worcester. The Lord and Lady Sandys mug has been attributed to the hand of James Rogers* but there are differences in minor details between this and the signed I. Rogers mug also in the British Museum.

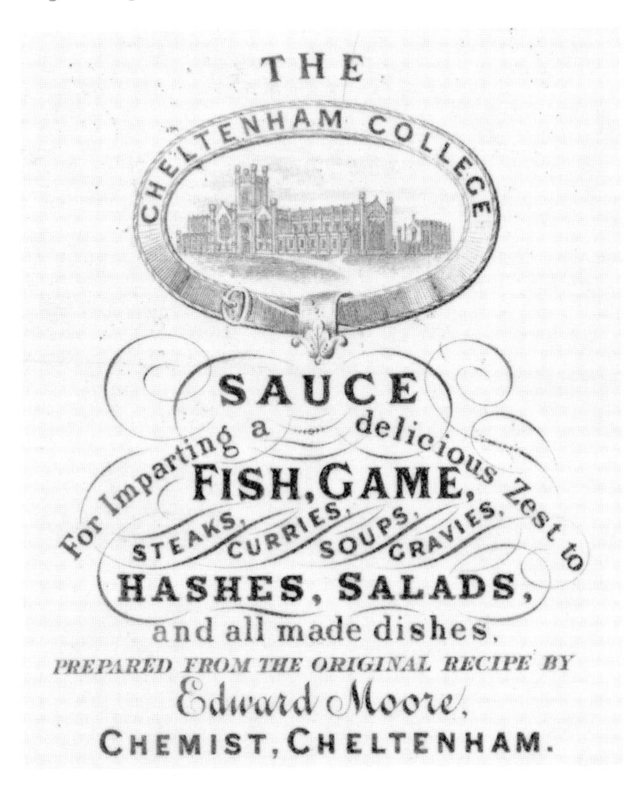

Sauce Bottles. *A pull from the original Grainger copper plate for printing a sauce bottle, c.1850. (Worcester Royal Porcelain Company.)*

Sauce Bottles
Two most curiously shaped Grainger bottles have been preserved, made for Edward Moore, a chemist in Cheltenham. They are printed in black with the elaborate legend 'THE CHELTENHAM COLLEGE SAUCE, for Imparting a delicious Zest to Fish, Game, Steaks, Curries, Soups, Gravies, Hashes, Salads and all made dishes'. The label also includes a view of Cheltenham College. The bottles were made c.1845-50 in the semi-porcelain* body and are unmarked, but the original copper plate for printing the label survives at the Worcester factory, confirming their Grainger origin.

Sauceboats. *A high-footed sauceboat of so-called silver shape with moulded rococo* panels, workman's mark*, c.1754-5, 7⅝in. (19.5cm) long. In this example the underglaze blue* Chinese style panel is previously unrecorded. (Private Collection.)*

Sauceboats
In the 18th century sauce was much more important than gravy and was used to disguise the rather bland and often stale taste of certain meats. Pairs of sauceboats were made in silver but rarely copied in Chinese porcelain. The English factories saw an opportunity to make a shape difficult to obtain elsewhere; by the 1740s many varieties of sauceboat were being made at Limehouse*, as well as at Chelsea and soon afterwards at Bow. The Bristol China Factory* were inspired by English rococo silver in their sauceboats; embossed with cornucopias of fruit hung from ribbon bows, together with high scrolling ring handles and a waisted spreading foot, these were described by Dr Richard Pocock* in 1750 as 'beautiful white sauceboats adorned with reliefs of festoons which sell for sixteen shillings a pair'. A few marked white examples are known and others were enamelled at Worcester shortly afterwards. One other shape of sauceboat known from embossed Bristol marks is shallow without a high foot, and has a plain handle with a pronounced thumb-rest. Smaller fluted or hexagonal boats were probably for cream rather than sauce and are discussed under creamboats*. Worcester continued to make high-footed as well as low sauceboats in great variety throughout the 1750s. In the London Warehouse c.1755-6 (*see* **London Shops**) they were selling 'Sauce-boats high footed' in three sizes for between 14s. and 27s. per dozen, a great deal less than the Bristol boats mentioned by Pocock five years before. The other varieties listed by the London Warehouse were 'Two Handle Boats' in three sizes (*see* **Two-handled Sauceboats**) and 'Leaf Sauce Boats Enamel'd' in two sizes (*see* **Leaf Sauceboats**).

A great variety of patterns were painted on the early sauceboat shapes, usually carefully contained within the moulded panels and not over-decorated to clash with the subtlety of the relief moulding. The panels in blue and white are always Chinese in origin while coloured patterns are mostly Chinese with the occasional European figure subject and rare flowers after Meissen. Workmen's marks are usually found on most blue and white sauceboats and occasionally on coloured examples. One interesting shape from c.1754-5 had

Colour Plate 76. ***Shell Decoration.*** *A collection of wares ranging from the Flight and Barr to the Flight, Barr and Barr periods. The shell painting is by a number of different hands including Samuel Smith* (marbled cups front left), Thomas Baxter* (pink-ground bouillon cup), and probably John Barker* (Gordon* service plate, centre left), c.1800-20. (Colin Harper Collection.)*

(Opposite) Colour Plate 78. ***Smith, Samuel.*** *A Barr, Flight and Barr jug and matching goblet with grey marbled ground*, the jug signed 'S.S.' and dated 1807, 6⅝in. (17cm). These pieces, which came down through the artist's family, are very important in attributing unsigned work by Smith. (Phillips.)*

Colour Plate 77. ***Shell Decoration.*** *A most impressive Flight, Barr and Barr pot-pourri vase painted with a continuous frieze of shells by a hand attributed to John Barker*, script mark Flight, Barr and Barr, c.1816-20, 18½in. (47cm). (Sotheby's, New York.)*

Sauceboats. *A sauceboat of helmet shape with gadroon rims* and unusual scale moulding*, painted in blue with the* Man with a Bomb *pattern, crescent mark*, 5½in. (14cm) long. (Godden of Worthing Ltd.)*

a monkey's or possibly a dog's head modelled as the thumb-rest (*see* **Monkey's Head Finial**), a feature also known on two-handled boats*.

The high footed boats were not made after c.1757 and other shapes from c.1760 become very much more uniform, both in design and decoration. The principal sauceboat shapes from the 1760s are a strap fluted* boat with rococo cartouche panels; a smaller ovoid panel-moulded boat which may have been a creamboat; a more elaborate lobed oval shape with a gadroon rim and either fine basket-weave or a scale moulded ground; and a larger version of the early fluted creamboats with a single spur handle. In the 1770s these shapes were joined by a shallow strongly fluted slipper-shaped sauceboat and a relief-moulded sauceboat embossed with a spray of roses and other flowers. The panel moulded and strap fluted shapes continued into the 1780s although the later examples have less detail in the moulding.

By the Flight and Barr period it was usual for dinner services to include sauce tureens with covers and stands although a few rare fluted oval sauceboats with narrow scroll handles have been seen in patterns such as *Royal Lily**. No Chamberlain or Grainger examples are recorded.

Scale Blue

A highly important part of the factory's production which can safely be claimed as a Worcester invention (Colour Plate 72). Slight scale patterns do occur in early Chinese blue and white porcelain but not with the underlying blue wash which distinguishes the Worcester pieces. The need to break up solid cobalt blue as an underglaze ground colour is evident from many Chelsea pieces where the 'mazarine' blue became dark, almost black, and dribbled badly. Worcester used powder blue* and cracked ice* as methods of lightening the blue ground, and discovered their most successful formula in about 1765. This was probably inspired to some extent by the coloured scale borders known as 'mosaic' grounds, used at Meissen.

Unglazed wasters from the Worcester factory site show clearly how the scale effect was achieved. First, the reserved rococo or mirror-shaped panels were marked out and then a light wash of cobalt oxide was applied over all of the ground area. Once dry, scales were carefully painted in the same cobalt oxide, but less diluted. When glazed and fired, the effect was an even and pleasing background, although at times the blue still came out smudgy, with ill-defined scales. Examples with very large scales in relation to the size of the object decorated tend to be earlier than those with very fine, small scales. Generalisation is difficult, however, and the nature of the coloured decoration within the reserves remains the best guide to dating a piece.

Most scale blue ground pieces were enamelled at the factory, although Giles* was undoubtedly responsible for many of the richest patterns, such as the *Lady Mary Wortley Montagu** pattern. Some faulty examples which fired particularly badly in the glaze kiln were decorated in a less elaborate manner, possibly outside the factory (*see* **Red Line Bordered Group**).

Caughley and Bow very rarely used an underglaze scale blue ground in direct imitation of Worcester, whereas Liverpool and Bristol used less successful scale grounds in overglaze blue. The *Robert Browne* pattern of Lowestoft used underglaze blue scales but not really in any attempt to copy Worcester. Worcester scale blue continued throughout the Flight period and reappeared at various times during the 19th century, always reproducing patterns from the 1770s. Chamberlain does not seem to have used this decoration,

Scale Blue. *A coffee cup of c.1768 together with two matching unfinished wasters* from factory site excavations*, and a recent trial by David Peplow to discover how the effect was achieved. (The cup, Dyson Perrins Museum.)*

however, although it was copied extensively, particularly at Coalport from about 1805-10. Graingers used a transfer printed scale blue ground but this was probably not introduced before about 1850. Worcester scale blue was universally copied during the later periods, not just by the notorious Samson of Paris. Some of the best copies were probably made at Tournai or at St-Amand-Les-Eaux in the second quarter of the 19th century. These were on ovoid vases bearing bird panels made in a creamy soft paste porcelain. Very rich gilding was a speciality.

The factory of Booth & Co. in Tunstall, Staffordshire, produced printed copies of Worcester blue scale in earthenware around 1900. These pieces are frequently referred to as Booths, Worcester, although the factory had no Worcester connection whatsoever. The Worcester Royal Porcelain Company continued to use scale blue in the 20th century and the technique has been used more recently by David Peplow in Worcester since the 1970s.

Scale Grounds

While Worcester can be credited with inventing scale blue*, other scale grounds were copied from abroad. The rococo borders of fine coloured scales were used at Meissen from c.1740 and were known as 'mosaic' grounds. Worcester factory versions are unknown but Giles* copied Meissen c.1770, mostly in pink or puce with flower or fruit centres. More elaborate versions in purple and yellow, red and yellow, or blue, puce and gold were used on rare porcelains, which have been described as peacock scale, a term which is hardly appropriate. These are amongst the most beautiful of all 18th century patterns. Somewhat crudely painted large yellow scales were used for a border on painted teawares attributed to Giles c.1768. The fine scale yellow ground* with rococo or mirror-shaped bird panels was decorated at the factory, however, c.1768-70, on at least two tea services, but examples are understandably rare today.

Scale Moulding. *A teabowl and saucer with very fine moulded petals or scales, the subtle decoration finished off with a simple gold line, c.1765. (Dyson Perrins Museum.)*

A curious class of teaware painted with Teniers figures* within a scale pink border has in the past been attributed to Giles but considerable doubt now hangs over this group (*see* **Scale Pink Grounds**). A large dish with figures within a dry blue* scale border seems to be totally authentic, however.

Replacements for Chinese export porcelain were made with brick-red coloured scale grounds (*see* **Scale Red Grounds**).

Scale Moulding

A small number of sauceboats* from the 1750s and 1760s incorporate scale motifs as backgrounds although the motif

Scale Grounds. *A finely decorated teacup and saucer, the scale border shaded in pink and puce, the flowers typical of the Giles* workshop, c.1770. (Phillips, New York.)*

***Scale Pink Grounds.** A fine hexagonal vase painted in the Giles* workshop with festoons and characteristic flowers, c.1770, 11½in. (29cm). The pink scales on authenticated Giles* pieces are usually of large size. (Dyson Perrins Museum.)*

***Scale Pink Grounds.** A small mug* painted in a distinctive hand which differs from other Teniers* style figure painting accepted as having originated in the Giles* workshop. The dating of this particular class with scale pink borders remains controversial, 3¼in. (8.25cm). (Kenneth Klepser Collection.)*

seems to have been more favoured at Liverpool. A very rare design from c.1765 known only on teabowls* and saucers features a very intricate pattern of moulded scales, the few surviving examples having been left mostly in white. The original block mould for a teabowl survives in the Dyson Perrins Museum and this shows how much of the crisp modelling became lost beneath the glaze.

Scale Pink Grounds

Copied from the 'mosaic' grounds of Meissen from the 1750s, borders of surprisingly large pink fish scales were used by Giles*, c.1770. Two tones of pale pink or puce were used, edged with narrow gold scrolls. The centres are usually painted with colourful fruit on dessert services and baskets, while flowers are more common on tea services. Some fluted teawares with dark pink scale borders are painted somewhat clumsily with flower spirals and appear to date from c.1785.

A most interesting class of teawares exists, painted with colourful Teniers figures* within fine scale pink borders. These have in the past been attributed to the Giles workshop but much uncertainty now exists. The same pattern and identical figures occur on Worcester and Caughley porcelain as well as a class of Staffordshire porcelain which has been linked to Neale and Co. The porcelain probably dates from c.1780-5 and, while there are signs of refiring, no previous decoration seems to have been removed. The finest piece in this class is a mug in the Dyson Perrins Museum (Colour Plate 73). Opinions are at present divided as to whether the decoration is by a contemporary outside artist, c.1780, or is a very much later deception (*see* **Redecoration**).

Scale Red Grounds

Several teapots and a range of fluted teawares are known with grounds of coarsely painted scales in brick-red. These initially copy Chinese export wares although the scale red designs seem to have been adapted somewhat. Whenever they occur the red scales are filled with painted brushstrokes instead of the solid washes of colour used with all other scale grounds. Two teapots are known decorated with scale red grounds and panels of formal puce flowers framed in gold, while a milk jug is known with similar pointed scales alternating with formal bands in overglaze blue and red. Both of these patterns seem to be related to the Giles* workshop, c.1770-5. Another pattern probably decorated at the factory includes only small panels of scale red between large Chinese figure panels. A pattern used on fluted teawares c.1765-70 includes underglaze blue borders and panels which are filled with Canton* style figures in thick enamels. The scale red ground is composed of rounded scales instead of the pointed scales found on Giles pieces.

Scale Yellow Grounds

Having developed a successful pattern of *Dishevelled Bird** panels on a scale blue* ground, the Worcester factory

Scale Yellow Grounds. *Three pieces from a remarkable tea service sold by Mrs Van Der Porter in 1956, the teapot showing the influence of Sèvres. The bird painting and gilding are typical of Worcester factory decoration, crossed swords marks, c.1768-70. (Sotheby's/Kiddell Papers.)*

attempted the same design using yellow enamel as the ground colour. The effect was totally different, perhaps softer and more feminine, but clearly it was unpopular. Two surviving teapots suggest that at least two tea services were made but it is unlikely that much more was produced c.1768-70. Parts of at least one such set had become worn and were repainted at a later date, when gilding and rubbed insects were replaced. These pieces show signs of this redecoration* but otherwise there is no doubt as to the authenticity of the scale yellow decoration.

Rare teawares c.1768 were decorated in the Giles* workshop with a border of large yellow scales on a white background hung with simple puce twigs. This also probably represents just a single service. *See also* **Scale Grounds.**

Scallopendrium Moulding

A rare embossed pattern first used at Chelsea in the late 1740s. Worcester initially copied Chelsea with a series of tall beakers with saucers as illustrated, usually marked with a red anchor, although the Worcester copies were not made until c.1765. The leaves are thickly enamelled in green and the rims are edged in brown exactly copying Chelsea. Subsequently a full range of teaware shapes was made, c.1770-5. These were usually decorated with painted flower sprigs placed between the moulded leaves, although one teapot has been recorded left entirely in white*.

Scallopendrium Moulding. *A beaker and saucer copying Chelsea and marked with a red anchor, but made at Worcester c.1765. (Phillips, Edinburgh.)*

Scratch Cross Class. A bell-shaped mug of strong shape on a spreading foot, with the handle form usually associated with this class, c.1754, 3¾in. (9.5cm). (Phillips.)*

Scarlet Grounds

The reference to scarlet grounds in the 1769 Worcester sale catalogue was thought to denote claret but is probably the deep orange used in conjunction with *Kakiemon* decoration. *See* **Scarlet Japan Pattern**.

Scarlet Japan Pattern

Lot 66 in the 1769 Worcester sale catalogue was a service decorated with a 'fine old scarlet japan pattern'. Twenty years later Chamberlain were decorating Caughley* porcelain with 'Scarllet & gold Japan'. The only form of decoration which is known to fit these descriptions is a pattern based on early Japanese porcelain (*see* Colour Plate 24). Vertical bands of a deep orange or coral colour are reserved with *mons* and gilded with a diaper pattern. These alternate with chrysanthemum, bamboo and prunus. The pattern appears to have originated at the Worcester factory c.1765-8 on plain teawares, and also occurs on fluted teawares made during the 1770s. Other versions include Chinese figures instead of plant motifs in the alternate panels. These are more likely to be decorated in the Giles* workshop. Identical decoration occurs on some Liverpool and many pieces of Chinese porcelain. It is possible that all were decorated in London as the Chinese are unlikely to have devised the pattern themselves. The early Chamberlain version which occurs on dessert services is divided into three radiating panels rather than four and does not include reserved white *mons*. Some examples of this version are on earlier Worcester porcelain of c.1780 and these will probably have been decorated by the Chamberlains some time during the 1780s.

Scent Bottles

While the Chelsea and Girl-in-a-Swing factories had made a great many scent bottles before 1760, Worcester seems to have made only a single model and the attribution of this to Worcester remains slightly in doubt. Of flattened lozenge form with scroll-shaped sides, examples are known with uncharacteristic coloured flower painting and probably date from the mid-1750s. Later 18th century scent bottles were mostly made of glass and some English examples were gilded and enamelled in the Giles* workshop as well as possibly at Chamberlains in the late 1780s. Chamberlain porcelain scent bottles from c.1795-1805 follow glass shapes and were sold with silver or gold caps mounted in Birmingham, as well as moroccan or shagreen cases. Usually decorated in blue and gold, frequently with ciphers, examples with views of Worcester were clearly popular, as well as classical figure panels. A slightly later model from c.1810 has a flattened arrowhead shape and an example in the Dyson Perrins Museum is painted with shells on a marbled ground. Like all Worcester scent bottles of this period, it is unmarked and may have been a blank merely decorated at Worcester. Many English porcelain bottles from the early 19th century are decorated in similar styles to the Worcester factories but it is difficult to accept most of the traditional attributions of these to Worcester, especially to Grainger. Flight's factory does not appear to have made any scent bottles and Grainger are known with certainty to have made only a single model around 1835, copied from Rockingham with encrusted flowers (*see* **Twigging**). Royal Worcester and the later Grainger factory made many scent bottles from the 1870s.

Scratch Cross Class

Many thrown and turned shapes dating from c.1753-5 are marked with either a cross or a single stroke incised into the clay of the base prior to firing. The cross mark is usually found on the base directly beneath the handle of a shape and it has been suggested that this is some kind of tally mark used by the 'repairer' who fitted the handles. Pieces bearing this mark have been grouped together into a so-called scratch cross family.

While not every piece is marked with a cross, there is a unity in the type of shape and especially the slightly creamy, almost grey-tinted body and glaze. Mostly mugs with spreading bases (Colour Plate 74) or bell-shaped mugs, the group also includes similar jugs ranging from small cream or milk jugs with sparrow-beak lips to large quart (1.1 litre) sized jugs. Other shapes such as water bottles* or guglets, mustard pots* and some large punch pots* can also be associated with this group. Decoration is almost exclusively Chinese, mostly in colours with limited gilding, although some scratch cross pieces are found in blue and white. Smoky Primitive* transfer prints and pencilling* also occur on this class, and three mugs enamelled with the *Bird and Snail** pattern are dated underneath 1754.

A cross is a very simple mark, of course, and occurs as a workman's symbol on many items of pottery and porcelain. It is much too dangerous to make any assumptions just because scratch crosses occur on Bow and many other early porcelains. It has been pointed out, however, that the old alchemist's sign for talc or soaprock* was a saltire cross.

Sea Green

The 1769 Worcester sale catalogue includes a reference to a sea green ground colour and this has not been satisfactorily identified with any known factory grounds. While it seems unlikely that Giles* porcelain was included in this sale, a number of pieces with a peculiar muddy green ground have decoration associated with Giles and the name sea green has been used for these. There is considerable uncertainty about this ground colour as, although it appears at first to be contemporary, all examples bearing the colour would be complete in themselves if the ground was taken away. Indeed, in certain cases involving plates with bird and fruit decoration, the painter has gone to most extraordinary lengths to squeeze the green ground around the existing painting, creating crosses or large trefoils of the colour. Where the colour could not go around flower sprigs or insects, these have been overdecorated in gold. Close examination reveals the underlying puce or coloured enamel. The only explanation is that this green ground was added subsequently, but only on Giles decorated porcelain. Probably a supply of Giles pieces was bought in one of the disposal auctions following Giles' bankruptcy, and the ground added by another painter in London, possibly a former employee of Giles.

Sebright Service
An exceptional instance of Worcester making an exact replacement for an oriental service, even to the extent of copying the shape of the plate. The painted peony design is in underglaze blue, bright colours and gold and the very narrow rims are painted with a blue whorl border. The copies date from c.1770. The original service was Japanese porcelain and belonged to Sir John Sebright in Worcestershire. When the service was sold in the early years of this century it was correctly recognised that some pieces were Worcester and these were separated and sold to collectors for a higher price. Ironically, while the Worcester pieces are still highly desirable today, the Japanese pieces now have the greater value. Both the Japanese and Worcester examples are marked with copies of Chinese marks.

Semi-Porcelain
A vitreous earthenware body and not strictly porcelain at all, this invention by George Grainger & Co.* was introduced in 1848. In November 1848 the *Art Journal* commented that

> for cleaness and beauty it is nearly equal to porcelain... it is vitrified throughout and has a sharp, clear fracture when broken, equal to the more expensive ware. It combines the beauty of china with the economy of ordinary earthenware, as the price is little beyond the cost of the latter...we can confidently recommend this new and beautiful fabric.

Used extensively for dinner services, the ware appealed particularly to hotels, clubs and regiments, thanks to its great durability. Also called chemical porcelain*, it was widely used in laboratories for all manner of scientific and analytical equipment. Dinner and dessert wares are frequently marked only with the impressed initials 'G G W S P', for George Grainger Worcester Semi Porcelain.

Sèvres Style Decoration
While the initial influence on Worcester's production was primarily Meissen*, during the 1760s Sèvres was to play an increasingly important role in inspiring Worcester decoration. The French coloured grounds, new formal patterns and a totally new rococo feeling was altogether different from Meissen, and only a very limited quantity of Sèvres was available for sale in London. The Chelsea factory during the Gold Anchor period in the 1760s was influenced mostly by the coloured grounds, especially the *gros bleu* which they called mazarine blue. Chelsea also copied certain Sèvres vase shapes. Worcester may have been introduced to the Sèvres style following Chelsea's success. By c.1768 a full range of new ground colours was in production, including wet blue*, and turquoise* which was directly taken from Sèvres and called sky blue after Sèvres' *bleu celeste.* During the period c.1768-75 the Worcester factory sold a great many patterns in Sèvres style, some with *Fancy Birds*,* others with formal flower patterns including the full range of *Hop Trellis** type patterns. Some will have been copied directly from Sèvres originals; others were adapted by Worcester where the style was taken up with such enthusiasm that they made almost more varieties of striped patterns than the Sèvres factory itself. Even simple patterns such as Sèvres' *Feuilles de Choux* with blue enamel shell-shaped panels were copied, and occasionally shapes such as ice cups* were made as direct copies also.

Shagreen Ground
It is unclear whether the Worcester factory were trying to imitate shagreen (green-stained sharkskin) or *cailloutė,* a background of different sized pebble effect popular at Sèvres. The ground known as shagreen was used on very rare dessert wares c.1765-8 with reserved rococo shaped panels of *Rich Kakiemon** beasts and vegetation. In addition panels of shagreen were sometimes incorporated into the borders and background patterns of elaborate *Rich Kakiemon* vases (Colour Plate 75). The effect was achieved by using a wash of transparent light green enamel and small black painted circles. A similar effect, although semi-matt rather than transparent, was used by Flight, Barr and Barr c.1815-20 as a rare ground on vases and cabinet wares.

Shakespeare Cup
When Michael Faraday visited Worcester in 1819 he was shown by Thomas Baxter* 'a specimen on porcelain entirely the work of his own hands'. This could possibly have been the 'Shakespeare Cup' which was in the possession of Thomas Baxter's son and had been shown by him to R.W. Binns*. This had long been claimed to have been made while he was at Swansea, but a few years ago I was shown a goblet from a private collection which had been loaned to the Dyson Perrins Museum for research. The plain circular bowl is painted with the head of Shakespeare and scenes from his work. The bowl is raised on a curious ribbed stem which had been turned on a lathe. Through the incredible skill of the potter the stem reveals the profile face of Shakespeare when viewed from the side. The painting is undoubtedly that of Thomas Baxter and the granular body suggests that it was made c.1815, potted by Baxter himself while engaged at Flight, Barr and Barr.

Shakespearian Subjects
A superb transfer print of Shakespeare, based on his monument in Westminster Abbey by Scheemakers (*see* illustration on page 308), sets the scene for a whole series of fine paintings of Shakespearian subjects. The engraving is attributed to Robert Hancock* but without a signature this cannot be confirmed. It was used in black on cylindrical or bell-shaped mugs from c.1765-75 and is always accompanied by prints of two standing female figures representing Comedy and Tragedy. The original copper plate survives at Worcester and was reused by Royal Worcester in the 1970s for a limited edition mask jug marking the inauguration of the Commemorative Collectors' Society.

Thomas Baxter* was well versed in English drama, having attended regularly at the London playhouses where he sketched all of the great actors and actresses of the day, often in Shakespearian roles. When he arrived at Worcester Baxter specialised in theatrical subjects, especially Shakespeare. Indeed, it was while at Flight, Barr and Barr's factory that Baxter made the Shakespeare cup* which remained in his possession until his death. Not all Shakespeare subjects on Flight porcelain are by Thomas Baxter, however, as figure subjects were continued by his pupils, Thomas Lowe* and Solomon Cole*, as well as Joseph Flight*. Several years before Baxter came to Worcester, Humphrey Chamberlain jun.* began to show great talent. As a boy of nine or ten he drew a portrait of Garrick, and it is worth mentioning that David Garrick as King Lear is one of the subjects in the Theatrical Tea Service* of c.1772-5.

Humphrey Chamberlain had possibly been taught by John

Shakespearian Subjects. *A cylindrical mug* transfer printed* in black, copied from the monument in Westminster Abbey, the engraving almost certainly by Robert Hancock*, c.1765, 4¾in. (12cm). (Phillips.)*

Shakespearian Subjects. *A Chamberlain cabinet plate painted with Pompey's ghost appearing to Caesar, signed below the panel 'H Chamberlain Pinxt', painted mark with elaborate quotation, c.1815, 9½in. (24cm). (Phillips.)*

Wood* whose speciality had been historical figure subjects. The young Humphrey caught the eye of the Prince of Wales in 1807 and was asked to work on a special service painted with historical figure centres. This is believed to have been the Shakespeare dessert service of forty-eight pieces which was given to the Los Angeles County Museum from the Walter T. Wells Collection. Humphrey Chamberlain's nephew, Thomas Chamberlain, later wrote that 'one small dessert service painted with subjects from Shakespeare by my uncle for the Prince Regent cost the latter 4000 pounds'. Scenes from twenty-six different Shakespeare plays are featured on this single set, all copied from engravings. Numerous other vases* and cabinet cups* as well as plates were painted by Humphrey Chamberlain in this manner, mostly on different marbled grounds*. His brother Walter Chamberlain* also painted Shakespearian scenes although he was not nearly so talented as a draftsman. Some of the two brothers' paintings were copied from Boydell's published prints which were used again in the Chamberlain & Co.* period, possibly by Luke Wells. Wells worked on the Kerr and Binns Shakespeare service in 1853.

Shanked Shape

On 14 September 1788 John Flight* recorded in his Diary* that he had been to Newcastle (in the Potteries) 'to seek after a modeller. I found one whom we have since agreed to take at Michae[lma]s for 3 years'. He then recorded a visit to France to see Porcelain factories there, aiming in particular 'to improve our shapes'. It was probably as a result of this and subsequent trips to France that the new spiral fluted shape was introduced at Flights, very likely during 1790. The shape was immediately popular and many finely potted teawares were made over the next decade. The Chamberlain account books show that they sent '1 complete sett, Worcr new shankered' to Thomas Turner* in July 1790. This was subsequently copied by Turner at Caughley for Chamberlain were once again selling Caughley porcelain of a shape called 'New Shankered' or 'new shank'd' by the end of 1792. This was a direct copy of some of Flights' basic forms. When Chamberlain began to manufacture their own porcelain they straight away introduced their own version. In December 1793 the inventory drawn up for stocktaking included '44 teapots, shanked & fluted' all in unglazed porcelain.

Most of the early Chamberlain shanked teawares are of the variation known as 'tramline' fluted by collectors today. These have a thin double line at the peak of each spiral flute, a feature not used on teawares at Flights. While tramline shanking does usually indicate a Chamberlain origin, it can also occur on Coalport and Grainger porcelain. Chamberlain also made a plain shanked shape but this is rarely seen. Both Chamberlain and Flight made a full range of spiral fluted dessert service shapes also, and these can often be very richly decorated. Occasionally Flight dessert shapes can be moulded with tramline flutes. In addition, Chamberlain made miniature or toy* tea services with tramline shanking but these are extremely rare.

A shanked or spiral fluted shape was probably the first Grainger shape introduced c.1805-6. By this time spiral fluted shapes had been around for a considerable time and were old-fashioned. Grainger made both plain and tramline versions but all are very rarely encountered. Shanked shapes were apparently not made at Worcester after c.1807-8.

Shell Decoration. *A pair of Flight, Barr and Barr serpent handled vases painted by Thomas Baxter* in his distinctive stippled technique, the rims applied with simulated pearls, script marks, c.1815, 5½in. (14cm). (Phillips.)*

Shape Books
Amongst the Grainger archives preserved at Worcester are a number of ornamental shape books in which vases, figures and other ornamental shapes were drawn, often in considerable detail. These records only begin in the 1820s but are fairly comprehensive after c.1830. They have proven invaluable in identifying many unmarked Grainger productions. Sadly no similar records survive from any of the other Worcester factories, nor are there any similar shape books for tea, dinner and dessert wares. Information on these can only be partially gleaned from the pattern books*.

Shell Decoration
Shells have always featured prominently in all branches of art but became of particular importance during the age of rococo*. From its earliest establishment the Worcester factory made modelled scallop shells as pickle* and sweetmeat* dishes and encrusted realistic modelled shells all around large sweetmeat stands*. These continued into the 1790s at Chamberlains and during the 1840s Chamberlain & Co.* made a variety of baskets*, trays and other vessels encrusted with very realistic modelled and coloured shells (*see* Colour Plate 17).

At the end of the 18th century keen shell collectors amongst the English gentry paid enormous sums for new and unusual specimens. These same wealthy patrons bought fine porcelain and the Worcester Flight factory realised that shells painted on porcelain would represent their customers' wealth. Flight and Barr introduced shell painting c.1800 and by the Barr, Flight and Barr period shells had become one of the factory's most important subjects (Colour Plates 76 and 77). Samuel Smith* was one of the two most prolific shell painters and his work is known from several signed pieces. Smith added particularly fine dendritic sprigs of weed behind his compositions, while another hand, presumed to be that of John Barker*, tended to group his weed into small clusters of filaments. This hand was responsible for the impressive Gordon service*. Thomas Baxter*, who arrived in Worcester in the Flight, Barr and Barr period, occasionally painted shells, placing his accurately observed groups in landscapes. These are sometimes titled by Baxter 'Shells from Nature'. There were many artists subordinate to these who also painted shells, but unfortunately the tendency in the past to attribute any shell painting to Baxter or Barker has led to much inaccuracy. (*See* illustration on page 310.)

Curiously, shell painting is very rare on Chamberlain porcelain and when it does occur is far inferior to most Flight painting. Marked Grainger examples are not recorded although some unmarked pieces which 'feel' Worcester have in the past been, probably incorrectly, attributed to Grainger.

During the Flight, Barr and Barr period a number of bat-printed* subjects were produced which seem to have been copied from painted pieces. These occur on tea and dessert services and can occasionally be coloured-in in an attempt to make a cheaper version of what was a costly subject to paint by hand. The fashion for shell painting declined by c.1820 and was not revived until the Kerr and Binns period in the 1850s.

Shell Dishes
The small dishes in the shape of scallop shells are described here under the heading **Pickle Dishes;** *see also* **Sweetmeat Shells.** It was standard for dessert services to include one shape of dish in the form of a shell although these became very stylised. Worcester's shell-shaped dishes from c.1768 onwards are based on shapes used at the Sèvres factory. They are of plain lobed shape with simple moulded scroll terminals. By the 19th century shell-shaped dessert dishes became so far removed from the shape of a real shell that it is difficult to relate them to the dishes called shell-shaped in the Chamberlain records.

Shell Decoration. *A Flight, Barr and Barr vase with dramatic dragon handles, the painted shells unusually placed on a bed of weed against a white ground, script mark, c.1820, 9½in. (24cm). (Phillips.)*

Sifter Spoons. *A rare example of the pierced rice spoon shape painted in bright blue with the* Compass Flower *pattern, c.1780-5, 5½in. (14cm). (Lawrence Branyan Collection.)*

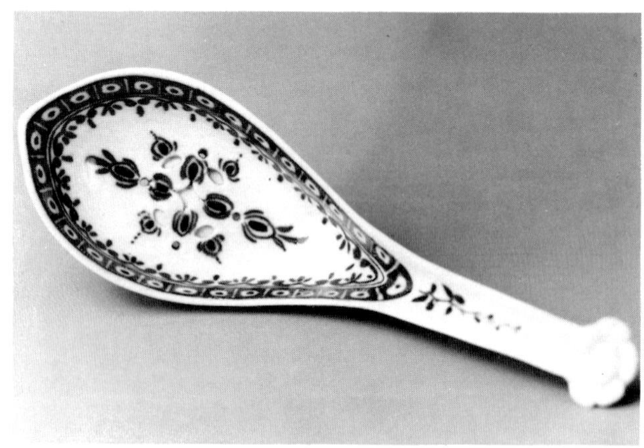

Sheriff, Charlotte and Samuel
A miniature or toy* tea service of *Prunus Root** pattern was inscribed under each piece with the initials 'C S' and the date 1758. These are believed through family tradition to have been made for Charlotte Sheriff who lived in Upton-on-Severn, Worcestershire. Apart from the teabowl and saucer in the Dyson Perrins Museum, only one other saucer is known to have survived from what was probably a complete tea service. A small mug painted in blue with the arms of the Foresters Company has been recorded with the inscription 'Saml. Sheriff in Upton 1771' (*see* **Dated Pieces**), presumably made for a relation of Charlotte Sheriff.

Sherwin, Ishmael
Solomon Cole's* account of decorators at Flight's factory* tells us:

> Ishmael Sherwin was chiefly engaged in designing patterns and in decorating the rich pieces with gems, &c., and attended principally to the embossed gold. He was a fine ornamental gilder.

The distinctive use of raised enamel jewelling* on many of Flight's richest productions has in the past been associated with Thomas Baxter* as it occurs on several pieces painted or modelled by him. Possibly there was some influence from Baxter but it is likely most of this ornamental work was by Sherwin. Pigot's 1841 *Worcester Directory* includes Ishmael Sherwin in a list of glass, china and earthenware dealers in the city.

Sifter Spoons
Plain shaped blue and white rice spoons* with flower terminals were frequently pierced with small holes in a geometric pattern. Their purpose is uncertain and they have also been described as egg drainers*. Usually painted with the *Maltese Cross* floral pattern and dated c.1770, a single later example of c.1780 has been noted with a formal *Compass Flower* pattern.

Sliced Fruit
A form of decoration copied from Meissen* and used on Worcester porcelain from c.1768-75. Virtually all examples in enamel colours can be safely attributed to the Giles* workshop, especially as one of the Grubbe plates* is painted with particularly fine sliced fruit. Sliced fruit is usually accompanied by rich coloured grounds, especially scale pink*, although in a simpler style the *Horner of Mells** pattern features

Smith, Samuel. *A watercolour signed by Samuel Smith and passed down through the family of the artist. The painting style is very similar to landscape painting on Flight porcelain, 12⅜in. x 9½in. (31.5 x 24cm). (Phillips.)*

fruit just in two tones of green. A certain care has to be taken as many expensive pieces with sliced fruit can show evidence of having been redecorated*. A fruit spray including a sliced apple occurs as a rare addition to a popular teaware pattern printed in underglaze blue c.1775-80.

Smith, Samuel

Considering the skill of this versatile artist it is very surprising that he was given only the slightest mention in the writings of Solomon Cole* and R.W. Binns*. His importance was recognised in 1976 when a descendant gave a number of signed pieces to the Dyson Perrins Museum. Made during the Flight and Barr and the Barr, Flight and Barr periods, these would appear to be special apprentice pieces or family presentation items as most are signed, either openly on the base or with a hidden signature. The pieces are dated between 1800 (a simple sprig pattern) and 1806 (a superb landscape beaker). Samuel Smith had been admitted Freeman of Worcester in March 1807 and so these pieces would fit in with the date of his apprenticeship. A Samuel Smith had worked previously in London as a china painter in 1790 in partnership with Samuel Fletcher but I feel these apprenticeship pieces make it very unlikely that this is the same Samuel Smith. The landscape painting is very similar to work ascribed by Binns to Thomas Rogers* and clearly great care has to be taken in attributing unsigned pieces. The two shell-painted pieces at Worcester, together with a jug and goblet signed 'S.S. 1807' (Colour Plate 78) sold at Phillips in 1990, give many clues to his technique of painting fine dendritic weed as a background to his shells. Other unsigned shell painting in this manner on Barr, Flight and Barr pieces can thus be attributed (*see* Colour Plate 76). A print of Worcester published in the 1820s is signed 'S. Smith Fecit', and an extensive sketch book along with other watercolours and pencil drawings which also came from a descendant, show the wide range of subjects Smith could attempt. From the same source came a Staffordshire mug of c.1825 bearing the initials 'S S', indicating that Smith also worked as a free-lance enameller at this time. He apparently remained at Flight's factory until 1840. The folder of drawings by Samuel Smith also included flower and fruit paintings by Eliza Smith although it is not known how she was related or if she also painted on porcelain.

Smoky Primitives. *An early hexagonal creamboat*, plain white except for small transfer prints* of buildings in the rococo* panels, c.1754, 4¼in. (10.8cm) long. (Sotheby's.)*

Smoky Primitives

A name given by early collectors to the first transfer prints used on Worcester porcelain (*see* Colour Plate 87, left). The name is appropriate as they can regularly appear slightly smudgy, and they lack, of course, the sophistication of later onglaze prints after c.1757. There has been much controversy as to where and when these prints were carried out. Some outline prints intended to be coloured-in (such as *Red Bull** and a design of 'Chinese Antiques') suggest that the printing must have been done within the factory, while other prints used also on Birmingham enamel might suggest equally that the printing was done in a Birmingham enamel workshop. There is no doubt that Robert Hancock* was involved with these prints before 1756 when he is believed to have arrived at Worcester. A number of engravings after L.P. Boitard* and engraved by Hancock for book impressions occur on porcelain from the 1753-55 period. The copper plates for these were probably acquired by Josiah or Richard Holdship* and printed at Worcester, justifying Josiah's claim to have invented printing on porcelain. When these occur in conjunction with painted borders, the palette and treatment is typically Worcester. The presence of early signed Hancock prints on Chinese porcelain and the *Red Bull* pattern on Chelsea complicates the matter, however.

In an important paper on Birmingham enamel printing given to the English Ceramic Circle in 1966, Dr Bernard Watney illustrated two very different treatments of the same two subjects, *The Fortune Teller* and *La Cascade**, printed in brown and black on Worcester coffee cups, c.1754. It is possible that one of each of these would have been factory printing while the other was printed at Birmingham. When

Smoky Primitives. *A two-handled sauceboat*, the interior with a print of waterfowl probably from an engraving supplied by Robert Hancock*, c.1755, 7½in. (19cm). (Phillips.)*

Lady Shelburne visited Mr Taylor's factory making enamel boxes in Birmingham she described a method of printing using paper to transfer the sticky impression and then dusting the colour on as a powder. It is likely that smoky primitives on Worcester porcelain were likewise printed in a kind of oil and then dusted with colour. Hand painting was then used to touch up any imperfect parts of the impression.

Snake in a Basket Pattern
A rare enamelled pattern used on teawares, small scratch cross* type mugs, and wine funnels, all from c.1753. The design includes a Chinese 'Long Eliza'* figure standing by a pine tree. Behind the tree is a basket containing what is probably meant to be a *ruyi* sceptre, a ceremonial stick often depicted in Chinese art. Rising from the basket in this way, the *ruyi* sceptre does indeed resemble a snake.

Snuff Boxes and Bonbonnières
Snuff boxes and bonbonnières were made extensively in Continental porcelain and in English enamel but are surprisingly rare in English porcelain. Worcester made circular boxes which can be dated c.1765-8 and from their size are more likely to have been for snuff. They have hinged metal mounts which have worn the flat bases. A spectacular example in the Schreiber Collection in the Victoria and Albert Museum has a shagreen* ground and flower panels with the arms and crest of Downes painted inside the lid.

A small circular box and cover moulded in the form of a peony flower appears to date from the late 1760s. The petals are strongly shaded in red and yellow (*see* **Peony Boxes**). Chamberlain made a small circular box with a loose flat top c.1798 which was probably intended as a patch box, although it could have been used for snuff. Larger flat circular boxes were listed as snuff boxes c.1820 and were richly decorated with fox-hunting scenes and other sporting subjects.

Soaprock
Also known as soapyrock, this is a granite, rich in steatite, which has decomposed into a soft, almost crumbly mineral which does literally feel soapy when rubbed. The purest source of steatite occurs naturally in the Lizard peninsula in Cornwall. As early as the 1720s it was discovered that this material could be used in the making of chinaware, although it was not until the mid-1740s that the technique for manufacturing porcelain from soaprock was discovered. Dr Richard Pocock* visited the Lizard in October 1750 and referred to the Bristol Porcelain Company* as having paid £5 a ton, far more than the rate for other pottery clays. Benjamin Lund* was granted a licence to mine at least twenty tons of soaprock a year at Gew Graze, near the Lizard, from 7 March 1749 for a period of twenty-one years. Soaprock had previously been used at Limehouse*. The Worcester factory was probably more interested in obtaining the soaprock licence when they bought the Bristol factory in 1752. Richard Holdship* controlled the licence and sold the soaprock to his partners for £18 per ton. The secret of soaprock was taken from Worcester to Liverpool probably by Robert Podmore* and accounted for the similarity between the porcelain of Worcester, Chaffers and Christian. Soaprock continued to be used throughout the Flight period until at least 1840 and is discussed by Henry Sandon in *Flight and Barr Worcester Porcelain.*

Soqui, Monsieur
References to a French artist employed at Cookworthy's Plymouth and Champion's Bristol factories have led to great confusion, especially concerning the role of this painter at Worcester. There is no evidence whatsoever to place the painter called Mons. Soqui at Worcester, or, it seems, any clear indication of what sort of painting he might have done at Bristol. He is believed to have come from Sèvres* although no artist by this name is listed in the extensive Sèvres archives. There does occur, however, a distinctive style of bird and landscape painting, very much in the French style, which can be found on early Cookworthy or Champion Bristol porcelain and which is very similar to a rare form of painting used at Worcester on dessert wares at about the same time, c.1770. *Fancy Birds** are placed among trees and foliage in a softer, more diffused style of painting with predominant grey-green tones. Fine gold dentil rims* suggest the painting was carried out at Worcester, probably by a Continental painter who joined the factory briefly before moving to Plymouth or Bristol.

Sparks, George
While many outside decorators used Coalport blanks, George Sparks is the only decorator to acknowledge this fact, adding 'Coalport Porcelain' to many of his marks. No Worcester porcelain is known with Sparks' name although some Minton teawares have been noted with his elaborate marks. Born in 1804, he joined Grainger probably as an apprentice and by the 1820s had become a senior decorator or supervisor, probably designing new patterns. By 1834 he had established his own retail shop in Broad Street, selling earthenware, glass and particularly Coalport porcelain 'at the same prices as charged at the manufactory'. Godden's *Encyclopaedia of British Porcelain Manufacturers* reproduces an advertisement from the 1851 Worcester directory where George Sparks lists the sort of wares he sold and the wide range of decorations he could provide for the nobility. Queen Adelaide gave him a Royal Warrant which he proudly used on his porcelain marks. Sparks specialised in landscape painting and very fine gilding, but also perfected transfer printing, not only for his marks but for delicate printed scenes or outlines for colouring-in. Sparks' work is uncommon but well worth seeking as the quality is always high.

Sparrow Beak Jugs
An appropriate name given by collectors to the shape of Worcester milk jugs from the early 1750s until c.1790. Most have plain baluster or pear-shaped bodies and the lip is a perfectly pointed triangle. Early examples from c.1752-54 generally have moulded handles and slightly larger lips in relation to the size of the jug. Otherwise there is very little variation in the form of Worcester sparrow beak jugs over the next thirty years. Small jugs usually have grooved handles and slightly flared rims and do not have covers, while larger jugs have plain round-sectioned loop handles and were normally sold with matching domed covers. With the exception of very early milk jugs, the sparrow beak jugs formed part of a tea service* with decoration to match the rest of the set. From c.1768-80 some milk jugs with similar sparrow beak lips can be barrel shaped and these were probably not sold with tea services. Many larger jugs, from a pint to two quarts (half to two and a half litres), have lips of similar shape to the small milk jugs but are not thought of as sparrow beak jugs.

Spill Vases. *A Chamberlain spill vase with Cardinal Wolsey in a scene from Shakespeare's King Henry VIII, painted by Humphrey Chamberlain jun*, script mark, c.1815, 3⅛ in. (8cm). (Lawrence Fine Art of Crewkerne.)*

Spill Vases
Pairs of small vases, roughly cylindrical in shape, were made by virtually every English porcelain factory during the first half of the 19th century. They seem to have been given a variety of names, mostly referring either to spills or matches in some way. Most confusing are names such as match cases, paper cases, match boxes and luminaries, all of which can be identified as holders for paper spills. These would have stood on a mantelpiece or recess in a fireplace and contained rolled-up paper sticks used for lighting a fire. Six different Grainger shapes are illustrated by Henry and John Sandon, *Grainger's Worcester Porcelain,* pls. 96-100. Grainger spill vases are often much more elaborate than Flight's or Chamberlain's who favoured plain cylinders or trumpet shapes to show off rich painted and gilded decoration. Mostly sold as pairs, some came as sets of three with a larger example in the middle, and sometimes spill vases were matched as the side vases in a garniture with a bough pot* or covered vase in the middle. They continued into the Kerr and Binns and Royal Worcester periods.

Spill Vases. *A Barr, Flight and Barr spill vase with popular eagle head and ring handles, the rim with finely modelled pearls, script mark, c.1810, 3½ in. (9cm). (Phillips.)*

Spinning Maiden Pattern
In reality there are two very different teaware patterns known as *Spinning Maiden,* both copied from Chinese Export *famille rose** porcelain. One dates from c.1768 and probably derives from a Chinese copy of Meissen.* Each piece bears two finely painted panels of a lady seated by a simple box and pole arrangement. The panels are framed with elaborate coloured *Laub und Bandelwerk* scrollwork popular at Meissen c.1730, and there is a red and gold spearhead border around the rim. The second design known by the same name, but also called *Lady at the Loom* pattern, depicts an older Chinese lady seated on a bench and working a circular frame in front of a very complicated loom (*see* illustration on page 314.) The reverse design shows green leafy plants growing from blue rockwork and the rims have a red and gold crow foot* border. This seems to date c.1772-5. Both *Spinning Maiden* patterns are rare but enough examples exist to confirm that they formed a Worcester factory production rather than being purely replacements for Chinese porcelain.

Spinning Maiden Pattern. *A milk jug with sparrow beak* lip, painted after a Chinese* famille rose* *original, the second of two versions of this pattern made at Worcester, c.1770, 3½in. (9cm). (Phillips.)*

Spittoons. *A spittoon complete with convenient carrying handle, printed in underglaze blue*, crescent mark*, c.1770, 4⅛in. (10.5cm). (Phillips.)*

Spiral Fluted Shape
See **Shanked Shape**

Spit-Out
Disfiguring blemishes in the glaze of many pieces of Worcester porcelain are usually unintentional and caused much concern to the proprietors. The wares of any period can be affected although mostly it is the very early pieces and the early Flight porcelain that is most affected. There are many causes, the most usual being sulphur in the firing. John Flight's Diary* records the trouble he had with 'Sulphuring', especially in 1789 when whole kiln-loads were spoilt. Evidence is small black specks which resemble eruptions in the glaze when viewed with a strong magnifying glass and taken together can give the effect of a cloudy dirt on the surface which will not clean off (*see* Colour Plate 16). Worcester were not alone in experiencing this trouble and both Pennington factories in Liverpool were affected far more. New small kilns from London and the use of lime proved to be John Flight's remedy and by the 1790s Flight's pieces were leaving the kiln in better shape than Chamberlain's who regularly experienced trouble with black specks in the glaze.

When a piece of porcelain is left in the atmosphere for any period of time it will absorb dampness and impurities, especially where the glaze is thin or absent on the rims and footrims. When such a piece is fired again in a decorating kiln the result is blackening where mainly carbon in the impurities stains the body or erupts in the glaze. Spit-out caused by re-firing can occur after only a few months but usually takes time to develop. Therefore heavy spit-out can be taken as a very likely sign that a piece has been redecorated*. Attempts to remove heavy spit-out with grinding are usually very obvious and confirm that a piece has been refired at a later date. Some early pieces exhibit small areas which seem to have been ground on the surface with a form of lapidary wheel and this attempt to clean up bad spit-out was probably done at the factory.

Spittoons
The wide neck on Worcester spittoons seems very precarious but thankfully many examples have survived, all in underglaze blue transfer prints. They were hand thrown shapes and finely turned and therefore must have been difficult to make. Most were plain but some have additional scroll handles applied at the side to enable the spittoon to be carried around. Worcester examples were mostly made in the *Fence** and *Three Flowers** patterns from c.1770-85. One example in *Fence* pattern is known with the impressed name 'FLIGHT'. Spittoons occur from the early 18th century in metal and Chinese porcelain as well as Continental porcelain and later in creamware and other pottery bodies. Enough evidence survives to show that their original purpose was as spittoons, the handle adding convenience when they needed to be carried around by their owner due to an ailment. Having said this, Geoffrey Godden made a convincing argument in his *Caughley and Worcester Porcelain* that when the Chamberlain family sold these shapes they referred to them as 'saffer pots'. Saffer could relate to saffron, a product of crocus plants, and the pots could have been used for bulbs, but most collectors find this difficult to believe. It is more likely that there was another meaning of the word saffer in the 18th century connected with spitting and that this was a nicer word than spittoon. *Saffe* was a little known derivative word meaning safe or safety and it is possible that it was considered 'safe' in society to keep a portable spittoon handy just in case.

Spoons
These are fragile items to attempt to make in porcelain and it is hardly surprising that relatively few have survived in early Worcester. The rarest of all are from the earlier Bristol factory

Spoon Trays. This standard shape of Worcester spoon tray accompanied most tea services. These examples all date from c.1768-70 and include the Hop Trellis* *pattern and* Rich Queen's* *pattern, each about 6in. (15cm). (Phillips.)*

and are tiny circular scoops on a gnarled twig handle, supplied with small blue and white baskets probably for cream. 18th century Worcester spoons are known in only a few small shapes and larger ladles*, almost all dating from the 1770s. One form copies a Chinese shape and is discussed here under **Rice Spoons**. The others are usually seen together with a wet mustard pot and this seems very logical for spoons with a long, plain, slightly curved handle which fits comfortably through the hole in the cover of the mustard pot.* The other types have either a flat circular bowl or a scallop shell bowl and a very flat leaf-moulded terminal to the handle. These just do not work inside a mustard pot as the delicate moulding usually becomes wedged in the cover. It is possible that these were sold as mustard spoons but it is more probable that they were for salt, especially as coloured spoons, although very rare, occur far more frequently than coloured wet mustard pots. One very rare version of a salt spoon has a plainer, flat handle copying a silver shape. Larger spoons were supplied with sugar and cream tureens from dessert services (*see* **Ladles**).

Spoon Trays

From contemporary paintings showing families at tea it is clear that, after stirring tea in a teabowl, the single spoon or occasionally several spoons would be placed on the spoon tray, never in the saucer. Worcester spoon trays date from about 1760 and seem mostly to have been intended for wealthy and more up-market customers. Consequently Worcester blue and white spoon trays are very rare and when they do occur they are usually in elegant moulded patterns with simple borders

Spoon Trays. A very unusual blue and white spoon tray painted in the style of a Kangxi *original, pseudo Chinese mark, c.1770, 5¾in. (14.5cm). (Phillips.)*

Spotted Fruit. *A teapot in the style of Sèvres* with typical spotted fruit decorated at the Worcester factory, crescent mark*, c.1770, 6⅞in. (17.5cm). (Phillips.)*

Staghunt Pattern. *The simple enamelled pattern is used most successfully on a strap fluted* teapot, the crisp modelling not affected by too much decoration, c.1755, 6½in. (16.5cm). (Phillips.)*

rather than Chinese patterns. The standard fluted hexagonal shape of the Worcester spoon tray hardly varies and continued until c.1785 when spoon trays became unpopular. The few other shapes which have been recorded are a plain oval spoon tray with a slight rim, seen in the *Eloping Bride** pattern from c.1768, and another oval shape with a fluted border, illustrated by H. Rissik Marshall, *Coloured Worcester Porcelain*, item 584, but not necessarily Worcester. Spoon trays with *Chrysanthemum** pattern moulding are of a different lobed lozenge shape. A very different form of spoon tray was moulded with the *Blind Earl** pattern of embossed rose leaves although these are usually ignored completely by the decoration (*see* Colour Plate 68). *Blind Earl* spoon trays have applied twig handles at each end and were made c.1770.

Although Caughley spoon trays were decorated by Chamberlain c.1790 (*see* Colour Plate 36), they were unfashionable by this time and none seems to have been made in Chamberlain's own porcelain or early Grainger. Some oval teapot-stands have become separated from a service, however, and these are sometimes incorrectly called spoon trays.

Spotted Fruit

A popular class of fruit painting in enamels which occurs on Worcester porcelain c.1770. The fruit is always somewhat stylised and painted in bright colours, using dark dots of colour to represent some sort of blight on the fruit. In the past this style has been attributed to a single 'Spotted Fruit Painter' but clearly many different hands are represented. The two most distinctive varieties of *Spotted Fruit* are both now believed to have been painted at the factory. One is represented by the Duke of Gloucester* service which is wonderfully bold and rich. The other occurs usually in conjunction with apple green grounds*.

Spurling, John
Thomas Mortimer's *Universal Director* of 1763 lists

> SPURLING, JOHN, Proprietor of Worcester China Manufactory, London-house, Aldersgate-street

Geoffrey Wills, writing in *Apollo*, discovered that Spurling was also in business as a glass-seller at Little Moorfields from 1755-61, and in 1770 traded from Gough Square. The Worcester China Warehouse had moved from Aldersgate Street to 12 Gough Square in 1768. *See* **London Shops.**

Square Marks
The curious mark of a fretted square was possibly originally intended for use on teawares painted in Chinese style but instead occurs on a variety of patterns from c.1766-8 until the late 1770s. Earlier examples are almost invariably on wide fluted teaware shapes, the patterns entirely in colours. By c.1770 the mark occurs on pieces decorated with underglaze scale blue* grounds, also solid wet blue* grounds and on patterns such as the *Queen Charlotte** in Imari* style. The individual formation of the square marks can vary but overall the mark is always carefully drawn. For this reason it has been an easy mark to copy and many fakes occur from the 19th century.

Staghunt Pattern
Searches for the original Chinese version of this popular pattern are complicated by the fact that most Chinese pieces are identical to English painting, suggesting that the pattern was painted in England. Evidence for this can be seen on many pieces where simple blue and white or *bianco sopra bianco* (white enamel only) Chinese patterns are covered over by the *Staghunt* pattern. Some early Worcester blue and white cups of c.1752-3 also bear underglaze blue patterns complete in themselves in addition to the overpainted *Staghunt* design which was possibly added outside the factory. It may even be that James Giles* was in some way connected with these pieces as he probably painted Chinese porcelain at this early period and was possibly living in Worcester at the time.

By c.1752-3 the pattern was in production at the factory on a series of rococo shapes based on English silver. The combination of a simple Chinese *famille rose** design and very English shapes works well together on teapots (*see* Colour Plate 69) and creamjugs. These shapes range from simple globular pots with moulded cartouches to wonderful and eccentric rococo versions like the example illustrated here. The compositions within the panels can vary considerably. The *Staghunt* pattern was also used on sauceboats, hexagonal creamboats and a plate of about 7in. (18cm). The pattern does not seem to have been produced at Worcester after c.1756 although it was copied in Liverpool and at Lowestoft subsequently. The *Staghunt* pattern was, however, reintroduced by Chamberlain on their early porcelain, c.1792. Chamberlain referred to the design as 'Hunting Pattern in Compartments', which was included as no. 9 in their pattern lists. Geoffrey Godden illustrates an extensive range of these wares in his *Chamberlain-Worcester Porcelain,* pp. 68-70.

Stephens, John
The only reference to this artist appeared in *Berrow's Worcester Journal* for November 1813:

> An inquest was on Thursday taken at the Curriers' Arms, Angel Street in this city by the coroner on the body of John Stephens, a china painter, who was seized by an apoplectic fit and instantly expired. Verdict — Died by the visitation of God.

Stinton, Charles. *A Flight, Barr and Barr vase with rich blue ground and applied pearls. The panel of* Fancy Birds* *is typical of the style attributed to George 'Doctor' Davis* but is more likely to be by Charles Stinton, c.1815, 9⅝in. (24.5cm). (Dyson Perrins Museum.)*

Stinton, Charles
The only information we have on this painter at Flight's factory is the note by Solomon Cole* that he painted 'Fancy Birds &c.' It is not known what the '&c.' were but *Fancy Birds** refers to exotic imaginary birds in the traditional Worcester style with landscapes behind. Most *Fancy Birds* are at present attributed to George Davis* and in the absence of any signed pieces by Stinton it remains impossible to distinguish his work from that of the better known Davis. Charles was almost certainly related to Henry Stinton*.

Stinton, Henry
A member of a great family of Worcester decorators, Henry Stinton is known from R.W. Binns' catalogue of his museum collection to have painted flower subjects on richly gilded Flight, Barr and Barr plates. These have insects in the smaller panels and Solomon Cole*, referring to artists around 1819, tells us that Samuel Astles* and Henry Stinton 'were painting groups of flowers....There were also flower-painters subordinate to them.' He adds that a beautiful vase 'painted on one side with exotic birds by Davis* and on the other a group of flowers by Stinton is in the possession of Mr R.C. Tennant of Kensington'. Because of Binns' attributions, most

Stirrup Cups. *Two views of a small beaker-shaped cup printed in underglaze blue* with additional painted shading, c.1780-5, 2½ in. (6.3cm). (Private Collection.)*

flower painting in traditional Worcester style with exotic insects is given to Stinton even though his pieces are indistinguishable from those that Binns attributes to Astles (*see* Colour Plate 20). Henry Stinton was admitted Freeman of Worcester on 13 March 1826, although he gave a London address when exhibiting flower paintings at the Royal Academy, 1830-1.

Stirrup Cups

Drinking cups in the shape of a fox's head were traditionally used at hunt meetings by riders while in the saddle, hence there was no need for a footrim on which to place the cup. Worcester examples are known only from Chamberlain's factory and appear in the records from the early 1790s until the 1820s. Usually examples are realistically coloured but some were just gilded or in blue and gold. Most are inscribed with the hunting cry 'Tally Ho'. Geoffrey Godden illustrates two different models in his *Chamberlain-Worcester Porcelain* (pl. 372) and refers to them by their original factory name as 'bumpers'. A hare's head was also made as a stirrup cup although surprisingly no hound's head cups which are so well known in Staffordshire porcelain. Silver, earthenware and Derby porcelain cups all pre-date the Worcester foxes and either could have inspired Chamberlain.

A very unusual cup with hunting connections was made in the early Flight period and has been referred to as a stirrup beaker. Only a single example is recorded dating from c.1780-5, transfer printed in blue with washed-in foreground. It shows a huntsman and dog running after a fox, the man with a speech bubble inscribed 'We Shall Catch him Anon' and 'Talio'. Dr Watney was unsure whether the beaker was Worcester or Caughley but, having inspected the piece, I have no doubt as to its Worcester attribution.

Stormont Service

One of the most original Worcester patterns, also known as Lord Stormont, which is believed to have been made for the seventh Viscount Stormont who died in 1796. The pattern comprises festoons of tasselled drapery suspended by simple knots from a gold dentil rim.* Two versions are known, one in bright turquoise as illustrated in Colour Plate 91, used only on teawares, the other in puce or carmine on tea and dessert wares. Most of the shapes upon which the turquoise version of the pattern was used are very unusual for Worcester. The main shapes are angular and the saucers have a moulded central well to hold the cups which can be either plain or of double-ogee shape with twisted handles. Because of the unusual shapes it is reasonable to accept that this service was a single special order, even if the puce version was a subsequent copy made for a different customer. Although difficult to date, both services were probably made c.1775.

Stowe Service

While armorial decoration was a speciality of the Flight factory, their greatest triumph in this area was the service made for Richard Temple-Nugent-Brydges-Chandos-Grenville, second Marquis of Buckingham, and his wife Anna Eliza,

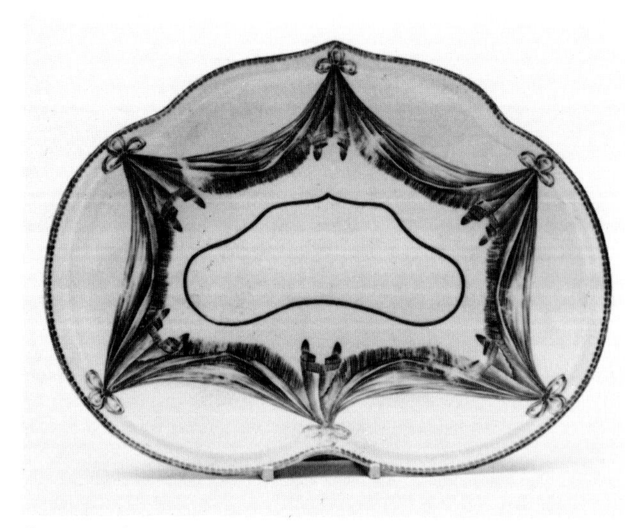

Stormont Service. *A heart-shaped dessert dish decorated in puce with dramatic hanging drapery, c.1775, 11¼ in. (28.5cm). (Sotheby's.)*

Strap Fluted Moulding. *Panels of monochrome landscape and coloured flowers combine with a strap fluted* ground to produce a European style of decoration. The handled teacup is very unusual at this period, c.1756. (Phillips.)*

Baroness Kinloss (Colour Plate 79). The service was made in 1813 when he succeeded, on the death of his father, to the fabulous estate of Stowe in Buckinghamshire, although it was not until 1822 that he was created first Duke of Buckingham and Chandos. No records remain of the original order which was for a dinner and dessert service, each piece painted with the full arms of the Marquis of Buckingham complete with supporters, within a border of the most wonderful gold scrollwork on a salmon ground. Most pieces are marked Flight, Barr and Barr although, as the name of the factory only changed in 1813, many pieces also bear impressed marks of 'BFB'. The set was sold at a bankruptcy sale at Stowe in 1848, although the third Duke of Buckingham and Chandos bought back eighty-two pieces which were sold again at Stowe in 1921. More recently forty-eight of these pieces were sold at Sotheby's in London, 12 March 1974 and eighteen pieces at Sotheby's, New York, 16 October 1987. Most pieces from the Stowe service have remained in immaculate condition, the gold surviving as a great testament to the qualities of the firm who made them.

Strap Fluted Moulding

One moulded motif derived from silver which enjoyed great popularity at Worcester was a background broken up into a texture of overlapping planks or straps. This has also been called pleat moulding. The earliest use was on a series of rococo teapots*, such as the example illustrated in Colour Plate 69, from c.1752, although gradually slightly less eccentric versions were introduced. Matching milk jugs and bowls were made for these teapots and then, by c.1755, a full range of cups and saucers to accompany the sets. Creamboats* and sauceboats* were occasionally modelled with strap fluted grounds as early as c.1754. By c.1758 a simple shape of sauceboat was introduced with a wide neck and rococo scroll panels reserved on a strap fluted ground. These were made in several sizes and during the 1760s replaced most other sauceboat shapes to become the principal form made at the factory. The usual decoration, a pattern known as the *Fisherman and Billboard Island,* painted in blue, was replaced c.1765 by a stylised floral pattern which was called by Branyan, French and Sandon the *Strap Flute Sauceboat Floral* pattern (I.E.37). Sauceboats bearing this pattern are amongst the most commonly seen pieces of Worcester porcelain from the 1770s. The shape was occasionally treated to richer forms of decoration, including scale blue* grounds which were unsuccessful on the heavy moulding. Copies of the sauceboat shape were made at Lowestoft and Caughley but as a rule the strap fluted shape can be claimed as a decoration unique to the Worcester potters.

Strawberry Dishes

The name cress dish is nowadays generally used incorrectly to describe a form of straining bowl which in the 18th century was called a strawberry dish. The shallow circular dish is raised on a footrim above a circular plate which has a matching barbed rim to confirm that they go together. The centre of the dish is pierced with rows of small circular holes and these were popular in the 1770s at Worcester and Caughley where an identical shape was made. The shape is more usual in English creamware and is listed in contemporary creamware catalogues as a strawberry dish. Examples are known in pottery painted with strawberries and Dutch Delftware dishes of related shape are also found painted with strawberries. The Worcester strawberry dishes are only known in blue and white, mostly printed with the *Pine-cone** pattern and occasionally painted with floral designs. None was made after c.1780. (*See* illustrations on page 320.)

Strawberry Dishes. *This shallow pierced bowl would have rested originally on a matching plate. The painting is in underglaze blue*, crescent mark*, c.1765, 9½in. (24cm). (Phillips.)*

Strutting Bird Patterns. *An early cream jug with a sparrow beak lip, painted in Worcester's adaptation of* famille rose* *enamels, c.1752-3, 3in. (7.5cm). (Phillips.)*

Strawberry Dishes. *The original use of this pierced dish is uncertain, but the addition of twig handles to a standard shape suggests that it was used as a drainer, possibly for strawberries, c.1768-70, 11¾in. (30cm). (Barrie Cathcart.)*

Colour Plate 79. ***Stowe Service.*** *Part of the fabulous dinner service made by Flight, Barr and Barr for the Marquis of Buckingham in 1813, the very detailed armorials* framed by quite superb gilding, printed and impressed* marks, c.1813-5. (Sotheby's, New York.)*

Sucriers and Covers. *This shallow covered bowl is believed to have been used originally as a sucrier although there is no evidence to support this. The strongly modelled shape and sparse sprigs confirm an early date, c.1752, 5in. (12.7cm) diameter. (Rous Lench Collection.)*

Sucriers and Covers. *The standard shape of sucrier from c.1765 until c.1780 has an ogee shaped cover and flower finial. This example has* Rich Kakiemon* *panels on a scale blue* ground, square mark*, c.1765-70, 4½in. (11.5cm). (Phillips.)*

Strutting Bird Patterns

A group of several early patterns painted in coloured enamels in Chinese style although none of Worcester's designs appears to have been copied directly from a Chinese original. The heron-like birds usually stand on one leg and look backwards, and are placed on the ground in simple landscapes with peonies and other plants. The designs mostly occur on fluted teabowls and saucers, sparrow-beak jugs with scroll handles, and dry mustard pots and date from c.1752-5. A strutting bird was also used on the neck of the fine large vase illustrated under **Vases.** Occasionally an overglaze enamel workman's mark* is seen underneath the bases. (*See* illustration on page 320.)

Sucriers and Covers

The French name is normally used today for the covered sugar bowl or sugar box which accompanied most tea services. Examples are particularly scarce in Worcester before c.1765-8. Early sucriers from c.1760 are reasonably shallow with flatter covers than sucriers of a decade later. They have a flower finial made from a closed bud which is associated with a Continental shape of teapot also dating from c.1760. Sucriers of this period are normally transfer printed* in black or in blue underglaze. The covers gradually became more domed with wider flanges by the 1770s. All are circular in section and can be moulded with different flutes or other patterns such as *Chrysanthemum** and *Scallopendrium.** By c.1785-90 a button finial replaced the flower and from c.1790 spiral-fluted or shanked shapes* were popular alongside straight flutes but rarely plain. Chamberlain from c.1792 and Flight from about the same date introduced oval sucriers to accompany the new oval teapot shapes. From this period and throughout the 19th century the sucrier or sugar box always matched the remaining shapes in the set. An early moulded form of covered bowl with a flame finial, c.1752, has been described as a sucrier and could have been for sugar, but its precise use is uncertain. *See also* **Sugar Boats** and **Sugar Bowls.**

Sugar Boats. *A Barr, Flight and Barr open sugar boat with a Barr's Orange* ground and fine picturesque* landscape, impressed mark*, c.1810, 5in. (12.5cm). (Phillips.)*

Sugar Boats

From c.1800-7 Flight's factory made open sugar bowls* which were oval in section with moulded classical handles at each end. These are often called 'sugar boats' today. They never came with covers and seem to have been restricted to just a few factories, principally Flight and Barr and Pinxton. The shape was not made by either Chamberlain or Grainger.

Sugar Bowls

Occasionally an open sugar bowl was preferred to a covered sucrier*, usually in more basic commercial services aimed at the less wealthy classes. Many cheaper Staffordshire porcelain services included one larger bowl as a slop bowl and a small bowl for sugar. Some Worcester tea services were supplied

Sundials. *The only known example of an English porcelain sundial, made for Josiah Holdship*, one of the partners in the Worcester company. The decoration is entirely painted and is dated 1766, 8¾ in. (22cm). (Dyson Perrins Museum.)*

with these two sizes of bowl from the 1760s and 1770s and it is possible that the 'Half pint basons' (*sic*) in the c.1755-6 price list of the London Warehouse (*see* **London Shops**) were not large teabowls but sugar bowls. This could help to explain the absence of covered sucriers before c.1760. *See also* **Sugar Boats.**

Sundials

Only a single example is recorded, made as a special production for one of the senior partners in the Worcester Porcelain Co. This specimen in the Dyson Perrins Collection was at one time believed to be enamel but careful examination shows that it is certainly Worcester porcelain. The sundial is

Colour Plate 80. **Sweetmeat Shells.** *A deep shell-shaped dish for sweetmeats or pickle*, usually decorated in blue and white and rare in full colours, c.1765, 5⅛ in. (13cm). (Colin Harper Collection.)*

Colour Plate 81. **Teapots.** *The plain shape of teapot is relatively uncommon in the 1750s. This example combines Chinese* famille rose* *with Meissen-style** indianische Blumen, *creating a restrained form of decoration which became a speciality of the Worcester factory, c.1752-3, 4½ in. (11.5cm). (Phillips.)*

Colour Plate 82. ***Teapots.*** *A strongly moulded design with rococo* panels left white to appear as windows through which to view the Chinese fishing scene painted in underglaze blue*, workman's mark*, c.1755, 5in. (12.5cm). (Phillips.)*

Sweetmeat Shells. *Three deep shell-shaped dishes probably used for serving sweetmeats, the decoration in underglaze blue*, crescent marks*, c.1765-70, 5½in. (14cm). (Phillips.)*

Sweetmeat Stands. *A triple shell sweetmeat stand surmounted by a single circular salt dish, the small white shells probably cast from actual specimens, c.1768-70, 8¼in. (21cm) wide. (Colin Harper Collection.)*

Sweetmeat Stands. *An early Chamberlain centrepiece corresponding with the 'Pickle stand, Apollo, glazed' priced at 10s.6d. in the 1795 stock list. It was modelled by John Toulouse* and the figure is standing beside flowers with hot cross bun buds*, c.1795-8, 9in. (23cm). (Godden Reference Collection.)*

inscribed with the name 'Josiah Holdship MDCCLXVI' for 1766. Because Josiah Holdship* was connected with the introduction of transfer printing* at Worcester it was presumed that the sundial is printed, but again careful examination reveals that it is instead finely painted in black. It is an incredible piece of precision decoration and a vital document as it shows Josiah was still at the factory in 1766 although Richard* had sold his share in the company in 1759.

Sweetmeat Shells

There is uncertainty whether some larger flat scallop dishes were for pickle* or sweetmeats. One particular deep shape of dish is generally referred to as a sweetmeat shell (Colour Plate 80), and this is somewhat stylised with a spreading lip and incurved scroll at one side. Most examples are in blue, either with printed flowers, or else a group of a marrow, mushrooms and a walnut, an unusual subject confirming that these, at least, would have contained pickles (*see* illustration on page 325.). The shape was made c.1765-70 and also occurs with coloured flowers painted in the Meissen style* within a shaded puce rim, and very rarely with scale blue.*

Sweetmeat Stands

It is probably true to say that it was entirely up to the original households what to serve in these complicated objects. They are generally known as sweetmeat stands today although in the 18th century 'pickle stand' was a more usual description. Pickles or sweetmeats were essential to disguise the taste of stale food in the days before refrigeration. Single pickle dishes* were amongst the earliest of all English porcelain shapes. Bow seems to have been the first factory to combine shell pickle dishes into stands, usually with three side dishes and occasionally a central smaller compartment, probably for salt. Worcester was much slower to introduce the shapes and probably waited until the arrival of John Toulouse* from Bow in the mid- to late 1760s. Several Worcester sweetmeat stands have been noted bearing the 'T' mark of John Toulouse and it is possible that he brought some of the moulds with him, for there is a great similarity between Bow and Worcester shell modelling. Some of the shells and coral supporting the pickle dishes were moulded from actual shells although it is clear that others were totally imaginary.

The most elaborate has five tiers of scallop shell dishes and a shell salt on the top. This size was clearly a special production and examples have been seen with blue* and apple green* grounds. The most usual have just the three side shell dishes and these are normally in blue and white, painted with formal rose sprays. Rare single shell dishes mounted on coral bases in the same manner as the triple stands are usually referred to as salts*, but it is more likely that they were used for serving individual pickles.

A very rare variant was made up of four circular pierced trellis baskets surrounded by modelled flowers. Two of these are illustrated by H. Rissik Marshall, *Coloured Worcester Porcelain*, items 864 and 958. The flower modelling and 'hot cross bun buds'* relate once again to John Toulouse. His departure to Bristol c.1772 marks an end to the production of sweetmeat stands at Worcester until his return as an old man at Chamberlains in the 1790s. Records for 1795 and 1798 include references to pickle stands with a figure of Apollo and Geoffrey Godden's surviving example, illustrated here, is an important link with Toulouse's earlier work at Worcester, the shell modelling unchanged in nearly twenty-five years.

T

Tambourine Pattern
A curious misnomer as nothing resembling a tambourine appears in this attractive composition, painted in underglaze blue c.1754-8. Instead the Chinese boy holds a circular dish which he appears to be striking with a stick. His female companion plays a drum and both figures are dancing in a landscape. The pattern is always painted with remarkable care and was used on teawares as well as mugs of various sizes. The *Tambourine* pattern was listed by Bernard Watney as one of the ten standard Chinese blue and white patterns used during the early period and it appears as I.A.18 in Branyan, French and Sandon.

Tankards
See **Mugs**

Tapersticks
See **Candlesticks**

Tart Pans
It is clear from 18th century records that the shapes we now call patty pans were originally called tart pans. These came in matching sets or else graduated sets called 'nests'. They were made in English glass and stoneware as well as Chinese porcelain, and examples are known from most English porcelain factories. Their original use is uncertain and they have been variously described as for pickle or for potted meats or pâté. The price list of Worcester's London Warehouse (*see* **London Shops**) c.1755-6 includes tart pans in three sizes selling for 4s., 6s. and 8s. per dozen. These early tart pans are plain circular shapes with sharply sloping straight sides. They are known only in blue and white and do not have a flanged rim. By c.1758 the shape had changed to a circular pan with straighter sides and a flat everted rim. These were painted with *Mansfield** and *Prunus Root** patterns as well as a simple landscape found only on this shape. Once again no coloured examples have been recorded. They continue only until c.1768-70 and were not made later. During excavations of the very earliest levels of the factory a different form of tart pan was found, the plain sloping side having a thick reinforced rim. This shape was made much later at Caughley in the 1780s but so far no finished early Worcester example has been seen.

Tart Pans. *An early tart pan or patty pan painted in underglaze blue**, *workman's mark**, *c.1753-4, 5½in. (14cm). (Christie's.)*

Tasters
See **Wine Tasters**

Taylor, William
The apprenticeship indenture survives binding William Taylor, the son of a weaver, to William Davis* to learn the 'art of painting of porcelain ware', for seven years from 14

Tambourine Pattern. *A drawing by Neal French of the full pattern on a teabowl, c.1757.*

Colour Plate 83. ***Three Dot Painter Style.*** *A large Bristol/Worcester* jug painted in the distinctive style which in this case includes numerous three dot motifs, c.1751-2, 7⅛ in. (18cm). (Dyson Perrins Museum.)*

Colour Plate 84. **Toddy Cups.** *This example of a rare thistle-shaped toddy cup was originally painted with the* Rich Queen's* *pattern. The landscape painting belongs to redecoration* Group VIb, square mark*, the porcelain c.1770. (Dyson Perrins Museum.)*

Colour Plate 85. **Toulouse, John.** *A fine pair of hexagonal frill vases* with applied female mask handles and festoons of modelled flowers complete with hot cross bun buds*, the flower painting and insects typical of Worcester factory decoration, one with impressed mark 'To'* for John Toulouse, c.1768-70, 15⅛in. (38.5cm). (Phillips.)*

Tea Party Patterns. *A saucer printed in underglaze blue* with the* Tea Party *version Number 3, c.1758-60, 4⅝in. (11.7cm). European subject prints are very rare in blue at this early date. (Dyson Perrins Museum.)*

June 1763. A William Taylor was listed by Chaffers as a painter at Flight's factory in 1819 doing blue paintings, and he also appears in a Board of Trade list for Worcester as a china painter living in London Road. R.W. Binns* described a book of patterns belonging to William Taylor, 'mostly imitations and modifications from the Japanese in colours, blue printed sprigs, and borders for gilding'. Sadly the present whereabouts of this book are unknown. Another William Taylor was a flower painter during the Kerr and Binns period and may have been related.

Tea Caddies
See **Canisters**

Tea Canisters
See **Canisters**

Tea Party Patterns
There are in fact several different transfer prints* used on Worcester porcelain, all known as the *Tea Party,* and in addition there are very many variations of some of these. It is therefore difficult to discuss the *Tea Party* as a single pattern. Cyril Cook, in *The Life and Work of Robert Hancock*, divided the pattern into three main versions. Number 1 (*see* **Birmingham Printing**) shows a lady and gentleman seated on a bench with a tea table directly in front of them. A page boy stands on their right and pours water from a kettle. This is probably the earliest version and signed examples by Hancock* have been recorded on enamel and on Bow and Worcester porcelain. These possibly all date before 1756. The *Tea Party* Number 2

Tea Services. *A complete tea service decorated with apple green* borders and spotted fruit* comprising all the principal shades, crossed swords marks*, c.1770. (Sotheby's/Kiddell Papers.)*

***Tea Services.** The principal shapes of a Grainger tea service of New Gadroon shape, c.1820. The standard components of a tea service remained unchanged throughout the period covered by this* Dictionary. *(Phillips.)*

is a very common pattern used from c.1757 until the 1770s. This shows a lady and gentleman seated on a bench with a high curving back and an attractive shaped tea table is fully set out just to their left. A statue can be seen in the far left distance and a spaniel-like dog is in the foreground. One very different variation of the *Tea Party* Number 2 includes a servant holding a kettle, standing behind the lady. Finally the *Tea Party* Number 3 shows a gentleman and lady in separate chairs either side of a circular table, while a dog in the foreground looks back towards the couple. This very rare version dates from c.1758-60 and is the only one of the three *Tea Party* prints which was also used in underglaze blue,* although only a single blue-printed saucer is recorded.

The 1769 Worcester sale catalogue included a tea service 'jet, enamel'd with a tea table', clearly referring to the *Tea Party* Number 2 which was the only version still in production at this date. This pattern was sometimes lightly heightened in gold or else fully coloured in.

It is puzzling why the Worcester factory should have used so many different versions of essentially the same subject. The examples of all three patterns signed by Hancock will certainly have been printed at Worcester but it is possible some of the variants may be copies printed at Liverpool or even in London.

Tea Services

The ability of Worcester's body to withstand hot liquid gave the factory something of a monopoly in the making of tea services in England. The result of this was that they were not under great pressure to compete and, having discovered a successful range of teaware shapes, were able to stick with these. It is disappointing, in a way, just how little variety there is in the shapes of Worcester's tea services, even though the range of decoration used on the standard shapes is very far from being uniform.

The earliest teawares do not fit into conventional sets easily. Far more teapots survive than cups and saucers, for example, suggesting these were sold by themselves. Milk jugs also seem to have been popular as single items while cups and saucers are rare before the later 1750s. By about 1762-5 the components of a tea service had become reasonably consistent and were to stay this way for considerable time. In 1769 Mainwarings, china dealers in Bath, were selling 'complete Tea Services of Blue and White Worcester China, from £1.15s. the set, consisting of 43 pieces'. Such a set probably comprised the following:

A teapot and cover	Two bread and butter plates
A sucrier and cover	Twelve teacups or teabowls
A milk jug	Twelve saucers
A slop or waste bowl	Eight or twelve coffee cups

In addition coloured services included a spoon tray and a stand for the teapot. Some services also included a coffee pot, and a pair of tea canisters was an optional extra. The same basic components of a tea service remained virtually unchanged until the middle of the 19th century, the only difference being the absence of spoon trays, coffee pots and canisters after c.1800. Tea plates were not included until c.1840-50 although some rare cup plates* were made in the 1830s. In contrast to tea services, breakfast services* included some different shapes and generally a larger size of cup.

Teabowls

A famous painting of a family taking tea in the 18th century illustrates three different ways to hold the Chinese porcelain teabowls. Oriental teabowls had been in use in England since the 17th century and Worcester introduced the shape from its outset as this was what customers had grown to expect. It was only after Continental porcelain from Meissen* began to exert an influence that we find the fashion for handles on cups. Generally speaking tea services decorated in oriental style were supplied with teabowls while European patterns were painted on handled teacups. There are of course a great many exceptions but the different influences are usually quite apparent. Most Worcester teabowls are plain circular shapes

Teapots. *A range of different Worcester teapot shapes from c.1760-75, mostly standard forms but including a very rare bucket shape decorated with the* Quail* *pattern. (Dyson Perrins Museum.)*

Teapots. *A very graceful and yet exceptionally rare teapot shape, the pierced handle influenced by Sèvres*, decorated with scale blue* and* Rich Kakiemon*, *square mark*, c.1765-8, 5⅛in. (13cm). (Dyson Perrins Museum.)*

Teapots. *A Meissen* shape with flat cover and faceted spout, popular c.1758-62. This example is painted in an unusual palette copying Chinese porcelain of the Yongzheng period, c.1760, 5½in. (14cm). (Phillips.)*

but occasionally reeded, fluted, feather-moulded* or *Chrysanthemum** pattern shapes are found. Octagonal teabowls or a very rare early shape with deep concave flutes may sometimes be found also. The size of a teabowl generally increased after the reduction of the taxation on tea in 1770 but it is difficult to see any direct changes caused as a result of the reduced tax. Teabowls continued into the 19th century as part of more traditional Chinese pattern services and shanked* services, for instance, although the fashion for drinking tea from bowls had mostly finished by c.1800.

Teapots

Collectors of teapots often complain about the lack of variation in Worcester shapes, but the reason for this is that the factory could not improve on such a perfect form. Worcester succeeded where all their competitors failed, a shape which poured well, was comfortable to use, simple to make and, above all, did not crack when hot liquid was poured in. No wonder Worcester specialised in teawares while many of the other factories concentrated on ornamental ware instead. Today surviving Worcester teapots far outnumber those of all the other English factories put together, and generally they remain in much better condition. One wonders if this was noticed by King George IV who was one of the first collectors of teapots.

During the first five years of the factory Worcester made a certain variety of teapot shapes (Colour Plates 81 and 82). Octagonal forms continued a tradition begun at Limehouse*, while Worcester added moulded rococo panels. Several large teapots were moulded with formal regular lobes while other shapes were influenced by the *rococo**. A number of basic teapot forms were moulded with a strap fluted* ground and these ranged from a very exciting asymmetric example with rococo panels (*see* Colour Plate 69), to more gentle globular shapes with crisp formal cartouches. Throughout this period they also made a plain, slightly squat, globular shape which originated at Bristol. By the late 1750s this had developed into the globular form of teapot which continued with little variation until the 1780s. Feather moulding*, fine reeding or chrysanthemum* moulding did not affect the basic shape, and even a widely fluted version retains the same overall plan. The factory did make other teapot shapes, of course. A baluster form was probably copied from Meissen* and usually had a finely fluted straight spout. A plain ovoid shape after Sèvres* accompanied the Duchess of Kent service* among others, and either plain or ribbed barrel shapes were used during the 1760s, some with embossed decoration. A few unusually eccentric shapes were made, such as a flat drum shape, a tall conical and also a double conical form, and a so-called bullet shape with a pierced scroll handle. These are regarded as exciting today but are very rare for the simple reason that they were not nearly as practical as the plain globular shape.

Early finials were turned on a lathe into elaborate stepped points or mushrooms, but by c.1755 the standard pointed finial was used. This continued until c.1770 although its use declined after 1760. Instead a slanting, closed bud used on baluster shaped teapots from c.1757 developed into the standard open flower finial from c.1765. Before 1760 all teapot covers were fully glazed underneath the flanged rim, and many continued to be glazed up until c.1765, but from the early 1760s it became usual to leave the flange unglazed.

The major development of the Flight period c.1790 was the shanked* teaware shape with a well-designed circular teapot. The advent of neo-classicism* saw the fashion for oval teapots and Flight and Barr made two distinctive forms, a fattened ovoid shape with a pronounced prow and flame finial, and a curious narrow flattened shape with a fluted shoulder. In the Flight, Barr and Barr period a squat circular teapot accompanied the gadroon edged teawares but these are great rarities, the factory preferring instead to concentrate on ornamental shapes.

Teapot Stands. *A rare rococo* teapot stand designed to accompany a strap fluted* teapot of the type illustrated in Colour Plate 69, decorated with the* Staghunt* *pattern, c.1755, 7½in. (19cm) wide. (Shand Kydd Collection.)*

Chamberlain started to make their own porcelain just as round teapots gave way to oval shapes. Their early shanked teapots are all oval in section and others were plain or had straight flutes. A plain 'Dejeune' shape with a double ogee base was used for most tea services up until c.1813-5. Another popular shape was plain ovoid with a sloping shoulder. Chamberlain's version of the London shape* was introduced by 1815 and teapots often had elaborately moulded ring finials. The London shape was replaced by a very squat circular shape after c.1825. Grainger followed a similar progression from plain, fluted or shanked 'New Oval' teapots up until c.1810-2, replaced by London shapes which were themselves replaced by a number of round shapes during the 1820s. During the 1830s and 1840s many elaborate Chamberlain and Grainger teapot shapes reflect the feelings for the rococo revival*. Grainger made several basic teapot shapes and sold these with different cup shapes causing much confusion today. At the Great Exhibition* of 1851 both factories showed double-walled reticulated* teapots which were well admired for their technical skill.

Teapot Stands

It is curious that while all of the early Worcester teaware shapes were round in section, the stand for the teapot was normally hexagonal. This fashion probably originated from Chinese porcelain when dealers in Europe sold lobed trays which had not previously been associated with teapots to customers who wanted to protect their furniture from the hot teapots. In Worcester the near absence of any blue and white teapot stands suggests that teapot stands were aimed at the wealthy families who owned furniture which was worth protecting. The earliest Worcester teapot stands are rococo* in form with strap fluting*, dating from c.1755, although examples are very rare. Stands from the late 1750s are mostly found with transfer prints* and are quite often of lobed square shape, this rare variation giving way to the standard

Telephone Box Pattern. *A pair of ovoid vases from a garniture, painted in bright Canton style*, c.1765-70, 7½in. (19cm).*

hexagonal shape from the early 1760s. Worcester teapot stands are usually well potted and always unglazed underneath. The hexagonal shape continued into the 1780s and was replaced only when shanked* or spiral fluted shapes became fashionable. The teapot stands with round Flight teapots can easily be mistaken for saucers as they are only slightly flatter than a saucer and much the same size. The oval teapots from the 1790s have matching oval teapot stands which can be mistaken for spoon trays*. During the 19th century some of the large moulded teapots can have equally large and elaborate stands.

Some early tea services of c.1760-5 include a *Blind Earl** moulded dish of a type known as a sweetmeat dish today. These dishes matched the services and are often rubbed. I have yet to see a service including a standard form of teapot stand as well as a *Blind Earl* dish and I suspect the dish acted as a form of stand for the teapot.

Tebo

When early researchers attempted to identify the modeller's mark 'To' used at Worcester c.1768-72, a name mentioned in Wedgwood correspondence seemed to fit. Mr Tebo was apparently a not very competent modeller who had done some work for Wedgwood. There was, however, no other evidence to attribute a whole class of Worcester modelling to him, but somehow this theory took hold. More recent research indicates that the mark 'To' relates to John Toulouse*.

Telephone Box Pattern

Although we have received much friendly criticism from collectors for the way we named this pattern when we were working on *Worcester Blue and White Porcelain*, Lawrence Branyan, Neal French and I were so struck by the resemblance of part of the design to a modern British telephone box that we could not think of any other name which satisfactorily described pattern I.A.8. The name has now entered general usage and I am proud to list it here. The pattern copies a Chinese original and was used on garnitures of baluster and beaker-shaped vases c.1770. Most surviving vases* are in underglaze blue* although a few identical coloured versions of the pattern have been seen from the same period. The groups of Chinese figures are always painted with very great care, spoilt only by occasional smudging of the cobalt blue.

Three Dot Painter Style. *A Bristol porcelain sauceboat painted in blue with many of the characteristics associated with the three dot painter style, c.1749-51, 7½in. (19cm). (Sotheby's.)*

Teniers Figure Subjects
The well-known paintings of tavern interiors by David Teniers the Younger are recalled by collectors of Worcester porcelain when referring to peasant figure subjects from c.1770. The actual inspiration is Meissen* from the 1740s where these rustic figures enjoyed great popularity. Worcester examples are very rare and always occur on Giles* decorated pieces. A fine tea service is in the collection of Her Majesty Queen Elizabeth II, painted with figures in vignettes of vegetation within gold dentil* rims. A well-known Giles decorated bowl with turquoise* ground and three 'harlequin' panels, and one of the two matching plates, both include a figure subject by the same hand as the Queen's service.

Most examples of Teniers figures are now treated with suspicion, however. A series with scale pink* borders occurs on porcelain made at Worcester, Caughley and an unknown Staffordshire factory. The painting is very convincing for the 18th century and there is usually little sign of refiring. These are possibly the work of a later 18th century decorator but could be much later (*see* Colour Plate 73). Several pieces are known with a claret* ground and Teniers panels and these are undoubtedly fakes, redecorated* at a much later date.

'T F' Marks
One of the most popular workmen's marks* used in the 1750s takes the form of the initials 'T F' combined in a number of ways. Like the 'I H' marks*, their true meaning is unknown. They certainly do not in any way relate to Thomas Frye, senior partner in the Bow factory. Similarly, it is highly unlikely that they are the initials of a single painter at Worcester. In the past a cursive 'I H' mark has been misinterpreted as an 'IR' monogram and associated with the mysterious painter James Rogers (*see* **Rogers, I.**).

Theatrical Tea Service
One of the more remarkable decorations found on Worcester from the early 1770s is a series of theatrical subjects which probably formed part of only a single tea service. Painted in colours and with slight gold dentil rims, the service has variously been ascribed to the Giles* workshop and the Worcester factory. I favour the latter on the strength of the dentil gilding*, but it is certainly uncharacteristic. All of the recorded subjects have been traced to a set of prints published by Robert Sayer of Fleet Street in 1772, entitled *Dramatic Characters, or Different Portraits of the English Stage, In the Days of Garrick &c.* These include David Garrick himself as 'King Lear', and as 'Don Felix'. The teapot in the Marshall Collection in the Ashmolean Museum depicts Miss Pope as 'Doll Snip' and Mr Smith as 'Jachimo'. The Theatrical Service is the subject of a paper by Babette Craven given to the English Ceramic Circle in December 1978.

Thimbles
Many very enthusiastic thimble collectors have been searching for years for definite examples of early Worcester thimbles but so far none can be dated to before the Royal Worcester period. There is evidence, however, that Chamberlain made and sold large numbers from as early as 1794 until the 1840s. Presumably all were unmarked. The only Flight thimble shape is known from a waster* found on the factory site, in biscuit*, fused to its firing support. It is spiral-fluted and would have been made c.1790. While Chelsea made thimbles in the 1750s it seems very unlikely that Worcester attempted these most difficult shapes at that time.

Thorneloe, John
John Thorneloe was listed as a 'Gent of the city of Worcester' in the Articles for Carrying on the Worcester Tonquin Manufacture* in 1751. He owned the fifth largest share of £337.10s. From the agreement there is no reason to assume he was anything other than a financial backer but according to tradition he acted as a representative for the company, travelling to Cornwall to search for soaprock*. A descendant of the Kempthorne family told R.W. Binns* that Renatus Kempthorne had offered accommodation to a Mr Thorneloe when he was staying near Mullion. Kempthorne would accept

Colour Plate 86. ***Tracy Mug.*** *The celebrated mug commemorating the election to Parliament of Robert Tracy in 1747. The mug has been attributed to the hand of Dr John Wall*. It is marked with a cross incised and therefore belongs to the Scratch Cross class*, c.1753-5, 3⅝in. (9.2cm). (Dyson Perrins Museum.)*

no payment and instead Thorneloe sent him a tea service of Worcester porcelain as a present (*see* **Kempthorne Pattern**).

Three Dot Painter Style
One of the most distinctive features of the earliest underglaze blue painting style is the placing of three dot-like rocks arranged as a triangle, frequently occurring several times on a single piece (Colour Plates 11 and 83 and page 335). The three dot motif is found on Chinese porcelain and was copied by the decorators at Bristol along with many other distinctive features which form a style of painting unique to this class of porcelain. Islands can be composed of solid mountains or open rocks with simple tufts of grass and plant motifs. Boats with tall masts and large sails ride on water drawn with strong horizontal lines. Buildings are very primitive and child-like while figures are reasonably sophisticated copies of Chinese 'Long Eliza'* types, standing and frequently pointing. This distinctive style was at one time felt to be the work of a single painter. This is most unlikely, however, although the name of a so-called three dot painter is closely associated with the style. There are indirect affinities with painting at Limehouse*, but the three dot painter style belongs to Bristol and the early days of the Worcester factory, as it is clear the style of painting is not restricted only to pieces decorated at Bristol. Round dots or cannonballs occur in later patterns but the three dot style itself does not continue after c.1752.

Three Flowers Pattern
A European floral print introduced c.1770, which achieved very great popularity, rivalling the *Fence** pattern as one of the

Thynne, Lord Henry, Pattern. *A dessert plate with one of many versions of this popular pattern, including flying birds in the border, crescent mark*, c.1776-82, 8¼in. (21cm). (Phillips.)*

Tiles. *A panel of four Chamberlain and Co. encaustic tiles making up the royal arms of Queen Victoria, impressed Chamberlains, c.1843, 12in. (30.5cm) overall. (Author's Collection.) different colour from that of the early 1770s. Because of the bright tone of the blue it has sometimes been suggested that the borders are in an overglaze 'royal blue', but this is quite incorrect.*

two most prolific blue-printed teaware designs. The name derives from the three small flowers in the centre of the main spray which always occurs within a narrow blue tramline border. The *Three Flowers* pattern was still in production c.1790 and examples sometimes bear the impressed mark 'FLIGHTS'. These later examples can sometimes be of very poor quality, however. The pattern was mostly used on teawares but has been noted on mustard pots*, spittoons*, custard cups*, in panels on potting pots* and on small tureens*. Lowestoft, Derby, Liverpool and Caughley all made a very similar pattern, the Caughley version being almost indistinguishable from Worcester. It is probable that Caughley teasets of this design were sold by Chamberlain and called 'Rose' pattern. Large quantities of Worcester's *Three Flowers* pattern appear to have been exported to Holland.

Thynne, Lord Henry, Pattern

A popular form of decoration used at Worcester from c.1775-85 has become associated with the name of Lord Henry Thynne, probably after the second son of the third Marquess of Bath who died in 1904. Evidently one dessert service of the design belonged to the Thynne family but this was by no means a unique production. Many sets must have been made over a period of about ten years, and almost all differed in some minor details of gilded borders and husk panels. All have a deep blue border with gilding, and circular landscape panels within frames of turquoise husks. The name of Lord Henry Thynne is correctly associated only with dessert wares bearing clusters of fruit and flying birds on the white ground. Other related designs omit the birds or have flowers instead of fruit. The name *Earl Dalhousie** is used when the pattern has festoons of fruit and flying insects, a version usually found on teawares. Examples are normally dated to c.1770-2 but in reality this is far too early. The blue borders are usually in the bright underglaze blue* of the late William Davis* and early Flight periods, c.1780, when the cobalt produced a distinctly different colour from that of the early 1770s. Because of the bright tone of the blue it has sometimes been suggested that the borders are in an overglaze 'royal blue', but this is quite incorrect.

Tiles

While tiles are mentioned in early Chamberlain accounts these are probably references to plaques. The fashion for pottery floor tiles swept England in the 1840s with architects and designers such as Pugin extolling the virtues of Gothic art and advocating the reproduction of medieval floor tiles for churches. Pugin himself is said to have preferred Chamberlain's mediaeval tiles to Minton as the Worcester specimens were closer to the traditions of the originals. This is readily apparent from surviving Chamberlain examples which are coarse and irregular and nothing like as perfect as their contemporaries. However, most of the public at the time did not share Pugin's enthusiasm for Worcester's irregularity and examples are now very uncommon. Chamberlain began tile production c.1836 and manufacture was transferred to the Warmstry House* site when the two Worcester factories amalgamated in 1840. Known as encaustic or tessellated tiles, they were made by pressing the design into a thick tile of brown clay and then filling the design with a light coloured slip. After eight weeks of drying the surplus clay was scraped off the surface and the tile then fired and glazed. A catalogue of the Worcester Encaustic Tile Works survives in the Prints and Drawings Department at the Victoria and Albert Museum and shows the extensive range of subjects, some attributed to known designers. Excavations* on the Warmstry House site found many unfinished examples as well as the base of the kiln used to fire the tiles. They were manufactured using

Colour Plate 87. Left: ***Transfer Printing.*** *A small onion-shaped bottle vase with a coloured-in smoky primitive* print, c.1753-5. Right:* ***Prunus Root Pattern.*** *A fluted teabowl and saucer painted with the popular blue and white* Prunus Root* *pattern, but using red enamel instead, c.1756. (Phillips.)*

a process called Prosser's patent and Worcester paid royalties to Samuel Wright and Herbert Minton. Tile production continued under Chamberlain & Co. until c.1850 when the tile works were taken over by Maw & Co.* Maws continued the same designs and subsequently moved to new premises in Worcester and then to Benthall, across the river from Ironbridge.

'To' Mark
An embossed or impressed mark of the letters 'To' occur on many pieces of Worcester porcelain, c.1768-72. At one time these were thought to be for a modeller named Tebo*, but are now attributed to John Toulouse*.

Tobacco Stoppers
H. Rissik Marshall recounted the discovery by the celebrated American collector Mrs Simund Katz that a porcelain pipe stopper in her collection was identical to the head and shoulders of the gardener's companion figure (illustrated under **Figures**) of Worcester porcelain, c.1770. The only

'To' Mark. *The base of a trellis-sided basket showing the embossed mark 'To'. This was incised into the mould and therefore probably relates to the modeller or mould maker, in this case John Toulouse*.*

Colour Plate 88. ***Transfer Printing.*** *A print of ruins in dark puce or lilac colour, the front inscribed 'Wm BARFOOT 1764', 4⅞ in. (12.5cm). (Phillips.)*

difference in the model is a bow placed around the neck of the pipe stopper. No other example has since come to light. The figures were probably modelled by John Toulouse* and it is possible the tobacco stoppers listed in production at Chamberlains in 1795 were a similar adaptation from one of Toulouse's models, maybe even the Apollo figure.

Toddy Cups

The name given to small thistle-shaped mugs made c.1768 and which were 2¼ in. (7cm) high or about the size of a coffee cup. They have plain rounded loop handles with a pointed kick at the base. These were possibly a special commission which failed, for all examples known to me were left unfinished by the factory. They were intended to be decorated in *Rich Queen's* pattern but were instead sold to an outside decorator with only the underglaze blue* bands. The painted *Kakiemon** decoration belongs to the 'red line bordered group'*. One well-known example now in the Dyson Perrins Museum (Colour Plate 84) was subsequently re-decorated* with the crude chrysanthemums ground away and replaced by a landscape.

Tokens

At a time when there was a national shortage of coin, many traders were allowed to make their own tokens which were used as cash and could be redeemed for goods locally. Porcelain tokens are very great rarities indeed. Worcester made two denominations, one shilling and two shillings, moulded roughly the same size as the coins they replaced. These were embossed on one side with the letters 'WPC' (for Worcester Porcelain Company) and are printed in black on the reverse 'I promise to pay the Bearer on demand one Shilling — W Davis At the China Factory'. John Wall* had retired in 1774 but William Davis* had been a senior partner

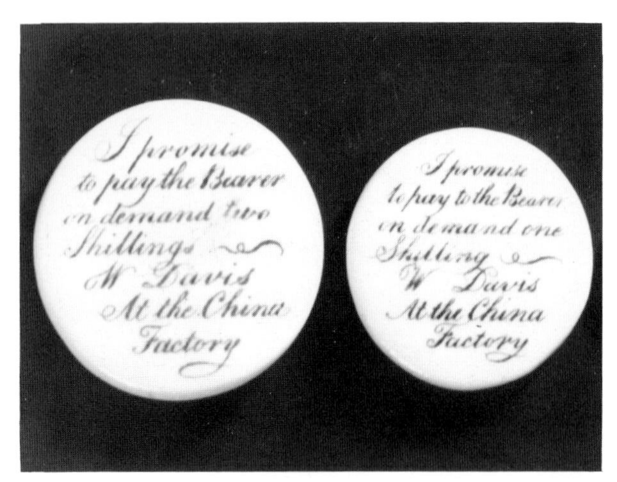

Tokens. *Two of the Worcester porcelain tokens to replace a two shilling and one shilling coin, printed in black, c.1768-80, the two shilling token 1⅛ in. (3cm) diameter. (Dyson Perrins Museum.)*

Tokens. *A Flight porcelain copy of a token struck to commemorate the visit of George III* to Worcester in 1788, printed in black, 1in. (2.5cm). (Dyson Perrins Museum.)*

for some time. The tokens are therefore impossible to date more precisely than c.1768-82. One example of the one shilling token is known in biscuit* only and thus without the inscription. A bronze medallion commemorating the visit of George III* to Worcester was struck in 1788. The King's visit to Flight's factory and the encouragement he gave to the ailing company was of such importance that they copied the medallion in porcelain the same year. The only surviving example is in the Dyson Perrins Museum.

Toulouse, John

Much mystery has surrounded the identity of an important figure in English porcelain whose mark of 'To', 'IT' or just 'T' was impressed underneath Bow, Bristol, Caughley and Worcester porcelain figures and vases. Because of a reference in Wedgwood's papers to a modeller named Tebo, early collectors incorrectly assumed that this was the name they had been looking for. Instead Geoffrey Godden presented the much more convincing argument in his *Chamberlain-Worcester Porcelain* that the mark refers to John Toulouse, a modeller employed by Chamberlain in the 1790s. The impressed 'T' mark occurs on Chamberlain porcelain of this period and there are many references to John Toulouse in the factory records. Godden has shown that Toulouse was employed as a potter during the day, presumably assembling pieces from the moulds, while he earned considerable overtime as a modeller. If we accept that the mark does refer to Toulouse, then he will have been known to the Chamberlains, having worked at Worcester from about 1765-8 until about 1772. Certain figures, encrusted vases and baskets bear these marks and usually exhibit, in the applied flower modelling, the distinctive feature of hot cross bun buds*. These occur on Worcester, Bristol and Caughley as well as early Chamberlain pieces, which suggests a common link. John Toulouse remained as a modeller at Chamberlains until 1807 when his death is noted in the records. Having probably worked at Bow fifty years earlier it is little wonder that elsewhere in the Chamberlain archives he is referred to as 'Old Toulouse'. I could not have chosen to illustrate a better example of the 'To' modeller's work than the frill vases* in Colour Plate 85. The flower modelling relates closely to this craftsman and virtually identical vases were made at Bristol shortly afterwards. Toulouse was certainly not another Joseph Willems — the great Chelsea modeller — for his work has an almost amateur feel to it. Even so, it is particularly distinctive and, as Geoffrey Godden points out, our understanding of Toulouse's career will benefit from much future study. *See also* **Figures** and **Cow Models.**

Toys

While the term is used today for a wide range of porcelain gallantryware, in the 18th and 19th century Worcester used the term 'toy' to refer to any miniature item. Many were very expensive and it is doubted whether all were strictly children's toys as opposed to novelties for the delight of grown-ups. Worcester porcelain miniatures were never intended to be 'travellers' samples', a mostly obsolete term nowadays but still used by some collectors and dealers with the romantic idea of factories lovingly making copies of full-sized pieces for their salesmen. In truth very few miniature pieces have exact full-size parallels.

Some coffee cans are sometimes referred to as miniature mugs, as are certain small sized teapots which were meant for use. True miniatures are much smaller than these and the only area where there ought to be confusion is between miniature punchbowls and slop bowls and small teabowls. Worcester

Toulouse, John. *A detail from the side of one of the frill vases* shown in Colour Plate 85. 'To' mark, c.1768-72. Identical mask handles occur on Bristol porcelain. Note the flowers with hot cross bun buds*. (Phillips.)*

Toulouse, John. *An early Chamberlain model of a kingfisher in white glazed porcelain, the flower modelling strongly suggesting this as the work of Toulouse, c.1795, 4½ in. (11.5cm). (Rous Lench Collection.)*

introduced toy copies of tea services c.1757 in blue and white, mostly using the popular *Prunus Root** pattern. A complete tea service in miniature is illustrated here and this was discovered recently in Holland where several identical sets have been found. The Dutch market was very important to Worcester for their blue and white and the Dutch have a long tradition of making their own miniature wares. The shapes include a tea kettle which follows a Dutch form, and the stand for this, a pierced dish for coals raised on three feet, is included as a very strange shape which has been the subject of much speculation as to its purpose, Worcester collectors not initially realising that it was a miniature copy of a purely Dutch object.

One slightly earlier miniature tea service of *Prunus Root* pattern was made with the initials and date 'C * S 1757' on each piece and this is believed to have been made for a girl named Charlotte Sheriff*. After this initial period of production the factory seems to have made far fewer miniatures until c.1780 when slightly larger miniature teawares were made in the blue printed *Three Flowers** pattern or painted with the *Gillyflower** pattern. Some others were just

Toys. *A miniature blue and white tea service of the* Prunus Root* *pattern, crescent marks*, c.1760-5. The exact shapes are mostly unknown in full-size versions and were probably made for the Dutch market. (Phillips.)*

Colour Plate 89. **Transfer Printing.** *A teabowl and saucer and matching wishbone-handled* coffee cup, printed in black and coloured in with the arms of Wilson impaling Langton, c.1760. (Fine Arts Centre, Cheekwood.)*

(Opposite above) Colour Plate 90. **Tureens.** *In terms of potting and elegance of decoration this massive tureen is a remarkable achievement by the Worcester factory. The underglaze blue* painting is particularly well controlled, workman's mark*, c.1753-5, 18⅛ in. (46cm) wide. (Dyson Perrins Museum.)*

Colour Plate 91. ***Turquoise Grounds.*** *Various different uses of turquoise from the 1770s. The square dessert dish was decorated in the Giles* workshop, the remainder were probably factory decorated, including a cup and saucer from the Stormont* service, c.1775. (Phillips and Author's Collection.)*

***Toys.** In spite of being only 1 ¾ in. (4.5cm) high, this Grainger, Lee and Co. jug is painted in sufficient detail to be able to recognise the city of Worcester in the distance, script mark, c.1825. (Private Collection.)*

gilded while only very occasionally are coloured patterns seen from the 1770s, such as a bird on a leafy branch or a design of formal flowers. During the 1780s the Caughley factory became the principal maker of English porcelain miniatures and the Chamberlain account books record numerous cases of the Chamberlains selling or decorating toys. By 1795 Chamberlains were making their own miniature tea services as well as baskets, followed by miniature ewers and basins from c.1815. Similar toy jugs and basins were also made at Graingers and by Flight, Barr and Barr.

Earlier Flight and Barr miniature sets tended to be in popular patterns such as *Royal Lily**. Chamberlain had complained to Thomas Turner* at Caughley that the toy sets were too small, and indeed Flight and Barr toys do tend to be larger than Caughley and also much finer, making them more costly when new and consequently rarer. Chamberlain produced a range of toy *déjeuner* sets* c.1820 with bird-handled shapes exactly copying French full-sized porcelain rather than shapes made previously at Chamberlains. Toy mugs, jugs, goblets and baskets continued until the 1840s. Grainger made very few toy shapes, mostly baskets or ewers in the 1820s.

Tracy Mug
One of the most significant pieces of early Worcester porcelain, made to commemorate the Worcester parliamentary election of 1747, is illustrated in Colour Plate 86. The shape is typical of the scratch cross class* and indeed the mark of a cross on the base indicates a date c.1753-5. It is painted in enamels with an armorial device on a pedestal inscribed:

> ERECTED To commemorate ye gratitude Freeman of Worcester owe Robert Tracy Esqr Who Restored their Liberty By defeating An arbitrary power in the year 1747

The monument is flanked by allegorical naked male figures representing 'Conquest' and 'Gratitude'. All are painted in a somewhat amateur style and may be the work of Dr John Wall* himself. Chambers' biography of Dr Wall written in the 1820s showed that Wall was closely acquainted with Robert Tracy. Tracy had stood in the 1747 election and finished last in the poll which had lasted for five days. The election was particularly corrupt, however, and the result was subsequently reversed so that Tracy was elected.

Tramline Flutes
See **Shanked Shape**

Transfer Printing
The process of transferring a design on to the surface of a piece of porcelain from an engraved copper plate appears to have been used first at Worcester, although a similar technique had been used to print on enamel prior to this. The earliest Worcester printed wares probably date from c.1753-4 and were certainly made before Robert Hancock* arrived in Worcester. Josiah Holdship* claimed to have first introduced the printing process and this is probably correct, although examples of printing are also known on Bow, Chelsea and Chinese porcelain, all of which could date from the early to mid-1750s.

There are two quite different methods of transferring a design from the engraved plate. One involves filling the engraving with a special oil and using a thin bat of a jelly-like glue to transfer the oil almost invisibly to the surface of the vessel. Very finely powdered enamel colour is then dusted on and sticks to the oil, completing the process which is then fired in a kiln. The earliest Worcester printed wares, the so-called Smoky Primitives* (Colour Plate 87) were probably transferred in this way.

The second technique involves filling the engraving with enamel colour already mixed with oil. The surplus is wiped away and then the copper plate is heated and covered with a thin sheet of tissue paper. Pressed between rollers, the design is transferred to the paper and can then be laid on the surface of the vessel to be printed. After rubbing-down to ensure a clear image, the paper is washed away leaving only the coloured design which is then fired. Both printing methods, when carefully controlled, can produce a perfect image and it is usually extremely difficult to determine which process has been used.

Successful printing relies on a finely engraved copper plate. Initially, Worcester obtained already engraved images, such as the set of the Seasons which Robert Hancock had engraved for the bookseller Robert Sayer after drawings by Boitard*. The presence of Boitard's name in reverse confirms that the plates had not been engraved for use on porcelain but had been reused. Hancock seems to have partly etched his plates using acid rather than engraving tools to cut out each line. Through the etching technique he could possibly have duplicated copper plates and thus it was probable for the same subject to be sold to Worcester, Bow and the Birmingham enamel manufacturers at the same time as Hancock was still in London. Josiah Holdship probably supervised the printing itself until Hancock came to Worcester c.1756.

By 1757, the date of the King of Prussia* prints, Worcester had totally mastered transfer printing overglaze and were just beginning to introduce underglaze printing. The oil and dusting method could not be used underglaze and paper pulls had to be used instead. From c.1757 paper transfers were likely to have been used for all printing, including overglaze.

Transfer Printing. A pull from the original copper plate of The Draw Well, *attributed to Robert Hancock*. Many 18th century copper plates survive at the Worcester factory, all still capable of producing a perfect impression.*

Transfer Printing. Amongst the most accomplished early prints used at Worcester were a series of the Elements copied from engravings after Boucher. Air is represented by the bird released from its cage. Printed in black on a feather moulded coffee pot*, c.1756-8, 9in. (23cm). (Dyson Perrins Museum.)*

The technique was no longer a secret and printing was carried out at most factories, with different degrees of success. Worcester employed the skills not only of Hancock, but also the engravers James Ross* and Valentine Green*, realising that successful printing depended on maintaining high quality copper plates. They remained market leaders until the development of fine printing on Wedgwood's creamware in the 1770s brought fierce competition and the eventual decline of Worcester's overglaze printing. Bat printing*, using oil transfers and delicate stipple engraving, revived the printing industry on porcelain in the early 19th century, although Worcester were to play only a minor role, far behind Spode and other Staffordshire makers. *See* Colour Plates 87 to 89.

Trembleuse Saucers

Saucers for coffee or chocolate cups in the style of early French blue and white porcelain were occasionally made with a raised ridge around the central well to prevent spillage during use by invalids or the infirm. The original idea came from the St Cloud factory some thirty or more years earlier, but Worcester still had a market for fairly exact copies, always moulded with fine reeding. These have only been seen with underglaze blue* borders of simple cells or *lambrequin* scrolls. Worcester examples date from c.1757-65 and were supplied with normal shapes of cups.

Tumblers

Tapering beaker shapes popular at many English porcelain factories from about 1780. Worcester tumblers are very rare before 1790 and tend to be quite small and thickly potted. By the 1790s Chamberlain and Flight were both producing fine half pint and pint (quarter and half litre) sized tumblers, the plain shapes suited to the classical styles of decoration. Flight and Barr examples are known with monochrome decoration including portraits of the King c.1792. Dated examples in the Dyson Perrins Museum which came from the family of Samuel Smith* provide useful clues, as do the Chamberlain account books which include numerous references to tumblers during the two decades either side of 1800. There is some confusion, however, as many tumblers are listed with covers, although these are unknown today except for ornamental versions with pierced tops for bulbs or pot-pourri, a smaller cover or stopper on the top. These were sometimes sold with matching saucer-like stands to accompany bough pots* and would not have been used for drinking. Most of the tumblers which survive today would not have had covers or stands although most came as pairs, often with a matching larger jug. Many Worcester tumblers are unmarked, especially Grainger examples of 1806-10. These are often painted with views of Worcester and are frequently confused with Chamberlain, although Grainger tumblers are not so thinly potted. (*See* illustrations on page 348.)

Tureens

Whilst it can generally be assumed that tureens were made to accompany dinner and dessert services, all examples surviving from the first decade or so of the factory are individual and do not match any existing plates and dishes. The price list of the London Warehouse (*see* **London Shops**) c.1755-6 includes 'Tureens round 1st and 2nd' (size) selling for 7s.6d. and 12s.6d. each while 'ditto Oval 1st and 2nd' sold for 21s. and 25s. each. These are far more expensive than any other items sold by the warehouse and this is quite understandable when you consider the difficulty the factory had in firing such pieces. The four or five surviving large oval tureens are all heavily misshapen, with a gap of more than an inch (2.5cm) between the cover and base on one example. They came with moulded

Colour Plate 92. ***Two-Handled Sauceboats.*** *A view looking into a two-handled sauceboat, the centre with a simple Chinese riverscape in pale underglaze blue*, workman's mark*, c.1756, 6½in. (16.3cm). (Phillips.)*

Colour Plate 93. ***Tynedale Plate.*** *Delicate painting and a soft palette combine to create a particularly beautiful specimen of early Worcester porcelain, c.1752-3, 8½in. (21.5cm). (Phillips.)*

Tumblers. *An early Chamberlain tumbler painted, probably by John Wood*, with an allegorical subject representing peace and including a view of the Nile, unmarked, c.1800, 3¾in. (9.5cm). (Phillips.)*

Tumblers. *A Grainger tumbler painted in grey monochrome with a distant view of Worcester, unmarked, c.1806-8, 3¾in. (9.5cm). (Phillips.)*

rococo* panels or else plain with lobed sides and can have either a dolphin or branch finial (Colour Plate 90). The circular tureens from this period are thrown rather than moulded and can be surprisingly thick and heavy. The most usual form has satyr mask handles joined by their ears while others have gnarled twigs as handles and finials or modelled roses as knops. All examples are great rarities, however. A variation which follows a Chinese form was made without handles and the centre of the cover is flat so that this can be inverted and used as a shallow dish.

The great novelty tureens which epitomise the Chelsea factory were not attempted at Worcester with the exception on a smaller scale of partridge tureens* and cauliflower tureens*. A much more exciting model is a tureen in the form of two billing doves which is now one of the rarest shapes found in early Worcester. Instead the small oval tureens which accompany most dessert services are very unoriginal at Worcester. Early examples from the 1760s have moulded rococo panels and thickened rims and it is unlikely that all were sold originally with covers as they are frequently encountered with open tops. A rarer version has heavy basket-weave moulding. By about 1770 the standard shape was of a quatrelobed oval tureen with scallop shell handles and an artichoke finial. These are often referred to today as sauce tureens but sauce tureens would have come with dinner services. Instead the standard pairs of Worcester dessert tureens were for sugar and cream.

Larger soup or vegetable tureens c.1770 have gadroon* moulded rims following silver prototypes and modelled twig handles usually with applied acorns, or else scallop shells. These would have accompanied dinner services with gadroon-edged plates although these are surprisingly rare. These tureens are found in blue and white printed patterns as well as rich scale blue. Very impressive examples were included in the Duke of Gloucester* service.

By the end of the 18th century and into the Regency period the standard dinner services from each of the Worcester factories would have included a soup tureen with cover and stand (*see* Colour Plate 64), four vegetable tureens with covers (probably in two different shapes, square and oval), and two or four sauce tureens with covers and stands. For larger services these numbers would be doubled up and there could be additional entrée dishes and covers which rested in shallow bases for hot water. Ladles* were optional extras. Tureens usually followed only a limited range of shapes within each factory and it should be remembered that most dinner services contained anything from a dozen to eighteen or more platters which were used to serve food.

Turner, Thomas

Born in 1749, Turner Thomas was the son of the Rector of Comberton, near Worcester. He was apprenticed to the Worcester Porcelain Company c.1765 as an engraver. Working alongside Robert Hancock*, Turner would have learnt all aspects of transfer printing*, as well as the full manufacturing processes. It is likely that he was principally involved in the development of underglaze transfer printing which was used in increasing quantities during the 1760s. It has been suggested that Turner acted as a dealer in Worcester porcelain but there is little evidence of this. He must have had good business sense as he felt able to leave his employment at Worcester and set up his own porcelain factory. He formed a partnership with Ambrose Gallimore who ran a pottery further up the river Severn at Caughley. It is likely that he had

Tureens. *One of a series of incredible large tureens made in the rococo* taste, the panels finely painted in underglaze blue*, workmen's marks*, c.1753-5, 17½in. (44.5cm) wide. The Worcester factory had to overcome great difficulties to fire and glaze pieces as large as this. (Rous Lench Collection.)*

Tureens. *Two early Grainger tureens featuring eccentric handles on plain shapes, the large tureen for soup, c.1812-4, the other for cream or sugar on dessert, c.1810, unmarked. (Jill Gosling Antiques and Phillips.)*

Twigging. *A Grainger perfume or scent bottle* with finely modelled flowers, the pattern of gold twigging providing the principal clue to a Grainger origin, confirmed by the factory shape books, c.1835, 6½in. (16.5cm). (Phillips.)*

planned this move with Robert Hancock who left Worcester himself on 31 October 1774 because of 'certain controversies, differences and disputes' with the other partners who bought Hancock's share of the stock for £900. Hancock was the senior figure at Worcester but lost his savings in a bank failure and was engaged by Turner merely as manager of the 'Salopian China Warehouse' through which Turner's Caughley porcelain was sold in Bridgnorth. Turner himself attended to the London trade.

The exact date of the commencement of the Caughley factory is uncertain. It could have been as early as 1772 although probably no porcelain was on sale until 1775. Turner would have needed to employ all manner of craftsmen and probably enticed a number of Worcester employees to join him at Caughley which would account for the great similarity between the two porcelains. While at Worcester Turner would have known the modeller John Toulouse*, who also worked for Turner at Caughley, and have been well acquainted with Robert Chamberlain sen.* who supervised the decorating at Worcester. When the Chamberlains left Flights to set up on their own in 1788 they looked to Thomas Turner to supply them with white porcelain. Turner had up until this time concentrated purely on the commercial blue and white porcelain and was happy for Chamberlain to provide him with enamelled and gilded wares for sale in his important London shop. Turner was a financial backer of the Chamberlains and probably encouraged their departure from Flights. A few years later, however, the Chamberlains treated Turner in the same way as he had treated the old factory, setting up as manufacturers in direct competition. Unable to compete with Staffordshire and rival Coalport, Turner blamed ill health and sold the Caughley factory to John Rose and Co. of Coalport in November 1799. He died in February 1809.

Turquoise Grounds

The origin of Worcester's most dramatic ground colour is the *bleu celeste* ground of Sèvres* rather than earlier Chinese or Meissen* turquoise grounds*. It was undoubtedly the colour called 'sky blue' in the 1769 Worcester sale catalogue. It was used as an all-over ground colour both at the factory and in the Giles* workshop, and it is only the gilding style which offers any clue as to which is which. Giles used the colour as a ground with reserved panels, although these wonderful rich forms of decoration are very rare. Giles also used two other shades of turquoise — a muddy colour found on pieces with heavily gilded turquoise cornucopia-shaped borders, and a paler version seen on the square dessert dish illustrated in Colour Plate 91. Some of the pieces with cornucopia-shaped

Two-Handled Sauceboats. *The combination of enamelled European figures and monkey head finials* on the handles makes this a particularly rare specimen, c.1756, about 8in. (20cm) long. (Present whereabouts unknown.)*

turquoise borders have been attributed to the Worcester factory but my feeling is to treat these with suspicion.

At Worcester the turquoise colour was mostly used as a background for border decorations in patterns such as *Hop Trellis**, *Jabberwocky** and designs with white pearls or chains reserved against thick turquoise enamel bands. These continued until c.1780. In the 19th century turquoise grounds became fashionable again with the rococo revival* and the renewed interest in Sèvres. Flight, Barr and Barr favoured a very pale turquoise ground and Chamberlain and Grainger pieces also tend to be lighter in colour when compared with Coalport or Minton for example.

A further distinctive class of 18th century Worcester porcelain occurs with thick turquoise borders and this is discussed as Group VIa in the section on redecoration*.

Twigging

A pattern in gold of hanging weed which was particularly popular at Graingers during the 1830s and 1840s. It was very easy for junior gilders to execute and was well suited to the fashion for rococo revival*. The presence of twigging can often be a vital clue to a Grainger origin although the motif does also sometimes appear on the wares of other factories, especially Samuel Alcock and Davenport. (*See* illustration on page 350.)

Two-Handled Sauceboats

Although very popular in silver and in Chinese and Continental porcelain during the first half of the 18th century, two-handled sauceboats were going out of fashion by the 1750s. Worcester specialised in sauceboats and they did make many two-handled examples between c.1753-7 (Colour Plate 92), although none was made after this date. Far fewer different mouldings were made compared with single-handled boats and while three sizes seem to have been made, the basic forms remain very consistent. Occasionally some of the large sized boats have monkey's head finials* on the handles.

Blue and white two-handled sauceboats far outnumber coloured examples, and virtually every one is painted with the same underglaze landscape pattern. Only five or six examples have been noted in a different pattern from all the others. There is far more variety in coloured decoration, but again this tends to differ from single-handled boats. Onglaze transfer prints* were often used, of Smoky Primitive* type but with clear and precise prints inside of shipping or aquatic birds. Enamel painting is frequently European rather than oriental, with some finely painted figures or further shipping scenes inspired by Meissen*. The primary painted decoration on these heavily moulded shapes is inside the base of the boats, although ironically this would be fully covered when the sauceboats were in use.

Tynedale Plate

A lucky purchase in a small auction in the Tyne Valley in northern England suggested the name for a remarkable early Worcester plate which was exhibited by Messrs Albert Amor in November 1982 (Colour Plate 93). The following year it was sold at Phillips and in now in the Paul Riley Collection. The importance of the plate is its early date, c.1753 or possibly as early as 1752, making it the earliest surviving Worcester coloured plate*. At the same time the quality of the decoration stands out as far superior to any other plates made in the 1750s. The decoration is in Worcester's own adaptation of *famille rose** and includes two birds among bamboo, peony and chrysanthemum, a popular combination in Chinese art.

U

Underglaze Blue

In the 18th century blue was the only colour which could be satisfactorily controlled in a single kiln firing along with the glaze, all other colours needing a separate enamel firing. Cobalt oxide, in the form of a black powder, was applied to the unglazed biscuit* surface of the vessel. When glazed and fired the cobalt reacts with the silicon in the glaze to become a form of cobalt silicate which is blue. Although sometimes difficult to control and needing a preliminary hardening-on firing, the advantage of underglaze blue is that the colour is sealed within the glaze for all time and never changes. Overglaze blue enamel, on the other hand, is very prone to discoloration and decomposition. Evidence confirmed by factory site excavations* indicates that initially Bristol porcelain and some of the earliest Worcester porcelain was painted in cobalt directly on to the fired biscuit and glazed straight away. It was then given a single glaze firing which accounts for the hazy appearance of these early pieces. Subsequently the technique was modified at Worcester — the cobalt-decorated biscuit was fired first to 'harden-on' the colouring prior to glazing. The excavations confirm that the use of a hardening-on firing dates back to c.1752. This was a crucial discovery: much greater detail could be achieved and the kiln wastage must also have been greatly reduced.

Underglaze blue grounds were introduced c.1760, first using powder blue* and subsequently scale blue* and wet blue*. The tone of blue was influenced by the quality of cobalt. Impurities resulted in the inky, slate-blue colour used up until the 1770s, whereas pure cobalt gives a much brighter, sharper colour with a hint of indigo. A significant change occurred c.1780 when the factory introduced a new purer form of underglaze blue. The colouring must have been popular and contrasted with Caughley and other English factories. When used for underglaze blue grounds the bright blue seems somewhat harsh but must have suited the taste of the time. Many patterns with borders in the bright blue are attributed to the 1770s but the pure tone of the cobalt shows that these were made after c.1780. *See also* **Blue and White**.

Underglaze Blue. *An early small mug or coffee can painted with an unusual effect of blue washes outlined in grey or black underglaze in the manner of* trekked *decoration on delft, c.1753, 2½in. (6.3cm). (Phillips.)*

Underglaze Green Decoration

Two wasters* found on the factory site in 1977 are painted in a pale green colour underglaze with a prunus pattern and probably date from the late 1750s. Tiny flecks of blue on the pieces suggest that they were intended to be green rather that a misfired blue. The green colour is pale and was probably unsuccessful, although it is of course possible some underglaze green was produced for sale.

V

Valentia, Lord, Service

When Lord Valentia travelled extensively in the East he took with him an artist named Page who made drawings of the landscapes, ruins and some of the people they encountered. These were published in an account of *Lord Valentia's Travels* between 1809 and 1811. A dessert service was made by Flight, Barr and Barr for Lord Valentia c.1815. Thomas Baxter* copied a series of Page's original drawings into the centres of each piece, while the borders were finely decorated in raised gold with anthemion and lotus motifs on a white ground. Two specimens kept for the factory's own collection can still be seen in the Dyson Perrins Museum and are illustrated in Colour Plate 7.

Valentine Pattern. *A saucer-dish exactly copied from a Chinese original, a most appropriate design for a marriage gift, c.1757, 6 7/8 in. (17.5cm). (Phillips.)*

Valentine Pattern

A most attractive pattern copied from Chinese export porcelain in the European taste. The original design was drawn by Piercy Brett for Commodore Anson and depicts a garlanded breadfruit tree on Tenian Island. The service made for Anson in 1743 led to many other Chinese services of the same pattern. The delicate colouring is well suited to this design of billing doves, hearts on an altar to Love and a quiver with arrows, symbols which make this an ideal design for a marriage gift. The pattern was used primarily on plain tea services from c.1756-60, but has also been seen on different leaf dishes, *Blind Earl** sweetmeat dishes and at least one oval basket. A version of the pattern was also adapted to fit into the panels of a hexagonal creamboat. A related pattern, adapted from another version of the Chinese patterns made initially for Anson, was painted in blue and white c.1765-75, the design including dogs by a tree with a shepherdess's hat, cloak and crooks. This is listed by Branyan, French and Sandon as I.C.30.

Vases

In the course of the period covered by this *Dictionary* the Worcester factories made so many vase shapes that it is virtually impossible to discuss them in a single entry. Early vases range from simple and really quite elegant small bottle shapes to some magnificent strongly moulded shapes inspired by silver but adapted to a style which was unique to the factory (*see* illustrations on page 354). The variety of vase shapes from the first five years is really quite surprising. By the later 1750s the range had been reduced considerably to just a few basic forms which copied Meissen* to a great extent, both in shape and decoration. Plain thrown and turned baluster vases have covers with flower finials and these were combined into garnitures with waisted shaped vases known as beaker vases, usually with bulbous moulded knops copying Meissen. These shapes continued until the 1770s.

The celebrated hexagonal vases were introduced c.1765-8 and came in a number of sizes. Initially the covered hexagonal vases had matching side vases with trumpet necks but these are very rarely seen. Larger versions have moulded panels and knops on basically octagonal trumpet shapes which can be 16in. (40.6cm) high and are usually badly distorted in the firing. Plain baluster shapes are standard c.1770 and again come in many different sizes, with or without rococo* scroll side handles. There is surprisingly little variation in shape at this period, and only the occasional moulded shape such as the pair of goblet shapes with putti by John Donaldson* in the Dyson Perrins Museum, and a number of shield-shaped vases which have upright scroll handles. New vase shapes were not high on the factory's list of priorities during the late 1770s and 1780s and vases become surprisingly uncommon at this time. The newly formed Chamberlain factory made some early vases but few before about 1800 by which time the factory had developed a reputation for rich decoration. Figure subjects, rich ground colours and gold competed with an even greater degree of richness at Flight and Barrs, culminating in some of the most wonderful vases imaginable made by Barr, Flight and Barr c.1810 and painted by Thomas Baxter* for Flight, Barr and Barr c.1815. An enormous variety of vase shapes were made, mostly inspired by the classical taste.

Grainger, who were slow to begin ornamental production, making very few vases before 1820, led the city in their adapting to the rococo revival*, producing some delightfully eccentric shapes in the 1830s. Chamberlain and Flight remained more firmly rooted in their past traditions and only began to compete with Coalbrookdale and Minton when it was too late in the 1840s and the quality of Worcester vase production had sadly declined.

Vases. *An exceptional early vase shape copied from the Chinese, c.1752-3, 10½in. (26.7cm). The decoration in* famille rose* *is very finely executed in a style unique to Worcester at this time. (Sotheby's/ Kiddell Papers.)*

Vermicelli Gilding

A continuous worm-like jig-saw pattern drawn in gold on a variety of coloured backgrounds. Vermicelli is a kind of pasta which was well known in England in the early 19th century. Both Chamberlain and Flight used the name vermicelli for their gold pattern even though they found several imaginative different ways to spell the word. An unexacting pattern which could easily be done by junior apprentice gilders, the design is nevertheless most effective and can be adapted to fit any shape. The earliest recorded Chamberlain pattern is 403 'Gold Vermicelli' used on Bute shape from c.1800-5. In 1812 Barr, Flight and Barr sold to the Earl of Coventry '1 Imperial form Ink Stand, blue and Gold Vermicilli [*sic*], green marble and views', priced at six guineas. The pattern was undoubtedly in use earlier than this, probably from c.1805, and continued into the Chamberlain and Co. period in the 1840s. Grainger used different versions of the design but only very occasionally copied the simple pattern used extensively elsewhere. Vermicelli probably originated on French porcelain and was used at many other English factories, although not as often as at Worcester.

Vases. *An important early vase, the shape inspired by metalwork, enamelled with* famille rose* *sprigs and the* Strutting Bird* *design below the lip, c.1752, about 6¼in. (16cm). (Sotheby's/Kiddell Papers.)*

Vernon, Rev. Thomas

Thomas Vernon, M.P., was brought in as a partner in the Worcester Porcelain Company in 1754 following the death of Edward Cave*. When the twenty-one year lease expired, the entire property of the company was sold by auction at the Hop Pole Inn in Worcester on 2 January 1772. The Reverend Thomas Vernon was the purchaser acting for a partnership which was formed into a company on 3 March 1772 and probably remained the largest shareholder, even though the firm traded as William Davis and Co.* Vernon and his remaining partners sold the company to Thomas Flight in 1783 (*see* **Flight Factory**). There is no evidence to suggest that Thomas Vernon was anything other than a sleeping partner providing much needed financial aid.

'W' Mark
It has always been puzzling why the 'W' mark should be so relatively uncommon while the crescent and square marks are so popular, as a letter 'W' seems a much more natural mark for the Worcester Porcelain company to have used. A workman's mark* resembling a 'W' was used in the 1750s, but it was not until the 1770s that the 'W' appeared as a mark on tea and dessert wares which include underglaze blue* as a ground colour. A printed mark of a cursive letter 'W' was used on floral and other European prints in underglaze blue c.1770-5 and this form of 'W' was later incorporated into the Kerr and Binns and Royal Worcester factory marks. One particular blue painted pattern, *The Floral Queen's* of c.1770, is marked with a letter 'W' within a square, a mark which seems unique to this pattern.

Waiting Chinaman Pattern
A very distinctive pattern which was simple to paint in strong underglaze blue* on teawares, c.1770-6. The single standing Chinaman by a triangular fence is presumably based on a Chinese original although the design was probably adapted by the Worcester factory into a more formal version for ease of production. Caughley made the same pattern c.1775-6, almost certainly painted by artists who had moved from Worcester. Consequently it is impossible to distinguish the two factories' versions without the help of the mark, as Worcester will always bear a painted open crescent while Caughley took care to add a serif to form a letter 'C', or else marked with an 'S'. The pattern is listed by Branyan, French and Sandon as I.A.6.

Wales, Prince of
See **Prince Regent Services**

Walker, Samuel
When William Billingsley's* porcelain manufactory at Torksey faced bankruptcy in 1805, one of the new backers was a young local farmer named Samuel Walker. Walker assisted Billingsley in the erection of new kilns and was clearly a very good pupil, developing a considerable interest and knowledge in the subject. Walker remained with Billingsley as he fled from Torksey in 1808, heavily in debt, travelling to Swansea in the hope of finding employment. In the summer of 1808 Samuel Walker accompanied William Billingsley to Worcester along with Billingsley's daughters, Sarah and Lavinia. Although not initially employed, Walker was in due course offered work in Barr, Flight and Barr's mixing room where he experimented to develop a new porcelain recipe.

R.W. Binns* wrote that Walker introduced a most important invention to the Worcester works. This was a 'reverberating enamel kiln' which worked by placing charcoal between the brick and iron structure of the kiln. This extended the heat evenly throughout, instead of initially heating the base of the kiln too greatly. The method of building these new enamel kilns was kept as a great secret, Walker always working by night. Binns tells us that Walker built similar kilns for both Flights and Chamberlains. The only other evidence which backs this up is a payment of £5 recorded in the Chamberlain account books, paid to 'Billingsley, Worcester' for a 'Plan of Building standing Kiln'.

William Billingsley and Samuel Walker remained very much partners and in 1812 Walker married Billingsley's eldest daughter Sarah at Clains Church near Worcester. She was twenty-five. In November 1812 a bond was drawn up by Martin Barr*, under which Billingsley and Walker received £200 for a 'secret relating to a new method of composing

Waiting Chinaman Pattern. *A drawing by Neal French of the full design on a coffee cup, c.1770.*

Wall, George, Service. *A coffee cup, teabowl and saucer from the tea service bearing the cipher of George Wall, a relative of Dr John Wall*, crescent marks*, c.1780. (Phillips.)*

porcelain'. A penalty of £1,000 was to be forfeited if Walker and Billingsley revealed this secret to any other persons. In spite of this, however, in November 1813 Walker and Billingsley left their employment without notice, taking the knowledge they had gained with them to Nantgarw. A year later Flight, Barr and Barr (the factory's name had changed in the meantime) caught up with Samuel Walker at Swansea. They wrote to him threatening legal action and then wrote to Lewis Dilwyn warning him not to employ the two fugitives, explaining also that Flights had no intention of using the new formula anyway.

Failure followed Billingsley and Walker at every step. Sarah Walker died on New Year's Day 1817 and Billingsley had to borrow £7 to pay for his daughter's funeral and medical costs. Samuel Walker received no reply to a pathetic letter to Wedgwood seeking employment, and instead joined Billingsley at Nantgarw where they made beautiful porcelain but incurred heavy losses. Money ran out in 1819 and after a severe winter they left their debts behind them once again and walked to Coalport. They worked for John Rose, Walker assisting with the kilns and perfecting new enamel colours. In due course Samuel Walker, together with his children, emigrated to America where he set up a factory making crude brown-glazed pottery in West Troy, New York. Many years later, in 1874, Walker wrote to the Royal Worcester factory offering to sell them some new discoveries. Walker added a cheeky postscript to his letter:

> I was employed by Messrs Flight and Barr 50 years ago makeing [*sic*] experiments. I made them a fine China — Mr Barr gave a £100 for it.

Wall, George, Service

A tea service of fluted shapes with a deep underglaze blue* border and formal coloured flower sprigs. Each piece was decorated with an elaborate scrolling gold cipher 'GW', the initials of George Wall who is believed to have been a relative of Dr John Wall*. The set passed by descent to John Henry Townsend Wall who died in 1968, and was subsequently sold by Messrs Albert Amor Ltd. in 1983. The underglaze blue border is in very bright blue suggesting a date c.1780. Therefore the set would probably have been decorated under the direction of the Chamberlains who specialised in similar gilded ciphers when they established their own works in 1788.

Wall, Dr John

John Wall M.D. (Colour Plate 94) was born in 1708 in Powick which lies half way between Worcester and the Malvern Hills. He attended the school at nearby Leigh Sinton and then the King's School in Worcester, the cathedral school founded by Henry VIII, where he studied the classics which were to influence much of his later painting. John Wall learnt Latin and Greek and won a scholarship to Worcester College, Oxford, to study medicine. In 1735 he was elected as a Fellow of Merton College, achieving his M.A. in 1736. He completed his medical training at St Thomas' Hospital in London, although he did not take his degree of Doctor of Medicine until 1757. As a qualified doctor he settled in Worcester in 1740 where he lived at 43 Foregate Street. John Wall's father had died in 1734 and from this time he had been technically in the hands of his 'guardian', Samuel Sandys* M.P. In 1740 John Wall married Lord Sandys' cousin, Catherine Sandys, and they had six children.

Chambers's Biographical Illustrations of Worcestershire gave details of Dr Wall's extensive medical practice and writings on the subject. One of his many published treatises covered the healing properties of Malvern water. Reading through this, one imagines Dr Wall as something of a quack, experimenting with this magical cure which he claimed had helped so many of his patients. For instance, he wrote of his preferred treatment:

> I always advise my patients to take the water internally for several weeks, then to bathe the affected parts under the tap and to immerse themselves in the water with the clothes on, allowing them to dry on their body. This has never killed anyone although used by many very tender patients. The affected parts smart at first which is the badness coming out.

The scientific basis of his explanations, on the other hand, reveal the depth of Dr Wall's medical knowledge. He had analysed Malvern spring water and found it to be almost totally pure, with virtually no mineral content. As a local wag put it

> The Malvern Water said Doctor Wall
> Was famed for containing just nothing at all.

John Wall was involved in the establishment of new wells in Malvern and also assisted in the setting up of the first infirmary in Worcester. Some of his cases make amusing reading:

> A patient had an opthalmic opthalmy in each eye and was unable to bear the light. She had been in this miserable condition for eight or nine months and I advised her at length to use Malvern Water. She had not used the water more than a week than she was so much recovered that she could see a flea leaping on her bed. This cure was performed 1754.

Clearly a man of many parts, he found time to be an accomplished amateur painter specialising in oil paintings of historical figure subjects. He exhibited at the Royal Academy and several fine large canvases by him hang in the Dyson Perrins Museum. Subjects such as 'Queen Eleanor Sucking the Poison from the Arm of Edward I' and the 'Head of John the Baptist on a Charger' are dramatic if not exactly masterpieces. He designed illustrations for books, including J. Hervey's *Meditations and Contemplations*, 1748, and R.O. Cambridge's *The Scribbleraid*, 1751. The engraving of Dr Wall's designs was carried out by the eminent hand of Ravenet, among others. Wall also designed the stained glass windows for a chapel at the Bishop's Palace in Hartlebury and a window of 'The Presentation of Christ in the Temple' for Oriel College, Oxford.

One of Dr Wall's medical tracts was on the subject of the effects of lead poisoning caused by drinking cider from lead-glazed earthenware vessels. Henry Sandon has suggested that Wall's research into this might have led him to experiment with lead-free glazes and the making of a more refined form of ceramics. William Davis* was an apothecary in Worcester who had a laboratory at 33 Broad Street near to Dr Wall's house and the site of the infirmary. Chambers's, op. cit., mentions their experiments using an iron pot round which the fire was heaped and kept up as near as possible to a furnace heat. It is probably here that Wall and Davis made their 'invention' of the secret of making porcelain, their experiments conjuring up an image of alchemy rather than serious scientific research.

In June 1751 they drew up the Articles for carrying on the Worcester Tonquin Manufacture* wherein Wall and Davis claimed to have discovered 'the secret of making the said porcelain'. The other subscribers in the new company paid for the inventors' shares and in return it was agreed that Dr Wall and William Davis would continue to work on perfecting their invention.

Whether they had in fact discovered the secret is uncertain, and is discussed in the opening historical review in this *Dictionary,* pages 11 to 13.

It is, however, most unlikely that John Wall played much of a part in the day to day running of the factory, because of

Wall, Dr John. *The engraved frontispiece to J. Hervey's* Meditations and Contemplations *published in 1748, the design by John Wall of Worcester. Curiously, this subject is known to have been later copied on to Birmingham enamel.*

his involvement in his medical work and other ventures. He was probably happy to leave the porcelain works in the hands of William Davis and the Holdship* brothers. An account in the *General Evening Post* for 6 October 1757 told how Dr Wall had been robbed of about four guineas by a highwayman on the way home from Ledbury. The report refers to the Doctor as 'an eminent Physician' of Worcester, not a porcelain manufacturer, and adds 'One William Lissimore was brought to our county gaol, being charged on suspicion of committing the said robbery.'

Dr Wall's name is only mentioned in connection with the porcelain works when the lease of Warmstry House* expired and he was one of the partners in a new company in 1772 which had temporarily been put in the name of Dr Wall's son, John Wall jun. Binns* discovered that in 1782 the son gave a detailed series of lectures at Oxford including 'The Qualities and Uses of *Soap Rock*' along with the history of porcelain making in China, Saxony and 'the other less perfect European Methods of making porcelain &c.' Clearly John Wall jun. had gained this knowledge working with his father at the Worcester porcelain works.

The retirement of John Wall sen. in 1774 marks the end of his involvement with porcelain and his shares were sold to the other partners. In spite of his advocacy of Malvern water,

John Wall chose instead to retire to the rival spa town of Bath. He died there in 1776 and his monument can be seen to the left of the west door of Bath Abbey. It proclaims that 'Nature gave him talents: a benevolent heart directed the application of them to a study and practise of a profession most beneficial to Mankind...' His monument mentions his 'genius for historic painting' but makes no reference to the porcelain venture. This is probably because, in spite of most claims to the contrary, Wall played a far less crucial role in the continuation of the factory, even though the First Period* of Worcester porcelain usually bears his name.

One important question concerns Dr Wall's painting on porcelain. As a talented artist connected with the porcelain works it is reasonable to assume that he tried his hand at painting on porcelain. Several pieces have been attributed to him but in truth there is very little evidence. The celebrated Tracy mug* (Colour Plate 86) is an early piece made for a local parliamentarian who would have been well known to Dr Wall. The painting has an amateur feel and is very different from other painting at the factory. Another kind of figure painting occurs on a mug inscribed 'Lord and Lady Sandys Health', painted c.1756 for John Wall's guardian (*see* **Sandys, Lord and Lady, Mug**). Both of these could have been by Dr Wall himself but there is insufficient evidence to make any firm attributions.

Wall Period
See **Doctor Wall Period** and **First Period**

Wall Pockets
See **Cornucopias**

Warbler Pattern
An underglaze blue* pattern of flowering rocks, named after the reverse design which features a bird on a rock. One of the first blue and white patterns identified by Dr Bernard Watney and used on teawares from about 1753 until the early 1760s, the pattern is listed as I.C.4 by Branyan, French and Sandon.

Warbler Pattern. *An unusual small mug with a rounded, unglazed base, painted in pale underglaze blue*, workman's mark*, c.1756, 3⅛ in. (8cm). (Phillips.)*

Warmstry House
A prominent manor house in the centre of Worcester dating back to the reign of Henry VII. It had formerly been the home of the Windsor family and the Earls of Plymouth and afterwards the Warmstry family in the 17th century, during which time it was largely rebuilt. The house and grounds were later used by the Reverend Thomas Blackmore as a place of worship for an independent church. In 1707 the premises were sold to William Evett, a glover, for the sum of £340. By this time the house was already divided into a number of tenements. It stood back from the River Severn beyond attractive formal gardens and early paintings of Worcester show these gardens complete with sandstone walls.

On 6 May 1751 William Evett leased all of the house and grounds to Richard Holdship* for a term of twenty-one years at an annual rent of £30, with an option to renew the lease for a further payment of £20 on termination. Holdship was a glover, like Evett, although for the purpose of leasing the site he represented the Worcester Tonquin Manufactory*. The original Articles of the company confirm that Holdship had leased 'a certain House with the Buildings, Gardens and appurtenances thereunto belonging situate in the Parish of St Alban'. By August 1752 when *The Gentleman's Magazine* reproduced an engraving, it is clear much building work had been carried out. Long blocks of biscuit* and glazing kilns ran at the side of the gardens along the length of the street called Warmstry Slip and the hovel of a bottle oven can be seen at the side of Warmstry house itself. The old Warmstry House building formed a quadrangle and was filled with various manufacturing processes and a yard for coal replaced some of the ornamental gardens. William Evett still occupied a large house alongside Warmstry House as landlord of the premises.

In 1756 Richard Holdship bought some houses to the south of Warmstry House and erected a large and elegant mansion in their place. This 'large commodious dwellinghouse' was described as 'Mr Holdship's new buildings' by Robert Hancock* when he engraved a view of the whole site in 1757. To make an attractive composition Hancock used a certain amount of artistic licence, moving Warmstry House itself to one side so that the masts of the river boats did not obscure the view.

In 1759 the freehold of Warmstry House became available and was bought jointly by Richard and Josiah Holdship* for £600. After Richard Holdship's bankruptcy in 1761 it is likely that his share was purchased by the remaining partners and became part of the assets of the company. The new dwelling house was eventually sold by Richard Holdship's mortgagees to Robert Hancock on 25 March 1769.

The Warmstry House factory was on the banks of the river which was still tidal at this time. A single door led to a slipway where the riverboats known as trows could be moored for unloading clay and coal directly into the yard. By a process of systematic dumping a large area of land was reclaimed from the river and a curved brick wall built around the perimeter. Excavations* on the factory site show that it was largely through dumping ash and debris from the kilns that this land was dried out and filled in, mostly during the 1760s. By the early 1770s the land had been flattened and compacted for use as a coal yard. This level was clearly visible in our excavations which show that it was prone to regular flooding. Below the successive dumpings of ash and porcelain wasters* we discovered the sharply sloping clay slipway and the original medieval sandstone wall. The curved brick wall from the 1770s is visible in views of the factory drawn by James Ross*

Warmstry House. *Robert Hancock's* 1757 engraving of the Worcester Porcelain Manufactory from the River Severn. Warmstry House can be seen in the background (moved to make room for the mast of the Severn trow riverboat). Richard Holdship's* imposing house stands alongside and this was eventually bought by Robert Hancock.*

for Flight and Barr and a ground plan drawn of the site in 1795 is reproduced in Henry Sandon's *Illustrated Guide to Worcester Porcelain*, pl.149. By this time Flight and Barr had added an arcaded frontage above what had been the original sandstone river wall and an imposing sign was built above the arches inscribed with the name of the factory.

After the amalgamation with Chamberlains in 1840 the Warmstry House site was used only for making tiles. In an attempt to sell the works many buildings were demolished and in subsequent periods the old factory was used to make a kind of Worcestershire sauce (not the 'Original and Genuine'). Dents glove manufacturers were still working there in the 1950s, in the same rooms used by William Evett for glove making in the 18th century. Incredibly, many of the original buildings were still standing in the 1950s but no detailed survey was made prior to their total demolition. The site is now a car park beside the Worcester technical college.

Warranted
The Chamberlain* and Grainger, Wood & Co*. factories c.1805 marked many of their teapots with their name and Worcester together with the word 'Warranted'. This indicates that their pots were warranted not to crack or discolour during use, a common fault with early English teapots. The so-called hybrid hard-paste bodies used by these two makers did indeed hold up well to use with boiling liquid. As Ann Chamberlain remarked in a letter sent in January 1796:

> On every painted teapot we write *Warranted* which never having in one instance failed think cannot be too much mentioned to our customers, flying being formerly a principal complaint but that will never happen to the goods of Messrs Chamberlain.

Warwick Vase
No other single object from antiquity had quite such an effect on English porcelain as the Warwick vase. When I saw the original for the first time in the Burrell Collection in Glasgow I was staggered by the scale of the monumental Roman marble urn. I had become so accustomed to seeing 19th century copies in porcelain and silver that I tended to forget these were merely miniatures. One senior silver specialist has claimed that the change from generally oval to round tureen shapes in England c.1815-20 was almost entirely due to this famous vase. Direct copies of the Warwick vase are rare, the modelled heads and ornament being difficult to reproduce. Chamberlain did, however make a number of exact copies complete with heads, at least by 1818 when they sold a pair for an incredible £31.10s. These were called ice pails* but probably did not have covers and would have been used as wine coolers*. The same form was still made in the Chamberlain and Co. period after 1840 (Colour Plate 95). Chamberlain's ice pails based on the Warwick vase varied in height and had added covers, but always copied the border of modelled vines and twisted handles. They accompanied standard dessert service shapes and are similar to ice pails made at Derby and Coalport. Flight, Barr and Barr introduced their version c.1815 as a vase or wine cooler. They chose to copy only the approximate form of the body and twisted handles of the Roman vase and made these in several sizes, some with tall plinths (*see* illustration on page 360). Grainger, Lee and Co. made a shape only very loosely based on the Warwick vase with a border of applied strawberries rather than vines.

Warwick Vase. A Barr, Flight and Barr vase, the general form inspired by the Warwick vase, painted with a fine picturesque landscape, 9½ in. (24cm). (Delomosne.)*

Wasters
Pieces of porcelain which went wrong during manufacture and were therefore discarded. Some wasters were ground up and reused in the body as grog*, but a vast number, usually fragmented, were dumped on or near the sites of the porcelain factories. Finding a waster on a kiln site is undoubted proof that such a piece had been made there. *See* **Excavations on the Factory Sites** and Colour Plate 1.

Watch Holders
It is said that families who could not afford to own a clock would place a pocket watch in a holder when it was not being worn. While this is a nice idea it is unlikely to have been the case in Worcester where Chamberlain watch holders would have been costly things in their own right. They did provide an attractive alternative to placing a watch on a dressing table. Most porcelain watch holders were made inexpensively in Staffordshire but Chamberlain made several versions, all very great rarities. The Apollo watch stand of c.1795 was one of the first early Chamberlain figures to be identified and helped Geoffrey Godden to piece together the career of John Toulouse*. Flight and Grainger watch holders are not recorded.

Watteau Figure Decoration
The so-called *Fête Galante* paintings by Watteau, Lancret and others were to have enormous influence on porcelain

Watteau Figure Decoration. *The* chinoiserie* *figures on this most impressive scale blue* ground vase have been attrbuted to John Donaldson*, although the foliage, birds and insects are likely to be by another hand, square mark*, c.1768-70, 11½ in. (29cm). (Dyson Perrins Museum.)*

decoration, not only in France at Sèvres* but especially at Meissen* where the name of Watteau had become associated with the style by the middle of the 18th century. In England the style was very important at Chelsea and it is likely that any Worcester Watteausque decoration was copied from Chelsea rather than Meissen directly. This very European style of figure painting is rare at Worcester. A series of leaf dishes c.1756 were painted with Watteau style figures in monochrome, but generally the style was not used until the late 1760s. There are two basic forms — European and chinoiserie* — as it must be remembered that Watteau also excelled in the Chinese taste.

The Worcester factory was probably responsible for the Lord Dudley* service of European musicians in a manner

Weed Gilding. *A Flight, Barr and Barr shell-shaped dessert dish with a ground of characteristic gold weed, impressed mark*, c.1825, 9in. (23cm). (Phillips.)*

Wet Blue Ground. *A scallop-edged dessert plate, with the typical solid underglaze blue ground known as wet blue. Painted with a fable of a cat and mouse in a very different hand from that of O'Neale*, crescent mark*, c.1775, 7½in. (19cm). (Phillips.)*

associated with Watteau. Other European figure painting was the work of Giles* and some fine examples were painted in monochrome c.1770. Chinese musicians, looking very fanciful and distinctly European in their manner and expressions, were painted on plain teawares, large chocolate cups, and most impressive hexagonal vases, all using reserved panels on scale blue* grounds. The male and female musicians differ little from piece to piece and are always placed among rococo* chinoiserie trellis or scrollwork and colourful foliage. The painting has been linked to John Donaldson* which may well be so, but there is little firm evidence, except that identical painting occurs more frequently on Chelsea porcelain of the Gold Anchor period. The painting was probably carried out at Worcester c.1768-70 by a painter who had come from Chelsea.

A distinctive range of pieces painted with panels of Watteau style figures reserved on claret* grounds is nowadays treated with considerable suspicion and is discussed here under **Redecoration,** Group VId.

Webster, Moses

A very fine flower artist who was born in Derby in 1792 and apprenticed at the Derby porcelain works. He was mentioned by Solomon Cole* as having been a pupil at Thomas Baxter's China Painting School in Worcester. There remains slight doubt as he had been in Derby until 1817 when he probably moved to London, working for Thomas Randall. Webster exhibited in London in 1818 and returned to Derby c.1820 where he died in 1870. It is probable Webster was only at Worcester for a very short time. The Derby historian Haslem reported that while at Worcester one of the other painters composed a verse about Moses Webster's flower painting:

If Moses composes
His posies of roses
Of sweeter he can't them
compose

No flower else that grows
Can compare with the rose
If you doubt it consult
your own nose

Weed Gilding

Weed or seaweed pattern was popular at Flights and Chamberlains from the early 19th century as well as at Graingers from c.1805. A very simple design in gold, it was applied to various ground colours and can range from very delicate filaments to heavy gnarled branches. A variation used at Graingers has hanging threads of weed and was known as twigging*.

Wet Blue Ground

A somewhat appropriate name used to describe the solid underglaze blue* ground introduced at Worcester c.1765-8, inspired, no doubt, by the *gros bleu* of Sèvres* and the 'mazarine blue' ground of Chelsea. Worcester managed the difficult task of controlling the cobalt blue to a considerable degree and were more successful than any other English factory in producing an even colour. Nevertheless, Worcester's wet blue ground can frequently smudge and dribble into the reserved panels. Scale blue* and powder blue* were therefore used as more costly but more reliable alternatives. It is apparent from the 1769 Worcester sale catalogue that the term mazarine was used for all of Worcester's blue grounds including scale blue. Wet blue as a term was first used by 19th century collectors and applies only to pieces made up until the early 1780s.

Wet Mustard Pots
See **Mustard Pots**

Wet Brush Style

One of the distinctive forms of painting associated with the Giles* workshop. The enamel colour is applied very thickly in bold blocks of colour with only minimal fine detail. Seen at its best with fancy birds on rockwork, the style was also used effectively for fruit. Very large, totally imaginary insects are another distinctive feature of the wet brush style. In the past this work has been attributed to a single hand, the so-called 'wet brush painter', although it is most likely that more than one artist would have been involved.

Colour Plate 94. ***Wall, Dr. John.*** *A portrait of Dr Wall, at one time believed to be a self-portrait but this is now considered most unlikely. Although he was only one of fifteen original partners, Dr Wall will always be regarded as the founder of the Worcester porcelain factory. (Dyson Perrins Museum.)*

Colour Plate 95. ***Warwick Vase.*** *A Chamberlain and Co. wine cooler* copying the famous Roman urn, brightly gilded on a grey marbled* ground, printed mark, c.1840-5, 9in. (23cm). (Dyson Perrins Museum.)*

Colour Plate 96. ***Wine Cisterns.*** *The largest and most impressive shape known from the early years of the factory, a powerful rococo* shape inspired by silver, c.1753-5, 24½in. (62cm) wide overall. (Phillips.)*

Colour Plate 97. ***Wine Funnels.*** *An elegant form belonging to the scratch cross* class, painted in* famille rose* *enamels, 3⅞in. (9.8cm). (Phillips.)*

Wheatsheaf Pattern
The name associated with a rich pattern popular around 1770 featuring alternate *Kakiemon** panels of foliage between deep underglaze blue* stripes, each containing an iron-red *mon* or circular badge. The contemporary name for the *Wheatsheaf* pattern was probably *Rich Queen's** pattern. *See also* **Banded Hedge** pattern.

White Porcelain
While some factories specialised in the production of white porcelain, Bow in particular, the Worcester factory seems largely to have avoided this area of the market. It concentrated on useful wares rather than sculptural ornaments and so needed forms of decoration which would compete with Chinese coloured wares and blue and white.

The Bristol factory, according to Dr Pocock*, was making in 1750 'beautiful white sauceboats adorned with reliefs of festoons which sell for sixteen shillings a pair'. Only two marked examples of these survive today although coloured ones are slightly more plentiful, the enamelling added at Worcester. Occasionally Worcester made white creamboats* or sauceboats* but these look unfinished, and indeed they tend to have firing faults which suggest they left the factory in an unfinished state rather than as white porcelain. Most surviving white Worcester is likely to be unfinished, with just a few exceptions, as the factory preferred at least a blue and white border to no decoration at all. Wigornia* type creamboats and some cornucopias* are crisply moulded with scenes and have only blue borders inside. Perhaps the factory was afraid of unauthorised outside decoration* such as that which now enriches virtually all the white Meissen and Chinese porcelain from the 18th century.

The earliest Worcester shape probably intended to be left white is a small lobed ovoid vase embossed with a Chinese figure by a fence, c.1752 (*see* Simon Spero's *Worcester Porcelain, The Klepser Collection*, item 12). The remarkable wine cistern* in Colour Plate 96 and a huge rococo tureen* (recorded by Binns* with just a date 1751) are from the same period but were probably intended to have been coloured. A barrel-shaped teapot* was made c.1760 with embossed moulded decoration of a Chinese fishing scene, and several white examples of these are known. A barrel-shaped milk jug* was likewise embossed with scrollwork. A number of dolphin ewer* creamboats are known just in white from c.1765-8, and moulded white cutlery handles* were made in *Chrysanthemum** pattern and another moulded pattern c.1758. From the late 1760s a number of elaborate ornaments have survived in white, such as several frill vases*, a pot of modelled flowers* and a small number of figures*. These are connected with the modeller John Toulouse* who also modelled a kingfisher and a figure of Apollo made in white at Chamberlains factory, c.1792.

Whitton Anglers Pattern
A popular overglaze transfer print attributed to Robert Hancock*. The subject was taken from part of a larger composition engraved by William Woollett entitled *A view of the Canal and of the Gothic Tower in the garden of His Grace the Duke of Argyle at Whitton in Middlesex*. The *Whitton Anglers*, which depicts two ladies dressed in the most inappropriate fashion to spend a day angling, was probably introduced c.1760 and continued into the 1770s. It was used on various sized mugs and jugs and coloured-in examples are recorded.

Whorl Pattern
See **Charlotte, Queen, pattern**

Whitton Anglers Pattern. *A finely detailed print in black on a cylindrical mug, c.1765, 4¾in. (12cm). (Phillips.)*

Wigornia Creamboat. *This celebrated creamboat is the only example surviving with the embossed mark 'Wigornia' on the base, c.1752, 2½in. (6.5cm). (Dyson Perrins Museum.)*

Wigornia Creamboat
The 'WIGORNIA' mark was inscribed in reverse into the mould of a creamboat so that it would appear embossed across the base. The potter who scratched the letters into the mould made a mistake with the final 'a' which appears back to front on the only creamboat recorded with this mark. Although eight different models of Wigornia-type creamboats* are recorded only one single example is known with this mark. First offered for sale in 1946 and rejected by C.W. Dyson Perrins as too expensive at £350, it was subsequently bought at Sotheby's in 1973 by the Dyson Perrins Museum for a record price of £20,000.

It is generally held that this is the first piece of porcelain made at Worcester, the name coming from the Latin name for Worcester. Embossed name marks were used at Bristol and the tradition could well have been continued at Worcester very

Wigornia Type Creamboats. *The subtle moulded decoration is shown to best effect when left plain white*. The border inside is in underglaze blue*, c.1752-4, 4½ in. (11.5cm). (Phillips.)*

early on. It is not a first piece in the same sense as the 'First Day' vases made at Etruria by Josiah Wedgwood and inscribed as such. More correctly, the celebrated cream jug should be regarded as a very early piece of Worcester bearing a unique mark. The fact that the Wigornia model is also found unmarked suggests that the mark was incised into an existing mould. The shape is derivative of English silver, where embossed chinoiserie* scenes are known from the 1740s, although no exact parallel between the jug and a silver piece has been recorded.

Wigornia Type Creamboats

It is really quite extraordinary how many different versions of these delightful creamboats were made within just a couple of years, c.1752-4. So far eight totally different embossed landscapes have been recorded although the hexagonal shape remains constant. Two different moulded scroll handles were used. Samuel Clarke, and subsequently Dr Paul Riley, have classified these boats according to the modelling as types A to H, although it should be remembered that only one single creamboat bears the Wigornia mark. Blue and white versions usually have plain white modelling on the outside accompanied by a painted inner border, although two examples are recorded with the modelling unsuccessfully picked out in blue. The enamelled creamboats are always in very bright colours reminiscent of enamelled Staffordshire saltglazed stoneware where embossed landscape decoration was also used. The interiors are painted either with ribboned emblems* or floral sprigs.

Wilkins, Stephen

Not a potter, but a vinegar merchant, he provided backing for the young Thomas Grainger* to enable the establishment of a china factory on his land in Lowesmoor in 1805 or 1806. The firm of Grainger, Wood and Wilkins* traded as Grainger and Co.* or Grainger, Wood and Co.* and Stephen Wilkins seems to have played little part in the running of the factory. His involvement probably terminated before June 1809 although part of his land was still leased to the factory in 1818.

William IV Service

In 1831 Flight, Barr and Barr won the commission for a dessert service to celebrate the accession of William IV. The King mostly patronised the Rockingham factory, but he possibly remembered the remarkable services Flights had made for him when he was Duke of Clarence*. The William IV service followed a traditional design with a deep blue ground. The royal arms were decorated by John Bly* whose particular speciality was giving a natural expression to the lion supporting the arms. All of the border panels contained heraldic devices against a soft primrose background and the panels were framed in raised gold and white enamel jewelling possibly by Ishmael Sherwin*. R.W. Binns* regarded the service as the most beautiful of all Flight's work.

Williams, Joseph

According to Geoffrey Godden in his *Chamberlain-Worcester Porcelain*, Joseph Williams was a traveller for Chamberlains from 1791, receiving expenses for a journey to Bath and Bristol and commission payments. He appears to have been partly responsible for the running of the factory's shop and also in some way connected with the burnishing of the gilding. A small mug is recorded inscribed in brightly burnished gold underneath 'JW November 5th 1797' and this may well refer to Joseph Williams. Another Joseph Williams, possibly a son, worked as a china painter for Kerr and Binns and was also probably engaged earlier at Chamberlains, specialising in fine landscapes. (*See* illustration on page 366.)

Wine Cisterns

The only example surviving from the mid-1750s (Colour Plate 96) was sold by Phillips in London in June 1989 and I was fortunate to have been able to recognise its significance. Based on a silver form and strongly rococo* in feel, it is plain white with heavy embossed scrollwork cartouches and borders, the handles modelled as Bacchic half-figures rising out of cornucopia shapes. Considering its size it had fired remarkably well. The handles show how far Worcester was

Williams, Joseph. *A Chamberlain small mug with yellow ground and panel of* Fancy Birds* *by George Davis*. The inscription dated 1797 in bright gold possibly relates to Joseph Williams. 3in. (7.5cm). (Phillips.)*

behind its contemporaries in the area of figure modelling in the 1750s. Chamberlain sold a 'pair wine cisterns, Queen Elizabeth pattern' for fourteen guineas in October 1813, but it is not known what form they took.

Wine Coolers

Many open shaped vases were actually made as wine coolers but this is not always apparent unless they have survived with a metal liner which some came with originally. They were used principally for cooling wine bottles, the glass bottle or decanter embedded in crushed ice. They served a quite different purpose from ice pails* and were not part of dessert services. The Chamberlain order books for 1810 include the following helpful entry: '2 ice pails complete/ 4 wine coolers, rather smaller than ice pails'. An earlier entry in April 1792 mentions '4 ice pails for decanters with plated pans', clearly referring to metal liners for the ice.

The earliest Worcester wine coolers date from around 1775 and are great rarities. An example in the Frank Lloyd Collection (catalogue no. 181) in the British Museum was decorated in the Giles* workshop with panels of classical urns and a deep blue ground. The shape is more waisted than an ice pail and has scallop shell handles. Flight's factory made far more wine coolers than any other factory, although they are still rarely seen as they were so costly when they were made.

Colour Plate 99. ***Yellow Grounds.*** *A group of wares with yellow grounds, comprising a junket dish, c.1760, 9in. (23cm); a coffee pot, c.1758, 8⅞in. (22.5cm); a butter cooler, c.1757, 5½in. (14cm) wide and a scale yellow cup and saucer, crossed swords marks*, c.1770. (Phillips.)*

(Opposite above) Colour Plate 98. ***Yellow Grounds.*** *A basket moulded serving dish modelled after a Meissen* original, the combination of yellow and puce with brightly enamelled leaves producing a dramatic effect, c.1758-60, 11¾in. (30cm). (Phillips.)*

Wine Coolers. *The modelled grapes below the handle confirm that this Flight, Barr and Barr vase was intended as a wine cooler, painted with a view of Buildwas Abbey within weed gilding*. Unmarked except for Davenport Longport printed as a retailer's mark, c.1820, 13¾in. (35cm). (Phillips.)*

Wine Ewers. *A most curious shape so far recorded only in a single blue and white printed pattern. This example has a particularly narrow neck and is unlikely to have had a cover, crescent mark*, c.1770, 7½in. (19cm). (Phillips.)*

The vase-shaped wine cooler in the Dyson Perrins Museum, painted c.1816 by Thomas Baxter* with a view of Carisbrooke Castle, must rank as possibly the finest of all pieces of Flight period Worcester. Usually thought of as a vase, the grapes and vine leaves underneath the handle confirm its actual purpose.

Chamberlain made an exact model of the Warwick vase* as a wine cooler, c.1840 (Colour Plate 95) and previously they produced a few truly magnificent wine coolers, undoubtedly painted by Humphrey Chamberlain jun.*, listed in the order books as '2 large ornamental wine coolers, with Baccanelian figures painted all round' (£170 in December 1811) and '1 ornamental wine cooler, rich with fine painting of Cardinal Wolsey and the Abbey of Leicester' (incredibly costly at £150 in February 1818).

Wine Ewers

The exact use of a curious shaped ewer of c.1770 is unknown, but it has been variously described as a wine ewer or a chocolate pot. The shape was made in several sizes and takes the form of a standard baluster vase applied with an additional moulded spout designed for a teapot. The handle is a loop or strap seemingly designed for a mug. One example is known with a wider neck which takes a cover. So far the shape has only been seen in a single pattern of blue printed 'Globe Flower Sprays'. The shape is so far removed from conventional coffee pot or teapot forms that an alternative use, such as for wine, seems much more likely.

Wine Funnels

Funnels must have been difficult shapes to make and fire in Worcester's early porcelain and, being so fragile, it is little wonder that these objects are such rarities today. Worcester funnels are very different from the usual cup shape of wine funnel found in silver and enamel which often contains a strainer. Instead the porcelain funnels are plain shapes thrown with great skill on a wheel, a process which probably accounts for the different sizes of the finished examples. Worcester funnels belong to the scratch cross class*. Two coloured designs were used c.1754, one depicting a 'Long Eliza'* figure holding a fan, the other with flowering hollow rockwork (Colour Plate 97). In addition, even rarer blue and white funnels are either painted with a bird and peony design or formal flowers. These are certainly from the mid-1750s although slightly larger examples with underglaze transfer printed* flowers appear to be from c.1770. The blue prints tend to be smudged and as a result these blue and white funnels have been attributed to Caughley. This would seem very unlikely, however, even though the absence of a mark makes it almost impossible to prove such a statement.

Wine Tasters

The exact use of these delightful objects is not known but they would certainly have functioned as a wine scoop with a handle suitable to raise the cup to drink from. A tiny lip allows the liquid to be poured out. Worcester examples exactly copy a Chinese shape, most likely a *Yixing* stoneware wine cup, in the

Wine Tasters. *A delightful small shape with strong colouring picking out the crisp moulding, c.1765-8, 3¾in. (9.5cm). (Phillips.)*

form of half a peach raised on leaves. It is not certain whether the moulded basketwork ground is a Worcester invention, however. Worcester examples date from c.1765-8, are about 3⅞in. (10cm) across and do not vary except for the painting of the inner border. All are painted in bright colours and none has been seen in blue and white.

Wishbone-Handled Cups
Although sometimes referred to as custard cups*, it seems most likely that the small bell-shaped cups were intended for coffee as they are known decorated with a great many different teaware patterns and some have survived as parts of services (*see* Colour Plate 89). None, however, has survived with a cover which seems to belong in any way. The shape is possibly derived from a very different handle used earlier at Meissen* and generally known as a *tau* handle because it resembles a letter 'T'. Alternatively, a pointed handle was used rarely in English silver. The Worcester cups date from c.1756-60 and occur in blue and white, coloured and overglaze printed patterns.

Wishbone-handled Cups. *A pleasing example painted in blue with the so-called* Walk in the Garden *pattern, workman's mark*, c.1756, 2⅜in. (6cm). (Phillips.)*

Wolfe, General
The victor of Quebec tragically died in 1759 and the Worcester mugs commemorating his exploits date from c.1760-5 and are probably the rarest of the series of Worcester commemoratives. General Wolfe's portrait was copied by Hancock* from an engraving by Richard Houston after a sketch by Captain Smith. He is shown in profile, usually flanked by Fame and Minerva. An exceptionally rare version in the Dyson Perrins Museum is transfer printed* in dry blue* enamel.

Wood, John
The identity of the artist responsible for the distinctive figure painting on early Chamberlain porcelain is provided by several references in the factory records. As early as 1793 the stocklist included '2 jarrs, 1 beaker, Wood's figures £1.4s', and in August 1805 the factory sold '2 chocolate & stands, figures, Woods, 4 guineas each'. Other references give his full name of John Wood. The painting of many classical figures has frequently been incorrectly attributed to Thomas Baxter* or else Humphrey Chamberlain jun.* but as a painter of figures Wood was accomplished rather than exceptional. Early examples, such as the two nymphs adorning Satyr, occur on Caughley porcelain as well as Chamberlain's own porcelain, as on the dish illustrated under the King of Hanover service*. This important service with different figure centres was probably made in 1796.

John Wood's work copied engravings and in 1798 the

Wood, John. *A set of three early Chamberlain beaker-shaped ornaments each in three sections with orange and gold grounds, painted with very typical classical subjects, unmarked, c.1800, central vase 7⅝in. (19.5cm). (Phillips, New York.)*

factory's stock of books and prints was valued by 'J. Wood' who was clearly well acquainted with them. The same subjects copied from prints occur on different shapes and are frequently titled in gold underneath the figure panels. One large group of figures representing 'Venus attired by the Graces' was painted by John Wood on vases* and also occurs as a series of Chamberlain bat prints*. These prints seem to convey the same mannerisms as Wood's paintings and it is possible Wood provided the etchings from which the prints were made.

The 'Wood' style of figure painting does not occur after c.1803-6 and by 1807 Humphrey Chamberlain jun. became the factory's principal figure painter. As a boy Humphrey may have been trained by John Wood but developed into a much more competent artist. This could have prompted Wood's departure at the end of 1805 or 1806 to join another Chamberlain employee, Thomas Grainger*, in establishing their own factory of Grainger, Wood and Co.* The John Wood who was in partnership with Grainger was listed as a 'China Painter'. There remains slight doubt about the correct identity of this John Wood as no pieces of Grainger porcelain are known with figure subjects resembling the Chamberlain 'Wood's figures'. Fine hunting subjects such as on the Grace mugs* illustrated could well represent John Wood's choice of a new style. The partnership of Grainger, Wood and Co. was dissolved in 1811 and Wood probably left the factory at this time.

'Worcester' Mark

The painted name of the city is incorporated into many factory marks but one particular form of marking presents great problems in identification. A class of porcelain from c.1840 is usually marked just with the word 'Worcester' painted on the base together with a relatively low pattern number. The wares themselves are of Staffordshire origin, many from the Bowers factory, and these were presumably decorated in Worcester by an independent artist or studio. Geoffrey Godden has suggested that these pieces could be the work of Conningsby Norris* and this theory would fit as Norris was decorating on his own in Worcester from about 1835 until the 1850s. There is no actual evidence apart from the similar date and the fact that no other group of decorated porcelain can be suggested as Norris' work.

Worcester Tonquin Manufacture

The original partnership deeds drawn up in June 1751 were entitled 'Articles for Carrying on the Worcester Tonquin Manufacture'. This is the sole reference to the company's intended name which was never used in any kind of advertisements. The Bow factory had chosen to style itself 'New Canton' and Worcester possibly had a similar idea in mind. They probably had a change of thought about this very soon afterwards and in 1752 were using the title 'Worcester Porcelain Manufactory'.

Wortley Montagu, Lady Mary. *A pair of lobed plates decorated in the Giles* workshop, with scale blue* ground and rich tooled gilding*, square marks*, c.1770, 9½in. (24cm). (Phillips.)*

Workmen's Marks

As part of the work for the revised edition of *Worcester Blue and White Porcelain*, Lawrence Branyan carried out a statistical analysis of all blue and white datable before c.1760. His conclusions still leave many questions unanswered and we cannot claim to begin to understand the true meaning of the painted marks which were used. They are not painters' marks in so far as they do not refer to a single craftsman who painted that piece. The same mark appears on pieces clearly painted by artists of differing abilities and there also seem to be far more different marks than there could possibly have been painters. Similarly, we felt it was impossible for the marks to relate to decorating sections, such as small teams of a foreman and his apprentices, as there are slightly more than sixty different marks known to us, some used far more often than others. Evidence precludes any weight being placed on the notion that the marks are date codes or linked to individual patterns. They are clearly some kind of tally mark using a form of factory code. One of the most frequently encountered marks, the monogram 'I H' in various forms, occurs on a trial waster along with other workmen's marks and is discussed here under a separate heading (*see* **'I H' Marks**). The theory that this mark is linked in some way with Josiah Holdship* is attractive but does not begin to explain all of the other marks. Page 24 of the revised edition of *Worcester Blue and White Porcelain* illustrates a large number of different variations of some of these 'workmen's marks' which occur on about fifty per cent of early blue and white Worcester as well as occasionally in coloured enamel on overglaze-decorated pieces. More work is still needed to explain fully their significance.

Wortley Montagu, Lady Mary, Pattern

Although Lady Wortley Montagu had died in 1762, before any pieces were made, a form of decoration from the Giles* workshop with bird panels on a scale blue* ground has for a long time been associated with her name. It was used on Worcester dessert wares c.1770-5 and can be distinguished principally by the wonderful tooled gold scrollwork and foliage surrounding the panels of typical Giles 'dishevelled'* birds and characteristic Giles flower centres. Gerald Coke, in his book *In Search of James Giles*, identifies seven different versions of the pattern which clearly did not comprise a single service. It is not clear, however, which of the versions matched the set once owned by Lady Mary's descendants. Therefore, the name has to be used with caution and 'Lady Mary Wortley Montagu type' would be a more correct form of identification for the several different patterns. The decoration is always of the highest quality, using finely potted 'blanks' with well controlled scale blue.

Y

Yates, James
The manager of Chamberlain's London shop at 155 New Bond Street which opened in 1816. From records which survive it is clear that he personally purchased the entire stock from the company in 1839, only to sell it back to the new partnership in 1840, in what turned out to be a shrewd move. Yates remained as manager at a salary of £400 plus £100 expenses per year, and continued to live rent-free on the shop premises. He clearly understood the London trade and proposed that the new company traded as Chamberlain and Co. instead of its new name Worcester Royal Porcelain Co. which he felt would be less successful for business. After argument over the value of the stock which was settled in Yates' favour, he resigned in June 1840, receiving just over £4,300 in cash rather than shares in the company. The stock included earthenware sets bought from other factories and a

Yellow Tiger Pattern. *A fine plate in the style of Meissen* but the pattern probably adapted slightly by Worcester, c.1765-70, 9¼in. (23.5cm). (Dyson Perrins Museum.)*

great quantity of glass. Unfortunately for the company, this glass in particular had been greatly overvalued and cost them nearly £1,250 from Yates. Four years later much still remained and it became clear that they had failed to allow for so many sets being incomplete as well as mostly old-fashioned stock and sample patterns which could never be sold for the price Yates had received.

Yellow Grounds
A successful yellow ground colour was difficult to control in the 18th century and consequently is scarce and desirable from any factory. Worcester probably produced more yellow ground wares than any other English factory prior to 1780, although it is likely that only a minority of the surviving pieces are totally authentic. So much controversy surrounds these wares that it is unlikely the true picture will ever be sorted out.

The first yellow ground at Worcester was probably introduced c.1757. H. Rissik Marshall was able to confirm this early date by examining the arms of Errol on a very fine armorial* yellow ground jug. These could only apply to the fourteenth Countess in her own right and she died in 1758. Significantly, the arms are enclosed in a panel framed with puce scrollwork. Indeed, most of the earlier examples of Worcester's yellow ground incorporate puce as a form of border or edging (*see* Colour Plate 98). Junket dishes*, bough pots* and other special shapes were made using strong yellow grounds during the 1760s, almost invariably edged in puce (Colour Plate 99). Teawares, however, were seldom decorated in this way, with the exception of some coffee pots* and sauceboats*. One popular pattern used on mugs* and large jugs* c.1760 combined a pale yellow ground with large panels of Chinese riverscapes in puce monochrome, a particularly successful combination and always of the highest quality.

Without a combination of puce and yellow ground, it is necessary to treat any piece with caution. The important criterion with which to assess such pieces is to judge whether the item would still be complete in itself if the yellow ground were taken away. Well-known patterns such as the *Two Quail** pattern, or any Chinese figure painting is likely to have been subject to redecoration*. Similarly, standard formal flower painting, in colours or dry blue*, is most unlikely to occur on a genuine yellow ground. It is important to look for evidence of re-firing, such as blackening of the unglazed footrims.

Yellow seems to have gone out of favour during the 1770s and convincing examples from this period are particularly scarce. There was a revival of interest c.1790 probably inspired by Derby where some very successful pieces were made. Flight and Barr used a strong yellow which tended to over-fire and can be uneven, somewhat matt, or covered with black specks. When fired successfully these Flight period wares can be quite stunning. Chamberlain had even more difficulty controlling their yellow ground which is usually very uneven. As a result they tended to restrict the use of yellow to borders only and all-over yellow grounds are rarely seen. By the 1820s, however, it was possible to control the colours very much more successfully and all factories made a number of different forms of yellow, mostly somewhat pale and closer to primrose than custard.

Yellow Scale Grounds
See **Scale Yellow Grounds**

Yeo, Admiral, Service. *A Chamberlain dessert tureen with very rich decoration including the Admiral's crest and motto, printed marks, c.1815-20, 7½in. (19cm). (Bearnes, Torquay.)*

Yellow Tiger Pattern
Originally a *Kakiemon** pattern which was very popular at Meissen*. At Worcester this occurs on lobed plates, c.1768-72, which follow a Meissen shape and so Worcester seems to have been copying Meissen rather than Japan* directly. The design features a pale yellow-coloured tiger entwined around a bamboo plant, and in the Worcester version there is usually an intricate floral scroll border in red. Variations on the design were also made by Barr, Flight and Barr and Chamberlain, probably as replacements for Meissen or Japan. In the past there has been considerable confusion over the name of this pattern. *Yellow Tiger* has sometimes been called *Bengal Tyger*, a name which is usually associated with the pattern called *Dragon in Compartments*.

Yeo, Admiral Service
One of the most important Chamberlain armorial* services was made for Sir James Yeo who had ordered a full breakfast, tea and dessert service in 1815. Like his famous predecessor, Admiral Nelson*, Yeo chose a pattern from stock, in this case number 298 which had a richly gilded deep blue border with panels of Japan* foliage. The painting of his crest and motto on every piece cost 10s. each time, and this accounted for a far greater amount than the cost of the porcelain and border decoration. The set was so lavish that it was not invoiced to Sir James' estate until 1820, two years after he was killed on a journey home from Jamaica.

Appendix 1

A Survey of Marks

It is fortunate that a very high proportion of Worcester porcelain bears a factory mark. Indeed, in the eighteenth century only Chelsea marked on a more regular basis. There are many anomalies concerned with Worcester's marking, however, leaving questions almost impossible to answer. Why, for example, did they mark the majority of their blue and white and patterns with blue grounds, while purely coloured wares were hardly ever marked?

The earliest mark used at Bristol, embossed in the mould, would have presented two significant problems. Firstly, being cut into the mould, these marks inevitably became worn. More importantly, the name of the factory so clearly inscribed would have prevented china dealers from passing off copies as true Chinese porcelain, their main competition. Worcester had to build up its reputation and sold primarily to dealers. The workmen's marks in blue or colours before 1760 must have been some sort of factory code rather than for actual identification, but they could be said to have an oriental appearance which some of the dealers must have welcomed.

The fame of Worcester's 'common sort of blue and white', unequalled in England for consistent quality, seems to have called out for a mark. Just why a crescent should have been chosen is unclear. It is frequently suggested that this derived from the arms of the Warmstry family whose house the factory had taken over, but there is no firm evidence for this. The crescent, printed by c.1757 and on painted wares after c.1760, was their first unique mark. The fact that the crescent was copied at Lowestoft and, indeed, on Chinese porcelain itself, indicates that the mark had come to represent a quality product.

The Meissen crossed swords, Chantilly hunting horn and mock Chinese marks were clear attempts to pass their wares off as foreign. The square mark was possibly a compromise, appearing vaguely oriental and yet, in England at least, uniquely Worcester. The letter 'W' seems a much more obvious choice for a Worcester factory mark, and yet was seldom used, certainly before the 1770s. While the crescent continued to be used throughout the 1780s on printed services, a new form of marking was employed on heavily printed Chinese patterns. It has been suggested that by using disguised numerals to resemble Chinese characters, Worcester's traditional customers would not have been aware of the low levels to which the factory had succumbed, but this seems a most unlikely explanation for what must have been a commercial decision.

The factory was the first English china maker to use the name of the proprietor as a mark rather than the place of manufacture. Thomas Flight possibly anticipated future competition in the city of Worcester and wished to build up the reputation of his porcelain using his own name, Flights, from c.1782. The arrival of Martin Barr was apparently commemorated by the new mark of an incised letter 'B', a most unlikely choice as it was very much a partnership, the firm always trading as Flight and Barr.

Before the 1790s Worcester porcelain had meant only one manufacturer but the break-away of Chamberlain and subsequently Grainger saw new competition, all keen to make the most of the reputation Worcester porcelain had attained. To publicise their products the rival firms had to mark the porcelain not only with their full names but also, frequently, the address of their principal showrooms in Worcester and in London. Changes of partnerships and shop addresses offer vital clues to dating Worcester porcelain. It is consequently very unusual to find any Chamberlain or Flight porcelain unmarked. Grainger on the other hand sold much of its more domestic ware through other china dealers and as a result only marked their more important products. Independent china painters in Worcester also seem to have avoided marks on the whole, probably to enable their wares to be offered just as Worcester Porcelain. Doe and Rogers and Sparks are exceptions, however.

The following pages do not set out to be a complete listing of every mark used at Worcester. I have tried to be as comprehensive as possible, but it has to be realised that the range of markings used over such a period is enormous and no volume could ever record them all. Printed marks will appear exactly the same on every piece, but painted marks will inevitably vary considerably, especially on smaller pieces where there was a problem accommodating every word of a long inscription. I have avoided repetitious copying of only slight variations of marks, and also accept that popular marks like the crescent, square and 'W' do occur in many other forms, although all are essentially the same. Research into the significance of the marks continues and I should be delighted to hear from collectors with details of any marks not recorded here.

No.	Mark	Description	Date
1.	Bristol	Embossed letters	c.1749-51
1a	Bristoll	ditto	c.1749-51
2.		Embossed letters, letter a reversed	c.1752-53
3.		'Scratch Cross' mark, incised on base usually below or opposite handle	c.1754-56
3a.		ditto	c.1754-56
3b.		ditto	c.1754-56
4.	Workmen's Marks (*see also page 378*)	Painted in blue, usually on base, occasionally under handle; sometimes more than one mark on a single piece. More rarely painted in colour	c.1753-60
5.		Painted in blue on large jugs or vases	c.1758-60
6.		Printed in blue on teaware	c.1757-60
7.		Painted in blue, many variations in size and form	c.1760-90
8.		Painted in red or gold on special productions or some Oriental patterns	c.1770-80
9.		Printed in blue	c.1762-85
10.		Printed in blue various letters or numbers used	c.1770-75
11.		Printed in blue on Fence pattern saucers only	c.1768-75
12.		Painted in blue, many variations in form	c.1762-75
13.		Painted in blue on one Chinese panelled pattern	c.1775
14.		Printed in blue	c.1770-75
15.		Painted in blue on pieces intended for overglaze European style decoration; slight variation in form	c.1765-75
16.	W P C	Painted in blue	c.1756-58
16a.	W P C	Embossed on tokens	
17.		Painted in red or brown mostly on outside-decorated wares but also some factory decoration	c.1765-78
18.		Painted in blue on copies of Chantilly	c..1775
19.		Painted in blue, many variations	c.1765-90
19a.		Square painted in blue, crescent in red, on blue-ground wares with Japan panels	c.1765-68
20.		Painted on blue on copy of a Chinese pattern	c.1755
20a.		Painted in blue on copy of a Chinese pattern	c.1758
20b.		Painted in blue on patterns with powder blue grounds	c.1760-70
20c.		Painted in blue, usually within two concentric rings	c.1770-75
21. / 21a.		Embossed or impressed on modelled or encrusted shapes, marks associated with John Toulouse. Also IT recorded on figures	c.1768-72
22.	R Hancock fecit	Printed in black, signature of Robert Hancock, various forms (with anchor of Richard Holdship)	c.1757-64
22a.	RH. Worcester		
22b.	RH		

No.	Mark	Description	Date
23.	RH	Printed in black. Possibly mark of Josiah and Richard Holdship	c.1760
24.		Printed in blue Numerals 1 to 9 disguised as Oriental characters	c.1780-90
25.	Flight	Painted in blue	c.1783-92
26.	FLIGHTS	Impressed	c.1783-92
27.	Flight	Painted in blue or enamel colours	c.1783-92
28.	Flight	Painted in blue on special productions	c.1788-92
29.	WORCESTER Manufactory FLIGHT	Printed in colour	c.1790
30.	F & B	Incised	c.1792-1804
31.	Flight & Barr. Worcester Manufacturers to their Majesties.	Painted in colour	c.1792-1804
32.	B	Incised, sometimes with added cross or single stroke	c.1792-1804
33.	BARR WORCESTER PORCELAIN MANUFACTURERS TO THE KING	Printed in colour, rare wording	c.1800
34.	BFB	Impressed	c.1804-13
35.	Barr, Flight & Barr. Worcester Flight & Barr Coventry St. London Manufacturers to their Majesties & Royal Family	Painted in colour	c.1804-13
36.	BARR FLIGHT & BARR. Royal Porcelain Works. WORCESTER. London House. No 1 Coventry Street.	Printed in colour various forms known	c.1807-13
37.	FBB	Impressed (sometimes just crown used without letters)	c.1813-40
38.	Flight, Barr & Barr Worcester	Painted in colour	c.1813-40
39.	Flight Barr & Barr Royal Porcelain Works Worcester London House 1 Coventry St.	Painted in colour various forms known	c.1813-40

CHAMBERLAIN FACTORY MARKS

No.	Mark	Description	Date
40.	CHAMBERLAIN	Painted in red on Caughley porcelain	c.1790-92
41.	Chamberlains	Painted, usually in red, sometimes with pattern no.	c.1790-1840
42.	Chamberlains Worcester	Painted in colour or sometimes gold	c.1790-1840
43.	Chamberlain, Worcester Warranted ~ No 66	Painted beneath covers	c.1790-1805
44.	T	Impressed or embossed, possible mark of John Toulouse	c.1795-1800
45.	Chamberlains Worcester & 63, Piccadilly, London.	Printed with Piccadilly address	c.1814-16
46.	Chamberlains Worcester Manufacturers to their Royal Highnesses The Prince Regent & Duke of Cumberland	Painted in colour	c.1815

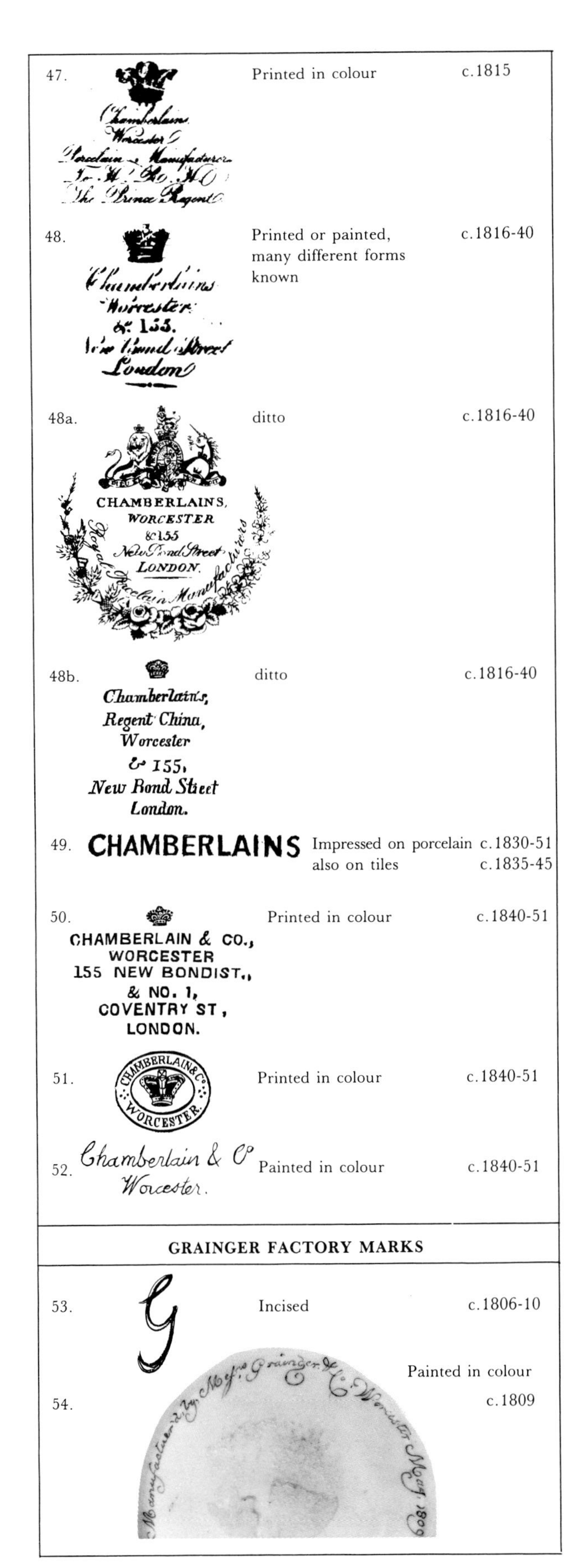

No.	Mark	Description	Date
47.	Chamberlains Worcester Porcelain Manufacturers To H.R.H. The Prince Regent	Printed in colour	c.1815
48.	Chamberlains Worcester & 155. New Bond Street London	Printed or painted, many different forms known	c.1816-40
48a.	CHAMBERLAINS, WORCESTER & 155 New Bond Street LONDON. Royal Porcelain Manufacturers	ditto	c.1816-40
48b.	Chamberlain's, Regent China, Worcester & 155, New Bond Street London.	ditto	c.1816-40
49.	CHAMBERLAINS	Impressed on porcelain also on tiles	c.1830-51 c.1835-45
50.	CHAMBERLAIN & CO., WORCESTER 155 NEW BOND ST., & NO. 1, COVENTRY ST, LONDON.	Printed in colour	c.1840-51
51.	CHAMBERLAIN & Co WORCESTER	Printed in colour	c.1840-51
52.	Chamberlain & Co Worcester.	Painted in colour	c.1840-51

GRAINGER FACTORY MARKS

No.	Mark	Description	Date
53.	G	Incised	c.1806-10
54.	Manufactured by Mess. Grainger & Co Worcester May 1809	Painted in colour	c.1809
55.	Grainger & co Worcester	Painted	c.1806-
56.	Grainger Wood & Co Worcester Warr. 232	Painted, usually under teapot covers	c.1806-11
57.	Grainger Lee & Co Worcester	Printed or painted various forms used	c.1814-37
58.	GRAINGER LEE & CO WORCESTER	Impressed on figure and animal models	c.1825-37
59.	Thomas Grainger & Co Royal China Works Worcester	Painted in colour usually red	c.1837-9 or possibly from 1830
60.	Published (date) by George Grainger Worcester	Incised on biscuit figures	c.1845
61.	G. Grainger Royal Porcelain Works Worcester	Printed in colour, below a crown	c.1840-60
62.	WORCESTER CORAL G G.	Initials included in name marks	c.1825-30
63.	G W Weed No.	Initials included in name marks	c.1820-50
64.	G G W S P	Impressed initials On Grainger 'Semi Porcelain' body	c.1848-60

MARKS USED BY OUTSIDE DECORATORS

No.	Mark	Description	Date
65.	Hopkins Worcester	Marked in gold Outside decorator	c.1805-10
66.	J Hadley	Painted in colour Outside decorator	c.1825
67.	Doe & Rogers Worcester	Painted in colour Outside decorators sometimes with 17 High Street address	c.1820-35
68.	Sparks Worcester	Painted in colour	c.1830-50s

No.	Mark	Description	Date
69.	SPARKS Broad St By Appointment to HER MAJESTY QUEEN ADELAIDE	Printed wording, various versions usually accompanied with 'Coalport Porcelain'	c.1830-50s
70.		Painted in red on Caughley porcelain using the blue 'S' of Caughley, possibly an outside decorator	c.1790
71.	Worcester.	Painted in red, often with pattern number, used by an outside decorator, possibly Conningsby Norris	c.1840
72.	New China Works Worcester	Painted in colour used by an outside decorator, possibly Doe & Rogers	c.1820s

4. A selection of workmen's marks. Painted in blue, usually on base, occasionally under handle; sometimes more than one mark on a single piece. More rarely painted in colour. c.1753-60.

Appendix 2

Contemporary accounts of visits to the Bristol and Worcester Porcelain Manufactories

These various accounts give a fascinating insight into the workings of a major porcelain factory. The details are at times confused, but reading these descriptions makes one realise just how little has changed in the porcelain industry, with many processes carried out in exactly the same fashion at the present day Worcester porcelain works.

2 November 1750 — Dr Richard Pococke

I went to see a manufacture lately established here, by one of the principal of the manufacture at Limehouse which failed. It is at a glasshouse, and is called Lowd'ns [word unclear] china house. They have two sorts of ware, one called stone china, which has a yellow cast, both in the ware and in the glazing, that I suppose is made of pipe clay and calcined flint. The other they call old china; this is whiter, and I suppose this is made of calcined flint and the soapy rock at Lizard Point which 'tis known they use. This is painted blue, and some is white, like the old china of a yellowish cast; another kind is white with a blueish cast, and both are called fine ornamental white china. They make very beautiful white sauceboats, adorned with reliefs of festoons, which sell for sixteen shillings a pair.

Dr Pococke's letter (Add. M.S. No. 15,800, British Museum) was first published by the Camden Society in 1888 in *Travels Through England of Dr Richard Pococke* and has since been quoted by many authorities.

1764 — Valentine Green

The Porcelain manufactory at Worcester, engages the attention of the curious, to explore the ingenious processes and apparatus made use of in the production of the finest ware in the kingdom. This factory is situate in Mardyke, near the Severn, having it on the West, Warmstry slip on the north, St Alban's church and Fish street on the east, and the Bishop's palace and the cathedral on the south. It was originally a large mansion-house, which, with its adjacent offices, is converted to a pleasing scene of art and industry. Upon the entrance of it, you are at first conducted into the counting house on the right-hand of the passage, and from thence into the throwing-room, where the ware is first formed from the clay. From this you are taken through a narrow passage, to the stove, which, a fire being placed in its centre, equally diffuses its heat to the whole; the ware is placed here to dry gradually, thereby preparing it for the succeeding operation. The next room shown is the great hall, where the ware is turned upon the lathe. In a little room adjoining, another method is carried on, called, pressing the ware on the wheel. In a great parlour of the opposite side of the building, is also turning on the lathe, with that part of the business called, handling and spouting, *i.e.* putting the hand to cups, &c, and the spouts to teapots, &c. From hence, you descend, by a flight of six or eight steps, into another pressing room, the action of which thus varies from the former; in this the clay is pressed by the hands only in the mould, but in the other by means of a wheel. From hence you are conducted to the lower regions of this work, where are the first sett of kilns; called the buisket-kilns, in which the ware is first burnt. After passing another stove, you enter the dipping or glazing room, in which the ware receives its glaze. From thence to another sett of kilns where the glazed ware is burnt. Then, crossing the coal-yard, you are shown a third sett, called streightening-kilns: in an adjoining room, the cases, or saggers, in which they burn the ware, are made. To the scraping room next shewn, all the buisket ware is brought from the first-mentioned sett of kilns, and there assorted. In the slip-house the different parts of the composition, being first levigated, are sifted thro' fine lawn seives and promiscuously blended together, afterwards dried in the slip-kilns, which are similar to the pans used in making of salt. In a room adjoining to the slip-house, you are shewn a large iron rowl, upwards of two tons weight, by the assistance of horses revolving in a grove, not much unlike a cyder mill. This rowl reduces all the hard bodies made use of in the composition to a fine powder, fit for levigation. You at length enter the painting room, where the ware receives the ornamental part of the process, and which, after burning and assorting, is completed for sale. The curious and valuable art of transferring prints on porcelain is, in this factory, arrived at, and carried on in the greatest perfection. This work is the employ and subsistence of a great number of people. . . .

This account, from Valentine Green's *A Survey of the City of Worcester* (J. Butler, 1764), concludes with a description of some of the ware, slightly adapted from an account which had appeared in the *Oxford Journal,* 7 May 1763. Green's account is reproduced in full by Dr Severne Mackenna, *Worcester Porcelain,* and also by Henry Sandon, *Worcester Porcelain.*

30 August 1766 — T. Falconer

The great improvements made in the Worcester manufactory of china would have afforded you great pleasure as it did me. It is hardly surpassed by the Vincennes, and much cheaper, they have not yet debased it by making vile attempts at human figures, but stick to the usefull.

From a letter sent from Chester by T. Falconer to C. Gray, discovered by C.W. Dyson Perrins in the Historical Manuscripts Commission, Round MSS, Birch Hall, Essex; quoted by Mackenna.

13 July 1770 — Lady Shelburne

After dinner we went to see the Manufactory of Worcester China, It is very curious, but easier to be imagin'd than that of the Pins (visited in Gloucester the day before), the Clay is first prepar'd of a White collour, & it is then turn'd, very much in the same method of any other Pottery; it then passes thro' other Hands who stamp it when it is to be fluted; or Ornamental, & it is afterwards smooth'd with a fine Tool previous to its being put into ye Oven, after Baking it is painted, & when quite dry dip'd into a White Liquid compos'd Chiefly of Arsenick, which Glazes it, & makes the collours disappear till a second burning brings them out and fixes them — Some of their China is painted with the Pencil, Others by a Copper Plate, but they make a secret of that Method, & will not let any body see it done. We saw some very fine Specimens of the Porcelaine, tho' there appears to me many things to be corrected in it, & their Sets so imperfect that I cou'd get nothing compleat to carry with me to Ireland (that was not of too great a Magnitude). I therefore bought only two Sallad Dishes of an Old China Pattern.

An added postscript on the opposite page reads:

They told us the China employ'd 600 people. If any pieces of it fail it can be Ground & mix'd up again into Clay.

Lady Sophia Shelburne kept a diary from 1766 until her death in 1771. This extract was published in a paper by John Mallet to the English Ceramic Circle, *Transactions,* Vol. 11, Pt.2, 1982, p.109. Lady Shelburne does not seem to have been nearly as observant as other visitors and her note of 600 employees has to be highly suspect. The following year Mrs Powys gives a far more believable account.

28 August 1771 — Mrs Philip Lybbe Powys

As to its china manufacture, 'tis more worth seeing than anything I hardly ever did see. They employ 160 persons, a vast number of them very little boys. There are eleven different rooms in which the employment is as follows: First room, a mill for grinding the composition to make the clay; second, the flat cakes of clay drying in ovens; third, the cakes work'd up like a paste, and formed by *the eye only* into cups, mugs, basons, tea-pots, their ingenuity and quickness at this appears like magic; fourth, making the things exactly by moulds all to one size, but they are seldom different so nice is their eye in forming; fifth, paring and chipping coffee-cups and saucers in moulds, a boy turning the wheel for each workman; sixth, making the little roses, handles, twists, and flowers one sees on the china fruit-baskets, all these stuck on with a kind of paste; seventh, scalloping saucers &c., with a pen-knife while the composition is pliable, and in this room they make the china ornamental figures; these are done in moulds, separate moulds for the limbs, and stuck on as above; eighth, the heat of this eighth room was hardly bearable, filled with immense ovens for baking the china which is put in a sort of high sieves about six feet long; ninth, glazing the china by dipping it into large tubs of liquor, and shaking it as dry as they can; tenth, some sorting the china for painting, others smoothing the bottom by grinding; eleventh, painting the china in the different patterns. I rather wonder'd they did not in one room exhibit their most beautiful china finished; but they did it seems, till finding people remain'd in it too long, and so took up too much of the men's time, so now they send it to the shops in Worcester for sale. You pay for seeing the manufacture by putting what you please in a box at the gate.

Mrs Lybbe Powys of Hardwick House wrote her account the day after her visit. It was published in 1899 in *Passages from the Diary of Mrs Lybbe Powys* and is quoted by Mackenna.

21 October 1771 — Capt. Joseph Roche R.N.

We went to the china factory, saw the whole process except the making of the composition, which is kept a secret... They make very fine figures or ornamental china, it being done much better and also cheaper at Derby: here they are obliged to mould it, but there it is cast, which is ten times as expedicious.

Capt. Roche passed through Worcester on his way by post-chaise from Liverpool. Extracts were published in the periodical *Notes and Queries,* February/March 1917.

6 and 9 August 1788 — King George III

On the afternoon of the same day [6 August], their Majesties and the Princesses attended by the Countess of Harcourt and Oxford, Lord Courtown, Colonels Goldworthy and Digby, walked to Messrs. Flight and Barr's elegant china shop in High Street, where they remained almost an hour, and greatly admired the beautiful porcelain manufactured under the direction of those gentlemen, and gave orders for an extensive assortment of it. . .

About 10 o'clock on Saturday morning, August 9th their Majesties and the three Princesses, attended by several of the nobility, visted Mr. Flight's china manufactory; as this visit was by appointment the proprietor had removed some of the branches of the manufactory for the convenience of showing the whole in three rooms; the workmen behaved with the utmost decency, and their Majesties expressed the highest satisfaction. The King gave Messrs Flight the liberty they had requested of styling themselves 'China Manufacturers to their Majesties', and wished success to the manufactory; Their Majesties giving at the same time some additional orders for their china. The King, as usual, showed great knowledge of trade and manufactures by the pertinent questions which he asked; and all the royal visitors were remarkable for their condescension, endeavouring to overcome that awe which so much honour could not but inspire. Their Majesties employed more than two hours in viewing the different departments, and left ten guineas with Mr Flight for the workmen.

This account was written by Valentine Green, and published seven years later in his *History and Antiquities of the City and Suburbs of Worcester,* 1795. Green made a mistake over the firm's name, as in 1788 the firm was still trading as Flights and only became Flight and Barr in 1792. In the same important book, Valentine Green gave an extensive account of the factory.

1795 — Valentine Green

By applying to Messrs Flight and Barr, the nobility and gentry who visit this city are conducted through their beautiful and extensive shew-rooms [no. 45 High St] and from thence have cards of admission to view the manufactory. The china works are usually shown in the following order. The first operation viewed, is that of reducing the hard bodies made use of in the composition of the china into powder, which is performed by an iron roller, upwards of two tons weight, revolving in a groove not much unlike a cider-mill. The materials are then calcined and afterwards ground at the water-mill; where by a late improvement they are levigated sufficiently fine to filter through sieves, made on purpose for this manufactory, through which no particle larger than a fifty-seventh thousandth part of a square inch can pass. The composition then in its liquid state, is dried upon the slip-kilns till it becomes of a consistency of clay; it is then taken to the throwing-room, where the ware is first formed, and from thence to the stove-room in which it is placed to dry gradually, thereby preparing it for turning and pressing. The articles being applied to the lathe, are reduced to less than half the substance in which they were at first formed; here also are seen the various methods used in pressing the different sorts of ware into their respective moulds. From this department of the works, the first set of kilns, called Buiscuit-kilns, receives the ware, and in which it is burnt near 60 hours. In the second kiln-house, is performed the ingenious operation of making straight such pieces of the china that may have been warped from a too great degree of heat in the buiscuit-kiln. Here also are made the cases, or saggars, in which the ware is burnt. On the opposite side of the building, the dipping or glazing room, in which the china receives its beautiful glaze, is next shewn. From hence it is committed to a third ordeal of fire, in another set of kilns, prepared for that purpose. The painting-room, a spacious apartment, lately enlarged to the length of near 60 feet, next exhibits its never-failing sources of entertainment and delight. After receiving here the embellishments of paintings and gilding, the ware is taken to the fourth set of kilns, called the Enamelling Kilns, wherein the gold and colours are intimately united to the substance to the glazing as to become equally durable with the ware itself. Lastly, from these kilns it is taken to the burnishing-room, where the gold receives that brilliant lustre, which has never yet been seen upon any foreign china.

In the course of the foregoing operations, many of the finer articles pass through the eight kilns several times, and are burnt, in the whole, near 200 hours. The process of printing the common ware, formerly kept a profound secret, is now openly shewn among the other operations of the manufactory.

From Valentine Green's *The History and Antiquities of the City and Suburbs of Worcester,* 1795, quoted by Henry Sandon, *Flight and Barr Worcester Porcelain.*

28 May 1796 — Charles Hatchett

We went to see the Porcelain Manufactory belonging to Messrs Flight and Barr. I have observed that the Steatites of Cornwall is used as an ingredient but could not learn the other component parts of the paste or clay (perhaps it is the decomposed Feldtspar from St Stephen in Cornwall). When the steatite is reduced to powder in a mill at Worcester, it is sent to some place about 10 miles distant to be mixed and washed: it is then brought back to W- and in a liquid state is passed through fine wire sieves, is dried and tempered with water for use.

When the ware is moulded it is of a brownish white or a very pale brown; it is then gently unperfectly dried. The bottoms and edges are then turned on a laithe and the Ribs if required are formed by pressing it in a mould, the edges are then scalloped with a knife.

The ware is then perfectly dried and is baked in a kiln, inclosed in pans of coarse clay. It then comes out in the state called Biscuit. If it is to be painted Blue (with cobalt) this is then done and the ware is again baked and then dipped into the glazing liquid which is of a pale red (perhaps contains Millium). The ware is then baked again and the blue colour strikes through the glazing. If gold or any other colour than blue is to be used these are applied after the ware is glazed. The colours appear to be glazed with oil of Turpentine. The gold appears to be used in the state of Cassius's Precipitate. When the ware is painted with this it is put into a small square brick furnace and is arranged in a square iron pan which has an iron cover with a Pipe. On this cover Kundled charcole is put till the top is full.

The gold when the ware comes out of this furnace is of a dead buff colour and is burnished by women with Burnishers made of Agate or Haematite.

The fuel used in the kilns is light Pit Coal in large masses with the appearance of charred wood in many places. Sometimes instead of pencelling the ware they use engraved copper plates which they fill up with the colouring matter, then with rollers take off the impression on a sort of soft tissue paper which they then apply to the ware and rub with cushions of flannel.

Charles Hatchett was a chemist and so was naturally more interested in the composition and materials than the processes. His diary was published by Arthur Raistrick and this extract was reproduced by Henry Sandon, *Flight and Barr Worcester Porcelain.*

1 June 1801 — Rev. Richard Warner

. . . the mixture above-mentioned consists of fifteen articles, the chief of which are, a white granite, from Cornwall, and a steatite or soap-stone, from Penzance . . . the whole quarry of which belongs to Mr Flight, who employs his own men there. The articles being first ground separately are afterwards mixed, and then calcined; the product of this process is the quantity of small blue and white lumps, which being thrown into a mill, and ground with soft water, a liquid of the consistence of thick cream is produced, perfectly white. This is passed through a lawn sieve, and then poured into vats, heated by outside flues in order to consolidate; the degree of heat applied to them being kept under the boilding temperature. The water being gradually evaporating by these means from the contents of the vats, an hard clay remains in the room of the liquid, which is brought into a stone apartment to be *tempered,* that is, wetted with water, beaten with a wooden mallet, and trodden by a man with his bare feet. The material is now fit for the thrower . . .

The articles thus prepared are then dried upon flues to consolidate their texture, and render them fit for the *vertical lathe* of the *turner.* Placed upon this machine they are reduced to their proper thickness and exact form; and if their pattern requires handles or spouts, they are here fitted with them by a workman called the *handler.* From this workshop they are carried into the *kiln-house* to be burned, and placed in *saggars,* or circular pans, made of Staffordshire crucible clay, open at the top, and about eight inches deep, the flat bottoms of which are strewed with calcined flint, to prevent the adhesion of articles to them. The kiln usually holds about one thousand five hundred of these saggers, and frequently from 25,000 to 30,000 pieces of ware. Here they continue 37 hours, exposed to such a violent heat as to render them red-hot, but carefully protected from flame. On coming out they are said to be in the *biscuit* state, that is, having the appearance of an unglazed tobacco pipe. If any blue be in the pattern of the articles, the figures are traced upon them at this time with a hair pencil, dipped in a mixture of a purple colour; and being suffered to dry, they are then immersed in a red liquid, called the *glaze,* of the consistency of cream, chiefly composed of white lead and ground flint. This adheres to every part of the articles, which are placed to dry in a room of a certain temperature, from whence they come out with a ground of a pale pink colour, and the pattern of a dingy purple. Being perfectly dry, they are given to the *trimmer,* who smoothes the surface of the article, and rubs off any little inequalities of the glaze; the most unwholesome part of the process, as he frequently inspires particles of the white lead, etc. to the great detriment of his stomach and lungs; which, indeed, he is obliged to relieve by frequent emetics. The articles are next placed in the *glaze kiln* and remain there 28 hours exposed to the fire; which being extinguished, the whole are suffered gradually to cool, and then taken out, when they exhibit a wonderful metamorphosis, effected by the chemical agency of fire. A vitrification having taken place on their surface, a beautifully glossy covering discovers itself within and without, and the figures of purple are converted into a vivid and beautiful blue. After passing through the *sorting room,* they are given to the painters, who with colours properly and nicely prepared (for the hues are all changed by a subsequent firing) trace those beautiful patterns, figures and landscapes, upon them . . . Again they are placed in the kiln, in order to fix the colours, and remain there for six hours. This completes the process of such articles as have no gold in their pattern; but those which are ornamented with this superb addition, undergo another burning after the enamel is laid on. They are also carried afterwards to the *burnishing shop,* where this final decoration is given them by a number of women, who soon change the dull surface of the gold into a most brilliant appearance, by rubbing the gilt part of the pattern with little instruments pointed with bloodstones and other polishing substances . . .

Many articles which could not be conveniently *thrown,* such as tureens, plates, and dishes, are made on moulds of plaister of Paris, and when dry are given to the *turner* as above-mentioned. The earnings of the workmen in this manufactory, who are all paid by the piece, are very considerable; throwers and turners making about 25s. per week; dippers and glazers, 21s.; and painters from 30s. to two guineas. *Pennington* is the inimitable artist who produces all these exquisite specimens of the perfection of the pencil, which the more expensive articles display.

This remarkably detailed and informative account, written from Dudley,

Worcestershire, was first published by the Rev. Richard Warner in *A Tour through the Northern Counties of England and the Borders of Scotland,* 1802. This extract was reproduced by Franklin A. Barrett, *Worcester Porcelain and Lund's Bristol.*

26 and 27 August 1802 — Lord Nelson

[Over the door of Chamberlain's factory had been thrown] a triumphal arch of laurel, ornamented with an elegant blue flag, with an appropriate inscription thereon. For more than an hour his Lordship viewed with the minutest attention every department of this highly improved work, so much the object of general curiosity; and on inspection of the superb assortment of china at the shop in High Street, honoured Messrs Chamberlain by declaring that, although possessed of the finest porcelain the courts of Dresden and Naples could afford, he had seen none equal to the productions of their manufactory, in testimony of which he left a very large order for china, to be decorated with his arms, insignia &c.

This account appeared in *Berrows Worcester Journal,* the local newspaper. For a separate description of this visit see the *Dictionary* entry for Nelson Service.

2 August 1819 — Michael Faraday

This day I did Wonders. Immediately after breakfast I went to Flight and Barrs House and presuming on the slight knowledge I had of Mr Martyn Barr, asked permission to see the porcelain works. Mr Barr himself was not there being at Malvern but his brother very politely instantly gave me admittance to the works. I went to them and found the old porter whose place it is to show them to strangers, and he immediately took me around regretting however I had come so early as the men generally had not yet come to work. He explained all he could to me and the workmen here and there left off what they were about to show me the series of operations. I was not very solicitous to see and examine at this time for I saw all was not yet in activity and I intended to have better opportunities in the course of the day.

Just in the entrance of the works was a box with an inscription over it forbidding any gifts to the workmen in the place but stating that whatever was put into the box was divided equally among them at the end of the year, so I of course at leaving the place paid my respects to the box. From thence I went to seek out Mr Bagster [Baxter] an artist employed at Chamberlains to whom I had words of introduction from several friends...

I went with him to Chamberlains, the Manufactory of Porcelain, where I believe he superintended the painting department and as Mr Bagster professed to be but a bad showman for all the operations, he placed me in the hands of another person who went over the works with me and showed me all very minutely. I will not here detail what I saw in the order which I saw it but endeavour briefly to describe the porcelain manufacture by and bye. Being later in the day Business had not yet got into its due order and velocity, and the place looked much fitter and more lively than Flight Barrs had done.

Michael Faraday subsequently met Mr George Barr once more and his brother Martin. He again saw their manufactory

...more minutely than before and found it far more lively and busy. After an hour or two spent here looking at the processes and some experiments, we left the place and I was persuaded to break my promise with Mr Bagster, that I might dine with Mr Barr and afterwards go with him and take tea at Malvern...

This account, from Dsfydd Tomos' *Michael Faraday in Wales,* is reproduced in full in Henry Sandon's *Flight and Barr Worcester Porcelain;* see also the *Dictionary* entry for Thomas Baxter.

Select Bibliography

A subject as wide ranging as Worcester porcelain has inevitably led to a great many books over the years. Each contributes new ideas and discoveries adding to our knowledge, while never fully superseding what has been written before. I have not attempted here to list every book which covers the period as to do so would be an impossibly long as well as meaningless task. Some general books on English porcelain do have significant Worcester sections containing important information and I have included a few which I feel make important contributions. I have not included catalogues, papers to learned societies or magazine articles in this list, but at the same time acknowledge the wealth of material which has been published in these forms. It is to be regretted that so many of the great books on Worcester porcelain were written so long ago as to be virtually unobtainable today.

Barrett, Franklin A., *Worcester Porcelain and Lund's Bristol,* Faber, 1966 2nd edn.

Binns, Richard William, *A Century of Potting in the City of Worcester,* B. Quaritch, 1865, 1877 revised edn.

Branyan, Lawrence. French, Neal. and Sandon, John, *Worcester Blue and White Porcelain, 1751-1790,* Barrie and Jenkins, 1981, 1989 2nd (enlarged) edn.

Catalogue of the Robert Drane Collection, *The collection of Old Worcester porcelain formed by the late Mr Robert Drane,* Albert Amor Ltd., 1922.

Catalogue of the Frank Lloyd Collection, Hobson, R.L., *The collection of Worcester Porcelain of the Wall Period,* British Museum, 1923.

Coke, Gerald, *In Search of James Giles,* Micawber, 1983.

Cook, Cyril, *The Life and Work of Robert Hancock,* Chapman and Hall, 1948, and *Supplement to The Life and Work of Robert Hancock,* 1955.

Fisher, Stanley W., *Worcester Porcelain,* Ward Lock, 1968.

Godden, Geoffrey A., *Caughley and Worcester Porcelains, 1775-1800,* Barrie and Jenkins 1969, reprinted by the Antique Collectors' Club, 1981.

Godden, Geoffrey A., *Chamberlain-Worcester Porcelain 1788-1852,* Barrie and Jenkins, 1982, reprinted 1992.

Godden, Geoffrey A., *Encyclopaedia of British Porcelain Manufacturers,* Barrie and Jenkins, 1988.

Handley, Joseph, *18th Century English Transfer-Printed Porcelain and Enamels,* Mulberry Press, 1991.

Hobson, R.L., *Worcester Porcelain,* B. Quaritch, 1910.

Honey, William B., *Old English Porcelain,* G. Bell & Son, 1928, revised by **Barrett, F.A.,** Faber and Faber, 1979.

Marshall, H. Rissik, *Coloured Worcester Porcelain of the First Period,* Ceramic Book Co., 1954, facsimile reprint 1970.

Mackenna, F. Severne, *Worcester Porcelain, the Wall Period and its Antecedents,* F. Lewis, 1950.

Sandon, Henry, *Flight and Barr Worcester Porcelain 1783-1840,* Antique Collectors' Club, 1978, reprinted 1992.

Sandon, Henry, *Worcester Porcelain 1751-1793,* Barrie and Jenkins, 1969.

Sandon, Henry and John, *Grainger's Worcester Porcelain,* Barrie and Jenkins, 1989.

Savage, George, *Eighteenth Century English Porcelain,* Rockliff Publishing, 1952.

Spero, Simon, *Worcester Porcelain, The Kenneth Klepser Collection,* Lund Humphries, 1984.

Watney, Bernard M., *English Blue and White Porcelain of the Eighteenth Century,* Faber and Faber, 1963, revised edn. 1973, reprinted 1979.

THE GRINDING MILL.
2 THE SLIP KILNS.
3 TEMPERING THE CLAY.
4 FORMING ON THE WHEEL.
5 TURNING.
6 MODELLING.
7 THE BISCUIT KILN.
8 DIPPING OR GLAZING.
9 THE GLAZE KILN.
10 PAINTING.
11 ENAMELLING KILN.
12 BURNISHING.